Securing Critical Infrastructures and Critical Control Systems:

Approaches for Threat Protection

Christopher Laing
Northumbria University, UK

Atta Badii
University of Reading, UK

Paul Vickers
Northumbria University, UK

T0338705

Information Science
REFERENCE

Managing Director:	Lindsay Johnston
Editorial Director:	Joel Gamon
Book Production Manager:	Jennifer Yoder
Publishing Systems Analyst:	Adrienne Freeland
Development Editor:	Austin DeMarco
Assistant Acquisitions Editor:	Kayla Wolfe
Typesetter:	Christina Henning
Cover Design:	Nick Newcomer

Published in the United States of America by
Information Science Reference (an imprint of IGI Global)
701 E. Chocolate Avenue
Hershey PA 17033
Tel: 717-533-8845
Fax: 717-533-8661
E-mail: cust@igi-global.com
Web site: http://www.igi-global.com

Copyright © 2013 by IGI Global. All rights reserved. No part of this publication may be reproduced, stored or distributed in any form or by any means, electronic or mechanical, including photocopying, without written permission from the publisher. Product or company names used in this set are for identification purposes only. Inclusion of the names of the products or companies does not indicate a claim of ownership by IGI Global of the trademark or registered trademark.

Library of Congress Cataloging-in-Publication Data

Securing critical infrastructures and critical control systems: approaches for threat protection / Christopher Laing, Atta Badii, and Paul Vickers, editors.
    p. cm.
  Includes bibliographical references and index.
  ISBN 978-1-4666-2659-1 (hardcover) -- ISBN 978-1-4666-2690-4 (ebook) -- ISBN 978-1-4666-2721-5 (print & perpetual access) 1. Buildings--Security measures. 2. Intelligent buildings. I. Laing, Christopher. II. Badii, Atta. III. Vickers, Paul, 1966-
  TH9705.S38 2013
  658.4'73--dc23
                            2012032808

British Cataloguing in Publication Data
A Cataloguing in Publication record for this book is available from the British Library.

All work contributed to this book is new, previously-unpublished material. The views expressed in this book are those of the authors, but not necessarily of the publisher.

Editorial Advisory Board

Alan Boulanger, *BlueRISC, USA*
Alvaro A. Cardenas, *University of Texas at Dallas, USA*
Tom Fairfax, *Security Risk Management Ltd, UK*
Ernie Hayden, *USA*
John Glover, *MayneStay Consulting Group Ltd, Canada*
Samuel A. Merrell, *Carnegie Mellon University, USA*
Paul Maliszewski, *Arizona State University, USA*
Chris Sandford, *Wurldtech, The Netherlands*
Corey Schou, *Idaho State University, USA*

List of Reviewers

Bill Bailey, *Edith Cowan University, Australia*
Esteban Garcia-Cuesta, *iSOCO, Spain*
Robert Doleman, *Edith Cowan University, Australia*
Ian Ellefsen, *University of Johannesburg, South Africa*
Tony H. Grubesic, *Drexel University, USA*
M. A. Hossain, *Northumbria University, UK*
Peter H. Jenney, *Security Innovation, USA*
Sean Lawson, *University of Utah, USA*
Gabriele Oliva, *University Campus Biomedico of Rome, Italy*
Neil Robinson, *RAND Europe, UK*
Bonnie Zhu, *University of California at Berkeley, USA*

Table of Contents

Detailed Table of Contents

Intelligent Buildings (IB) are facility-wide systems that connect, control, and monitor the plant and equipment of a facility. The aim of IB is to ensure a facility is more efficient, productive, and safe, at a reduced cost. A typical IB integrates diverse subsystems into a common and open data communication network, using both software and hardware; however, IBs suffer from diverse generic vulnerabilities. Identified vulnerabilities may include limited awareness of security threats and system vulnerabilities, physical access to parts of the system, compromise of various networks, insertion of foreign devices, lack of physical security, and reliance on utility power. IB risks are contextual and aligned with the threat exposure of the facility. Nevertheless, there are generic mitigation strategies that can be put in place to protect IB systems. Strategies include threat-driven security risk management, an understanding of system criticality, greater integration of departments, network isolation, layered protection measures, and increased security awareness.

Chapter 2

Nowadays, critical infrastructure plays a fundamental role in our modern society. Telecommunication and transportation services, water and electricity supply, and banking and financial services are examples of such infrastructures. They expose society to security threats. To safeguard against these threats, providers of critical infrastructure services also need to maintain the security objectives of their interdependent data networks. As an important part of the electric power system critical infrastructure, Supervisory Control and Data Acquisition (SCADA) systems require protection from a variety of threats, and their network infrastructures are potentially vulnerable to cyber attacks because security has not been part of their design. The diversity and lack of interoperability in the communication protocols also create obstacles for anyone attempting to establish secure communication. In order to improve the security of SCADA systems, anomaly detection can be used to identify corrupted values caused by malicious attacks and injection faults. The aim of this chapter is to present an alternative technique for implementing anomaly detection to monitor electric power electric systems. The problem is addressed here by the use of rough set theory.

Chapter 3

Bill Bailey, Edith Cowan University, Australia
Robert Doleman, Edith Cowan University, Australia

The belief that a static alarm system will safeguard critical infrastructure without additional support mechanisms is misplaced. This complacency is no longer satisfactory with the increase in worldwide threat levels and the potential social consequences. What is required is a more proactive, comprehensive security management process that adds to the ability to prevent, detect, deter, respond, and defeat potential harmful events and incidents. The model proposed here is proactive and grounded upon current operational procedures used by major companies in hostile and dangerous environments. By utilising a clearly defined comprehensive risk management tool, a more systematic security, threat, risk, and vulnerability assessment (STRVA), process can be developed. This process needs to identify deliberate targeting of assets through multiple intelligence gathering capabilities, plus defeat testing to probe existing security defences. The consequence approach to a potential breakthrough is at the essence of this methodology.

Chapter 4

Antony Bridges, QinetiQ, UK

As industrial control systems (ICSs) have been connected to wider organisational networks and the Internet, the threat from unauthorised access has increased. Protecting these systems from attack requires not just the use of appropriate technological solutions but also an understanding of the humans within the wider system. It is not sufficient that the human knows what they need to do. They must also be willing and able to do it. This chapter highlights some of the human vulnerabilities within Industrial Control Systems and suggests that greater consideration of and adaptation to the human limitations will enhance the future security of these systems.

Chapter 5

Rafal Leszczyna, ENISA, European Union & Gdansk University of Technology, Poland
Elyoenai Egozcue, S21sec, Spain

In 2011, the European Network and Information Security Agency (ENISA) conducted a study in the domain of Industrial Control Systems (ICS). Its objective was to obtain the current view on the ICS protection primarily in Europe but also in the international context. The 'portrait' included threats, risks, and challenges in the area of ICS protection as well as national, pan European, and international initiatives on ICS security. The study was performed through desktop research, survey and interviews, and a meeting with all involved stakeholders. This chapter highlights the most relevant parts of the final report of the study. It focuses on the challenges to securing ICS identified during the research, but also presents the context and the methodology of the study. In response to the challenges, the seven recommendations of ENISA for protecting ICS are proposed.

Matthew Brundage, The University of Tulsa, USA
Anastasia Mavridou, The University of Tulsa, USA
James Johnson, The University of Tulsa, USA
Peter J. Hawrylak, The University of Tulsa, USA
Mauricio Papa, The University of Tulsa, USA

SCADA systems monitor and control many critical installations around the world, interpreting information gathered from a multitude of resources to drive physical processes to a desired state. In order for the system to react correctly, the data it collects from sensors must be reliable, accurate, and timely, regardless of distance and environmental conditions. This chapter presents a framework for secure data acquisition in SCADA systems using a distributed monitoring solution. An overview of the framework is followed by a detailed description of a monitoring system designed specifically to improve the security posture and act as a first step towards more intelligent tools and operations. The architecture of the Smart Grid is used to analyze and evaluate benefits that the proposed monitoring system can provide. Finally, the effects and use of Radio Frequency Identification (RFID) and ZigBee as data acquisition platforms are discussed in the context of the proposed solution.

Sean Lawson, University of Utah, USA

Based on an analysis of key policy documents and statements from civilian policymakers, military leaders, and cybersecurity experts, this chapter demonstrates that although there is still concern over cyber threats to critical infrastructure, other threat objects have begun to figure more prominently in public policy discourse about cybersecurity in the United States. In particular, intellectual property and government secrets are now identified most often as the primary object of cyber threats. When critical infrastructure is mentioned, it is often used as a motivational tactic, with collapse of critical infrastructure serving as a central theme of hypothetical scenarios meant to motivate a policy response. This chapter documents and critically evaluates this shift in U.S. cybersecurity discourse.

Konstantin Knorr, Trier University of Applied Sciences, Germany

Worm epidemics such as Stuxnet and Conficker have raised great interest in the public and media lately and stressed the question of how our critical infrastructure can be protected against such attacks. Besides reactive measures like incident response, pro-active counter measures are required. Patch management is such an essential pro-active measure for the secure operation of our critical infrastructure. It is an indispensable activity which is required in many standards. This chapter focuses on patch and update management for industrial control systems that are part of our critical infrastructure. Standards for the automation of patch management and selected operational security standards are discussed in the context of patch management. The main contribution of the chapter is the definition and description of a standard conform patch management process for industrial control systems with special focus on the interaction between operator and vendor of such systems.

Chapter 9

Peter H. Jenney, Security Innovation, USA

Industrial Control System (ICS) cyber security is weak and exploitable. As evidenced by STUXNET's attack on the Iranian Natanz nuclear facility in 2010 and others since global critical infrastructure is in danger of cyber attack. The problem stems from the growth of industrial management systems over three distinct generations that moved process management systems from manual to fully networked controls and sensors. In many cases the transition has been poorly managed and proper IT management techniques were not employed. In others, the software and hardware systems are so fragile that any change or unexpected access can crash or otherwise render them useless. These instabilities, both caused by poor management and weak equipment open large security holes that allow hackers to exploit critical systems with potentially disastrous results. For example, a petroleum distillery could be made to vent and burn excess gas at a time where it could potentially destroy the facility or perhaps take down entire electrical grids, inconveniencing and possibly causing significant harm.

Chapter 10

Ian Ellefsen, University of Johannesburg, South Africa
Sebastiaan von Solms, University of Johannesburg, South Africa

Developing countries are fast becoming players in an increasingly interconnected world. Many developing countries are making use of technological solutions to address unique challenges. However, in many cases, this growth is not accompanied with the development of appropriate information infrastructure protection structures. As technological solutions are deployed in developing countries, there will be a large number of new users gaining access to Internet-based systems. In many cases, these new users might lack the skills necessary to identify computer security threats. Inadequate cyber security measures can increase the risk and impact of cyber attacks. The development of internal structures to address Critical Information Infrastructure Protection (CIIP) is dependent on the environment in which it will be deployed. Therefore, traditional CIIP structures might not adequately address the technological challenges found in developing countries. In this chapter, the authors aim to address the development of CIIP structures in developing regions by elaborating on the set of unique challenges that exist. Furthermore, they aim to present a community-oriented structure aimed at providing CIIP, in what they refer to as a "bottom-up" manner. The larger aim of CIIP structures in developing regions is to support the future development and deployment of cyber security mechanisms and to allow developing countries to play a trusted role in global cyber security efforts.

Chapter 11

Eduardo E. Gelbstein, Webster University, Geneva, Switzerland

Critical Information Infrastructure Infrastructures (CII) have been recognized as potential targets for cyber-attacks since the late 1990s and many have already been successfully attacked since then. The attacks that took place on September 11, 2001 have increased the concerns of the impact such attacks could have and many governments, professional bodies, and vendors have put in place advisory and co-ordination mechanisms to share and encourage such good practices. Critical infrastructures are monitored and controlled by information systems, and this makes it increasingly difficult to distinguish a Critical Infrastructure from a Critical Information Infrastructure. It is also acknowledged that such information systems are complex, interdependent, and convergent as they share components that use a small number of products and standards. All of these systems and the products with which they are built are known to have known and unknown vulnerabilities that could be exploited by attackers.

This chapter describes vulnerabilities related to safety and security in distributed process control systems integrated with information and communication technology (ICT). The author describes key vulnerabilities and how to mitigate these vulnerabilities by current best practices, which have worked in an industrial setting in Norway. Distributed process control systems are denoted as SCADA systems, i.e. supervisory control and data acquisition systems. Increased networking and increased use of ICT impacts the complexity and vulnerability of the SCADA systems. To improve safety and security, there must be a focus on systematic knowledge generation between ICT and process experts and a focus on exploring resilience as a strategy to manage risks and support continuity of operations (resilience seen as the ability to bounce back and sustain operations). Best practices in risk management in this area are to establish policies, improve risk awareness, perform risk assessment in collaboration between ICT and SCADA professionals, focus on segregation of networks, focus on active protection against malicious software, improve reporting and sharing of incidents, and establish and explore disaster/recovery plans. In addition, there should be focus on certification and testing of components in ICT and SCADA systems and improvement of resilience to mitigate uncertainty and complexity.

Large scale, geospatial networks—such as the Internet, the interstate highway system, gas pipelines, and the electrical grid—are integral parts of modern society, facilitating the capability to communicate, transport goods and services between locations, and connect homes and businesses to basic necessities like water and electricity. The associated management and protection of this critical infrastructure is a challenging task because it is often compromised or damaged by natural disasters, human error, or sabotage. Further, the cascading effects associated with disruptions can impact related interdependent infrastructure, such as supervisory control and data acquisition systems (SCADA). In this context, although the protection and/or hardening of network elements can reduce disruptive impacts, the cost to protect all equipment in the system is prohibitive. The purpose of this chapter is to detail an optimization approach for selecting elements on a network to be protected, under budget constraints, in order to maximize system performance if one or more components are damaged or destroyed. Applications results for a large scale, geospatial network are explored and presented, illustrating problem complexities as well as the potential for informed strategic investment decision making. The implications for SCADA systems relying on large scale geospatial networks, including the public Internet, are also discussed.

This chapter describes and contrasts policy, economic theory, and insights concerning the establishment and operation of Information Exchanges (IE). In the context of this chapter, IEs are specific mechanisms meant to stimulate the exchange and sharing (aside from pure disclosure) of a range of confidential information relating to security between owner-operators of critical infrastructure. Information shared in IEs may be of varying types but is reported to generally be of a non-technical nature. In the Supervisory Control and Data Acquisition (SCADA) community, a number of nations have established IEs; for example, European SCADA and control systems exchange has been operating since 2005. The chapter primarily considers these issues through the perspective of efforts to address the security of the Critical Information Infrastructures (CII). Despite IEs being seen by policy-makers as important to tackle CIP issues, limited empirical operational evidence exists to suggest that IEs constitute a useful mechanism to successfully overcome the economic incentives governing the disclosure of information. The chapter concludes by identifying opportunities to further explore the disparities and reasons for the indicative disjuncture between economic theory, policy, and practice. The chapter is thus aimed primarily at managers, policy-makers, and non-technical personnel considering participation in an IE.

Designed without cyber security in mind, most existing Supervisory Control And Data Acquisition (SCADA) systems make it a big challenge to modify the conventional Information Technology (IT) intrusion detection techniques, both to counter the threat of cyber attacks due to their standardization and connectivity to the Internet, and to achieve resilient control without fully retrofitting. The author presents a taxonomy and a set of metrics of SCAD-specific intrusion detection techniques by heightening their possible use in addition to explaining the nuance associated with such task and enumerating Intrusion Detection Systems (IDS) that have been proposed to undertake this endeavor. She identifies the deficits and voids in current research and offers recommendations on which strategies are most likely to succeed, in part through presenting a prototype of her efforts towards this goal. Specifically, she introduces an early anomaly detection and resilient estimation scheme consisting of a robust online recursive algorithm, which is based on the Kalman Filter in a state space model setting. This online window limited Robust Generalized Likelihood Ratio Test (RGLRT) that the author proposes identifies and detects outliers among real-time multidimensional measurements of dynamical systems without any a priori knowledge of the occurrence time or distribution of the outliers. It attains a low detection delay and an optimal stopping time that yields low rates in false alarm and miss detection while maintaining the optimal online estimation performance under normal conditions. The author proposes a set of qualitative and quantitative metric to measure its optimality in the context of cyber-physical systems.

Preface

The increasing prevalence of cloud services in the context of the future Internet heralds the emergence of a new pervasive technology environment. In the future, all users, and in particular both attackers and protectors of critical infrastructure, will be able to exploit new degrees of freedom based on the convergence of cloud services, smart grid, and mobile telecommunications. This will be supported by the provision of anywhere anytime computation services particularly to serve big data processing, simulation, and data intelligence. This trend provides a timely motivation for this book concerned as it is with the exploration of the critical infrastructure domain and the study of its vulnerabilities, as well as the protection and mitigation against attacks and failure-recovery emergency response policy-making at national and international strategic levels.

As their name suggests, industrial control systems (ICS) are made up of components and architectures that control industrial processes. It is a broad church taking in distributed control systems (DCS), programmable logic controllers (PLC), and supervisory control and data acquisition (SCADA) systems. Such control systems are to be found in numerous industrial sectors (manufacturing, power generation, refining, etc.,), critical infrastructures (water treatment and distribution communication systems, transportation etc.,), and environmental control systems (HVAC – heating, ventilation & air conditioning –, physical access and energy consumption, etc.,). ICS are evolving from closed and proprietary technologies to become increasingly interconnected; indeed, current trends are seeing ICS making more use of networking technologies, with Ethernet and TCP/IP protocols beginning to replace the older, more proprietary standards. It is anticipated that this trend will continue and accelerate. Application specific ICS systems are already being remotely hosted, with the use of web-based products, thin clients and web portals increasing. The advantages of this approach – specifically, the convenience of viewing industrial processes remotely – are, of course, obvious. Unfortunately, the increasing application of TCP/IP protocols to ICS may have made such systems more vulnerable.

It is difficult to prescribe generic hard and fast solutions for ICS security, so instead the book's editors and authors have striven to provide a full and detailed understanding of the security threats and vulnerabilities that exist within industrial control systems. Consequently, the rationale for the book is simple:

1. Security through obscurity has pervaded the ICS community, but compromises such as the Modbus protocol and the Stuxnet worm have changed all that.
2. ICS are long lived and are now being connected across the Internet; such systems were never originally designed with cyber security in mind.
3. Terrorists, organized criminals, and hostile governments are using this lack of cyber security to attack the critical infrastructures of nation states.

4. Given the highlighted vulnerabilities with ICS systems, national governments are actively promoting cyber security and the protection of the national infrastructure.
5. These same national governments are also involved in investigating ways to identify potential cyber threats to their critical infrastructures, and to conduct pre-emptive military cyberspace operations.

While the book offers practitioner case studies and academic research to provide a technical, procedural, and managerial response to securing industrial control systems, it should be noted that awareness raising and training are also essential components in securing ICS. This is all the more so given cultural and historical beliefs that still exist within some sections of the ICS community, the key elements of which can be set out in contra-distinction with the current realities as follows:

- **Belief:** ICS are secure because they use protocol and interface obscurity.
- **Reality:** The use of commercial off-the shelf technology (COTS) solutions, and the integration of technologies such as Microsoft operating systems, and TCP/IP protocols mean that ICS are now vulnerable to the same viruses, worms and trojans that affect mainstream IT systems. Furthermore, the use of Internet protocols opens ICS up to bespoke malware targeted specifically at infrastructure degradation.
- **Belief:** ICS are secure because they are physically secure.
- **Reality:** The intended target of Stuxnet was the Natanz plant, a highly secure hardened fuel enrichment plant situated in the Isfahan province of Iran. The physical security of the Natanz plant was compromised and Stuxnet introduced. The malware initially spread using infected removable drives, and then via peer-to-peer RPC, thereby infecting other systems within the Natanz network.
- **Belief:** ICS are secure because they are not connected to the Internet.
- **Reality:** Increasing demands for enterprise integration and remote access mean that TCP/IP protocols are replacing the older, more proprietary standards, and it is anticipated that this trend will continue and accelerate.

U.S. President Barack Obama has been quoted as equating the outcomes of a cyber attack on Industrial Control Systems, to that of nuclear and biological attacks. While in the UK, the Director General of GCHQ, Ian Lobban, has identified a "real and credible" threat to the UK's critical infrastructure from terrorists, organized criminals, and hostile governments (BBC, 2010).

Speaking to business leaders on USS Intrepid, US Defence Secretary Panetta said that attacks such as Shamoon[1] on the Saudi Arabian state oil company, ARAMCO, "mark a significant escalation of the cyber threat … we know that foreign cyber actors are probing America's critical infrastructure networks … they are targeting the computer control systems that operate chemical, electricity and water plants, and those that guide transportation throughout the country" (Defense News, 2012).

The security of ICS that control and monitor industrial, infrastructure, and environmental processes is important; the compromise of such a system, will have an effect far removed from an initial security breach. A power outage, caused by a compromised electrical ICS, could be a minor inconvenience for some, a financial loss for others, and for some, death. However, what about a compromised air-traffic control system, or a compromised water treatment plant? What would be the outcomes then? This is difficult to assess, as are the security implications of legacy ICS being coupled with networking technologies, such as Ethernet and TCP/IP, and increasingly reliant on remote monitoring and decision support applications and convergence of cloud services, smart grid and mobile telecommunications.

A PwC report entitled 'The Global State of Information Security® Survey 2013' makes for interesting reading, especially when the focus is directed at critical sectors such as Energy (Oil & Gas), Power and Utilities. In all cases these sectors are 'trying to catch up to known cyber-security problems' and, more importantly, less than half of them 'have programs in place to combat advanced persistent threats' (APTs)1. Furthermore, within these sectors, the adoption of new technologies appears to be outpacing the implementation of any security measures. The report also details the level of security incidents suffered by the Energy, Power and Utilities sectors. Interestingly, and in line with the concerns of the both the UK and US governments, is that attacks directed at these critical sectors are rising.

Readers of this book will no doubt be aware of the issues surrounding the protection of critical infrastructures, and the editors suspect that even the non-practitioner members of the general public will also have some awareness. Indeed the general public cannot fail to be aware, what with daily headlines such as:

Leon Panetta warns of 'cyber Pearl Harbour' (BBC, 2012)

The picture painted by the US Defense Secretary was one of doom and destruction on a massive scale; derailing "trains loaded with lethal chemicals" contaminating the "water supply in major cities" and causing "physical destruction and loss of life" (Defense News, 2012). Is this picture full of cold hard realities or political hype? Only time will tell, but in the mean time the editors and authors of this book present a mixture of theoretical and practical themes on the securing of ICS. These themes are (i) policies and risk management, (ii) protection models, frameworks and processes, and (iii) security audits for critical infrastructures (CI), critical information infrastructure protection (CIIP), industrial control systems (ICS), and supervisory control and data acquisition (SCADA) systems.

In the first chapter David Brooks considers the security threats and risks to intelligent building systems. Such systems connect, control, and monitor the plant and equipment of a facility, thereby ensuring a facility is more efficient, productive, and safer at a reduced cost. He explains how a building's diverse subsystems are integrated into a common and open data communication network, using both software and hardware. He goes on to point out that such an arrangement may have limited awareness of security threats and system vulnerabilities. This is followed by a detailed discussion on how generic mitigation strategies that can be put in place to protect such systems.

In the next chapter, a theoretical discussion on detecting cyber attacks on critical infrastructures is presented by Maurilio Pereira Coutinho, Germano Lambert-Torres, Luiz Eduardo Borges da Silva, Horst Lazarek, and Elke Franz. They detail how anomaly detection can be used to identify corrupted values that have been caused by malicious attacks and go on to discuss an alternative technique (using Rough Set Theory) for the implementation of anomaly detection to monitor electric power systems.

In their chapter, Bill Bailey and Robert Doleman look at the proactive security protection of critical infrastructure and propose a process driven methodology. They argue that the current belief that a static alarm system will safeguard critical infrastructure is misplaced, and that what is required (given the increasing threat levels) is a more proactive, comprehensive security management process. They have developed an approach that is grounded in current operational procedures used by major companies in hostile and dangerous environments.

Next, Antony Bridges considers the human element in the protection of ICS. He suggests that while attention has been focused on using appropriate technological solutions to protect ICS, more consideration must be given to understanding how humans interact with the systems being protected, and the technical means used to protect them. He is advocating a greater consideration of, and adaption to, human limitations, and that such consideration will enhance the future security of these systems.

Rafal Leszczyna and Elyoenai Egozcue present a European Network and Information Security Agency (ENISA) study on challenges in securing ICS. This study highlights the current situation in Europe on protecting ICS. While this study has a European perspective, the editors feel that the challenges that have been identified have an international resonance. ENISA, in responding to those challenges, has made a number of pertinent recommendations to protecting ICS.

This is followed by Matthew Brundage, Anastasia Mavridou, James Johnson, Peter J. Hawrylak, and Mauricio Papa's discussion of the use of distributed monitoring. They present a framework for secure data acquisition in SCADA systems. A smart-grid architecture is used to analyze and evaluate the benefits that the proposed monitoring can provide. This evaluation takes into account the use of radio frequency identification (RFID) and ZigBee as data acquisition platforms.

Sean Lawson assesses the status of critical infrastructure as an object of cyber threats. He suggests that while concern should still be given to protecting critical infrastructures, other threat objects (such as intellectual property and government secrets) have now begun to figure more prominently in cybersecurity discourse. The central premise is that the protection of critical infrastructure is part of a motivational tactic, with collapsing critical infrastructure as a central theme of hypothetical scenarios designed to motivate a policy response.

Taking a look at patching critical infrastructure, Konstantin Knorr discusses the need for an efficient patch and update management for ICS. Knorr considers the need for standards in the automation of patch management. He then goes on to define and describe a standard patch management process for ICS, which focuses on the interaction between the operator and the vendor of such ICS.

Peter Jenney's treatment of ICS assesses the status of ICS software protection. It is Jenney's view that such software protection is often weak and exploitable, and that IT best practices should be applied to current ICS software. Jenney acknowledges that the operational parameters of ICS would require some modification to these best practices, and goes on to suggest a framework that allows for the protection of ICS software, while at the same time providing a stable and secure ICS environment.

In their chapter Ian Ellefsen and Sebastiaan von Solms look at a community-oriented approach to critical information infrastructure protection in developing countries. They point out that expanding information infrastructures allow for developing countries to have an increasingly important role within an interconnected world. They also observe that this growth is often not accompanied (because of legal, political and social reasons) by appropriate protection mechanisms. In order to overcome these difficulties, they present a community-oriented structure aimed at providing protection to critical information infrastructures in a bottom-up manner.

The next chapter deals with the design of a security audit plan for critical information infrastructures. Here, Eduardo Gelbstein assesses the security performance of critical information infrastructures, and then focuses on how to design the scope of a security so that the audit can be conducted in a reasonable time, but still able to deliver valuable and actionable recommendations.

Stig Johnsen's chapter deals with how SCADA safety and security can be improved through resilience based risk management. He argues that to improve safety and security, there must be a greater focus on exploring resilience as a strategy to manage risk and support continuity of operations.

Continuing the SCADA theme, Alan Murray and Tony Grubesic consider the fortification of large scale geospatial networks, and the implications for SCADA systems. They acknowledge that although the hardening of geospatial networks such as gas pipelines, and the electrical grid would reduce disruptive impacts, the cost is prohibitive. However, they present an optimization approach for selecting elements on a network to be protected, thereby maximizing system performance if one or more components are damaged or destroyed.

In the penultimate chapter, Neil Robinson looks at information sharing for critical infrastructure protection, in particular the distinction between policy, theory, and practice. Robinson presents an analysis of the establishment and operation of information exchanges set up to stimulate the exchange and sharing of a range of confidential information relating to security of critical infrastructure.

Bonnie Zhu and Shankar Sastry close out the book by presenting a theoretical approach to intrusion detection and resilient control for SCADA systems. This new approach focuses on early anomaly detection and resilient estimation. A Generalized Likelihood Ratio Test is used to detect anomalous measurements from among real-time multidimensional measurements of dynamic systems. Such an approach offers low detection delay, low false alarm rates and misdetection, while at the same time maintaining optimal online performance.

Taken together the authors' various contributions offer both a pragmatic and theoretical approach to securing critical infrastructures, and, it is hoped, offer something to both the theorists and the pragmatists. The book is not an 'academic text', neither must it be seen as a 'how to fix it' manual – the intention was to gather expertise from within the critical infrastructure protection community, and present different approaches as to how the protection of critical infrastructure could be improved. We, the editors, trust this volume will find much use, become well thumbed, littered with penciled suggestions and comments, and not be gathering dust on some half forgotten shelf.

Yours in appreciation,

Christopher Laing
Northumbria University, UK

Atta Badii
University of Reading, UK

Paul Vickers
Northumbria University, UK

REFERENCES

BBC. (2010, 12 October). *UK infrastructure faces cyber threat, says GCHQ chief.* Retrieved from http://www.bbc.co.uk/news/uk-11528371

BBC. (2012, October 12). *Leon Panetta warns of cyber Pearl Harbour.* Retrieved from http://www.bbc.co.uk/news/technology-19923046

Defense News. (2012, October 12). *Text of speech by US Defense Secretary Leon Panetta.* Defense News. Retrieved from http://www.defensenews.com/article/20121012/DEFREG02/310120001/

ENDNOTES

1. Shamoon is a computer virus discovered in 2012, and is being used for cyber espionage in the energy sector. Once a system is infected the virus compiles a list of specifically selected files. It then sends that information to a command and control server after which it will erase the files from the system. Once that is complete, Shamoon then overwrites the system's master boot record, in effect thereby preventing the system from re-booting.

2. An advanced persistent threat (APT) normally refers to a group (e.g., a hostile foreign government, terrorist organization) having the capability and the intention to direct an attack against a target, which is both persistent and effective. It should be noted that individuals (whether monitored by political or criminal desires) rarely have sufficient resources to be referred to as an APT. The term usually refers to cyber threats, in particular those that make use of the Internet to conduct intelligence gathering operations and/or denial of service attacks to distribute the provision of financial, media, logistic, telecommunications and energy provision.

Acknowledgment

In editing this book we did not work unaided, and we would like to gratefully acknowledge the tireless and diligent work of the reviewers and Editorial Advisory Board.

Chapter 1

Security Threats and Risks of Intelligent Building Systems:
Protecting Facilities from Current and Emerging Vulnerabilities

David Brooks
Edith Cowan University, Australia

ABSTRACT

Intelligent Buildings (IB) are facility-wide systems that connect, control, and monitor the plant and equipment of a facility. The aim of IB is to ensure a facility is more efficient, productive, and safe, at a reduced cost. A typical IB integrates diverse subsystems into a common and open data communication network, using both software and hardware; however, IBs suffer from diverse generic vulnerabilities. Identified vulnerabilities may include limited awareness of security threats and system vulnerabilities, physical access to parts of the system, compromise of various networks, insertion of foreign devices, lack of physical security, and reliance on utility power. IB risks are contextual and aligned with the threat exposure of the facility. Nevertheless, there are generic mitigation strategies that can be put in place to protect IB systems. Strategies include threat-driven security risk management, an understanding of system criticality, greater integration of departments, network isolation, layered protection measures, and increased security awareness.

INTRODUCTION

Intelligent Buildings (IB) or Building Management Systems (BMS) are building-wide control systems that connect, control and monitor the fixed plant and equipment of a facility. Increasingly into the future, such systems will be installed and operated in many building types, from Critical Infrastructure facilities to residential buildings.

These systems allow the facility users to have a much better experience. For example, when a person first arrives at work in the morning and uses their RFID tag to enter the building, the IB system will call the lift to the foyer, allow access to their designated floor, and their office lights and Heating, Ventilation and Air-Conditioning (HVAC) will turn-on. The IB system keeps the lights and HVAC operating while it detects move-

DOI: 10.4018/978-1-4666-2659-1.ch001

Copyright © 2013, IGI Global. Copying or distributing in print or electronic forms without written permission of IGI Global is prohibited.

ment in their office and the adjacent area, turning these off when that person leaves for the day.

While there is no single definition for IBs, the following one summarises elements commonly associated with IBs:

A system that supports the flow of information throughout the building, offering advanced services of business automation and telecommunications, allowing furthermore automatic control, monitoring management and maintenance of the different subsystems or services of the building in an optimum and integrated way, local and/or remote, and designed with sufficient flexibility to make possible in a simple and economical way the implementation of future systems (Lafontaine, 1999).

IBs integrate and enable connectivity within the plant and equipment subsystems of a facility, including security systems. In the last ten years or so, IBs have become a significant factor in the design, build, operation and maintenance of commercial buildings. Such systems have become popular due to the need to save energy, provide more reactive and safer facilities, and reduce operational costs. Many of these facilities contain classified material or critical assets. As SCADA system vulnerabilities have been exposed, IBs suffer similiar vulnerabilities. Whether the system is an IB or SCADA system, both may control and monitor Critical Infrastructure.

The ability of IBs to integrate diverse subsystems is achieved through common and open data communication protocols and hardware. Such an open approach leaves facilities vulnerable to both external and internal threats and risks. Depending on the threat environment of a facility, vulnerabilities can be diverse and occur throughout many parts of the IB such as vulnerable hardware devices, insecure software and various insecure networks. From a security perspective, IBs are still at an early stage of understanding and the feasibility of such technological solutions should be considered from the onset, as privacy, information control and security are often neglected (Gadzheva, 2008, p. 6).

Many of these systems are designed and installed by building engineers, and owned and operated by facility managers, with both groups generally having limited secuity awareness.

IB vulnerabilities cover a broad range of potentially exploitable systems. These vulnerabilities open up many approaches for using IB systems for covert or illegal activities. Being able to log into most parts of an IB system, in particular, the automation network level will allow a "picture" of the facility to be built up. For example, when a person first arrives at work in the morning and uses their RFID tag to enter the building, this is communicated throughout the IB System. It is possible to then track that person as various systems turn on or off triggered by various room sensors. When the CEO is in their office and as they leave, it becomes a relatively easy monitoring task to track their movements. When and where security guards patrol the facility and their current location after hours can also be tracked. Finally as security devices such as detectors and CCTV are incorporated into IBs, this allows these devices to be turned off for a period of time to allow illegal access.

Therefore, the objectives of this chapter are to provide:

- An overview of Intelligent Building systems and their architecture, both software and hardware.
- Present generic Intelligent Building systems vulnerabilities.
- Provide generic mitigation strategies to protect Intelligent Building systems.
- Raise awareness of Intelligent Building systems vulnerabilities and the need for directed mitigation strategies.

BACKGROUND

Intelligent Buildings (IB) are becoming increasingly popular, driven through the need to save energy, provide more reactive and safer facilities, and reduce operational costs. These systems integrate and enable connectivity within all building systems and subsystems. In contrast to automation, which can be traced back a couple of hundred years, IB systems only started to evolve over the last three decades. There is no single point in time when these systems were introduced; instead, they developed from different areas of automation that merged over time to result in what could be considered as being an IB. Nevertheless, there have been three main influences that have aligned to support the development of IBs.

These three influences have been:

1. The emerging trend for energy management systems (EMS),
2. Expanding process control systems (PCS), and
3. The drive to reduce staffing and operational costs.

IBs have become a significant factor in the design, build, operation and maintenance of commercial buildings. There is also a trend to retrofit existing buildings in increasing numbers, where reduced maintenance costs and greater energy savings to all stakeholders lead to positive cost returns. For example, the Empire State building installed an integrated IB system with the aim of reducing energy use by 40% (Schneider & Rode, 2010, Spring). IBs are primarily about creating operational efficiency and effectiveness of the multiple and disparate systems that make up a modern building. Such systems include fire and life safety, Heating, Ventilation and Air-Conditioning (HVAC), standard and emergency lighting, emergency warning and intercommunication (EWIS), elevators and security such as access control, intruder detection and Closed Circuit Television (CCTV). The list of the building systems and subsystems now being integrated is extensive and growing, including all security systems.

WHAT ARE INTELLIGENT BUILDING SYSTEMS?

Intelligent Buildings (IB) could be considered to be buildings that integrate technology and processes to create a facility that is safer, more comfortable and productive for its occupants, and more operationally efficient for its owners and operators. Many of the building functions operate automatically with minimal human intervention.

According to Smart Accelerate (n.d), an IB incorporates available concepts, materials, systems and technologies, and by integrating these, meets or exceeds the performance requirements of the building stakeholders including the owners, managers and users. Therefore, the environment of the building should be productive, safe, healthy, and thermally, aurally and visually comfortable. It should have the potential to serve future generations, through sustainability or adaptability over the life cycle of the building and safeguarding environmental resources. Furthermore, the building can be built within some cost constraints, whilst retaining market value. These can be achieved through optimising a building's four basic components, namely its structure, systems, services and management.

There is no standard consensual definition of what constitutes an integrated IB; however, most consider that they are a centralised common user interface that integrates disparate building systems using a shared network (Madsen, 2008). Kujuro (1990) summarised that an IB comprises of key elements, being a building-wide local area network (LAN) with advanced communications capabilities and effective integration. IBs provide significant benefits to building owners, property and facility management professionals, and end-users, maximising building performance and efficiency by integrating building systems. Finally, the system uses technology and strategies that add long-term, sustainable value to the property.

Further to this view, the Asian Institute of Intelligent Buildings (AIIB) adopted a definition for an integrated IB as the inclusion of nine environmental modules (Table 1). These elements resulted in a definition that an "Intelligent Building is designed and constructed on an appropriate selection of quality environment modules to meet the users' requirement by mapping with the appropriate building facilities to achieve long-term building value" (So & Wong, 2002, pp. 288-289).

The concept of modern integrated IBs has received widespread acceptance in the marketplace. Such acceptance, in both commercial and industrial buildings, is due to their ability to "reduce energy costs while improving system performance, operability and reliability" (Langston & Lauge-Kristensen, 2002). Nevertheless, it is important to note that integrated IBs may also be known by several different names including building management system (BMS), smart building, building automation system, high-performance building and energy efficient building.

ARCHITECTURE OF INTELLIGENT BUILDING SYSTEMS

A typical Intelligent Building (IB) integrates many component parts into a common network, using both software and hardware architecture. The European Committee for Standardization (CEN) divides IB communications into three layers: *management level, automation level* and *field level*. These three levels of architecture are used in the

Table 1. Intelligent buildings environmental elements

Environmental elements		
Environmental friendliness	Flexibility	Space utilisation
Construction process & structure	Human comfort	Culture
Technology safety & security measures	Working efficacy	Life cycle costing

(So & Wong, 2002, pp. 288-289)

following sections to provide an overview of IB and also discrete vulnerabilities of both software and hardware devices.

Network Architecture

Network architecture can be divided into the three levels of management, automation and field (Figure 1). At the field level, sensors and actuators communicate with each other via Controllers without sending information to higher levels. Controllers and the central supervisor—which monitors and controls the intelligent devices—belong to the automation level. Management information between supervisors is passed on separately in the management layer. The advantages of this model are a clear separation of duties and a reduction of network traffic; however, for smaller systems a separation of networks is expensive.

In order for IBs to function, there is a requirement for some form of common protocol that links and integrates the many discrete devices. The network needs to be "real-time and have simple device interfaces comparable with the cheap nature of existing building devices such as light switches" (Sharples, Callaghan, & Clarke, 1999, p. 136). Such a requirement has led to a number of specific IB network standards and protocols (Table 2), although IBs also use more generic IT and computing protocols such as TCP/IP, 802, etc.

The industry has embraced Ethernet connectivity with all IB devices, whether they are primary network or sub-network devices. Connectivity encompasses Direct Digital Controllers (DDC) along with open protocols such as BACnet, LonWorks and Modbus (Figure 2). Contemporary IB control supports many of these protocols, while providing universal input/output connections to temperature sensors, actuators, life safety devices, lighting devices (Automated Buildings. com, n.d.) and security devices.

Figure 1. Three layered IB network architecture

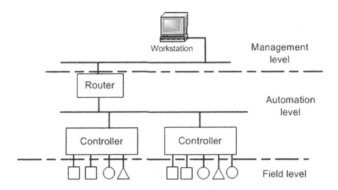

Hardware Architecture

A typical IB system is made up of various hardware components (Figure 3) within both the automated system, and facility plant and equipment. As with the software architecture, a typical system can be divided into the three levels of IB architecture of management, automation and field level. In general, the management level contains the human interface (workstations), server and routing device, all connected via an Ethernet communication LAN/WAN using TCP/IP/BACnet. The automation level provides the various primary controls and secondary room automation, connected via

Table 2. IB industry standards and protocols

Standards and Protocols		
BACnet[1]	Dynet	Modbus
C-Bus	Energy Star[3]	oBIX
CIBSE[2]	EnOcean[4]	OpenTherm
DALI	KNX	ZigBee[5]
DSI	LonTalk	
Midac	OpenWebNet	

Notes:

1. ASHRAE (American Society of Heating, Refrigerating and Air Conditioning Engineers).

2. CIBSE (Chartered Institute of Building Services Engineers).

3. Energy Star. Program created by the United States government to promote energy efficient consumer products.

4. EnOcean. A batteryless, interoperable and wireless standard.

5. ZigBee. A short range, low-powered wireless communication standard targeted at Building Automation.

networked Controllers using twisted-pair cables and operating BACnet, LonWorks or KNX, to name a few. Finally, field level devices are connected to specific plant and equipment sensors or activators operating such protocols as Modbus or their own proprietary protocol.

There is no single approach to IB hardware application, as the integration of devices will depend on the user and building requirements, and their complexity. For example, the division of IB into three architecture levels could be considered abstract and from a hardware perspective, better divided into two levels. A two-level approach does provide greater hardware demarcation, but this approach does not effectively consider software. Nevertheless, a typical three-level division of hardware devices is presented, consistent with the general network architecture approach.

The management device level primarily consists of a Workstation that has a software package to allow a human-system interface, in general, operating on a standard PC with software such as Microsoft Windows. The software system primarily allows human interface to control, adjust and monitor the IB. Many of the manufacturers provide such software packages in various modules, allowing users to select what most suits their building and future upgrades.

The second level of an integrated IB system is the automation level. The automation level comprises of Controllers that provide an interface

Figure 2. IB software architecture

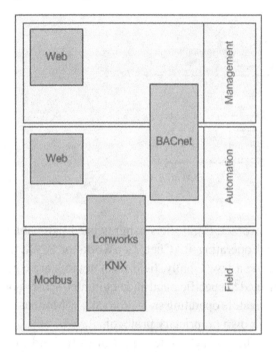

Figure 3. Typical IB system

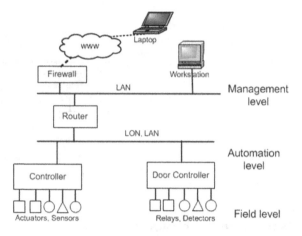

between the upper and lower levels of the IB system, and contains some distributed intelligence. Controllers are typically designed to either provide specific application functionality or generic functionality, although most still contain some degree of multi-functionality.

The third level of an integrated IB system is the field device, which in general comprises of actuators and sensors that operate the building plant and equipment. Field devices are the elements that connect the IB to its physical environment, providing the system with information and the means to continually adjust the building environment and safety conditions.

INTELLIGENT BUILDING VULNERABILITIES

When using an Intelligent Building (IB) system, the plant and equipment of the facility are integrated through common and open data communication protocols and hardware, leaving them

vulnerable to both external and internal threats. Common protocol and hardware devices have to be freely available to allow designers, manufactures and system integrators to build systems where each subsystem will communicate with the greater system. For example, today Chillers will have the functionality to interface not only with its propriety HVAC system, but also the generic IB system.

Furthermore, the intent of the IB is to connect and integrate, allowing local and/or remote control and monitoring; however, many of these systems are designed, installed and operated by service engineers, with restricted consideration of security. The service focus is to maintain the environmental and operational capability of the facility, rather than protect the various IB parts beyond locking plant rooms or enclosures.

An IB, being similar to an IT network, requires there to be a data network throughout the facility. Nevertheless unlike an IT network, the IB network has to be extended into almost every part of the facility, such as plant rooms, service areas, ceiling spaces, etc. In addition, many IBs use the IT network as its primary data network. In each component location, there will be a Controller. In essence, the Controller is a computer that has all the functionality of a desk computer excluding the user interface i.e., screen and keyboard.

However, there is functionality to allow a laptop or other programming devices to be plugged into the Controller, giving access to the greater IB system and in some instances, the greater IT network.

Until recently there has been limited consideration of the vulnerability of IB systems, either from such bodies as the International Organization for Standardization (ISO), the IB manufacturers, integrators or maintainers. Their focus has been to ensure that the many subsystems in the plant and equipment of a facility are integrated and effectively communicate, with little additional interfacing required. Underlying program coding and interface hardware is freely available.

IB Vulnerabilities

IB suffers from generic vulnerabilities, with their level of risk directed by the contextual application of the facility. A facility that is likely to be exposed to a greater threat will result in an IB that is exposed to a greater threat. For example, a nuclear power station will have a significantly higher threat profile than a standard multi-storey office building. Identified vulnerabilities that have been identified include:

- Physical access to the Workstation and its operating software, comprising the management level.
- Compromise of the management level and automation level Ethernets via physical network wiretapping.
- Compromise of the automation level software, such as LonWorks and BACnet.
- Insertion of a foreign Workstation and/or Controller into the network (i.e., "rogue" device).
- Embedded system memory and functionality modification.
- Compromise of open and standardised operating software.
- Use of a locally connected but *foreign* Service Tool or Handheld Programmer.
- Lack of robust Controller enclosures.

- Compromise of any form of anti-tamper function.
- Loss of power supply.
- External access and compromise of wireless networks in the IB.

Physical access to the Workstation with common management level software is a significant threat against the IB and greater facility. Such access allows the attacker to alter the IB program with their own coding, for example write to a Controller to allow an extended time delay before a detector sets off an alarm to support covert entry. In addition, physical access allows an attacker to install malicious code on the system, for example a key logger.

Furthermore physical access to any part of the Ethernet cable allows wiretapping, for example using insulation-displacement connectors (Figure 4). Fibre-optics networks, when compared to Ethernet cabling, are less susceptible to such wiretapping although far from impossible. Fibre-optics wiretapping requires significantly greater knowledge and equipment, and data extraction is more difficult. Furthermore, detection techniques can be applied to monitor for such wiretapping. Once an attacker is connected to the automation level network, freeware such as BACnet4Linux enables full monitoring capability; however, this software (at time of writing) could not write-back to gain control of the IB system. Nevertheless professional automation level software could not only monitor, but also write back to the IB system. At the management level, the MS/TP protocol is readable using freeware such as Wireshark.

A number of significant vulnerabilities of IB protocols have been identified. One such software protocol, LonWorks, suffers vulnerabilities ranging from Denial of Service (DoS) attacks on the OSI layer 1 to layer 7 attacks on management messages. The more significant vulnerabilities are the lack of encryption technology and the use of the same short-shared secret for network authentication.

Figure 4. Wiretap covertly using single pair insulation-displacement connectors

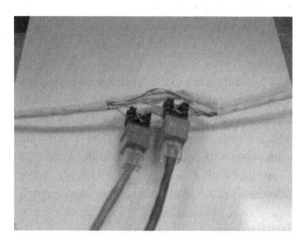

Figure 5. Service port on a typical controller

Most IB Controllers contain some form of service port—either physical or infrared—where a readily available handheld Service Tool can be connected (Figure 5). With a Service Tool and access to the Controller, changes to the automation level program can be carried out. For example, such program changes could switch inputs and outputs on or off at a predefined time, thereby turning off a detector or series of detectors to allow illegal covert entry. Another example could be turning off the HVAC and disabling any alarms, allowing server rooms to overheat and eventually trip-off.

Controllers are supplied with a light-weight cover that is designed to provide protection for the internal circuitry, but not to protect against an attacker. The cover clips on or off by a simple depression of its sides, with no anti-tamper function. Finally, various Controllers had their literature reviewed for additional add-on wireless functionality. A wireless adaptor that plugs directly into the service port was found and such a device was covertly inserted within the Controller's enclosure. Such a device could allow remote access into the IBs automation level to access building use, turn devices on or off and carry out many other actions.

PROTECTING THE INTELLIGENT BUILDING

Intelligent Building (IB) risks are contextual; in other words, directly aligned with the threat exposure of the facility. If the facility contains sensitive or other highly protected information, the IB threat should be considered significant. However, there are a number of generic mitigation strategies that can be taken, such as:

- **Security Risk Management:** A sound, holistic security risk management strategy considering physical and cyber situational threat assessment, system criticalities and identified vulnerabilities.
- **Information System and Communication Protection:** Provide some degree of network isolation and partitioning, both internal and external, between the IB, operating systems and wider networks.
- **Physical and Environmental Security:** Control and validate access to the various and critical IB parts, with layered protection measures wherever possible.

- **Personnel Security**: Ensure personnel are vetted who use and maintain the IB system, including third parties such as the IB system Vendor.
- **Continuity of Operations**: Provide a degree of emergency power and redundant networks to the more critical IB functions and devices.
- **Security Awareness**: Provide training to increase awareness of IB and their vulnerabilities across the organisation. In addition, ensure greater integration of the various stove-piped departments such as IT and Computing, Physical Security, Personnel Security and Facility Management functions.

A more extensive listing of the top 20 mitigation approaches (Table 3) is provided, presenting greater detail to the above points. Mitigation strategies provide factors such as security effectiveness, user resistance, upfront costs, ongoing maintenance costs and defence mechanisms. The upfront cost factor considers the initial cost of resources, such as staffing, consultancy fees and capital equipment costs, whereas the maintenance cost considers the ongoing annual cost to the organisation. The defence mechanism considers how the strategy interrelates to prevention (P), detection (D) and delay (DElay) security elements.

The top 20 mitigation strategies were chosen based on their ability to provide a degree of protection against a broad range of vulnerabilities at management, automation and to a lesser degree, device levels. As discussed, IB vulnerabilities are contextual so risks are directly aligned with the facility's threat exposure. For efficacy in protection, an understanding of the threat, what is critical and where the vulnerabilities lie needs to be established. Such an approach allows the more critical functions and their supporting facilities to be zoned within a traditional layered protection manner directing security strategies.

FUTURE VULNERABILITIES OF INTELLIGENT BUILDINGS

There needs to be some consideration of the future of Intelligent Building (IB) systems, to provide an operational outlook on developing and changing technologies likely to be used in the next decade. Such a review should provide some understanding of potential and developing threats and vulnerabilities of IB technologies. Therefore, future considerations include the greater use of wireless devices and telecommunications for ease of connectivity, open architecture, plug and play to facilitate connectivity, single design approach, artificial intelligence and finally, smart and multi-functional sensors (Table 4).

Wireless Technology

Perhaps one of the greatest concerns will be the increasing use of mobile technologies to allow greater communications, interconnectivity and flexibility. As Gadzheva states "wireless building automation promise to revolutionize home and commercial and building management [IB] where fast deployment, increased building efficiency and optimal occupancy comfort and convenience are top priorities" (2008, p. 1). Greater device mobility will be incorporated into static devices, using communication protocols such as Bluetooth, Wireless 802.11x, WiFi, ZigBee, cellular (CDMA, GSM, LTE), etc. The drive by users, operators and owners to make IB systems more adaptable will further increase the use of wireless IB systems (Reyes, Barba, Callaghan, & Clarke, 2001). For example, the cost of wiring sensors and their devices can vary widely from about 20% to as much as 80% of a cost of a sensor to its control point (Brambley, Kintner-Meyer, & Katipamula, 2006, p. 2). It is expected that in the near to medium future wireless will significantly replace existing wired solutions due to their many advantages such as network convergence, reduced costs, greater mobility, increased flexibility and simple convenience (Gadzheva, 2008, pp. 2-4).

Table 3. Top 20 security mitigation strategies

Mitigation Strategy	Overall Security Effectiveness	User Resistance	Upfront cost	Maint. cost	Prevent, Detect or DElay
Security risk management: Apply a documented risk management security policy that addresses: i. The objectives, roles and responsibilities for the program as it relates to protecting the personnel and assets of the organisation; ii. The scope of the program as it applies to all of the organisational staff, contractors, and third parties; and iii. Management commitment to compliance.	Average	Low	Medium	Medium	P
Security risk management: Apply a threat assessment to inform risk management and decision-making that: i. Specifies the threat assessment methodology and levels; ii. Documents the threat results (including supporting rationale) in the security plan for the IB system; and iii. Reviews the IB and threats on an organisation-defined frequency.	Good	Low	Medium	Medium	P
Security risk management: Apply a criticality assessment to inform risk management and decision-making that: i. Identifies the critical IB functions and supporting devices based on maintaining operational IB objectives; ii. Documents the criticality results (including supporting rationale) in the security plan for the IB system; and iii. Reviews the IB and its devices criticality on an organisation-defined frequency.	Excellent	Low	Low	Low	P
Security risk management: Apply a vulnerability assessment that: i. Monitors and evaluates the IB according to the risk management plan on an organisation-defined frequency to identify vulnerabilities that might affect the security of the IB; ii. Document the vulnerabilities results (including supporting rationale) in the security plan for the IB system; and iii. Analyse vulnerability reports and remediate vulnerabilities within an organisation-defined time frame based on the management of risk.	Excellent	Low	Medium	Low	P, D
Information system and communication protection: Physical or logical separation of the IB from other networks.	Excellent	Low	High	Medium	P, D, DE
Physical and environmental security: Control physical access to all IB parts, such as Workstations, Controllers, by: i. Enforcing physical access authorisations for all IB access points in the facility; ii. Verifying individual access authorisations before granting access to the facility; iii. Securing keys and other physical access devices; iv. Inventory physical access devices on a periodic basis; and v. Changing combinations, keys and authorisations credentials on an organisation-defined frequency or when keys are lost, combinations are compromised, individual credentials are lost, or individuals are transferred or terminated.	Excellent	Medium	High	High	P, D, DE
Physical and environmental security: Validate physical access authorisation to IB parts, such as Controllers, by: i. Develop and maintain lists of personnel with authorised access to IB and issue appropriate authorisations credentials; and ii. Designated officials within the organisation to review and approve access lists on an organisation-defined frequency, removing from the access lists personnel no longer requiring access.	Excellent	Medium	Medium	High	P
Physical and environmental security: Emergency power to all critical IB parts to maintain functionality that: i. Provides a long-term alternate power supply for the IB that is capable of maintaining minimally required operational capability in the event of an extended loss of the primary power source; and ii. Detection, operational and other critical devices have local emergency power supply i.e., battery back-up.	Good	Low	High	Low	P, D, DE

continued on following page

Table 3. Continued

Mitigation Strategy	Overall Security Effectiveness	User Resistance	Upfront cost	Maint. cost	Prevent, Detect or DElay
Information system and communication protection: IB network functionalities are partitioned by: i. Partition the communications for telemetry/data acquisition services and management functionality; and ii. Isolate security functions from non-security functions.	Excellent	Low	Medium	High	P, D, DE
Access control: Enforce access authorisation to the IB Workstation and other critical parts of the IB. In addition, consider the implementation of a controlled, audited and manual override of automated mechanisms in the event of emergencies.	Excellent	Medium	Medium	High	P, DE
Access control: External access to the IB is strictly controlled, monitored and managed by: i. Authenticating remote access and use of cryptography to protect the confidentiality and integrity of remote access sessions; ii. IB routing all remote accesses through a limited number of managed access control points; iii. IB protecting wireless access to the system using authentication and encryption, where authentication applies to user, device or both as necessary; and iv. Monitoring for unauthorised remote connections to the IB, including scanning for unauthorised wireless access points on an organisation-defined frequency and takes appropriate action if an unauthorised connection is discovered.	Good	Medium	Low	Medium	P, D, DE
Information system and communication protection: Protect all external points into the IB such as hard (Controller) and soft (network) parts. External IB access connections need to be secured, including externally connected communication end point i.e., dial-up modems, etc.	Good	Medium	Medium	Low	P, DE
Security awareness: Provides basic security awareness training and general information to relevant users, operators and maintainers of IB vulnerabilities. In addition: i. IB design and procedure changes are reviewed for inclusion in the security awareness training; and ii. Practical exercises in security awareness briefings simulate actual IB attacks.	Average	Medium	Low	Medium	P, D, DE
Security assessment and authorisation: Connections made to the IB network, Controllers or devices, both physical and logical, are authorised. To support connection control: i. Authorises all IB connections to other information systems; ii. Documents the IB connections and associated security requirements for each connection; iii. Monitors the connections on an ongoing basis, verifying enforcement of documented security requirements; and iv. All external IB communication connections are protected from tampering or damage.	Good	Low	Low	Medium	P, D, DE
Planning: Develop security policy and plans that define the corporate expectations of the IB, maintain optimal operations and to prevent or recover from undesirable interruptions to IB operations that address: i. Objectives, roles and responsibilities for the planning program as it relates to protecting the organisation's personnel and assets; ii. Management commitment with the security policy and other regulatory requirements; iii. Alignment with the enterprise wide risk appetite of the organisation; iv. Explicitly defining the components and describes relationships with and interconnections to other IB; v. Providing an overview of the security objectives for the IB; vi. Review and approval prior to plan implementation; and vii. Revision to address changes to the IB or environment or problems identified during plan implementation or security requirement assessments.	Average	Low	Medium	Medium	P

continued on following page

Table 3. Continued

Mitigation Strategy	Overall Security Effectiveness	User Resistance	Upfront cost	Maint. cost	Prevent, Detect or DElay
Personnel security: Apply personnel security vetting policy and procedures requiring access to the IB before access is authorised. Basic vetting requirements should include: i. Employment history; ii. Verification of the highest education degree received; iii. Residency; iv. References; and v. Law enforcement records.	Good	Medium	Medium	Medium	P
Development and maintenance: Only trusted maintainers to access the IB, achieved by: i. Documenting authorisation and approval policies and procedures for maintaining a list of personnel authorised to perform maintenance on the IB; and ii. Supervision of maintenance personnel during the performance of maintenance activities on the IB by personnel with appropriate access authorisations when maintenance personnel do not have access authorisations.	Average	Medium	Low	Medium	P
Information integrity: Monitor events on the IB to detect attacks, unauthorised activities or conditions. IB monitoring capability can be achieved through a variety of tools and techniques i.e., intrusion detection systems, intrusion prevention systems, malicious code protection software, log monitoring software, network monitoring software and network forensic analysis tools. The granularity of the information collected can be determined based on its monitoring objectives and the capability of the IB to support such activities. In addition: i. IB notifies a defined list of incident response personnel; ii. Protect information obtained from intrusion monitoring tools from unauthorised access, modification and deletion; iii. Test intrusion monitoring tools on a defined time period; iv. Interconnects and configures individual intrusion detection tools into a IB-wide intrusion detection system using common protocols; v. Provide a real-time alert when indications of compromise or potential compromise occur; and vi. The IB prevents users from circumventing host-based intrusion detection and prevention capabilities.	Average	Low	Medium	Medium	P, D, DE
Continuity of operations: Develop and implement a IB continuity management plan in case of system failure or loss of service. The continuity management plan should: i. Address roles, responsibilities, assigned individuals with contact information and activities associated with restoring IB operations after a disruption or failure; and ii. Provide management authority.	Average	Low	Medium	Medium	P, D, DE
Audit and accountability: To monitor conformance, apply regular audits of the IB mitigation strategies. Audits can be either in the form of internal self-assessment (first-party) or independent (third-party) audits.	Average	Medium	Medium	Medium	P, D, DE

Open Architecture

Open architectures have many advantages (Wojnarowicz, Klamra, Rzecki, & Romanska, 2005), having greater connectivity and more commonality including out-of-the-box interoperability and the ability to replace components without having to adapt a system. Such open architecture will be driven and promoted by the industry and bodies such as the International Organization for Standardization, where commonality results in greater efficiency, safer products, reduced costs and increased markets. Such open systems are easier to learn and therefore, hack into. There is a call to make IB architecture and technologies more open using Universal Mobile Telecommunications System (UMTAS), Internet Protocol and other open platforms such as COBRA and

Jini (Reyes, et al., 2001). As IB architecture develops and becomes more open there will, in the initial instance, be limited issues; however, as use increases and more people become aware, the threat will increase. This threat aspect has already begun with current industry standard protocols such as LonWorks, BACnet, etc.

Extended IB System Communications

The focus on many developing IBs is to integrate all aspects of that building to form a panoptic model. In general, panopticism is cited when considering surveillance and control in areas such as prisons (see Foucault's Panopticism). In an IB context, panopticism is considered all-embracing and all-controlling. Users like to be connected at all times and wherever they may go, and the *office* is now mobile and such mobility is likely to increase. The use of this technology is highly likely to be incorporated into IB systems, as discussed in past paragraphs; however, in the midterm it is likely that buildings will also become far more connected. For example, buildings within a central business district are likely to "talk" to each other, driven to improve services such as communications bandwidth, transfer of self-generated energy and other utilities. In addition, from a safety and emergency management perspective, there could be an ability to better manage the flow of traffic, both people and vehicles, during peak rush hour or in a crisis. When the car parks are full in one building, the IBs redirect vehicles to other local buildings that have available parking spaces and transfer the parking fees.

Plug and Play

The ability of systems to readily accept additional devices is likely to increase, driven by the need for less technical expertise on a particular system, straight forward installation, ability to use a greater diversity of devices, the increasing rise of single

companies that act as the principal installer and maintainer, system flexibility, reduced cost of manufacturing such functionality, and reduced costs of installation. As Porteous stated, the intent of modern systems is that they are "plug and play" (1995, p. 188). Plug and Play devices offer some degree of protection, often as part of the component configuration, but these require an awareness, activation, monitoring and response to detected threats.

Common Device Design Approach

Manufacturers currently design and manufacture many functions integrated into a single device, which have these various functions activated depending on the level of service the client purchased or the building may require. This manufacturing approach allows a single device to be built for an international market and for local integrators to up-sell functionality, for a minimal initial build cost. Such functions are later activated through installing an integrated circuit, setting on-board toggle switches or more commonly, installer software settings. Nevertheless *hidden* functionality may be included that users are not aware of, for example embedded wireless connectivity, whereas attackers are aware of this and can therefore, exploit it.

Increasingly Smart Sensors and Single Sensors

Devices and sensors are likely to gain more *intelligence* in the future. Current white devices, such as fridges, ovens, microwaves, etc., have limited functionality and input/output; however, brown devices such as HVAC systems, emergency warning and intercom systems (EWIS), lighting systems, etc., have greater autonomous intelligence (Reyes, et al., 2001). Brown devices will become more intelligent as microprocessors become cheaper, greater connectivity becomes the norm and users gain greater benefits from such

Table 4. Future IB threats and risk

Future threat	Descriptor
Wireless	Increasing use of wireless for ease and cost of connectivity
Open architecture	To aid increasing connectivity, both software and hardware architecture will become more open source. This will result in greater vulnerabilities
Extended interconnectivity	Large systems will have multiple connectivity, both internal and externally, extending to other networks and cloud computing
Plug & play	Devices will be easier to install through plug and play functions
Common design approach	A single Controller circuit will be supplied with multiple application use and functions. Functions may be software disenabled, such as wireless, various inputs & outputs, etc
Smarter & single sensor	Systems and sensors will become "smarter", leading to greater complexity and more difficulty in identifying vulnerabilities. Sensors will perform multiple functions such as light, HVAC and security detection, making them more prone to spoofing or masking

connectivity. Nevertheless as sensors become smarter, they require greater external network capability, leading to greater complexity and increasingly complex and hidden vulnerabilities.

The ability to use a single sensor to achieve multiple functions will be a strong driver, with many perceived and actual benefits. For example, the use of a passive infrared detector that is used to trigger room lights will, after working hours, become an intruder detector. Such dual functionality will have a direct cost benefit in the initial construction and reduced maintenance costs, leading to an improved whole of life cost. Nevertheless, taking such an approach will result in a number of vulnerabilities. With current dual technology security detectors, there is a reduction in nuisance alarms as both detector sensors have to be activated to trigger an alarm output; however, this reduction in nuisance alarms decreases the detector's sensitivity, reducing probability of detection. An intruder only needs to defeat one of the sensors to defeat the detector (Garcia, 2001, pp. 74-75) and any increase in nuisance alarms will result in entropic security decay (Coole & Brooks, 2009), where alarm response is reduced or not carried out. In addition, the most effective sensor positioning for automation building monitoring may not be the most suitable to detect a likely intruder, leading to severe comprise in sensor locality and detection capability.

FUTURE RESEARCH DIRECTIONS

Further research into Intelligent Building (IB) vulnerabilities could consider three areas, namely the:

- Dynamic technology of IB systems.
- Changing approaches to IB systems application.
- The IB industry.

The dynamic technology of IBs needs to be divided into the two distinct domains of networks and hardware, although these two are increasingly converging. Directed studies into the misuse of the IB automation level and management level infrastructure networks need to be considered, with ethical hacking to ensure that these systems are secure. The vulnerabilities of hardware and firmware on various IB devices such as routers, controllers and field devices need to be identified and understood.

The changing approach to systems application needs to gain an understanding of how users, operators and integrators configure, install, operate and maintain IB. What other facilities, systems and subsystems are converging onto IB and what is the approach? In addition, what are the drivers for IB and what types of buildings are installing IB? Finally, there needs to be consideration of the industry perspective and awareness of current and future security issues. What is the industrial approach to installing IBs, is there a security awareness or culture, and what are the perspective and awareness for industry of future security issues?

Protecting IB: The Way Forward?

There are a number of issues that need to be considered to mitigate current and future IB vulnerabilities, beyond the technical and application issues of IB. Such issues include:

- Increasing the awareness of IB vulnerabilities to the various communities, such as security management, IT and computing, infrastructure and facilities, etc.
- Increase research into IB vulnerabilities, considering the dynamic nature of IB such as developing technical issues, changing approaches to application and the industrial approach to these issues.

CONCLUSION

Intelligent Buildings (IB) are facility wide systems that connect, control and monitor the plant and equipment of a facility. An IB enables a facility to be more efficient in its energy use, provides greater productivity and a safer environment, enables it to be more reactive to its users and operate at a reduced cost to achieve a greater profit. A typical IB integrates many systems, subsystem, devices and other component parts onto a common and open data communication network, using both software and hardware architecture over some form of network.

IBs suffer from many and diverse generic vulnerabilities; nevertheless, these are contextual inasmuch as they are directly aligned with the threat exposure of the facility. Identified vulnerabilities may include limited awareness or consideration of security threats and system vulnerabilities, common and known protocols, physical access to many parts of the system, compromise of the various networks, insertion of foreign devices, lack of physical security and reliance on utility power.

There are generic mitigation strategies that can be adopted to protect IB systems. These strategies include security risk management that considers situational threat assessment, system criticalities and identified vulnerabilities; need for increased integration of the various departments that install, operate and maintain IBs; that some degree of network isolation should be applied and there needs to be an increased awareness of IB vulnerabilities across the greater security domain. A list of 20 mitigation approaches (see Table 3) has been provided, presenting additional detail and considering factors such as security effectiveness, user resistance, upfront costs, ongoing maintenance costs and defence mechanisms.

Future vulnerabilities of IB need to be considered to provide some understanding of potential and developing threats and vulnerabilities of technologies. Future considerations include the greater use of wireless devices and telecommunications for ease of connectivity, increasingly open architecture, plug and play to facilitate connectivity, single design approach, artificial intelligence and finally, smart and multi-functional sensors. Research needs to address these issues, relative to their security considerations, such as emerging and dynamic IB technologies, the application of IB and the industry.

REFERENCES

Brambley, M. R., Kintner-Meyer, M., & Katipamula, S. (2006). Wireless sensor applications for building operation and management. In Capehart, B. L., & Capehart, L. C. (Eds.), *Web based energy information and control systems: Case studies and applications* (pp. 341–367). Lilburn, GA: The Fairmont Press Inc.

Buildings, A. com. (n.d.). *Networks*. Retrieved July 22, 2010, from http://www.automatedbuildings.com/frame_products.htm

Coole, M., & Brooks, D. J. (2009). *Security decay: An entropic approach to definition and understanding.* Paper presented at the 2nd Australian Security and Intelligence Conference. Perth: Security Research Centre.

Gadzheva, M. (2008). Legal issues in wireless building automation: An EU perspective. *International Journal of Law and Information Technology, 16*, 1–17. doi:doi:10.1093/iijit/ean001

Garcia, M. L. (2001). *The design and evaluation of physical protection systems.* Boston, MA: Butterworth-Heinemann.

Kujuro, A. (1990). *Trend of system technology in intelligent buildings in Japan.* Singapore: Asia-Pacific Exhibitions and Conventions Pte Ltd.

Lafontaine, J. (1999). *Intelligent building concept.* Ontario, Canada: EMCS Engineering Inc.

Langston, C., & Lauge-Kristensen, R. (2002). *Strategic management of built facilities.* Boston, MA: Butterworth-Heinemann.

Madsen, J. (2008). *The realization of intelligent buildings.* Retrieved May 28, 2010, from http://www.buildings.com/ArticleDetails/tabid/3321/ArticleID/5736/Default.aspx

Porteous, J. M. (1995). Intelligent buildings and their effect on the security industry. *Proceedings Institute of Electrical and Electronics Engineers 29th Annual 1995 International Carnahan Conference* (pp. 186-188). New York, NY: IEEE.

Reyes, A., Barba, A., Callaghan, V., & Clarke, G. (2001). *The integration of wireless, wired access and embedded agents in intelligent buildings.* Paper presented at the The 5th World Multi-conference on Systemics, Cybernetics and Informatics, Orlando, Florida.

Schneider, D., & Rode, P. (2010, Spring). Energy renaissance. *High Performance Building Magazine, 13-16.*

Sharples, S., Callaghan, V., & Clarke, G. (1999). A multi-agent architecture for intelligent building sensing and control. *Sensor Review, 19*(2), 135–140. doi:10.1108/02602289910266278

Smart Accelerate. (n.d). *Intelligent building assessment methodology.* Retrieved May 24, 2010, from http://www.ibuilding.gr/definitions.html

So, A. T. P., & Wong, K. C. (2002). On the quantitative assessment of intelligent buildings. *Facilities, 20*(7/8), 288–295. doi:10.1108/02632770210435206

Wojnarowicz, J., Klamra, M., Rzecki, K., & Romanska, A. (2005). *Security threats in open protocols for intelligent buildings.* Krakow, Poland: Cracow University of Technology.

ADDITIONAL READING

CIBSE. (2000). *Building control systems: CIBSE Guide H. Oxford, UK: Butterworth-Heinemann. Standards Australia. (2006). HB 167:2006 Security risk management.* Sydney, Australia: Standards Australia.

The Smart Grid Interoperability Panel, & the Cyber Security Working Group. (2010). *Guidelines for smart grid cyber security: Vol. 1, Smart grid cyber security strategy, architecture and high-level requirements.* National Institute of Standards and Technology, US Department of Commerce.

Chapter 2
Detecting Cyber Attacks on SCADA and Other Critical Infrastructures

Maurilio Pereira Coutinho
Itajuba Federal University, Brazil

Luiz Eduardo Borges da Silva
Itajuba Federal University, Brazil

Germano Lambert-Torres
Itajuba Federal University, Brazil

Horst Lazarek
Technische Universität Dresden, Germany

Elke Franz
Technische Universität Dresden, Germany

ABSTRACT

Nowadays, critical infrastructure plays a fundamental role in our modern society. Telecommunication and transportation services, water and electricity supply, and banking and financial services are examples of such infrastructures. They expose society to security threats. To safeguard against these threats, providers of critical infrastructure services also need to maintain the security objectives of their interdependent data networks. As an important part of the electric power system critical infrastructure, Supervisory Control and Data Acquisition (SCADA) systems require protection from a variety of threats, and their network infrastructures are potentially vulnerable to cyber attacks because security has not been part of their design. The diversity and lack of interoperability in the communication protocols also create obstacles for anyone attempting to establish secure communication. In order to improve the security of SCADA systems, anomaly detection can be used to identify corrupted values caused by malicious attacks and injection faults. The aim of this chapter is to present an alternative technique for implementing anomaly detection to monitor electric power electric systems. The problem is addressed here by the use of rough set theory.

DOI: 10.4018/978-1-4666-2659-1.ch002

Copyright © 2013, IGI Global. Copying or distributing in print or electronic forms without written permission of IGI Global is prohibited.

INTRODUCTION

Critical infrastructure services are essential to the society. Their continuous and reliable operation and increasing use of Information Technology (IT) have made these critical infrastructures increasingly complex and interdependent, exposing the society to security vulnerabilities and threats. The protection of these services relates to the protection of the cyberspace at the most fundamental level, due to its dependency on the use of computer networks, routers, switches, cables and the entire infrastructure to ensure its functionality.

The great complexity and the resulting interdependence have led to the creation of a layered approach where each of the layers relates to the others and with others infrastructures. There are three main layers, named: physical, cybernetic and operational layer. Although the problems with security and protection traditionally exist in the physical and operational layers, the biggest concerns of providers of such essential services currently reside in the cybernetic layer. The main reason is because of the increased number of vulnerabilities present in this layer.

Due to the scope and influence of these infrastructures in Society throughout the globalised world, several initiatives have been taken by public and private sectors, building new guidelines at governmental level, and establishing best practices and standards for the industry as a whole. In the paper "Cybersecurity standards for the electric power industry- a survival kit", the authors presented and commented on some industry standard initiatives such as ISO/IEC 2700x Series, the IEC62351 Technical Specifications, the IEEE P1711 & P1689 drafts, the ANSI NASI/ISA 99 Technical reports and Standards Series, the NERC CIP Standards, the NIST SP800-53 and SP800-82 Special Publications and the British CPNI Guidelines (Pietre-Cambacedes et al., 2008).

Regarding the electricity sector, the infrastructure consists of several facilities such as: generating units, transmission lines, substations, transmission and distribution substations, national, regional and local control centres, remote terminal units (RTUs), intelligent electronic devices (IEDs) and communications links. The various control centres that make up this infrastructure are arranged hierarchically and each contain one or several workstations, connected via Local Area Network (LAN), running different applications, such as Energy Management Systems (EMS) and database applications. These control centres interact with the supervisory and control systems, called SCADA (Supervisory Control and Data Acquisition) systems, which consist of specialised software to interface with the hardware units, such as RTUs and IEDs, which in their turn monitor sensors and interface with the various physical devices from the electric power system, such as circuit breakers, breakers switches, transformers, protection relays, etc.

The RTUs and IEDs are connected with the Control Centre networks via Wide Area Network (WAN). These connections can be owned by the electric power utilities (private) or by telecommunication service utilities (public). All these facilities make up the national interconnected electric power system (National Electric Grid). This system is highly dynamic and interconnected, consisting of several utilities, private or public, which perform services of generation, transmission, distribution and marketing of electric power, constituting the so-called market deregulated electricity sector. Figure 1 presents a diagram with the interrelationships of these various sectors. In this way, these facilities and applications provide important functions for essential services of the electrical system as part of the National Critical Infrastructure and require special protection against a variety of threats, physical or cybernetic.

Problem Definition

The operation of an electric power system is inherently complex due to the high degree of uncertainty and the large number of variables involved. The

Figure 1. Power system control centre interactions

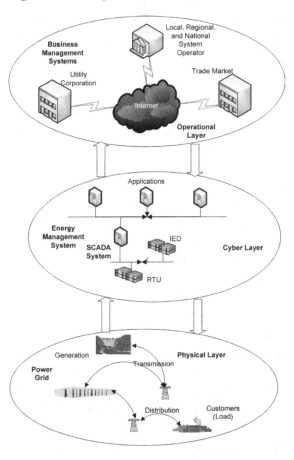

various actions of supervision and control request the presence of an operator, who should be able to respond effectively to diverse needs through the treatment of various types of data and information. These data are from the SCADA measurement systems and computational processes.

The increase use of control centre databases in recent years is related to the fact of the growing use of new technologies and network communications. However this has meant that the control systems have become more vulnerable to attackers. In order to improve the security of industrial control systems, several measures can be taken, such as the use of firewalls, access control, encryption, etc. Several examples are found in the industrial control systems security literature (Stouffer et al, 2011, and Krutz, 2006). One of the

solutions by way of "defence-in-depth" is the use of intrusion detection systems (IDS) to identify corrupted information by attacks and fault injection from a malicious source. An example can be found in "Recommended Practice: Improving Industrial Control Systems Cybersecurity with Defense-In-Depth Strategies" in http://www.us-cert.gov/control_systems/practices/documents/Defense_in_Depth_Oct09.pdf.

The IDS is similar to an "anti-theft residential alarm". This type of device has been widely studied in the last 20 years and an extensive bibliography can be found on the subject. These systems can be characterised by different proposals for monitoring and analysis. With respect to the type of monitoring they can be employed on three levels: network, host and application. With respect to the analysis of the events there are two basic models: detection by abuse or signature and anomaly detection. The first type looks for network activities that are similar to the set of events that describe, in a unique way, a type of attack. This is the method most often used in commercial systems. The anomaly detectors determine attacks by identifying the system behaviour. If this behaviour deviates from what is considered to be a normal profile, an alarm is triggered. The assumption of this model is based on the observation that attackers behave differently from an ordinary user and they can be detected by systems that identify these differences. The main difference between these two models is the ability to adapt to new types of attacks: anomaly detectors have dynamic behaviour, differently from systems by signatures. There are currently several versions for commercial systems, public domain and those resulting from research.

In the 90sintrusion detection became a "hot topic" and commercial applications began to appear for this purpose. There are also several prototypes resulting from research, some of which have evolved into commercial products. One of the most used is the SNORT, open source software and distributed site: http://www.snort.org/. In (Lundin & Jonsson, 2002) and (Axelsson, 2000), there is an interesting "survey" of this topic with an extensive bibliography. There is also a wide ranging literature survey found in the work of Peddabachigari et al., (2007) and Mé & Cédric, (2001). A practice available intrusion detection technology report is presented in Allen et al., (2000). A good text book on the subject can be found in Northcutt & Novak, (2000). In McHugh et al., (2000), a list of commercial IDS products and public domain research is found. The NIST document "Intrusion Detection Systems" presents an excellent study of IDSand technical considerations for selection and implementation of IDS (Bace & Mell, 2002). An evolution of the IDS is presented in ITL Bulletins of National Institute of Standards and Technology, from the US Department of Commerce, called Intrusion Detection and Prevention Systems (IDPS) (http://www.itl. nist.gov/lab/bulletns/b-02-07.pdf). In addition to detecting the intrusion, these systems are capable of attempting to stop a possible incident. IDPSs are well described in the "NIST Special Publication 800-94 - Guide to Intrusion Detection and Prevention Systems", accessible sitehttp://www. nist.gov.

As we can see from the previous paragraph much research has been done to implement metrics for analysis in detection systems: threshold limits, statistical measures, measures based on rules and models using machine learning techniques, such as classification techniques, neural networks and immune systems. According to Allen et al., (2000), there is considerable advantage to using machine learning techniques: computational efficiency, the need for scarce resources and storage capacity to adapt to the new data (events).

Proposed Solution

Many solutions have been found in the literature for implementing anomaly detection using intelligent techniques, for the reasons outlined above. Even some of these solutions apply directly to the problem of infrastructure protection of the electrical system.

The electric power grid is controlled by the exchange of control signals between control centres and the RTUs and IEDs, which in turn control circuit breakers, transformers, switches, etc. The tasks of data acquisition and supervisory control are performed through the SCADA systems. The data collected by these systems are, in most cases, incomplete and subject to being corrupted. Two types of anomaly intrusion detection can be defined: (1) by identifying attacks that use the infrastructure of the data communication network and (2) by modelling the flow of data and control operations in SCADA systems in order to detect anomalies caused by attempts to cause damage to the system, such as changes in the amounts of transmitted data, change of control signals, opening breakers, fraud, and so on.

One of the major difficulties encountered in monitoring of electric power systems is the nonlinear characteristic of its behaviour, forcing the use of numerical methods which generally consume time and resources and are not suitable for on-line monitoring. Power electrical systems currently use an application called State Estimator, which is used to deal with these problems. As the state estimator cannot work well with large data losses, it assumes that its information on the network is always correct. This is a risk assumption, because in general there are configuration errors and there is always the chance that an attacker could be mediating between the control centre and the electrical system. This work proposes and implements an application to monitor and protect electrical power systems in the case of cyber threats using smart techniques. The proposed technique is based on the database knowledge extraction using the Rough Set Theory. This approach was created by Zdzisław Pawlak (Pawlak, 1982) and can be classified as another powerful technique of the theory of knowledge.

The proposal is to build an application capable of performing the online monitoring in power substation, collecting the measures from RTUs and informing the occurrence of anomalous events through the anomaly detector, as shown in Figure

2. This detection can be undertaken in two steps: designing and implementing a classifier to detect corrupted and normal measurements, and the design and implementation of a classifier for the type of attack or error injected. In both cases the detector should trigger an alarm in the presence of an abnormality.

Attacks on Critical Infrastructure of Electric Power Systems

The electric power industry can be considered as one of the more sensitive critical infrastructures as it incorporates potentially key objectives for the correct functioning of other infrastructures. Despite the existence of backup resources and procedures for the continuity of operations if the electricity sector collapses, communications are disrupted, trains stopped, planes grounded, and the economy may be seriously impaired. Unlike other types of energy, electricity cannot be stored, so interruptions in the electricity supply produce immediate effects.

There have been dozens of cases where control systems – in electrical systems, water, sewage, oil, gas, and pulp and paper industries-have been impacted intentionally or unintentionally by electronic means, in accordance with operators and industry experts. A very good text book describing such vulnerabilities can be found in Weiss, (2010). The author describes many situations where such

Figure 2. Model of the proposed anomaly detector

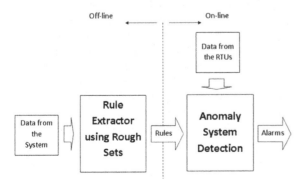

control systems do not operate properly, and result in impacts ranging from the minor to catastrophic. In addition, online attackers are seeking to use the corporate information system of electric power utilities as an input port to the control systems. This information shows how the electricity sector can be vulnerable to the cyber attacks of terrorists, hackers, hostile nations, and so on.

It is not clear what consequences could result from a cyber attack on control systems in the electricity sector. However, from the reports of accidents and mistakes that led to interruptions or failures, local or regional, we can conclude that it is relatively easy for an experienced hacker to perpetrate such attacks. Coordinated attacks on regional electricity systems are also likely to occur, given the current vulnerabilities found in these systems. For example the 2003 US blackout was a huge blackout in Ontario, the Midwest and Eastern United States. It affected an estimated 10 million people in the Canadian province of Ontario and 45 million people in eight U.S. states (https://reports.energy.gov/). In the paper "Creating Large Disturbances in the Power Grid: Methods of Attack After Cyber Infiltration" the author describes how an attacker who is able to infiltrate an Energy Management System (EMS) can instruct elements of the grid to function improperly or can skew the state information received by the control programs or operators (Sands-Ramshaw, 2010). In Naedele & Dzung, (2005), some incidents are listed and they are related to types of cyber attacks to critical infrastructures. One of them occurred in March 2000 where a disgruntled former contractor gained access to the control system of a sewage treatment plant in Maroochy Shire in Queensland/Australia. He flooded the surrounding environment with millions of litres of untreated sewage. More recently, Kabay, (2010) lists a series of attacks to critical infrastructures around the world.

With the rise of the Stuxnet malware in June 2010, much has changed with respect to the real cyber threats in industrial control systems. Stuxnet is a threat that was primarily written to target an industrial control system or set of similar systems, such as gas pipelines and power plants. In the work of Fallere et al, (2011) the authors take a detailed look at Stuxnet and its various components and particularly focus on the final goal of Stuxnet, which is to reprogram industrial control systems. Stuxnet is a large, complex piece of malware with many different components and functionalities.

Structure of Electric Power System

The electric power system is highly dynamic and interconnected, consisting of several utility companies, private or public. This system has a hierarchical feature, being subdivided into more regional systems, as shown in Figure 3 (Rossi, 2000). In addition, there is the subdivision of the sector in the generation, transmission, distribution and marketing of electric power market.

The interconnection and hierarchical organisation of national, regional and local operation control centres are also shown in Figure 3. They monitor the data acquired by RTUs to ensure the system is working properly. Control centres also dispatch control messages for the generating units and power substations to regulate the flow of power and voltage levels. Computational systems that allow operators to control the power flow

(generation, transmission and distribution) are called Electric Power Management Systems (EPMS) or EMS. In general, operators and system administrators use the EPMSs, while protection engineers and automation/integration use and are responsible for the SCADA systems.

Control systems contain computers and applications that perform important functions for the essential services of the electrical system. As such, they are part of the national critical infrastructure and require protection against a variety of threats. As these systems are based on proprietary hardware and networks, they have been erroneously considered immune from cyber attacks and security. This is a neglected topic in the design of such systems. If they are included in the project, they are very limited on various issues, but mainly for economic reasons which make these potentially vulnerable systems. The interruption of service, distributed denial of service, process redirection, or manipulation of operational data can lead to destabilisation of critical infrastructure.

Cyber attacks on systems of production and distribution of electrical energy pose a risk to public safety and welfare, and can cause serious environmental damage. The introduction of IT, Internet-based strategies and new business integration with the little knowledge on IT security in

Figure 3. Hierarchical system of control

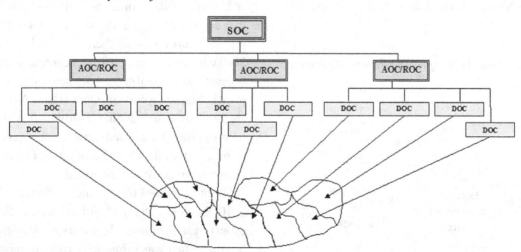

this environment has become even more control systems for industrial processes vulnerable to cyber attacks.

The trend in the Control and Operation Centres has been towards the use of remote access using the public communication system, Internet and wireless technology, as shown in Figure 4 (Oman et al., 2002). Due to the economic advantages to perform the functions of management and maintenance, this increased connectivity has led to greater automation of transmission and distribution substations and therefore an increase in connections between the systems of monitoring and corporate information systems. This trend brings with it the risk of cyber attacks perpetrated by "hackers" and/or terrorists. Invasions can produce disastrous effects if control devices are manipulated maliciously. In order to protect the electrical system against such threats, it is necessary to identify vulnerabilities and, then make it more robust ("hardened") against intruders and attackers.

Currently, the major challenge for the electric power industry is the integration of diverse equipment and protocols used in communication and in control of electrical systems. Examples of protocols found in control systems in power substations include Ethernet protocols and proprietary protocols, FastEthernet, EIA232/485, UCA - Utility Communication Architecture, and UCA2, TCP/IP, ControlNet, v. 32, WAP, WEP, IEC60870, DNP3, Modbus, Profibus, IEC61850 and Fieldbus, among others. These protocols are used to connect the sensors and IEDs, the control equipment, such as programmable logic controllers (PLC business), RTUs, communications processors, local PCs and devices of the SCADA system. Figure 5 shows an example of this structure.

The diversity and lack of interoperability of these communication protocols creates obstacles to establishing a secure link of communication between power substations. In addition, there is also a variety of means of communication used to access these equipment and systems. It is common to find public telephone, wireless network,

Figure 4. Remote access electric power infrastructure

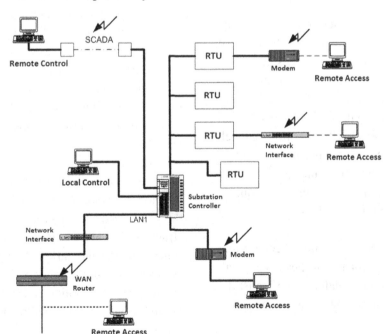

Figure 5. Typical architecture of a SCADA system (source: Areva T & D)

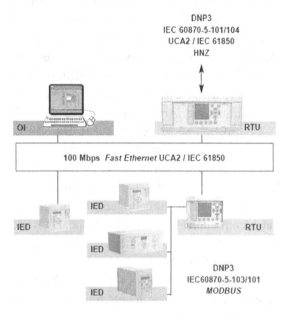

microwave link, fibre optic cables, and connection to the Internet in the power substations interconnections with the control centres.

Electrical Power Infrastructure in the European Union

In Europe the transmission services of electricity, bilateral or multilateral, agree with the rules of the energy industry and best practices laid down by the "European Network of Transmission System Operators for Electricity-ENTSO-E" (http://www.entsoe.eu/). Being the body of transmission system operators of electricity at European level, the mission of ENTSO-E is to promote important aspects of energy policy in the face of significant challenges in the fields of security, adequacy, market, and sustainability of the European Electricity System.

Therefore the ENTSO-E must become and remain the focal point for all European, technical, market and policy issues related to the Transmission System Operators (TSOs), and interfacing with the power system users, EU institutions, regulators and national governments. This mission contributes to security of supply, a pan-European electricity market, a secure integration of renewable resources and a reliable future-oriented grid, adequate to achieve energy policy goals.

The ENTSO-E coordinates the operation and development of the electricity transmission network from Portugal to Norway and the Netherlands to Romania and Greece. It has been fully operational since 2009. This is an association of 42 Transmission System Operators from 34 countries of continental Europe, providing a reliable market for all participants of "*Internal Electricity Market – IEM*". Its assets consist of 525 million customers, 828 GW generation capacity, 305,000 Km of transmission lines and electricity trade volume of 400 TWh/year (http://www.iene.gr/5thSEEED/articlefiles/sessionIII/kabouris.pdf). The synchronous interconnection means that individual systems are connected and work together on the same frequency (50 Hz). The TSO is the pilot of the system: it is responsible for the safe operation of the system. This means:

- Monitoring the security of the system of transmission of electricity;
- Monitoring the reliability and stability of the system;
- Balancing supply and demand at any moment; and
- Maintaining and developing the infrastructure: networks and related technical facilities.

In the liberalised electricity market that is developing in the European Union, the TSO is the provider of management services and infrastructure that are essential prerequisites for the functioning of the market. As a provider of these services to the components of the market (producers, traders and suppliers of electricity), the TSOs do not only have technical responsibility for the operation of the system, but are also responsible for fair and non-discriminatory access to these services by market participants.

The excessive increase in flow across borders and the restructuring of the electricity sector, separating vertically integrated utilities previously in separate businesses of generation, transmission and distribution, resulted in the need to create European standards of security and reliability required for all TSO interconnected, and finally, for all customers of the system.

The System Operations Committee (SOC) ensures a high standard of operability, reliability and security of the European electricity transmission systems within the framework of liberalised energy markets. As depicted in Figure 6, the System Operations Committee has five permanent groups based on the synchronous areas (Continental Europe, Nordic, Baltic, Great Britain, and Ireland- Northern Ireland), and two voluntary Regional Groups (Northern Europe and Isolated Systems). Having a permanent character, these Regional Groups ensure compatibility between system operation on the one hand and market solutions and system development issues on the other.

The network generation capacity of the ENTSO-E System in 2010, according to data provided by ENTSO-E (https://www.entsoe.eu/resources/data-portal/production/) was approximately 3,400 TWh. Figure 7 shows the contribution made by each country.

The operation of this highly interconnected system operation requires a much closer between the TSOs involved according to pre-set rules. The set of these rules form the "*Operation Handbook*" (https://www.entsoe.eu/resources/publications/system-operations/operation-handbook/), comprising the technical rules and principles laid down in the past by the former UCTE (Union for the Coordination of the Transmission of Electricity) for the operation of interconnected networks. For the avoidance of doubt in relation to the importance of the "*Operation Handbook*", each member must

Figure 6. UCTE system (source: http://www.entsoe.eu/)

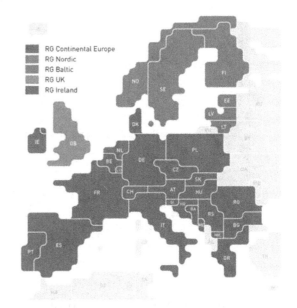

sign a multilateral agreement (MLA), assuming your acquiescence to the manual.

Electric Power Infrastructure in Brazil

The Brazilian electricity sector has made major changes by migrating from a configuration centred on state monopoly with a single provider and investor services to a new market model, with the participation of multiple agents and shared investments with private capital. The main structural adaptations include:

- Exploration of electrical energy services by third parties;
- Control and operation of electrical systems in a centralised manner;
- Free access to and use of electrical networks;
- Segmentation of activities (generation, transmission, distribution and marketing);

Figure 7. Monthly production for the year of 2010 (data provided by ENTSO-E)

Country	Sum	1	2	3	4	5	6	7	8	9	10	11	12
AT	70685	6013	5404	5694	4627	5916	6458	6099	6122	6034	5901	5844	6573
BA	15554	1657	1504	1609	1251	1409	1074	903	847	934	1167	1365	1834
BE	89864	8312	7676	8071	7293	7511	6901	7174	7417	7104	7409	7493	7503
BG	41027	3876	3631	3592	2900	2699	2973	3336	3369	3225	3521	3635	4270
CH	68252	5554	4895	5036	4738	5893	6186	6663	5534	4980	5533	5336	5904
CY	5235	437	393	379	341	381	448	549	620	507	411	365	404
CZ	79482	7872	7031	7472	6565	5748	5634	6325	5687	6214	6957	6699	7278
DE	573150	55498	52245	51662	45094	44063	43923	45002	42605	42668	49133	49502	51755
DK	36762	4041	3769	3809	3036	2570	1899	1895	2006	2692	3328	3560	4157
EE	11328	1092	1001	1048	754	841	838	851	800	836	988	1045	1234
ES	279481	25170	23381	24350	21448	21819	21973	25078	23092	22347	22558	23524	24741
FI	76967	8264	7483	7560	6640	5553	4825	4689	4676	5393	6469	7082	8333
FR	550309	56545	50416	51077	41685	39848	40225	41075	39498	39233	42015	49634	59058
GB	332569	30909	29544	29708	25206	25951	23789	24535	23630	25271	28688	30772	34566
GR	47880	4482	3770	3806	3285	3556	3739	4723	4805	3751	3903	3727	4333
HR	13251	1347	1249	1338	1162	1034	930	940	830	846	938	1120	1517
HU	33781	3310	3009	3086	2499	2463	2407	2395	2553	2661	2872	3146	3380
IE	26819	2541	2281	2419	2140	2038	2004	2066	1985	2128	2214	2421	2582
IS	16679	1458	1327	1455	1376	1386	1323	1338	1351	1348	1414	1419	1484
IT	290706	25241	23241	24505	22165	23390	23851	27291	22305	23979	24334	24091	26313
LT	5328	801	705	594	325	331	298	312	308	302	401	446	505
LU	4515	399	375	392	389	347	361	335	317	339	396	407	458
LV	6444	728	541	692	988	582	399	238	330	330	413	590	613
ME	4005	509	393	439	360	319	294	214	145	199	230	362	541
MK	6598	676	637	568	547	593	592	543	461	398	464	485	634
NI	7325	787	667	634	563	594	625	491	503	509	612	631	709
NL	113685	11258	10029	10622	8466	8354	7910	7648	7780	8750	11181	10729	10958
NO	123445	14827	12591	11185	8657	7420	6888	7866	7768	8814	11242	12121	14066

- Creating and regulating the marketing of electric power; and
- Creation of a free consumer.

The Brazilian laws 10,847 and 10,848 of March 15, 2004 established:

- **Electric Energy National Agency -ANEEL (www.aneel.org.br):** Regulatory agency responsible for standardisation of the policies and guidelines and the monitoring of the services provided
- **National System Operator - ONS (www. ons.org.br):** Company responsible for coordination and supervision of centralised operation of generation and transmission of the interconnected system; and
- **Electric Energy Trading Chamber – CCEE (www.ccee.org.br)**
- **The Energy Studies Company – EPE (www.epe.org.br):** Linked to the Ministry of Mines and Energy (MME), aims to provide services in the area of studies and research intended to support the planning of the energy sector.

In addition, these laws also established the National Council for Energy Policy – CNPE and the Monitoring Committee of the Electricity Sector - CMSE. Figure 8 presents the main institutions of the current Brazilian electric sector model.

The national electrical system is composed of the National Interconnected System (SIN) and the Isolated Systems, mainly located in the north of the country. Figure 9 shows the main Brazilian system interconnections.

The SIN is formed by companies of South, Southeast, Midwest, Northeast, and part of the North region. Only 3.4% of the electricity production capacity of the country is out of SIN. The system of production and transmission of the electric energy of Brazil is a large hydrothermal system, with a strong predominance of hydroelectric power and with multiple owners. According to data from the ONS, the SIN is responsible for servicing approximately 98% of the Brazilian market of electric energy. At the end of 2010, the installed capacity of SIN reached the power of about 96,201.00 MW, of which approximately 70,000 MW are generated by hydroelectric plants. The basic network transmission (voltages above

Figure 8. Main institutions of the current model Brazilian electric sector: CNPE – National Council for Energy Policy, MME – Ministry of Mines and Energy; CMSE - Monitoring Committee of the Electricity Sector, EPE - The Energy Studies Company, ANEEL - Electric Energy National Agency, ONS - National System Operator, and CCEE - Electric Energy Trading Chamber

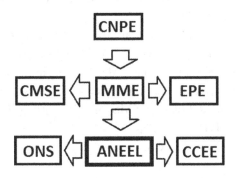

230 kV) peaked in December 2010 approximately 96,000 km, encompassing 851 transmission circuits. The geographic information cadastral system (SINDAT) provides relevant information from the system. According to SINDAT, there are 560 power plants and substations indexed and 1079 transmission lines forming the operating network of ONS.

The integrated operation of the SIN is within the standards established in the Grid Procedures, aimed at meeting both the requirements of electrical safety and to minimising operating costs. The Grid Procedures are normative documents drawn up by the ONS, with the participation of agents and approved by ANEEL. They define the requirements necessary to carry out planning activities of the power system operation, administration of the transmission and operation in real time as part of the SIN.

During theSECGOV-2006 (http://www.secgov.com.br), ONS presented a series of projects for electrical security. In particular one of them is the "Plan for Expansions and Reinforcements SIN Basic Network", which will evaluate the security conditions for the next three years and will propose works for expansion and reinforcement of existing facilities, as well as new works in the line of the planned expansion of SIN" (Tolmasquim, 2009). Another project discussed was the "Electrical Planning of the Operation" with the goal of deepening and detailing the securities studies.

Characteristics of Electrical Systems Networks

Due to the benefits offered by data communication networks, many companies and industries have shown interest in implementing this technology with the purpose of industrial control and automation. In Dzung et al. (2005) and Tipsuwan & Chow (2003), there are interesting reviews of this technology in industrial control including examples of the use of these technologies in industries such as manufacturing, generation and distribution of electric power, gas and water supply, transport, oil and chemical industries, among others. Depending on the type and purpose of the automation system, its components can be local, spread across a geographic area or even on a global scale (Arango & Lambert-Torres, 2004).

There are two types of configuration for this network type: direct and hierarchical (Lambert-Torres et al., 1992). Typically, communication networks for industrial automation are built using the hierarchical model (Dzung et al., 2005), with levels varying from sensors and actuators at the bottom of the hierarchy to local networks (LAN – "*Local Area Network*") and, possibly, WAN networks ("*Wide Area Network*") at the top. The use of hierarchical levels is necessary due to the need to handle large amount of data, not always relevant to all levels.

The structure of a typical distributed control system is shown in Figure 10. At the top of the structure there is a corporate network that runs the management applications and manufacturing processes. In the middle part of the structure there is the control network that connects the man-machine interface workstations (IHM), used by supervisory systems, to the process controllers. This control network can be divided into different segments. The process controllers are in turn connected to the lower level of the structure, called the field or process level. At this point there are field buses connecting the field devices, such as sensors and actuators. From the lower level to the top of the structure, the data traffic is filtered and aggregated to specialised servers situated between levels.

There are several communication protocols associated to the different hierarchical levels. The networks of higher levels of the hierarchy use in most cases the TCP/IP suite of protocols. In Mission-critical connections there are the predominance of the fieldbuses or dedicated connections, although the Ethernet technology is also

present. Fieldbuses have specific protocols, therefore necessitating gateways to perform protocol conversion and to provide a common interface to the upper levels. Examples of these industry standard interfaces are the "*Manufacturing Message Specification – MMS*" (ISO 9506) (SISCO, 2005) and the standards defined by the "*Open Process Control OPC Foundation*" (OPC Task Force, 1998).

One of the functions of these standards is to hide the interfaces of the fieldbus protocol details, allowing you to design and implement automation applications efficiently. Many of the implementations of MMS and OPC are built on the TCP/IP suite of protocols. See the example of MMS interface in Figure 11.

Figure 9. National electrical system (source: www.ons.org.br)

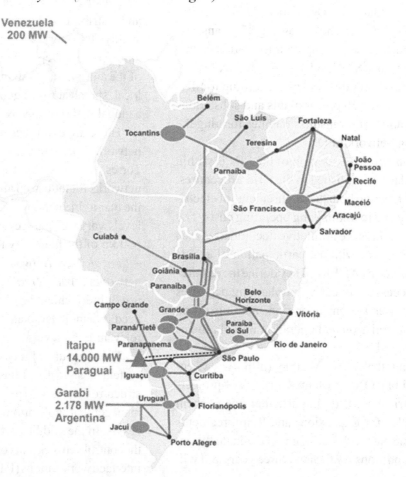

Figure 10. Hierarchical structure of an industrial network

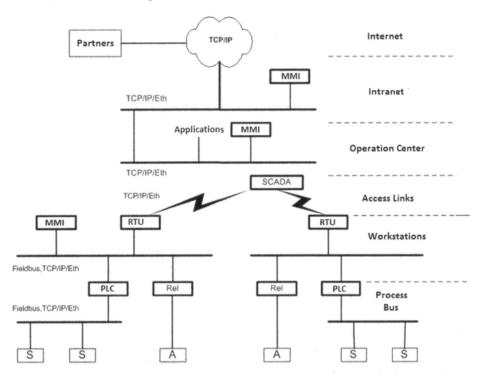

The fieldbus is the generic term that describes digital data communication networks used by the industry. They are used to connect field devices, such as, controllers, transducers, sensors and actuators. They are divided into two major groups, depending on the features that they offer:

- **Control Buses:** For example, "*High Speed Ethernet-HSE*", ControlNet, Foundation Fieldbus, Profibus, DeviceNet, Profibus DP, Interbus-S, SDS, DNP3, MODBUS, EtherNet/IP; and
- **Sensor Bus:** For example, CAN, ASI, Seriplex, LonWorks.

Attack Detection by Anomaly in Electrical Power Systems using Smart Techniques

Previous sections have stressed the importance of SCADA systems in electric power infrastructure, as well as their vulnerability. This section makes a study of the published work in this area and which guided the proposition of anomaly detection model using smart techniques for information systems of electric power systems.

Bases of the Development

Gamez et al., (2000) describe the development of the project SAFEGUARD whose goal is to improve the dependability and survivability of critical infrastructure by monitoring and protection using autonomous agents. In general the security, integrity, and availability goals in critical infrastructure are monitored and maintained by operators. The SAFEGUARD Project uses agent technology to perform the functions of automatic control and to support the operators to make the right decisions at the right time. In its architecture, the project combines knowledge-based detection and behaviour-based detection in a hybrid detection model that levels the existing knowledge and seeks significant deviations from normal operation the system.

Figure 11. Vision MMS network application (SISCO, 2005)

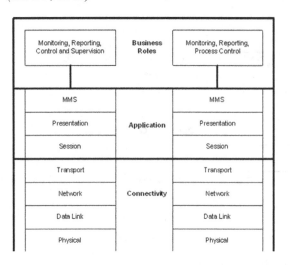

Figure 12. SAFEGUARD project architecture

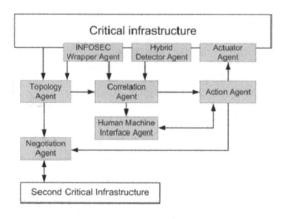

The model is implemented by agents with the data type related to the fields of telecommunications and electric power systems. For example, an agent could be monitoring the IP packets, while another checks timing differences in SCADA systems and another examines the electric network power readings. The detection is designed to be used in lower levels of the structure of the system. The second phase in the identification of the problems is the correlation of this information to form the basis of a combined response. SAFE-GUARD strategy uses distributed agents to carry out this event correlation for the operator. The architecture of the project is presented in Figure 12. This figure highlights the block of the Hybrid Detection agent and the block correlation agent. The Hybrid Detection agent monitors the network data and seeks to identify corruption of information using a combination of methods of detecting signatures and anomalies. The correlation agent collects information from other agents, such as the hybrid detection, makes approximations of assumptions about the state of the system and suggests an appropriate response.

The challenge of this correlation in the field of electrical power systems is the complexity of the system and the large number of possible sce-

narios. Several papers published within the framework of this project involved Queen Mary College, University of London, Aplicaciones em Informática Avanzada, ENEA, Linköping University and Swisscom.

In the work of Bigham et al., (2003), they set out how SCADA systems can be improved by using anomaly detection to identify false values produced by attacks and faults. The paper uses data from the Electric Power System to demonstrate the performance of two anomaly detection methods: induction Invariant and N-Gram. By considering a promising area of research, the authors have used the template to detect anomalies in the data flow and control signals of the SCADA system, rather than monitor the behaviour of the system through sequences of function calls and connections between the machines.

The model chosen has the advantage of detecting unknown attacks and malicious actions of people inside the organisation, although it can generate many false alarms if not handled carefully. The techniques described in the paper are parts of the IST SAFEGUARD project (Gamez et al., 2000) and they were incorporated inside of agents that are used to detect and repair anomalies within large and complex critical infrastructures.

The two techniques discussed in the text are used to model SCADA systems in electric power system networks: a technique treats the data as text and learns the normal patterns displayed by the text (N-Gram). The other technique treats the data as numbers and searches for invariants, such as mathematical relationships between numbers (Induction Invariant). The N-Gram technique was modified to be applied to data from power electric systems (Manning & Schütze, 1999). Rather than tolerate errors in electric power systems it is necessary to detect them. In electrical measures, lack of a decimal point or the exchange of the signal measured value results in an entirely different reading. This technique is very tolerant to error because it is essentially a statistical technique that measures the distributions of N-Gram in the data.

The technique of the Inducing Invariant constructs the normal data template looking for relationships between different readings. These relationships are expressed as invariants, for example, facts that must always maintain the current context. On the data present in electrical networks, this model is particularly effective, because much data is interrelated in a systematic way. Viaload flow application, the measures of active and reactive powers for a network of 6 bars were calculated and the total system loads for a given annual cycle using the specification of the network of 24 bars test("*IEEE Reliability Test System*"). This produced 8736 files containing network reads for every hour of every day of the year.

To test the rate of false positive of anomaly detectors, one among ten of these files was chosen and then the techniques of N-Gram and Invariant Induction were used to learn the normal model of the network. Next was introduced from 1 to 44 errors, such as exchange of signal, move the decimal point and an exchange of digits randomly, in each of the selected files. The ability to identify errors by two techniques was evaluated. Two experiments were conducted using two techniques: the first experiment measured the false positive rates and actual values per file. The second experiment measured the ability to identify true errors

in each file corrupted. Both techniques have been successful in the first experiment. N-Gram identified 19.8% with 1% false positive rate. 19.1% of invariant induction identified corrupted files with a 4% false positive rate. In the second experiment using the technique of N-Gram proved to be best when used to identify a small number of errors within each file. However when the number of errors increased, false positive rates became meaningless.

The induction invariant performed this task with better results, to identify corrupt lines within files. The results of these tests suggest that the best way to detect anomalies in electric power systems is to combine more than one anomaly detection technique. An effective way of accomplishing this is suggested in Bigham et al. (2005), where the authors use a Bayesian network to correlate the outputs with other data sources. This would reduce the number of false positives and reduce the errors.

The work of Martinelli et al., (2004) proposes a model to monitor and protect electrical power systems using learning techniques of the normal behaviour of the system at the level of substations and indicating a condition of abnormality through the use of alarm signals. The techniques described in the paper are part of the project "SAFEGUARD (Gamez et al., 2000). The paper proposes to build a system capable of performing online monitoring in substations which are part of an electric power system, to read measurements of RTUs and to inform the occurrence of anomalous events through an anomaly detector. One of the major difficulties encountered in monitoring large critical infrastructure is the nonlinear characteristic of its behaviour, forcing the use of numerical methods that consume time and resources and are not suitable for online monitoring.

According to the authors the peculiarities presented by the electrical power systems and the specific features of the problem suggest the use of neural networks for the continuous monitoring of data collected by SCADA systems. The model uses a *self-encoder* for each substation. The *self*-encoder is a *Self-associative Neural Network Encoder* which presents 2 main features: the self-associative and the bottleneck-layer. Due to the particularities of each substation in terms of its components, geographic location, function of transmission and/or distribution, specific training is necessary for each neural network deployed. The architecture of anomaly detection system proposed is presented in Figure 13. The pre-processor function organises the data for each *self-encoder* in sliding time windows. The *self-encoder* properly trained is able to reproduce the set of data considered normal behaviour.

The post-processing through the technique of "*novelty assessment*" does not use training to inform the learning system (Markou & Singh, 2003). In this technique, "negative" entries are recognised as being of a different nature – abnormal-("*novel*") compared with positive entries, considered normal and who are more familiar, because they belong to the class that was used for training. In this way "*novelty detection*" differs from other conventional techniques of classification, because it attempts to recognize the right sample concept rather than distinguish it between samples of both classes (Japkowicz, Myers & Gluck, 1995).

Threshold values are defined for the normal behaviour of the system and used to indicate the occurrence of an abnormal condition or not indicated by an alarm. The experimental results were conducted by implementing the IEEE electrical system model RTS-96 (Grigg et al., 1999) in a simulator of electrical networks. The training, using an algorithm of "*back-propagation*" took 72 hours, consisting of 432 training patterns. To test the self-encoder with non-normal values were made the following modifications to the original data set: introduction of random noise on each vector measures, changes in the format of the demand curve and load changes in the network topology or electrical components.

These changes aim to simulate errors in the sensor measurements or intentional data corruption, intentional faults or not, in the electric network components, interruption of transmission lines and demand trend of unexpected load. The results showed that the proposed model detected successfully the simulated anomalies. After training of data relating to the normal activity of the components, the *self-encoder* became able to map the system behaviour.

A new class of attacks, called *false data injection attacks*, against state estimation in electric power grids is described in the work of Liu et al (2009). In this case an attacker can exploit the configuration of a power system to launch attacks to successfully introduce *arbitrary* errors into certain state variables while bypassing existing techniques for bad measurement detection. The authors demonstrated the success of these attacks through simulation using IEEE test systems. The results indicate that security protection of the electric power grid must be revisited when there are potentially malicious attacks.

In the reference Dawson (2009) the author investigated attacks against state estimation algorithms that are undetected given currently-used fault detection algorithms and proposed new detection algorithms that are better for identifying false data injection attacks.

The work of Kosut et al (2010) describes malicious attacks against power system state estimation. For the authors if an adversary is able to manipulate the measurements taken at several meters in a power system, it can sometimes change the state estimate at the control centre in a way that will never be detected by classical bad data detectors. However, in cases when the adversary is not able to perform this attack, it was not clear what attacks might look like. An easily computable heuristic is developed to find adversarial attacks in all cases.

In Xie et al (2010), the authors presented a class of cyber attack, named *false data injection attack*, against the state estimation in deregulated

Figure 13. Anomaly detector architecture

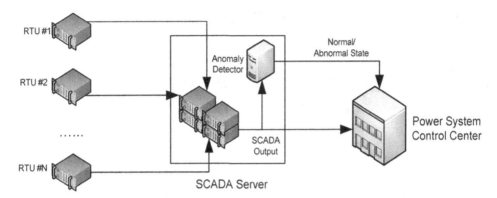

electricity markets. With the knowledge of the system configuration, they demonstrated that such attacks will circumvent the bad data measurement detection equipped in present SCADA systems, and lead to profitable financial misconduct such as virtual bidding against the ex-post locational marginal price (LMP).

Data Communication in SCADA Systems

SCADA systems are used to collect data from sensors and instruments located in remote locations and transmit the same to a control centre for the purposes of control and supervision. These systems can monitor and control hundreds to hundreds of thousands of points of input/output. The RTUs and PLCs are located between the remote sensors and control centre with the function of collecting data from sensors and field devices, as shown in Figure 14. The sensors are analogue or digital input/output that are not easily transmitted over long distances. Thus the RTUs and PLCs are used to digitise and pack signals from the sensors so that they can be transmitted digitally through the use of industrial communication protocols over long distances. Some examples of these protocols are Modbus, DNP 3.0, ICCP. The standard protocols used by the physical layer are of the serial type, such as RS485, RS422 and RS232.

The SCADA system is located in an industrial PC, or workstation, containing the Human-Machine Interface (HMI) software. This software is used to read the remote stations and store the data collected in a centralised database. This way data acquisition is initiated first by RTUs or PLCs, reading the input fields connected to them. Once the data is read they are transmitted to the workstation where the data will be processed. There are 3 types of data collected: analogue, digital, and pulse (counter).

Communication employed by the SCADA system uses several physical means, such as public lines, dial-up lines, fibre optics, ADSL, etc, and wireless media such as radio, spread spectrum, mobile (GSM), WLAN, or satellite, as shown in Figure 15.

The IEC 61850 *"Communication Networks and Systems in Substations"* (Baigent, Adamiak, &

Figure 14. Communication model in SCADA systems

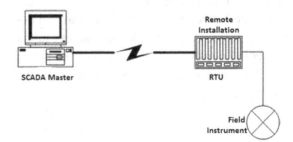

Figure 15. UTR Model using integrated radio

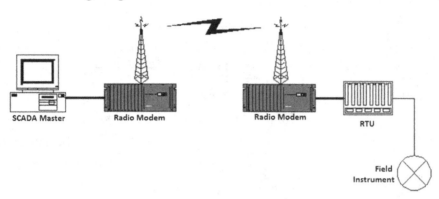

Mackienwicz, 2004) defines a standard model of communication architecture in substations using Ethernet technology and the Internet, as shown in Figure 16. In the process layer level, data from current and voltage sensors, as well as state information of the equipment, are collected and digitised through "*Merging Units*" (MUs). From these units, the data are transferred to the layer of "Substation" using Ethernet technology with redundancy.

Figure 17, taken from the reference (Conte de Leon et al., 2002), presents the example of a control system of a hypothetical substation. This figure shows the various connections between power equipment such as transformers, circuit breakers, and relays connected to their respective RTUs, through local network connection or serial transmission. These RTU devices are connected to the Main Substation Controller. In turn, the substation controller is connected to the SCADA Master using dedicated fibre optic, or via corporate network through the connection to the Internet network (TCP/IP) using WAN technology. Through vulnerability analysis study there are several attack routes where internal and external attackers could use to gain access to the substation power equipment, such as the public telephone network, the corporate network, the wireless network, etc.

In the structure shown in Figure 17, there are many scenarios where the attackers (external or internal) could gain access to the RTUs or IEDs and therefore to the substation power equipment and the collected measurements.

Anomaly Detector Algorithm

The basis of the anomaly intrusion detector proposed is the Rough Sets algorithm. In this section it is introduced a brief description of the algorithm and how it is used to implement the intrusion detector.

The Rough Set theory was proposed in 1982 by Z. Pawlak (Pawlak, 1982). The fundamental idea of this theory is to find a set representing the examples (data set) through two approximation sets named the upper approximation set and the lower approximation set. Thus, through the knowledge available in the examples, the upper approximation set must be reduced; while through this same knowledge the lower approximation set should be expanded. In this work, the idea is to represent the final set through a set of production rules that can detect intrusions into the system.

An information system may be defined as being a 4-tuple as $K = (U, R, \rho, V)$, where U is a finite set of objects (the search space), R is a finite set of attributes (strings, state of the equipment and lines,

Figure 16. Model communication in substation by the standard IEC61850 (Baigent, Adamiak, & Mackienwicz, 2004)

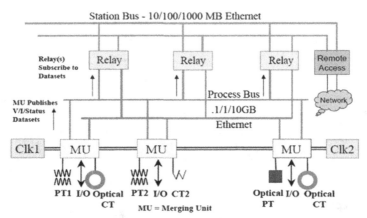

among others), V is the domain of each attribute of R, and ρ is a total function (called information function) that defines the following application: ρ: R × U → V, i.e. the examples.

The concept of information system is not exclusive of Rough Set Theory and has extensive use in Information Theory. One of the major contributions of Rough Set Theory is to automatically transform data in knowledge (Pawlak, 1991).

The upper and lower approximation sets are denoted by $\bar{R}X$ and $\underline{R}X$. So the three regions are created and called: positive region, $POS_R(X)$, boundary region, $BN_R(X)$, and negative region, $NEG_R(X)$, as shown in Figure 18. Below, these regions are defined mathematically.

Let the $X \subseteq U$, R an equivalent relationship, and $K = (U, \{R\})$, a knowledge base. In this way, two subsets can be associated with:

1. **R-Lower:** $\underline{R}X = \cup \{Y \in U/R: Y \subseteq X\}$
2. **R-Upper:** $\bar{R}X = \cup \{Y \in U/R: Y \cap X \neq \emptyset\}$

These definitions indicate that all elements that belong to $\underline{R}X$ set (lower approximation) with certainty belong to the solution sought; while the elements $\bar{R}X$ set (upper approximation) may belong to the solution. Also, the regions $POS_R(X)$, $BN_R(X)$, and $NEG_R(X)$ express:

3. $POS_R(X) = \underline{R}X \Rightarrow$ all points in this region are member of X
4. $NEG_R(X) =) \ U - \bar{R}X \Rightarrow$ all points in this region are certainly not member of X
5. $BN_R(X) = \bar{R}X - \underline{R}X \Rightarrow$ the points in this region can (or can't) be member of X

There are two important concepts that must be submitted before the presentation of the algorithm, which are reduction set and core set. Let R be a family of equivalent relations. The reduction set of R, $RED(R)$, is defined with a reduced set of relationships that retains the same inductive classification of set R. The core set R, $CORE(R)$, is the set of relationships that appear throughout the reduction of R, i.e. the set of all essential relationships to characterize R.

The main idea of the algorithm is simplifying the set of samples through the following actions:

1. Calculate the core set of the problem;
2. Delete (or replace) a variable using another; and
3. Redefine the problem using new basic categories.

An algorithm that follows the procedure above can be represented by the following steps:

Figure 17. Example of a control System of substation (Conte de Leon et al., 2002)

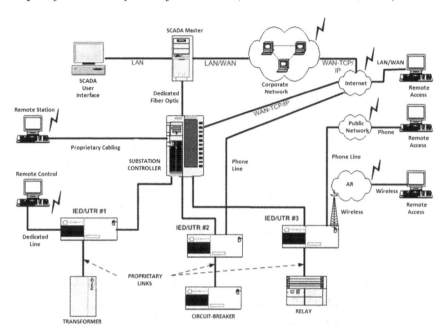

Step 1: Delete the attributes expendable.

Step 2: Compute the core set of each example.

Step 3: Compose the table of examples with the values of reduction.

Step 4: Merge possible redundant examples.

Scenarios of Attacks

Taking into account the Figures17 and 19, the following attack scenario can be drawn:

- IED/RTU # 2 can be considered a potential object of attack because of their Internet connectivity, which allows remote access, either directly via the controller of the substation as via the corporate network.

- If the attacker (internal or external) can access the IED/RTU# 2, two probable situations may occur:
  - Attacker will take control of the circuit breaker;
  - The attacker will change/corrupt the information in the database of the RTU.

In the first case the attacker could block control signals from the SCADA Master and send false confirmations. The operator could think that the switch is closed when it is open, or that it is malfunctioning when it is not. The attacker could also take direct control of the equipment and send control signals to shut it down. The operator attempts to reconnect the equipment could be blocked by a denial of service attack.

Figure 18. Definition of upper and lower approximate sets and their regions of interest

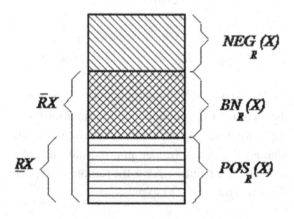

In the second case the attacker could manipulate data readings and corrupt the SCADA Master database. Figure 19 presents the master-slave relationship ("*Master/Outstation*" in DNP3 nomenclature), taken from (Curtis, 2005). The RTU is represented with a dataset, in the form of vectors, coming from the sensors and stored in the local database and commands that are being sent to the output devices. The same procedure occurs on the side of the *master* server, where the server uses these values in its database for specific purposes, such as charts, trend analysis, system equipment status, alarms, etc. The goal of the master server is to keep the database updated. Thus it sends "*request messages*" to the RTU asking for it to return the values from your database. This method is called "*polling*". The RTU responds by sending the contents of your database. For the Brazilian ONS procedures, measurements are made separately and periodically transferred to the operation centres. The transfer period is configurable, and supports periods of at least 4 sec.

As shown in Figure 19 when the RTU # 2 is invaded with a change of DNP3 user code with some sort of "exploit", the collected data could be corrupt and false information would be sent to the SCADA Master.

If the electric power system operator takes any action based on these corrupted information from his SCADA Console User Interface, the whole power grid could be in danger. In short, the database of the SCADA Master does not anymore depict the reality of the Electric Power System. For example, a line could indicate an overload, leading the operator to take steps to turn it off. This manoeuvre, taken as a result of false information, could lead the Electric Power System as a whole to collapse.

In such a way to detect these attack scenarios, it is proposed to implement an anomaly detector to identify and report these threats through an alarm of an attempted attack, as well as the type of attack. The proposed method should model the

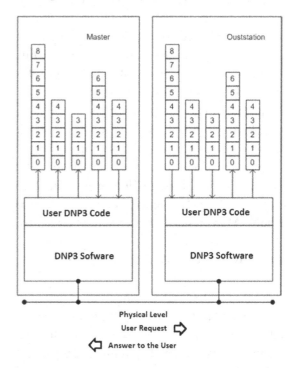

Figure 19. "Master-Outstation" relationship in DNP3 protocol (Curtis, 2005)

normal dataflow and control operations within the SCADA system through intelligent techniques to detect anomalies produced by changes in information gathered from the electrical power system.

Anomaly Detector Architecture

The proposed solution for the problem of detecting anomalies, presented in the previous attack scenarios, uses intelligent techniques to extract knowledge of the SCADA system. The approach proposed is divided into 2 stages. The first stage, named the knowledge extractor, generates a set of rules that determine the normal or abnormal system behaviour. This set of rules is obtained through the information collected in an offline SCADA data treatment, such as measurements from different parts of the system, state of the switches and the transformer taps, circuit breakers status, etc. and by the analysis of an expert, to determine its normality or not. In the second step, the data from the real-time RTU passes through this set of rules, thereby defining normalcy or not of the collected information. The diagram in Figure 20 describes the proposed model. In this step the anomaly detector established by the rules previously extracted should recognise the condition and may also undertake the abnormality with some kind of classification of the type of attack occurred for example, when considering the attack scenarios proposed in the previous section. The alarm condition of Figure 17 indicates whether the state of the circuit breaker is maliciously altered or if the SCADA master database has been corrupted.

Implementation of Anomaly Detector

In the face to the large volume of information in the SCADA Master database, the proposed model reduces the number of input variables and the number of cases, providing a more compact set of rules for the anomaly detector. The proposed model is based on the Rough Set theory, and has the following main advantages:

- Reduction of the number of rules without reducing system knowledge base;
- Dynamic behaviour, because the rules that have not been informed by the expert can be extracted from the system;
- Reduction of the necessity for large computational resources and large memory capacity.

The main disadvantage is the necessity of an expert to classify the system data.

A database control centre, represented by the SCADA Master in Figure 13, composed of a set of values related to the measurements collected by the RTU/IED. These values are presented in Table 1. The operational state of the electrical power system relies on four hypothetical elements:

Table 1. Reduced database SCADA master

U	Attributes				S
	A	B	C	D	
1	0	57	82	1,07	A
2	0	37	32	0,97	A
3	1	0	87	0,95	A
4	1	72	31	1,07	A
5	0	28	39	1,02	A
6	0	42	82	1,07	A
7	0	52	59	1,01	N
8	1	62	67	1,04	A
9	0	57	45	0,99	N
10	0	45	58	1,00	N
11	0	32	57	0,94	N
12	0	0	57	1,08	A
13	1	58	87	1,03	A
14	0	58	56	1,07	A
15	0	25	57	1,03	N
16	0	56	54	1,08	A
17	1	59	72	1,08	A
18	0	32	0	0,93	A
19	0	32	45	0,94	N
20	1	72	67	0,96	A
21	0	57	45	1,01	N
22	0	32	45	0,94	N
23	0	29	43	1,08	A
24	1	0	72	0,95	A
25	1	57	79	1,07	A
26	0	31	43	0,99	N
27	0	32	42	0,94	N
28	0	17	32	0,92	A
29	0	23	22	1,00	A
30	0	23	57	0,91	N

the status of the circuit breaker, the transmission capacity of the lines B and C and the voltage on D Bus. These attributes are represented by the columns A, B, C, D of Table 1 and correspond to:

- The state of the circuit breaker: 0 (closed) and 1 (open);
- The values of transmission lines B and C are percentages of the actual power flow according to their maximum capacities, in percentages;
- The bus voltage D is expressed in PU.

The classification of each condition to the operational state of the electrical power system, S, is made according to the expert in two possible outputs: Normal (N) and Abnormal (A). The ab-

Figure 20. Knowledge extraction algorithm using rough set theory

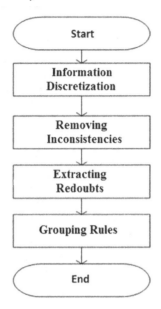

normal level might represent malicious actions in the RTU/IED, according to the attack scenarios proposed previously.

The algorithm that provides the conditions for the reduction is represented by the diagram in Figure 20.

The information discretisation process (first step), considered the following operational ranges for each attribute:

- **Attribute A:** 0 and 1
- **Attributes B and C:**
  - Between 0 and 40: L
  - Between 40 and 60: M
  - Between 60 and 100: H
- **Attribute D:**
  - Between 0 and 0.95: L
  - Between 0.95 and 1.05: N
  - Above 1.05: H

Table 2 represents the final step of the process of extracting knowledge, using the algorithm of Figure 20. This table represents the set of rules that form the knowledge base from the original table. This knowledge base can be used now by an expert system that will analyse the information in the database of the SCADA Master and detect whether or not an attack occurred, caused by the change of information from the SCADA Master database.

The rules specified for this case based on the Table 3 are the following:

IF C = H THEN OUTPUT = A;

IF D = H THEN OUTPUT = A;

IF C = L THEN OUTPUT = A;

IF C = M AND D = N THEN OUTPUT = N;

IF C = M AND D = L THEN OUTPUT = N.

Example for a Six-Buses Electric Power System Test

This section presents an example of the anomaly detection algorithm for detecting malicious actions in SCADA systems, using a six-buses test system, described in Wood & Wollenberg, (1996) and shown in Figure 21. Some results are carried out and an analysis of the responses obtained is made.

Methodology

In this case, a test environment containing some key components present in a control centre has been created with: load-flow, SCADA system and state-estimator. In addition, the proposed

Table 2. Reduced set of examples

Attributes				Output
A	B	C	D	S
-	-	H	-	A
-	-	-	H	A
-	-	L	-	A
-	-	M	N	N
-	-	M	L	N

Table 3. Summary of the results of the test: Anomaly detector module versus state-estimator module

IMW4 Pu	IMW6 pu	LINE 4 TO 1 MW	LINE 4 TO 2 MW	LINE 4 TO 5 MW	LINE 6 TO 2 MW	LINE 6 TO 3 MW	LINE 6 TO 5 MW	STATUS ANOMALY DETECTOR	TYPES OF INTRODUCED ERRORS
-0.63	-0.73	-39.83	-28.75	5.58	-27.17	-43.82	-2.02	Normal	Without error
+0.63	-0.73	-21.41	2.92	15.91	-33.59	-43.58	-2.54	Abnormal	Change signal
-0.53	-0.83	-37.75	-22.69	7.44	-31.44	-47.32	-4.24	Normal	Without error
-0.53	+0.83	-36.69	-31.06	5.85	-4.3	-10.45	13.77	Abnormal	Change signal
-0.77	-0.61	-43.38	-36.76	3.13	-22	-39.62	0.62	Normal	Without error
0.77	+0.61	-20.03	-4.36	14.59	-10	-12.8	13.28	Abnormal	Change signal
-0.71	-0.52	-37.46	-36.69	3.15	-18.47	-36.45	2.92	Normal	Without error
-0.71	+0.52	-36.8	-41.9	2.14	-1.37	-13.35	14.26	Abnormal	Change signal
-0.45	-0.95	-37.32	-16.9	9.23	-36.48	-51.54	-6.98	Out-of-Range	Without error
+0.45	-0.95	-24.17	5.8	16.63	-41.03	-51.38	-7.36	Abnormal	Change signal
-0.83	-0.78	-51.62	-35.05	3.69	-28.8	-45.61	-3.57	Normal	Without error
-0.83	+0.78	-50.68	-42.91	2.18	-3.27	-10.97	13.34	Abnormal	Change signal
-0.56	-0.88	-40.82	-22.65	7.47	-33.41	-49.09	-5.49	Normal	Without error
0.56	+0.88	-23.29	-3.39	15.01	-10.54	-9.75	13.14	Abnormal	Change signal
-0.56	-0.56	-30.87	-30.25	5.11	-20.41	-37.84	2.25	Normal	Without error
+0.56	-0.56	-14.3	-2.24	14.26	-26.12	-37.62	1.79	Abnormal	Change signal
-0.6699	-0.8599	-45.85	-27.22	6.18	-32.38	-48.4	-5.21	Normal	Without error
-0.6699	+0.8599	-44.79	-35.89	4.43	-4.29	-10.21	13.43	Abnormal	Change signal
-0.601	-0.7661	-39.4	-26.82	6.17	-28.69	-45.88	-2.83	Normal	Without error
-0.601	+0.7661	-38.48	-34.54	4.7	-3.61	-11.05	13.8	Abnormal	Change signal

rule extractor module and the anomaly detector is implemented using the extracted rules. The architecture of this test environment is presented in Figure 22. This figure is composed of the following components:

- **Load-Flow Computation Module:** This module is used to compute the power flow through the transmission lines of the system.
- **SCADA Simulator Module:** This module mimics the functions performed by the SCADA. The idea is to simulate the electrical network, compute bus voltages, total the power flows and system loads and then associate them with the meters previously specified. It was adapted from programs in Wood & Wollenberg, (1996).
- **State-Estimator Module:** This module adapted from Wood & Wollenberg, (1996) is used to perform the process of state-estimation functions. A successful cyber-

attack needs to pass through this module without substantial modification.

- **Rule Extractor Module:** This module is used to create the knowledge base expressed by rules, using the proposed algorithm based on the Rough Set theory.
- **Anomaly Detection Module:** This module uses the rules created in the Rule Extractor Module to determine the state of system using data from the SCADA system.

So that the electrical power system can operate correctly, it is necessary that all data of voltage and power flow, collected by SCADA system, keep inside their security boundaries. The state-estimator process consists in obtaining these quantities in real-time (Lambert-Torres et al., 1992). This process assigns a value to an unknown state variable based on the measures obtained from that system in accordance with certain criteria. This process tries to rebuild the system measures in case of measurement errors,

Figure 21. Six-buses power system (Wood & Wollenberg, 1996)

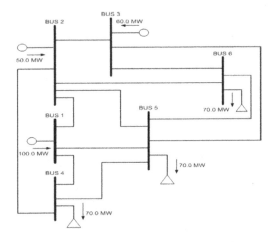

data loss and/or corruption. This model, however, does not address the problem of providing the normal or abnormal state assessment system, and, in some cases, it could hide evidence of an attack or other anomalies. This is an assumption of risk, since in general configuration errors occur, and there is always the possibility of an attacker to be between the control centre and the electrical power system.

Case 1: Corrupting Power Values

In this test, a data set test was generated through the corruption of the values produced by SCADA Simulator Module. According to Wood & Wollenberg, (1996) the state-estimator process is subject to three types of errors: errors in analogue measures (rough errors); errors due to erroneous information regarding states of switches or circuit breakers (topological errors); and errors caused by erroneous information of some system parameter (parameter errors). According to Jin et al., (2006), there is the possibility of 5 types of errors: "bias" constant with deviations normally distributed, the loss of the decimal point (mantissa), signal switching, fixed value for a fixed period of time and random value for a fixed period of time. These 5 types of errors are attributed to the fact

that electrical measures may be changed due to noise, attacks, software errors, failure of meters, EMI and transmission errors.

The ability of the anomaly detection model proposed to identify normal and abnormal conditions is evaluated in relation to state-estimator module capacity to provide a reasonable result, even considering that the data has been corrupted somehow.

In this test, the SCADA Simulator Module uses a set of 29 meters represented in Figure 23. The location and the type of meter (voltage or power) are specified in a specific file of SCADA Simulator module meters, as shown in Figure 22. As shown in Figure 17, in a real environment these meters are connected to RTUs which send the collected data to the control centre, where the operator parses the results produced by the State-Estimator Module and takes the necessary actions to keep the system operating conditions.

To build the knowledge base of the first test, initially, 25 examples are generated by varying the value of the load in buses 4 and 6. The range of variation of active power values in absolute value is $0.5 \leq$ active power ≤ 0.9 pu, in intervals of 0.05 pu. In the test environment, represented in Figure 22, these examples are assembled by the SCADA Simulator Module. Each example consists of 57 values, each one refers to a measure carried out by meters specified in the configuration file of meters. Then the knowledge base totalises 64 examples, which 39 examples are generated from the corruption of the sign on the values of active power. To facilitate the preliminary analysis of this first test case, the errors are applied only in buses 4 and 6. The type of error introduced involved only the switching of the sign of active power values in the output file of the SCADA Simulator Module, as shown in the list of Figure 24. The values pointed to were initially -8.9991317636e-01 and -6.9994161078e-01. This file contains one sample of the knowledge base.

Regarding the file, besides the modification of the active and reactive power values, indicated

Figure 22. Environment for tests of the proposed anomaly detector

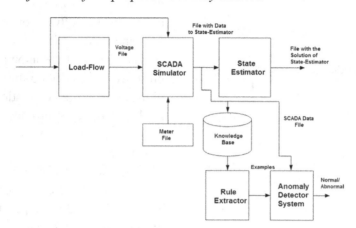

by the letter I, there is also the possibility of changing the values of voltage (indicated by the letters V and A) and the active and reactive power flows in lines, indicated by the letter F.

The knowledge base is established by 64 samples, and each sample with 57 values. As shown in the test environment in Figure 22, these 64 examples are handled by the Rules Extraction Module generating the rules shown in Figure 25.

Figure 23. Six-buses power system with meters (Wood & Wollenberg, 1996)

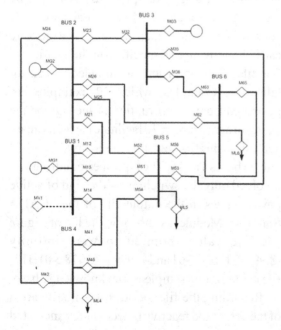

These rules show as well how the data reduction occurred: the Rule Extractor Module extracted 8 rules for a total of 3648 samples.

In order to evaluate this generated rule set, a test with 20 examples is created and subjected to the same anomaly detection module. The type of error introduced into the file generated by the module is an exchange of signal for all examples. Table 3 lists the comparison of the results obtained by the Anomaly Detector Module and the State-Estimation Module. The values IMW4 and IMW6 correspond to the load values in buses 4 and 6, respectively. The flows on lines 4-1, 4-2, 4-5, 6-2, 6-3 and 6-5 are obtained by State-Estimation Module. Each group of 2 examples shows a normal entry and an entry corrupted by changing a sign. The output of the anomaly detector shows 3 possible states: normal, abnormal and out-of-range. The last output state expresses out of range values for the examples generated in the knowledge base. For example, values as-0.45 pu for IMW4 and -0.95 pu for IMW6 are outside of predefined initial range: abs (0.5 pu) $\leq$ active power $\leq$ abs (0.9 pu). It is very important the correct generation of examples that make up the knowledge base, so that such errors do not occur. This is only an example to demonstrate the validity

Figure 24. File with the first attack in the active power values of buses 4 and 6 – type of attack: inversion of signal

```
SIXBUS POWER FLOW SAMPLE SYSTEM
-----------------------------------
6
11
LINE    1    2    1.00000E-01    2.00000E-01    2.00000E-02
LINE    1    4    5.00000E-02    2.00000E-01    2.00000E-02
LINE    1    5    8.00000E-02    3.00000E-01    3.00000E-02
LINE    2    3    5.00000E-02    2.50000E-01    3.00000E-02
LINE    2    4    5.00000E-02    1.00000E-01    1.00000E-02
LINE    2    5    1.00000E-01    3.00000E-01    2.00000E-02
LINE    2    6    7.00000E-02    2.00000E-01    2.50000E-02
LINE    3    5    1.20000E-01    2.60000E-01    2.50000E-02
LINE    3    6    2.00000E-02    1.00000E-01    1.00000E-02
LINE    4    5    2.00000E-01    4.00000E-01    4.00000E-02
LINE    5    6    1.00000E-01    3.00000E-01    3.00000E-02
V    1         1.0500000000E+00    1.000E-04
A    1         0.0000000000E+00    1.000E-04
I    1         1.2926382831E+00    1.000E-02         2.5547635626E-01    1.000E-02
I    2         4.9990173678E-01    1.000E-02         1.0004148677E+00    1.000E-02
I    3         5.9995430599E-01    1.000E-02         5.9999305592E-01    1.000E-02
I    4        +8.9991317636E-01    1.000E-02        -7.0000930338E-01    1.000E-02
I    5        -6.9994125684E-01    1.000E-02        -6.9999348948E-01    1.000E-02
I    6        +6.9994161078E-01    1.000E-02        -6.9998235508E-01    1.000E-02
F    1    2    3.5417726409E-01    1.000E-02        -1.5040670241E-01    1.000E-02
F    1    4    5.4460436822E-01    1.000E-02         2.4278040036E-01    1.000E-02
F    1    5    3.9385665081E-01    1.000E-02         1.6310265830E-01    1.000E-02
F    2    1   -3.4130497589E-01    1.000E-02         1.3231241138E-01    1.000E-02
F    2    3    1.2609734643E-02    1.000E-02        -6.7821822666E-03    1.000E-02
F    2    4    4.1365251965E-01    1.000E-02         4.7143716966E-01    1.000E-02
F    2    5    1.5270749550E-01    1.000E-02         1.8889744167E-01    1.000E-02
F    2    6    2.6223696287E-01    1.000E-02         2.1455002730E-01    1.000E-02
F    3    2   -1.2571647608E-02    1.000E-02        -5.7969124298E-02    1.000E-02
```

Introduced Errors: inversion of signal – to +

of the proposal. In real cases the knowledge base is extremely large and produces a few variations.

The graphic of Figure 26 shows a comparison of values obtained through the State-Estimator Module for the first two examples in Table 3. In this case the value of the load of the bus 4 is inverted (from -0.63 to +0.63), signifying a change in given originally generated by the Load Flow Module and by SCADA Simulator Module. This modification means that the values that are delivered to the State-Estimator are corrupted.

Observing the graphic of Figure 25, the power flow values of transmission lines 6-2, 6-3 and 6-5 are virtually unchanged, even in the presence of errors. However the lines 4-1, 4-2 and 4-5 have presented disparate values with respect to the original value. If, for example, the nominal capacities of lines 4-1, 4-2 and 4-5 are 50 MW, 40 MW and 10 MW, respectively; the line 4-5 would be roughly 60% beyond their nominal capacity (i.e. 15.91/10 = 1.59). If the operator

were to consider these results, this would lead them to think of an overhead line capacity in 4-5. In this case they could adopt measures to solve the "false problem", endangering the stability of the system. Unlike, the Anomaly Detector qualified this example as abnormal, pointing to a possible corruption of the values read from the SCADA system.

Another example can be seen in Figure 27. In this case the lines 4-1, 4-2 and 4-5 present compatible values between the original case and the corrupted case. However, the lines 6-2, 6-3 and 6-5 presented disparate values between the original case and the corrupted case.

In the same way, if the nominal capacities of transmission lines 6-2, 6-3 and 6-5 are 40 MW, 50 MW, and 10 MW, respectively, the value displayed by the line 6-5 would be around 37% beyond nominal capacity (i.e. 13.37/10 = 1.37). This fact could lead to a wrong decision by the operator, if it is based on the values delivered by

Figure 25. Rule obtained from the attack of inversion of signal in buses 4 and 6

- If (Active Power in Bus4 >=-0.62)&(Active Power in Bus4 <-0.3)&(Active Power in Bus6 >=-0.9)&(Active Power in Bus6 <-0.6) then (RESULT = NORMAL)

- If (Active Power in Bus4 >=-0.9)&(Active Power in Bus4 <-0.6)&(Active Power in Bus6 >=-0.6)&(Active Power in Bus6 < -0.3) then (RESULT = NORMAL)

- If (Active Power in Bus4 >=-0.6)&(Active Power in Bus4 < -0.3)&(Active Power in Bus6 >=-0.6)&(Active Power in Bus6 < -0.6) then (RESULT = NORMAL)

- If (Active Power in Bus4 >=-0.9)&(Active Power in Bus4 < -0.6)&(Active Power in Bus6 >=-0.9)&(Active Power in Bus6 <-0.6) then (RESULT = NORMAL)

- If (Active Power in Bus4 >= 0.3)&(Active Power in Bus4 < 0.6) then (RESULT = ABNORMAL)
- If (Active Power in Bus6 >=0.6)&(Active Power in Bus6 < 0.95) then (RESULT = ABNORMAL)
- If (Active Power in Bus6 >= 0.3)&(Active Power in Bus6 < 0.6) then (RESULT = ABNORMAL)
- If (Active Power in Bus4 >= 0.6)&(Active Power in Bus4 < 0.95) then (RESULT = ABNORMAL)

Figure 26. Case 1: IMW4 =-0.63 and IMW6= -0.73   *Figure 27. Case 1: IMW4 =-0.53 and IMW6 = -0.83*

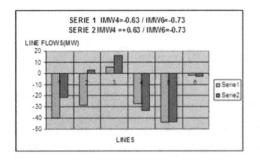

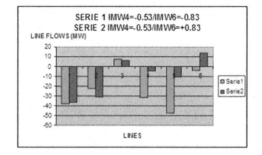

Figure 28. Rule obtained from the attack of extended operating range in buses 4 and 6

- If (Active Power in Bus4 >=-0.7333) & (Active Power in Bus4 < -0.3667) & (Active Power in Bus6 >=-0.7333) & (Active Power in Bus6 <-0.-0.3667)then (RESULT=NORMAL)
- If (Active Power in Bus4 >=-1.1) & (Active Power in Bus4 < -0.7333)&(Active Power in Bus6 >= -0.7333)&(Active Power in Bus6 < -0.3667) then (RESULT=NORMAL)
- If (Active Power in Bus4 >=-0.7333) & (Active Power in Bus4 < -0.3667) & (Active Power in Bus6 >=-1.1) & (Active Power in Bus6 < -0.7333) then (RESULT=NORMAL)
- If (Active Power in Bus4 >=-1.1) & (Active Power in Bus4 < -0.7333) & (Active Power in Bus6 >= -1.1) & (Active Power in Bus6 <-0.7333) then (RESULT=NORMAL)
- If (Active Power in Bus4 >= 0.3667) & (Active Power in Bus4 < 07333) then (RESULT=ABNORMAL)
- If (Active Power in Bus6 >=0.3667) & (Active Power in Bus6 < 1.101) then (RESULT=ABNORMAL)
- If (Active Power in Bus4 >= 0.7333) & (Active Power in Bus4 < 1.101) then (RESULT=ABNORMAL)
- If (Active Power in Bus6 >= 0.7333) & (Active Power in Bus6 < 1.101) then (RESULT=ABNORMAL)
- If (Active Power in Bus4 >=-0.3667) & (Active Power in Bus4 < 0.0) & (Active Power in Bus6>= -0.7333) & (Active Power in Bus 6<-0.3667) then (RESULT=NORMAL) & (Active Power in Bus4 < -0.3667) & (Active Power in Bus6>=-03667) & (Active Power in Bus6 < 0.0) then (RESULT=NORMAL)
- If (Active Power in Bus4 >=-0.3667) & (Active Power in Bus4 < 0.0) & (Active Power in Bus6>= -0.3667) & (Active Power in Bus6 <0.0) then (RESULT=NORMAL)
- If (Active Power in Bus4 >= 0.0) & (Active Power in Bus4 < 0.3667) then (RESULT=ABNORMAL)
- If (Active Power in Bus6 >= 0.0) & (Active Power in Bus6 < 0.3667) then (RESULT=ABNORMAL)
- If (Active Power in Bus4 >=-0.3667) & (Active Power in Bus4 < 0.0) & (Active Power in Bus6 >=-1.1) & (Active Power in Bus 6 <-0.7333) then(RESULT=NORMAL)
- If (Active Power in Bus4 >=-1.1) & (Active Power in Bus4 <-0.7333) & (Active Power in Bus 6 >= -0.3667) & (Active Power in Bus6 < 0.0) then (RESULT=NORMAL)

the State-Estimator Module. In turn the Anomaly Detection Module has detected that this example shows an abnormal condition, indicating that there was some form of corruption of values.

Case 2: Extending Operating Range

The second test case expands the operational ranges of active power values of buses 4 and 6. The new sample file has 162 examples with values ranging from 0.3 to 1.1 pu in intervals of 0.05 pu. The error introduced in the output file of the SCADA Simulator Module again involved the exchange of signal. The knowledge base generated for this new case contains 162 examples, each one

Figure 29. Results of the classification made by the new set of rules

```
» rulesdb
Input:    -0.630    -0.730    Result: NORMAL
Input:    -0.530    -0.830    Result: NORMAL
Input:    -0.770    -0.610    Result: NORMAL
Input:    -0.710    -0.520    Result: NORMAL
Input:    -0.450    -0.950    Result: NORMAL
Input:    -0.830    -0.780    Result: NORMAL
Input:    -0.560    -0.880    Result: NORMAL
Input:    -0.560    -0.560    Result: NORMAL
Input:    -0.670    -0.860    Result: NORMAL
Input:    -0.601    -0.766    Result: NORMAL
Input:    +0.630    -0.730    Result: ABNORMAL
Input:    -0.530    +0.830    Result: ABNORMAL
Input:    +0.770    +0.610    Result: ABNORMAL
Input:    -0.710    +0.520    Result: ABNORMAL
Input:    +0.450    -0.950    Result: ABNORMAL
Input:    -0.830    +0.780    Result: ABNORMAL
Input:    +0.560    +0.880    Result: ABNORMAL
Input:    +0.560    -0.560    Result: ABNORMAL
Input:    -0.670    +0.860    Result: ABNORMAL
Input:    -0.601    +0.766    Result: ABNORMAL
```

Table 4. Summary of the results of the test: Anomaly detector module versus state-estimator module

IMW4	IMW6	Line 4 to 1	Line 4 to 2	Line 4 to 5	Line 6 to 1	Line 6 to 3	Line 6 to 5	Type of Introduced Error	Detector Status
-0.310	-0.700	-22.19	-17.74	+8.93	-26.59	-42.73	-0.67	Without Error	NORMAL
+0.310	-0.700	-12.99	-2.21	+14.00	-29.73	-42.61	-0.93	Change signal	ABNORMAL
-0.700	-0.430	-34.18	-38.43	+2.61	-14.84	-33.29	+5.13	Without Error	NORMAL
-0.700	+0.430	-33.63	-42.74	+1.78	-0.67	-14.19	+14.52	Change signal	ABNORMAL
-0.480	-0.423	-22.47	-30.55	+5.01	-15.03	-33.03	+5.72	Without Error	NORMAL
+0.480	+0.423	-7.54	-10.93	+12.02	-6.04	-14.01	+14.60	Change signal	ABNORMAL
-0.9799	-0.610	-54.20	-44.56	+0.77	-21.58	-39.65	+0.23	Without Error	NORMAL
-0.9799	+0.610	-53.48	-50.68	-0.41	-1.53	-12.56	+13.49	Change signal	ABNORMAL
-0.999	-0.6399	-56.08	-44.59	+0.77	-22.76	-40.71	-0.52	Without Error	NORMAL
+0.999	-0.6399	-27.12	+5.59	+17.17	-33.16	-40.32	-1.35	Change signal	ABNORMAL
-0.420	-1.078	-39.75	-12.78	+10.52	-41.75	-56.05	-10.0	Without Error	NORMAL
-0.420	+1.078	-38.38	-23.68	+8.47	-6.73	-8.16	+13.32	Change signal	ABNORMAL
-1.045	-1.089	-72.10	-35.94	+3.54	-40.99	-56.56	-11.35	Without Error	NORMAL
+1.045	+1.089	-40.92	+5.81	+18.87	-16.74	-7.74	+11.25	Change signal	ABNORMAL
-1.0678	-1.000	-70.52	-38.87	+2.61	-37.32	-53.42	-9.26	Without Error	NORMAL
+1.0678	-1.000	-39.94	15.14	20.29	-48.26	-53.06	-10.20	Change signal	ABNORMAL
-1.0678	-1.0395	-71.73	-37.95	+2.91	-38.93	-54.82	-10.20	Without Error	NORMAL
+1.0678	+1.0395	-39.94	+5.42	+18.69	-16.48	-8.18	-11.33	Change signal	ABNORMAL
-1.045	-1.0899	-72.10	-35.94	+3.54	-40.99	-56.56	-11.35	Without Error	NORMAL
-1.045	+1.0899	-70.95	-46.95	+1.46	-5.61	-9.19	+12.14	Change signal	ABNORMAL

Figure 30. Other results of the classification made by the new set of rules

```
» rulesdb
              IMW4      IMW6
Input:    -0.310    -0.700    Result: NORMAL
Input:    +0.310    -0.700    Result: ABNORMAL
Input:    -0.700    -0.430    Result: NORMAL
Input:    -0.700    +0.430    Result: ABNORMAL
Input:    -0.480    -0.423    Result: NORMAL
Input:    +0.480    +0.423    Result: ABNORMAL
Input:    -0.980    -0.610    Result: NORMAL
Input:    -0.980    +0.610    Result: ABNORMAL
Input:    -1.000    -0.640    Result: NORMAL
Input:    +1.000    -0.640    Result: ABNORMAL
Input:    -0.420    -1.078    Result: NORMAL
Input:    -0.420    +1.078    Result: ABNORMAL
Input:    -1.045    -1.089    Result: NORMAL
Input:    +1.045    +1.089    Result: ABNORMAL
Input:    -1.068    -1.000    Result: NORMAL
Input:    +1.068    -1.000    Result: ABNORMAL
Input:    -1.068    -1.040    Result: NORMAL
Input:    +1.068    +1.040    Result: ABNORMAL
Input:    -1.045    -1.089    Result: NORMAL
Input:    -1.045    +1.089    Result: ABNORMAL
```

Figure 31. Comparing results without data corruption (series 1) and with corrupted data (series 2)

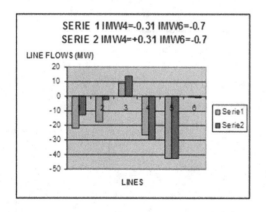

with 57 measures, defined by meters configured in the SCADA Simulator Module.

The examples considered as normal operation were classified as Normal and those who had signal corruption were classified as Abnormal. The Knowledge Base so established has been treated by the Rule Extraction Module, which generated the following rules presented in Figure 28.

A set of 15 rules from 162 examples are generated to represent the knowledge base. Figure 29 shows the same file of test examples of the previous case with this new set of rules.

It is possible to note that the anomaly detection module performed the correct detection of the examples where the signal was corrupted. With the expansion of the operating range of the examples of the knowledge base, the case classified "out-of-range" in the first case has now been correctly classified as a typical example.

A new set of tests is created for this anomaly detection model containing 20 examples as shown in Figure 30. In this output is highlighted the exchange of signals of 1 and 2 measures. These measures correspond to the values of active power at bus 4 (IMW4) and active power at bus 6 (IMW6).

Table 4 summarises the values of the flows in the lines attached to the bars 4 and 6 and obtained via State-Estimator Module.

Figure 32. File with the second attack in the voltage values of buses 4 and 6 – type of attack: change values

```
LINE   1   2   1.00000E-01   2.00000E-01   2.00000E-02
LINE   1   4   5.00000E-02   2.00000E-01   2.00000E-02
LINE   1   5   8.00000E-02   3.00000E-01   3.00000E-02
LINE   2   3   5.00000E-02   2.50000E-01   3.00000E-02
LINE   2   4   5.00000E-02   1.00000E-01   1.00000E-02
LINE   2   5   1.00000E-01   3.00000E-01   2.00000E-02
LINE   2   6   7.00000E-02   2.00000E-01   2.50000E-02
LINE   3   5   1.20000E-01   2.60000E-01   2.50000E-02
LINE   3   6   2.00000E-02   1.00000E-01   1.00000E-02
LINE   4   5   2.00000E-01   4.00000E-01   4.00000E-02
LINE   5   6   1.00000E-01   3.00000E-01   3.00000E-02
V      1       1.0500000000E+00   1.000E-04
V      4       9.9757488501E-01   1.000E-04
V      6       9.8744382133E-01   1.000E-04
A      1       0.0000000000E+00   1.000E-04
A      4      -3.1603824341E-02   1.000E-04
A      6      -7.2849142749E-02   1.000E-04
I      1       6.5929218705E-01   1.000E-02   2.6187809122E-01   1.000E-02
I      2       5.0000093699E-01   1.000E-02   8.8506883860E-01   1.000E-02
```

> Corrupted voltage values in buses 4 and 6 changed from 0.89775 (V4) and 0.8886 (V6) 10 % less than the original value).

Figure 33. Rule obtained from the attack of voltage value changed in buses 4 and 6

- IF (V4>=0.9217) & (V4<0.9977) & (V6>=0.9071) & (V6<1.0007) Result = Normal
- IF (V4>=0.8459) & (V4<0.9217)   Result = Abnormal
- IF (V6)>=0.8135) & (V6<0.9071) Result = Abnormal
- IF(V4>=0.77) & (V4<0.8459)   Result = Abnormal
- IF (V6>=0.72) & (V6<0.8135)   Result = Abnormal

The graphic of Figure 32 presents a comparison of the values obtained through the State-Estimation Module for the first two examples of Table 4. The discrepancy between the values obtained in the two series presented in this graphic for the lines 1-4 (column 1), 4-2 (column 2) and 4-5 (column 3). Considering the nominal capacities for lines 4-1, 4-2 and 4-5 respectively 50 MW, 40 MW, and 10 MW; the line 4-5 would be approximately 40% in addition to its nominal capacity (141/10 = 1.40). The same previous observations are also valid here (See Figure 31).

Case 3: Corrupting Voltage Value

In this new test case, corruption of the voltage values of buses 4 and 6 are addressed and their influence in the proposed operational model is studied. The idea is to change the voltage values in these buses, and check if the anomaly detector classifies this new situation as abnormal and how the state-estimator sees this new situation.

Initially, in the test environment, several examples are produced through the values of active power in buses 4 and 6. The range of this variation is between 0.3 until 1.8 pu, at intervals of 0.1 pu. After that, the voltage values are corrupted in the file produced by SCADA Simulator. The type of error introduced changes the value 10% less than the original value. Figure 32 shows an example with the corrupted values.

A knowledge base with 170 examples, each example with 59 values, is produced. These samples are classified as a normal or abnormal as a case, depending on the values of voltage. This knowledge base is read by the Rule Extractor Module and produced the rules shown in Figure 33.

Figure 34. Results of the classification made by the set of rules for voltage attack

```
» rulesdb1
                    V4            V6
Input:     1     +0.994   +0.985   Result: NORMAL
Input:     2     +0.900   +0.850   Result: ABNORMAL
Input:     3     +0.982   +0.960   Result: NORMAL
Input:     4     +0.882   +0.910   Result: ABNORMAL
Input:     5     +0.929   +0.916   Result: NORMAL
Input:     6     +0.829   +0.906   Result: ABNORMAL
Input:     7     +0.922   +0.926   Result: NORMAL
Input:     8     +0.902   +0.826   Result: ABNORMAL
Input:     9     +0.921   +0.946   Result: ABNORMAL
Input:    10     +0.721   +0.846   Result: ABNORMAL
```

Figure 35. Comparison the output results to state-estimator tests without corruption (series 1) and with corruption (series 2) voltage in buses 4 and 6

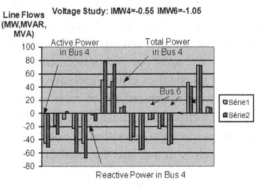

The output for this test case is presented in Figure 34; while the Figure 35 shows the comparison of the output results to state-estimator tests without corruption (series 1) and with voltage corruption in buses 4 and 6 (series 2).

The analysis of the results shows that the reactive power and apparent power Bus 4 has the biggest discrepancies between the original values and corrupted values by changing the value of the voltage. The real power in the two buses not presented variations that might draw attention. This is due to the fact that there is, in this case, the corruption of the voltage magnitude values in buses 4 and 6, unlike previous cases, where there is corruption of active power flow values on lines connected to the buses 4 and 6. It is known that active power suffers strong influence of the angle of the voltage while the reactive power suffers direct action of the magnitude of the voltage.

CONCLUSION

Critical Infrastructures are vital for modern society. In the case of the electric power system, protection is required for a variety of threats and vulnerabilities and their control centre networks must pay special attention of the possibility of cyber attacks. Scenarios demonstrating situations where the security of the electric power system critical infrastructure is in danger are set out. The Anomaly Detection System is an important tool to increase the security of the Control Centre Networks, improving the operator system trustiness of the data coming from the SCADA System. The chapter shows an implementation of a security mechanism called Anomaly Detector Module using a reduced set of rules extracted from an Electrical Data Base Knowledge using Rough Classification Algorithm. The objective of this research is to increase the reliability of the Electric Power System Critical Infrastructure, offering a new tool to increase the confidence of the operator system, in the case of the corruption of the system data by a cyber attack.

This fact will enforce the security objective of the integrity of the Information System. A test environment was implemented and two types of corruption data were successfully tested. The examples demonstrated that the technique has many advantages, such as simplicity of implementation and favourable performance, especially for the SCADA System environment requirements. In a future work it is planned to use a hybrid intelligent algorithm, combining the techniques: fuzzy logic, rough sets, and genetic algorithms. The idea is to combine the three techniques in order to explore the advantages of each one in order to classify the type of detected error.

ACKNOWLEDGMENT

The authors would like to express their thanks to the financial support of this work given by the DAAD and the Brazilian research agencies: CNPq, CAPES, FINEP and FAPEMIG. The authors also would like to thank the reviewers for their comments and suggestions about the chapter.

REFERENCES

Allen, J., Christie, A., Fithen, W., McHugh, J., Pickel, J., & Stoner, E. (2000). *State of the practice of intrusion detection technologies*. Technical Report CMU/SEI-99-TR-028 ESC 99-028, Software Engineering Institute, Carnegie Melon University.

Arango, H. G., & Lambert-Torres, G. (2004). Spatial electric load distribution forecasting using simulated annealing. *WSEAS Transactions on Systems, 1*(3), 14–19.

Axelsson, S. (2000). *Intrusion detection systems: A survey and taxonomy*. Götebrog, Sweden: Department of Computer Engineering, Chalmers University of Technology.

Bace, R., & Mell, P. (2002). *NIST special publication on intrusion detection system*. Retrieved October 15, 2011, from http://csrc.nist.gov/publication/nistpubs/800-31/sp800-31.pdf

Baigent, D., Adamiak, M., & Mackienwicz, R. (2004, November). *IEC 61850 communication networks and systems in substations: An overview for users*. Paper presented at the meeting of the Iberoamerican Symposium on Power System Protection, SIPSEP 2004, Monterrey, Mexico.

Bigham, J., Gamez, D., & Ning, L. (2003, September). *Safeguarding SCADA systems with anomaly detection*. Paper presented at the meeting of the Second International Workshop on Mathematical Methods, Models, and Architectures for Computer Network Security, St. Petersburg, Russia.

Bigham, J., Jin, X., Gamez, D., & Phillips, C. (2005). Hybrid workflow and Bayesian networks to correlate information in protection of large scale critical infrastructures. *Electronic Notes in Theoretical Computer Science*, *121*, 87–99. doi:10.1016/j.entcs.2004.10.009

Conte de Leon, D., Alves-Foss, J., Krings, A., & Oman, P. (2002, November). *Modeling complex control systems to identify remotely accessible devices vulnerable to cyber attack*. Paper presented at the meeting of the ACM Workshop on Scientific Aspects of Cyber Terrorism, SACT 2002, Washington DC, USA.

Curtis, K. (2005). *DNP3 primer*. Revision A, 20 March 2005, DNP User's Group. Retrieved September 11, 2011, from http://www.dnp.org

Dawson, J. (2009). *Identification of bad data*. TRUST Program, Jackson State University, 2009. Retrieved from http://www.truststc.org/reu/09/Reports/DawsonReport.pdf

Dzung, D., Naedele, M., Von Hoff, T. P., & Crevatin, M. (2005). Security for industrial communications systems. *Proceedings of the IEEE*, *93*(6), 1152–1177. doi:10.1109/JPROC.2005.849714

Fallere, N., Murchu, L. O., & Chien, E. (2011). *W32.Stuxnet dossier - Version 1.4*. Retrieved February 07, 2012, from http://www.symantec.com/content/en/us/enterprise/media/security_response/whitepapers/w32_stuxnet_dossier.pdf

Gamez, D., Nadjm-Tehrani, S., Bigham, J., Balducelli, C., Burbeck, K., & Chyssler, T. (2000). Safeguarding critical infrastructures. In Diab, H. B., & Zomaya, A. Y. (Eds.), *Dependable computing systems: Paradigms, performance issues, and applications* (pp. 479–500). Hoboken, NJ: Wiley.

Grigg, C. Reliability Test System Task Force of the Application of Probability Methods Subcommittee. (1999). IEEE reliability test system – 1996. *IEEE Transactions on Power Systems*, *14*(3), 1010–1020. doi:10.1109/59.780914

Japkowicz, N., Myers, C., & Gluck, M. (1995, August). *A novelty detection approach to classification*. Paper presented at the meeting of the 14th International Conference on Artificial Intelligence, Montreal, CA.

Jin, X., Bigham, J., Rodaway, J., Gamez, D., & Phillips, C. (2006, March). *Anomaly detection in electricity cyber infrastructure*. Paper presented at the meeting of the International Workshop on Complex Network and Infrastructure Protection, CNIP 2006, Rome, Italy.

Kabay, M. E. (2010). *Attacks on power systems: Data leakage, espionage, insider threats, sabotage*. Retrieved October 15, 2011, from http://www.networkworld.com/newsletters/sec/2010/090610sec2.html?page=1

Kosut, O., Jia, L., Thomas, R. J., & Tong, L. (2010, March). *Limiting false data attacks on power system state estimation*. Paper presented at the meeting of the 2010 44th Annual Conference on Information Sciences and Systems, CISS 2010, Princeton, USA.

Krutz, R. L. (2006). *Securing SCADA systems*. Hoboken, NJ: Wiley Publishing, Inc.

Lambert-Torres, G., Rossi, R., Ribeiro, G. M., Valiquette, B., & Mukhedkar, F. (1992, August). *Computer program package for power system protection and control*. Paper presented at the meeting of the CIGRÉ Biennale Congress, Paris, France.

Liu, Y., Ning, P., & Reiter, M. K. (2009, November). *False data injection attacks against state estimation in electric power grid.* Paper presented at the meeting of the 16th ACM Conference on Computer Communications Security, CCS'09, Chicago, USA.

Lundin, E., & Jonsson, E. (2002). *Survey of intrusion detection research.* Technical Report No. 02-04, Department of Computer Engineering, Chalmers University of Technology, Götebrog, Sweden.

Manning, C. D., & Schütze, H. (1999). *Foundations of statistical natural language processing.* Cambridge, MA: MIT Press.

Markou, M., & Singh, S. (2003). Novelty detection: A review – Part 2: Neural network based approaches. *Signal Processing, 83*(12), 2499–2521. doi:10.1016/j.sigpro.2003.07.019

Martinelli, M., Tronci, E., Dipoppa, G., & Balducelli, C. (2004, September). *Electric power system anomaly detection using neural networks.* Paper presented at the meeting of the 8th International Conference KES 2004, Wellington, New Zealand.

McHugh, J., Christie, A., & Allen, J. (2000). The role of intrusion detection systems. *IEEE Software, 17*(5), 42–51. doi:10.1109/52.877859

Mé, L., & Cédric, M. (2001). *Intrusion detection: A bibliography.* France: SUPÉLEC.

Naedele, M., & Dzung, D. (2005). Industrial information system security part 1. *ABB Review, 2*, 66–70.

Northcutt, S., & Novak, J. (2000). *Network intrusion detection – An analyst's handbook* (2nd ed.). Indianapolis, IN: New Riders Publishing.

Oman, P. W., Risley, A. D., Roberts, J., & Schweitzer, E. O., III. (2002, April). *Attack and defend tools for remotely accessible control and protection equipment in electric power systems.* Paper presented at the meeting of the Texas A & M Annual Conference for Protective Relays Engineers, College Station, TX.

OPC Task Force. (1998). *OPC overview.* Retrieved June 7, 2011, from http://www.opcfoundation.org/Archive/72e9fbfa-6a89-4ef2-9b6d-3f746fd7eb05/General/OPC%20Overview%201.00.pdf

Pawlak, Z. (1982). Rough sets. *International Journal of Information and Computer Sciences, 11*, 341–356. doi:10.1007/BF01001956

Pawlak, Z. (1991). *Rough sets - Theoretical aspects of reasoning about data.* Dordrecht, The Netherlands: Kluwer Academic Publishers.

Peddabachigari, S., Abraham, A., Grosan, C., & Thomas, J. (2007). Modeling intrusion detection system using hybrid intelligent systems. *Journal of Network and Computer Applications, 30*(1), 114–132. doi:10.1016/j.jnca.2005.06.003

Pietre-Cambacedes, L., Kropp, T., Weiss, J., & Pellizzoni, R. (2008, August). *Cybersecurity standards for the electric power industry – A survival kit.* Paper presented at the meeting of the 42nd CIGRE Biennale Conference, Paris, France.

Rossi, R. (2000). *Systemic hierarchical classifier for high-voltage electric systems.* PhD Thesis, Itajuba Federal University, Itajuba, Brazil (in Portuguese).

Sands-Ramshaw, L. (2010). *Creating large disturbances in the power grid: Methods of attack after cyber infiltrations.* Dartmouth College Computer Science Technical Report TR2010-668, Dartmouth College.

SISCO - Systems Integration Specialists Company, Inc. (2005). *Overview and introduction to the manufacturing message specification (MMS).* Retrieved October 12, 2011, from http://www.sisconet.com/downloads/mmsovrlg.pdf

Stouffer, K., Falco, J., & Scarfone, K. (2011). *NIST special publication 800-82: Guide to industrial control systems (ICS) security.* Retrieved February 7, 2012, from http://csrc.nist.gov/publications/nistpubs/800-82/SP800-82-final.pdf

Tipsuwan, Y., & Chow, M. Y. (2003). Control methodologies in network control systems. *Control Engineering Practice, 11,* 1099–1111. doi:10.1016/S0967-0661(03)00036-4

Tolmasquim, M. T. (2009). *SIN - National interlinked system.* Retrieved October 15, 2011, from http://www.senado.gov.br/sf/comissoes/ci/ap/AP20091210_Dr_Mauricio_Tolmasquin.pdf

Weiss, J. (2010). *Protecting industrial control systems from electronic threats.* New York, NY: Momentum Press.

Wood, A. J., & Wollenberg, B. F. (1996). *Power generation operation and control* (2nd ed.). Hoboken, NJ: John Wiley & Sons, Inc.

Xie, L., Mo, Y., & Sinopoli, B. (2010, October). *False data injection attacks in electricity markets.* Paper presented at the meeting of the 2010 First International Conference on Smart Grid Communications, Maryland, USA.

ADDITIONAL READING

Braendle, M. (2011, April). *Cyber security for power systems — A closer look at the drivers and how to best approach the new challenges.* Paper presented at the meeting of the, 2011 64th Annual Conference forProtective Relay Engineers.

Brasch, W. (2005). *America's unpatriotic acts: The federal government's violation of constitutional and civil rights.* New York, NY: Peter Lang Publishing.

Chen, D., Chang, G., Jin, L., Ren, X., Li, J., & Li, F. (2011, August). *A novel secure architecture for the internet of things.* Paper presented at the meeting of the 2011 Fifth International Conference onGenetic and Evolutionary Computing, ICGEC 2011.

Cole, D., & Dempsey, J. X. (2002). *Terrorism and the constitution: Sacrificing civil liberties in the name of national security* (2nd ed.). New York, NY: W.W. Norton & Co.

Dogrul, M., Aslan, A., & Celik, E. (2011, June). *Developing an international cooperation on cyber defense and deterrence against cyber terrorism.* Paper presented at the meeting of the 2011 3rd International Conference on Cyber Conflict, ICCC 2011.

Dong, Y., & Kezunovic, M. (2011, July). *Communication infrastructure for emerging transmission-level smart grid applications.* Paper presented at the meeting of the, 2011 IEEE Power and Energy Society General Meeting.

Fadul, J., Hopkinson, K., Sheffield, C., Moore, J., & Andel, T. (2011, January). *Trust management and security in the future communication-based "smart" electric power grid.* Paper presented at the meeting of the 2011 44th Hawaii International Conference on System Sciences, HICSS 2011.

Ferragut, E. M., Darmon, D. M., Shue, C. A., & Kelley, S. (2011, April). *Automatic construction of anomaly detectors from graphical models.* Paper presented at the meeting of the, 2011 IEEE Symposium on Computational Intelligence in Cyber Security, CICS 2011.

Fletcher, K.K., & Liu; X. (2011, June). *Security requirements analysis, specification, prioritization and policy development in cyber-physical systems.* Paper presented at the meeting of the 2011 5th International Conference on Secure Software Integration & Reliability Improvement Companion, SSIRI-C 2011.

Government, U. S. A. (2003). *National strategy for the physical protection of critical infrastructures and key assets.* Retrieved October 13, 2010, from http://www.dhs.gov/xlibrary/assets/Physical_Strategy.pdf

Government, U. S. A. (2003). *The national strategy to secure cyberspace*. Retrieved October 13, 2010, from http://www.dhs.gov/xlibrary/assets/National_Cyberspace_Strategy.pdf

Guan, J., Graham, J. H., & Hieb, J. L. (2011, July). *A digraph model for risk identification and management in SCADA systems*. Paper presented at the meeting of the 2011 IEEE International Conference on Intelligence and Security Informatics, ISI 2011.

Haack, J. N., Fink, G. A., Maiden, W. M., McKinnon, A. D., Templeton, S. J., & Fulp, E. W. (2011, April). *Ant-based cyber security*. Paper presented at the meeting of the, 2011 Eighth International Conference on Information Technology: New Generations, ITNG 2011.

Hahn, A., & Govindarasu, M. (2011, July). *An evaluation of cybersecurity assessment tools on a SCADA environment*. Paper presented at the meeting of the 2011 IEEE Power and Energy Society General Meeting.

Hajian, S., Domingo-Ferrer, J., & Martinez-Balleste, A. (2011, April). *Discrimination prevention in data mining for intrusion and crime detection*. Paper presented at the meeting of the, 2011 IEEE Symposium on Computational Intelligence in Cyber Security, CICS 2011.

Harvey, R., & Volat, H. (2006). *De l'exception à la règle: USA Patriot Act*. Paris, France: Lignes.

Husheng, L., Lai, L., & Djouadi, S. M. (2011, June). *Combating false reports for secure networked control in smart grid via trustiness evaluation*. Paper presented at the meeting of the 2011 IEEE International Conference on Communications, ICC 2011.

Kuljaca, O., Gadewadikar, J., & Horvat, K. (2011, May). *Network structure for low level control systems designed to prevent cyber attacks*. Paper presented at the meeting of the 2011 34th International Convention MIPRO.

Lambert, J. H., Karvetski, C. W., Hamilton, M. C., & Linkov, I. (2011, April). *Energy security of military and industrial systems: Multicriteria analysis of vulnerability to emergent conditions including cyber threats*. Paper presented at the meeting of the 2011 IEEE International Systems Conference, SysCon 2011.

Linda, O., Manic, M., & McJunkin, T. R. (2011, August). *Anomaly detection for resilient control systems using fuzzy-neural data fusion engine*. Paper presented at the meeting of the Resilient, 2011 4th International Symposium on Control Systems, ISRCS 2011.

Linda, O., Manic, M., Vollmer, T., & Wright, J. (2011, April). *Fuzzy logic based anomaly detection for embedded network security cyber sensor*. Paper presented at the meeting of the, 2011 IEEE Symposium on Computational Intelligence in Cyber Security, CICS 2011.

Luiijf, E. A. M., & Klaver, M. H. A. (2005, May). *International Interdependency of C(I)IP in Europe (Internationale Verflechtung von C(I) IP in Europa)*. Paper presented at the meeting of the Clingendael Center for Strategic Studies, CIP Europe 2005/Informatik 2005, Bonn, Germany.

Mailman, S., Merritt, J., Van Vliet, T. M. B., & Yale-Loehr, S. (2002). *Uniting and strengthening America by providing appropriate tools required to intercept and obstruct terrorism*. Newark, NJ: Matthew Bender & Co., Inc.

Malviya, A., Fink, G. A., Sego, L., & Endicott-Popovsky, B. (2011, April). *Situational awareness as a measure of performance in cyber security collaborative work*. Paper presented at the meeting of the 2011 Eighth International Conference on Information Technology: New Generations, ITNG 2011.

Michaels, C. W. (2005). *No greater threat: America since September 11 and the rise of the national security state*. New York, NY: Algora Publishing.

Mulwad, V., Li, W., Joshi, A., Finin, T., & Viswanathan, K. (2011, August). *Extracting information about security vulnerabilities from Web text*. Paper presented at the meeting of the 2011 IEEE/WIC/ACM International Conference on Web Intelligence and Intelligent Agent Technology, WI-IAT 2011.

Musman, S., Tanner, M., Temin, A., Elsaesser, E., & Loren, L. (2011, April). *Computing the impact of cyber attacks on complex missions*. Paper presented at the meeting of the 2011 IEEE International Systems Conference, SysCon 2011.

Ravindran, K. (2011, August). *Cyber-physical systems based modeling of dependability of complex network systems*. Paper presented at the meeting of the 2011 Sixth International Conference on Availability, Reliability and Security, ARES 2011.

Rigoni, A., Fovino, I. N., Di Blasi, S., & Casalicchio, E. (2011, June). *Worldwide security and resiliency of cyber infrastructures: The role of the domain name system*. Paper presented at the meeting of the 2011 Second Worldwide Cybersecurity Summit, WCS 2011.

Ronchi, C., Khodjanov, A., Mahkamov, M., & Zakhidov, S. (2011, February). *Security, privacy and efficiency of Internet banking transactions*. Paper presented at the meeting of the 2011 World Congress on Internet Security, WorldCIS 2011.

Scott, A., Hardy, T. J., Martin, R. K., & Thomas, R. W. (2011, August). *What are the roles of electronic and Cyber Warfare in cognitive radio security?* Paper presented at the meeting of the 2011 IEEE 54th International Midwest Symposium on Circuits and Systems, MWSCAS 2011.

Van Bergen, J. (2004). *The twilight of democracy: The Bush plan for America*. Monroe, ME: Common Courage Press.

Wong, K. C. (2007). *The impact of USA Patriot Act on American society: An evidence based assessment*. New York, NY: Nova Press.

Wong, K. C. (2007). *The making of USA Patriot Act: Legislation, implementation, impact*. Beijing, China: Law Press.

Chapter 3

Proactive Security Protection of Critical Infrastructure:
A Process Driven Methodology

Bill Bailey
Edith Cowan University, Australia

Robert Doleman
Edith Cowan University, Australia

ABSTRACT

The belief that a static alarm system will safeguard critical infrastructure without additional support mechanisms is misplaced. This complacency is no longer satisfactory with the increase in worldwide threat levels and the potential social consequences. What is required is a more proactive, comprehensive security management process that adds to the ability to prevent, detect, deter, respond, and defeat potential harmful events and incidents. The model proposed here is proactive and grounded upon current operational procedures used by major companies in hostile and dangerous environments. By utilising a clearly defined comprehensive risk management tool, a more systematic security, threat, risk, and vulnerability assessment (STRVA), process can be developed. This process needs to identify deliberate targeting of assets through multiple intelligence gathering capabilities, plus defeat testing to probe existing security defences. The consequence approach to a potential breakthrough is at the essence of this methodology.

INTRODUCTION

Over the last few years the level of threat has increased substantially throughout the world. The need to ensure the protection of critical infrastructure has taken on a new dynamic as the capabilities of adversaries have become more sophisticated. The threats are not just terrorist or criminally based, but also from natural phenom-ena and catastrophic events. New methods and approaches are required that can assist in dealing with this increased anxiety from these threats. However, first is necessary to define what exactly needs to be protected and why.

Critical infrastructure as laid out by "The "Marsh Report" (1997- US) and the subsequent executive order EO-13010 (1998)...*a network of* independent, mostly privately-owned, and-made

DOI: 10.4018/978-1-4666-2659-1.ch003

Copyright © 2013, IGI Global. Copying or distributing in print or electronic forms without written permission of IGI Global is prohibited.

systems that function collaboratively and synergistically to produce and distribute a continuous flow of essential goods and services" (Lewis, 2006, p. 3). A piece of infrastructure is considered critical when it is vital to national security and to the country. But as Lewis points out, the Marsh Report did not define critical. However, this has evolved since 1998 and most countries have a structured definition that allows them to encompass what they consider to be part of their critical infrastructure. This approach will often include parts controlled by the government and by private industry. This is where the heart of the problem often lays as the resources required to protect are not unified and are asymmetrical in approach (Lewis, 2006, p. 3).

A more widely accepted definition is:

Critical infrastructures involve multi-dimensional, highly complex collections of technologies, processes, and people, and as such, are vulnerable to potentially catastrophic failures on many levels. Moreover, cross-infrastructure dependencies can give rise to cascading and escalating failures across multiple infrastructures (Tolone et al., 2004, p. 214).

Based upon these definitions, it is clear there are multiple cross-overs that need to be considered, requiring a multi-layered approach involving more than one facility, organisation or regional authority. Because of the complexity of systems and structures involved, it is necessary to have a much more integrated and comprehensive methodology to identify where weaknesses might occur or be targeted. The potential consequences that such a dislocation could cause needs to be firmly understood and dealt with accordingly. By adopting the proposed integrated assessment process, a more proactive approach can be used to increase readiness, improve the systems and put mitigation measures in place.

This chapter brings together a series of methods, which are currently being used by many security professionals' operationally in hostile and dangerous operations in the field, but have not been documented, into a single methodology. Therefore, the approach presented here is to advance this all-inclusive method as part of the process that should be used when dealing with complex multi-dimensional organisations that need to harmonise their security operations to make them more robust. Working directly in hostile environments requires a more comprehensive approach than most security mangers have hitherto experienced. Hence, by incorporating the hostile-based- methodology to the process, it adds a broader dimension to assessing the protective measures required for critical infrastructure. However, when so many disparate organisations are also involved, a more unified approach is required. The template presented here should provide a useful guide to putting this into place by identifying what areas need to addressed and how the process can operate successfully.

The goal of this chapter is to demonstrate how organisations can improve their overall protection by increasing the information that is required to produce a more comprehensive risk and threat identification audit. The audits should also include vulnerability and consequence assessments, together with additional inputs such as computer generated modelling techniques, red teaming and penetration tests. A comprehensive intelligence gathering structure should underpin the whole process capable of producing a formidable output that is organic and evolving, but highly useable.

This comprehensive model is based upon a recognised approach by security professionals operating in volatile and hostile situations where oil and gas recovery is taking place such as: Algeria, Sudan, Nigeria, Angola, Iraq and Equatorial Guinea. Experience has shown it is possible to manage potentially dangerous situations if the right approach has been taken to mitigate the risks. The Risk Assessment process being discussed consists of seven sequential sub-elements:

1. Threat,
2. Criticality,
3. Vulnerability (Likelihood),
4. Detection, Response and Recovery Capabilities,
5. Impact (Consequence),
6. Overall Risk, and
7. Mitigation.

By adopting these tried and tested measures into security management generally, there is a potential to assist in improving the robustness of the protection of critical infrastructure. The potential breakthrough might be e process is controlled by what is called 'adaptive and proactive security management'. Both terms will require a substantial change in the mind set for many organisations if they are adopt this proposed revised methodology. Furthermore, they will require highly qualified security professionals to manage, operate and mitigate the security threats using this recommendation.

BACKGROUND

The basic premise behind proactive protection is linked back to military and police structures of operational working practices. These practices require prevention ahead of reaction, which is the common approach to security when working with more dynamic threats. In countries where the threat is not as recognisable or so immediate, a more complacent approach is taken. Typically an alarm system is built into a facility and when it is activated then a reaction takes place to deal with the alarm. This type of approach is more commonly called 'fire fighting'. Such an approach may be satisfactory for many organisations with budget restraints or in low threat regions, but this should not be the case when dealing with critical infrastructure.

The critical problem is that by the time the 'reaction' has taken place the system may be irrevocably damaged or destroyed with all the ensuing negative dimensions this will place on the community. Furthermore, because infrastructure is linked at several levels, this will cause chain reactions that compound the initial failure to potentially becoming catastrophic. Reaction has to be changed to being proactive, which means working to prevent an event ever taking place in the first place. This proactive approach requires on-going intelligence gathering capabilities that have to be linked to known and perceived threats in an effort to mitigate their potential damage to assets and capabilities. Intelligence thus augments the whole threat assessment process with the consequence that sound intelligence is the basis of sound tactics, without it we are merely working in the dark.

Why is it Even Necessary?

Accepting that the measures put in place to safeguard the assets are always going to be sufficient to maintain the security required is one that is fraught with potential failure. Not only should decay of the system be considered, but also how much more likely has that threat become. The process whereby a security system is no longer capable of maintaining its required level of efficiency needs to be addressed regularly with actions to ensure its functionality in place (Coole & Brooks, 2009). The evolution of threats into actual incidents needs to be constantly assessed based upon known and perceived capabilities.

- Is the threat real and likely to be acted upon? Intelligence can assist in this assessment process.
- Has knowledge of the systems that are in place been compromised to the point where it could now be defeated? Once again additional targeted intelligence can assist with this question.

The key to mitigating this deficiency is to establish a reliable and competent intelligence gathering capability for the particular infrastructure concerned. This will require access to a wide and varied range of sources that can provide layered pieces of data. When these are collated correctly they then need to be presented in a structured organic picture that is capable of highlighting the known and perceived threats. Based upon a methodology that has been used by many 'Special Branch' police forces and often called 'ground cover', it incorporates a myriad of information that is constantly updated using various sources to comprehensive picture of the total environment within which a facility or organisation is operating. Sources will be varied and include government and private agencies, as well as informants and social contacts, which will have to be nurtured to ensure time valuable material is being fed into the matrix.

Even if we deal with risks in our day-to-day life, it is not always clear what risk actually is. Risk has been, and is still used in many different contexts with an equally wide variety of definitions (Ritchie, 1993). However, Holton (2004, p. 22) explains that risk entails two essential components: exposure and uncertainty. Accordingly, risk is exposure to "something" of which the outcome is uncertain. For example, if a person jumps out from an airplane without a parachute and is certain that fatality will be the outcome, there is no risk, since there is no uncertainty. Hence, risk requires both exposure and uncertainty. Furthermore, the Australian standard (Standards Australia, 2004b, p. 4) defines risk as "the chance of something happening that will have an impact on objectives"

There are many ways to approach the assessment process, as it needs to look at multiple aspects to have any degree of reality. This approach will include what Kaplan has called the risk a triplet: scenario, likelihood, and consequences (1997). The important aspect of this idea is the relationship to consequence, and its effects in real time, as opposed to modelling affects; this could mean severe outcomes for a city or region. Ezell argues this further where "vulnerability highlights the notion of susceptibility to a scenario, whereas risk focuses on the severity of consequences within the context of a scenario"; proposing a series of definitions to accommodate this concept (2007, p. 571). Although "Vulnerability assessments are not the same as risk assessments", because "risk assessments are employed to help understand what can go wrong, estimate the likelihood and the consequences, and to develop risk mitigation strategies to counter risk."(Ezell, Farr, & Wiese, 2000, p. 114). Garcia highlights that a vulnerability assessment is part of a much larger process and goes on to point out that,

Security is only one facet of risk and therefore must be considered in the context of holistic risk management across the enterprise, along with other categories such as market, credit, operational, strategic, liquidity and hazard risks (2006, p. 3).

By accepting this as a necessary additional requirement, if all aspects are to be assessed in relation to the others, then this chapter develops an alternative model from an operational perspective. Furthermore, the inclusion of vulnerability should be incorporated into the full process. Therefore, the proposed model will become the Security, Risk, Threat and Vulnerability assessment (SRTVA). The benefits of this type of methodology allows for a more comprehensive assessment to take place and support the subjective approach that is utilised by security professionals in the field. From an operational perspective, no mathematical model has achieved acceptance to date in dealing with front line security. The subjective and critical nature of the SRVTA appraisal process is based upon sound operational security experience. This requirement is necessary to manage the protection of critical assets and requires a dedicated professional security management team. The central theme utilised to provide a reliable and robust Risk Management matrix lies within *AS/NSZ ISO 31000:2009 (Standards Australia, 2009).*

ISO 31000:2009, Risk Management – Principles and Guidelines: In Context

To fully comprehend the purpose of infrastructure security methodology it is considered important to fully understand the application of the basic risk management standard. The ISO 31000 standard has been embedded as the primary thread for the creation of the 'critical infrastructure security risk management methodology' and provides a holistic overview of the risk management process (Figure 1). The Standard provides a common multiple over layering foundation upon which risk management protocols can be built. The generic attributes of ISO 31000 allow adaptation for any organisational risk process to be undertaken.

In many respects, security risk management involves analysing and understanding the threat context of organisational exposures, the application of resources, and the scrutiny of systems quality to achieve a level of security commiserate with risk that is cost-effective and as low as realistically practical according to (Talbot & Jakeman, 2009, p. 97).

Benefits of the Risk Management Process

Risk management forms an integral part of good business practice and quality management within an organization. Today, a lot more organisations utilize an integrated approach to risk management by using "common language, shared tools, techniques and periodic assessments of the total risk profile for the entire organisation" (Standards Australia, 2004a, pp. 7-8). In the end it depends upon the nature and complexity of the Risk Management approach taken within an organisation that decides how integrated this process will actually become. Moreover, an integrated risk management approach requires people, at all levels, to manage risks, commiserate with their responsibilities (Standards Australia, 2004a, 2004b).

Some of the specific benefits include:

Figure 1. Risk assessment process

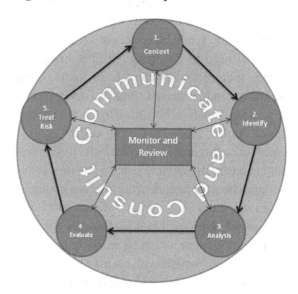

- **Fewer Surprises:** Control of adverse events is enhanced by identifying and taking actions to minimize their likelihood and reduce their effects.
- **Exploitation of Opportunities:** Opportunity seeking behaviour is Enhanced if people have confidence in their understanding of risks and have the capabilities needed to manage them.
- **Economy and Efficiency:** Benefits in economy and efficiency can be achieved in the targeting of resources, protection of assets, and avoidance of costly mistakes.
- **Improved Stakeholder Relationship:** Encourages an organisation to identify its internal and external stakeholders and develop a two-way dialog between them.
- **Improved Information for Decision-Making:** The process provides a more accurate information and analysis in support of strategic decision making.
- **Personal Wellbeing:** Effective risk management of personal risk generally improves health and wellbeing of self and others (Standards Australia, 2004b).

All organisations exist in environments of uncertainty; whether internal, external, political, socio-cultural, economic, technological, legal, which may impact on organisation objectives. To increase the probability of success organisational risk processes and strategies must be established. Some processes are naturally evolving within the organisations context but need to be formalised in standards such as ISO 31000:2009, Risk management – Principles and guidelines.

Figure 1, is an interpretation of the ISO 31000:2009 (Standards Australia, 2009) and outlines the assessment processes to be created to establish communication and reporting mechanisms to facilitate the framework development. These include risk analysis and modelling, decision making, risk communication and perception management. Initially it is important to establish the terms of reference. An important step refers to the identification of objectives for the risk assessment process. A key element of security risk management, that distinguishes it from other forms of risk management, is that the risk management process is often separated in practice into two elements - a security risk assessment and security risk management according to Talbot & Jakeman (2009, p. 138).

Using the flow chart process as shown in Figure 1, a basic understanding of what is required is now discussed, before an organisation could adopt the proposed methodology.

Establishing the Context

Establishing the context is a fundamental component of the risk management process as the context defines the considerations for the Risk Management process. The definition of context varies from one organisation to another even within the modern organisational environment context can change rapidly and suddenly within the same organisation. Modern organisations are evolving entities and therefore context within

the organisation may be fluid with a current risk assessment not be identical to the prior risk assessment or future assessments.

Organisational assets are human: people, skills and training, financial: cash and investments, physical: buildings, plant and equipment, intellectual property: products, services and patents, information and IT: data, information systems and market knowledge, and relationships: brand reputation, publicity and suppliers (Diaxion., 2010, p. 2).

Risk Identification and Analysis

There are a number of steps in the generic risk management process, which have been outlined in Figure 1, and correspond to those suggested by ISO 31000: 2009. One of the initial steps in the process is "communicate and consult". It is important to remember that risk management takes place in a social context, which means the information needs to be shared and discussed by people who are affected differently by a set of risks. Not all risks affect people in the same way and many may have different views regarding their likely affect. (Standards Australia, 2010, p. 4). Communication and consultation is therefore a continual and repetitive process that an organisation is required to conduct to provide, share or obtain information and to constantly engage in dialogue with stakeholders regarding the management of risk.

According to Talbot and Jakeman (2009, p. 140) the importance of fully and comprehensibly establishing the security risk management context cannot be understated, and stakeholders should be engaged to identify the following: external context, internal context, security risk management context, process/program structure, evaluation, criteria and risk appetite, security agendas of stakeholders & security business case. Talbot & Jakeman (2009, p. 138) emphasise the importance of this process, as this foundational step is often glossed over in their view, by inexperienced practitioners in a desire to identify and treat the risks before they have been adequately assessed. It is imperative that some risks are not over looked or misjudged, as this will have a serious outcome on the risk assessment and treatment plans.

It is at this stage that the additional stages come into play and need to be addressed as in Figure 2: Security, Risk, Threat and Vulnerability Assessment (SRTVA) process. The ability to characterise threats in relation to vulnerabilities will now be analysed first before presenting the full sequence required to undertake the whole process.

How to Assess Vulnerabilities

Security management has developed a wide range of capabilities to assess what is vulnerable and how important this is to overall infrastructure and especially its level of inter-dependence. By using a variety of risk management and assessment tools, the level of threat can be identified and measures taken to mitigate the risk. Additional tools are also available, such as threat and risk modelling visualisation techniques to aid the development of acceptable mitigation strategies. All these strategies will be discussed as they from part of the overall process required to undertake a comprehensive Security, Risk, Threat and Vulnerability Assessment (SRTVA). Consideration needs to be given to what essentials are included to ensure that all the risks are identified for each part of the infrastructure. Otherwise the analysis will be faulty.

Often untrained people have been used to carry out the risk management for security operations. In most cases this happens as there is confusion over a risk analysis used for health and safety, and one required for security. The preferred option is to have a team that is made up of a series of specialists from different disciplines that fully understand the operational requirements of the organisation. The team should always include a senior health and safety specialist as the assessment proposals will need to be accepted at the highest level, which should always include health and safety. It will then be possible to accurately identify what is in fact critical giving it an identifier of criticality for the matrix. By undertaking the SRTVA, as a team, the outcomes will have greater validity with senior management as it reflects a combined approach, rather than a single individual from the security department (Boeing, Masek, & Bailey, 2008).

The identification of the threat is a critical part of the process as once identified then a proactive assessment can begin, which will then add additional information regarding the known and perceived threats into a new matrix. The Matrix will need to be interactive as it must be capable of running a number of scenarios to establish multiple scenario threats and weaknesses.

SECURITY, RISK, THREAT AND VULNERABILITY ASSESSMENT (SRTVA) PROCESS

Risk management explicitly addresses uncertainty (Standards Australia, 2009) and protecting critical infrastructure is fundamentally about how to ensure that this uncertainly can be addressed both defensively and offensively. The proposed process here unites two accepted practices, Risk and Threat and combines them with Vulnerability to make them in to a single methodology. The other added component is Consequence, as this allows prioritisation of strategies. If the consequence is low then it can be moved lower down on the level for mitigation. Priority is normally given to the highest consequence. The formula:

Risk = Threat × Vulnerability × Consequence.

This is an accepted generic formula used to identify risk. Using this approach Risk Analysis and Management for Critical Asset Protection (RAMCAP TM), has developed a structured assessment process (ASME, 2006). This methodol-

Figure 2. Security risk, threat and vulnerability assessment (SRTVA) process

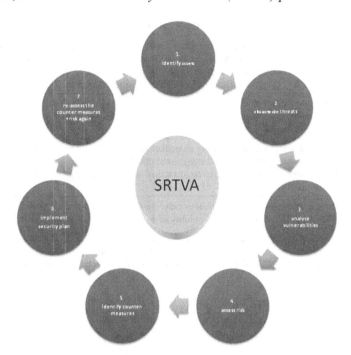

ogy together with those developed by organisations such as the Scandia research laboratories "Critical infrastructure systems of systems assessment methodology" (DePoy et al., 2006) identify the problems associated with using some models including that proposed by RAMCAP TM. These problems are centred around the difficulty in assessing and quantifying threat (Cox, 2008). However, the RAMCAP TM does provide a useful starting point for the development of a more comprehensive assessment process (See Table 1).

A working template has been developed to illustrate the methodology required to be taken to conduct the process and is presented here to assist security managers apply the concepts proposed. The template in Figure 2, although adapted from the ISO 31000:2009, Risk Management – Principles and Guidelines, is not identical, it has additional aspects that will be discussed later, namely: (2) characterise threats and (3) analyse vulnerabilities before returning to the cycle as shown in Figure 1. By first working through what is required to conduct and apply the proposed assessment process, the reasons for the additions should become more understandable. Communicate and consult widely is at the core of the process.

The risk assessment process provides a mechanism that:

- Reviews potential threats to security interests;
- Determines appropriate levels of protection for assets;
- Emphasizes back-up systems and in-depth protection;
- Addresses cost-risk benefit-analysis tradeoffs;
- Promotes action to reduce risks that are not acceptable ;
- Promotes decisions that accept certain levels of risk; and
- Provides a means to judge whether the resultant risks meet acceptability criteria.

Table 1. Terms used in RAMCAP^{TM}

Term: RAMCAPTM Definition
Risk: the potential for loss or harm due to the likelihood of an unwanted event and its adverse consequences. It is measured as the combination of the probability and consequences of an adverse event, i.e., threat. When the probability and consequences are expressed numerically, the expected risk is computed as the product of those values with uncertainty considerations. ... In security, risk is based on the analysis and aggregation of three widely recognized factors: threat, vulnerability, and consequence.
Conditional risk: A measure of risk that focuses on consequences, vulnerability, and adversary capabilities, but excludes intent. It is used as a basis for making long-term risk management decisions. The adversary capabilities, countermeasures, and residual vulnerability are often combined into a measure of likelihood of adversary success
Consequence: The outcome of an event or occurrence, including immediate, short- and long-term, direct and indirect losses and effects. Loss may include human casualties, monetary and economic damages, and environmental impact, and may also include less tangible and therefore less quantifiable effects, including political ramifications, decreased morale, reductions in operational effectiveness, or other impacts.
Threat: Any indication, circumstance, or event with the potential to cause the loss of, or damage to, an asset or population. In the analysis of risk, threat is based on the analysis of the intention and capability of an adversary to undertake actions that would be detrimental to an asset or population.
Vulnerability: Any weakness in an asset's or infrastructure's design, implementation, or operation that can be exploited by an adversary. Such weaknesses can occur in building characteristics, equipment properties, personnel behaviour, locations of people, equipment and buildings, or operational and personnel practices.

(Cox, 2008, p. 1749)

Stage 1: Identify Assets

To correctly identify the level of protection required it is essential to understand what is being protected. Facility characterization includes:

- Identifying the key assets
- Reviewing information that describes the technical details of those assets
- Capable of supporting the analysis
- Identifying the consequences based upon potential break-throughs to the site and the surrounding area
- Lastly determining the target attractiveness as a basis of likelihood for malicious action

Stage 2: Characterise Threats

Target Attractiveness is estimated during the facility characterization, based on several factors:

- Key assets need to be identified and assessed to define the potential targets for consideration.

- Multiple source Intelligence

The characterization should consider consequences that are consistent with the anticipated motivation and capabilities of the adversaries to achieve their objectives, assuming they are successful.

Existing systems to mitigate undesired events need to be identified and analyzed in terms of effectiveness. An understanding of the potential/likelihood of successful attack must be developed based on analysis of available or projected data and information, including:

- Consideration of previous incidents,
- Target uniqueness,
- Projected severity/consequences of attack,
- Difficulty for such an attack to take place
- Existing security and response measures, and
- Other factors (e.g. media attention, visibility, proximity to other locations, historic, community, environmental, or political significance).

Intelligence

Fundamental to the whole process is the ability to harness a wide range of intelligence gathering capabilities and use them diagnostically to assess the threat characterisation. The capabilities, likelihood and target attractiveness can be better assessed when based upon a multiplicity of intelligence sources. A wide range of methods are discussed later in this chapter, suffice it to say that this is core to the whole SRTVA process, which cannot be effective without intelligence.

Physical and Operational Characteristics

The facility characterization includes physical characteristics such as site boundaries, perimeter barriers, locations of buildings, business critical operating units, physical and technical protection features, on site process flow, and infrastructure details. Operational issues need to be well understood in order to effectively design a security system capable of protecting the key assets, without unduly impeding operations.

In this approach, assets and essential elements that are associated with assets must be identified and assessed as to their importance within the overall operating environment. Identification of those assets is accomplished through interviews with asset owners and personnel, data reviews, facility tours/inspections, and a variety of other sources. Asset owners are generally the most knowledgeable about the assets in need of protection and what would be the consequence to operations should they be unable to function. .

Security Data Development

It is important to develop information about as many aspects of the facility or operation as possible. The security audit team should spend time at the facility observing the overall operation; preferably both in daylight and at night, reviewing facility data relevant to regulatory requirements, safety, labour or collective bargaining issues, movement of contractors and historical legal concerns.

An additional means of gathering data during the on-site stage security audit is to conduct a series of interviews with site personnel including all contractors, with outside individuals, especially from government agencies or other neighbouring facilities. Developing a wide network of contacts is essential if proactive security is to be successful. This network should be as wide and as varied as possible to ensure all shades of opinion and diversity can be captured for incorporation into intelligence gathering process.

Analysis of threat intelligence gathered is critical to the security audit process. Threats need to be evaluated in terms of insider threats, outsider threats, and potential threats posed by collusion between insiders and outsiders. Threats should be rated as severe, high, medium, or low. This ranking will correspond to the Threat Matrix which should be in use for all facilities and act as a constant guide to the actual status at any given time. The initial threat characterization should be based on sound local knowledge from those who are familiar with the region where the facility is located. Sources of threat data include, but are not limited to, archival incidents, crime statistics, police sources, government agencies and incident data from neighbouring facilities/operations. Threat, at its simplistic level, is defined by intent and capability. Input from other security companies operating in the same region should also be included to ensure local industry benchmarking for all operators in the region. Combined post SRTVA's with other companies and operators to evaluate and harmonise outcomes should be encouraged. If working on overseas operations, then embassy or other local or national government data sources should always be consulted. Local threat data and local inputs should be added to the overall multiple-layered-picture to ensure this produces a comprehensive output.

Identifying the Threat

To determine the appropriate threat ratings, the team should ask the following questions:

- What are the goals and objectives of the threat adversary?
- What does the adversary gain by achieving these goals?
- How will the adversary achieve these goals?
- Are there other means or easier means of achieving these goals?
- Which means will the threat most likely choose?
- What events might provoke a threat?
- What are the capabilities of the adversary?
- To what degree is the adversary motivated?
- What organizational flaws create threat or can be exploited by adversaries?
- Historical trend analysis- looking at other incidents

A threat identification process is then required dealing with the following:

- Threat Source
- Threat Risk
- Likelihood
- Risk Impact
- Risk Rating
- Risk Management Measure

Normal procedure would be to address all of these topics in a systematic and comprehensive manner before attempting to assess them in the risk matrix process.

A summary statement should be developed in the form of an Executive summary that personifies the actual status snap shot. These summary statements should depict the primary threats to the facility's key assets, but do not consider the existing safeguards provided by security countermeasures. These security countermeasures will be accounted for when the risk of individual scenarios is calculated and laid out for each defined area or facility.

Stage 3: Analyse Vulnerabilities

Analysing vulnerabilities is the core stage of the Security Risk, Threat and Vulnerability Assessment (SRTVA) process. Vulnerability analysis identifies flaws, limitations and weaknesses that, if exploited, could result in a security incident.

Vulnerability analysis should begin with a gap assessment. The vulnerability analysis should include an even more thorough evaluation of existing security countermeasures, including an evaluation of recommendations implemented from previous SRTAs.

Analysis vulnerability flow process:

1. **Identify Vulnerabilities**
   a. Pair the assets to the threats
   b. Identify vulnerabilities and undesired events - develop scenarios
   c. Determine the causes of vulnerabilities
2. **Assess Vulnerabilities**
   a. Determine severity
   b. Determine probability
   c. Decide to accept, eliminate, or control associated risk
3. **Resolve Vulnerabilities**
   a. Determine severity
   b. Determine probability
   c. Decide to accept, eliminate, or control associated risk
4. **Follow Up**
   a. Monitor for effectiveness
   b. Monitor for any changes
   c. Assess any changes against the outcomes of the SRVTA
   d. Communicate and consult widely

Evaluation of Existing Counter Measures

Existing security countermeasures should be fully understood and evaluated. These will have been considered by security when they have conducted a gap analysis of the facility. Each subsequent gap analysis from the time the initial audit will have been recorded and this should be evaluated to ensure it still meets the requirements. All recommendations should be re-assessed, particularly if they have not been implemented to ascertain whether they are still valid

General areas of vulnerability may be included in Table 2.

The process should address security vulnerabilities by pairing assets with threats to identify flaws, limitations and weaknesses that could be exploited by an adversary. The process can be greatly improved by using a brainstorming session with all those that are involved with the SRTVA. It is important to have a team that is made of more than just those from the security department. The more knowledgeable and experienced the makeup of the group is the more informed the final outcome will be. On large scale facilities this requirement is essential if all aspects of the proposed action are to be measured, as very often countermeasures may impede parts of the facility from actually functioning. It is highly unlikely that an un-representative team will have sufficient working knowledge of the complexity of the whole operational requirements to avoid such mistakes. During the brainstorming session, attention should be given to developing and refining realistic scenarios with clear security consequences. The scenarios should attempt to address the most-credible and worst-case outcomes in terms of consequence. Scenarios should then be used to help the team recognize how security incidents occur, in terms of causes and effects and how to deal with them.

Consequence is a preferred measure of dealing with risk when used by security professionals. Understanding what the potential consequences may be to the whole operation allows priorities to be set and ranked. It will be the role of senior management to assess the consequences of not implementing measures against possible budget constraints. Very often it is possible to present alternatives which could also accomplish similar outcomes but not be as expensive.

As far as possible, the scenarios should correspond with asset owners' priorities and with any threats identified in previous steps. Consideration of existing and planned security countermeasures must also be evaluated. Questions to ask and things to look for include:

- Identifying the existing layers of protection, including potential points of failure.
- What type of protection do existing systems provide, and what do they safeguard against? Can this be improved?
- When and where are the existing systems effective? Have they enhanced effectiveness since installation?
- Have they prevented or caused program or project problems?
- Have they been defeated during actual incidents or during penetration or red team testing? If so, how were the systems defeated? What is the remedy?
- Is there a history of flawed operations or on-going maintenance issues?
- Does this involve obsolete or faulty equipment? Is this a system decay issue?
- Is the equipment sufficiently integrated?
- Is the equipment properly maintained?
- Is the equipment secure and protected?
- Are the system users properly and adequately trained? How are they assessed?
- Is human error a recurring factor?
- The effectiveness of existing countermeasures that have been put in place, especially as perceived by potential adversaries.

Once the answers have been assessed then the team is prepared to develop final, refined scenarios. Refined scenarios should generally be written so

Table 2. Assessing vulnerability

To be assessed:	What can be done?
Nature of the locality	
Road access	
Building character-istics	
Equipment properties	
Operational practices	
Personnel practices	
Employee / Contractor behaviours	
Management / Leader-ship	
Guard force practices	
Locations of people, equipment, and build-ings	
Nature of operations	

that they clearly indicate how the event would unfold, what would happen and what would the consequence likely to be. A flow chart and event matrix aids with this exercise.

Stage 4: Assess Risk

The team should then conduct deliberations to analyze cause-effect relationships from the perceived and verified threats to provide the initial estimation of risk using the risk matrix and the probability / consequence severity tables. In order to establish an understanding of exposure to the risk, scenarios must be assessed in terms of severity of consequences and likelihood of occurrence. These are subjective judgements based upon qualitative estimations with limited quantitative data. It is necessary to have knowledgeable and experienced security team members to accomplish this task.

In the context of communication, *trust* is an important factor. According to Slovic (Slovic, 1999, p. 697) "trust in risk management, like risk perception, has been found to correlate with gender, race, worldview, and affect". Stakeholder

relationships rely heavily on trust, and one reason why stakeholders may reject to proposals, is lack of trust. If stakeholders trust management and the organisation as a whole, communication will be relatively easy. If trust however is lacking, no form or process of communication will be satisfactory. Hence, it is essential that the organisation build a strong and trustworthy consultative relationship with all the stakeholders (Slovic, 1999, p. 697).

Consultation is a two-way process of informed communication between an organisation and its stakeholders on an issue prior to making a decision or determining direction on that issue HB 327:2010 (2010, p. 4). Communication and consultation should facilitate truthful, relevant, accurate, and understandable exchanges of information, taking into account confidential and personal integrity aspects. It is important to remember stakeholders are likely to make judgements about risk based on their perceptions, which if left uninformed or unacknowledged can have a significant impact on the management of risk HB 327:2010 (2010, p. 4).

The objective of scenario brainstorming is to focus on vulnerabilities from the threats, risks and vulnerabilities that are not already mitigated or clearly dealt with by existing countermeasures. Scenarios should not be developed and worked for the sole purpose of justifying perceived security enhancements; this type of approach can prove to be counter-productive and alienate management.

Risk is the product of scenario probability and severity using the threat analysis process. The risk and threat matrix categorizes levels of risk that provide guidance to management and establish a basis for the stewardship of identified risks. The acceptable level of risk for an asset does not remain constant and varies with time, circumstances, and management's attitude toward risk. Ultimately this is a consultative process whereby senior management must take the responsibility for either accepting the risk or taking measures to mitigate that risk. The SRTVA is a tool to assist with the protection of the critical infrastructure and unless the authority is vested in the highest level then it remains just that, a tool. Ensuring that senior management understand the outcomes of the assessment is core to this proactive approach.

Risk Matrix

The standard process for assessing the actual risk is by using a Risk Matrix, which incorporates a number of variables indicating levels of risk. Once the agreed level has been placed into the matrix it can then be assessed against the acceptance criteria. The criteria will be based upon the standard set by the organisation at which it is prepared to tolerate potential unfavourable outcomes. There are a substantial number of matrixes which are in use and a company will need to adopt one that suits its own requirements. The Risk matrix models that are used in this chapter are therefore generic and only indicative.

Risk ratings within the Risk Matrix provide a basis for prioritizing one risk over another.

During the process of security risk analysis, where the threat scenario being considered involves human intervention, three elements need to be considered in order for a specific event to be realised. Without any one of these elements the event cannot occur; that is:

- Motivation
- Capability
- Opportunity

Threat assessment is based upon an assessment of both Motivation and Capability, and by association Opportunity.

Motivation requires an assessment of both desire and expectation.

Capability is a combination of resources and knowledge of the target.

Motivation is the degree to which the threat source has demonstrated adversarial aims against you or a history of even minimal activity hostile to your interests. Their desire is measured in terms

of their agenda, activity history, current activities or merely hostile interests. Their expectation of success is largely dependent on their will as well as their ability to overcome security controls you have in place to protect you.

Motivation is expressed as nil, limited, significant or complete. Motivation is a direct indicator of Likelihood an event will occur, as in Nil (totally unlikely>every 100 years), Limited (possible> 10 - 100 years), Major (probable>1 – 10 years), or Complete (likely>within a year)

Capability encompasses the adequacy of the threat's structure, size, organization, modus operandi, disposition and finances, and opportunities available to them. Their resources include organization, presence and location within your business sector and market. Their knowledge includes not only availability of information, but also technical and professional operating capacity.

If the Capability of the threat is considered to be either "Stated or known" or "General or Suspected", the potential consequence will be the anticipated magnitude of impact the relevant threat is capable of inflicting on the operations.

If the Capability of the threat is considered either "None Suspected", or "None Confirmed", the assessed Consequence should be reduced to the next lower category.

Mitigation is the ability to deny Opportunity to carry out the threat.

Risks that must be taken into considered:

- Reputational risks
- Business culture risks
- Legal and institutional risks
- Economic risks
- Political risks
- Security of financial assets
- Security of physical assets
- Security of personnel

There are also four principal types of consequence to consider: Financial, Health & Safety,

Environment and Reputation out of a potential of eight risks as shown above. These consequences are placed into a Risk Matrix, which allows for a visual representation based upon the factors included in the assessment. The rating of the risk is made by reference to an assessment of the severity of the potential consequences and the frequency at which those consequences are estimated to occur.

The process of Risk Rating must be used as follows:

- The consequence severity rating must be selected first based on the most likely potential adverse consequence with current Controls, or in the case of a new Business Element the intended controls to be put in place.
- The likelihood of the Consequence must then be selected.

The "Threat Assessment Matrix" shown in Figure 7 can be used once the various potential factors have been assessed. These include Figure 3, Consequence looking at the Extent and the Duration together with Figure 4, Motivation versus Capability and finally Figure 5, Likelihood and Impact

Where security threats are considered, the "Threat Assessment Matrix" is to be used as an additional tool designed to qualify a determination of Likelihood. Consistent with this system, correlation of the relationship between Motivation and Capability is expressed as either: Low (L), Medium (M), High (H) or Almost Certain (AC). The purpose of this process is to gauge how likely the threat is to the organisation, based upon capability. Do they have the resources to actually cause harm?

The table is used to identify the Risk Index (RI) of a scenario, based on its placement on the risk matrix. RI ratings are used to determine whether a recommendation is Critical, High, Medium, or Low priority. Figure 5 helps determine the level of impact caused by an event and assessed against the likelihood this could happen. Table 3 is to be used when determining the criticality of assets to be protected:

The criticality assessment is made in relation to the potential effect on the business operations. The crucial element is to ascertain the consequences to business continuity and the impact this would have too. Recovery is linked to consequences, which lie at the foundation of using the proposed methodology.

Figure 6 looks at three further indicators required as part of the assessment process: costs, health & safely impact and time to recovery. In order to calculate the probability of future events, a definable end date is selected, usually a 10-year period, upon which to base the analysis. Table

Figure 3. Consequence matrix

EXTENT	NATIONAL	MODERATE	MAJOR	CATASTROPHIC	CATASTROPHIC
	WIDESPREAD	MINOR	MODERATE	MAJOR	CATASTROPHIC
	REGIONAL	MINIMAL	MINOR	MODERATE	MAJOR
	LOCAL	MINIMAL	MINIMAL	MINOR	MODERATE
		SHORT TERM	MEDIUM TERM	LONG TERM	SUSTAINED
		DURATION			

Figure 4. Motivation versus capability

		CAPABILITY			
		None	Limited	Restricted	Unrestricted
MOTIVATION	Totally				
	Highly				
	Slightly				
	Low				

4 identifies how to categorize undesired event probability

The final stage in assessing the risk requires the use of the *Risk Matrix*. There are any number of matrixes that are in use today, as companies attempt to copyright their own version. Each organisation will need to identify which one suits their needs and adopt that one for all future use. In addition, it is beneficial to adopt the same matrix to be used by security as that used by the Health and Safety department. Using five levels allows for more flexibility but this is not an essential requirement. The generic Matrix shown in Figure 7 has combined both asset protection and safety on to the same Figure so they can be assessed together. No organisation today should be ignoring the safety issues when they are dealing with security protection measures. Legal consequences are severe for failure to appreciate the potential to cause injury and should remain upmost in minds at all times.

Security Risks – Rating Look-Up Matrix Table

An overall rating for each risk is obtained by assessing the factors that influence risk. For each of the combinations, there is an overall risk rating of Low, Moderate, High, or Extreme as shown in the matrix in Figure 7.

The matrix in Figure 7 is used to estimate risk as the product of probability and severity of consequence, from both a Business and a Health and Safety perspective.

Stage 5: Identification of Countermeasures

Once the initial estimation of risk has been completed, then recommendations of countermeasures that would either prevent or mitigate the risk of the scenario should be considered. After listing the relevant recommendations, the risk matrix should again be consulted to recalculate the risk of the

Figure 5. Likelihood and impact

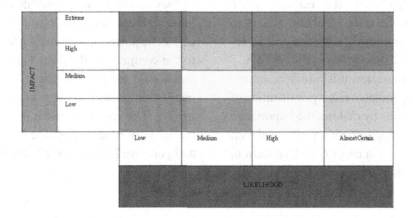

IMPACT	Extreme				
	High				
	Medium				
	Low				
		Low	Medium	High	Almost Certain
		LIKELIHOOD			

Figure 6. The consequences to the operations

CRITICALITY	Low	Medium	High	Extreme
Capital: Total insured value of the facility	< $1 M - $10 M	$10 M - $50 M	$50 M - $100 M	> $100 M
OSHE: Impact to people, community & environment, reputation	Lower	Medium	Higher	• Significant community impact • Hazardous Product Release • Corporate impact
Business Continuity: (Incident recovery time)	< 3 Months	3 - 6 Months	6 - 12 Months	> 12 Months

scenario based on successful implementation of their recommendations (See Table 5).

Countermeasures, or corrective actions, mitigate the causes and effects of scenarios. Their effectiveness must be evaluated by the team in terms of their impact primarily on reducing the probability of event occurrence or, to a lesser extent, on lessening the severity of consequence. Their effectiveness is then measured in terms of probability and severity. The effectiveness or otherwise of the measures is then considered and either accepted or rejected. If the latter then the process begins again in order to find an acceptable mitigation measure that will work and is suitable to the situation. Cost benefit analysis will have to be undertaken at this stage to make certain the mitigation measure can be achieved within the budget. Although this should not be the only factor as if it is the best and most effective measure then steps need to be taken to obtain budget to cover the costs. Supporting evidence will be required including all the data from the SRTVA.

In order to facilitate stewardship of recommendations and management of risks, prioritisation of the recommendations by ranking the importance of each against the appropriate scenario and then ranking the scenarios in order of risk reduction. These should be then labelled as Critical, High, Medium, and Low priority using the following criteria: The results of the team deliberations for each scenario are captured for assessment.

Using the Tables

The tables provide a methodology to assess the risks, capabilities, consequences and the threats. Although many organisations have tried to make this a simple input process, unfortunately this cannot be done successfully. It is necessary to have trained professional who is capable of assessing the levels of risk and subjectively applying the rank of each of these risks in the table before obtaining a numerical output. Many companies sometimes attempt to restrict the outcomes by imposing tight definitions as to the level of number allowed to be used, as in 5 critical. The reason for this is so they can continue to operate even against the highest threat identifications. For example, a risk cannot be placed as extreme if it has not happened to the company in the past. This is ridiculous as that would tend to indicate it is never likely to happen either, which does not stop it actually happening. The risk assessment must be conducted realistically based on all the known, calculated and perceived threats (See Table 6).

Figure 7. Risk Matrix

Safety		Occurs often	Previously occurred more than once	Occurred once in the last year	Experience of previous occurrences	Never occurred before	Asset Protection
		A: Frequent	B: Likely	C: Possible	D: Unlikely	E: Rare	
Multiple fatalities to >25 people	1. Critical						Irreparable damage to highly valued assets
Single fatality to >10 persons	2. Major						Wide spread long term damage to assets
Permanent disability or impairment >1 or more persons	3. Serious						Medium term damage to assets
Medical treatment requiring hospitalization	4. Moderate						Minor local damage to assets
Treatment with first aid only	5. Minor						Limited damage to assets. No lasting effects

Stage 6: Implement Security Plan

When concluding the risk assessment, Management must be made aware of the observations and recommendations developed during the assessment and to solicit their input. The briefing should:

- Provide a summary of the Threat Characterization Statement,
- Discuss the effectiveness of the current safeguards and security program, including a catalogue of gaps in the baseline countermeasures,
- Provide an overview of the risk assessment, reviewing all recommendations to be contained in the audit report,
- Establish expectations for the timing and review of the SRTVA report.

After the vulnerability analysis is complete, the vulnerabilities can be resolved by deciding to: accept the risk associated with the vulnerability, eliminate it completely or control the source of the vulnerability. Various methods can be used to reduce the risk to an acceptable level.

Design to Eliminate Vulnerabilities

This strategy generally applies to the design and acquisition of new subsystems and equipment or the expansion of existing subsystems; however, it can also be applied to any change in equipment or individual components.

Design to Minimize Vulnerabilities

A major goal during the subsystem design process is to include features that are fail-safe or have capabilities to handle contingencies through redundancies of critical elements. Complex features that could increase the likelihood of a loss should be avoided.

Safety Devices

Known vulnerabilities that cannot be eliminated or minimized through design may be controlled through the use of appropriate safety devices. The use of such countermeasures can help reduce risk to an acceptable level. Safety devices must be integrated into a part of the safeguards and security system.

Table 3. Criticality assessment

Facility	A site or location controlled or managed or conducts work activities OR has employees or "staff contractors" OR property or information considered important to the overall critical infrastructure
criticality of assets are to be determined based on categories found in the table below	
Capital	The capital consequence factor is based on the total insured value of the asset.
	Consider factors that include location, terrain including the built environment, proximity to and size of human population; factors associated with the natural environment and issues of sensitivity in the area of operation.
	Higher: Loss of operation would cause catastrophic consequences to the company and or its reputation Operation is susceptible to or has a history of focused public, media, activism, or unwanted NGO attention.
	Medium: Damage to operation would cause serious to severe consequences to the company and or its reputation Operation has a limited history of public, media, activism, or NGO attention.
	Lower: Damage to operation would have limited or minor consequences to the company and or its reputation Operation has a very limited history of public, media, activism, or NGO attention.
Business Continuity (BC)	The business continuity factor in the criticality matrix below is based on the estimated time it would take to fully recover from a major incident or replace capacity/capability using alternate operations/facilities.

Access Control and Warning Devices

Warning devices and access control measures for timely detection of conditions that precede the actual occurrence of the event. The complexities of systems that can be used for this role are substantial requiring detailed knowledge before implementation. The ability to match access cards to visual identification through CCTV (Closed circuit television) of the person using the card, to finger print or retina identification are just some of the options that need to be considered. Expert advice should be sought to ensure the most effective systems are installed.

Procedures and Training

Where it is not possible to totally eliminate or control safeguards or security-related vulnerabilities using one of the above methods, detailed procedures for responding to the resulting undesired event should be developed and formally implemented. These procedures should be standardized and used in all protective system tests, operations, and maintenance activities. Personnel should receive proper training to enable them to carry out these procedures.

Vulnerability Acceptance

Where it is not possible to reduce the probability of safeguards or security vulnerabilities by any means, a decision must be made to either accept the risk associated with the vulnerability or re-evaluate the requirements for the particular asset being protected.

Stage 7: Re-Assess the Risk

The last step in the vulnerability resolution process is follow up. It is necessary to monitor, check and audit the effectiveness of recommended countermeasures; this ensures that the measures do not introduce any new vulnerability. Whenever changes are made to any of the system elements (equipment, procedures, people, or environment), then a vulnerability analysis should be conducted again to identify and resolve any new weakness that may occur.

The entire process needs to be tracked in a way that can be audited (for compliance) until the risk can be permanently addressed. This means the system must provide useful and accurate findings while recording key decisions that can be shared with multiple teams and maintained as part of the

Table 4. How to categorize undesired event severity using five probabilities

Impact	Probability	Frequency
Extreme	Almost certain	Possibility of repeated incidents (> 1 event per year)
High	Likely	Possibility of isolated incidents (1 event in 5 years)
Medium	Possible	Possibility of occurring sometime (1 event in 10 years)
Low	Unlikely	Not likely to occur (10% chance of occurrence in 10 years)
Very Low	Rare	Very highly unlikely (1% chance of occurrence in 10 years)

assessment lifecycle to demonstrate compliance. While taking the steps to remediate risks is necessary to improve security, the final step of the process is to ensure reporting that improves audit readiness, demonstrates compliance and supports continued improvement. Successful organizations use this step to develop specialized show progress over time and promote accountability.

Any changes to the integrity of the critical infrastructure must be notified back to the security management team to assess their impact on the security measures currently in place. In the same way that any changes made to the security need to be fed back up the management chain. Involving security at the highest level of any 'management of change' processes will help to alleviate potential conflicts of interest in securing the assets. Normal practice in big organisations is to always involve the security team in the managing change through development adjustments.

Proactive Security

The essence of being proactive requires the security team to be aware of all developments that affect the organisation. Attention to detail and changes that may seem insignificant need to be incorporated into the overall security plans. Con-

stant liaison is the key to being proactive. This has two major benefits: one, this gets the security personnel known to everyone in the organisation, making them more accessible and two; more good intelligence will be sourced by this greater contact with personnel (See Figure 8).

A summation of a threat driven risk based design is graphically condensed in (Figure 6). The holistic method combines as many elements as possible including systems based approaches together with security best practices to support the planning, organization and execution of the security function (Coole & Brooks, 2011). In essence this process has to be managed constantly, which involves an on-going assessment of what is the nature of the threat and what can be done to mitigate it using the resources available.

THE ROLE OF INTELLIGENCE

It is impossible to conduct a comprehensive STRVA without input and information from a multitude of sources, which is known as intelligence. Gathering of Intelligence is a fundamental process generally accepted as part of warfare and in the domain of national security as well as foreign policy, law enforcement and the broader areas involving governance and compliance. However, intelligence is now a core aspect of business activity involving all sections of the organisation, including marketing strategies as well as gaining knowledge of competitor's activities too. It is now a critical element in 'effective decision' making at all levels of business. Intelligence describes both a product and a process. For all aspects of the security function it is now an essential element in compiling comprehensive SRTVA's and operational strategies.

Intelligence is the umbrella term referring to the range of activities – from planning and information collection to analysis and dissemination

Table 5. The methodology sequence

Methodology sequence	Explanation
Understand the infrastructure	This requires knowledge of all aspects of operations, including sub-contractors.
Identify all appropriate risks	Many risks have associations that must be considered too.
Estimate the likelihood and	Careful evaluation of the probability that it could happen is required.
The impact of each risk	The knock on effect must be considered.
Assess vulnerability to risks	What would be the consequences if it happened?
Assess and identify risk solutions	How good are the mitigation measures and countermeasures?
Manage and observe the risks as events change	This is an ongoing essential process

Table 6. Recommnedations to deal with risk

Level of priority given to the risk	Recommendations to be adopted
If it is critical	Action must be taken immediately to remedy the situation. If this cannot be done then reduction of staff, evacuation or even complete shutdown must be considered.
If the situation is considered high risk	Undertake risk reduction exercise looking at alternatives or elimination. This is a priority that must be signed off at high level before proceeding with operations.
Risk is considered to be medium	Consider what actions can be used to lower the risk, ensuring the severity is reduced. Consider the potential consequences.
Risk is considered to be low	Look at improving the situation to ensure the risk does not increase. Consider improvements and barriers to reduce the risk still further.
No consequence to the operations	Monitor and consider what could change

– conducted in secret, and aimed at maintaining or enhancing relative security by providing forewarning of threats or potential threats in a manner that allows for the timely implementation of a preventative policy or strategy, including, where desirable, covert activities (Gill & Phythian, 2006, p. 2)

Intelligence encompasses a range of activities including planning and information collection, analysis and dissemination in support of formal decision making. It is the latter that defines the word for security management, as it allows decisions to be made based upon information that is pertinent to the operation. The word secret needs to be defined for the purpose of supporting operations and covert would be more appropriate. However, it should be noted the gathering process is not done by an underground network of spies but open source gathering techniques that any organization can use. Checking and verifying the

data remains a constant requirement to ensure its veracity and reliability. A difficult process as much is obtained by word of mouth.

Collection planning is the process of establishing a collection program with the primary purpose of collecting information in accordance with defined security management requirements. The direction of the collection process is continuous with a primary objective of controlling, coordinating and monitoring efforts of collection assets. Included in this is the compilation of all data, which must be in an accessible and useable form.

The intelligence requirements need to be clearly identified and allocated as some aspects will need more resources and time to acquire. The requirements can alter depending on the sensitivity of the asset, and based on incoming intelligence that may vary or alter the priority. In the business world resources can be limited

Figure 8. Threat driven risk based design philosophy for security systems (Coole & Brooks, 2011)

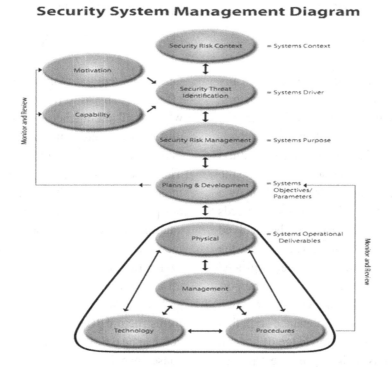

Security System Management Diagram

so priority allocation is an important part of the security manager's role.

Verification Process

The factoring in of redundancy into the collection process and acquiring the same information through differing collection assets provides an opportunity to test the veracity of information reported, whilst also supporting the security of more sensitive collection assets. To ensure maximum utilisation of intelligence, a collection management system is required; this should be a centralised function preventing unnecessary duplication. Coupled with this requirement is the need to cross-reference material to ensure as far as possible how reliable or correct this intelligence maybe? For most organisations intelligence collection is sensitive with resources scarce, therefore, flexibility of approach is required to modify the demands dependent upon the nature of the threat

or based upon new information that requires more data (See Table 7).

How Can we Protect the Infrastructure Using Proactive Measures?

- Maintain a time constant intelligence gathering capability linked to a interactive matrix
- Sound security risk management strategies considering situational threat, system criticality and asset vulnerability
- A series of layered protection measures should be used wherever possible incorporating the whole integration of the infrastructure
- Utilise government and private agencies to acquire up-to date data
- Increased awareness of the status of the Assets and their vulnerabilities within the infrastructure capability
- Greater integration of the Threat and Risk analysis into the overall IT and Computing,

Physical Security, Personnel Security and the Facilities functions

Meetings with Staff

One of the greatly under-utilised resources in any company are the staff, including all contractors. However, it must also recognised that they are potentially a threat because of their inside knowledge of how the organisation functions. A method to overcome this is to get the staff to buy into the need to protect the organisation and their own welfare at the same time. The management needs to ensure that they portray the need to be involved in security in all corporate literature outputs to the staff. In addition, the security department will need to back this up by establishing a working rapport with all members of staff, at all levels. Very often it will be the cleaning and maintenance staff, that have the greatest working knowledge of how an organisation functions, including any weak points. The ancillary staff also tends to know what is happening across the sites, as they interact with their fellow workers daily. The ability to incorporate this rich source of intelligence gathering into the proactive security process is crucial. Many security managers ignore this resource at their peril, as staff can also be quickly alienated too, by not directly involving them in the company security structure. It will require time and effort to manage this resource, which involves regular unofficial meetings, listening to gossip and ensuing that they feel part of the overall security structure of the company as valued members.

It is an unfortunate fact that as far as security is concerned every person within the organisation knows how security should be conducted and will always have an opinion on what should be done and why this is not being done. Nonetheless, this can be turned to an advantage rather than a distraction. Invite the staff to comment on the situation through setting up a web based comments page, where their observations can be registered. A reply should always be given back to them, even if the information is of little value;

allowing the member of staff the feeling that have not 'wasted their time'.

Ground Coverage Status

Ground coverage involves a concept developed effectively by the Rhodesian Police Force, whereby all intelligence; every snippet with every nuance is collected and collated regularly into a multi-dimensional composition (Bailey, 2010). The process is on-going and requires regular interpretation of the links and sources to ensure any productive leads can be followed through. By adapting this concept an organisation can greatly increase its intelligence capabilities.

Known personalities can be profiled building up a picture of their affiliations, known habits and propensity to commit overt acts against the infrastructure. It should be understood these overt acts can be politically biased as well motivated to cause financially harm or damage to the reputation of the organisation concerned. Reputation for a publically listed company is of vital importance, as bad publicity can affect the share value.

Note that the threat is not just criminal involving financial loss; it may also be political or reputational. Therefore, political activists, environmental campaigners or union agitators will also need to be monitored, as they too can have a potential impact on the organisation.

Additional Resources to Support the SRTVA

The objective of using this comprehensive SRTVA is to quantify the risk vis a vis the consequences. The appropriate preventative measures then need to be assessed and analysed and align against the cost and risk benefit to the organization against its overall strategic goals. Can it afford not to put mitigation into place and continue to carry the risk? Once the consequence of the potential outcome is firmly understood then management is better able to deal with implementing measures at the highest level. Unfortunately in the past the concerns

Table 7. Sources of intelligence

Controlled sources.	Security personnel, management, contractors and confidential informants.
Commercial sources	Information may be purchased and can include commercial information brokers, academics and private intelligence sources.
Open sources.	Open sources are generally not tasked but researched by analysts and can include public records, newspapers, journals, libraries and the internet.
Official sources.	Includes government agencies: police, customs, council offices, Local authorities, service providers The Nature of Sources and Agencies
Sensitive sources.	May include informants and individuals in the community
Technical sources.	In the private sector we might include CCTV, data acquisition, such as Access control systems
Casual sources	One off informants and chance encounters. Information from such is often difficult to verify. However, may be a valuable source
Liaison	Between other security agencies. A rapport needs to be developed and nurtured if this is to be successful.

raised by security have not been presented in a format which transfers easily upwards to those that need to make the decisions. Very often they do not have the experience or the expertise to understand what the consequences might be for the operation. Once this can be explained and presented in a more comprehensive visual manner this process becomes a lot simpler.

Modelling, Table-Top Exercises, and Red Teaming

There are a number of additional tools that can be used to test the existing structures and procedures that are already in place. The use of the table-top exercise is a theoretical work shop bringing together various stake-holders under the guidance of a facilitator. A scenario will be played out requiring the participants to react to each additional piece of information as it is introduced to them. The intention is to intensify the incidents requiring the participants to draw on their problem solving skills at greater and greater levels to deal with the situation All actions are recorded and then discussed in a debrief to assess how each performed and what actions could be improved for real time events. These sessions are a very effective way of testing the command and control procedures showing up any weaknesses that may be present. Making them part of a regular training program for all key staff has been shown to be

very beneficial for team building and preparing for the real thing.

Another useful tool is 'Red Teaming'. Effectively it means attacking your own defences to see if they can withstand the offensive. Although developed for the military purposes to simulate an attack by the enemy, who are the *red team*, hence the name; it is now used by security operatives and often called defeat testing. The 'Red-Teaming' concept is quite common amongst the technological community, and is a means to ensure that the systems are tested and changed regularly. However, in the context of general security it means far more as it includes the gathering of intelligence as well as running penetration tests utilising such terms as red and blue teaming, (blue is the defensive team) assessing decay in systems and monitoring weaknesses. "Exploiting vulnerabilities to mitigate risk can be done by human-based red teaming, where a force is divided into two teams; one simulating the enemy (red team) while the other simulating friends (blue team)" (Moteff, 2005, p. 268).

Within the overall risk assessment process 'Red Teaming' can be very useful in assessing how capable the security systems and practices are when put to the test. It is method to assess likely adversary modus operandi. In essence it is the ability to create multiple scenarios based upon defined parameters assessing potential threats and how these evaluate as risks to the operations.

Once the weaknesses have been exposed, then it is possible to improve and defend against them with a greater understanding of how they could be breached in the first place (Yang, Abbass, & Sarker, 2006).

There are limitations to using staff that are acquainted with the overall complex as they will have a good knowledge of how the systems work; this can skewer the outcomes. Using a variety of outside contractors can overcome this limitation but this will depend on budget constraints as to whether it is cost effective. Another method is to use staff from differing departments as part of the management team building exercises for conducting penetration tests.

A further instrument that can be used is an interactive prototyping tool. This is useful in playing out scenarios and simulating the effect of change using a multitude of scenarios; however existing simulators in the critical infrastructure area are typically limited in the visual representation and limited inter-activity. Masek et al have suggested an additional method using games technology for scenario modelling and assessment (Masek, Boeing, & Bailey, 2010).

Using Simulation Support Techniques

At present the common approach is to use graphical visualization simulations when attempting to deal with critical infrastructure. By using a single user graphic display, the nodes can be connected up to show their interdependencies, often using integrated Geographic Information Systems (GIS), such as Google maps, then overlaying the connected node diagram for a 2D effect. Such displays are useful for traditional risk-based analysis in the design and analysis of critical infrastructure systems, but not for identifying local security vulnerabilities. The current requirement is to improve upon this and create an interactive 3D capability (Boeing, et al., 2008, p. 28).

Games technology appears to be able to remedy this problem, as it is an interactive tool, whereby the "intruder" can be manipulated independently within the scenario to complete tasks based upon varying inputs (Cardoso & Diniz, 2009; Liu, Wang, & Camp, 2008). Changing the scenarios and implementing the mitigation measures tests whether the target hardening actually improves the capacity to prevent access. By using such technology it greatly reduces the cost of applying actual mitigations in situ, if in fact they will not improve the robustness of the protection measures. Alternatively, it can demonstrate where mitigation measures need to be applied, if at all. Furthermore, the process of conducting SRTVA's using these methods improves the mindset of those involved to test varying hypotheses to the point of defeat (Boeing, et al., 2008).

Simulation starkly represents the importance of understanding the realities of 'consequence' in the overall security risk mitigation process. It becomes more obvious because of the visualisation process. Being able to see what went wrong makes it easier to put it right. Appreciating the nature of the actual consequence also helps in ascertaining what needs to be done to rectify the weakness. In addition, a cost-analysis-benefit should be preformed assessing the outlay involved in comparison with the feasible mitigation strategies. The assessment should include the potential consequences of not implementing any changes at all; doing nothing is a decision in itself under certain conditions. A return on investment matrix should be produced to assist with the management decision regarding the proposed changes.

The ability to test all the possible measures that could be used relative to the cost makes it easier to identify the preferred option. The use of this visualisation technology presents a substantial improvement over the outlay of conducting a series of real time risk assessments in the field. In addition, maintaining a relative real-time working model of the whole complex allows a company to test any proposed or suggested improvements prior to implementation; a considerable cost saving benefit coupled with avoiding costly mistakes.

FUTURE RESEARCH DIRECTIONS

The development of risk based modelling through games technology and image creation technology will enhance the capabilities of security risk and threat management identification. Security requires harnessing multiple technologies to combat potential threats and this can only be achieved by ensuring that every possible application is assessed to see if it can be utilised.

A large amount of research and development is available from the US. Homeland security web site: http://www.dhs.gov/index.shtm. Depending on which countries you are dealing with, will depend on where you can access more defined information on particular support structures. In Australia for example the following are useful: http://www.securitymanagement.com.au/critical_infrastructure_protection.php, http://future-directions.org.au/publications.html, http://www.securityresearch.org.au/, and the research centre at Edith Cowan University, Perth, Australia, which looks at all aspects of securing infrastructure: http://www.ecu.edu.au/schools/computer-and-security-science/research-activity/secau-security-research-centre/overview

CONCLUSION

For many organisations using the SRTVA, which incorporates a structured intelligence gathering capability too, is a new and uncertain concept; especially if it needs to be formalised within the overall managerial structure. Security for many organisations is considered as a one off budget expense, which normally means purchasing a static alarm and access control system operated by low maintenance security guards. Involving security departments into a wider role will have to be managed carefully and encouraged, especially as the threats to infrastructure have wide ranging consequences to the country and for all concerned. Although this concept of utilising security intelligence in a more proactive role is not new to a number of security operations, particularly those operating in hostile environments: oil, gas and mining sectors, it will be a very new and different approach to the majority of infrastructure operations in less hostile environments.

This chapter has looked at the use of proactive security management as a holistic process based upon sound intelligence gathering capabilities and effective dissemination systems. Furthermore, it has identified how new methods can be incorporated into the risk, threat and vulnerability analysis procedures, explained penetration testing based upon the scenario outcomes and produced a detailed work sheet for operations to establish this proactive approach. The use of red-teaming has been explored and shown to be capable of incorporating both computer based modelling techniques with real time penetration testing and using trained security personnel or contractors in an attempt to defeat the systems in place. Future developments in this area of technology are set to produce far more effective methods of testing security; resulting in cost benefits too.

By combining all these processes into a single methodology allows the protection of critical infrastructure to move from response based mode to proactive mode; by taking the initiative to forestall potential breaches or genuine penetrations to the actual critical infrastructure security. The argument put forward here is that major corporations worldwide, particularly oil companies, are currently operating in difficult, daunting and hostile environments and they are able to manage their security by using this type of methodology. Therefore, the logical progression is that if this methodology allows them to operate, then all major critical infrastructure complexes should be implementing a similar methodology too. By adopting a more proactive security management strategy now will assist in mitigating future risks, threats and vulnerabilities before they have dire consequences.

REFERENCES

ASME. (2006). *RAMCAP: The framework (Vol. Version 2.0)*. Washington, DC: ASME Innovative Technologies Institute, LLC.

Bailey, W. J. (2010). *Hearts and minds, psuedo gangs and counter-insurgency: Based upon experiences from previous campaigns in Kenya (1952-60), Malaya (1948-60) & Rhodesia (1964-1979)*. Paper presented at the 1st Australian Couter Terrorism Conference, Perth, Australia.

Boeing, A., Masek, M., & Bailey, B. (2008). *Protecting critical infrastructure with games technology*. School of Computer and Information Science, Edith Cowan University, Perth, Western Australia (9th Australian Information Warfare and Security Conference).

Cardoso, J. M. P., & Diniz, P. C. (2009). Why both game theory and reliability theory are important in defending infrastructure against intelligent attacks game theoretic risk analysis of security threats. *International Series in Operations Research & Management Science, 128*, 1–11. doi:10.1007/978-0-387-87767-9_4

Coole, M., & Brooks, D. (2009). *Security decay: An entropic approach to definition and understanding*. Paper presented at the 2nd Australian and Security conference, Perth, Australia.

Coole, M., & Brooks, D. (2011). *Mapping the organizational relationships within physical security body of knowledge: A management heuristic of sound theory and best practice*. Paper presented at the 4th Australian Security and Intelligence Conference, Perth, Australia.

Cox, J. L. A. (2008). Some limitations of "risk = threat × vulnerability × consequence" for risk analysis of terrorist attacks. *Risk Analysis, 28*(6), 1749–1761. doi:10.1111/j.1539-6924.2008.01142.x

DePoy, J., Phelan, J., Sholander, P., Smith, B. J., Varnado, G. B., Wyss, G. D., et al. (2006). *Critical infrastructure systems of systems assessment methodology*. Livermore, CA: Technical Report SAND2006-6399, Sandia National Laboratories (October 2007).

Diaxion. (2010). *Understanding IT governance – Part two*. Retrieved from http://www.diaxion.com/blog/2010/05/04/understanding-it-governance-%e2%80%93-part-two/

Ezell, B. C. (2007). Infrastructure vulnerability assessment model (I VAM). *Risk Analysis, 27*(3), 571–583. doi:10.1111/j.1539-6924.2007.00907.x

Ezell, B. C., Farr, J. V., & Wiese, I. (2000). Infrastructure risk analysis model. *Journal of Infrastructure Systems, 6*, 114. doi:10.1061/(ASCE)1076-0342(2000)6:3(114)

Garcia, M. L. (2006). *Vulnerability assessment of physical protection systems*. Burlington, MA: Elsevier Butterworth-Heinemann.

Gill, P., & Phythian, M. (2006). *Intelligence in an insecure world*. London, UK: Polity.

Holton, G. A. (2004). Defining risk. *Financial Analysts Journal, 60*(6), 19–25. doi:10.2469/faj.v60.n6.2669

Kaplan, S. (1997). The words of risk analysis. *Risk Analysis, 17*(4), 407–417. doi:10.1111/j.1539-6924.1997.tb00881.x

Lewis, T. G. (2006). *Critical infrastructure protection in homeland security: Defending a networked nation*. Monterey, CA: John Wiley & Soms. doi:10.1002/0471789542

Liu, D., Wang, X. F., & Camp, J. (2008). Game-theoretic modeling and analysis of insider threats. *International Journal of Critical Infrastructure Protection*, *1*, 75–80. doi:10.1016/j.ijcip.2008.08.001

Masek, M., Boeing, A., & Bailey, W. (2010). Critical infrastructure protection risk modelling with games technology. *What Kind of Information Society? Governance, Virtuality, Surveillance, Sustainability* . *Resilience*, *328*, 363–372. doi:doi:10.1007/978-3-642-15479

Moteff, J. (2005). *Risk management and critical infrastructure protection: Assessing, integrating, and managing threats, vulnerabilities and consequences*.

Ritchie, B. (1993). *Ritchie and Marshall (1993) business risk management* (*Vol. 1*). London, UK: Chapman & Hall.

Slovic, P. (1999). Trust, emotion, sex, politics, and science: Surveying the risk-assessment battlefield. *Risk Analysis*, *19*(4), 689–701. doi:10.1111/j.1539-6924.1999.tb00439.x

Standards Australia. (2004a). *HB 221:2004 Business continuity management*. Sydney, Australia: Standards Australia International Ltd.

Standards Australia. (2004b). *HB 436:2004 Risk management guidelines: Companion to AS/NZS 4360*. Sydney, Australia: Standards Australia International Ltd.

Standards Australia. (2009). *AS/NZS ISO 31000:2009. Risk management - Principles and guidelines: In context*. Sydney, Australia: Standards Australia International Ltd.

Standards Australia. (2010). *HB 327: 2010 Communicating and consulting about risk: Companion to AS/NZS ISO 31000:2009*. Sydney, Australia: Standards Australia, International Ltd.

Talbot, J., & Jakeman, M. (2009). *Frontmatter. Security Risk Management* (pp. i–xxiv). London, UK: John Wiley & Sons, Inc. doi:10.1002/9780470494974.fmatter

Tolone, W., Wilson, D., Raja, A., Xiang, W. N., Hao, H., Phelps, S., & Johnson, E. (2004). In Chen, H., Moore, R., Zeng, D., & Leavitt, J. (Eds.), *Critical infrastructure integration modeling and simulation: Intelligence and security informatics* (*Vol. 3073*, pp. 214–225). Lecture Notes in Computer Science Berlin: GermanyL Springer. Retrieved from.

Yang, A., Abbass, H. A., & Sarker, R. (2006). Characterizing warfare in red teaming. *IEEE Transactions on Systems, Man, and Cybernetics. Part B, Cybernetics*, *36*(2), 268–285. doi:10.1109/TSMCB.2005.855569

Chapter 4
Industrial Control Systems:
The Human Threat

Antony Bridges
QinetiQ, UK

ABSTRACT

As industrial control systems (ICSs) have been connected to wider organisational networks and the Internet, the threat from unauthorised access has increased. Protecting these systems from attack requires not just the use of appropriate technological solutions but also an understanding of the humans within the wider system. It is not sufficient that the human knows what they need to do. They must also be willing and able to do it. This chapter highlights some of the human vulnerabilities within Industrial Control Systems and suggests that greater consideration of and adaptation to the human limitations will enhance the future security of these systems.

INTRODUCTION

In the past employees stationed in remote huts or signal boxes manually adjusted valves and switches to maintain production or support the running of transportation systems. As technology advanced these standalone control points were connected and manual controls were replaced with remotely operated controls. This allowed just a few individuals to monitor and make prompt interventions to any part of the system, reducing disruption to production, decreasing operating costs and improving safety. Over time, the systems have grown in scale and complexity, from closed networks to those operating across large distances through corporate networks and the Internet. As the use of Industrial Control Systems (ICSs) has grown, system providers have moved to standard system platforms and off-the-shelf software using standard operating systems. This has increased their vulnerability to the cyber security threat and reduced the ability of organisations to understand the potential consequences of an attack.

The US Industrial Control Systems Cyber Emergency Response Team (ICS-CERT, 2011) highlighted a significant growth in incidents

DOI: 10.4018/978-1-4666-2659-1.ch004

Copyright © 2013, IGI Global. Copying or distributing in print or electronic forms without written permission of IGI Global is prohibited.

impacting on US organizations' that own and operate control systems associated with critical infrastructure. In 2009 four incidents were confirmed. In 2010 this had risen to 41 reported incidents involving the deployment of onsite response teams on eight occasions. In 2011, 198 incidents were reported. This increase may be partially attributable to greater awareness and better reporting nonetheless the incidents included genuine threats. Cases included spear-phishing e-mail campaigns that successfully compromised and copied data from the business enterprise network, the Stuxnet virus on engineering workstations and several machines connected to manufacturing control systems network and the infection of a remote terminal server. In 2005 13 US DaimlerChrysler plants employing 50,000 workers were shut for an hour after becoming infected by the Zotob worm (United States General Accounting Office, 2007). When ICS stops functioning there is an immediate and direct cost in terms of loss production or service.

The Human in the System

Those that design technologies and processes have the advantage that the human is very adaptable and will tend to find a way of getting the system to work for them. This adaptability will often come at some cost however, from personal injury, to significantly lower levels of overall productivity and performance than could be achieved from a better designed system.

The human errors associated with poorly designed Industrial Control Systems have been reduced as a result of findings from human factor research and accident investigations such as the Three Mile Island disaster. However, human factors have not been considered in the same way in the security domain. In the safety context steps have included:

- Developing a better understanding of the workload that a system places on the human operator. For example, understanding

individuals' limits in terms of the information they can process from visual and audio sources.
- Selecting individuals with the appropriate skills and traits to operate, manage or maintain the system and providing effective training to develop and maintain relevant skills.
- Enhancing the operator's ability to remain vigilant, respond quickly and make effective decisions by quantifying the time that an individual can remain effective on a given task as well as their overall shift length and the time of day.
- Considering how information should be presented. ICS interfaces have been enhanced so they assist the operator in interpreting the information and making decisions. The use of automated monitoring that sets off alarms when systems fall outside of the expected ranges has allowed the time that human operators spend monitoring to be reduced, and allowed them to control bigger networks.

Human Factors supports the development of security systems so that they provide an acceptable degree of security in a form that does not overburden the users or impact unduly on operations. Security spending has tended to fall into two distinct groups: the employment of security guards and the purchase of security equipment. Less thought has been given to how the security system involves the complex interaction of technology, process and the human. This includes operators, maintenance personnel, administrators, software designers and where the system is linked to the Internet; all those who may for whatever reason seek to access the system. Turk (2005) noted that, "Knowledge of human factors and human reliability concepts can be used to strengthen the design of cyber security training and awareness, and ensure getting systems back online with the least amount of damage to property and human life" (Turk, 2005, p. 16).

This Chapter highlights the need for ICS security systems to be designed to enable humans to complete their tasks efficiently and effectively, rather than expecting the human to cope unaided with an increasingly complex and sophisticated world of cyber security. This Chapter also addresses the human behaviours that make ICSs and Information Communication Technology systems vulnerable to attack. The ICS-CERT Incidents Response Summary (2011) highlighted the human threat. Successful attacks had occurred as a result of employee behaviour either through sophisticated Spear-Phishing when employees had followed links or opened attachments on e-mails that appeared to be from corporate executives or other trusted sources. In another case a number of organisations had been exposed to a virus from contracted from employees using a USB stick to load presentations at an industry conference. The Chapter concludes with actions that organisations could take to alert them to potential risks and reduce the likelihood of the risk occurring.

Industrial Control Systems Are Vulnerable to a Changed World

Remote access and monitoring of parts of the system have provided significant cost savings for industries such as manufacturing or oil and gas. The system can be operated by fewer operators in a central location and much of the maintenance monitoring can be conducted remotely avoiding the costs of sending crews to check units. The integration of the industrial control systems with other corporate systems means that information from production or operations can be fed directly into corporate systems.

However, whilst these systems have brought significant benefits they have also created greater vulnerabilities. The integration of ICS with other corporate ICT systems means that the ICS are vulnerable to attack using the same tools and methods as are used in more traditional information theft attacks. As the European Network and Information Security Agency (ENISA) noted,

"one of the biggest issues that ICS operators have to face is to build security programmes that integrate all aspects of cyber security, incorporating desktop and business computing systems with industrial automation and control systems (European Network and Information Security Agency, 2011, 6.1.3).

According to ENISA (European Network and Information Security Agency, 2011, p. 15) "ICS systems and other corporate IT systems are nowadays interconnected". A survey of 134 individuals responsible for security and/or operations within industrial automation environments found that 71% were expecting the connectivity between industrial endpoints and corporate IT infrastructure to increase over the next 3-5 years (Industrial Defender, 2011). Information Communication Technology (ICT) describes the wider business enterprise software, data storage and data transmission systems. The interconnectivity between ICSs and ICT systems, and the ability to access ICSs using the ICT systems means that both need to considered when addressing the human threat within ICSs. In the case of a European utility, a virus entered the ICS through the ICT network and prevented 30-40% of communications between ICS and the control centre. The utility lost visibility of a number of substations and 40 man weeks of effort were required to remove the virus from the system (Turk, 2005).

The workforce for many industrial organisations has changed, with an increased reliance on contractors who move between employers and locations. This has created new security risks. A transient workforce requires operating systems that are easily understood or are supported with user guides. It encourages the use of standard passwords or password sharing that risks letting unauthorised individuals have access. It also results in a workforce that is not as effectively monitored or understood by supervisors and managers as permanent employees are, reducing the organisations ability to detect the early signs of employee disengagement and discontent.

The use of standardised systems as a result of the increase in construction of industrial facilities across the globe also brings new vulnerabilities. Rather than creating bespoke control processes, utility companies are increasingly using off-the-shelf ICS. The result, as Shea (2003) noted is that individuals have opportunities to learn about the design of ICS by breaking into systems in a different company and country far away from their ultimate target. Organisations may therefore not get an early warning of threat activity. Their own safeguards for documentation and user guides for the ICS may be undermined if other organisations fail to protect information in the same way, where they are using the same off-the-shelf system.

Lessons from Other ICS Incidents

Industrial incidents have highlighted how minor errors can lead to significant incidents that result in the loss of service, productivity or result in major incidents. They highlight the unpredictable impact that a modest cyber attack could have on an organisation.

On August 14, 2003 the North American power grid experienced its largest blackout ever (NERC Steering Group, 2004). The blackout affected an estimated 50 million people in the USA and Canada. For most customers power was restored within a few hours. However, some areas in the United States experienced a blackout lasting two days and parts of Ontario suffered from rotating power cuts for up to two weeks.

As already discussed, ICS provide monitoring and control over thousands of sensors and control points allowing a limited number of personnel to operate complex networks. To manage their workload systems will set off an alarm in the event that a particular sensor reading falls outside of an acceptable range, alerting the operator to the need to make an intervention.

At the beginning of the North American power grid blackout incident, as a result of a processor stalling, the control room operators lost the alarm function that provided audible and visual indications of a problem with an important element within the ICS. As the Technical Analysis report noted, "with the software unable to complete that alarm event and move to the next one, the alarm processor buffer filled and eventually overflowed. After 14:14, the FE control computer displays did not receive any further alarms, nor were any alarms being printed or posted on the EMS alarm logging facilities" (NERC Steering Group, 2004, p. 32). The lack of an alarm contributed to a misunderstanding of the status of the system and allowed the situation to further deteriorate. The system then created further errors by presenting an inaccurate description of the situation following a warm reboot of the system. As the report noted, the start-up diagnostics "verified that the computer and all expected processes were running. Accordingly, the FE computer support staff believed that they had successfully restarted the node and all the processes it was hosting. However, although the server and its applications were again running, the alarm system remained frozen and non-functional, even on the restarted computer" (NERC Steering Group, 2004, p. 34). It is wrong to assume that in the early stages of an attack or a malfunction that those responsible for making the correct decisions have a clear picture of what they are facing. Human operators do not cope well with uncertainty. By moving a valve to an incorrect position and denying the human operator an alert, the first they may become aware of the problem is when a second part of the system becomes disrupted. At this point the direction of attention has been drawn to the secondary part of the system with the actual cause still hidden. Responses to the problem can therefore be incorrect. In the case of Three Mile Island poor interface design was the key issue. Operators were unable to read the control room displays due to poor positioning and poor design. A hidden indicator light led an operator to manually override the automatic emergency cooling system of the reactor. The lack of initial warning due to the fact the indicator was obscured, led the operator to incorrectly believe that the cause of the malfunction was too much coolant water present in the reactor. (Jewell & Siegal, 1990).

These two examples indicate the challenges faced by human operators using ICS. They are expected to intervene after periods of fairly low or routine activity and make critical decisions based on the information provided to them. Incidents that could have been relatively easily managed can quickly escalate if the information made available leads to incorrect action being taken. In both cases described here the malfunction that triggered a more serious series of events was manageable but the confusion caused by the lack of initial alarm led to incorrect actions. Such confusion can be created by providing apparently contradictory information. This could include removing the warning signal associated with the valve attacked, or removing faith in the system by ensuring that a few indicators provide false information or provide incorrect information on an intermittent basis. To address this risk consideration needs to be given to the typical problem solving procedures to account for a more considered human attack rather than a potentially more manageable and logical component failure.

Examples of Attacks

There are a number of well publicised cases that have at least demonstrated that ICS can be attacked and that these attacks can result in disruption with serious implications and additional costs for the organisations involved. Each case highlights the human element of the threat. As a US Government Accountability Office (GAO) report noted, "there has been a growing recognition that control systems are now vulnerable to cyber attacks from numerous sources, including hostile governments, terrorist groups, disgruntled employees, and other malicious intruders." (United States General Accounting Office, 2004, p. 11).

Charney (Hearing before Subcommittee, 2002) reported a case when a juvenile had remotely taken control of a telecommunications switch. The switch serviced the unmanned control tower of a regional airport. As planes approached the airfield they would radio the tower and a signal would be sent automatically across the telecommunications network to turn on the landing lights on the runway. The juvenile had disabled the telecommunications switch so when the next plane approached the airfield the landing lights did not turn on, forcing the plane to divert. The airport had been effectively shutdown through an indirect attack on the telecommunications system: the key lesson being that significant disruption can be achieved by taking control of a relatively small element of the control system.

The Davis-Besse nuclear power plant attack in Ohio highlights the challenges faced by organisations in making timely interventions once their system has been attacked. The Davis-Besse private computer network was infected by the Microsoft SQL Server worm, known as Slammer. The virus disabled a safety monitoring system for nearly 5 hours and the plant's process computer failed. It took six hours to make the system available again. According to the GAO report, Slammer also "affected communications on the control networks of at least five other utilities by propagating so quickly that control system traffic was blocked" (United States General Accounting Office, 2004, p. 34).

The last two examples involve an attack by individuals outside the organisation, however, of equal concern is the threat from within. In 2000 Vitek Boden attacked the Maroochy Shire sewage control system and caused millions of litres of raw sewage to spill out into local parks and rivers polluting the water system, killing marine life and upsetting local residents. Vitek, angry at the rejection of his job application to the council, had used knowledge he had gained by working for the company that had installed the system to gain access and open critical valves. Vitek's laptop hard drive contained software for accessing and controlling the sewage management system (Smith, 2001). Another factor in this case was the time it took Maroochy Water Services to identify that an individual was attacking their system. Initially it was believed that problems such as pumps not running when they should have been and alarms not being reported to the central computer were caused by installation errors (Abrams & Weiss, 2008). The security by obscurity approach, which assumes a system is protected because it is complex or archaic, becomes significantly less effective when those that helped install or maintain the system seek to attack it. It also demonstrates how an organisation can become the victim of an attack driven by a desire to harm another organisation, in this case the individual's frustration with the council led to an attack on the sewage control system.

One of the first reported cases of a cyber attack on industrial production was on Allen-Bradley DH+ in 1988. According to Bryes and Hoffman (n.d.) a frustrated worker changed the system password to an obscene word. This locked all other users out of the system. As discussed earlier, given the importance of maintaining operations and productivity such changes can have a significant impact on the organisation. The worker had been able to log in to the system as the original password had been written down and left in a visible location by an authorised user.

THE HUMAN COMPLICATION

Addressing the ICS security challenges described above requires an understanding of the complexity of the human and their interaction with other elements of the system. Systems are often based upon rules and logic. A certain input will be processed in a certain way and, based on the rules, result in a certain outcome. Whilst human behaviour is to some extent predictable, training or instructing an

individual to follow an unusable process is unlikely to result in the desired behaviour. People will not necessarily behave as the organisation would like just because certain behaviour is enshrined in the organisational process. They will inevitably seek the simplest way of completing their tasks. Ignoring this in the design of a security system creates points of failure.

Jeannot suggests that, "the greatest vulnerabilities come from people. Most of the time the technology is actually pretty robust but people click on a link when they are not supposed to, choose a simple password, or write the password down on a piece of paper" (Homeland Security Newswire, 2011, p. 1). However this behaviour is to some extent the inevitable consequence of some system designs.

Humans may not behave as the system design requires because they are unable to e.g. the system requires the human to do things which are beyond most peoples cognitive or physical abilities. Alternatively they may not behave as expected because they do not have the motivation or inclination to. Finally, in some cases people are not aware that certain behaviours are expected or needed. This section considers the implications of all three factors on system performance.

The attack examined by Pfleeger (2010) provides a useful case study. It concerns a large multinational company with a central server in the US with thousands of end user systems and 200 to 300 other servers with staff and clients requiring access to parts of the system. The company were infected by a sophisticated Trojan attack. The Trojans had arrived through e-mail attachments and malicious. It had been designed to avoid being detected by automated tools. Staff had all completed security awareness training; however the attackers used trusted sources for e-mails e.g. the hotel employees were due to stay in and other colleagues. Staff found it hard to distinguish between non threat and threat e-mails. Pfleeger also suggested there was a lack of focus or willingness on behalf of the employee to focus on security.

"Knowing that IT support staff employs a great deal of cybersecurity technology, many workers felt the technology would protect them – so they focussed more on getting their jobs done than on protecting their equipment and data" (Pfleeger, 2010, p. 22). Support staff had all been using the same password to access different servers and the attackers took advantage of common local admin passwords.

People Can't do It

The human is a very adaptable part of any process; however there are limits to his or her performance. Many security systems do not appear to have considered human limitations and expect the human to adapt to poorly designed processes and tools.

Passwords do not Consider User Requirements

Passwords frustrate users when they are unable to complete their tasks because they are unable to recall their passwords. Sasse, Ashenden, Lawrence, Coles-Kemp, Fléchais, and Kearney (2007) concluded, "The cumulative effect of the demands of several such security mechanisms (e.g. passwords and PINs) at work and at home means that many individuals simply cannot cope and make mistakes. This negative experience of security antagonises people, reduces their motivation to follow security policies, and creates negative attitudes towards security" p. 3. As a result individuals will make it as easy as possible to recall the password which results in the use of a common set of passwords e.g. Admin, Password, 12345 or qwerty. These passwords make recall simpler and reduce the likelihood of problems accessing data or controls. Engineers and security experts may consider such behaviour to be a demonstration of human foolishness, however from a user's perspective it is a perfectly sensible activity. It reduces cognitive load and increases the likelihood of being able to access the protected system without delay. The United States General Accounting Office (2004) report referred to the tendency for passwords to be shared (p. 18). The need for the human operator to complete their tasks and minimise delay or inconvenience drives behaviours that create security weaknesses. Designing a security system without considering the needs and pressures placed upon those who are expected to use it inevitably created potential vulnerabilities.

Creating longer passwords reduces the likelihood of an individual guessing or breaking the protection. To improve the effectiveness the password should make use of numeric keys, characters and symbols, ideally using alternative scripts to Latin such as Chinese or Arabic. However, this does nothing to help the human operator recall the password. When designing a system it is not enough to dictate that it must involve a complex sixteen character password and then expect the users to memorise it instantly. The reality is that they will be unable to recall it and will therefore resort to writing it down where it can be relatively easily accessed. In the case of Allen-Bradley DH+ the employee had obtained the original password he needed to enter the system from a note on another employee's desk. Employees writing passwords down is a behavioural issue that creates weaknesses within the security system. It is also in some cases the inevitable outcome of designing a security system that most humans are unable to comply with.

Individuals will look for way for simplifying tasks. The Burton report highlighted the risk of wide access to information as a result of individuals backing information up in order to have easy access. "Data is replicated without due consideration. This can range from individuals saving duplicate copies of shared area files within their own personal drives, to large scale data replication" (Burton, p. 3). In the case of user documents this can lead to sensitive system documents being copied to hard drives or backed up on other servers.

Security Performance is not Managed

Employees are not always able to complete tasks, for example they are not trained to distinguish threat from non-threat e-mails.

In order to enhance security officers' performance in the detection of physical threats (for example improvised explosive devices), security officers are provided with random, typically daily, tests where amongst the non threat items they view, there will be what appears to be a genuine threat (Cutler and Paddock, 2009). This regular exposure maintains vigilance, helps the individual quantify their performance and provides regular exposure to the types of devices that they could come across in their duties.

In the case of e-mails being used to place a Trojan virus on an organisation' system, organisations should assess how well their staff perform in that threat detection task and quantify performance against a range of typical attack profiles. This test could range from e-mails from an unknown source announcing love or the offer of easy money to highly sophisticated attacks. In a description of an attack on a large organisation, Pfleeger (2010, p. 22) describes how, "staff about to attend an upcoming workshop received emails with three attachments, each purportedly containing information about workshop attendance and accommodation, but each also contained a separate, hidden Trojan". In order to detect such well hidden attacks from apparently legitimate e-mail addresses individuals would need to adopt a very cautious approach to opening e-mail attachments. Whilst some malicious software could be detected by automated algorithms, the human is still required to detect more sophisticated attacks. However, as there is no widespread testing programme to test and enhance individuals' ability to identify threat e-mails very few organisations know the baseline level of performance of their personnel in identifying suspicious e-mail attachments.

Organisations have the opportunity to build intelligence on the type of attacks being aimed at them and the employees most commonly targeted. Chien and O'Gorman (2011) described the techniques used in an attack directed companies involved in the research, development, and manufacture of chemicals and advanced materials. In some cases a small number of employees received targeted e-mails, in such cases the e-mails, "purported to be meeting invitations from established business partners" (Chien & O'Gorman, 2011, p. 2). In other cases, "when the emails were being sent to a broad set of recipients, the mails purported to be a necessary security update" (Chien & O'Gorman, 2011, p. 2). Having security procedures that require employees to just ignore or delete suspect e-mails without any reporting denies the opportunity for other employees to be made aware of the latest threat or for the organisation to build up a picture of individuals or groups of individuals within the organisation that are most likely to be exposed to attacks.

Staff are not Recruited Because They are Good at Security

Some organisations will operate a vetting system such as a criminal record check to identify individuals who, due to previous activities in their lives, pose a potential security risk (Centre of Protection for National Infrastructure, 2009). This is an active selection out of those who pose a threat but it not a positive selection of those that are likely to actively enhance security.

Individuals who do not like adhering to rules, who prefer not to spend time trying to understand procedures and regulations and who are set business objectives that ignore or even conflict with security requirements, are unlikely to be able to behave as the security system requires. The various roles within a diverse organisation will require a range of skills. If security is critical to an organisations success, not being clear in the initial interview that certain security behaviours are expected and required, creates future challenges in the management of these staff.

Even in the case of the IT security professional at the heart of the security system there is often little thought to their role as a business enabler, as part of a team whose mission is to let the business operate securely and efficiently. Glover and Bowyer (2011, p. 3) highlighted the wider skills that are required of specialist security staff. Being an effective cyber security professional involves more than just applying technical skills: it also involves working well in a team, making effective decisions, using information appropriately, and responding quickly to issues that arise. Glover and Bowyer included in their paper a range of skills required for many cyber security specialists including the ability to work under pressure, ability to make decisions and initiate action and the ability to work with others.

Staff do not Know How to Respond

Organisations conduct regular fire alarm tests and periodically require staff to evacuate the building and follow the full fire alarm drill. Once evacuated, fire wardens may remind staff that there were faster routes to leave the building or comment on the speed of response. Individuals that failed to respond in an appropriate manner may receive a more direct warning and reminder that they are to follow the evacuation procedure should the alarm sound. Very few organisations adopt a similar rehearsal process for a cyber attack. Pfleeger (2010) highlighted the serious impact of this failure to prepare in a paper examining an organisation's response to a cyber attack. Recognising that employees' passwords had been compromised the IT department e-mailed all staff mandating them to reset their passwords. The organisation had not rehearsed this activity. At a time when the IT Department's resources were already stretched as they attempted to protect the organisation from a significant attack, the message resulted in the

help-desk call volume increasing to over 3000 calls with callers either asking why the request had been made or for guidance on how to change the password. It would clearly be unacceptable in the event of a fire for employees to phone their Estate office to ask for guidance. Just as organisations may have an alarm for a fire consideration should also be given to a cyber threat alarm. Whatever system is used to create the alarm, staff should be clear about how they should respond and have the skills to respond appropriately.

Staff do not React as You Expect Them to

In the book 'On War' Clausewitz (Griffith, 1997) emphasised the confusion that battle brings, the effect of uncertainty and the impact of chance. The loss of sensitive information or control of systems will not always come in the form of a clear 'enemy' or assault. It brings with it confusion, uncertainty and distrust as to whether the attack has come from outside the organisation or has been instigated by individuals within it. This can increase existing tensions and distrust within the leadership team.

The uncertainty caused by information known by a small trusted group leaking is significant. Take for example the testimony from the recent UK investigation into phone hacking. The actress Sienna Miller commented, "I remember one occasion where I sat my family and friends down in a room, and I accused them of leaking stories to the press as a story had come out that only they had known about. Looking back, it makes me extremely angry that I was forced into being so suspicious of people that I love and care for, and that I had to suffer such feelings of betrayal, especially by those who had done nothing wrong" (The Leveson Inquiry, 2011). The lesson that organisations should draw is that their cyber defence plans may not survive contact with an attack and that in the fog of the moment they should also plan for the management of the secondary damage that such an attack brings. An attack could destroy trust between key individuals and departments. The cause will not immediately be known nor will it be immediately clear whether or not there is an insider element to the attack.

Future attacks may well be more subtle with the attackers attempting to prevent the organisation from realising that the problems it has been experiencing are due to an attack. In the case of Viteks' attack on Maroochy Water Services (Abrams & Weiss, 2008), the issues were not recognised as a cyber attack when they first emerged. Attackers may seek to undermine confidence in systems, cause managers to distrust critical production or financial information, unsettle investors who become concerned by the apparent disorganisation or lack of control within the business. The attack may last weeks, months or even years slowly eroding confidence before being finally discovered.

People Won't do It

The humans within any system will seek ways of making their lives simpler. A key question for any security manager is to what extent do the security systems support individuals' primary tasks and to what extent do they create additional burdens or barriers.

Architects refer to the concept of 'lines of desire' or 'desire paths' (AJ The Architects' Journal, 2012), referring to the paths worn away by people seeking to find the shortest route between two points. This concept can be also applied to security processes. The 'human failings' or abuse of security processes or procedures where the security system has prevented employees or users completing their task in the most direct way is a way of identifying obstacles within the system.

During a QinetiQ Penetration Testing project for a client operating an industrial control system, the team searched for unsecured ports and found a modem that allowed them access into the organisations systems. The subsequent investigation revealed that the modem had been put in by a maintenance engineer. The engineer had become increasingly frustrated by the number of occasions he had been woken up during the night and called to the client's site to resolve technical issues. To make life easier he installed his own modem allowing him to make the correction from his own home saving the journey time to the client's site. The engineer had found his own 'line of desire' and in the process opened up a significant security risk for the organisation. His approach had demonstrated a more cost effective way of providing support but it had not been implemented as part of the formal process with the appropriate level of security creating news risks for the organisation concerned.

Tail gating is following an individual who has the correct swipe card or code to open a door or gate by getting them to hold the door open or pushing in behind. A variety of techniques are used from the tail gaiter dressing or behaving in such a way that they appear to be seniority or authority, appearing to be in hurry or overburdened or blending with a crowd (Hadnagy, 2011). The end result is that an individual with authorised access allows unchallenged someone who is not authorised to enter a secure area. On most occasions the individual is probably someone who has forgotten their pass or has been asked to attend a meeting in part of the building that they are not normally in and therefore do not have access. In other words there has been no negative organisational impact by letting the individual in. However, each a breach encourages further breaches. Members of staff do not want to challenge as they notice others are not challenging, and doing so causes embarrassment and discomfort for all involved. Such procedures need to be supported by the technology within the system that encourages compliance through, for example, airlock doors that prevent tail gating or a culture in which preventing an individual from tail gating is not seen as anti-social behaviour.

As Stajano and Wilson (2009, p. 10) observed, "It's not that the users are too lazy to follow the prescribed practice on how to operate the security mechanisms, but rather that their interest is principally focused on the task, much more important to them, of accessing the resource that the security mechanisms protect".

It's not How we do Things Here

If the level of security required to protect a system will require the human to put in considerable additional effort, consideration should be given to how the importance of that process is conveyed.

Security culture reflects the attitudes, assumptions, values, procedures and artefacts of the organisation. To what extent do the Board members and senior managers set and review security goals? Are these supported by clear policies and procedures? Do senior managers reinforce these by having specific measures of security performance as key business metrics and by asking their subordinates about security? Do senior managers follow the security processes themselves or is a blind eye turned to their tendency to connect their personal devices, transport sensitive documents without encryption? As Nath (2011) noted, failure to achieve a robust security culture is often seen as a weak link in organisations' security.

Adherence to security procedures is influenced by the employees' perception of threat and whether or not they understand the need for security. If employees of an organisation have received letter bombs or staff have been threatened at their homes or in public spaces, the need for security will be well understood by staff. In most organisations this will not be the case, and organisations will tend to want to play down any security failings concerned that their clients or regulators will lose confidence in them. As a result, unless an individual was personally involved in a security breach, he or she will not to know about incidents within their organisations. Security becomes a rather academic subject with security managers briefing staff on the need to follow processes but employees never coming across an event that suggests security is an issue. In the safety domain

potential risks are quickly communicated to others who may be affected. The need for safety is continually reinforced by making individuals aware of near misses and accidents within their own workplace or accidents elsewhere involving the same equipment and processes. This information helps the employees understand why safety is important. It challenges previously held assumptions that a task is not dangerous or that safety is not relevant. Introducing the procedures or artefacts of security, for example swipe access or passwords without the continually communication of relevant examples is unlikely to have any real impact. If an organisations requires staff to adhere to security processes the staff will need to have the attitudes, values and assumptions that make adhering to those processes a logical decision. Rader, Wash and Brooks (2012) highlighted the importance of 'story telling' both in terms of the tendency for certain stories to spread by word of mouth and also because of the impact it has on individual perceptions. They found that respondents changed their thinking about security issues and their behaviour. "52% of respondents said that they changed their behavior as a result of hearing the story they reported. 94% of the respondents reported changing the way they think about security after hearing the story" (Rader et al, 2012, p. 7).

Adherence to security will also be linked to the relative costs and benefits of not complying with security policy. How easy is it for staff to steal from an organisation? Can employees print key documents such as user guides to the ICS and simply walk off the site with them? Are there other criminal activities on the premises, for example wallets or bags? Does the use of sticky tape increases twenty or thirty fold during December? Even the unusual increase in use of company stationery during a period when across many homes in the country people are busy wrapping presents indicates something about the culture of security within the organisation. In the 'The Tipping Point', Gladwell describes the 'broken window' theory. "If a window is broken and left unrepaired, people walking by will conclude no one cares and no one is in charge. Soon, more windows will be broken and the sense of anarchy will spread' (Gladwell, 2009, p. 141). Taking sticky tape to wrap personal Christmas presents is perhaps one of those 'broken windows', those that take it might feel it is a very small contribution by their employer given all the extra unpaid hours they had put in or the problems they had solved for the organisation over the year. Those that take copies of the reports or models when they leave to work for another employer might feel that this is merely them having what is owed to them.

Ignoring the personal use of company materials or making a comment during the Exit Interview about returning company documents is not sufficient. Following the 'broken window' principle there is a need to demonstrate the seriousness with which the organisation treats security with every opportunity from sticky tape to the reviewing of logs of individuals leaving the organisation. This will help create a culture within the organisation where security is valued and the required behaviour reinforced even in the case of relatively minor breaches.

There is a significant cultural and communication gap between those in the security profession whose outlook on life tends to be one of recognising security threat and risk and those focussed on other aspects of the business. The differences can be seen not just in the background of the individuals but also the language used. As Malcolmson, Brown, Way, Abdi, Brennen and Walters (2010) noted, the difference in culture between departments in an organisation, "which consists of the social norms, attitudes, values and beliefs of organisational members, may actually influence the extent to which people and organisations effectively interoperate and share information between each other" (Malcolmson et al, 2010, p. 7). Security managers who cannot bridge the gap between the language and detailed considerations of the organisations

security challenges and the needs and attitudes of those responsible for operations and production will quickly find themselves increasingly isolated within their own organisation. In turn security becomes seen as a problem just for the security department not the business as noted in the case study given by Pfleeger (2010).

People do not Believe in It

Security is not the core business of most organisations and most employees' technical or professional training will not have focussed on security. Employees will give a number of reasons why they should not adhere to security processes. These might include the need to focus on the core job or an assumption that there is no real security risk. They may not be aware or choose to down play the risk associated with loading personal photos on to the corporate system as a screensaver, listening to music files from a personal USB stick, or loading personal software onto the corporate system.

Festinger (1957) coined the phrase 'cognitive dissonance' to refer to the tension that an individual experiences when their attitudes, emotions or beliefs are not consistent. For example, those that enjoy smoking are likely to hold views about the risks they face that in some way support their smoking habit or take on a belief that they are gaining benefits that outweigh these risks.

Transferring this concept to the security domain, staff who do not adhere to security rules and procedures avoid the discomfort of cognitive dissonance by changing their beliefs as to the risk of the behaviour. They form the view that the security rules are unnecessary and bureaucratic or put in place by people who do not understand the business. There may on occasions be genuine business reasons to challenge the security solutions adopted by an organisation. Security managers should also be aware that in some cases these views have been formed by employees in order to justify their lack of adherence and reduce cognitive dissonance. By reinforcing the adoption and following of effective and efficient security procedures the organisation in turn is able to help change individual beliefs about the importance of security.

The Insider Attack

There are those that for a range of reasons seek to disrupt their organisation's systems or take information that is commercially sensitive to their employer. Typically such actions are driven by a sense of injustice or a feeling that they are owed something by their employer.

The Psychological Contract is a term used to describe the idea that people tend to balance their inputs to the organisation with what the organisation does for them (Rosseau, 1998). The organisation gives employees far more than just a salary. Included in an individual's assessment of the balance could be flexibility, the value and trust that the organisation places in them and the job role. When these become unbalanced, (i.e. the individual feels that their efforts and contributions are no longer balanced by the organisation's rewards), the individual is likely to respond by complaining to managers or their colleagues, decreasing their loyalty or increasing neglect (reducing their effort, working hours etc) or even exiting the organisation.

Within the ICT domain there are some patterns in terms of the profile of those that have intentionally removed commercially sensitive information. However, this also represents a typical profile of those who work in the organisations concerned and have through the nature of their work access to more confidential information. Shaw and Stock suggest that IP theft is typically committed by current male employees averaging about 37 years of age who serve in mainly technical positions including engineers or scientists, managers, salespersons and programmers" (Shaw & Stock, 2011, p. 4). These individuals clearly have access to more sensitive documents and, as approximately 65% of those that have committed the insider

theft had a job offer that they had accepted with another organisation, they were individuals who had disengaged from their employer.

Shaw and Stock's report makes a second interesting observation, that individuals had taken, "the data they know, work with and often feel entitled to" (Shaw & Stock, 2011, p. 4). In 75% of cases the individuals had taken information that they had authorisation to access as an employee during their normal activities.

Finally, Shaw and Stock (2011) note that whilst technical means are used to steal IP, (in 54% of cases the organisation's e-mail system, remote network access channel or network file) most theft was discovered by non-technical employees.

These findings are relevant to those concerned with ICS. The discontented employee that feels that after possibly years of work for an organisation that contacts, code or databases that he or she had spent many days, weeks or months working on in some way belonged to them or was owed to them, is not isolated to the ICT world. The desire to revenge a perceived injustice was a factor behind the Maroochy Water Services attack.

Supervisors and line managers play an important role within any organisation in terms of having a reasonable understanding of individuals' perceptions of their employers and general attitude towards the organisation. Discontented staff are typically vocal in their views. A change in policy on overtime or changes in processes can contribute to the psychological contract being put out of balance. This could in turn, as Shaw and Stock (2011, p. 5) note, lead to a point when "a perceived professional set-back or unmet expectations" pushed an individual from thinking of taking action against their employer to taking action.

The insider threat needs to be addressed as much with a human response as with data monitoring. Data monitoring might indicate potentially suspicious behaviour from an individual, however as Chaffey (2011) notes this information is often in silos so not effectively shared (physical security databases are rarely integrated with IT monitoring or concerns raised by colleagues with Human Resources). In addition, as individuals are generally taking information that they have access to there also needs to be recognition that data monitoring will miss certain activity and inevitably result in false alarms. A human is therefore required to engage with any individual whose behaviour has triggered an alarm from data monitoring software. This human intervention needs to be conducted by someone who can manage it with the tact needed to maintain an individual's engagement. It should not make them feel distrusted by their own employer.

Line managers and colleagues are frequently aware of their close colleagues' levels of engagement, even their job hunting activity. The behaviour described earlier around individuals' perceptions of a violation in their psychological contract are relatively easy to detect. They include, complaining to managers or colleagues, decreasing loyalty or increasing neglect (reducing their effort, working hours etc). Organisations need to be able to take actions to protect the organisation and individual from the risk and consequences of rash decisions made by disengaged staff.

Understanding Personal Risk

Bossler and Holt (2009) conducted a relevant study building upon Cohen and Felson's (1979) Routine Activities Theory. This theory suggested that, "direct-contact predatory victimisation occurs with the convergence in both space and time of three components: a motivated offender, the absence of a capable guardian, and a suitable target" (Bossler & Holt, 2009, p. 402).

Bossler and Holt consider the importance of social guardianship that Spano and Nagy (2005) described as, "the availability of others who may prevent personal crimes by their mere presence or by offering assistance to ward off an attack" (Spano & Nagy, 2005, p. 418). Social guardianship in the work place may include colleagues, security managers or experts from the IT department. In

individuals' home life there is less social guardianship to protect individuals from cyber threat. A neighbour can see an individual climbing over a fence but cannot see malware being downloaded on to a home computer. However as an attack may begin by targeting an employee's vulnerable home system employers can make themselves available to at least offer guidance on home security. After all, in industries where kidnap or physical violence are risks employers will advise their employees on home security.

Social guardianship is also relevant within the workplace. If an employee engagement survey indicates that in a particular location or amongst a particular team engagement is consistently low, it is an indication that staff may be less likely to find colleagues in their area who will express concern about individuals not following procedure. Discontent and withdrawal of effort will be more prevalent.

Employees are unlikely to ask their employer or indeed anyone about the risks associated with the use of sites that may provide access to pirated media. However, accessing such sites makes the individual more vulnerable, or as described in Routine Activities Theory, a potential target. They begin to expose the individual to individuals involved in criminality. Bossler and Holt (2009) suggest other activities are an example of risky behaviour. These include guessing other peoples passwords in order to access accounts of files, looking at information or files without the consent of knowledge of the owner and sharing 'pirated' media. Decisions about what an individual does in their home life may be down to that individual, but the employer can at least advise them of the risks they may be unknowingly exposing themselves to.

The recent BBC report on police disciplinaries (BBC News, 2011) following comments by officers on social networking sites, highlights the challenges many organisations face in managing staff behaviour that takes place in their own time, in the privacy of their own home yet reaches large networks and places their views on record and in the public domain. The report highlights disciplinary action taken against officers including those who commented on colleagues, colleagues' partners or posted 'inappropriate material'. The article includes a comment attributed to Roger Baker, who led the Her Majesty's Inspectorate of Constabulary's 'Without Fear or Favour – A review of police relationships' review into police corruption. "We found a significant blurring between people's professional lives on social networking sites and their private lives which may be in the public domain and private lives which probably should remain extremely private" (as cited in BBC News, 2011). The concept of a public and private life is becomingly increasingly blurred. A new generation are now working in organisations, which regularly use updates of their locations and activity to help organise their social lives, to define who they are or aspire to be and to develop social cohesion amongst their friendship groups. Burton commented in the MoD report, "the Department recruits from, and exists within, a culture where the rapid and often uninhibited exchange of information is the norm" (Burton, 2008, p. 1).

Many organisations are unaware of the information that is publically available about their systems and system security. Hadnagy & O'Gorman (2011) found an organisation that had an unencrypted 60 page document containing logins, usernames and passwords available online. In other cases organisations have placed photographs of employees wearing their ID badges on their websites, allowing those seeking to disrupt the organisation the opportunity to study and copy the badge designs. In another case an employee had blogged details of IT procedures and methods for circumventing them apparently unaware that he was not only providing his colleagues with methods for accessing their personal software but also creating significant organisational security vulnerabilities.

Obtaining confidential information, gaining access or getting an individual to take an action by deceiving or manipulating them is known as 'social engineering'. Even where personal or corporate data is intended to be protected employees may be deceived into revealing it. The techniques used appeal to basic human behaviours and emotions. As Hadnagy (2011) noted typical human responses that have individuals elicit information:

- People tend to have a desire to be polite to strangers;
- Professionals like to appear informed and intelligent;
- Individuals will often divulge more if praised;
- Most people will not lie for the sake of lying; and
- Most people respond kindly to people who appear concerned about them.

Mitnik and Simon (2002) highlight common techniques used to manipulate individuals. For example, the social engineer will create a problem for the employee then offer them a solution playing on the employee's gratitude to extract the necessary information.

In many cases employees may not know the value of the information they hold. Relatively innocuous information regarding an organisations terminology, the name of subcontractors or departments ID codes can be used by social engineers to create believable cover stories for asking for additional information. Mitnik and Simon (2002) provide an example of a social engineer initially calling a bank to check on terminology. That information is then used to allow the social engineer to call another part of the bank and obtain additional information before finally calling the target organisation a credit check agency to obtain information on an individual's financial position. This lack of knowledge of the security risks provides attackers with valuable sources of information on vulnerabilities as well as information to support social engineering attacks.

SOLUTIONS AND RECOMMENDATIONS

Define What is Needed

In order to create an effective security system, organisations need to clearly define what security is required to enable the business to deliver its objectives. The people involved with the system need to be able to use it appropriately, have the willingness to adhere to the processes and know what is expected of them. These security objectives, as agreed by the Board, need to be clearly conveyed to, and be understood by, all those that are required to access and use the systems. Potential design flaws and processes that create unnecessary burdens can be identified by monitoring the systems to identify employee 'lines of desire'. Failures to comply with the designed path or process can indicate that processes are inhibiting efficient business practice.

The implication for the human in the technologies and processes that form the security system need to be fully thought through. Has everything that people need to do been made clear to them? In other words do they know what is required? Is the system designed in such a way that it is easy for them to use it? How are they motivated to follow the procedures and adhere to the system requirements? Do all those that need to interact with the system have the skills and abilities needed? How has their competence been verified?

There is an argument for accepting that an organisation's systems are compromised. Assuming that all that is needed is a physical and cyber perimeter fence will create internal weaknesses. Rather than continually building more and more complex walls around a system, consideration should be given to the monitoring and control of access to key documents within the organisation. These could include system user guides and help documents. Users are often unaware of the importance of the information they hold and how their

behaviours make it relatively simple for others to obtain it and use it as part of an attack on the organisation. Hadnagy (2011) highlighted the sources of information available to those prepared to search through organisations rubbish or conduct more targeted observations such as collecting details of service providers or of personnel through social media sites. With many subcontractors and sub-contracting organisations requiring some degree of access and understanding of the system there has been a need to in some way document how the system can be commanded. These documents might sit within the organisations that originally created the component or system parts or those that maintain them. For those prepared to spend the time looking, there will be help documents, user guides or development documentation. The knowledge exists, and the chances are the knowledge exists on an ICT system. Once available within the right communities such information can be rapidly promulgated across sites and accessed by those with an interest in understanding how to control the system.

As Gershwin noted, many organisations are not fully aware of exactly who has access to their systems. With reference to US firms he commented, "opportunities for foreign placement or recruitment of insiders has become legion … access to US proprietary networks by subcontractors … is creating virtual insiders whose identity and nationality often remain unknown to US network operators" (Joint Economic Committee, 2001). In the case of the Maroochy Shire sewage control system attack, the attack came from a sub-contractor who had the knowledge needed to access the system not a current employee (Abrams & Weiss, 2008).

Access control is a critical issue and addressing it involves getting back to a fundamental understanding of the business. What needs to be stored, for how long does it need to be stored and who needs access to it? Pfleeger (2010) description of an attack highlighted the usefulness of apparently low value information about the hotel that employers were attending a course at and the name of the attendees. This was used to send an e-mail apparently from the hotel with a virus embedded in a document attached. Balancing the need to know with the appropriate access employees need in order to run an effective and efficient organisation across a range of potential scenarios, is a significant challenge for all organisations. There is no point basing access on standard daily operations only to find that on regular occasions additional access is required and, for example, members of the production team fed up with getting asked for information have provided the finance department with an unauthorised link to production numbers.

Embed Security in Wider Systems

Merely using the word security risks isolating an individual within a business whose fundamental objective is to deliver energy supplies, provide clean water or maximise production. As examples in this Chapter have illustrated, if security matters to a business it needs to be embedded in the wider systems.

To what extent are the skills needed to perform effectively at the security tasks required of personnel considered in the recruitment process? How does the Security Department engage with the wider organisational employee engagement surveys? Disengaged and de-motivated employees do not enhance security so security departments should have an active role in engagement survey projects and use the results in their risk analysis and action plans. Whilst Human Resources is seen as the department responsible for staff behaviour the reality is that line managers have the greatest ability to judge and act on engagement survey results. The security department need to create appropriate mechanisms to support the level of communication and interaction. As Burton (2008) and Malcolmson et al (2010) noted, the security culture of an organisation has a significant impact on the attitudes, values and social norms of staff.

There is an additional risk for those organisations driven by a requirement to comply with regulators or international standards. Attention and energy tends to be diverted to whether or not the organisation can demonstrate compliance. In such cases Security Managers should in addition seek to provide to the Board monthly security audit reports based on security outcomes, e.g. number of times passwords were found, tests on access controls. By moving attention to the security outcomes, Board attention can be focussed on actual performance rather than having security as a tick box compliance exercise. In order for security to be understood, security departments should, wherever possible, provide clear metrics. These will highlight performance improvements or failings, highlight differences between teams or locations and attract the interest of senior management.

The right individuals need to be involved in the design of the security system, including security experts, software designers, those responsible for business processes and the users. The desired security behaviours should be exhibited by those at the top of the organisation as much as those involved in day to day operations, as the International Atomic Energy Agency (IAEA) noted, "Managers have a key role in ensuring that staff members are appropriately motivated, and that their role in enhancing nuclear security is recognized and valued within the organization" (IAEA, 2008, p. 13). The British North American Committee (2007) reported that IT security was only represented at Board level in 55% of US companies surveyed. If security is considered secondary to other business priorities then individuals will focus their effort on the elements of their task that are most valued by their managers.

A useful metric for an organisation is noting the number of calls made to security reporting security concerns. Do staff feel able to report concerns? Will they be put off by the fact that they find themselves getting dragged into meeting by managers concerned more about their own reputation than helping to overcome a genuine flaw in organisational process? Is there the ability to alert the organisation to potential problems anonymously or in confidence? Do staff know who they should go and talk to if they have a concern?

Creating an effective security culture requires more than putting in place the processes or artefacts associated with security e.g. an IT security policy, controlled access or a firewall. It also requires Security staff to have attitudes, assumptions and values that support the adherence to the security procedures.

Prepare Staff

Organisations rarely conduct regular testing or rehearsals for a cyber attack. There is not the monthly fire alarm test or systems in place that would allow regular testing of employees' behaviour. Staff should be aware of the various approaches that attackers might use such as embedding programmes within e-mail attachments or links. Whilst some attack e-mails may be picked up by automated detection programmes, more sophisticated attacks require a human to identify non threat e-mails linked to normal business activity with those that pose a threat. Individuals can be trained to look for suspicious signs. To be effective in this task, individuals need to be regularly reminded of what the threat could look like and receive feedback on performance in correctly detecting it. They also, as Siponen, Pahnila and Mahmood (2010) noted, need to have a belief in their own ability to make that decision and correct judgement. If staff leave training courses not confident that they are able to apply the skills they have been instructed in they are unlikely to perform to acceptable standards in the workplace.

Organisations need to understand how to support their staff in safe social network behaviour. Would identifying their employer put them at any risk? Would identifying their role put them at any risk? Given that individuals may wish to use social networking sites to help them build professional networks, what guidance should they be given on managing approaches from other individuals through such networks?

Most organisations, understandably, treat accessing sites that contain pirated material as a disciplinary offence. There are good security reasons for not accessing such sites e.g. presence of malicious software and risks of providing personal data. Internet search statistics suggests that there are a significant number of individuals who might be making themselves vulnerable to these risks through activities conducted from their homes in their own time. Whilst this falls out of most organisations remits, there is an opportunity in organisational security training to at least provide members of staff with a better understanding of the risks they face. Staff vulnerability at home may well create organisational vulnerability.

Monitor and Intervene

Pfleeger (2010) suggests that honey traps are used to lure insiders attacking the system to interesting sounding files and alert the security team to suspicious activity. Such approaches may provide useful indications, however a clumsy internal security process will do more to disengage staff than reduce the threat. Close monitoring will result in alarms, many of which will turn out to be constructive employee activity that the organisation will not want to discourage by accusing members of staff of 'suspicious activity'. People change working patterns for many reasons. It might be because the organisation needs them to work longer on a particular problem or project; because they wish to impress their manager in the hope of a promotion; because they need more money or because they are intending to leave and are seeking to access sensitive documents when there are fewer colleagues around. When the organisation is interested in understanding a change in work pattern, the first engagement is critical. If individuals are left feeling accused of wrongdoing when they were providing additional support for the organisation they may feel further distanced from their employer.

Many organisations require staff to click on a window indicating they accept the company's policies and terms of use. This is a lost opportunity and other than being used to discipline a member of staff should they intentionally or inadvertently break those rules or procedures is of relatively little value. This touch point between security and all employees could be used to illustrate a current threat or recent error. For example, a reminder on disclosing personal information over the phone as during the last three days the organisation had received a number of unusual phone calls.

Adapt

Security processes and technology will need to evolve as new personnel with different attitudes and behaviours join the organisation, business requirements change and new threats appear. Security is not a static process or policy as illustrated by the changing attitudes and behaviours of a new generation of employees and the constantly evolving technology.

In most organisations security systems that log physical access and provide software monitoring are already installed but they are not being effectively monitored. The system should include ongoing monitoring of systems and activity to identify changes in behaviour, new threats and new system vulnerabilities. The users' lines of desire will highlight parts of the system where, for whatever reason, there is poor compliance.

Depending upon what the system is protecting (valuable data, access to critical control systems) those seeking to take that information or take control may well be prepared to use techniques that harm the organisations employees. This might include exploiting personal financial difficulties or encouraging employees to get involved in relationships that make them vulnerable to coercion. With many organisational policies the employee is encourage to take his or her own responsibil-

ity for performance, for example, encouraging individuals to take responsibility for their career development or adherence to safety rules. Whilst a similar approach can to some extent be adopted in security, security is a threat to humans from humans. As such those that seek to compromise the system will exploit insecurity, embarrassment and vulnerability. The organisation therefore needs to be far more proactive in its support and defence of the employees, including providing guidance on how they can protect themselves in their personal use of IT.

CONCLUSION

There are a range of constraints on any security system. Security is in place to reduce the risks that organisations face from disruption or theft and in some cases to meet regulatory requirements. It needs to be delivered within financial constraints and in a way that does not unacceptably hinder business processes. A highly effective security system that almost entirely removes the threat of an external attack or disruption to the ICS is not going to be acceptable if it makes the organisation uncompetitive or prevents the business from operating.

Security is a business enabler and as such its performance, effectiveness and efficiency should be managed like other business metrics. Poorly implemented it introduces inefficiencies, encourages individuals to ignore company policies and procedures and still leaves organisations open to unnecessary and unacceptable risk.

The following actions will make a significant contribution to security effectiveness and the perception of security within the business. They focus on ensuring people know what they need to do, are able to do and are motivated to do.

• Do those that interact with any element of the ICS know what to do?

- Clearly define what security is required to enable the business to deliver its objectives.
- Create and maintain an effective security culture reinforce the right behaviours and continually highlight the need for the security system through relevant examples of risks.
- Security needs to be dynamic, quickly adapting to new threats and changes in technology, new connections and human behaviour. Use monitoring and feedback to identify new risks and vulnerabilities and make staff aware of new requirements.

Do they have the skills, knowledge and abilities needed to comply?

- Embed security within selection, employee engagement and performance management processes. If a recruitment process selects staff who do not follow rules, like to take shortcuts and get the job done at any cost, they are unlikely to adhere to security processes.
- Prepare for an attack. Consider the physical and psychological impact of an attack on staff and customers. Use this to create a plan that will still function during the 'fog of war'.
- A perimeter security system is not sufficient; an organisation will require defence in depth (within and beyond the physical fences of the organisation). This requires effective staff training and preparation.

Are they willing to comply, what are the costs and benefits of complying?

- Monitor systems to identify where employee 'lines of desire' indicate processes may be inhibiting efficient business practice and creating security weaknesses.

- Consider employee engagement not just as a productivity issue but also a security issue. Demotivated and disengaged staff do not enhance security.

ICSs have evolved to enable organisations to monitor and control key elements of production remotely, providing productivity, security and safety benefits. Whilst the archaic, proprietary nature of such systems may have helped protect them in the past, this is an ineffective defence against a persistent, motivated and patient attacker. Previous attacks demonstrate systems can be accessed and damage can be caused and accidents have demonstrated how relatively minor errors can lead to much more significant events.

The solution to this challenge involves more than the introduction of additional security software. Effective security systems need to take into account the humans who interact with any element of the process, from the control room operators and maintenance staff to business administrators. Not only do those individuals need to know what the appropriate security processes and procedures are, they also need to be willing and able to comply with them.

REFERENCES

Abrams, M., & Weiss, J. (2008). *Malicious control system cyber security attack case study- Maroochy Water Services, Australia*. Retrieved 2 January, 2012, from http://csrc.nist.gov/groups/SMA/fisma/ics/documents/Maroochy-Water-Services-Case-Study_report.pdf

AJ The Architects' Journal. (2012). *Oxford circus gets Japanese style 'desire-line' crossing*. Retrieved 9 August, 2012, from http://www.architectsjournal.co.uk/news/daily-news/-oxford-circus-gets-japanese-style-desire-line-crossing/5210489.article

Bossler, A. M., & Holt, T. J. (2009). On-line activities, guardianship, and malware infection: An examination of routine activities theory. *International Journal of Cyber Criminology*, *3*(1), 400–420.

British-North American Committee. (2007). *Cyber attack: A risk management primer for CEOs and directors*. Retrieved 10 August 2012 from http://www.acus.org/docs/071212_Cyber_Attack_Report.pdf

Bryes, E., & Hoffman, D. (n. d.). *The myths and facts behind cyber security risks for industrial control systems*. Retrieved 19 December, 2011, from www.isa.org/link/cyber_myth_fact

Burton, E. (2008). *Final report into the loss of MOD personal data for Permanent Undersecretary Ministry of Defence*. Retrieved 10 December 2011 from http://www.mod.uk/nr/rdonlyres/3e756d20-e762-4fc1-bab0-08c68fdc2383/0/burton_review_rpt20080430.pdf

Centre of Protection for National Infrastructure. (2009). *Risk assessment for personnel security*. Retrieved 22 January 2012 from http://www.dft.gov.uk/publications/personnel-security-resource-list/

Chaffey, N. (2011). *Cyber security: Managing people risk and the insider threat through strategic protective monitoring*. Retrieved 2 March 2012 from http://www.paconsulting.com/our-thinking/managing-people-risk-and-the-insider-threat/

Charney, S. (2002). *Hearing before the Subcommittee on Government Efficiency, Financial Management and Intergovernmental Relations, Committee on Government Reform, House of Representatives. Critical Infrastructure Protection Significant Challenges Need to Be Addressed: Statement of Scott Charney Chief security strategist, Microsoft Corp*. Retrieved 20 December, 2011, from https://house.resource.org/107/org.c-span.171444-1.raw.txt

Chien, E., & O'Gorman, G. (2011). *The nitro attacks: Stealing secrets from the chemical industry*. Retrieved 2 March, 2012, from http://www.symantec.com/content/en/us/enterprise/media/security_response/whitepapers/the_nitro_attacks.pdf

Cutler, V., & Paddock, S. (2009). *Use of threat image projection (TIP) to enhance security performance*. 43rd Annual 2009 International Carnahan Conference Security Technology, 5-8 Oct. 2009. doi: 10.1109/CCST.2009.5335565

European Network and Information Security Agency. (2011). *Protecting industrial control systems, recommendations for European and member states*. Retrieved 16 January, 2012, from http://www.enisa.europa.eu/activities/Resilience-and-CIIP/critical-infrastructure-and-services/scada-industrial-control-systems/protecting-industrial-control-systems.-recommendations-for-europe-and-member-states

Festinger, L. (1957). *A theory of cognitive dissonance*. Stanford, CA: Stanford University Press.

Gershwin, K. L. (2001). *Cyber threat trends and US network security: Statement of L.K. Gershwin, National Intelligence Officer for Science and Technology*. Retrieved 20 December 2011 from https://www.cia.gov/news-information/speeches-testimony/2001/gershwin_speech_06222001.html

Gladwell, M. (2009). *The tipping point*. St Ives, UK: Abacus.

Glover, P., & Bowyer, S. (2011). *Who will secure your organisation in the future? Selecting for cyber-security personnel*. Retrieved 20 April 2012 from https://cybersecuritychallenge.org.uk/files/info-downloads/Who_will_secure_your_organisation_in_the_future.pdf

Griffith, T. (Ed.). (1997). *On war*. Chatham, UK: Wordsworth Editions Limited.

Hadnagy, C. (2011). *Social engineering: The art of human hacking*. Indiana: Wiley

Hadnagy, C., & O'Gorman, J. (2011). *Social engineering: Capture the flag results*. Retrieved 4 January 2012 from http://www.social-engineer.com/downloads/Social-Engineer_Defcon_19_SECTF_Results_Report.pdf

Homeland Security Newswire. (2011). *Greatest cyber vulnerabilities are people, says cybersecurity expert*. Retrieved 15 December 2011 from http://www.homelandsecuritynewswire.com/bull20111019-greatest-cyber-vulnerabilities-are-people-says-cybersecurity-expert

Industrial Control Systems Cyber Emergency Response Team. (2011). *ICS-CERT incident response summary report*. Retrieved 20 July, 2012, from http://www.us-cert.gov/control_systems/pdf/ICS-CERT_Incident_Response_Summary_Report_09_11.pdf

Industrial Defender. (2011). *Managing automation systems: Critical infrastructure operators' challenges and opportunities*. Retrieved 20 July 2012 from www.industrialdefender.com/icsreport/ICSurveyReport.pdf

International Atomic Energy Authority. (2008). *Nuclear security culture*. Retrieved 10 August, 2012, from http://www-pub.iaea.org/MTCD/publications/PDF/Pub1347_web.pdf

Jewell, L. N., & Siegal, M. (1990). *Contemporary industrial organizational psychology*. St Paul, MN: West Publishing Company.

Leveson Inquiry. (2011). *Witness statement of Sienna Miller*. Retrieved 17 April 2012 from http://www.levesoninquiry.org.uk/wp-content/uploads/2011/11/Witness-Statement-of-Sienna-Miller.pdf

Malcolmson, J., Brown, P., Way, R., Abdi, S., Brennen, S., & Walters, J. (2010). *Improving interoperability by understanding information-sharing culture: A scoping study*. QINETIQ/10/00888.

Mitnik, K., & Simon, W. (2002). *The art of deception*. Indiana: Wiley Publishing.

Nath, C. (2011). *Cyber security in the UK*. Number 389 September 2011. Retrieved 2 August 2012 from http://www.parliament.uk/business/publications/research/briefing-papers/POST-PN-389

NERC Steering Group. (2003). *Technical analysis of the August 14, 2003 blackout: What happened, why, and what did we learn?* Retrieved 10 December 2011 from http://www.nerc.com/docs/docs/blackout/NERC_Final_Blackout_Report_07_13_04.pdf

News, B. B. C. (2011). *150 officers warned over Facebook posts*. Retrieved 14 January, 2011, from http://www.bbc.co.uk/news/uk-16363158

Pfleeger, S. L. (2010). Anatomy of an intrusion. *IT Pro, July/August 2010*, 21-28.

Rader, E., Wash, R., & Brooks, B. (2012). *Stories as informal lessons about security*. Symposium on Usable Privacy and Security (SOUPS). Symposium on Usable Privacy and Security (SOUPS) 2012, July 11-13, 2012, Washington, DC, USA.

Rousseau, D. M. (1989). Psychological and implied contracts in organizations. *Employee Responsibilities and Rights Journal, 2*, 121–139. doi:10.1007/BF01384942

Sasse, A. M., Ashenden, D., Lawrence, D., Coles-Kemp, L., Fléchais, I., & Kearney, P. (2007). *Cyber security KTN human factors white paper: Human vulnerabilities in security system*.

Shaw, E. D., & Stock, H. V. (2011). *Behavioral risk indicators of malicious insider theft of intellectual property: Misreading the writing on the wall*. Retrieved 15 December, 2011, from http://www.symantec.com/about/news/release/article.jsp?prid=20111207_01

Shea, D. A. (2003). *Critical infrastructure: Control systems and the terrorist threat*. Retrieved 15 April, 2012, from www.fas.org/irp/crs/RL31534.pdf

Siponen, M., Pahnila, S., & Mahmood, M. A. (2010). *Compliance with information security policies: An empirical investigation.*

Smith, T. (2001, 31 October). Hacker jailed for revenge sewage attacks. *The Register*. Retrieved 2 April, 2012, from http://www.theregister.co.uk/2001/10/31/hacker_jailed_ for_revenge_sewage/

Spano, R., & Nagy, S. (2005). Social guardianship and social isolation: An application and extension of lifestyle/routine activities theory to rural adolescents. *Rural Sociology, 70,* 414–437. doi:10.1526/0036011054831189

Stajano, F., & Wilson, P. (2009) *Understanding scam victims: Seven principles for systems security.* University of Cambridge Computer Laboratory. UCAM-CL-TR-754

Turk, R. J. (2005). *Cyber incidents involving control systems.* Idaho National Laboratory. Retrieved 2 August, 2012, from http://www.inl.gov/technicalpublications/Documents/3480144.pdf

United States General Accounting Office. (2004). *Critical infrastructure protection: Challenges and efforts to secure control systems.* Retrieved 7 January 2012 from www.gao.gov/new.items/d03233.pdf

United States General Accounting Office. (2007). *Critical infrastructure protection: Multiple efforts to secure control systems are under way, but challenges remain.* Retrieved 18 December 2011 from www.gao.gov/assets/270/268137.pdf

Chapter 5
ENISA Study:
Challenges in Securing Industrial Control Systems

Rafal Leszczyna
ENISA, European Union & Gdansk University of Technology, Poland

Elyoenai Egozcue
S21sec, Spain

ABSTRACT

In 2011, the European Network and Information Security Agency (ENISA) conducted a study in the domain of Industrial Control Systems (ICS). Its objective was to obtain the current view on the ICS protection primarily in Europe but also in the international context. The 'portrait' included threats, risks, and challenges in the area of ICS protection as well as national, pan European, and international initiatives on ICS security. The study was performed through desktop research, survey and interviews, and a meeting with all involved stakeholders. This chapter highlights the most relevant parts of the final report of the study. It focuses on the challenges to securing ICS identified during the research, but also presents the context and the methodology of the study. In response to the challenges, the seven recommendations of ENISA for protecting ICS are proposed.

INTRODUCTION

Industrial Control Systems (ICS) are command and control networks and systems designed to support industrial processes (Igure, Laughter, & Williams, 2006). These systems are responsible for monitoring and controlling a variety of processes and operations such as gas and electricity distri-bution, water treatment, oil refining or railway transportation. The largest subgroup of ICS is SCADA (Supervisory Control and Data Acquisi-tion) systems. Industrial control systems constitute a strategic asset of critical infrastructures.

Since the potential for catastrophic terrorist attacks that affect critical infrastructures is increas-ing (Commission of the European Communities,

DOI: 10.4018/978-1-4666-2659-1.ch005

Copyright © 2013, IGI Global. Copying or distributing in print or electronic forms without written permission of IGI Global is prohibited.

2004), in 2004 a series of actions were launched to address this issue. These activities were driven by the European Commission, the Council and the Justice and Home Affairs Council and resulted in the adoption of the conclusions of a European Programme for Critical Infrastructure Protection (EPCIP) (Commission of the European Communities, 2006) by the Council of the European Union, in April 2007. The key element of EPCIP is the Directive on the Identification and Designation of European Critical Infrastructures (Commission of the European Communities, 2008). In parallel, the information security issues for vital infrastructures in Europe are addressed by The Digital Agenda for Europe (DAE) (Commission of the European Communities, 2010) and the CIIP action plan (Commission of the European Communities, 2009).

Recognising the importance of assuring the security of industrial control systems in the protection of critical infrastructures, in 2011 the European Network and Information Security Agency (ENISA) launched a series of activities, which aimed at bringing together the relevant stakeholders and engaging them into an open discussion on ICS protection. The principal goal of the open dialogue was to identify the main concerns regarding the security of ICS[1] as well as to recognize and support national, pan European and international initiatives on ICS security. The involved stakeholders included ICS security tools and services providers, ICS software/hardware manufactures and integrators, infrastructure operators, public bodies, standardisation bodies and academia, R&D.

Furthermore, in order to help the stakeholders get a deeper insight on the issue, ENISA decided to further explore this problem by delivering a research and survey-based study on this topic. The objective of the study was to obtain the current perspective of ICS protection primarily in Europe, but also in the international context. This view includes threats, risks and challenges in the area of ICS protection as well as national, pan European and international initiatives on ICS security.

The outcomes of the study were gathered into the report "Protecting Industrial Control Systems: ENISA Recommendations" (ENISA, 2011), which is divided into the main part (the main report) and 5 annexes. The main report summarises the results of the study, while the annexes contain the detailed information on the results. Annex I presents the main results coming from a desktop research phase. It provides a comprehensive overview of the current panorama of ICS security. Annex II provides a detailed analysis of the data gathered from the interviews and the survey in which ICS security experts participated. Annex III is a compilation of current security guidelines and standards for ICS.

Annex IV includes a complete list of initiatives related with ICS security. Annex V provides detailed descriptions of the Key Findings which make up the knowledge base on which recommendations are built upon. Annex VI includes the minutes of the Workshop. The distribution of content among the appendices is illustrated in Figure 1.

This chapter highlights the most relevant parts of the report to present the study of ENISA and its core results. It starts with an overview of Industrial Control Systems and continues with the description of the study and the research approach applied to it. After that the selected results of the study are demonstrated, which includes the interesting outcomes of the literature study and the survey and the interviews of the experts. Based on the findings the seven recommendations of ENISA for the protection of Industrial Control Systems were derived. The recommendations call for:

1. Developing national and pan-European ICS security strategies
2. Creating a good Practices Guide for ICS Security
3. Developing ICS security plan templates
4. Raising awareness and training
5. Creating a common test bed or ICS security certification framework

Figure 1. The distribution of the content of enisa report among the appendices

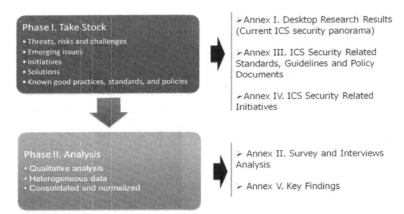

6.   Establishing national ICS-CERCs
7.   Fostering research in ICS Security

The details of the recommendations are presented in the concluding section of the chapter as they follow the description of the key findings of the study, from which they were derived.

ENISA STUDY

Industrial Control Systems are core components of many nations' critical infrastructures, and thus they have been recognised as a strategic asset against the rising potential for catastrophic terrorist attacks affecting critical infrastructures (Commission of the European Communities, 2004). Following the European initiatives regarding the protection of Critical Infrastructures (CI) and the Critical Information Infrastructure (CII) (Commission of the European Communities, 2006) (Commission of the European Communities, 2008) (Commission of the European Communities, 2010) (Commission of the European Communities, 2009), ENISA launched a series of activities, which aim at bringing together the relevant stakeholders and engaging them into an open discussion on ICS protection. The principal goal of the open dialogue was to identify the main concerns regarding the security of ICS and the possible ways to address them. In order to help the stakeholders get a deeper

insight on the issue, ENISA conducted a research and survey-based study on this topic. The objective of the study was to obtain the current perspective of ICS protection primarily in Europe, but also in the international context. This obtained image includes threats, risks and challenges in the area of ICS protection as well as national, pan European and international initiatives on ICS security.

The study comprised two main phases. The first phase, a 'stock-taking', was intended to gather all the data that will make up the work base for the study. The second phase was based on the analysis of the data in order to develop recommendations for the different types of stakeholders involved with cyber security aspects of ICS.

The activities carried out during the first phase of the study included the so called 'desktop research' and the survey and interviews with the domain experts. The desktop research aimed at analysing the available documents relevant to the topic of the study. In this part high reputation documents (guidelines, recommendations, reports etc.) coming from various organisations (such as public bodies, companies, consortiums or research centres), as well as the most influential books in the field, and the latest news (using forums, discussion groups, news feeds, etc.) were processed. The full list of information sources used in the study comprises around 150 references and is available in the report of the study (ENISA, 2011).

The second crucial part of the 'stock taking' was the survey and interviews with the domain experts aimed at obtaining their opinion on the most important ICS security subjects. In this part six dedicated questionnaires for the following groups of stakeholders were prepared:

- ICS security tools and services providers
- ICS software/hardware manufactures and integrators
- Infrastructure operators
- Public bodies
- Standardisation bodies
- Academia, R&D

Each questionnaire comprised a mixture of around twenty six open ended and multiple- or single- choice questions which addressed the security of ICS from different points of view: political, organizational, economic/financial, dissemination/awareness, standards/guidelines, and technical. Dedicated tools were developed to process the answers (ENISA, 2011).

Interviews were conducted in a personal basis by means of audio conferences. The goal of the interviews was to:

- Discuss in detail some of the answers of the survey
- Exchange of points of view on several hot topics in the field of ICS security
- Short questionnaire for those who did not participate in the poll

The interviews allowed for exploring in more depth the details of the answers of the survey as well as to discuss several hot topics in the field of ICS security. Around half of the interviews was conducted with new experts.

The survey and the interviews are very important part of the study not only as a source of expert knowledge but also because their participants – the experts involved in the ICS security – are the final addressees of the study. Participation in the survey and the interviews allows them to shape its final results. It is worth to mention that over one hundred fifty experts were contacted for the study, fifty of which participated in the poll. More than twenty personal interviews were carried out. The proportions of how many experts were contacted from each type of respondents and how many of them responded are illustrated in Figure 2 and Figure 3.

The second phase of the study was based on the qualitative analysis of the findings and the development of recommendations for different categories of stakeholders. As the result of the previous stage, it means of the stock taking, a large data source was created. This database comprised various information, unstructured and very heterogeneous. Thus, in order to be analysed, it needed to be first consolidated and normalized, for which dedicated, proprietary tools developed specially for this purpose, were used.

The process resulted in a structured set of information, the basic elements of which were, so called –"key findings", which are defined as the most relevant and influential observation from the desktop research, the survey and the interviews.

Key findings represent one of the following:

- An emerging issue,
- An initiative undertaken or believed to be undertaken,
- An agreement/disagreement level between stakeholders,
- Values or tendencies in the answers,
- A relevant line of opinion,
- Or any other piece of elaborated information that might have any impact in the field of ICS security.

Key findings are obtained from any of the data sources already presented, and are linked to these sources to assure information traceability and good reasoning. Those "information elements" are

Figure 2. The proportions of experts from 6 groups of stakeholders contacted during the survey

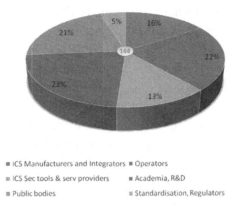

- ICS Manufacturers and Integrators ■ Operators
- ICS Sec tools & serv providers ■ Academia, R&D
- Public bodies ■ Standardisation, Regulators

always classified based on different criteria. It is important to explain that they are not necessarily exclusive, so a key finding may be related to one, several or even all fields[2] and stakeholders, so any possible number of classifying "labels" can be assigned simultaneously. After the key findings had been identified and treated, they were analysed thoroughly in order to ultimately derive the recommendations.

Finally, the results of the study were presented for a validation during a thematic workshop.

In the next section the results of the ENISA study, coming from the desktop research, the survey and the interviews are described.

DESKTOP RESEARCH RESULTS

The desktop research performed in the framework of the ENISA ICS Security Study resulted, among the others, in the identification of current challenges to ICS security (including threats, risk factors and vulnerabilities); determination of the current policy context; analysis of different technical solutions that are currently being applied for securing ICS; stock taking of standards, guidelines, regulatory documents as well as active groups and initiatives in the field of ICS security; and the designation of emerging issues on the context of ICS security. As this chapter concentrates on the

Figure 3. The response ratio in each group of survey respondents

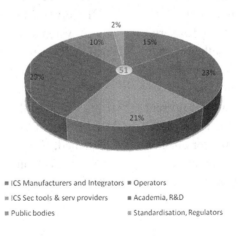

- ICS Manufacturers and Integrators ■ Operators
- ICS Sec tools & serv providers ■ Academia, R&D
- Public bodies ■ Standardisation, Regulators

challenges to securing the ICS, this section focuses on the description of the current vulnerabilities and risk factors, as well as the issues which may pose a problem in the future if not properly addressed in advance.

Vulnerabilities and Risk Factors

Most Industrial Control Systems were not designed with cyber security in mind. Additional to that, with the years passing, new factors contributed to the current state of cyber security of these systems. The main risk factors include the following:

- Vulnerable communication protocols
- Use of commercial off the shelf operating systems and applications and general-purpose hardware
- Increased interconnection
- Insecure connections
- Use of standard ICT security technology and procedures
- Widespread availability of ICS technical information
- Evolving threat landscape

Vulnerable Communication Protocols

The majority of ICS communication protocols in use doesn't contain protective measures. The protocols don't use encryption or message integrity mechanisms, which makes them exposed to eavesdropping, session hijacking or manipulation. Many of the protocols were initially conceived as serial protocols with no built-in message authentication (which means that devices accept connections from any device trying to communicate).

Additionally to these vulnerabilities present already for years, new factors contribute to the increased exposure of ICS to computer attacks. For example, ICS vendors publish protocol specifications to enable third-party manufacturers to build compatible accessories (National Institute of Standards and Technology (NIST), 2011). Organizations are also transitioning from proprietary systems to common networking protocols such as TCP/IP (i.e. Modbus/TCP, IEC 104, etc.) or new standard open protocols such as OPC to reduce costs and improve performance (National Institute of Standards and Technology (NIST), 2011). The introduction of common protocols is making these systems susceptible to the same software attacks and hacking tools already present in business desktop devices and networks (American National Standard (ANSI), 2007). Moreover ICS devices are very prone to simple denial of service attacks and buffer overflows due to the limited capability of communication stacks which were tailored for handling only SCADA-specific, relatively scarce (comparing to open networks) data and communications (IBM Global Services, 2007).

Use of Commercial Off-the-Shelf Operating Systems and Applications and General-Purpose Hardware

Not only communication protocols have been modified or replaced by common solutions. For the same reasons of reducing the costs and increasing performance, operating systems and applications in ICS have also transitioned from dedicated, specific-purpose and proprietary, to 'de facto' standard, widely used operating systems (e.g. MS Windows or Unix-like) and applications (e.g. MS SQL Server, MS Excel, etc.). This in turn makes these systems prone to the same software attacks that are present in business and desktop devices (American National Standard (ANSI), 2007). Moreover most of these systems are not patched (this would violate the vendor's service contract (IBM Global Services, 2007)) or cyber security hardened. At the same time, general-purpose hardware is being used in RTU, PLCs, Industrial PCs, and other control components.

Increased Interconnection

Since it is already quite common to have Internet Protocol-based ICS communications, interconnectivity capabilities have been drastically improved. As the result, ICS systems and other corporate IT have become highly interconnected in recent years in order to simplify service operation and reduce associated costs. Remote administration of control systems and associated network devices has become a common practice. Even for the critical functions of monitoring and control, the ICS engineers and support personnel are often authorised to perform them from the outside of the usual company perimeter (National Institute of Standards and Technology (NIST), 2011). Many organisations have enabled connections between corporate networks and ICS networks to allow the organizations' decision makers to monitor the status of their operational systems or to control the manufacturing or distribution of a product (National Institute of Standards and Technology (NIST), 2011). It happens very often that even if in theory these connections should be protected (usually by using firewalls), in reality the security is illusive, as the devices or software intended for its provision are misconfigured. Then it is sufficient to breach the perimeter of the ICS, to render it open to external access (IBM Global Services, 2007).

Partially because of the fact that the original ICS systems were isolated due to their architecture, most of the operators of critical infrastructures don't have network segmentation strategies. Nowadays, when the networks of infrastructures are connected to open networks, this results in that all the network parts, including the most critical, like ICS, are fully interconnected with the open networks.

This situation has become even more complex due to the proliferation of joint ventures, alliance partners, and outsourced services in the industrial sector in recent years, which led to the increased number of organizations and groups contributing to security of ICS. Now vendors, maintenance contractors, other CI operators, etc. have wide access to critical ICS elements and are more exposed to IT threats than ever before (American National Standard (ANSI), 2007).

Insecure Connections

It is a usual practice that ICS vendors deliver systems with dial-up modems, which serve to enable remote connections for the maintenance of the systems. Sometimes organizations use similar access links for remote diagnostics, maintenance, and monitoring. These access links are usually not sufficiently protected. They lack strong authentication and/or encryption mechanisms.

The scarcity of protection mechanism concerns also the connections between corporate and ICS networks. This is because control engineers have little awareness of cyber security issues while IT security personnel are often not involved in ICS security design. In result, access controls designed to protect control systems from unauthorized access through corporate networks are usually minimal (National Institute of Standards and Technology (NIST), 2011). Communications are exposed to eavesdropping and session hijacking what worsens the connectivity risk panorama described above (IBM Global Services, 2007).

Use of Standard ICT Security Technology and Procedures

Standard security procedures and technologies which are effective inside business and desktop devices and networks expose specific vulnerabilities when applied to ICS. Initially, many vendors did not support anti-virus applications as their incorporation would require testing, impact assessments, compatibility checking and so on, and might imply many change management issues (National Institute of Standards and Technology

(NIST), 2011). Since ICS very often are customer-tailored the above processed would need to be performed for each customer.

Similar situation regards patching. They need to be adequately tested (e.g., off-line on a comparable ICS) as it is not uncommon for them to have an adverse effect on other software (National Institute of Standards and Technology (NIST), 2011). Moreover, to the contrary to the typical business or home use, the upgrading and patching tasks of ICS are usually delegated to vendors.

Intrusion Detection Systems (IDS), Intrusion Prevention Systems (IPS) and firewalls are another example of how well-proven technologies in the office environment cannot be directly applied to ICS. These systems are effective in detecting and preventing well-known Internet attacks, but don't address ICS protocol attacks. The work on adapting IDS and IPS to the ICS protocols has started only recently (National Institute of Standards and Technology (NIST), 2011).

Likewise, firewalls are generally not designed for ICS protocols and packet filtering of ICS protocol messages is not common. Moreover firewalls operate in real-time mode, which might have an impact on ICS protocols, introducing unacceptable latency into time-critical systems. This applies also to IPS (Centre for the Protection of National Infrastructure (CPNI), 2005).

Widespread Availability of ICS Technical Information

It is quite easy to find publicly available information on ICS applications and systems design, characteristics, communications, etc. This information is intended to help a potential end user to decide among several options. It also creates a competitive advantage – the more detailed characteristics of the product are provided in comparison to the product of a market competitor, the more attractive the product is for a potential buyer.

The technical information on the ICS is also often available in the vendors' news sections in their websites, which gives an attacker a good way to gather initial knowledge on a potential target. Additionally, ICS vendors sell toolkits and provide, without a charge, Application Programming Interfaces (APIs) to help integrators or sometimes the end users to develop their own ad-hoc application enhancements. At the same time, based on the available sources, the potential attackers can develop targeted attack toolsets.

Other valuable sources of information on the ICS are contractors, employees and other stakeholders from the sector. Moreover, since security of critical infrastructures became a main research topic, an increasing number of technical papers, research results, laboratory tests, etc. are available. More and more attention is paid to ICS and as a result more and more people are becoming orientated in their specific security aspects.

This leads to the significant increase in the number of potential attackers. Finally, Stuxnet (see the description in the next section) has provided malware developers an excellent reference model for their new developments (National Institute of Standards and Technology (NIST), 2011).

Evolving Threat Landscape

During the last years a high-scale proliferation of malicious software on businesses and personal computers has been observed. In parallel ICS incidents have evolved from unintentional and casual (e.g. launched by amateur 'script-kiddies') to directed attacks from disgruntled employees, organized crime, terrorists, and even foreign governments. Moreover hacking tools are now commonly available on the Internet and start to include ICS-specific extensions.

Stuxnet is the most evident example of a threat which encompasses all the previously mentioned features. Being considered one of the most advanced malware ever created, it was developed by a well prepared, funded and coordinated organisation. Stuxnet was designed to target Siemens' industrial control systems. The worm was the first to simultaneously exploit four zero-day vulnerabilities for propagation, infection and hiding purposes. It also used stolen digital certificates to sign and legitimize its malicious content and avoid operating system malware protection mechanisms. It was demonstrated that the authors of Stuxnet had also a deep knowledge of their targets, their control systems as well as the process being controlled and monitored by these control systems. Stuxnet did not collect personal information, such as online banking data or user account credentials, nor infected systems to convert them into zombie stations as part of a botnet. It has been speculated that its main motivation could have been sabotage, probably of the Iranian nuclear programme. It was a directed weapon (probably the first one ever), presumably against the Uranium centrifuges in Iran. It contained dedicated code aiming at specific ICS applications and devices. Today Stuxnet is considered as a step by step guide for the development of new malicious software targeting control systems. Moreover there is a danger that hackers can create hybrid variants of the virus which may be able to avoid detection and attack other installations (Department of Homeland Security (DHS), 2011).

Emerging Issues

According to the research, the main issues which have emerged recently are the following:

- ICS-targeted cyber attacks
- Cloud computing in the industrial control environment
- Smart Grids

ICS-Targeted Cyber Attacks

Targeted attacks drew attention of security experts to the area of industrial control systems and opened a vivid discussion on the concepts of cyber war and cyber terrorism.

Most of targeted attacks aim at critical infrastructures, thus they pose a high risk to the society. A disruption of a critical infrastructure may lead to severe or catastrophic adverse effects on individuals, organizations or nations.

Targeted attacks employ a large variety of techniques designed to compromise the integrity, confidentiality and availability of industrial control systems. These techniques range from sophisticated rootkits[3] hiding running processes on the SCADA equipment, or simply well-known attacks that create backdoors on computers of control centres.

The two most 'famous' attacks of this type directed towards critical infrastructures are Stuxnet (described shortly in the previous section) and Night Dragon.

The 'Night Dragon' alias was assigned collectively to a number of targeted attacks which main objective was to compromise the information systems of several energy companies in the United States. According to the report of McAfee (McAfee, 2011), attacks are believed to have their origin in China. These attacks relied on a combination of several techniques, tools and vulnerabilities (i.e. spear-phishing, social engineering, windows bugs and remote administration tools). Although the attacks were not very sophisticated and did not exploit any zero-day vulnerability, the information obtained by attackers was of very high value for competitors. That information included financial documents, related to oil and gas field exploration and big negotiations, as well as operational details of production supervisory control and data acquisition systems.

Cloud Computing in the Control Environment

Cloud computing is a technology and a paradigm which calls for a user-involvement-free provision of computation, software, data access, and storage services. This technology responds to the need for the capability of increasing computational capacity or extending system functionalities on the fly, without investing into new infrastructure, training new personnel, or licensing new software. Cloud computing encompasses any subscription-based or pay-per-use service that, in real time over the Internet or intranets, extends existing ICT capabilities. The principal benefits of cloud computing are the augmented storage, flexibility, availability and mobility.

Currently, experts are beginning to debate if cloud computing technology could be applied to the ICS domain, arguing that the fundamental reason for its adoption, as with virtualization, would be availability. However it must be understood that the adoption of cloud computing in industrial control systems will not be easy due to the existence of several problems which have to solved first. For example, many contemporary industrial control systems still run on machines with obsolete operating systems (such as Windows 95) and software applications able to operate only on the old operating systems. Also the applications available in clouds may not be necessarily useful for the industry. While 'on demand' accounting software and office functionality might be ideal for the back office, much of the software used in the manufacturing environment is highly specific and specialised. Besides the applicability of the technology and the business case behind it, the are several security issues which must be properly addressed before 'going into the cloud' (Gartner, 2008):

- **Privileged User Access:** If cloud computing is implemented mainly for providing outsourced services, it is of major importance to understand that these services by-pass the physical, logical and personnel controls defined in the corporate security policy. It would be of crucial importance to ask providers to oversight privileged administrators.

- **Regulatory Compliance:** Customers are ultimately responsible for the security and integrity of their own data, even when it is held by a service provider.

- **Data Location:** Users of the cloud will usually be unaware of the geo-political location of where the services are hosted (i.e. in which country) and therefore what jurisdictions are they being affected by.

- **Data Segregation:** Cloud is a shared environment, therefore encryption schemes are applied to guarantee segregation of data among different customers. However, encryption accidents can make data totally unusable giving raise to availability problems.

- **Recovery:** In case of a disaster it would be important to get guarantees from the provider on used redundancy schemes and backup procedures.

- **Investigative Support:** Cloud services are especially difficult to investigate, because logging and data for multiple customers may be co-located and may also be spread across an ever-changing set of hosts and data centres.

- **Long-Term Viability:** Cloud computing providers might go bankrupt or get acquired by a larger company which might affect the services being offered.

Smart Grids

Smart grid is a new type (still under development) of electrical grid where it is attempted to predict and intelligently respond to the behaviour and actions of all electric power users connected to it, in order to efficiently deliver reliable, economic, and sustainable electricity services.

There is no consensus in relation to the composition of smart grids. Some experts consider smart grids being composed only of smart meters with the associated communication infrastructures and head-end systems. Others add to it the whole part of automation, and supervisory control devices and applications which are essential for the distribution of electricity – industrial control systems.

From the point of view of information security, smart grids introduce new entry points for attackers and new threats in comparison to traditional grids. This is because a smart grid directly connects customer houses with the information infrastructure of the energy distribution system, which may potentially give the customers a direct access to the infrastructure. Moreover, in the configurations where smart metering systems and head-end systems share a common underlying infrastructure, the risks will be propagated to the energy providers.

Smart grids is an emerging technology, so there is still time to avoid the mistake which was made for industrial control systems, it means of not designing it with security in mind. It is essential to pay proper attention to the security of smart grids already at the stage of their design, in order to avoid future problems which can be very expensive or impossible to solve.

Security solutions that have been proved effective for ICS can be adopted for smart grids. One example could be the use of encrypted communications based on digital certificates to secure the connections existing between smart grid devices. Also the existent good practices, guidelines and standards on the security of ICS can be applied to smart grids.

SURVEY ANALYSIS RESULTS: KEY FINDINGS

In this section the key findings discovered during the desktop research and the analysis of the results of the survey and interviews are presented.

The details regarding the weight of agreement or consensus on each issue across the respondents can be found in *Annex II. Survey and Interview Analysis* of the ENISA report (ENISA, 2011). Apart of descriptive text, charts illustrating the division of opinions between the respondents are presented. An exemplary chart is brought in Figure 4.

The key findings have been grouped into various thematic categories, starting with the biggest challenges in ICS security, and continuing with a multiplicity of topics on ICS security, including:

* Standards, guidelines, and regulatory documentation,
* Information sharing,
* Public-private partnerships and other initiatives,
* Dissemination and awareness,
* Technical security aspects,
* Present and future of research,
* Pending debates and other related issues.

The Biggest Challenges in ICS Security

Challenge 1: The Lack of Specific Initiatives on ICS Security

At the EU level there are policy areas addressing Critical Infrastructure Protection and Critical Information Infrastructure Protection. However, none of them is addressing ICS specifically. COM(2011) 163 recognizes that new threats have emerged mentioning Stuxnet explicitly. However, new activities proposed by this Communication on CIIP do not include anything specific to ICS. ENISA has formally declared that after Stuxnet, currently prevailing approaches to CIIP will have to be reconsidered. At the same time, United States Department of Homeland Security established the Control Systems Security Program (CSSP) as a cohesive effort between government and industry to improve the security posture of control systems within the nation's critical infrastructure.

Challenge 2: The Lack of a Common Reference in Europe

Most experts consider that there should be a European reference point in regard to security standards, guidelines or regulations. This is particularly an issue when there are operators with presence in several countries with several control centres and autonomous organizational structures, which is often the results of companies' fusions or mergers. These companies might have to deal with different regulations. Moreover, standards or guidelines being followed might not be the same in every division of the company. There is a need for a European trustworthy authority for ICS security, which would be the reference on which standards, guidelines and regulations should be followed, providing useful and practical information.

Challenge 3: The Lack of an Integrated Management of ICS Security

It has been found, both during the desktop research and the questionnaire analysis that one of the biggest issues that ICS operators have to face is to build security programmes that integrate all aspects of cyber security, incorporating desktop and business computing systems with industrial automation and control systems. Many organizations have fairly detailed and complete cyber security programmes for their business computer systems, but cyber security management practices are not as fully developed for ICS. Additionally, these companies normally have physical security programmes focused on preventing unauthorised access to facilities accommodating critical machinery which is part of the process being controlled or of the ICS itself. However, nowadays many cyber attacks can be combined with physical attacks to ICT systems to which access is not restricted. These systems might have not been considered critical for the process but they might be logically interconnected with critical

Figure 4. Sample chart from annex ii. survey and interview analysis of the enisa report: most effective ways to address the challenges based on the opinion of stakeholders. The chart shows the distribution of respondents' opinions.

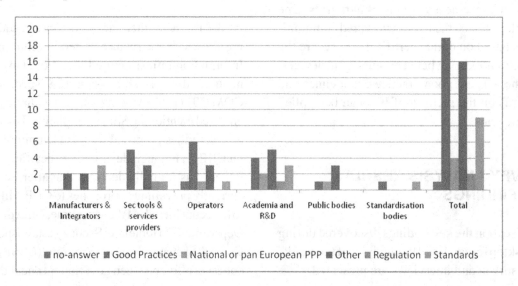

systems. In fact, the boundary between 'critical' and 'non-critical' is fading as some attacks (and risks) that needed physical action years ago may be perpetrated in the cyber space nowadays.

Challenge 4: Lack of Involvement of the Top Management

Operators' top management is not considered to be involved enough in ICS logical security. Experts expressed that top managers usually consider cyber security as a cost rather than as an investment. Moreover most of them share the view that their involvement into the area of ICS logical security is already sufficient. Thus it is essential to create awareness among them that securing ICS is a key aspect to be considered in modern organisations, also from the economical point of view (security is a business driver today).

Challenge 5: Amortization of ICS Investments

ICS systems technology has been developed in many cases for a very specific use and its implementation is different for each use case. This in turn has implied high investments from operators that are normally amortized during the next 15-20 years, or even more. Most of these components do not include appropriate security mechanisms to protect them from today's threats and less from tomorrows'. As a result, security staff will have to deal with ICS with little or no security capabilities for the next 10 – 15 years, and this will have to be taken into account when designing security plans.

Challenge 6: A Long Path for ICT Security Tools and Services Providers

Traditional ICT security companies have tried to penetrate the control and automation market in the last years. However, the ICS world is different from classic ICT systems and there are challenges that force them to adapt existing – or even create new

– solutions and services. A fundamental difference is in the very basic guiding principles. The ruling security paradigm in classic ICT systems is based in the CIA model (Confidentiality, Integrity, Availability), but in the ICS environment what rules is the SRA model (Safety, Reliability, Availability). As a result, even though many security strategies, technologies and services may be exported from one world to the other, this transition must be first thoroughly analysed before the implementation and accompanied with ICS-oriented trainings for the ICT security industry.

Challenge 7: Adaptive Persistent Adversaries as the Threat of the Future

As ICS systems are often behind critical infrastructures, many self-organized, well supported and technically skilled adversaries may see ICS as the perfect target to sabotage for many possible reasons (e.g. terrorist attack, unfair competition, etc.). Terrorists, criminal organizations, rival companies, foreign states or independent groups can make use of different means (e.g. ad-hoc malware, highly qualified hackers, etc.) to attack these systems thanks to the increasing integration with ICT technology and other corporate systems. This is an increasing phenomenon and most experts think it will grow during the following years.

Challenge 8: The Security Technical Challenges of the Smart Grid: Size, Third Party Networks, and Customer Privacy

The most challenging security factors of the adoption of the Smart Grid have been identified as: the overwhelming size of the networks, the trustfulness of third party networks for data transmission, and how to guarantee end customer privacy. Additionally, security challenges were commonly related with the deployment of secure smart meters. The remote control of these devices, together with a higher number of interdependencies and a distribution of control are considered factors that might increase the probability of weak points and cascade effects.

Current Standards, Guidelines, and Regulations

Not All Sectors Addressed by EU Policies

The Council Directive 2008/114 defined the procedure for identifying and designating European critical infrastructure and a common approach to assessing the need to improve the protection of such infrastructure. This directive articulated the pillars of the EU framework for the protection of critical infrastructures that were defined in COM(2006) 768. However, this Directive only concentrates on the Energy and Transport sectors (excluding also Nuclear Power plants) leaving place for a future review to include other sectors within its scope.

Current Documents, Usually Generic

During the desktop research phase, 35 different documents were studied: 24 guidelines, 9 standards and 3 regulatory documents. Most of them can be considered as "generic", in the sense that they focus on security aspects affecting ICS from a general perspective.

Standards and Guidelines Target: ICS Communications, ISMS and the Definition of Security Profiles

Several guidelines provide advice based on industrial security good practices for relevant issues specific to ICS security and important efforts regarding the improvement and standardisation of the security of SCADA and DCS communications. A very important aspect of cyber security is to establish inside the company an Information Security Management System (ISMS). To this regard there are several documents that have been studied which guide operators on how to include industrial control systems into their ISMS. Finally, there is a very useful set of documentation which addresses the security requirements/profiles and characteristics that new ICS components should include to comply with critical infrastructure protection programmes.

Energy, the Sector with a Larger Number of Specific Guidelines

Some of the documents studied during the Desktop Research phase focus on specific sectors, being the Energy sector (including here oil, gas and electricity subsectors) the most active one. Moreover, inside the Energy sector, it is the electricity subsector the one which presents by far the larger number of specific guidelines, standards and regulatory documents.

Transportation, Water Supply, or Agriculture within the Less Active Sectors

Sectors like transportation (e.g. railway transportation or airports), water supply (e.g. water distribution and waste water), or agriculture (e.g. food production) were not seen as active as the Energy sector with regard to the creation of security guidelines and standards for ICS protection.

Guidelines: "Fresh" and "Final"

Many new publications or updates have arrived in the last three years, from 2009 onwards. Actually, 18 of the 35 identified documents were published during that period. Additionally, most documents are in a final state, even though there are important initiatives that are yet in a draft version such as the ANSI/ISA 99 and of IEC 62443 standards.

Lack of Coordination among European Countries

Many documents do come from the United States of America or from international organizations such as IEEE, ISO, etc. At the same time, there are some countries in Europe that have defined on their own guidelines or even industrial mandates, some of the most active ones have been the United Kingdom, Germany, and Norway.

Acceptance and Use of Standards, Guidelines, and Regulations

Good Practices and Standards are Considered to be the Most Effective Measures

Most survey respondents agree that the most effective mechanisms to secure ICS are Good Practices and Standards. There was a significant part of them stating that it must always be addressed as a combination of standards and guidelines together with awareness raising initiatives.

The Most Valued Characteristics of Security Standards: A Holistic Approach, Risk Management Guidance, and Business-Orientation

Standards that had a holistic approach, that helped in risk management, and which have a business orientation were more appealing for the experts since they consider that their implementation turned to be more successful.

Little Acceptance of Too Technical Standards

Too comprehensive or technical standards are normally not taken so much into consideration. Some respondents even warn about the danger of providing too much useful information for potential attackers.

The Costs of Implementing Guidelines Considered Acceptable

Most of the interviewed stakeholders considered that implementing security "minimum" measures proposed by security guidelines is not very expensive. Operators are the ones that consider them assumable –probably due to the tender offer strategy they use to follow for product acquisition - while Security Tools and Services Providers and Manufacturers tends to consider them more expensive.

Low Level of Adoption of Security Guidelines and Standards

Survey respondents showed that their current level of adoption of ICS security good practices was between low and medium, being Operators the best positioned. Most of them are in the early stages of implementing security good practices, since they declared that they are currently developing a security plan or even performing the initial risk analysis. Among the problems they are facing they highlight the low level of involvement of Top Management or the lack of a common framework to follow.

Implementation of Non-European Regulations, Standards, or Good Practices in Industrial Environments

International, non country-specific standards and United States' guidelines are being followed widely. Moreover, companies are starting to comply with different aspects considered in regulations that are not of application in Europe, probably as a result of a lack of leadership in European authorities.

Some sectors are already starting projects to improve the security of their ICS due to the fact that there are specific regulations in place in the USA, like the NERC CIP standards for the bulk electricity transportation or the NRG 5.71 for nuclear power plants. However, there are other sectors that seem to be waiting for a specific mandate from public organisms before accomplishing such tasks.

Mistrust of Guidelines
Causing Heterogeneity

A wide variety of ways to deal with security threats, risks and challenges has been observed within the different participants of the survey and interviews. The most relevant reason for this heterogeneity is the lack of confidence in existing guidelines. This lack of confidence stems from various reasons that range from not being included into the "addressed audience" to not trusting the organisms, companies or groups behind those guidelines.

Disagreement between Stakeholders
on the Effectiveness of Regulations

Opinions are divided regarding the effectiveness of regulations, especially in Europe. Most Manufacturers and Operators' experts believe that this is not the best way to address security issues. Some others emphasizes that there is a big difference between being compliant with a regulation and being really secure. Only Security Tools and Service Providers and Academia have expressed direct support to it.

Manufacturers' Negative Attitude
towards Good Practices and Standards

Manufacturers participating in the survey and interviews are very little interested or even show a negative attitude towards most security standards of the industry. Some experts stated that since vendors are global companies, they are not strongly influenced by unilateral efforts and suggested that a joined European approach could be useful. ENISA was pointed out like an appropriate organism to do so.

Compliance: Not a Market
Driver in ICS Security

As there are no specific regulations to be compliant with in the European ICS environment, it is not a driving factor for operators to invest in security technology even if most Security Tools and Service Providers think that it could help them foster the adoption of their solutions and the selling of their services.

No Need for a Specific Law to
Prosecute Cyber Criminal Targeting ICS

Stakeholders do not think that a specific law to prosecute ICS attacks is necessary as this is mostly covered by general regulation on cyber crime. Some of them state that some kind of amendment could be done to include aggravating factors. Some experts state that, at this respect, the USA are more advanced than European countries, but not all of them consider this to be better as they might have done it too fast.

Need for a European ICS Security
Good Practices Documents

A majority of respondents consider that it is important, and even urgent, to have a European collection of documents on ICS security good practices. Most respondents spontaneously said that it not necessary to "reinvent the wheel" and it would be desirable to cooperate with European Member States, US, Asia or Oceania to quickly have a collection of European ICS security good practices. However, there are some experts that do not feel comfortable with cooperating with USA organisms. Furthermore, cooperation within European affected stakeholders will be much appreciated. Several respondents pointed to ENISA and Euro-SCSIE as catalyst organisms to create/compile a collection of ICS security good practices.

Operators/Infrastructure Level Security Plans

Need for an Operator/Infrastructure Level Security Plan Template

There is high agreement about the need for creating a reference security plan for each operator and/or infrastructure. Most believe a general template could be useful as a first step.

Sections to be Included in the Operator/Infrastructure Level Security Plan

Most respondents believe that the plan should include operational and physical security, technical issues, training and awareness, security governance (roles and responsibilities), business impact measures, and crisis management.

Risk Management to be Included in the ICS Security Plan

ICS on-field stakeholders should establish a process for assessing the current security posture of industrial control systems and for conducting risk analysis. It is important to understand what the information flows and system dependencies are, based on the consequences that a fault or disrupted function could have, both for the physical process being controlled and the organization itself.

Awareness Topic to be Included in the ICS Security Plan

On-field staff should have guidance regarding: a) proper understanding of the current information technology and cyber security issues; b) differences between ICT and ICS technologies, along with the process safety associated management processes and methods; c) Developing practices that link the skill sets of all the organizations to deal with cyber security collaboratively.

Security Plans Needed to be Adapted for Every Operator

ICS usually consist of highly specialised deployments, designed for very specific purposes and to fulfil very precise requirements. Security projects deriving from the security plan normally include the implementation of technical, operational and management security controls. These controls should be tailored for each ICS since their applicability widely differ from their classic IT counterparts. Some examples of security controls that need some tailoring are: account management, separation of duties, least privilege principle, concurrent session control, remote access, auditable events, configuration change control, contingency plan testing and exercises, maintenance tools, remote maintenance, malicious code protection, security functionality verification, etc.

Developing Security Programs Too Costly for Operators

Developing and Implementing complete security programmes that incorporate ICS can be very costly. Many large operators are making use of compensatory controls to avoid investing lots of money in renewing old insecure devices, operating systems and software applications. However, smaller end users might find even this approach unaffordable.

Attitude towards Information Sharing and Other Collaborative Initiatives

Interest in Sharing Initiatives

Most stakeholders have expressed their interest in the creation or promotion of information sharing and mutual collaboration initiatives. They referred to the benefits coming from information sharing and collaboration within partners, such as the exchange of specific expertise and tools, the possibility of creating integrated solutions and promoting awareness. The information exchange may benefit from the participation of Academia and Public bodies as this provides a desirable, more objective point of view.

Excessive Size, Constraints, or Private Interests Are the Main Disadvantages and Risks of Sharing Initiatives

Although the attitude is usually positive, several experts warned about negative aspects of this kind of initiatives, such as:

- Loss of efficiency if they become too big
- Potential undesired constraints introduced by states
- Private companies' participation focusing only on defending their own interests instead of acting for the common good

Unbalanced Interest in Cooperation between Each Group of Stakeholders

There are big differences regarding the interest that each type of stakeholder has in cooperating with other types. Operators are the most demanded by the rest, and they keep the interest in others too. Academia is the stakeholder type with more interest in cooperating with others, but at the same time they do not receive much attention from the rest. Manufacturers seem to be very focused in cooperation with Operators even though all other stakeholder types would like to cooperate more with them.

Active Collaboration between the ICT Security Sector and ICS Manufacturers, Essential to Improve ICS Security

The ICT security sector and ICS manufacturers' organizations should work collaboratively and bring their knowledge and skills together to tackle security issues. This is important since, in some cases, the security practices are in opposition to normal production practices designed to maximize safety and continuity of production. Vendors might need to consider differentiating their ICS products based on the security functionalities they include.

Bilateral Cooperation Preferred to Multilateral

A few experts stated that bilateral cooperation is usually more effective and efficient than multi-lateral initiatives.

Public Private Partnerships (PPP)

PPP Sharing Initiatives Demanded by Most Stakeholders

The majority of experts believe that public-private information sharing and collaboration initiatives are useful and necessary, as eventually they will lead to the improvement of the situation in the ICS security domain, even if they show different, sometimes contradictory, interests. Some experts even consider that without a facilitator (i.e. public sector), it is unlikely that private companies will get together. It is interesting however to highlight that both Manufacturers and Security Tools and Services Providers prefer other mechanisms to address ICS security challenges. In addition to usual sharing initiatives, public support can help long term funding, which is not always evident for companies, usually looking for short-term results and where true costs can be initially underestimated.

Not Involving All Stakeholder Types and Slowness: Main Critics Regarding Public-Private Partnerships

Experts signalled several negative points of PPP's:

- Public entities do not always take all stakeholder types into account.
- Public guidelines that arrived late.

National or European Funded Security Programs to be Improved

A slight majority of stakeholders is participating in public programs to improve security in ICS. Participation is high particularly in research activities and also in Smart Grid issues, but more practical, better articulated, longer and more ICS oriented programs are demanded by interviewees.

Trust: An Essential Ingredient for the Success of Sharing Initiatives

Several respondents had a good impression on some ICS security successful PPP initiatives. They consider them a facilitator for cooperation and they particularly highlighted the importance of classifying information based on confidentiality levels. Privacy is of paramount importance for the success of these kinds of sharing initiatives.

Common Test Bed

Need for Independent Evaluations and Tests of ICS Security Products

According to the operators, there is no difficulty in finding technical information on particular ICS security technologies or products. The problem is that the information comes from various sources, which are not really trustful. Operators indicate that independent evaluations and tests are missing.

Interest in Creating a Common Test Bed

A vast majority of participants were interested in the creation of a common test bed to certify technologies regarding ICS Security and interoperability.

PPP, of European Scope and Supported by Academia: The Desired Characteristics of the Common Test Bed

Respondents supporting the creation of a test bed believe that funding should come from public and private organisms and that the test bed should operate on a European level. A minority of respondents even think that technology certification by this test bed should be mandatory. Academia is willing to participate, as they have experience in creating minor test beds and have the knowledge about methodologies.

Concerns Regarding a European Common Test Bed

Some respondents, and in particular ICS Manufacturers, are reluctant to the creation of a European test bed. They do not think that Public Bodies should be very involved into technological aspects and that they do not like the kind of bounds that are derived from such participation. Others think that it is unlikely that such an organism could work fast enough to be useful.

Security Reference Model as an Alternative to a European Common Test Bed

A few experts signalled different options that could have more support than a European common test bed. It would be the definition of a security model, such as Common Criteria or Federal Information Processing Standards 200, adapted for ICS and which those already existent certifying organisms in each Member State are responsible for the certifying process. The reference standard would be used for this purpose and facilities should be available and configured and appropriate detailed test procedures should be defined.

ICS Operators, Manufacturers, certifying companies, etc. would need to verify and validate security configuration aspects, capabilities and interoperability of ICS including security features.

Dissemination and Awareness Initiatives

Space for Improvement in Dissemination and Awareness Forums

Only two thirds of participants were aware of the existent dissemination and awareness initiatives.

High Interest in Participating in Dissemination and Awareness Forums

A large number of stakeholders which were aware of dissemination and awareness forums were actively participating on them, following their high interest in such initiatives.

Quality of ICS Security Events Low-Rated

Participants stated that ICS security events quality could be improved. They consider that they are too commercial (so too general) or too academic (without the presence of Manufacturers, Operators or Security Tools and Services Providers). Moreover, some interviewees stated that there are far too many conferences where it is too easy to get a paper published, in all domains not only in the security domain. Many experts think that there is a need for events addressing specific problems, existing standards or focused to Senior Management audiences.

Top Management Awareness to be Fostered

Many experts agreed that one of the main difficulties in improving ICS security is to defend security costs before the Top Management. There is a current of opinion that states that it has to be presented as a business driver, providing economic reasons such as that, if considered during the PDCA cycle, it can be good for efficiency purposes. Incidents in industrial control systems should serve as a basis for risk assessment updates and to lead corrective measures and reprioritizing resource allocation. Organisations should address the challenge of establishing a group that meets regularly to discuss incidents and risks. This group should evaluate how these risks could impact security in the organisation's control systems. It should be composed by representatives from Management as well as from process control and IT.

Discussion on Technology-Centric Forums

A few experts stated that Dissemination and Awareness Forums do focus too much in security technologies or generic security aspects, not giving too much attention to the business aspects, such as the specific ICS implementations used in different activity sectors. Moreover, technologies may be adapted for several functionalities, but specific issues come from productivity and business objectives. Therefore, there is a need for dissemination and awareness initiatives focusing in specific activity sectors and which consider technology as a horizontal subject.

The Usefulness of an ICS-CERT or Equivalent Alternatives

Creation of an ICS-CERT

According to a large number of experts there should be an ICS-CERT established.

PPP and European as Desired Characteristics of an ICS-CERT

Most respondents think that the ICS-CERT should work at a European level and associate public and private bodies. It should be promoted by ENISA. Respondents proposed that providing guidelines and a vulnerability model could be some of the activities of the ICS-CERT.

Characteristics of the ICS-CERT

Some of the experts consider that this ICS-CERT should address ICS security issues by sector. This means that there should be specialised divisions for Energy, Transportation, Water, etc. that should work in a coordinated manner.

Means for a European ICS-CERT

A new EU-CERT is being established. Its role is not completely specified. This EU-CERT could either assume the role of the potential ICS-CERT or coordinate the different national or sector/business-oriented CERTs.

Current Situation of Technologic Threats and Solutions

About the Technical Threats Identified by Experts

According to the respondents, the biggest technical challenges regarding ICS security are: legacy issues, ICS and ICT convergence issues (including common viruses, Stuxnet-like malware and increasing interest in hacking), practical difficulties in patching/vulnerability management, and human unintentional errors due to a lack of interest or understanding of ICS security issues.

ICS Security "Taken in their Own Hands"

Operators normally rely on third parties on issues that are not considered their core business for efficiency reasons. However, this is not the case as far as the ICS security is concerned.

IDS/IPS, DPI, VPN and NAC, the Most Recommended Security Technologies

IDS/IPS, DPI, VPN and NAC technologies are the most popular security technologies for Operators, Academia and Security Tools and Service Providers. The subsequent on the list of most applied solutions are: conventional firewalls, application white listing, host bastioning, wireless security and multi-factor authentication.

Discrepancies among Stakeholders on the Most Appropriate Security Technologies

Operators usually use IDS/IPS, VPN, Firewalls or Host bastioning technologies, while other tools pointed out by Security Tools and Service Providers and Academia (such as NAC, Wireless Security or DPI) are not widely adopted.

Discrepancies within Most Demanded/Acquired Security Services

According to the survey, developing cyber security plans, performing penetration tests and risk analysis are the most recommended security services for the Operators. At the same time, Operators declare that they are only demanding security network (re)design and penetration tests. On the contrary, ICS Security Services Providers are providing risk analysis, security products deployment, compliance audits and host bastioning.

Legacy Related Risks

Untrusted and Legacy Devices and Protocols: The Biggest Threat Nowadays

According to the survey, the biggest threat to the security of ICS is the existence of untrusted devices and devices. This is very often related to the use of legacy or proprietary technologies that often include security breaches (e.g. backdoors).

Legacy Devices Working under Invalid Assumptions and the Long Lifecycle of ICS

Obsolete technologies were designed with invalid assumptions such as that "devices are isolated", or "these systems are only known by a reduced number of experts". These assumptions are no longer true. Built-in security is the appropriate approach for protecting these systems, but for economic reasons a compensating, multi-layer approach is being implemented in most networks. The situation is worsened by the fact that ICS technologies lifecycle is much longer than the usual ICT ones. As a result, many current ICS systems may remain vulnerable for long.

Built-In Security Needed

Security requirements should be included from the beginning in system specifications. It is always much more difficult and expensive to implement compensating controls that solve the security deficiencies of these products designed and developed with no security requirements in

their specifications. Often this is impossible, since many of the 'old' solutions do not have enough computing resources available to accommodate current security mechanisms. Additionally, third-party security solutions are not allowed due to ICS vendor license and service agreements.

Most Manufacturers Already Produce Built-In Security Functionalities

During the interviews the majority of Manufacturers stated that their products were currently providing built-in security functionalities such as communication or password storage encryption.

Modular Approach to Built-In Security Requested by Most On-Field Stakeholders

Most experts agree that for economic end reusability reasons it is more reasonable to design devices in modular way. So, if a module needs to be updated or replaced, it can be done at lower cost. This is also the recommended approach to be able to cope with the evolving threat panorama in the long life-cycles of ICS components.

ICT and ICS Convergence Problems

ICS Importing the ICT Solutions and the ICT Problems

During the last years ICT solutions have been becoming more and more common in ICS environments. Field devices evolved from mechanical to electronic, relays have been replaced with microprocessors, computer operating systems and high level programming languages have been introduced to ICS. Control systems used to be built up on proprietary software but now many of them utilise standard applications or OS, or use IT systems such as TCP/IP networks. With this adoption of ICT solutions, ICS have inherited also their vulnerabilities. Additionally the increased complexity of software raises the likelihood of implementation flaws (such as software bugs).

Regular ICT Solutions Need to be Adapted Further to the ICS Scenario

ICS tool providers still need to do an effort in adapting some of their technologies to the ICS world. For instance, Deep Packet Inspection in industrial firewalls is limited to a small subset of control protocols. Professional IDS/IPS solutions should start to commit with ICS protection, developing professional signatures and including new integral techniques. Data Loss Prevention is another technology with little acceptance in the ICS domain but which might become useful in the data exploitation process from historical and other business information processing applications and servers. Finally, data diodes are compatible (and not all commercial available solutions) with a very small set of industrial protocols while they are still focusing on traditional ICT protocols such as FTP, SMTP, CIFS, etc.

ICT Staff Does Correctly Understand ICS Requirements

A common problem mentioned by the ICS Security respondents was to make the ICT personnel, often in their own companies, to properly understand the real needs and requirements of ICS environments. Some approaches regularly used in the ICT context can have catastrophic consequences if applied to ICS environments. Proper education must be performed.

ICS Providers Are Not Aware of Security Good Practices of the ICT World

Many ICS software and hardware vendors are not aware of programming good practices and methodologies. Penetration tests and white box audits in controlled laboratories have shown that there are basic security bugs in devices and applications that could be properly identified if security development good practices were included into the development cycle.

Warnings about ICT Security Vendors into ICS

Many respondents expressed their concern regarding the appearance during the last years of conventional ICT security vendors, trying to sell their technologies to ICS operators without deeply understanding their requirements.

Potential Role in ICS-ICT Security Integration

To correctly adapt security requirements and functionalities into the ICS environments, Academia stakeholders may play an important role as they have the necessary resources. Developing theoretical frameworks to help both vendors and customers to understand what is needed and how to address it.

Other Technology Issues

Hardening Often Requires Support from Vendors and Security Tools and Services Providers

Hardening (e.g. restricting the permissions of running ICS applications) of computer solutions implies reducing the attack surface and therefore risks. ICS components cannot normally be hardened without a strong support from vendors and often requires Security Tools and Service Providers.

Difficulties with Vulnerability Management in the Operators Side and in the Commitment of Manufacturers

New vulnerabilities in ICS software and devices are discovered every day. Operators are often not prepared to address this issue in their systems. At the same time, ICS vendors don't provide quick enough and effective response to this demand. Sometimes there are tensions between security researches (who disclose vulnerabilities) and Manufacturers.

ICS Security Dependence of the ICT QoS

Quality of Service (QoS) parameters of the underlying ICT communication infrastructure are of paramount importance since many of the ICS need real-time performance, where delay and jitter are not acceptable, rely on it.

Security in Remote Accesses

Enabling remote accesses to a control system by vendors, maintenance contractors, management staff accessing from their homes, etc. increases the exposure of the system to the external threats. Thus it is necessary to introduce security for remote access. At the same time it must be assured that the introduced security measures do not impede or degrade the normal operational processes that are critical for the control system to function normally. This sometimes may constitute a challenge.

Cloud Computing Not to be Adopted in Core ICS Technologies

Cloud Computing is perceived by respondents as promising from some points of view, as for instance for computational needs. But the majority stated that it is yet too immature or even not valid by nature for the Control System itself, considering uses of QoS or real time functionalities. Even for valid use cases, some experts warned that every detail must be very clearly stated in Contract Agreements. One of the respondents indicated that standardized requirements at a European level would foster the adoption of this paradigm.

Present and Future Research

Current Research Lines

Currently and during the last years, ICS security research has been focused on: testing methodologies and tools for system interdependencies, security and functionality metrics, access controls for devices, security in wireless networks, vulnerability analysis, Intrusion Detection Systems, study and test performance of current Smart Grid installations, Smart Grid standards and measures of effectiveness.

Future Research Lines

During the following years, research lines are planned to focus in: more robust and flexible architectures, early anomaly detection by Network Behaviour Analysis (NBA) and Security Information and Event Management (SIEM) systems, patching and updating equipment without disruption of service and tools, methodologies to manage and integrate logic and physic threats, and improve forensic techniques for supporting criminal law enforcement.

Future Threats a Research Topic

Experts considered that in the future their biggest technical challenges will be to deal with external targeted attacks, internal threats (both intentioned and unintentional) as well as increased difficulties in the vulnerability management and privacy issues, due to the growth of Smart Grids.

Pending Debates on ICS Security and Other Related Issues

The Security by Obscurity Debate

There is a strong debate about the suitability of the "security by obscurity" approach. Many manufacturers and some other experts of different fields believe that this security philosophy is correct and even necessary. On the other hand, most ICT specialists and academia consider this is not an acceptable practice. For example, Standardization groups consider that the Industry should adopt a single cryptographic system rather than a diverse mix of systems that have not undergone public expert review. The system should be flexible to permit the introduction of new algorithms (ciphers) and new technologies after they are validated to be cryptographically secure.

The Debate about Regulation Enforcement by Penalties

A slight majority of respondents think that the regulation enforcement in Europe should not follow the NERC-CIP approach of the US.

Reasons against Regulation Enforcement by Penalties

Several experts stated that it is not in the European culture to apply a regulatory approach, and that Good Practices and Standards should be used instead. Some pointed out that being compliant does not always mean being secure, with the former being often the only objective of Senior Management. They brought in the example of US companies trying to bypass the regulation and, hence, compromising security.

Reasons for Regulation Enforcement by Penalties

Some experts believe that introducing penalties for not implementing regulations is an effective way to proceed at least to make the Senior Management aware, because the lack of compliance with the regulations will have a direct economic impact (and will be visible in the accounting reports). Others state that if Operators were more aware of the cascading effects that other Operators' security failures may have, they would prefer this type of enforcement for their own confidence.

Debate Regarding Smart Grid Dependency on Third Party Telecomm Operators

A majority of stakeholders perceive as negative the dependency on third parties when providing Smart Grid services. However, there are a number of voices, especially from Academia, that consider it could provide benefits for Operators.

Concerns Regarding Smart Grid Dependency on Third Party Telecomm Operators

Respondents are concerned because Operators don't have control or knowledge on the status of the network. Operators cannot identify, neither solve any problem independently of the telecommunication operator. Many agree to require encryption and signatures to prevent information leaks.

Positive Points Regarding Smart Grid Dependency on Third Party Telecomm Operators

A few respondents consider a benefit for operators to rely on specialized telecommunication companies, as this allows to Smart Grid Operators' to focus on their core business. At the same time there is a need for IT security monitoring technologies that allow maintenance personnel to quickly solve the problem or even to trigger automated actions that can minimize the impact. Relying on third party telecommunication operators might make possible to ask for this service.

ENISA SEVEN RECOMMENDATIONS FOR THE ICS PROTECTION

In response to the challenges identified during the study ENISA proposes seven recommendations to the public and private sector involved in the area of Industrial Control Systems. These recommendations intend to provide useful and practical advice aimed at improving current initiatives, enhancing co-operation, developing new measures and good practices, and reducing barriers to information sharing.

Recommendation 1: Creation of Pan-European and National ICS Security Strategies

The European Union should create a pan-European Strategy for European ICS Security activities and each Member State should develop a National Strategy for ICS Security. The strategies must be coherent with the European Union Council Directive 2008/114/EC for Critical Infrastructures, and leverage the existing initiatives addressing the problem of ICS Security (e.g. EuroSCSiE) as well as the national and Pan-European Public Private Partnerships (e.g. EP3Rs). The strategies have to serve as references for all state-members stakeholders, act as facilitators for sharing initiatives and foster research and education.

For the implementation of the recommendation the following steps are advised:

- At the EU level, recommend Member States to create a National Security Strategy on ICS security.
- Current Member States' procedures to establish national strategies on ICS security should be followed.
- The most relevant stakeholders, both public and private, should be invited to take part on a Working Group (WG).
- Define a process to incorporate in the WG any other actor willing to participate once the WG is operative.
- Define the process of cooperation in the WG, with regular meetings and defining short-medium and long term objectives as well as developing a network of trust.
- Define the National ICS security strategy: scope, objectives, guiding principles, etc.
- Develop the Pan-European ICS security strategy.

In this process public bodies should assume the leadership and cooperate with manufacturers and integrators, ICS Security tools and services providers and operators. Academia and R&D as well as standardisation bodies will have a consulting role.

Recommendation 2: Creation of a Good Practices Guide for ICS Security

The European Union should assume leadership and develop a consensus-reached guide or set of guides regarding security good practices, integrating both physical and logical security aspects, to serve as a reference for all stakeholder types. This guide or set of guides should help every stakeholder to ensure that good security practices are applied in the industry. There are already international and member-state efforts, so it is not necessary to build this kind of documentation from scratch, but in a cooperative manner. Moreover, this Good

Practice document should make clear reference to existing international standards supported by CEN/CENELEC.

In order to make these guidelines useful over time it is necessary to:

- Contact international and national peers that already have experience in developing these kinds of guidelines to speed things up and make the most of previous experiences. ENISA, or any other competent organisms, could be in charge of this.
- Establish a working group including all stakeholders, to receive cooperation from both Public and Private sector expertise.
- Publish the Good Practices document but providing mechanisms to receive future inputs and subsequently updating it.

In the development process it is necessary that all the groups of stakeholders will cooperate with each other under the coordination of public bodies.

Recommendation 3: Creation of ICS Security Plan Templates

The different National ICS Security Strategies introduced in Recommendation 1 should consider within their tasks the creation of ICS security plan templates, both for Operator and Infrastructures, which security experts could adapt to their particular situation. These plans should include operational and physical security, technical issues, training and awareness, security governance with roles and responsibilities, business impact measures and crisis management. Furthermore, these templates should be coherent with the set of good practices documents defined in Recommendation 2.

Security plans can be reached by the following steps:

- Establish a working group comprised especially of industry experts to identify all generic needs, understand the problems

that operators are facing when preparing such plans, study success stories in other Member States and select the most appropriate ones as a reference model.
- Prepare a set of templates for each activity sector including examples of security projects. These templates should be coherent with the set of good practice documentation defined in Recommendation 2.
- Publish the Template, with proper documentation to adapt to current situations.
- Consider the possibility of preparing a web-based support tool as guidance for the first steps: classification, prioritising, definition of the different security projects, etc.
- Provide mechanisms to collect experiences and update the document.

In this process public bodies should assume the leadership and cooperate with manufacturers and integrators, ICS Security tools and services providers and operators. For the consultation academia and R&D environments will be referred to.

Recommendation 4: Foster Awareness and Training

As part of national ICS-Security strategies, the Member States should foster dissemination and awareness activities through high quality events involving all types of stakeholders and with special attention to top management commitment. Training and awareness programmes and events should be created for all end user types and other stakeholders such as manufacturers and integrators. These initiatives can focus among other things on existing standards and good practices on ICS security, to disseminate their content and raise end user awareness. Other possible topics can be the discussion about the suitability of the "security by obscurity" paradigm and other pending debates affecting the security of ICS.

Several events could be created, targeting real security problems in each sector. These initiatives should be mainly vertical (i.e. sector-based) with some others focusing on horizontal aspects: technology, security solutions, etc., but with the common guiding principle of differentiating different activity sectors. Special attention should be given to the quality of these initiatives, avoiding duplicated work programmes, and assuring the quality of the speakers.

For the implementation of the recommendation the following stages are advised:

- Member States should create or get actively involved in the organisation of existing forums and events regarding ICS security. This could be leaded by the competent National authority.
- Identify experts among each stakeholder type that are able to differentiate myths from realities and to provide reliable arguments and expose them in an understandable manner for any kind of stakeholder.
- Focus on top management by showing real security problems that could affect their business.
- Look for cooperation from ICS leading-companies' managers and show how security gestures may (positively) affect business results.

In the process the leadership should be shared between public bodies and operators, which will cooperate with manufacturers and integrators, ICS Security tools and services providers and academia and R&D.

Recommendation 5: Creation of a Common Test Bed, or Alternatively, an ICS Security Certification Framework

The Common ICS security strategy should lead to the creation of a common test bed(s) at European level, as a Public-Private Partnership that leverages existing initiatives (e.g. EuroSCSiE). This test bed would make use of realistic environments

with the appropriate resources for conducting independent verification and validation tests. These tests should include, at least:

- Check the compliance of applications and systems with specific security profiles.
- Verify and validate that programming good practices and methodologies are being applied.
- Certify that ICT security tools and services are compatible with specific ICS systems, applications and specific setups.
- Product/services certification would not be mandatory but should also be considered as an option.
- The creation of the common test bed may follow the given steps:
- Coordinate a group to clearly define the purpose of such a test bed.
- Identify the requirements and design the organisation of such a test bed.
- Get involved the main actors: ICS manufacturers, security tools and services providers.
- Develop the test bed: infrastructures, procedures, metrics, etc. Academia may be particularly helpful as they have experience in such kind of environments. Moreover, standardisation bodies could help standardising such procedures, metrics, etc.

An alternative option to a European common test bed is the definition of a security framework model, such as Common Criteria or FIPS, adapted for ICS. In each Member State a national certifying authority exists which, based on a certification framework (e.g. Common Criteria or FIPS), is in charge of checking the compliance of applications and systems with specific security profiles.

Therefore, Member State existing certifying organisms would be responsible for the certification process: verify and validate security configuration aspects, capabilities and interoperability of ICS devices and security tools. Moreover, a

European coordination group could be defined to avoid duplicated work. For instance, once a product is certified in a Member State's national laboratories, it wouldn't be necessary to certify it once again.

As far as the roles of the stakeholders in the implementation process are concerned, the leadership should be assumed by public bodies, while the main operational tasks should be performed by standardisation bodies, academia and R&D and manufacturers and integrators. ICS Security tools and services providers and operators will assume a consulting role.

Recommendation 6: Creation of National ICS-Computer Emergency Response Capabilities

Following the national ICS Security Strategies, national ICS-computer emergency response capabilities should be established, in cooperation with an adequate number of public and private CERTs. The capabilities should leverage on the initiatives deriving from previous recommendations being the visible reference for ICS stakeholders.

They should structure their activity by business/sector rather than by technologies. This means that there should be specialised divisions for Energy, Transportation, Water, etc. Some experts consider that, usually, problems are more related to production functionalities than with the technology itself. Especially, in cases such as ICS environments in which systems based on the same solutions can vary heavily on the functionality they are designed for. An advantage of this division is that top management would be more likely to become involved if they can see business orientation in the initiative.

Reasoning on the previous ideas, the ICS-computer emergency response capabilities should be focused on the following services:

- Centralising ICS security good practice set of guides.

- Centralising security plan templates.
- Fostering of awareness and training events and programmes.
- ICS components and applications vulnerability disclosure coordination.
- Coordinate ICS security incidents: information sharing, crisis management, etc.

In order to create such a structure it would be necessary to:

- Consider other initiatives to find synergies and avoid duplicated efforts.
- Contact Member State authorities to coordinate the collaboration with national public and private CERTs. The contributions from every public and private actor involved should be clearly defined.
- Define the ICS-computer emergency response capability functional and operational duties.
- Create the ICS-computer emergency response capability, providing budget.

In this process public bodies will take the leadership and cooperate with manufacturers and integrators, ICS Security tools and services providers and operators. Academia and R&D as well as standardisation bodies will have a consulting role.

Recommendation 7: Foster Research in ICS Security Leveraging Existing Research Programmes

The National and Common ICS Security Strategies should foster research to address current and future threats and challenges such as ICS-ICT integration, legacy/insecure equipment, targeted attacks or Smart Grid issues. This should be done by leveraging existing European or National research programmes, such as the European Framework Programme.

A future work programme for research in ICS security should include the following topics at least:

- Robust and flexible architectures (e.g. modular approach for security)
- Early anomaly detection by Network Behaviour Analysis (NBA) and Security Information and Event Management (SIEM) systems
- Patching and updating equipment without disruption of service and tools
- Methodologies to manage and integrate logic and physic threats
- Improved forensic techniques for supporting criminal law enforcement
- Adaptation of current ICT security solutions to ICS environments
- Implementation of the recommendation can comprise the following actions:
- Establish priorities for the different research objectives in accordance with the National and Common ICS Security Strategies.
- Making contact with existing security programmes at EU and National levels, such as the European Framework Programme.
- Working together with appropriate organisations and bodies (e.g. Framework Programme Committee and Advisory Groups, Technology Platforms, etc.) to define an appropriate Work Programme.
- Emphasizing results dissemination, especially those that can help to shed light on pending debates.

In this process the leading role will have the academia and R&D together with public bodies. They will cooperate with manufacturers and integrators, ICS Security tools and services providers as well as operators.

CONCLUSION

The ENISA study analysed the situation of the ICS protection in Europe. To obtain the most possibly comprehensive picture, survey and interviews with 150 experts in the field were performed, and a broad literature study was conducted. Also a dedicated workshop was held in order to intensify the discussion between the experts. The extensive ENISA report which presents the results of the study is divided into the core part – the main report, and 5 annexes which comprise the details of the findings. This chapter highlighted the most relevant part of the report.

The study shows that there is much room for improvement in the area of ICS security. In particular actions have to be undertaken in the following areas in order to improve the security:

- Developing national and pan-European ICS security strategies,
- Creating a good Practices Guide for ICS Security,
- Developing ICS security plan templates,
- Raising awareness and training,
- Creating a common test bed or ICS security certification framework,
- Establishing national ICS-CERCs,
- Fostering research in ICS Security,

The real state of security of Industrial Control Systems can be only achieved with a common effort of all involved stakeholders. The effort which is based on equilibrated contribution, cooperation, knowledge exchange and mutual understanding. The ENISA contribution to this endeavour is the facilitation of the dialogue between the interested parties. For this the involved stakeholders were invited to the common discussion on how to improve the security of ICS. The report presented in this chapter not only shows a detailed picture of ICS security situation in Europe, but also served as a facilitator of this discussion.

REFERENCES

American Gas Association (AGA). (2006). *AGA report No. 12, cryptographic protection of SCADA communications. Part 1 background, policies and test plan*. American Gas Association.

American Gas Association (AGA). (2006). *AGA report No. 12, cryptographic protection of SCADA communications. Part 2 performance test plan*. American Gas Association.

American National Standard (ANSI). (2007). *ANSI/ISA–99.00.01–2007 security for industrial automation and control systems. Part 1: Terminology, concepts, and models. International Society of Automation*. ISA.

American National Standard (ANSI). (2007). *ANSI/ISA-TR99.00.01-2007 security technologies for industrial automation and control systems. International Society of Automation*. ISA.

American National Standard (ANSI). (2009). *ANSI/ISA–99.02.01–2009 security for industrial automation and control systems. Part 2: Establishing an industrial automation and control systems security program. International Society of Automation*. ISA.

American Petroleum Institute (API) energy. (2005). *Security guidelines for the petroleum industry*. American Petroleum Institute.

American Petroleum Institute (API) energy. (2009). *API standard 1164. Pipeline SCADA security*. American Petroleum Institute.

Amin, S., Sastry, S., & Cárdenas, A. A. (2008). *Research challenges for the security of control systems*.

Asad, M. (n.d.). *Challenges of SCADA*. Retrieved from http://www.ceia.seecs.nust.edu.pk/pdfs/Challenges_of_SCADA.pdf

Bailey, D., & Wright, E. (2003). *Practical SCADA for industry*. Newnes.

Berkeley, A. R. III, & Wallace, M. (2010). *A framework for establishing critical infrastructure resilience goals. Final report and recommendations by the council*. National Infrastructure Advisory Council.

Boyer, S. A. (2004). *SCADA supervisory and data acquisition*.

Boyer, S. A. (2010). *SCADA: Supervisory control and data acquisition. Iliad Development Inc.* ISA.

CI2RCO Project. (2008). *Critical information infrastructure research coordination*. Retrieved from http://cordis.europa.eu/fetch?CALLER=PROJ_ICT&ACTION=D&CAT=PROJ&RCN=79305

Centre for the Protection of Critial Infrastructure (CPNI). (n.d.). *Meridian process control security information exchange (MPCSIE)*. Retrieved from http://www.cpni.nl/informatieknooppunt/internationaal/mpcsie

Centre for the Protection of Critical Infrastructure (CPNI). (n.d.). *CPNI*. Retrieved from http://www.cpni.gov.uk/advice/infosec/business-systems/scada

Centre for the Protection of National Infrastructure (CPNI). (2005). *Firewall deployment for SCADA and process control networks*. Centre for the Protection of National Infrastructure.

Centre for the Protection of National Infrastructure (CPNI). (2011). *Configuring & managing remote access for industrial control systems*. Centre for the Protection of National Infrastructure.

Centre for the Protection of National Infrastructure (CPNI). (2011). *Cyber security assessments of industrial control systems*. Centre for the Protection of National Infrastructure.

Centre for the Protection of National Infrastructure (CPNI). (n.d.). *Process control and SCADA security- Good practice guidelines*. Retrieved from http://www.cpni.gov.uk/advice/cyber/business-systems/scada/

Commission of the European Communities. (2004). *Communication from the Commission: Critical Infrastructure Protection in the Fight against Terrorism, COM(2004) 702 final.*

Commission of the European Communities. (2004). *Communication from the commission to the council and the European parliament. Prevention, preparedness and response to terrorist attacks COM(2004) 698 final.*

Commission of the European Communities. (2004). *Communication from the commission to the council and the European parliament. Prevention, preparedness and response to terrorist attacks COM(2004) 698 final.*

Commission of the European Communities. (2004). *Communication from the commission to the council and the European parliament. Critical Infrastructure Protection in the fight against terrorism COM(2004) 702 final.*

Commission of the European Communities. (2005). *Green paper on a European programme for critical infrastructure protection COM(2005) 576 final.*

Commission of the European Communities. (2006). *Communication from the Commission on a European programme for critical infrastructure protection COM(2006) 786.*

Commission of the European Communities. (2006). *Communication from the Commission on a European programme for critical infrastructure protection COM(2006) 786.*

Commission of the European Communities. (2006). *Communication from the commission to the council, the European parliament, the European economic and social commitee and the commitee of the regions. A strategy for a Secure Information Society – 'Dialogue, partnership and empowerment' COM(2006) 251.*

Commission of the European Communities. (2008). *Council decision on a Critical Infrastructure Warning Information Network (CIWIN) COM(2008) 676.*

Commission of the European Communities. (2008). *Council directive 2008/114/EC of 8 December 2008 on the identification and designation of European critical infrastructures and the assessment of the need to improve their protection.*

Commission of the European Communities. (2009). *Communication from the Commission: Protecting Europe from large scale cyber-attacks and disruptions: enhancing preparedness, security and resilience, COM(2009) 149.*

Commission of the European Communities. (2009). *Communication from the commission to the European parliament. Protecting Europe from large scale cyber-attacks and disruptions: enhancing preparedness, security and resilience.*

Commission of the European Communities. (2010). *Communication from the Commission: A Digital Agenda for Europe, COM(2010) 245.*

Commission of the European Communities. (2011). *Communication from the commission to the European parliament, the European economic and social commitee and the commitee of the regions. Achievements and next steps: towards global cyber-security.*

CRUTIAL Project. (2006). *Critical utility infrastructural resilience.* Retrieved from http://crutial.rse-web.it

Department of Energy (DoE). (2002). *Energy infrastructure risk management checklists for small and medium sized energy facilities.* Department of Energy.

Department of Energy (DoE). (2008). *Hands-on Control systems cyber security training of national SCADA test bed.* Retrieved from http://www.inl.gov/scada/training/d/8hr_intermediate_hand-son_hstb.pdf

Department of Energy (DoE). (2010). *Cybersecurity for energy delivery systems peer review.* Retrieved from http://events.energetics.com/CSEDSPeerReview2010

Department of Energy (DoE). (n.d.). 21 steps to improve cyber security of SCADA networks. *Department of Energy.*

Department of Energy (DoE). (n.d.). *Control systems security publications library.* Retrieved from http://energy.gov/oe/control-systems-security-publications-library

Department of Homeland Security (DHS). (2003). *Homeland Security Presidential directive-7.* Retrieved from http://www.dhs.gov/xabout/laws/gc_1214597989952.shtm#1

Department of Homeland Security (DHS). (2009). *Catalog of control systems security: Recommendations for standards developers.*

Department of Homeland Security (DHS). (2009). *National infrastructure protection plan: Partnering to enhance protection and resiliency.* Department of Homeland Security.

Department of Homeland Security (DHS). (2009). *Recommended practice: Improving industrial control systems cybersecurity with defense-in-depth strategies.* Department of Homeland Security.

Department of Homeland Security (DHS). (2011). *Cyber storm III final report.* Department of Homeland Security Office of Cybersecurity and Communications National Cyber Security Division.

Department of Homeland Security (DHS). (2011). *DHS officials: Stuxnet can morph into new threat.* Retrieved from http://www.homelandsecuritynewswire.com/dhs-officials-stuxnet-can-morph-new-threat

DigitalBond. (n.d.). *DigitalBond.* ICS Security Tool Mail List. Retrieved from http://www.digitalbond.com/tools/ics-security-tool-mail-list

Energiened. (n.d.). *Energiened documentation.* Retrieved from http://www.energiened.nl/Content/Publications/Publications.aspx

ENISA. (2011, December). *Protecting industrial control systems: ENISA recommendations.* (R. Leszczyna, Ed.). Retrieved from https://www.enisa.europa.eu/activities/Resilience-and-CIIP/critical-infrastructure-and-services/scada-industrial-control-systems/

Ericsson, G. (2001). *Managing information security in an electric utility.* Cigré Joint Working Group (JWG) D2/B3/C2-01.

ESCoRTS Project. (2008). *Security of control and real time systems.* Retrieved from http://www.escortsproject.eu

ESCoRTS Project. (2009). *Survey on existing methods, guidelines and procedures.* eSEC. (n.d.). *eSEC.* Plataforma Tecnológica Española de Tecnologías para Seguridad y Confianza. Retrieved from http://www.idi.aetic.es/esec

European Network and Informations Security Agency (ENISA). (2010). *EU Agency analysis of 'Stuxnet' malware: A paradigm shift in threats and critical information infrastructure protection.* Retrieved from http://www.enisa.europa.eu/media/press-releases/eu-agency-analysis-of-2018stuxnet2019-malware-a-paradigm-shift-in-threats-and-critical-information-infrastructure-protection-1

Falliere, N., Murchu, L. O., & Chien, E. (2011). *W32.Stuxnet dossier*. Symantec.

Gartner. (2008). *Assessing the security risks of cloud computing*. Retrieved from http://www. gartner.com/DisplayDocument?id=685308

Ginter, A. (2010). *An analysis of whitelisting security solutions and their applicability in control systems.*

Glöckler, O. (2011). *IAEA coordinated research project (CRP) on cybersecurity of digital I&C systems in NPPs*. Retrieved from http://www. iaea.org/NuclearPower/Downloads/Engineering/meetings/2011-05-TWG-NPPIC/Day-3.Thursday/TWG-CyberSec-O.Glockler-2011.pdf

Goméz, J. A. (2011). *III curso de verano AMETIC-UPM 2011 hacia un mundo digital: Las e-TIC motor de los cambios sociales, económicos y culturales.*

Holstein, D. C., Li, H. L., & Meneses, A. (2010). *The impact of implementing cyber security requirements using IEC 61850.*

Holstein, D. K. (2008). *P1711 "The state of closure"*. PES/PSSC Working Group C6.

Huntington, G. (2009). *NERC CIP's and identity management*. Huntington Ventures Ltd.

IBM Global Services. (2007). *A strategic approach to protecting SCADA and process control systems.*

Igure, V. M., Laughter, S. A., & Williams, R. D. (2006). Security issues in SCADA networks. *Computers & Security, 25*(7), 498–506. doi:10.1016/j. cose.2006.03.001

Iinternational Atomic Energy Agency (IAEA). (2011). *IAEA technical meeting on newly arising threats in cybersecurity of nuclear facilities*. Retrieved from http://www.iaea.org/NuclearPower/Downloads/Engineering/files/InfoSheet-CybersecurityTM-May-2011.pdf

INSPIRE Project. (2008). *Increasing security and protection through infrastructure resilience*. Retrieved from http://www.inspire-strep.eu

Institute of Electrical and Electronics Engineers (IEEE). (1994). *IEEE standard C37.1-1994: Definition, specification, and analysis of systems used for supervisory control, data acquisition, and automatic control*. Institute of Electrical and Electronics Engineers.

Institute of Electrical and Electronics Engineers (IEEE). (2000). *IEEE PES computer and analytical methods subcommittee*. Retrieved from http://ewh.ieee.org/cmte/psace/CAMS_taskforce.html

Institute of Electrical and Electronics Engineers (IEEE). (2007). *IEEE standard for substation intelligent electronic devices (IEDs) cyber security capabilities.*

Institute of Electrical and Electronics Engineers (IEEE). (2008). *Transmission & Distribution Exposition & Conference 2008 IEEE PES: Powering toward the Future*. Institute of Electrical and Electronics Engineers. Institute of Electrical and Electronics Engineers (IEEE). *WGC1 - Application of computer-based systems*. Retrieved from http://standards.ieee.org/develop/wg/WGC1. html.

Institute of Electrical and Electronics Engineers (IEEE). *E7.1402 - Physical security of electric power substations*. Retrieved from http://standards.ieee.org/develop/wg/E7_1402.html.

Institute of Electrical and Electronics Engineers (IEEE). (n.d.). *IEEE power & energy society*. Retrieved from http://www.ieee-pes.org

Institute of Electrical and Electronics Engineers (IEEE). *WGC6 - Trial use standard for a cryptographic protocol for cyber security of substation serial links*. Retrieved from http://standards.ieee. org/develop/wg/WGC6.html

International Electrotechnical Commission (IEC). (2007). *IEC TS 62351-1: Power systems management and associated information exchange – Data and communications security. Part 1: Communication network and system security – Introduction to security issues*. International Electrotechnical Commission.

ENISA Study

International Electrotechnical Commission (IEC). (2007). *IEC TS 62351-3: Power systems management and associated information exchange – Data and communications security – Part 3: Communication network and system security – Profiles including TCP/IP*. International Electrotechnical Commission.

International Electrotechnical Commission (IEC). (2007). *IEC TS 62351-4: Power systems management and associated information exchange – Data and communications security – Part 4: Profiles including MMS*. International Electrotechnical Commission.

International Electrotechnical Commission (IEC). (2007). *IEC TS 62351-6: Power systems management and associated information exchange – Data and communications security – Part 6: Security for IEC 61850*. International Electrotechnical Commission.

International Electrotechnical Commission (IEC). (2008). *IEC TS 62351-2: Power systems management and associated information exchange – Data and communications security – Part 2: Glossary of terms*. International Electrotechnical Commission.

International Electrotechnical Commission (IEC). (2009). *IEC TS 62351-5: Power systems management and associated information exchange – Data and communications security – Part 5: Security for IEC 60870-5 and derivatives*. International Electrotechnical Commission.

International Electrotechnical Commission (IEC). (2010). *IEC 61850-7-2: Communication networks and systems for power utility automation – Part 7-2: Basic information and communication structure – Abstract communication service interface (ACSI)*. International Electrotechnical Commission.

International Electrotechnical Commission (IEC). (2010). *IEC TS 62351-7: Power systems management and associated information exchange – Data and communications security. Part 7: Network and system management (NSM) data object models*. International Electrotechnical Commission.

International Federation for Information Processing (IFIP). (n.d.). *IFIP TC 8 International Workshop on Information Systems Security Research*. Retrieved from http://ifip.byu.edu

International Federation for Information Processing (IFIP). (n.d.). *IFIP technical committees*. Retrieved from http://ifiptc.org/?tc=tc11

International Federation for Information Processing (IFIP). (n.d.). *IFIP WG 1.7 home page*. Retrieved from http://www.dsi.unive.it/~focardi/IFIPWG1_7

International Federation of Automatic Control (IFAC). (n.d.). *TC 3.1. Computers for control — IFAC TC websites*. Retrieved from http://tc.ifac-control.org/3/1

International Federation of Automatic Control (IFAC). (n.d.). *TC 6.3. power plants and power systems — IFAC TC websites*. Retrieved from http://tc.ifac-control.org/6/3

International Federation of Automatic Control (IFAC). (n.d.). *Working Group 3: Intelligent monitoring, control and security of critical infrastructure systems — IFAC TC websites*. Retrieved from http://tc.ifac-control.org/5/4/working-groups/copy2_of_working-group-1-decentralized-control-of-large-scale-systems

International Instruments Users' Association (WIB). (2010). *Process control domain - Security requirements for vendors*. EWE (EI, WIB, EXERA).

139

International Organization for Standardization (ISO). I. E. (2005). *Information technology — Security techniques — Code of practice for information security management*. International Organization for Standardization, International Electrotechnical Commission.

International Society of Automation (ISA). (n.d.). *ISA99 Committee - Home*. Retrieved from http://isa99.isa.org/ISA99 Wiki/Home.aspx

International Society of Automation (ISA). (n.d.). *LISTSERV 15.5 - ISA67-16WG5*. Retrieved from http://www.isa-online.org/cgi-bin/wa.exe?A0=ISA67-16WG5

INTERSECTION Project. (2008). *Infrastructure for heterogeneous, resilient, secure, complex, tightly inter-operating networks (INTERSECTION)*. Retrieved from http://www.intersection-project.eu

Interstate Natural Gas Association of America (INGAA). (2011). *Control systems cyber security guidelines for the natural gas pipeline industry*. Interstate Natural Gas Association of America.

IRRIIS Project. (2006). *Homepage of the IRRIIS project*. Retrieved from http://www.irriis.org

Jeff Trandahl, C. (2001). *USA Patriot Act (H.R. 3162)*. Retrieved from http://epic.org/privacy/terrorism/hr3162.html

Masica, K. (2007). *Recommended practices guide for securing ZigBee wireless networks in process control system environments*.

Masica, K. (2007). *Securing WLANs using 802.11i*. Draft. Recommended Practice.

McAfee. (2011). *Global energy cyberattacks: "Night dragon"*. Retrieved from http://www.mcafee.com/us/resources/white-papers/wp-global-energy-cyberattacks-night-dragon.pdf

Meridian. (n.d.). *Meridian*. Retrieved from http://www.meridian2007.org

National Infrastructure Security Coordination Centre (NISCC). (2005). *Firewall deployment for scada and process control networks. Good practice guide*. National Infrastructure Security Coordination Centre.

National Infrastructure Security Coordination Centre (NISCC). (2005). *Good practice guide on firewall deployment for SCADA and process control networks. British Columbia Institute of Technology*. BCIT.

National Infrastructure Security Coordination Centre (NISCC). (2006). *Good practice guide process control and SCADA security*. PA Consulting Group.

National Institute of Standards and Technology (NIST). (2004). *NISTIR 7176: System protection profile - Industrial control systems*. Decisive Analytics.

National Institute of Standards and Technology (NIST). (2009). *NIST SP 800-53: Information security*. National Institute of Standards and Technology.

National Institute of Standards and Technology (NIST). (2010). *NISTIR 7628: Guidelines for smart grid cyber security. Smart Grid Interoperability Panel–Cyber Security Working Group*. SGIP–CSWG.

National Institute of Standards and Technology (NIST). (2011). *NIST SP 800-82: Guide to industrial control systems (ICS) security*. National Institute of Standards and Technology.

North American Electric Reliability Corporation (NERC). (2009). *Categorizing cyber systems. An approach based on BES reliability functions. Cyber security standards drafting team for project 2008-06 Cyber security order 706*.

North American Electric Reliability Corporation (NERC). (2010). *CIP-001-1a: Sabotage reporting.* North American Electric Reliability Corporation.

North American Electric Reliability Corporation (NERC). (2011). *CIP-002-4: Cyber security — Critical cyber asset identification.* North American Electric Reliability Corporation.

North American Electric Reliability Corporation (NERC). (2011). *CIP-003-4: Cyber security — Security management controls.* North American Electric Reliability Corporation.

North American Electric Reliability Corporation (NERC). (2011). *CIP-004-4: Cyber security — Personnel and training.* North American Electric Reliability Corporation.

North American Electric Reliability Corporation (NERC). (2011). *CIP-005-4: Cyber security — Electronic security perimeter(s).* North American Electric Reliability Corporation.

North American Electric Reliability Corporation (NERC). (2011). *CIP-006-4: Cyber security — Physical security.* North American Electric Reliability Corporation.

North American Electric Reliability Corporation (NERC). (2011). *CIP-007-4: Cyber Security — Systems security management.* North American Electric Reliability Corporation.

North American Electric Reliability Corporation (NERC). (2011). *CIP-008-4: Cyber security — Incident reporting and response planning.* North American Electric Reliability Corporation.

North American Electric Reliability Corporation (NERC). (2011). *CIP-009-4: Cyber security — Recovery plans for critical cyber assets. North American Electric Reliability Corporation.* NERC.

Norwegian Oil Industry Association (OLF). (2006). *OLF guideline No. 104: Information security baseline requirements for process.* Norwegian Oil Industry Association.

Norwegian Oil Industry Association (OLF). (2006). *OLF guideline No. 110: Implementation of information security in PCSS/ICT systems during the engineering, procurement and commissioning phases.* Norwegian Oil Industry Association.

Norwegian Oil Industry Association (OLF). (2009). *Information security baseline requirements for process control, safety, and support ICT systems.* Norwegian Oil Industry Association.

Open Smart Grid. (n.d.). *Open smart grid.* Retrieved from http://osgug.ucaiug.org/default.aspx

Oracle Security 1998 O'Reilly *PLC manual.* (2011). Retrieved from http://www.plcmanual.com/

Rijksoverheid. (2009). *Scenario's nationale risicobeoordeling 2008/2009.* Retrieved from http://www.rijksoverheid.nl/documenten-en-publicaties/rapporten/2009/10/21/scenario-s-nationale-risicobeoordeling-2008-2009.html

Rinaldi, S. M., Peerenboom, J. P., & Kelly, T. K. (2001). Identifying, understanding, and analyzing Critical Infrastructure Interdependencies. *IEEE Control Systems Magazine.* doi:10.1109/37.969131

SANS. (1989). *SCADA security advanced training.* Retrieved from http://www.sans.org/security-training/scada-security-advanced-training-1457-mid

SANS. (2011). *The 2011 Asia Pacific SCADA and Process Control Summit - Event-at-a-glance.* Retrieved from http://www.sans.org/sydney-scada-2011

Smart Grid Interoperability Panel (SGIP). (n.d.). *SGIP Cyber Security Working Group (SGIP CSWG)*. Retrieved from http://collaborate.nist. gov/twiki-sggrid/bin/view/SmartGrid/CyberSecurityCTG

Smith, S. S. (2006). *The SCADA security challenge: The race is on.*

Stouffer, K. A., Falco, J. A., & Scarfone, K. A. (2011). *Guide to industrial control systems (ICS) Security - Supervisory control and data acquisition (SCADA) systems, distributed control systems (DCS), and other control system configurations such as Programmable Logic Controllers (PLC)*. National Institute of Standards and Technology. doi:10.6028/NIST.SP.800.82

Suter, M., & Brunner, E. M. (2008). *International CIIP handbook 2008/2009.*

Swedish Civil Contingencies Agency (MSB). (2010). *Guide to increased security in industrial control systems*. Swedish Civil Contingencies Agency.

Technical Support Working Group (TSWG). (2005). *Securing your SCADA and industrial control systems*. Department of Homeland Security.

The 451 Group. (2010). *The adversary: APTs and adaptive persistent adversaries.*

The White House. (2001). *Executive order 13231*. Retrieved from http://www.fas.org/irp/offdocs/eo/eo-13231.htm

The White House. (2007). *National strategy for information sharing*. Retrieved from http://georgewbush-whitehouse.archives.gov/nsc/infosharing/index.html

Tsang, R. (2009). *Cyberthreats, vulnerabilities and attacks on SCADA networks.*

United States Computer Emergency Readiness Team (US-CERT). (n.d.). *Control systems security program: Industrial control systems cyber emergency response team*. Retrieved from http://www.us-cert.gov/control_systems/ics-cert/

United States Computer Emergency Readiness Team (US-CERT). (n.d.). *Control systems security program: Industrial control systems joint working group*. Retrieved from http://www.us-cert.gov/control_systems/icsjwg/index.html

United States Computer Emergency Readiness Team (US-CERT). (n.d.). *US-CERT: United States computer emergency readiness team*. Retrieved from http://www.us-cert.gov

United States General Accounting Office (GAO). (2004). *Critical infrastructure protection. Challenges and efforts to secure control systems*. United States General Accounting Office.

United States Nuclear Regulatory Commission. (2010). *Regulatory guide 5.71: Cyber security programs for nuclear facilities.*

VIKING Project. (2008). *Vital infrastructure, networks, information and control systems management*. Retrieved from http://www.vikingproject.eu

Water Sector Coordinating Council Cyber Security Working Group. (2008). Roadmap to secure control systems in the water sector.

Web application Security Consortium. (2009). *Web application firewall evaluation criteria*. Retrieved from http://projects.webappsec.org/w/page/13246985/Web Application Firewall Evaluation Criteria

Weiss, J. (2010). *Protecting industrial control systems from electronic threats*. Momentum Press.

West, A. (n.d.). *SCADA communication protocols*. Retrieved from http://www.powertrans.com.au/articles/new pdfs/SCADA PROTOCOLS.pdf

ZigBee. (n.d.). *ZigBee home automation overview.* Retrieved from http://www.zigbee.org/Standards/ZigBeeHomeAutomation/Overview.aspx

Zwan, E. v. (2010). *Security of industrial control systems, what to look for.* ISACA Journal Online.

KEY TERMS AND DEFINITIONS

ENISA: European Network and Information Security Agency.

ICS: Industrial Control Systems.

ENDNOTES

1. On different levels: legal and regulatory, organisational, dissemination and awareness, economic/financial and technical.

2. Fields include: organizational and policy, standards, awareness and dissemination, economic/finance, and technical.

3. A rootkit is software that enables continued privileged access to a computer while actively hiding its presence from administrators by subverting standard operating system functionality or other applications.

Chapter 6
Distributed Monitoring:
A Framework for Securing Data Acquisition

Matthew Brundage
The University of Tulsa, USA

James Johnson
The University of Tulsa, USA

Anastasia Mavridou
The University of Tulsa, USA

Peter J. Hawrylak
The University of Tulsa, USA

Mauricio Papa
The University of Tulsa, USA

ABSTRACT

SCADA systems monitor and control many critical installations around the world, interpreting information gathered from a multitude of resources to drive physical processes to a desired state. In order for the system to react correctly, the data it collects from sensors must be reliable, accurate, and timely, regardless of distance and environmental conditions. This chapter presents a framework for secure data acquisition in SCADA systems using a distributed monitoring solution. An overview of the framework is followed by a detailed description of a monitoring system designed specifically to improve the security posture and act as a first step towards more intelligent tools and operations. The architecture of the Smart Grid is used to analyze and evaluate benefits that the proposed monitoring system can provide. Finally, the effects and use of Radio Frequency Identification (RFID) and ZigBee as data acquisition platforms are discussed in the context of the proposed solution.

INTRODUCTION

Supervisory Control and Data Acquisition (SCADA) systems (NCS, 2004) form the backbone of industries in the areas of electric power, oil and gas, water, and rail transportation. They have been identified by the EU Commission and the U.S. Department of Homeland Security as a core component of most critical infrastructures (Brunner, & Suter, 2008). SCADA systems provide real-time centralized monitoring and control of industrial processes through a combined use of data acquisition and transmission systems and Human-Machine Interfaces (HMIs). In the past, SCADA systems were considered to be secure due to the use of proprietary equipment and soft-

DOI: 10.4018/978-1-4666-2659-1.ch006

Copyright © 2013, IGI Global. Copying or distributing in print or electronic forms without written permission of IGI Global is prohibited.

ware as well as the limited network connectivity and isolation of these systems. However, during recent years, continued SCADA modernization and increased interconnection have resulted in a transition from closed, isolated networks to open, IP-based networks. Therefore SCADA systems are now considered to be part of the cyber infrastructure (DHS & DoE, 2007). The increased interconnection has made SCADA systems more vulnerable to attacks and has introduced new security risks. As a result, there is a pressing need to mitigate these risks.

Currently, in industry, there are several SCADA protocols in use. In the electric sector, the most popular are the International Electrotechnical Commission (IEC) 60870-5-101 (IEC, 2003), commonly referred to as 101, and the Distributed Network Protocol version 3 (DNP3) (Curtis, 2005). IEC is also developing 61850 to provide guidelines for the secure automation and operation of electrical substations. Security in SCADA implementations is a major concern because many SCADA protocols in use today are still operating in unauthenticated clear text. While there is a significant effort to enhance SCADA protocols with security functionality, for example the DNP3 SA (secure authentication) (Gilchrist, 2008), the majority of systems in the industry sector still use clear text. As a result, in order to enhance the security of SCADA systems and detect any suspicious behavior, SCADA communication networks need to be monitored to provide operators with accurate and timely information about the network devices and their interactions. In particular, a distributed monitoring system will be able to verify that the incoming information is accurate, as well as provide a foundation to support development of more powerful tools such as intrusion detection systems and packet filtering components.

This chapter uses the Smart Grid domain and relevant components in the energy sector to illustrate security concerns in SCADA systems. Although utilities in the electric sector require 24x7 availability, they may not be able to recover quickly and efficiently from all security breaches. Thus, a cyber-attack in this sector can have destructive results. Such an attack on SCADA systems located in the power grid can have a significant impact in the functionality of the grid. In fact, the massive North East Blackout has been linked to the propagation of the MSBlaster worm in 2003 (Verton, 2003; CERT, 2003). Also, the recently discovered W32.Stuxnet rootkit (Falliere, Murchu, & Chie, 2011) is an example of malware targeting Industrial Control Systems (ICS). Falliere (2010) notes that, "Stuxnet has the ability to take advantage of the programming software to also upload its own code to the PLC in an industrial control system that is typically monitored by SCADA systems."

In particular, this chapter contributes a recommended security practice of a monitoring structure for the purpose of improving SCADA security. The proposed distributed monitoring system addresses the important issue of secure data acquisition. This will provide system operators with the information needed for (i) a more intelligent response to incoming information and (ii) increased awareness of possible malicious activity in an environment outside of the control of the SCADA system. The Smart Grid is used as a case study to demonstrate the benefits such a distributed monitoring system could provide.

BACKGROUND

SCADA systems and their communications are currently at a critical point in time, as cyber-attacks become more common and these systems are becoming increasingly interconnected (Craig, Mortensen & Dagle, 2008). A brief overview of the security risks, standards, encryption and authentication, and functionality of the systems will be given.

SCADA Systems

SCADA systems (NCS, 2004) are used to monitor and control critical infrastructures such as energy, oil and gas, water, transportation, and telecommunications. The main components of a SCADA system are (See Figure 1):

- Data field devices such as Remote Terminal Units (RTUs) and Programmable Logic Controllers (PLCs) that interface with local sensors and actuators
- The communication network between the SCADA master and the field devices (slaves).
- The SCADA master station located in the control center
- The Human Machine Interface (HMI) devices

Data collected by field sensors and system commands are, when needed, transmitted between a SCADA master and units in the field such as Remote Terminal Units (RTUs) and Programmable Logic Controllers (PLCs). Both RTUs and PLCs are embedded computers that perform industrial automation functions, reading data from sensors, applying control inputs, and reporting data. The information is collected from the field devices and relayed to the control center, where the SCADA master station will determine the appropriate response to the situation and environment. The data acquisition framework consists of remote sensors and the necessary communication paths to transmit gathered information back to the control center. In some cases, data will also flow in the other direction, providing information and control signals to the field stations.

In particular, the data will travel from the sensors and gathering devices, to the RTUs, to the Gateway, then to the control center where the data is finally displayed by an HMI. At the core of the SCADA system is the control room, where the data will be collected and stored in the data warehouse. This is the backend of the system, where much of the information used to determine the course of action is located. The various tools and applications in the control center use this information, not only to display the current system status in the HMI but also to implement the automated responses of the system. This data is often used by the utility to plot historical trends and to monitor long-term operating conditions and efficiency of a particular system.

SCADA systems used to connect to and monitor field devices through the Public Switched Network (PSN) (NCS, 2004). Today, the infrastructure of the corporate Local Area Network (LAN) is used. In general, the accuracy and integrity of the messages transmitted and collected for monitoring purposes are of paramount importance.

Security Risks

In the past, ICS were physically isolated from the Internet and therefore were considered to be safe. Lately, however, ICS have been connected to internet-facing networks, and many security specialists believe that connecting industrial control systems to the Internet, even indirectly, exposes these systems to grave risk (Oman, Schweitzer & Frincke, 2000; Igure, Laughter & Williams, 2006). By sending a control message from a computer

Figure 1. SCADA system components

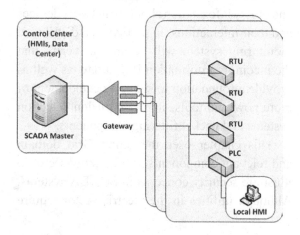

connected to the Internet, an unauthorized intruder could manipulate the operation of electric power substations, sewage-water valves, control systems of chemical plants or other critical infrastructures.

NIST, in its document "Guide to Supervisory Control and Data Acquisition (SCADA) and Industrial Control Systems Security", states that there are three broad categories of SCADA incidents including intentional attacks, unintentional consequences or collateral damage from viruses or control system failures, and unintentional internal security consequences, such as inappropriate testing of operational systems or unauthorized system configuration changes (Stouffer, Falco, & Ken, 2006). Possible attack scenarios for SCADA systems include:

- Delaying or blocking the flow of information through corporate or control networks (Denial of Service)
- Changing programmed instructions in PLCs, RTUs, or SCADA controllers
- Sending false information to control system operators either to disguise unauthorized changes or to initiate inappropriate actions by system operators.
- Modifying control system software or configuration settings
- Introducing malicious software into the system

Addressing these security issues requires solutions that are interoperable and backward compatible with existing technology. Standardization will play a key role in ensuring interoperability. Regulations are necessary to define what information must be included in a standard and how to react to a given set of conditions. Many standardization efforts are underway simultaneously in an attempt to cover all SCADA application domains.

Regulations and Standards

There is significant effort to enhance the cyber and physical security of SCADA systems and power grids through the development of security requirements and standards to address the aforementioned security issues. The following are the main organizations developing security regulations and standards:

- The Institute of Electrical and Electronics Engineers (IEEE) is an organization that has been involved in standardization for many years. It has developed Electrical and IT-related standards that are used internationally. With respect to SCADA systems, the following standards have been published:
  - IEEE Std 999-1992 – IEEE Recommended Practice for Master/Remote Supervisory Control and Data Acquisition (SCADA) Communications (IEEE, 1992),
  - IEEE Std 1379-2000 – IEEE Recommended Practice for Data Communications Between Remote Terminal Units and Intelligent Electronic Devices in a Substation (IEEE, 2000), and
  - IEEE Std C37-1-2007 – IEEE Recommended Practice for SCADA and Automation Systems (IEEE, 2007).

These recommended practices introduce a set of guidelines for the communication activities between SCADA masters and geographically distributed RTUs and also for the communication of IEDs and RTUs in power substations.

- ISA99 is the Industrial Automation and Control System Security Committee of the International Society for Automation (ISA). Since 1949, ISA has been recognized as the expert source for automation and control systems and has developed a large number of standards and technical reports. In particular, the first two of the following standards include foundational information such as security concepts, models, terminology and technologies concerning Industrial Automation and Control Systems (IACS), while the third addresses how to establish an IACS security program from the asset owner point of view.

  ◦ ANSI/ISA-TR99.00.01-2007 Security Technologies for Industrial Automation and Control Systems(ANSI/ISA, 2007)

  ◦ ANSI/ISA-TR99.00.01-2007 Security for Industrial Automation and Control Systems Part 1: Terminology, Concepts, and Models (ANSI, 2007)

  ◦ ANSI/ISA–TR99.02.01–2009, Security for Industrial Automation and Control Systems: Establishing an Industrial Automation and Control Systems Security Program (ANSI/ISA, 2009)

- The National Institute of Standards and Technology (NIST), especially after the publication of NISTIR 7628 (NIST, 2010), has significantly contributed in shaping the Smart Grid Cyber Security Research. SCADA systems are considered as a significant part of the Smart Grid. According to this document, increasing the complexity of the power grid could also affect the exposure to potential attackers and unintentional user errors. Furthermore, interconnected networks increase the risk of private data exposure, while systems with a large number of entry points are more vulnerable to attackers.

- The Federal Energy Regulatory Commission (FERC) is responsible for protecting the reliability of the bulk (high voltage) transmission system. In particular, FERC's mission is to "assist consumers in obtaining reliable, efficient and sustainable energy services at a reasonable cost through appropriate regulatory and market means" (FERC, 2009). FERC designated the North American Electrical Reliability Corporation (NERC) as the Electric Reliability Corporation (ERO).

- NERC on the other hand, has developed a number of reliability standards that specify the minimum requirements in order to ensure the reliability of the bulk electric system. These standards are known as NERC Critical Infrastructure Protection (CIP) Standards 002-009 (NERC, 2011). NERC CIP standards (See Table 1) provide requirements for communications within an Electronic Security Perimeter (ESP).

Encryption and Authentication in SCADA Protocols

In a typical SCADA system, messages are sent using a clear text, unsecure protocol (Hamoud, Chen and Bradley, 2003). Anyone who can read traffic (eavesdrop) between hosts can see what information is being transferred. On the other hand, in encrypted SCADA communication systems not only are messages encrypted, but they are padded with random data to prevent an attacker from estimating the size or type of the transmission. Moreover, using authentication methods helps with proving the identity of SCADA users and access control. Control messages affect the

Table 1. Version 4 of NERC CIP standards (NERC, 2011)

CIP-002-4	CS - Critical Cyber Asset Identification	Requires the identification and documentation of the Critical Cyber Assets associated with the Bulk Electric System.
CIP-003-4	CS - Security Management Controls	Requires that Responsible Entities have minimum security management controls in place to protect Critical Cyber Assets.
CIP-004-4	CS - Personnel & Training	Requires that personnel having authorized cyber physical access to Critical Cyber Assets have an appropriate level of personnel risk assessment, training, and security awareness.
CIP-005-4a	CS - Electronic Security Perimeter(s)	Requires the identification and protection of the Electronic Security Perimeter(s) inside which all Critical Cyber Assets reside, as well as all access points on the perimeter.
CIP-006-4c	CS - Physical Security of Critical Cyber Assets	Requires the implementation of a physical security program for the protection of Critical Cyber Assets.
CIP-007-4	CS - Systems Security Management	Requires methods, processes, and procedures for securing those systems determined to be Critical Cyber Assets.
CIP-008-4	CS - Incident Reporting and Response Planning	Requires the identification, classification, response, and reporting of Cyber Security Incidents related to Critical Cyber Assets.
CIP-009-4	CS- Recovery Plans for Critical Cyber Assets	Requires that recovery plan(s) are put in place for Critical Cyber Assets and that these plans follow established business continuity and disaster recovery techniques and practices.

system's behavior and operation, and therefore, it is exceedingly important to verify that a message came from an authorized user by challenging the sender's identity.

In order to meet the aforementioned security and reliability standards, encryption and authentication are needed to better secure SCADA communications. There are two main open standards for enforcing SCADA communication with these security mechanisms.

The first is a suite of open standards developed by the American Gas Association (AGA) 12 Cryptography Working Group. In particular, the IEEE 1689 standard, also known as AGA 12 (West, 2008), aims to protect the data transmitted in SCADA networks using encryption, to authenticate the senders and the receivers of the SCADA messages, and to ensure data integrity.

The second is the IEC62351 standard (IEC, 2011), developed by the International Electrotechnical Commission (IEC) Technical Committee 57. This standard was mainly developed for enhancing the security of the IEC 60870-5 protocol (IEC, 2003), which is widely used in Europe and other non-US countries for SCADA masters to RTUs communications, and also was used as a basis for DNP Secure Authentication (Gilchrist, 2008), which is mainly used in the U.S. The DNP Secure Authentication is an addition to the DNP3 protocol (Curtis, 2005) that permits the receiver of a DNP3 message to verify that the message came from an authorized user and was not tampered with during transit.

Although, a number of solutions have been developed to augment the initial SCADA protocols with security functionality, legacy systems still use clear-text. Even if measures to better secure SCADA systems have been implemented, the communication channels still need to be monitored. A distributed monitoring system will contribute to the defense in depth security approach.

DISTRIBUTED MONITORING FOR SCADA SYSTEMS

A distributed monitoring system is proposed to provide additional situational awareness in SCADA systems (Mavridou & Papa, 2011). A brief overview of the system is presented, followed by implementation details and a discussion of the benefits it would bring to these systems.

Overview

Wireless networks as well as utilization of corporate networks and the Internet provide many locations for intruders to gain access to an interconnected system. Deployment of a distributed monitoring system will improve overall situational awareness in these situations. The proposed monitoring system consists of four major components: network sensors deployed in the field, a gateway to facilitate communications, a database in the control center, and an application suite. It will be able to detect messages being passed along the data acquisition framework and gather information about those transmissions.

- **Network Sensors:** The sensors will be deployed alongside the data acquisition devices in the SCADA system. By operating in promiscuous mode, the data traffic can be monitored to determine what information is being sent to and from the control center. The messages containing information such as event notification, service quality, network topology and other important pieces of information can be logged and sent to the database to be stored for later use.
- **Gateway:** The gateway facilitates communication between the sensors and the control center. The transmissions from the sensors must be formatted and stored in the database. Also, various commands such as changes to configuration settings will be forwarded from the control center to the sensors.
- **Database:** The database acts as the interface for the control center and storage of information from the sensors. It will also store state and configuration settings for the network and sensors. This information will allow analysis of the state and information flow from the data acquisition system through the application suite.

- **Application Suite:** The application suite consists of the various tools which can utilize the information gathered by the monitoring system. These provide facilities for alert reporting, event correlation, auditing and policy enforcement, intrusion detection, and forensics. This data can be used to determine the validity and system responses to the messages received through the data acquisition framework.

Implementation

One of the main goals in the design and implementation of a monitoring system is to cover the system access points and provide a comprehensive view of the information flow from the remote units of the SCADA system to the control center (See Figure 2). The most remote sensors can be connected through Home Area Networks (HAN), short range wireless networks. The communication from those sensors and aggregators will use more public means, such as cellular technology or the Internet (Gungor, Sahin, Kocak, Ergut, Buccella, Cecati, & Hancke, 2011). These are the main components of the increasingly interconnected data acquisition system. Monitoring both will ensure a full view of the information flow within the network.

Deployment locations of sensors should coincide, for the most part, with the topology of the data acquisition network. The most important pieces of information to monitor are the inputs and outputs of each component in the system. The HAN should be monitored to observe what data is flowing between the sensor and the aggregator. The aggregator, gateway, and entry to the control network should be monitored as well, as this information may flow through public networks. By comparing the data monitored at each of these locations, messages can be verified to have passed through all required stages of the data acquisition framework.

Figure 2. SCADA monitoring system

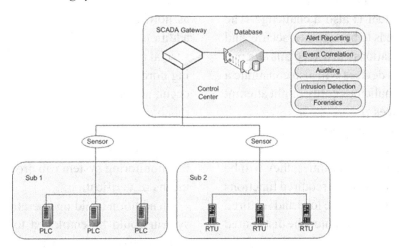

The database will then be updated with the logs from the monitoring system to provide the data necessary for use by the application suite. At a minimum, collected information should contain: the ID of the sensor that collected the information, a timestamp, and the type of message, as well as any other information deemed necessary by the specific implementation. This will provide the raw data that applications which form the final part of the monitoring system will use. The logs can be utilized for the purposes of forensic analysis, auditing, and policy enforcement. Reports can be generated for these purposes using the data gained from the monitoring system. Real-time applications such as intrusion detection, event correlation, and alert reporting can use the information gathered to improve awareness and security within the system.

Challenges

Several challenges exist in the implementation of SCADA security mechanisms. These derive mainly from the unique characteristic of SCADA systems in comparison with traditional IT environments. The monitoring should be continuous, in real time, distributed but also holistic, and should have knowledge and intelligence of SCADA applications and protocols (Mavridou & Papa,

2011). Additionally, in industrial control systems, availability is the primary security concern. As a result, it is important to ensure that protection mechanisms do not themselves become attack vectors and also have minimal impact on real-time plant operations. The risk and impact associated with anomalous events (malicious or not) in a SCADA environment are significant and may result in loss of production, equipment and even lives. It may also catastrophically disrupt critical infrastructures.

As a result, the main challenges for the proposed distributed monitoring system include the computation power necessary to collect and analyze the information received from the multitude of sensors, the communications infrastructure of the monitoring system itself, and the means of securing the devices and transmissions. With a large inflow of data from the sensors, a powerful computer is required to quickly process it. If collected information arrives at a rate faster than it can be analyzed and organized, this will result in a backlog of monitored traffic. In addition, the sensors will require a communication channel to provide the information back to the control center. In some cases this will be the same channel that the data acquisition units utilize to communicate with the SCADA system. The bandwidth usage for monitoring must not impede the necessary activity of the data acquisition. The security of the monitoring system is also a challenge. The communication needs to be accurate, secure, and reliable. Implementations must keep this as a priority. The deployed devices will also constitute a vulnerability, as a malicious entity might attempt to subvert the devices.

A possible means of addressing some of these issues lies in the abilities of the sensor. If they are deployed with more capabilities, they will be able to accomplish some of the required functions themselves. In order to ease the load and required computations at the control center, the distributed sensors could include more processing power. This would allow the units to conduct some of the analysis in the field. For example, if the distributed sensors handle most of the data processing, the control center will only be responsible for coordination and collecting alerts such as security related traffic (e.g. any critical states identified). This can help in saving bandwidth and lessening the amount of data transmitted (Berthier, Sanders, & Khurana, 2010). When a large number of sensors each provide a contribution, it will result in a much reduced workload at the control center. The bandwidth usage of the communication channel can also be minimized by utilizing some local storage to collect multiple transmissions to send in one larger message. These more powerful devices will also have a greater ability to implement secure systems through encryption and other means. However, the power of the device would need to be balanced against cost of being deployed in large numbers.

Benefits to the SCADA System

In some cases, the information gathered and transmitted to the SCADA system includes notifications of events. These events range from sensor condition warnings to failures in the system, and are an ideal message for the monitoring system to act upon. The system has automated responses, which can include drastic measures to limit harm

or redirect the normal flow of operations, as well as notification to individuals who can provide additional actions. These events are designed for special circumstances, and should not occur during normal operation. However, when one does occur, actions must be taken quickly. Therefore, reliable event notification becomes important to maintaining control of the system. While alternative means exist to authenticate transmissions, the monitoring system can provide an additional means of verification.

In addition to aiding operations, a monitoring system could be employed to log and analyze observed traffic. The situational awareness gained from this system would enable the implementation of more intelligent responses and activity of the control center and personnel. The ability to monitor the traffic will allow logging of the messages, which in turn can be used for many other functions. Analysis of these logs will enable correlation of messages, events, and responses. Making connections between these will provide the information to determine if the correct actions were taken, as well as the status of the system throughout the situation. These tools will be able to give accurate feedback on how well the architecture is working in both data gathering and system response. Monitoring the message through its genesis, transmission, and reception along with the status of the system and the reaction to the data provides very useful understanding of the operation of the system. Security tools will also find this information very helpful in implementing more advanced features.

Whenever undesirable events occur, it is important to understand why it happened in order to prevent such a reoccurrence. In order to do this, logs of the monitoring system will be utilized to determine the state of the SCADA system throughout the event and the triggering message. The distributed monitoring system will allow investigations to follow that transmission back to its entry into the system. The information will be very helpful in determining the perpetrator or cause as well as increasing awareness of the system and its responses. The basic requirement for these forensics tools to be useful is to have accurate logging with adequate information for obtaining a full image of the event. Event correlation will use the same logs to determine how connected various events are in the system. This will enable analysts to determine if widespread events could in fact be part of the same attack on the system. While this information will only be determined after the fact, the knowledge can be utilized to implement an intrusion detection system to prevent such an attack from being successful in the future.

With the information that the monitoring system provides, and also the data on normal traffic flow in the network, an intrusion detection system (IDS) becomes a very useful security feature to add. An anomaly-based IDS will be able to determine when abnormal messages enter the network and flag them as possible attacks. The distributed monitoring system will assist in determining what the normal traffic looks like to determine what the anomalies are. It will also provide an abundance of information to intelligently analyze what traffic should be accepted. Determining where a message enters the network and whether that is an authorized origin for that message is one instance where monitoring can determine whether the message should be accepted. All of the information collected by the monitoring system and stored in the database can be used to determine the intelligence of the IDS and prevent undesirable events from occurring.

In addition to these automated tasks, the monitoring system can also be used for auditing and policy enforcement. By logging the traffic and connections to the network, verification that policy is being followed becomes a much simpler task. Security policies are put in place to assist in the prevention of unauthorized activity in the system. When it is not being followed, additional vulnerabilities can occur. Therefore, enforcement of the policy becomes necessary for the sake of the safety of the SCADA system. Logs of the activities of users will provide alerts in these cases so that changes can be made. Compliance with these policies is necessary for assurance of the system as well as from the legal perspective of the companies involved. Implementing an automated system for increasing awareness and enforcing the policies will limit the capabilities of those not following the policy and increase the desire to follow correct procedure.

SMART GRID

The Smart Grid is an improvement to the current power grid that uses bidirectional communication links throughout the infrastructure. They facilitate information gathering and control over the system by expanding and improving data flow in the entire grid. It is an ideal example case for the monitoring system as it implements many new connections to the SCADA system. An overview of the Smart Grid will be given, as well as a discussion on some security risks and how the monitoring system could be of use.

Overview

The traditional electric power grid is responsible for providing power to residential, commercial, and industrial users. This grid also consists of SCADA systems which help control the processes of electricity generation, transmission, and distribution. The key elements and principles for these systems were established before the 1960s, before the emergence of the commonplace networks that exist today (Massoud Amin & Wollenberg, 2005). The nature of the current grid is unidirectional, converting fuel energy into electricity and transmitting it to customers. It is a product of the rapid urbanization and development of infrastructure throughout the world in the past century (Farhangi, 2010). Due to the degree of interconnection within the grid, any change in conditions can have impacts over a wide area. In addition, the congestion and demand for higher reliability and service threaten to overwhelm the aged system (Massoud Amin & Wollenberg, 2005). The Smart Grid development is designed to address these issues through the integration of intelligent networks and communication. It will be able to efficiently deliver reliable, economical, and secure electricity as well as provide bi-directional communication throughout the system (Yu, Cecati, Dillon, & Simoes, 2011).

By upgrading the existing grid, many new features will be added into the system to improve its capabilities and efficiency. The Smart Grid will be able to intelligently integrate all of the users and equipment connected to it in order to do so (Yu, Cecati, Dillon, & Simoes, 2011). The development of this system is focused most on the distribution network, as the causes of nearly 90% of all power outages and disturbances have roots there (Farhangi, 2010). Advanced metering projects are already in progress, typically using a network of smart meters, which are capable of communication with the consumer as well as the utility company. The information transmitted from these meters to the utilities consists of power quality, usage, and event notification. Power outages will be immediately noted in the control center so that restoration activity can begin without delay. In addition, these meters will provide consumers with real-time information on pricing to allow intelligent decisions on power usage. The additional benefit to user's awareness is that their decisions will likely lead to a decrease in load during peak hours, as the consumers reduce usage during high price periods of the day (Yu, Cecati, Dillon, & Simoes, 2011).

The Smart Grid will utilize intelligent systems to improve performance by enabling decision making at all levels. The connectivity of the grid will provide information to the systems in order to respond to events in the best manner. For example, power can be redirected in the event of a damaged power line to prevent outages. The automated activities will also be better able to integrate renewable energy resources into the grid with improved awareness of the amount being generated (Yu, Cecati, Dillon, & Simoes, 2011). These improvements will also make it a self-healing system. Failures are predicted and corrective actions are taken to avoid or mitigate the problems. The gathered information will be used to continually optimize the system while minimizing costs (Farhangi, 2010).

Implementation of the Smart Grid will have many key components to be fully functional. At its core, the current system will be utilized with upgrades to the hardware to allow more capabilities. The key functions will be based on the additional information flow in the more connected network and the data acquisition framework of the SCADA system. The basis of these connections will be the integration of intelligent microgrids, networks of distributed energy systems (Farhangi, 2010). In order to facilitate these connections, the communication technologies play a crucial role. The amount of data necessary for the desired function of the Smart Grid is immense, so the communication infrastructure must be designed well. There are two types of infrastructure needed for correct information flow. The first is between sensors or appliances and the smart meters, the second is between the meters and the utility's data center. The options for communications consist of ZigBee, 6LowPAN, Z-wave, cellular technologies, and the Internet (Gungor, Sahin, Kocak, Ergut, Buccella, Cecati, & Hancke, 2011) (See Figure 3).

Microgrids are smart networks capable of stand-alone power supply and distribution which are designed to also function while connected to the grid. There are several key components to a fully functional microgrid, which will create a system capable of handling power for a smaller area. It includes power plants capable of meeting local demand as well as being able to feed excess power to the grid. It will use local and distributed power-storage to smooth delivery. Residential, office, and industrial loads can be serviced. Smart

Figure 3. Smart Grid system overview. Information flows between the Smart Meters and the Data Aggregator through the Home Area Network such as ZigBee. The Data Aggregator will communicate with the Utility's MDMS through a long distance network such as the Internet.

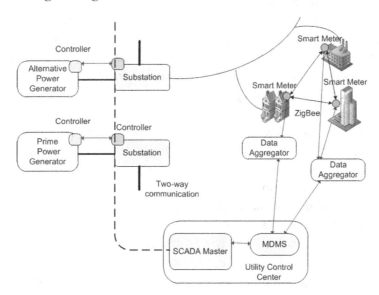

devices such as smart meters and appliances should be incorporated, along with a communication infrastructure to enable information exchange. An intelligent core should be implemented in the form of energy management software for command and control. Evolution of the Smart Grid will come through integration of many of these intelligent microgrids (Farhangi, 2010).

There are several devices deployed in the Smart Grid, based on the focus of an interconnected communication infrastructure. Smart meters, data aggregators, gateways, and the Meter Data Management System (MDMS) make up the framework of the system. The smart meter will gather information such as usage and power quality and transmit it to the data aggregator. The received information is then aggregated with that from any other meters in the area and sent to the gateway where the messages are then forwarded to the control center at the utility. The MDMS is the software which forms the database and tools for the utility to utilize the data gathered from the Smart Grid. This information flow also works in reverse, bringing data to the consumer as well (NETL, 2008).

The first stage of communication exists at the smart meter and data aggregators. The Home Area Network (HAN) is utilized to send information over short distances, as well as connect various other devices in the home. These other devices consist of visual displays, smart appliances, and home automation equipment (NETL, 2008). The ZigBee wireless protocol has been realized by the U.S. National Institute for Standards and Technology (NIST) as the most suitable for this communication in the Smart Grid. Meanwhile, the communication between the gateway and the utility will consist of longer ranged mediums such as the Internet or cellular technology (Gungor, Sahin, Kocak, Ergut, Buccella, Cecati, & Hancke, 2011).

Security Risks

The development and implementation of the Smart Grid will greatly assist the progress towards a more capable and efficient infrastructure. However, the security of such a distributed system should be considered and reviewed prior to deployment (Cardenas, Roosta & Sastry, 2009). In this situation, the network providing the necessary communications infrastructure acts as the backbone of the Smart Grid. It entails a number of connections, which are necessary for the correct functioning of the system. Unfortunately, they will also create many opportunities for vulnerabilities and entry points to the system (Baumeister, 2010). The potential repercussions of a cyber-attack on the SCADA system of the Smart Grid can be quite damaging.

The publicly exposed nature of the data gathering process of the Smart Grid has many security risks (Ralston, Graham & Hieb, 2007). Access control is very limited as both wireless networks and public networks are part of the communication. Increasing numbers of deployments are using these communication environments. The lack of adequate security in the rush to deploy compounds the problem (Khurana, Hadley, Lu, & Frincke, 2010). The data acquisition process also suffers from vulnerabilities that malicious attackers could exploit. Denial of service through signal jamming or resource exhaustion could easily prevent relevant data from reaching the SCADA system. Compromising the various networks can also provide information to the intruder, such as a consumer's billing and usage information, if data is not appropriately protected while in transit. An attacker could also use that access to inject traffic to cause certain automated responses (Berthier, Sanders, & Khurana, 2010). The devices themselves also make for attractive targets. Hacked smart meters can be a means for consumer fraud as well as remote penetration for more sophisticated attacks (McDaniel & McLaughlin, 2009). These are vital security issues to address, as the Smart Grid operates under the assumption that it is a trusted environment, which includes accurate data and secure devices. Past systems have had strict physical access control, but the distributed nature of this system makes that difficult (Khurana, Hadley, Lu, & Frincke, 2010).

Advantages of the Monitoring System

The monitoring system presented previously provides the situational awareness to prevent many of the possible attacks on this network. In the event of fraud attempts, the monitoring system can compare previous reports from the meters and realize the change and notify the technicians of an anomaly to be investigated. The scrutiny brought to such an instance will be more than enough to determine the culprit in that instance. The monitoring system will make it simple to identify these cyber-attacks and alert authorities.

In the case of more sophisticated attacks, the monitoring system can provide much more information to act intelligently upon. With the architecture of the Smart Grid, information is collected at the aggregators before being sent to the utilities. An attack at this location could tamper with the data from many sources. In this case, monitoring the data transmitted from each source and comparing it with what is received at the control center will alert the system to a breach. In this case the system can avoid reacting to falsified information, which may include false event reports.

With the distributed nature of the Smart Grid, attacks could also come in a distributed fashion. If malicious messages are sent from many different sources, having the situational awareness to correlate all of the transmissions to determine the cause to be malicious could be vital to preventing great harm in the system. Rather than blindly reacting to the received information, the IDS can alert the control center to the incident and prevent the system from entering into a dangerous state. The benefits from such a monitoring system can not only provide a vast amount information, but can also be used by the previously mentioned security tools to reinforce the system to prevent disastrous results throughout the power grid.

DATA ACQUISITION FROM THE SENSORS

The data acquisition framework of the SCADA system entails the gathering of information from the many distributed sensors. That network of information can be implemented in several ways. This section focuses and analyzes two technologies of interest in the Smart Grid: RFID and ZigBee. Security risks for both technologies are also discussed along with the benefits a monitoring system can provide.

Radio Frequency Identification (RFID) Sensors

Radio frequency identification (RFID) technology has been used to track retail goods (Bustillo, 2010), track shipments, in healthcare (Hawrylak, Ogirala, Norman, Rajgopal, & Mickle, 2011; Jara, Zamora, & Skarmeta, 2011) and even monitor the environment via sensors (Emond, 2008; Becker, Metsis, Arora, Vinjumur, Xu, & Makedon, 2009; Chen, Gonzalez, Leung, Zhang, & Li, 2010; Hoque, Dickerson, & Stankovic, 2010). RFID systems are composed of RFID reader, RFID tags, and a suite of software controlling operation: usually some form of enterprise resource planning (ERP) software. An overview of RFID systems is provided by Hawrylak, *et. al* (Hawrylak, Cain, & Mickle, 2008).

RFID systems are divided into one of three classifications: active, battery assisted passive (BAP), and passive. The category that a technology falls into depends on how the RFID tag is powered. Passive tags have no on-board power supply and harvest the power required for their operation from the reader's transmission (electromagnetic waves or field). Passive tags communicate using backscatter. The tag communicates using backscatter by altering the impedance of its antenna. This alteration in the antenna results in more or less of the reader's transmitted energy, termed *carrier wave* or CW, being reflected back to the reader, thus providing amplitude modulation

(AM) of the reader's signal. BAP tags have an on-board battery that powers a microprocessor and/or a sensor, but not the communication circuitry. BAP tags communicate using backscatter and can harvest energy for operation from the reader's carrier wave (CW). Thus, BAP tags offer a fail-safe mode where they can provide some functionality once their battery has been depleted or fails. Active tags are entirely battery powered and can communicate over distances of several hundred meters or over shorter distances in environments with large amounts of interference, e.g. other wireless signals or large amounts of metal. Once the battery in an active tag is depleted, the tag is rendered non-functional, and thus, does not offer a fail-safe mode. Replacing the battery can enable the user to retrieve all information stored up to the time that the battery was depleted.

Passive RFID tags with large memories have limited operating ranges, which may prevent them from being viable solutions for SCADA monitoring systems needing long range communication. Sensors have been standardized in two types of RFID tags: BAP tags following the ISO 18000-6 Type C standard (ISO, 2010), and active tags following the ISO 18000-7 standard (ISO, 2009). An overview of the EPC Gen-2 protocol (EPCglobal, 2008), which the ISO 18000-6 Type C protocol is based on is provided by Hawrylak and Mickle (Hawrylak & Mickle, 2009). These sensor equipped tags can be used as part of a SCADA system to collect data. Here the RFID protocol offers a communication channel to provide the "last-mile" connection between the backbone SCADA network and the sensors at the edge. RFID tags provide an economical location to place the sensor because the tag can be used to track and identify the piece of equipment in addition to providing the sensor readings.

RFID based sensor networks are adhere to a master-slave architecture, where the reader acts as the master and the tag the slave. In these networks the tags contain the sensors and provide information on-demand to the reader. Tags typically do not send alerts in the ISO communication protocols. Such networks are found in cargo container monitoring and food shipment tracking (Wessel, 2007; Emond, 2008). However, other RFID based sensor networks enable the tag to transmit alerts. Having a tag that can send alerts without being asked by the reader appears to be the future trend in RFID based sensor networks.

Passive ISO 18000-6 Type C tags support on-demand sensors that can take a reading only when being read or interrogated (powered) by a reader. Such tags have significant uses in SCADA systems because they are economical and have a long life. For example, these tags can be deployed in a power plant and can provide sensor readings on demand from an engineer with a handheld RFID reader or from a fixed RFID reader. BAP and active tags can support sensors that can log readings when not being interrogated (powered) by an RFID reader. In these cases the RFID reader can periodically query the tag to collect the sensor readings.

Machine-to-Machine Communication

Machine-to-machine (M2M) communication is a key component in SCADA systems. Many utilities are moving towards automation and the remote control of facilities, such as electric substations, to reduce costs. Facilities must manage themselves and be capable of responding to changing conditions. The increase in computing power available in embedded platforms enables construction of advanced intelligent electronic devices (IEDs). These IEDs communicate with each other using M2M communication.

The Smart Grid will employ IEDs to automate and provide remote control capabilities to substations. The IEC 61850 family of standards defines the higher layers of the network protocol to link the IEDs together and to the human-machine interface (HMI) and ultimately the human operator. In the Smart Grid, the IEDs will share information with each other to provide the optimal amount of power based on current and forecast demand.

This architecture introduces several security issues that must be addressed. The insertion of a fake IED into the system can cause significant problems. For example, the fake IED can transmit false information to cause the substation to adjust the power output, potentially leading to a blackout (Dondossola, Deconinck, Garrone, & Beitollahi, 2009). Another attack scenario is to have the fake IED impersonate a central network device, such as an Ethernet switch, to become a central link in a local network and then stop relaying messages, fragmenting the network (Dondossola, Deconinck, Garrone, & Beitollahi, 2009). Both of these attacks can be addressed with a distributed monitoring system.

A denial-of-service (DOS) attack is another threat to M2M communication. The Smart Grid has hard-real-time limits on response time and a DOS attack could prevent messages from reaching their destination in time. This could result in a blackout or damage to electric equipment. Several studies of the IEC 61850 protocol have raised significant questions about the ability of the IEC 61850 network to meet the hard-real-time deadlines necessary for controlling the electric grid (Dondossola, Deconinck, Garrone, & Beitollahi, 2009; Kanabar & Sidhu, 2011). DOS attacks are difficult to prevent on the Internet, but they can be kept out of the substation LAN using a strong firewall with a proper rule set.

ZigBee Wireless Protocol

ZigBee is a communications standard developed by the ZigBee Alliance as a low-cost, low-power-consumption, two-way solution for embedded devices, home and building automation, industrial controls, and M2M communication. This standard forms the top layers of a communication protocol riding on top of the IEEE 802.15.4 standard (ZigBee Alliance, 2008). The design is based on utilizing a low-data-rate wireless network during which devices will spend a majority of their time in low-power or sleep mode, often being active less than 1% of the time. This allows battery operated devices to function for months or years without replacing the battery (Farahani, 2008).

The IEEE 802.15.4 standard defines the Physical (PHY) Layer and the Medium Access Control (MAC) Layer. The PHY layer is responsible for the control of the radio, which includes access to the transceiver and low-level control mechanism. These mechanisms allow transmission, reception, and channel assessment to see if a transmission can occur. Meanwhile, the MAC layer provide the most basic network services, including acknowledgement frames, association and disassociation from the network, and beacon management. Beacon frames are used to determine when devices are allowed to transmit (IEEE, 2006).

The ZigBee standard defines the higher levels of the communication stack. This includes the Network (NWK) Layer and the application layer. The NWK layer is responsible for managing the network and routing. ZigBee utilizes mesh wireless networking to provide self-healing when problems exist by dynamically reconfiguring routes. The application layer exists as the Application Support Sublayer (APS), ZigBee Device Object (ZDO), and Application Objects. These provide access points to the device and user specific applications in order for them to connect and utilize the ZigBee standard (ZigBee Alliance, 2008).

Implementing ZigBee into sensors is an ideal way to utilize the technology. For example, a security system can utilize motion detection sensors, glass-break sensors, and cameras. By communicating through ZigBee, these sensors can share a complete image of the property without placing a large drain on the batteries of the devices (Farahani, 2008). Previously, the Smart Grid section also mentioned use of ZigBee as a HAN for the acquisition of data from the smart meters. SCADA systems can utilize these types of sensors as an ideal means of gathering data from distributed areas without placing too much of a strain on the power required to operate the sensors.

Security Risks

BAP and active RFID tags suffer from energy draining attacks (Louthan, Hardwicke, Hawrylak & Hale, 2011; Brownfield, Gupta & Davis, 2005; Buennemeyer, Jacoby, Chiang, Marchany & Tront, 2006; Raymond, Marchany, Brownfield & Midkiff, 2009), while passive tags do not because of their lack of a battery. In ZigBee as well, the desire to prolong battery life through spending time in a low-power mode can provide a ripe target for these attacks. Energy draining attacks are defined as any set of actions taken by a malicious actor to drain the tag's battery. In the case of ISO 18000-7, this could be repeatedly transmitting the wake-up command to prevent the tags from returning to their low-power sleep mode. Other attacks include issuing normal commands to the tags causing them to perform tasks that are useless to the larger system.

From the perspective of the SCADA system, while the possibility of losing power on a sensor can disrupt the information that is received, that is an issue whether these technologies are used or not. However, there are several vulnerabilities that the addition of these connections brings. Devices can be compromised, and begin transmitting malicious messages through the data acquisition framework. These transmissions will seem reliable to the SCADA system, as they are originating from a trusted device. These networks also provide an additional access point to the system. Malicious attackers may use this to either eavesdrop on communication or inject messages into the system to cause harm.

Monitoring System Benefits

Due to the limited capabilities of the RFID tags, sophisticated monitoring techniques cannot be deployed on the RFID tags. Thus, the monitoring must be done on the RFID reader side. The readers can monitor the communication channels and can overhear other reader and tag messages. One method is to use logs to define what normal operation looks like. This is most likely a given set of commands being transmitted each day. If abnormal communications are taking place then an alert can be raised that a rogue device may have entered the network. Employing strong authentication, such as a challenge-response method, on the readers can be used to enable each reader to verify itself to the system. If the reader initiating the abnormal traffic is authenticated then the traffic is acceptable; otherwise a rogue reader has been inserted or an authentic reader has been compromised. The sensors from the monitoring system will be able to analyze this traffic to determine if any new devices are to be trusted or not.

These sensors will be able to analyze the traffic on the network and determine the normal flow of operations, so that hacked devices can also be identified. The logs and standard flow of information will show what should be expected, and deviations will call for closer analysis to determine what is causing the change in behavior. The monitoring system will provide a degree of security in networks which cannot have the same strict access control as SCADA systems previously operated with.

FUTURE RESEARCH DIRECTIONS

Technology evolves continuously and work in this area must continue to ensure system operators keep operational risks at an acceptable level. In the next section, discussions will focus on expected changes in the future of these SCADA connections. Interconnection will continue to grow in size and complexity, embedded device security will become more important, and the last mile of the SCADA connection will grow. In addition, the Internet of Things concept will become more common and compose part of the network connecting SCADA systems together.

Future Trends

As SCADA systems are linked to the Internet to satisfy increased demand for detailed information for use in the enterprise network, security and infrastructure costs become key issues. SCADA systems, previously constructed as isolated networks limited to a factory or electric power plant are now being connected to the Internet. This connection requires a reevaluation and redesign of many systems to incorporate Internet security features and accepted practices into SCADA hardware, software, and applications. The delicate nature of the TCP/IP stacks deployed by most field devices requires that solutions be designed specifically for this environment. It is well known that many of the security tools frequently used in IT networks do not work well in an industrial network. In addition, it may be prohibitively expensive for facility operators to reinstall and reconfigure their entire SCADA system; in this case, data connections and trust boundaries must be closely audited and strictly controlled.

Further, because SCADA systems link the cyber (computer) and physical (machinery) worlds these linkages and their interaction must be evaluated; the impact of vulnerabilities in information services takes on an entirely new dimension when the exploitation of those vulnerabilities may have physical consequences. The remarkable convenience of wireless technologies makes them attractive for deployment in large portions of the network while reducing maintenance costs at the same time.

In addition to giant leaps in connectivity, SCADA systems are also broadly increasing in size and scope. In the past, SCADA systems have stayed largely out of the public eye, managing the operation of backbone infrastructure in remote locations. However, new innovations such as the smart grid have brought SCADA to the public's attention, and have placed potential access points to SCADA networks within easy reach of the general population. As such, the trust level of connections between various SCADA devices will need to be radically redesigned. As the devices comprising the SCADA network will also be easily within the grasp of the general population, special attention must also be paid to avoiding and patching implementation-level vulnerabilities in SCADA devices, as the ease of access to these devices will gravely increase the impact of these vulnerabilities.

Embedded Device Security

As a consequence of the increased connectivity and complexity of SCADA networks and the devices that comprise them, increased attention must be paid to security practices in the devices themselves. In years past, the serial networks connecting the devices were very difficult to access, and the devices themselves were so simple that the gains of exploiting them were minimal.

That age is now firmly in the past. Incidents such as the intrusion of the Slammer Worm into the Davis-Besse power plant network in 2003 demonstrate the possibility of intrusions into production networks by a clever attacker (or a careless operator), and SCADA devices today are sufficiently complex and powerful that a successful exploit may be as dangerous as compromising a control system computer, if not more so because of the difficulty of forensics and monitoring device memory.

Several steps must be taken in order to mitigate this threat. The first, and most important, step is a cultural shift in the development of software that runs on embedded devices. Secure software engineering practices have become an industry standard in development for workstation platforms; these same standards must be adopted by the embedded device programming community. Not only must the practices be adopted, but the importance of security must truly be taken to heart by the community and given top priority in design decisions.

The second step is that monitoring software must take into account the possibility that embedded devices are now legitimate targets for exploitation. Intrusion detection systems on enterprise networks have signatures that detect likely attack strings for common architectures in that space such as x86. Similarly, SCADA network intrusion detection systems must now be designed to detect attack strings targeting common embedded device architectures such as ARM.

A third step that is related to step two is the development of incident response plans that account for the possibility of the compromise of embedded devices. Incident response plans must include forensic techniques that can record device data in a forensically sound manner, both to recognize the compromise of a device and to investigate its source. In addition to detection, they must also include provisions for reconfiguring the devices with trusted firmware and software to quickly return the production network to a secure, trusted, functional state.

Economic Last-Mile Connection

The last-mile connection represents the connection between the main network and the end-point, and often represents a significant amount of the total cost of deployment. In this case, this is the sensor or actuator and the SCADA controller. RFID is one wireless technology capable of providing the last-mile connection. RFID systems have been widely deployed in the retail and supply chain industries. Many supply chain applications require monitoring of different physical phenomenon, such as the temperature of fresh fruit (Wessel, 2007) and wine (Swedberg, 2010). RFID is a logical place to incorporate sensors into a SCADA system because the sensor equipped RFID tags can be placed on the equipment for the purposes of tracking it during production, shipment, and maintaining the operating or maintenance history. ZigBee is another option for a wireless technology to incorporate into this stage of the SCADA system. It will provide a low-power means of communication among devices to collect information and transmit it to the next stage of the data acquisition framework. These devices will be able to remain connected despite individual device failures and continue to provide the necessary information to the system. This last-mile connection continues to grow in both scale and quality of information provided to the control center. It is important to continue to realize the importance of both gathering additional information and securing the means of that process as it is not necessarily possible to limit access to the location.

Internet of Things

The Internet of Things (IoT) is a term used to describe the connection of all manner of devices (e.g. climate control, smartphone, and home appliances) together to form a network. Usually this network is connected to the Internet via some portal, e.g. a smartphone. The IoT provides a means to connect SCADA devices together and to the human operators. For example, near-field communication or NFC technology is one form of RFID found in many smartphones that could be used to read sensors on machinery. Many other protocols provide similar possibilities for these growing connections of devices, such as ZigBee, Bluetooth, and WiFi. Research is required to develop the human-machine interfaces (HMIs) and applications to interact with the sensors. Further, research is required to secure the devices providing the HMI and the link between the sensor and the HMI. Securing the sensor is particularly problematic due to the power and computing power limitations of the sensor. As these technologies expand in their uses, more and more devices will be connected, providing both greater collections of data, but also additional possible access points for a malicious intruder.

CONCLUSION

SCADA systems control a vast number of important resources and function in an increasingly automated manner. The triggers for various responses are based on the data gathered throughout the distributed sensors of the system. While this provides excellent results and quick responses to many situations, it is completely dependent on the timeliness and integrity of the data received from these distant devices. The trust placed in this information and the ramifications of a response to incorrect data make the security of these distributed data acquisition systems a high priority.

Communications from the data gathering devices travel through a wide range of protocols and networks. Information collected by a distributed monitoring system can be used to verify and validate messages and, more generally, to provide information assurance. The proposed monitoring system uses a network of sensors strategically positioned to observe data flow throughout the system. Secure data acquisition within the distributed monitoring system is achieved by implementing secure communication channels and mutual authentication. The logs of this traffic would be collected at the control center and securely stored in a database. In addition, situational awareness, which is a key feature in intelligent systems, grows tremendously from implementing such a monitoring system. They provide all the raw data required by applications to implement sophisticated tools that are capable of analyzing the system from a higher, more abstract level.

Furthermore, the distributed monitoring system could then be used as the first step in the development of a security tool set that integrates resources and ensures a more secure operating environment. The information gathered by the monitoring system will be also be able to assist with policy auditing and enforcement, event correlation, forensic analysis, and intrusion detection systems. These tools will increase the security inside the SCADA system in a way that will not impede operation, i.e., it preserves system availability. In addition, tools using data collected by the monitoring system can mitigate overall risks and improve the security posture of the environment.

REFERENCES

ANSI. (2007). *TR99.00.01-2007, security for industrial automation and control systems, part 1: Terminology, concepts and models.*

ANSI/ISA. (2007). *TR99.00.01-2007, security technologies for industrial automation and control systems.*

ANSI/ISA. (2009). *TR99.02.01-2009, Security for industrial automation and control systems: Establishing an industrial automation and control systems security program.*

Baumeister, T. (2010). *Literature review on smart grid cyber security.* University of Hawaii, Department of Information and Computer Sciences. Retrieved January 23, 2012, from http://csdl.ics. hawaii.edu/techreports/10-11/10-11.pdf

Becker, E., Metsis, V., Arora, R., Vinjumur, J., Xu, Y., & Makedon, F. (2009). *SmartDrawer: RFID-based smart medicine drawer for assistive environments.* 2nd International Conference on PErvasive Technologies Related to Assistive Environments (PETRA '09). New York, NY.

Berthier, R., Sanders, W., & Khurana, H. (2010). Intrusion detection for advanced metering infrastructures: Requirements and architectural directions. *First IEEE International Conference on Smart Grid Communications (SmartGridComm),* (pp. 350-355). Gaithersburg, MD.

Brownfield, M., Gupta, Y., & Davis, N. (2005). Wireless sensor network denial of sleep attack. *Sixth Annual IEEE Information Assurance Workshop* (pp. 356-364). West Point, NY: IEEE.

Brunner, E., & Suter, M. (2008). *International CIIP handbook 2008/2009: An inventory of 25 national and 7 internation critical information infrastructure protection policies.* Zurich, Switzerland: ETH.

Buennemeyer, T., Jacoby, G., Chiang, W., Marchany, R., & Tront, J. (2006). *Battery-sensing intrusion protection system. In 2006* (pp. 176–183). IEEE Information Assurance Workshop.

Bustillo, M. (2010, July 23). Wal-Mart radio tags to track clothing. *Wall Street Journal.* Retrieved February 18, 2011, from http://online.wsj.com/article/SB1000142405274870442130457538321306119 8090.html

Cardenas, A. A., Roosta, T., & Sastry, S. (2009). Rethinking security properties, threat models, and the design space in sensor networks: A case study in SCADA systems. *Ad Hoc Networks, 7*(8), 1434–1447. doi:10.1016/j.adhoc.2009.04.012

CERT. (2003). *Advisory CA-2003-20 W32/Blaster worm.* Carnegie Mellon University's Computer Emergency Response Team. Retrieved January 23, 2012, from http://www.cert.org/advisories/CA-2003-20.html

Chen, M., Gonzalez, S., Leung, V., Zhang, Q., & Li, M. (2010). A 2G-RFID-based e-healthcare system. *IEEE Wireless Communications, 17*(1), 37–43. doi:10.1109/MWC.2010.5416348

Craig, P., Mortensen, J., & Dagle, J. (2008). *Metrics for the National SCADA Test Bed Program, PNNL-18-31.* Richland, WA: Pacific Northwest National Laboratory. doi:10.2172/963242

Curtis, K. (2005). *A DNP3 protocol primer (Revision A)*. Retrieved May 25, 2011, from http://www.dnp.org/AboutUs/DNP3%20Primer%20Rev%20A.pdf

DHS & DoE. (2007). *Energy: Critical infrastructure and key resources, sector-specific plan as input to the national infrastructure protection plan.* Department of Energy. Retrieved January 23, 2012, from http://energy.gov/oe/downloads/energy-critical-infrastructure-and-key-resources-sector-specific-plan-input-national

Dondossola, G., Deconinck, G., Garrone, F., & Beitollahi, H. (2009). Testbeds for assessing critical scenarios in power control systems. In Setola, R., & Geretshuber, S. (Eds.), *Critical Information Infrastructure Security* (*Vol. 5508*, pp. 223–234). Lecture Notes in Computer Science Berlin, Germany: Springer. doi:10.1007/978-3-642-03552-4_20

Emond, J. P. (2008). Resolution and integration of HF and UHF. In Miles, S. B., Sarma, S. E., & Williams, J. R. (Eds.), *RFID technology and applications* (pp. 144–156). New York, NY: Cambridge University Press. doi:10.1017/CBO9780511541155.012

EPCglobal. (2008). *EPC^TM radio-frequency identity protocols class-1 Generation-2 UHF RFID protocol for communications at 860 MHz - 960 MHz version 1.2.0.* EPCglobal, Inc.

Falliere, N. (2010). *Stuxnet introduces the first known rootkit for industrial control systems.* Symantec Official Blog. Retrieved September 5, 2011, from http://www.symantec.com/connect/blogs/stuxnet-introduces-first-known-rootkit-scada-devices

Falliere, N., Murchu, L., & Chie, E. (2011). *W32. Stuxnet dossier version 1.4.* Symantec Security Response. Retrieved September 5, 2011, from http://www.symantec.com/content/en/us/enterprise/media/security_response/whitepapers/w32_stuxnet_dossier.pdf

Farahani, S. (2008). *ZigBee wireless networks and transceivers*. Oxford, UK: Elsevier Ltd.

Farhangi, H. (2010). The path of the smart grid. *IEEE Power and Energy Magazine, 8*(1), 18–28. doi:10.1109/MPE.2009.934876

FERC. (2009). *Smart grid policy*. Federal Energy Regulatory Commission. Retrieved January 20, 2012, from http://www.ferc.gov/whats-new/comm-meet/2009/071609/E-3.pdf

Gilchrist, G. (2008). Secure authentication for DNP3. *IEEE Power and Energy Society General Meeting - Conversion and Delivery of Electrical Energy in the 21st Century*, (pp. 1-3).

Gungor, V. C., Sahin, D., Kocak, T., Ergut, S., Buccella, C., Cecati, C., & Hancke, G. P. (2011). Smart grid technologies: Communication technologies and standards. *IEEE Transactions on Industrial Informatics, 7*(4), 529–539. doi:10.1109/TII.2011.2166794

Hamoud, G., Chen, R., & Bradley, I. (2003). Risk assessment of power systems SCADA. *IEEE Power Engineering Society General Meeting.*

Hawrylak, P. J., Cain, J. T., & Mickle, M. H. (2008). RFID tags. In Yan, L., Zhang, Y., Yang, L. T., & Ning, H. (Eds.), *The internet of things: From RFID to pervasive networked systems* (pp. 1–32). Boca Raton, FL: Auerbach Publications, Taylor & Francis Group. doi:10.1201/9781420052824.ch1

Hawrylak, P. J., & Mickle, M. H. (2009). EPC Gen-2 standard for RFID. In Y. Zhang, L. T. Yang, & J. Chen (Eds.), *RFID and sensor networks: Architectures, protocols, security and integrations* (pp. 97-124). Boca Raton, FL: Taylor & Francis Group, CRC Press.

Hawrylak, P. J., Ogirala, A., Norman, B. A., Rajgopal, J., & Mickle, M. H. (2011). Enabling real-time management and visibility with RFID. In Kolker, A., & Story, P. (Eds.), *Management engineering for effective healthcare delivery principles and applications* (pp. 172–190). Hershey, PA: IGI Global. doi:10.4018/978-1-60960-872-9.ch008

Hoque, E., Dickerson, R. F., & Stankovic, J. A. (2010). Monitoring body positions and movements during sleep using WISPs. *Proceedings of the 2010 International Conference on Wireless Health*, (pp. 44-53). New York, NY.

IEC. (2003). *International Standard IEC 60870-5-101, second edition, Telecontrol equipment and systems - Part 5-101: Transmission protocols - Companion standard for basic telecontrol tasks.*

IEC. (2011). *IEC/TS 62351: Security*. Retrieved October 1, 2011, from http://www.iec.ch/smargrid/standards

IEEE. (1992). *IEEE recommended practice for master/remote supervisory control and data acquisition (SCADA) communications.*

IEEE. (2000). *IEEE recommended practice for data communications between remote terminal units and intelligent electronic devices in a substation.*

IEEE. (2006). *802.15.4-2006 wireless medium access control (MAC) and physical layer (PHY) specifications for low-rate wireless personal area networks (LR-WPANS)*. Retrieved from IEEE 802.15 WPAN TG4: http://www.ieee802.org/15/pub/TG4.html

IEEE. (2007). *IEEE recommended practice for SCADA and automation systems.*

Igure, V., Laughter, S., & Williams, R. (2006). Security issues in SCADA networks. *Computers & Security*, 25(7), 498–506. doi:10.1016/j.cose.2006.03.001

ISO. (2009). *ISO/IES 18000-7 Information technology -- Radio frequency identification for item management -- Part 7: Parameters for active air interface communications at 433 MHz.*

ISO. (2010). *ISO/IEC 18000-6: 2010 FDIS Information technology -- Radio frequency identification for item management -- Part 6: Parameters for air interface communications at 860 MHz to 960 MHz.*

Jara, A. J., Zamora, M. A., & Skarmeta, A. F. (2011). An internet of things-based personal device for diabetes therapy management in ambient assisted living (AAL). *Personal and Ubiquitous Computing*, 15(4), 431–440. doi:10.1007/s00779-010-0353-1

Kanabar, M., & Sidhu, T. (2011). Performance of IEC 61850-9-2 process bus and corrective measure for digital relaying. *IEEE Transactions on Power Delivery*, 26(2), 725–735. doi:10.1109/TPWRD.2009.2038702

Khurana, H., Hadley, M., Lu, N., & Frincke, D. (2010). Smart-grid security issues. *IEEE Security & Privacy*, 8(1), 81–85. doi:10.1109/MSP.2010.49

Louthan, G., Hardwicke, P., Hawrylak, P., & Hale, J. (2011). *Toward hybrid attack dependency graphs*. Paper presented at the 7th Annual Cyber Security and Information Intelligence Research Workshop, Oak Ridge.

Massoud Amin, S., & Wollenberg, B. (2005). Toward a smart grid: Power delivery for the 21st century. *IEEE Power and Energy Magazine*, 3(5), 34–41. doi:10.1109/MPAE.2005.1507024

Mavridou, A., & Papa, M. (2011). A situational awareness architecture for the smart grid. *7th International Conference in Global Security Safety and Sustainability (ICGS3)*. Thessaloniki, Greece.

McDaniel, P., & McLaughlin, S. (2009). Security and privacy challenges in the smart grid. *IEEE Security & Privacy*, 7(3), 75–77. doi:10.1109/MSP.2009.76

NCS. (2004). *Supervisory control and data acquisition (SCADA) systems, technical information bulletin NCS TIB 04-1*. Arlington, VA.

NERC. (2011). *Reliability standards for the bulk electric systems of North America*. Retrieved January 23, 2012, from http://www.nerc.com/docs/standards/rs/Reliability_Standards_Complete_Set.pdf

NETL. (2008). *Advanced metering infrastructure*. Retrieved January 23, 2012, from http://www.netl.doe.gov/smartgrid/referenceshelf/whitepapers/AMI%20White%20paper%20final%20021108%20%282%29%20APPROVED_2008_02_12.pdf

NIST. (2010). *NISTIR 7628, guidelines for smart grid cyber security*. National Institute of Standards and Technology.

Oman, P., Schweitzer, E., III, & Frincke, D. (2000). Concerns about intrusions into remotely accessible substation controllers and SCADA systems. *Twenty-Seventh Annual Western Protective Relay Conference*, (p. 160). Spokane, WA. Retrieved January 18, 2012, from http://www.selinc.com/literature/literature.aspx?fid=282

Ralston, P. A., Graham, J. H., & Hieb, J. L. (2007). Cyber security risk assessment for SCADA and DCS networks. *ISA Transactions, 46*(4), 583–594. doi:10.1016/j.isatra.2007.04.003

Raymond, D. R., Marchany, R. C., Brownfield, M. I., & Midkiff, S. F. (2009). Effects of denial-of-sleep attacks on wireless sensor network MAC protocols. *IEEE Transactions on Vehicular Technology, 58*(1), 367–380. doi:10.1109/TVT.2008.921621

Stouffer, K., Falco, J., & Ken, K. (2006). *Guide to supervisory control and data acquisition (scada) and industrial control systems security, Recommendations of the National Institute of Standards and Technology*. NIST.

Swedberg, C. (2010). UC Davis winery tracks fermentation via RFID sensors. *RFID Journal*. Retrieved October 9, 2011, from http://www.rfidjournal.com/article/view/8033

Verton, D. (2003). Blaster worm linked to severity of blackout. *Computerworld*.

Wessel, R. (2007). RFID keeps cherries fresh. *RFID Journal*. Retrieved October 9, 2011, from http://www.rfidjournal.com/article/view/3554

West, A. (2008). *Securing DNP3 and Modbus with AGA12-2J*. IEEE Power and Energy Society General Meeting - Conversion and Delivery of Electrical Energy in the 21st Century, Pittsburgh, PA.

Yu, X., Cecati, C., Dillon, T., & Simoes, M. (2011). The new frontier of smart grids. *IEEE Industrial Electronics Magazine, 5*(3), 49–63. doi:10.1109/MIE.2011.942176

ZigBee Alliance. (2008). *ZigBee specification*. Retrieved September 17, 2011, from http://www.zigbee.org/Specifications/ZigBee/download.aspx

KEY TERMS AND DEFINITIONS

Data Acquisition Framework: The information gathering component of the SCADA system. This consists of the sensors and the communication path to the control center.

Distributed Monitoring System: A large scale distribution of sensors deployed to monitor communication over a large number of collection points, feeding that information back to a central computer.

Distributed Network Protocol (DNP3): A set of communication protocols used in industrial SCADA systems.

Human Machine Interface (HMI): A system designed to gather information from the backend and display it in a format that is easily readable by humans.

Industrial Control Systems (ICS): These systems will operate based on information received from remote locations, they can send commands to field devices which control components such as valves and sensors.

Machine to Machine (M2M): Machine-to-machine (M2M) communication is defined as any two machines communicating with each other without human interaction. An example of this in a SCADA system includes a sensor communicating with a controller unit.

Microgrid: A small cell of the smart grid, which contains everything needed to run. It has the ability to control and distribute power locally and communicate effectively. By integrating several of these, the Smart Grid will develop.

Programmable Logic Controller (PLC): A computer designed to interact with physical components in order to obtain information about or to control a physical system as well as communicate with other computers.

Radio Frequency Identification (RFID): RFID stands for Radio Frequency Identification and is a wireless system used to identify objects, which may be people or assets. RFID systems contain RFID readers and RFID tags. Tags are attached to the objects and readers provide the means for the user to interact with the tag.

Remote Terminal Unit (RTU): This unit controls a physical object and communicates that status with the control center. It acts as a means to send digital commands to the physical object.

Situational Awareness: The intelligence and ability to recognize what events are occurring in the system. It includes monitoring, recognizing, and analyzing activity.

Smart Grid: An initiative to upgrade the power grid to modern standards by incorporating current technology and networking to improve communication, situational awareness, and information flow to both customers and providers.

Supervisory Control and Data Acquisition (SCADA): An industrial control system to monitor a plant or equipment in industry. It entails the control center where decisions are made, remote locations where sensors are placed to gather information, and the communication to connect them.

ZigBee: A communication standard designed for low-cost, low-power-consumption wireless communication. Devices generally spend a majority of time asleep, leading to batteries lasting for months or years before requiring a replacement.

Chapter 7
Motivating Cybersecurity:
Assessing the Status of Critical Infrastructure as an Object of Cyber Threats

Sean Lawson
University of Utah, USA

ABSTRACT

Based on an analysis of key policy documents and statements from civilian policymakers, military leaders, and cybersecurity experts, this chapter demonstrates that although there is still concern over cyber threats to critical infrastructure, other threat objects have begun to figure more prominently in public policy discourse about cybersecurity in the United States. In particular, intellectual property and government secrets are now identified most often as the primary object of cyber threats. When critical infrastructure is mentioned, it is often used as a motivational tactic, with collapse of critical infrastructure serving as a central theme of hypothetical scenarios meant to motivate a policy response. This chapter documents and critically evaluates this shift in U.S. cybersecurity discourse.

INTRODUCTION

As advanced Western societies and economies have become increasingly dependent upon networked information and communication systems, concern over the security and reliability of those systems has also increased. This concern with

cybersecurity has gone hand-in-hand with increased concern about the security and reliability of critical infrastructures. For most of the 1990s and early 2000s, cybersecurity experts, military leaders, and policymakers in the United States identified critical infrastructure as the primary object of prospective cyber threats either from

DOI: 10.4018/978-1-4666-2659-1.ch007

Copyright © 2013, IGI Global. Copying or distributing in print or electronic forms without written permission of IGI Global is prohibited.

state or non-state actors. While public policy discussion of cybersecurity in the United States waned during the wars in Afghanistan and Iraq, a number of well-publicized cyber attacks since 2007 against Estonia, Georgia, and Iran have focused attention once again on cybersecurity. In the process, however, critical infrastructure has slipped from its position as the primary object of the cyber threat. Although there is certainly still concern over cyber threats to critical infrastructure, other threat objects have begun to figure more prominently in public policy discourse about cybersecurity in the United States. In particular, intellectual property and government secrets are now identified most often as the primary object of cyber threats. When critical infrastructure is mentioned, it is often used as a motivational tactic, with collapse of critical infrastructure serving as a central theme of hypothetical scenarios meant to motivate a policy response. This chapter documents and critically evaluates this shift in the U.S. cybersecurity discourse by analyzing a collection of significant policy documents and public statements from policymakers, military leaders, and cybersecurity experts.

The next section of this chapter explains the sources that were examined for this study, as well as the theories and methods used to analyze those sources. The bulk of the chapter addresses the past and present status of critical infrastructure as an object of concern in the ongoing U.S. public policy debate about cybersecurity. In particular, it demonstrates that, since 2009, significant policy documents, as well as statements from military leaders, policymakers, and cybersecurity experts in the United States, most often identify private intellectual property, government secrets, and the economy as the primary objects of cyber threats. It also examines the status of critical infrastructure as an object of cyber threats in these same documents and statements. The final section of this chapter identifies potentially negative impacts of this shift in U.S. cybersecurity discourse and provides suggestions for how these can be overcome.

BACKGROUND

This chapter is informed by the results of an ongoing research project that is monitoring, documenting, and analyzing the evolving public policy discourse about cybersecurity in the United States. Previous studies of U.S. cybersecurity discourse (discussed in more detail below) have noted that perceptions of cyber threats have changed over time. With renewed interest in cybersecurity coinciding with several well-publicized cyber attacks and the election of a new president in the United States, this project has worked to determine the degree to which dominant perceptions of cyber threats may have changed across a number key categories. This chapter focuses on the relationship of critical infrastructure to two of those categories: the object and impact of cyber threats.

This chapter is based on an analysis of what have been called "discourse events." Discourse events are documents or statements that are reflective of or have the power to shape the overall public policy debate about cybersecurity in the United States. While there are thousands of news stories, blog posts, discussion forum posts, and more each week about cybersecurity, these are not necessarily representative of dominant perceptions of cyber threats, and very few have the power to shape the overall discussion of the issue. They do not count as discourse events. Discourse events are produced by high-ranking policymakers, military leaders, Internet security companies, security experts, or veteran journalists and include accounts from influential media sources, government policy documents, industry and think-tank reports, military strategy and doctrine publications, and speeches, op-eds, or Congressional testimony by civilian policymakers, military leaders, or experts. This chapter is informed by the collection and analysis of over one hundred such documents since 2009.

The analysis of these documents has been shaped by the critical constructivist tradition of scholarship in security studies (Peoples and Vaughan-Williams, 2010), and in particular the body of scholarship that has examined the role of language, discourse, and perception in identifications of and responses to cyber threats (Bendrath, 2001, 2003; Dunn Cavelty, 2008; Eriksson, 2002; Hansen & Nissenbaum, 2009). Drawing heavily from "securitization theory," this work begins with the observation that it is not predetermined which security threats will make it onto the political agenda. Identifying, understanding, and responding to security threats is the result of political discourse—i.e. security threats are "constructed." Securitization theory describes the process of constructing security threats as involving a "securitizing actor" (usually a political leader or decision maker) identifying "threat subjects" (the source of the threat), "referent objects" (that which is threatened), and the prospective impacts of a threat. Securitization of an issue often results in taking "extraordinary measures" outside the normal political process in response to a newly identified threat (Buzan et. al., 1998). In short, securitization involves diagnosing a threat, offering responses, and motivating action, what Myriam Dunn Cavelty has called diagnostic, prognostic, and motivational framing (Dunn Cavelty, 2007, 2008).

This chapter builds on this theoretical foundation by adding insights from the field of argumentation theory. Scholars of public policy debate note that diagnosis of a problem usually involves providing both a quantitative and qualitative assessment of the problem. This involves assessing a problem's significance—how pervasive or widespread it is—but also its harmfulness—the severity of its impacts. It is possible for a problem to be significant but not necessarily harmful or harmful but not necessarily significant. Ideally, we expect public resources to be expended on problems that are both significant and harmful (Inch et. al., 2006, pgs. 252-253). This chapter examines the interplay between diagnosing and motivating a response to cyber threats by looking

at the role of critical infrastructure as an object of cyber threats and the potential impacts ascribed to cyber attacks on critical infrastructure. What it will demonstrate is that there is a divergence in the current diagnosis of the cyber threat between the way that significance and harmfulness are assessed, between the identification of the primary object of the cyber threat and the prospective impacts of that threat. It will demonstrate that while the currently dominant framing of cyber threats diagnoses private intellectual property and government secrets as the most significant or pervasive object under threat, fear of the potentially more dangerous but perhaps less likely impacts of cyber attacks upon critical infrastructure is leveraged as a means of motivating a response.

The following section will provide historical background on the linking of concerns about cyber threats with concerns about critical infrastructure protection. It offers empirical examples from significant discourse events that will demonstrate the divergence in assessing significance and harmfulness when diagnosing and motivating a response to cyber threats. The chapter will end with a discussion of the potentially negative impacts of this divergence and how it might be corrected.

CRITICAL INFRASTRUCTURE AS AN OBJECT OF CYBER THREATS, PAST AND PRESENT

Cyber Threats and CIP Converge

Concern with cybersecurity has grown over the last three decades as modern societies have become increasingly dependent upon networked information and communication systems. During that time, however, cybersecurity proponents have found it difficult to identify and then communicate clearly and precisely what it is that is threatened, by whom, and with what potential impacts, in and through cyberspace. Dominant perceptions of cyber threats have shifted over time and, as they have, so have claims about the primary subjects (e.g. foreign spies, criminals, terrorists, insiders), objects (e.g. business data, state secrets, critical infrastructure), and impacts (e.g. monetary loss, diminished competitiveness, catastrophe) of those threats.

While it is now common to link cyber threats and critical infrastructure protection, concern with cybersecurity actually predates this linkage. In the United States, cybersecurity concerns date to the 1980s and were focused on what Dunn Cavelty (2008) has called "the hostile intelligence threat" (p. 41)—i.e. the potential for foreign espionage conducted via exploitation of networked information and communication systems. It was not until the mid 1990s that cyber threats and critical infrastructure were linked as a national security concern. In the United States, this was primarily a result of the 1995 Oklahoma City bombing (Dunn Cavelty, 2008, p. 91). One response to the attack was the formation of the President's Commission on Critical Infrastructure Protection (PCCIP). The 1997 report of a PCCIP study that assessed the vulnerabilities in and threats to U.S. critical infrastructures clearly linked cyber threats and critical infrastructure protection (CIP) and has remained one of the "most influential of all studies" on the subject (Dunn Cavelty, 2008, p.117). Thus, in the late 1990s, the dominant U.S. perception of cyber threats underwent a transformation. As prospective cyber threats to critical infrastructure became predominant, "the focus on the foreign intelligence threat further decreased" (Dunn Cavelty, 2008, p. 115). As the object of the perceived threat shifted from state secrets to civilian critical infrastructure, so did the supposed subject of the threat. Where the "hostile intelligence threat" had perceived foreign intelligence agencies as the primary threat subjects, from the mid 1990s through the presidency of

George W. Bush, terrorist groups were identified as most likely to engage in cyber attacks against critical infrastructure (Dunn Cavelty, 2008, p. 103; Conway, 2008).

But it was not just the subjects and objects of the cyber threat that underwent a transformation in the mid 1990s. Fear about the potential impacts of cyberattacks increased exponentially as critical infrastructure emerged as the primary object of such attacks. The linking of cyber threats and critical infrastructure meant that "the magnitude of the threat was expanded considerably" as it was "linked to the possible destruction of the whole of society. As a consequence, cyber-threats are treated as being equally dangerous as nuclear weapons" (Dunn Cavelty, 2008, p. 98). This greatly heightened fear of cyber threats resulted in the proliferation of what some have called "shut-down-the-power-grid scenarios" (Conway, 2008, p. 113) and others "cyber-doom scenarios" (Dunn Cavelty, 2008, p. 2; Lawson, 2011), which typically involve "a cyberattack disrupting or destroying critical infrastructure" (Lawson, 2011, p. 5). Conway (2008) has noted that such scenarios played a prominent role in U.S. public discourse about CIP in the late 1990s and early 2000s. Two scenarios in particular were popular and cited widely, including John Arquilla's essay hypothesizing what "The Great Cyberwar of 2002" would look like, as well as a *FOX News* documentary that warned of the "Dangers of the Internet Highway: Cyberterror." Both scenarios featured cyber attacks against power, communications, and transportation systems leading to traffic accidents, plane crashes, colliding trains, nuclear meltdowns, and disruption of military command and control (Conway, 2008, p. 113-114). These concerns were echoed in the 1997 PCCIP report, which warned that cyber attacks could be "devastating" and could "paralyze or panic large segments of society, damage our capability to respond to incidents (by disabling the 911 system or emergency communications, for example), hamper our ability to deploy conventional military forces, and otherwise limit the freedom of action of our national leadership" (Marsh, 1997, pgs. 17-18).

Though there were a number of shifts in assessments of the primary subject of the cyber threat during the administration of President George W. Bush, critical infrastructure retained its place as the primary object of concern. In the opening months of the Bush administration, attention shifted briefly from non-state to state-level cyber threats, back to non-state actors in the wake of the terrorist attacks of September 11, 2001, and then to states once again in the run-up to war with Iraq in 2003 (Weimann, 2005, p. 133–134; Bendrath, 2001; Bendrath, 2003; Dunn Cavelty, 2008). While the wars in Afghanistan and Iraq led to a brief decline in U.S. public policy discussion of cyber threats, a number of high-profile cyber attacks since 2007 have led to renewed interest. These have included two large-scale cyber attacks, one against the country of Estonia in 2007 (Blank, 2008; Evron, 2008) and the other against the country of Georgia in 2008, both of which are widely believed to have been the work of state-sanctioned Russian hackers (Bumgarner & Borg, 2009; Korns & Kastenberg, 2008; Nichol, 2008). In January 2010, Google's claims to have been the target of a Chinese cyber attack received a great deal of press attention and were featured prominently in Secretary of State Hillary Clinton's speech on "Internet Freedom" (Clinton, 2010). Finally, speculation continues to swirl around the Stuxnet computer worm that many believe was used to deliberately sabotage the Iranian nuclear program (Mills, 2010).

From Infrastructural to Informational Cyber Threats

Though there were shifts in perceived cyber threat subjects during the period between 1997 and 2008, the prevailing cyber threat perception was consistent in its focus on critical infrastructure

as the object of prospective cyber attacks (Dunn Cavelty, 2008, p. 90). But with the election of President Barack Obama in November 2008, the cyber threat perception began to shift once again. As a result, critical infrastructure has slipped from its position as the primary object of cyber threats. The first indication of this shift appeared in December 2008 when the Center for Strategic and International Studies (CSIS) released a report titled, *Securing Cyberspace for the 44th Presidency* (Langevin, et. al., 2008). The report was the result of a year-long effort by the CSIS Commission on Cybersecurity for the 44th Presidency, which was co-chaired by two Congressional representatives, James Langevin (D-RI) and Michael McCaul (R-TX), the Corporate Vice President for Trustworthy Computing at Microsoft, Scott Charney, and a retired United States Air Force officer, Lt. General Harry Raduege. The project was directed by James Lewis, the head of the CSIS Technology and Policy Policy Program and a respected expert on cybersecurity policy. After "examin[ing] existing plans and strategies" for cybersecurity, the Commission "assess[ed] what a new administration should continue, what it should change" (Langevin, et. al., 2008, Preface). The report clearly identified a need for change in perceptions of the primary object of cyber threats:

In 1998 [sic], a presidential commission [PCCIP] reported that protecting cyberspace would become crucial for national security. In effect, this advice was not so much ignored as misinterpreted—we expected damage from cyber attacks to be physical (opened floodgates, crashing airplanes) when it was actually informational. (Langevin, et. al., 2008, p. 12)

But what is "informational" damage? The report focused primarily on theft of intellectual property and government secrets. It argued that "the immediate risk lies with the economy" and that the U.S. had already suffered from the theft of billions of dollars worth of intellectual property and government secrets, including crucial data related to military technologies. Ultimately, the report warned that "America's power, status, and security in the world depend in good measure upon its economic strength; our lack of cybersecurity is steadily eroding this advantage" (Langevin, et. al., 2008, p. 13). Although the report acknowledged that "exploiting vulnerabilities in cyber infrastructure will be part of any future conflict," it was quick to provide the caveat that "depriving Americans of electricity, communications, and financial services may not be enough to provide the margin of victory in a conflict, but it could damage our ability to respond and our will to resist" (Langevin, et. al., 2008, p. 13). Informational threats were presented as having already been realized and as having had identifiable impacts. Infrastructural threats, while not discounted as a possibility, were framed as existing only in the future and exhibiting uncertain potential impacts.

Two years later, after being confirmed as the first commander of the newly-formed U.S. Cyber Command, Gen. Keith Alexander acknowledged that the CSIS report "served as a key thread of continuity across two administrations and really set the foundation for crafting this administration's strategy for cyber and security" (Alexander, 2010). While Gen. Alexander is correct that the CSIS report was an important influence on the new administration's vision of cybersecurity, it did not represent a "thread of continuity," but rather, the beginning of an important shift in what had otherwise been a stable perception of the primary object of cyber threats. Official Obama administration statements of cybersecurity policy and strategy, both civilian and military, have echoed the CSIS framing of the primary objects and impacts of cyber threats and have, therefore, focused primarily on the negative economic impacts of stolen intellectual property and government secrets.

The impact of the CSIS report was seen only five months after its publication, in May 2009, when the Obama administration released its *Cy-*

berspace Policy Review. While the overall goal of the review was to set the stage for formulating and implementing policies and strategies for *"assuring a trusted and resilient information and communications infrastructure,"* much of the document's "case for action" focused on the threat to intellectual property and economic competitiveness. The CSIS report was referenced directly on the first page of the White House document, which was prefaced by a statement that framed the cybersecurity threat in exactly those terms outlined by the CSIS report:

Our digital infrastructure has already suffered intrusions that have allowed criminals to steal hundreds of millions of dollars and nation-states and other entities to steal intellectual property and sensitive military information. Other intrusions threaten to damage portions of our critical infrastructure. These and other risks have the potential to undermine the Nation's confidence in the information systems that underlie our economic and national security interests. (The White House, 2009, p. i)

As in the CSIS report, threats to intellectual property and military secrets leading to monetary loss were identified as having already occurred, while threats to critical infrastructure had yet to be realized but were still of concern. Variations of the phase "economic and national security," which can be read as either putting economy first and security second or as conflating the two, were used consistently throughout the *Cyberspace Policy Review.* As evidence to support its "case for action," the document cited two economic-related threats—"exploiting global financial services" and "systemic loss of U.S. economic value"—in addition to "failure of critical infrastructures" (The White House, 2009, p. 2). President Obama's speech introducing the *Cyberspace Policy Review* reiterated this framing. He led the speech by highlighting the costs of stolen credit card information, stolen intellectual property, and manipulations of the financial system emanating from cyberspace to emphasize that "America's economic prosperity in the 21st century will depend on cybersecurity." Only then did he turn to the potential for cyber threats to civilian critical infrastructures and military information and communication networks (White House Press Office, 2009).

This framing has served as the foundation of the United States' vision for global "Internet freedom" and norms of international behavior in cyberspace. In her January 2010 speech on "Internet freedom," Secretary of State Hillary Clinton made special note of Google's accusations that it had been the victim of a Chinese government cyber attack. While she noted the increasing use of Internet filtering and censorship worldwide as a means of repressing political dissent and violating religious freedoms, she used the Google case to warn that "Our ability to bank online, use electronic commerce, and safeguard billions of dollars in intellectual property are all at stake if we cannot rely on the security of our information networks." Addressing these threats, she said, "demand[s] a coordinated response by all governments, the private sector, and the international community" (Clinton, 2010). Critical infrastructure went unmentioned in her speech.

It is not surprising, therefore, that "respect for property," including "respect for intellectual property rights, including patents, trade secrets, trademarks, and copyrights," was listed as a key principle upon which to build international norms of cyberspace behavior in the Obama administration's May 2011 *International Strategy for Cyberspace* (The White House, 2011, p. 10). While protecting critical infrastructure by "reduc[ing] intrusions into and disruptions of U.S. networks" was identified as a policy priority (The White House, 2011, p. 17), economic priorities, including "protect[ing] intellectual property, including commercial trade secrets, from theft" were identified first and foremost. This prioritization of economy and property is rooted in the belief that

Cyberspace can be used to steal an unprecedented volume of information from businesses, universities, and government agencies; such stolen information and technology can equal billions of dollars of lost value. [...] Results can range from unfair competition to the bankrupting of entire firms, and the national impact may be orders of magnitude larger. The persistent theft of intellectual property, whether by criminals, foreign firms, or state actors working on their behalf, can erode competitiveness in the global economy, and businesses' opportunities to innovate. (The White House, 2011, pgs. 17-18)

Finally, the economic framing of the objects and impacts of cyber threats has been at the heart of a number of recent pieces of cybersecurity legislation proposed in the U.S. Congress. Senators Sheldon Whitehouse (D-RI) and Jon Kyl (R-AZ) explained the need for their proposed Cyber Security Public Awareness Act of 2011 by claiming that cyber attacks have not only resulted in stolen intellectual property and government secrets, but also the "loss of countless American jobs" (Committee on Homeland Security and Governmental Affairs, 2011b). In an accompanying op-ed piece, Senator Whitehouse argued that while cyberattacks have the "potential" to "sabotage our critical infrastructure," cyberattacks have already put the United States "on the losing end of what could be the largest illicit transfer of wealth in world history" (Whitehouse, 2011). Similarly, the Cyber Security and American Cyber Competitiveness Act of 2011, which was introduced by Senate Majority Leader Harry Reid (D-NV), echoes Senators Whitehouse and Kyl's concern that "Businesses in the United States are bearing enormous losses as a result of criminal cyber attacks, depriving businesses of hard-earned profits that could be reinvested in further job-producing innovation" (Committee on Homeland Security and Governmental Affairs, 2011a).

Perhaps most surprising is that this focus on short-term monetary and long-term economic impacts of stolen intellectual property and government data has been just as pronounced in statements by U.S. military leaders, both civilian and uniformed, as well as in official Department of Defense cybersecurity policy documents. In fact, in many cases they have been even more explicit than civilian policymakers in stating that cyber threats to private intellectual property and sensitive government data have taken precedence over cyber threats to critical infrastructure. This view has been expressed most clearly by William Lynn III, who served as Deputy Secretary of Defense from February 2009 to October 2011 and who led efforts to create the U.S. Cyber Command and to develop the first *Department of Defense Strategy for Operating in Cyberspace*. In a 2010 article for *Foreign Affairs*, Lynn explained that

Although the threat to intellectual property is less dramatic than the threat to critical national infrastructure, it may be the most significant cyberthreat that the United States will face over the long term. Every year, an amount of intellectual property many times larger than all the intellectual property contained in the Library of Congress is stolen from networks maintained by U.S. businesses, universities, and government agencies. As military strength ultimately depends on economic vitality, sustained intellectual property losses could erode both the United States' military effectiveness and its competitiveness in the global economy. (Lynn, 2010)

Like the CSIS report and subsequent reports and statements from the Obama administration, Lynn framed threats to critical infrastructure as still in the future and of uncertain potential impacts. Although such threats were still cause for concern because they "could have an impact analogous to physical hostilities," he noted repeatedly that "the vast majority of malicious cyber activity today does not cross this threshold" and that, therefore, current attention should focus first and foremost on informational threats (Lynn, 2011).

The commander of U.S. Cyber Command, Gen. Keith Alexander, has echoed this framing

in explaining the *raison d'etre* and mission of his command. He explained that there is enough evidence "to be concerned about the potential effects of an actual attack" on critical infrastructure, but admited that "no one has seriously attacked these yet" (House Committee on Armed Services, 2010, pgs. 7-8). Thus, while serious threats to critical infrastructure have yet to be realized, "economic espionage for commercial and technological advantage is an everyday event" with impacts that "can take on hitherto unimaginable scale; a conqueror once had to capture a city before his army could loot it" (House Committee on Armed Services, 2010, p. 4).

With the dominant perceptions of the primary objects and impacts of cyber threats shifting from critical infrastructure and physical impacts to intellectual property, government data, monetary loss, and economic competitiveness, it might seem odd that the primary response measure taken by the United States thus far has been the formation of a military command. But by thoroughly linking economic competitiveness with military effectiveness and national security, Lynn and Alexander have been able to turn informational objects and impacts, often in the private sector, into matters of military concern. Because private defense contractors have been among those companies that have suffered cyberattacks leading to losses of intellectual property and sensitive weapons-related information, Lynn has proposed that "policymakers need to consider…applying the National Security Agency's defense capabilities beyond the '.gov' domain" and "look for innovative ways to use the military's cyberdefense capabilities to protect the defense industry" (Lynn, 2010). Gen. Alexander agreed. Though he admitted that theft of intellectual property is crime, not war, and therefore "belongs more properly in law enforcement than military channels," he justified military involvement nonetheless by arguing that "when a prime target of such crime is our defense industrial base, we in the Department of Defense have a role to play in the response" (Alexander, 2011, p. 6).

This focus on private intellectual property, government data, and economic competitiveness has been a direct driver of the United States' policy response during the Obama administration. For example, Gen. Alexander has explained that it was not a major cyber incident involving critical infrastructure that led to the creation of U.S. Cyber Command, but rather, a 2008 breach of military computer networks that involved infected thumb drives (Alexander, 2010). Finally, and most importantly, Lynn's identification of intellectual property theft as "less dramatic" but "the most significant cyber threat" in his 2010 *Foreign Affairs* article is repeated almost verbatim in the July 2011 *Department of Defense Strategy for Operating in Cyberspace* in the section of the strategy that describes current threats and the need for action by DoD (Department of Defense, 2011, p. 4).

Motivating Cybersecurity with Cyber-Doom Scenarios

To be sure, though informational objects and impacts have emerged as the primary objects and impacts of cyber threat perceptions over the last three years, concerns over prospective cyber threats to critical infrastructure have not disappeared from public policy discourse. As mentioned above, "shut-down-the-power-grid" or "cyber-doom" scenarios are not new and are exemplary of the deep concerns that modern societies have over their increasing dependence upon complex, interlinked, and interdependent socio-technical systems of all kinds (Lawson, 2011). As early as 1994, futurist and best-selling author Alvin Toffler claimed that cyberattacks on the World Trade Center could be used to collapse the entire U.S. economy and even to "'shut down America… [by] clos[ing] down all the automated teller machines, the Federal Reserve, Wall Street, and most hospital and business computer systems'" (Elias, 1994). The 1997 PCCIP report reflected these fears when it warned that "the impact of an Internet attack could be devastating" and could "paralyze or panic large segments of society" (Marsh, 2997, pgs. 17-18).

Pundits and policymakers alike continue to indulge such scenarios. In a 2010 book co-authored with Robert Knake, Richard Clarke presented a scenario in which a cyberattack destroys or seriously disrupts all U.S. infrastructure in only fifteen minutes, killing thousands and wreaking unprecedented destruction on U.S. cities (Clarke & Knake, 2010, pgs. 64-68). A year later, he called Chinese intrusions into critical infrastructure systems an "act of war" and likened them to "digital bombs" that are equivalent to having planted "explosives… throughout our national electrical system" (Clarke, 2011). Others have gone so far as to compare the hypothetical impacts of cyberattacks to the terrorist attacks of September 11, 2001, the use of nuclear weapons, the 2004 Indian Ocean tsunami, and have even warned that cyberattacks could pose an existential threat not only to the United States but to all of global civilization (Lawson, 2011, pgs. 6-7). In 1999, *Fox News* warned of "Danger on the Internet Highway: Cyberterrorism" (Conway, 2008); in February 2010, *CNN* televised the "Cyber Shockwave" war game in which malware spreading among cell phones resulted in serious disruptions of critical infrastructure across the United States (Gaylord, 2010).

While policymakers like William Lynn III readily admit that informational threats have become more "prevalent" and "significant" than infrastructure threats, they continue to maintain that potential cyberattacks on critical infrastructure are "the most dangerous threat" (Whitehouse, 2011). In his 2008 essay for *Foreign Affairs*, Lynn warned that "Such attacks may not cause the mass casualties of a nuclear strike, but they could paralyze U.S. society all the same" (Lynn, 2008). The *Department of Defense Strategy for Operating in Cyberspace* echoed this view, claiming that "computer-induced failures of power grids, transportation networks, or financial systems could cause massive physical damage and economic disruption" (Department of Defense, 2011, p. 4). Even President Obama has warned that cyberattacks could be used as a "weapon of mass disruption" that could "cripple society" (White House Press Office, 2009).

DISCUSSION AND FUTURE RESEARCH

As we saw in the previous section, leading policymakers in the United States have readily admitted that we have yet to experience serious cyberattacks against critical infrastructures; we have not come anywhere close to cyber-doom. What's more, others have made strong arguments that such scenarios are highly unlikely if not impossible (Stohl, 2007; Sommer, 2011; Lawson, 2011; Rid, 2011). After all, terrorists did not attack the World Trade Center and the U.S. economy with a cyberattack as Alvin Toffler predicted. Instead, they used "kinetic" means of attack. Even then, the closure of the New York Stock Exchange and halting of air travel for an entire week, as well as all of the other associated disruptions, did not "shut down America." Western societies have experienced failures of critical infrastructure in the past, such as the 2003 blackout that affected the entire northeastern part of the United States. Modern cities have come under attack from the air during wartime, and from hurricanes and other forces of nature during peacetime. Even these events have not historically resulted in the kind of panic, paralysis, and collapse that often feature prominently in hypothetical, cyber-doom scenarios involving cyberattacks against critical infrastructure (Lawson, 2011). As such, a recent report from the Organization for Economic Cooperation and Development (OECD) was skeptical of the ability of cyberattacks by themselves to cause systemic global shocks on par with the 2004 Indian Ocean tsunami, the ongoing financial crisis, or other such events (Sommer, 2011).

So why do such scenarios persist in public policy discourse? James Lewis has been critical of those who rely on such scenarios. Though he is sympathetic to the frustrations of those who perceive a lack of attention to cybersecurity threats on the part of the public and policymakers, he nonetheless worries that this frustration results in a belief that "exaggeration" and "appeals to emotions like fear can be more compelling than a rational discussion of strategy" (Lewis, 2010, p. 4). In short, in the use of cyber-doom scenarios, not only does motivational framing end up trumping diagnostic framing, but the claims used to motivate a policy response are out of sync with the diagnosis of the actual problem to be addressed.

There are a number of potentially negative implications to this situation. First is that this blurring of diagnostic and motivational framing, significance and harmfulness, is yet one more problem with a public policy discourse about cybersecurity that has suffered from a number of similar deficiencies. Several observers have noted that not only has the story about who threatens what, how, and with what potential impact shifted on a number of occasions over the last three decades, but that it has done so with very little evidence provided to support the claims being made (Bendrath, 2001, 2003; Walt, 2010; Brito and Watkins, 2011). Others have noted that many of those who are most outspoken in warning of the threat of "cyberwar" are reluctant to even define what the term means, what counts as war in/through cyberspace (Lawson, 2010). One result of this tendency towards equivocation has been a tendency also to conflate many different types of problems—e.g. espionage, crime, critical infrastructure protection, etc.—under the moniker of "war" (Lewis, 2010). Additionally, cybersecurity discourse often suffers from conflation of vulnerabilities and threats. That is, many assessments jump from the existence of vulnerabilities to the inevitability of attack, merely assuming the existence of actors possessing both the means and motivation to carry out such attacks (Dunn Cavelty, 2008, p. 103).

In the case examined here, we see a confusion between diagnostic and motivational framing, between assessing the significance and harmfulness of a threat. This additional confusion is, in fact, made possible by the others. The currently dominant threat perception combines the significance and prevalence of the admittedly less harmful problem of economic espionage with the potentially more harmful but less prevalent problem of cyberattacks against critical infrastructures to call for action against a generic cyber threat. The conflation of economic espionage and critical infrastructure protection is what allows for this confusion between significance and harmfulness. As James Lewis (2010) points out, we face a number of different problems in/through cyberspace. Economic espionage is one; potential cyberattacks on critical infrastructure is another. Only by conflating them into one problem do cybersecurity proponents make the strongest possible case for action; only together do they seemingly meet the test of both significance and harmfulness.

Second, there are a number of potentially negative policy implications to continued reliance upon cyber-doom scenarios as a rhetorical tactic to motivate a policy response. The most obvious negative impact is the potential for policy responses to be driven by the motivational frame as opposed to the diagnostic frame, that is, to be geared towards preventing the more frightening but less likely threat as opposed to adopting measures that are most appropriate for addressing more likely dangers. With public policy discourse about cybersecurity in the United States increasingly dominated by talk of "cyberwar," combined with cyber-doom scenarios that mirror the effects of strategic attack or large-scale natural disaster, it seems little wonder that the most significant policy response to date has been the creation of a military Cyber Command.

But even those policymakers most closely associated with the creation of this command readily admit that the most significant cyber threat is related to private intellectual property and government data, not the kinds of threats for which one would normally create a military command.

This development should at least encourage further investigation into whether policies are being driven more by the dominant diagnosis of the problem or by the rhetorical tactics being used as a call to action. Because the two refer to quite different problems in this case, a policy response to one is not necessarily appropriate for the other—i.e. policies appropriate for responding to cyber-doom scenarios are likely not appropriate for responding to crime and espionage, and vice versa.

Indeed, there is strong evidence to suggest that cyber-doom scenarios have already had the effect of distorting policymaker views of the threats actually facing the United States. For example, when reflecting upon the terrorist attacks of September 11, 2001, a member of the President's Critical Infrastructure Protection Board during the George W. Bush administration said that

We were very shocked in the federal government that the attack didn't come from cyberspace... Based on what we knew at the time, the most likely scenario was an attack from cyberspace, not airliners slamming into buildings... We had spent a lot of time preparing for a cyber attack, not a physical attack. (Quoted in Conway, 2008, p. 124)

While U.S. policymakers were awaiting the fulfillment of Alvin Toffler's hypothetical cyberattack on the World Trade Center, we know from the report of the 9/11 Commission, as well as other work done since that time, that there were a number of indicators pointing to what al-Qa'ida was actually planning.

What's more, reliance upon cyber-doom scenarios for motivational purposes is also potentially counterproductive for responding to those critical infrastructure-related cybersecurity threats that do exist. Certainly there are very real cybersecurity challenges, some of which really do affect critical infrastructures. One need only look to the Stuxnet worm to know that this is the case. Nevertheless, James Lewis has warned that "either overreaction or miscalculation, or a blasé dismissal of risk after hearing 'wolf' cried too many times" are "the most likely outcomes" of relying upon cyber-doom scenarios (Lewis, 2010, p. 4). Overreaction in this case could involve over-regulation of private critical infrastructure owners and operators or highly centralized, military-led responses in the event of cyberattacks against critical infrastructure. There are already provisions for Cyber Command to assist the Department of Homeland Security in the event of a major domestic cyberattack (Ackerman, 2010), and some have even explored legal options for the U.S. Government to "conscript companies" as a means of "compelling civilian cooperation in cyberwarfare" (Brenner and Clarke, 2010, p. 1011).

At the other end of the spectrum is the possibility for a blasé under-reaction. Based on his analysis of media portrayals of cyber threats, Francois Debrix argued that "Being conditioned to such a degree of generalized panic, any real cyberterrorist attack that does not follow the simulated scenario and produce the anticipated amount of casualties will fall short of being worthy of people's attention and worry" (Debrix, 2001, p. 156). Continued traffic in cyber-doom scenarios for motivational purposes could ultimately have exactly the opposite of their intended effect, one in which we do not take real threats seriously because they fail to live up to imagined threats. For example, some have worried that cyber-doom scenarios encourage a fortress mentality and the misallocation of resources away from the repair, maintenance, and modernization of critical infrastructure that is essential for creating the resilience needed "to mitigate the effects of a cyberattack should it occur, and…to deter cyberattacks by providing a would-be attacker with fewer valuable and vulnerable targets" (Lawson, 2011, p. 27). A spate of recent infrastructure failures in the United States, including the 2003 northeast blackout and the 2007 I-35 bridge collapse in Minnesota, indicate that U.S. infrastructure systems are aging and are becoming more prone to failures of various kinds. These and other incidents

that are occurring with alarming regularity were the result of a lack of repair, maintenance, and modernization, not intentional attack (Nye, 2010, p. 180; Patterson, 2010). Just as investments in the public health system are beneficial regardless of whether a disease outbreak is natural or the result of malicious activity, repair, maintenance, and modernization is the key to resilient systems. Such activities help to prevent failures in the first place, but also increase the ability of systems to recover from failures when they do occur, whether accidental or the result of attack, by promoting learning and adaptation among operators who are the first responders when failures occur (Graham & Thrift, 2007, p. 5, 14; Nye, 2010, p. 189). David Nye, who has written about the history of blackouts, has argued that instead of "think[ing] of the grid as a fortress to be protected at every point" (Nye, 2010, p. 197), we should invest in the more mundane, ongoing, and decentralized work of repair, maintenance, and modernization. Currently, the United States risks under-reacting to the threats and vulnerabilities that do exist if it chooses to focus instead on preparing for hypothetical, cyber-doom scenarios. In short, it is currently in danger of simultaneously over- and under-reacting to prospective cyber threats against critical infrastructure.

Concerns about the possibility for over- and/ or under-reaction are not unfounded. There have been a number of recent incidents that demonstrate the way that expectations of CI-related cyber-doom can distort our understanding of real incidents when they do occur. First among those, of course, is Stuxnet. It is one of the most destructive industrial control system (ICS)/critical infrastructure cyber attacks that we have seen to date. It has rightly caught the attention of media, policymakers, and citizens around the world and helped to raise legitimate concerns about CI cybersecurity. Nonetheless, it is important to point out that for as effective as it was, it has not ended concern over the possibility of an Iranian nuclear weapons program. What's more, the current consensus is that Stuxnet required a significant amount of money, time, and effort to create and was, therefore, most likely created by an advanced nation like the United States or Israel. As such, Stuxnet is a classic example of a CI-related cyber threat that is harmful but not pervasive—i.e. it is dramatic in its effects, but it is not representative of the most pervasive cyber threats. Thus, looking to Stuxnet as a model of cyber threats to CI systems is potentially misleading.

We have already seen an example of how the expectations and fears raised by Stuxnet can cloud perceptions of other incidents. In mid October 2011, the Laboratory of Cryptography and System Security (CrySyS) of the Budapest University of Technology and Economics and the computer security firm Symantec broke the news of a what they called a "Stuxnet-like malware" (Benscath et. al., 2011) that they believed to be "the precursor to a future Stuxnet-like attack" (Symantec, 2011). In response, the United States' ICS-CERT issued an alert that repeated Symantec's claims that what was being called the Duqu worm was "an information-gathering threat targeting specific organizations, including ICSs manufacturers" (ICS-CERT, 2011a, p. 2).

But within a week of this alert, a number of other analyses began to cast doubt on the initial characterization of Duqu, including its purpose and relationship to Stuxnet. Dale Peterson of Digital Bond, a control system security firm, noted the contradiction in Symantec's claim that Duqu was "'nearly identical to Stuxnet, but with a completely different purpose'" and countered that "to most in the ICS community it appears nothing like Stuxnet" (Peterson, 2011). Similarly, Dennis Fisher of Kaspersky Labs argued that the code-level similarities between Stuxnet and Duqu did not prove that the latter was the "spawn" of the former and noted, like Peterson, that the two had very different end goals. Likewise, on October 26, Dell SecureWorks released its own analysis that contradicted several key claims made by CrySyS and Symantec and reported by ICS-CERT.

First, they questioned the link between Stuxnet and Duqu, arguing that "supporting evidence is circumstantial at best and insufficient to confirm a direct relationship." Second, not only did they claim that "Unlike Stuxnet, Duqu does not contain specific code" targeting ICS, they also called into question whether Duqu, as an information-stealing trojan, was targeted at ICS-related organizations at all (SecureWorks, 2011).

Thus, within two weeks of initial reports about Duqu, ICS-CERT reported "after additional analysis that neither industrial control systems (ICSs) nor vendors/manufacturers were targeted by Duqu" (ICS-CERT, 2011a, p. 1). They reiterated that assessment a week later, saying that it had "found no evidence that Duqu targeted owners and operators, vendors, or manufacturers of industrial control systems (ICSs)" ICS-CERT, 2011b, p. 1).

Nonetheless, as of November 23, Symantec was still claiming that "Duqu's purpose is to gather intelligence data and assets from entities such as industrial infrastructure and system manufacturers…including industrial control system facilities" (Symantec, 2011, p. 1). The last word from Symantec about Duqu came in a December 12, 2011 blog post, which repeated the claim that Duqu was "the son of Stuxnet" and that it was targeted against "suppliers to industrial facilities" (Parker, 2011).

At minimum, the initial (and continued) framing of Duqu in terms of Stuxnet has resulted in unresolved confusion about the origins and nature of Duqu. That initial framing obviously raised a lot of legitimate concerns. But since those initial fears were laid to rest, we have not seen efforts by the initial parties to the controversy—Symantec and ICS-CERT in particular—to resolve the remaining confusion over Duqu's relationship to Stuxnet and whether or to what degree it does or does not target ICS-related organizations. Dennis Fisher of Kaspersky Labs correctly called Duqu and Stuxnet together "words of mass disruption" and warned that "in the current climate, simply invoking the name of Stuxnet immediately triggers a set of assumptions and conclusions about the nature of the threat. Saying that Duqu or any other piece of malware is the 'son of Stuxnet'... has overtones of the often hysterical discussions about cyberwar." He urged his fellow security experts "to be careful about using Stuxnet as the basis for comparison. It clouds the issue and drowns out any substantive discussions that might take place" (Fisher, 2011).

But the inaccurate and possibly distracting use of Stuxnet to frame Duqu is an indicator of a larger phenomenon, which is the tendency to see any CI-related cybersecurity incident through the lens of long-anticipated and feared cyber-doom scenarios. Only days after ICS-CERT's final update on the Duqu incident, Joe Weiss of Applied Control Solutions caused a national stir when he leaked details of an Illinois Statewide Terrorism & Intelligence Center (STIC) report that claimed that a cyberattack originating in Russia had destroyed a pump at the Curran-Gardner Public Water District just outside of Springfield. Less than twenty-four hours after Weiss' initial blog post about the supposed cyber-attack (Weiss, 2011), national newspapers like *The Washington Post* ran headlines proclaiming that "Foreign hackers targeted U.S. water plant in apparent malicious cyber attack" (Nakashima, 2011a), and the incident was covered in dramatic fashion on CNN's *The Situation Room* with Wolf Blitzer (Todd, 2011). Steven Bellovin, a computer science professor at Columbia University, proclaimed that the debate over the possibility of cyber-attacks leading to physical damage of CI "is now over." He saw in the supposed Illinois water hack "an existence proof. All future debate has to start from this fact: the threat is real. We can argue over magnitude, but not over the possibility" (Bellovin, 2011).

But less than a week after Weiss leaked the information from the STIC report, ICS-CERT issued a response that unequivocally stated that a joint ICS-CERT/FBI investigation "found no evidence of a cyber intrusion," "no evidence to support claims made in the initial Illinois STIC report," and "no malicious or unauthorized traffic from Russia or any foreign entities" (ICS-CERT, 2011c, p. 1). In a correction to its earlier story, *The Washington Post* reported that the incident was mistaken for a cyber-attack "because a plant contractor traveling in Russia remotely logged in to the plant's computer system" (Nakashima, 2011b).

Joe Weiss' response to the ICS-CERT/FBI conclusions provides a glimpse of the powerful hold that cyber-doom scenarios can have upon the thinking of even well-informed and well-meaning experts. He told reporter Brian Krebs, "something doesn't smell right" and suggested that "DHS is covering something up" (Krebs, 2011). More recently, he pointed to the 2003 blackout in the American northeast, which was not caused by a cyber-attack, as evidence that cyber-attacks could cause "havoc," leave people in the dark for "nine to 18 months" and cause "incalculable" financial loss (Wingfield, 2012). In this most recent case, the anticipation and fear of cyber-doom results in turning a known, non-cyber-attack-related incident into an historical counterfactual to motivate a response to hypothetical, future scenarios with impacts out of all proportion to the real-world incident being referenced.

Finally, in the case of the so-called "Night Dragon" cyber attacks we see a legitimate set of CI-related cyber attacks that should be cause for concern in their own right, but which get hyped anyway for the purpose of motivating a policy response to cyber threats more generally. In early 2011, McAfee released a white paper detailing the results of its investigation into a series of "coordinated covert and targeted cyberattacks [that] have been conducted against global oil, energy, and petrochemical companies." The white paper reported that Chinese hackers had routinely collected "competitive proprietary operations and project-financing information with regard to oil and gas field bids and operations...email archives and other sensitive documents" (McAfee, 2011,

p. 3-4). These attacks are clearly cause for serious concern. But in a recent op-ed for *The Wall Street Journal*, former White House cybersecurity czar, Richard Clarke, equated the Night Dragon attacks—along with a laundry list of others—with an "act of war" (Clarke, 2011). Such rhetoric hypes the actual impacts of the Night Dragon and other attacks and, in so doing, invites over-reaction.

Media reporting, expert analyses, and policymaker responses to each of these incidents has exhibited a sort of confirmation bias. They illustrate the twin dangers of possible under- and over-reaction when fears and expectations of what could or might happen unduly cloud our perceptions of what has happened or is happening. First, initial hyping of a CI-related failure, including speculations of cyber attack, followed by reversals of claims about the incident's origin or impact can contribute to the-boy-who-cried-wolf phenomenon. It can contribute to a mentality that only takes CI threats and attacks seriously if they can or do have catastrophic consequences. Second, in the case of Clarke's deployment of Night Dragon, we see the danger of possible over-reaction as a result of fears and expectations distorting our view of reality. We should not need to distort the nature of Night Dragon, Duqu, or any other incident for CI cybersecurity to be taken seriously. Continued incidents of distortion, which the above cases illustrate are all too common, increase the risk that we will either under or over react to legitimate cyber threats to critical infrastructure.

While there are real cyber threats that need to be taken seriously, including the daily occurrences of crime and espionage in/through cyberspace conducted by both state and non-state actors (Dunn Cavelty 2010), effective response requires disaggregating and distinguishing among the various threats that have been conflated under the term "cyberwar" (Dunn Cavelty 2010; Dunn Cavelty and Rolofs 2011; Lewis 2011). Each threat should be addressed first and foremost by the institutions and using the techniques most appropriate to it.

One normative framework that may be of use in this process is one suggested by Rita Floyd (2011) in her attempt to bring a policy-relevant, normative edge to securitization theory. She has argued that not all problems are national security threats; not all are deserving of the "extraordinary measures" associated with responding to such threats, measures that often trade a degree of democracy, freedom, civil liberties, and transparency for security. Threats deserving of such attention, she argues, should be existential in nature, should be directed towards an object that is a legitimate national security concern, and measures taken in response should be congruent with and appropriate to the severity and object of the threat. Based on the preceding analysis, it is doubtful at best that the currently dominant cyber threat perception and associated policy response in the United States meets this criteria. Theft of intellectual property and government secrets, though damaging, is not an existential threat, and certainly not a problem for which we would traditionally create a military command in response.

Some basic principles of good public policy argumentation and debate can be of use when evaluating claims for a security threat and whether or not they meet Floyd's criteria. In addition to expecting that policymakers offer a case for action that includes congruence between the problem and the proposed solution—i.e. between diagnostic and prognostic framing—we should also expect assessments of significance and harmfulness to refer to the same problem rather than shifting from one to the other and back again as a rhetorical tactic that serves the interests of motivational framing but which, ultimately, can undermine our understanding of the various problems that we confront and our options for response. In a time of increasingly scarce resources, those threats that meet the test of both significance and harmfulness—with priority given to loss of human life or the creation of human suffering—should be prioritized. This should be followed by those threats that exhibit a great potential for harmfulness but are perhaps less prevalent. Problems that are significant/ prevalent but not as harmful should receive less attention. Thus, although cyber-doom scenarios are unlikely, threats to critical infrastructure would still seem to have more potential to cause human loss or suffering than threats to intellectual property. Nonetheless, this still does not mean that a centralized, military-led response is most appropriate. Prioritizing critical infrastructure does not require securitizing it. Just as the creation of a military command is likely inappropriate if the dominant objects of cyber threats are informational and economic, it is also likely inappropriate for dealing with infrastructural threats.

These assessments should eschew hypothetical scenarios in favor of empirical research and insight from a wide variety of subject-matter experts. Several prominent voices in the current cybersecurity debate have decried the quality of that debate and have called for a public policy discourse around cybersecurity that would mirror the depth, diversity, and dynamism of the debates that led to the development of a strategy of nuclear deterrence during the 1960s (Clarke, 2009; Clarke and Knake, 2010, p. x; McConnell, 2010). While it is hard to disagree with their call for more and better quality public policy debate about such an important issue, it is important to remember that more debate does not necessarily translate into better debate. As scholars of rhetoric and persuasion have demonstrated, the tools of persuasion can just as easily be appropriated for purposes of deception as they can for increasing clarity and understanding, especially in the area of national security policy (Mitchell, 2000; 2006). As such, more work is needed on what Mitchell has called "public-argument driven security studies" (Mitchell, 2002), in particular studies that examine how the process of argumentation and debate about security matters goes astray and how those failings can be avoided.

CONCLUSION

This chapter has explored the current status of critical infrastructure in the dominant U.S. perception of cyber threats. It has demonstrated that while critical infrastructure was consistently identified as the primary object of cyber threats from the mid 1990s through the presidency of George W. Bush, intellectual property and government data are now clearly and consistently identified by Obama administration officials as the primary objects of perceived cyber threats. Although the 1990s and early 2000s saw a dramatic increase in concern over possible cyber-doom scenarios in which cyberattacks on critical infrastructures caused panic, paralysis, and collapse of society, the most significant and prevalent impacts of cyberattacks are now said to be "informational," including monetary loss and decreased economic competitiveness. Despite this shift in perceived objects and impacts, and despite the fact that we have not and likely will not experience cyberattacks that approach the impacts predicted in cyber-doom scenarios, nonetheless, policymakers and pundits alike continue to deploy such scenarios when making a case for action to address cyber threats. This tendency represents a confusion in the current public policy discourse between diagnostic and motivational framing, between assessing the significance and harmfulness of a threat.

In the case of cyber threats, theft of intellectual property and government data, monetary loss, and decreased economic competitiveness are problems that are significant but not as harmful as prospective destruction or disruption of critical infrastructure. Conversely, cyberattacks on critical infrastructure, while potentially more harmful, are less prevalent than "informational" threats. In the United States, policymakers diagnose informational cyber threats as being more significant and prevalent, but rely upon the fear generated by cyber-doom scenarios as a rhetorical tactic for motivating a response. This confusion in assessing significance and harmfulness results in a blurring of diagnostic and motivational framing that threatens to further diminish the quality of a public policy debate that has already been criticized by outside observers and participants alike. In turn, the poor quality of this debate poses serious challenges for formulating appropriate and effective responses to cyber threats of all kinds, including threats against critical infrastructure.

Public policy debate about cybersecurity can be improved by reserving calls for the "extraordinary measures" typical of responses to security threats for only those threats that are existential and that threaten an object of legitimate national security concern. Additionally, responses should be appropriate to the diagnosed threat. In short, diagnostic and prognostic framing should be congruent. What's more, we should strive for congruence between assessments of significance and harmfulness as a check against allowing fear-based motivational frames to drive policy responses. In a time of scarce resources, policy priorities should focus on threats that are either significant and harmful or have the potential to bring great harm to human life. Based on the analysis provided here, there is good reason to believe that diagnostic, prognostic, and motivational frames are currently incongruent in U.S. cybersecurity policy. The diagnosis focuses on informational objects and impacts; the motivation is fear of cyber-doom; and the response thus far has been the creation of a military command that seems an inappropriate response to both. At the present moment, U.S. cybersecurity policy risks simultaneously over- and under-reacting to the challenges it seeks to address. Ultimately, we must improve the quality of public policy debate about cyber threats if we are to improve our ability "to navigate the rocky shoals between hysterical doomsday scenarios and uninformed complacency" (Dunn Cavelty, 2008, p. 144).

REFERENCES

Ackerman, S. (2010, 13 October). Doc of the day: NSA, DHS trade players for net defense. *Danger Room*. Retrieved on February 6, 2011, from http://www.wired.com/dangerroom/2010/10/doc-of-the-day-nsa-dhs-trade-players-for-net-defense/

Alexander, G. K. (2010). *U.S. cybersecurity policy and the role of U.S. CYBERCOM*. Presentation to Center for Strategic and International Studies, 3 June.

Alexander, G. K. (2011). Building a new command in cyberspace. *Strategic Studies Quarterly*, *5*(2), 3–12.

Bellovin, S. (2011, 18 November). Water supply system apparently hacked, with physical damage. *CircleID*. Retrieved on February 6, 2011 from http://www.circleid.com/posts/20111118_water_supply_system_apparently_hacked_with_physical_damage

Bendrath, R. (2001). The cyberwar debate: Perception and politics in U.S. critical infrastructure protection. *Information & Security: An International Journal*, *7*, 80–103.

Bendrath, R. (2003). The American cyber-angst and the real world–any link? In Latham, R. (Ed.), *Bombs and bandwidth: The emerging relationship between information technology and security* (pp. 49–73). New York, NY: The Free Press.

Benscath, B. (2011). *Duqu: A Stuxnet-like malware found in the wild*. Budapest, Hungary: Laboratory of Cryptography and System Security, Budapest University of Technology and Economics.

Blank, S. (2008). Web war I: Is Europe's first information war a new kind of war? *Comparative Strategy*, *27*(3), 227–247. doi:10.1080/01495930802185312

Brenner, S. W., & Clarke, L. L. (2010). Civilians in cyberwarfare: Conscripts. *Vanderbilt Journal of Transnational Law*, *43*, 1011–1076.

Brito, J., & Watkins, T. (2011). Loving the cyber bomb? The dangers of threat inflation in cybersecurity policy. *Mercatus Center Working Paper No. 11-24* April.

Bumgarner, J., & Borg, S. (2009). Overview by the US-CCU of the cyber campaign Against Georgia in August of 2008. *US-CCU Special Report,* August.

Buzan, B., Wæver, O., & Wilde, J. D. (1998). *Security: A new framework for analysis.* Boulder, CO: Lynne Rienner Pub.

Clarke, R. (2009). *War from cyberspace. The National Interest.* October/November.

Clarke, R. (2011, 15 June). China's cyberassault on America. *Wall Street Journal.* Retrieved February 6, 2011, from http://online.wsj.com/article/SB10001424052702304259304576373391101828876.html

Clarke, R. A., & Knake, R. (2010). *Cyber war: The next threat to national security and what to do about it.* New York, NY: HarperCollins.

Clinton, H. R. (2010). *Remarks on internet freedom.* Presentation to The Newseum [January.]. *Washington D., C,* 21.

Committee on Homeland Security and Governmental Affairs. (2011a). *Cyber security and American cyber competitiveness act of 2011 (S.21).* 112th Congress, 1st Session, United States Senate, 25 January.

Committee on Homeland Security and Governmental Affairs. (2011b). *Cyber security public awareness act of 2011 (S.813).* 112th Congress, 1st Session, United States Senate, 13 April.

Conway, M. (2008). Media, fear and the hyperreal: The construction of cyberterrorism as the ultimate threat to critical infrastructures. In Dunn Cavelty, M., & Kristensen, K. S. (Eds.), *Securing the 'homeland': Critical infrastructure, risk and (in) security* (pp. 109–129). London, UK: Routledge.

Debrix, F. (2001). Cyberterror and media-induced fears: The production of emergency culture. *Strategies, 14*(1), 149–168. doi:10.1080/10402130120042415

Department of Defense. (2011). *Department of defense strategy for operating in cyberspace.* Washington, DC: Department of Defense.

Dunn Cavelty, M. (2007). Cyber-terror—Looming threat or phantom menace? The framing of the US cyber-threat debate. *Journal of Information Technology & Politics, 4*(1), 19–36. doi:10.1300/J516v04n01_03

Dunn Cavelty, M. (2008). *Cyber-security and threat politics: U.S. efforts to secure the information age.* New York, NY: Routledge.

Dunn Cavelty, M. (2010, 29 October). The real cyberwar is about beating the crooks and the spooks. *Parliamentary Brief Online.* Retrieved February 6, 2011, from http://www.parliamentarybrief.com/2010/10/the-real-cyberwar-is-about-beating-the-crooks-and-the#all

Dunn Cavelty, M., & Rolofs, O. (2011). *From cyberwar to cybersecurity: Proportionality of fear and countermeasures.* Presentation to Munich Security Conference, 5 February.

Elias, T. D. (1994, 2 January). Toffler: Computer attacks wave of future. *South Bend Tribune.*

Eriksson, J. (2002). Cyberplagues, it, and security: Threat politics in the information age. *Journal of Contingencies and Crisis Management, 9*(4), 211–222.

Evron, G. (2008). Battling botnets and online mobs: Estonia's defense efforts during the internet war. *Georgetown Journal of International Affairs, 9*(Winter/Spring), 121–126.

Fisher, D. (2011, 20 October). Using Stuxnet and Duqu as words of mass disruption. *Threat Post.* Retrieved February 6, 2011, from http://threatpost.com/en_us/blogs/using-stuxnet-and-duqu-words-mass-disruption-102011

Floyd, R. (2011). Can securitization theory be used in normative analysis? Towards a just securitization theory. *Security Dialogue, 42*(4-5), 427–439. doi:10.1177/0967010611418712

Gaylord, C. (2010, 16 February). Cyber shockwave cripples computers nationwide (sorta). *Christian Science Monitor.* Retrieved February 6, 2011, from http://www.csmonitor.com/Innovation/Horizons/2010/0216/Cyber-ShockWave-cripples-computers-nationwide-sorta

Graham, S., & Thrift, N. (2007). Out of order: Understanding repair and maintenance. *Theory, Culture & Society, 24*(3), 1–25. doi:10.1177/0263276407075954

Hansen, L., & Nissenbaum, H. (2009). Digital disaster, cyber security, and the Copenhagen school. *International Studies Quarterly, 53*(4), 1155–1175. doi:10.1111/j.1468-2478.2009.00572.x

House Committee on Armed Services. (2010). *Statement of General Keith B. Alexander Commander United States Cyber Command.* United States House of Representatives, 23 September.

ICS-ALERT. (2011a, 1 November). ICS-ALERT11-291-01E-W32.Duqu: An information-gathering malware. *ICS-ALERT.* Retrieved February 6, 2011, from http://www.us-cert.gov/control_systems/pdf/ICS-ALERT-11-291-01E.pdf

ICS-CERT. (2011b, 8 November). JSAR-11-312-01-W32.Duqu-Malware. *Joint Security Awareness Report.* Retrieved February 6, 2011, from http://www.us-cert.gov/control_systems/pdf/JSAR-11-312-01.pdf

ICS-CERT. (2011c, 23 November). Icsb-11-327-01-Illinois water pump failure report. *ICS-CERT Information Bulletin.* Retrieved February 6, 2011, from http://www.us-cert.gov/control_systems/pdf/ICSB-11-327-01.pdf

Inch, E. S., Warnick, B., & Endres, D. (2006). *Critical thinking and communication: The use of reason in argument* (5th ed.). Boston, MA: Allyn & Bacon.

Korns, S. W., & Kastenberg, J. E. (2008). Georgia's cyber left hook. *Parameters,* (Winter): 60–76.

Krebs, B. (2011, 22 November). DHS blasts reports of Illinois water station hack. *Krebs on Security.* Retrieved February 6, 2011, from http://krebsonsecurity.com/2011/11/dhs-blasts-reports-of-illinois-water-station-hack/

Langevin, R. J. R. (2008). *Securing cyberspace for the 44th presidency.* Washington, DC: Center for Strategic and International Studies.

Lawson, S. (2010, 23 April). Cyberwar: We don't know what it is or if we're in one, but. *Forbes.com.* Retrieved February 6, 2011, from http://www.forbes.com/sites/firewall/2010/04/23/cyberwar-we-dont-know-what-it-is-or-if-were-in-one-but/

Lawson, S. (2011). Beyond cyber-doom: Cyberattack scenarios and the evidence of history. *Mercatus Center Working Paper, No. 10-77.*

Lewis, J. A. (2010). *The cyber war has not begun.* Unpublished manuscript. Retrieved February 6, 2011, from http://csis.org/files/publication/100311_TheCyberWarHasNotBegun.pdf

Lewis, J. A. (2011). *Thresholds for cyberwarfare. IEEE Security and Privacy, 99.* PrePrint.

Lynn, W. J. III. (2010). Defending a new domain: The Pentagon's cyberstrategy. *Foreign Affairs*, *89*(5), 97–108.

Lynn III, W. J. (2011). *Remarks on the department of defense cyber strategy*. Presentation to National Defense University, 14 July.

Marsh, R. T. (1997). *Critical foundations: Protecting America's infrastructures: The report of the president's commission on critical infrastructure protection*. Washington, DC: The White House.

McAfee Foundstone Professional Services and McAfee Labs. (2011). *Global energy cyberattacks: "Night dragon*. Santa Clara, CA: McAfee Foundstone Professional Services and McAfee Labs.

McConnell, M. (2010, 28 February). Mike McConnell on how to win the cyber-war we're losing. *Washington Post*, p. B01.

Mills, E. (2010, 15 November). Symantec: Stuxnet clues point to uranium enrichment target. *CNET News*. Retrieved on February 6, 2011 from http://news.cnet.com/8301-27080_3-20022845-245.html

Mitchell, G. R. (2000). Placebo defense: Operation desert mirage? The rhetoric of patriot missile accuracy in the 1991 Persian Gulf War. *The Quarterly Journal of Speech*, *86*(2), 121–145. doi:10.1080/00335630009384286

Mitchell, G. R. (2002). Public argument-driven security studies (review essay). *Argumentation and Advocacy*, *39*, 57–71.

Mitchell, G. R. (2006). Team B intelligence coups. *The Quarterly Journal of Speech*, *92*(2), 144–173. doi:10.1080/00335630600817993

Nakashima, E. (2011a, 18 November). Foreign hackers targeted U.S. water plant in apparent malicious cyber attack, expert says. *Washington Post*. Retrieved February 6, 2011, from http://www.washingtonpost.com/blogs/checkpoint-washington/post/foreign-hackers-broke-into-illinois-water-plant-control-system-industry-expert-says/2011/11/18/gIQAgmTZYN_blog.html

Nakashima, E. (2011b, 25 November). Water-pump failure in Illinois wasn't cyberattack after all. *Washington Post*. Retrieved February 6, 2011, from http://www.washingtonpost.com/world/national-security/water-pump-failure-in-illinois-wasnt-cyberattack-after-all/2011/11/25/gIQACgTewN_story.html

Nichol, J. (2008). *Russia-Georgia conflict in South Ossetia: Context and implications for U.S. interests*. Washington, DC: Congressional Research Service.

Nye, D. E. (2010). *When the lights went out: A history of blackouts in America*. Cambridge, MA: MIT Press.

Parker, M. (2011, 12 December). Beyond Stuxnet and Duqu: Security implications to our infrastructure. *Symantec Connect*. Retrieved February 6, 2011, from http://www.symantec.com/connect/blogs/beyond-stuxnet-and-duqu-security-implications-our-infrastructure

Patterson, T. (2010, 15 October). U.S. electricity blackouts skyrocketing. *CNN.com*. Retrieved February 6, 2011, from http://www.cnn.com/2010/TECH/innovation/08/09/smart.grid/index.html?hpt=Sbin

Peoples, C., & Vaughan-Williams, N. (2010). *Critical security studies: An introduction*. London, UK: Routledge.

Peterson, D. G. (2011, 19 October). Duqu and ICS? *Digital Bond*. Retrieved February 6, 2011, from http://www.digitalbond.com/2011/10/19/duku-and-ics/

Rid, T. (2011). Cyber war will not take place. *Journal of Strategic Studies,* iFirst.

SecureWorks. (2011, 26 October). Duqu questions and answers. *SecureWorks.com.* Retrieved February 6, 2011, from http://www.secureworks.com/research/threats/duqu/

Sommer, P., & Brown, I. (2011). *Reducing systemic cybersecurity risk.* Paris, France: OECD.

Stohl, M. (2007). Cyber terrorism: A clear and present danger, the sum of all fears, breaking point or patriot games? *Crime, Law, and Social Change, 46*(4-5), 223–238. doi:10.1007/s10611-007-9061-9

Symantec. (2011). *W32.Duqu: Precursor to the next Stuxnet.* Mountain View, CA: Symantec.

The White House. (2009). *Cyberspace policy review: Assuring a resilient information and communications infrastructure.* Washington, DC: The White House.

The White House. (2011). *International strategy for cyberspace: Prosperity, security, and openness in a networked world.* Washington, DC: The White House.

Todd, B. (2011, 18 November). Water pumping station hacked? *The Situation Room with Wolf Blitzer, CNN.* Retrieved February 6, 2011, from http://situationroom.blogs.cnn.com/2011/11/18/water-pumping-station-hacked/

Walt, S. M. (2010, 30 March). Is the cyber threat overblown? *Foreign Policy.* Retrieved February 6, 2011, from http://walt.foreignpolicy.com/posts/2010/03/30/is_the_cyber_threat_overblown

Weiss, J. (2011, 17 November). Water system hack—The system is broken. *ControlGlobal.com.* Retrieved February 6, 2011, from http://community.controlglobal.com/content/water-system-hack-system-broken

White House Press Office. (2009, 29 May). Remarks by the president on securing our nation's cyber infrastructure. *White House Press Office.* Retrieved February 6, 2011, from http://www.whitehouse.gov/the_press_office/Remarks-by-the-President-on-Securing-Our-Nations-Cyber-Infrastructure/

Whitehouse, S. (2011, 7 March). Cybersecurity needs complete plan. *Politico.* Retrieved February 6, 2011, from http://dyn.politico.com/printstory.cfm?uuid=8D587513-F55D-BEB0-A25C03B5B2018326

Wingfield, B. (2012, 13 January). Power-grid cyber attack seen leaving millions in dark for months. *Bloomberg.* Retrieved February 6, 2011, from http://www.bloomberg.com/news/2012-02-01/cyber-attack-on-u-s-power-grid-seen-leaving-millions-in-dark-for-months.html

ADDITIONAL READING

Alexander, G. K. (2011). Building a new command in cyberspace. *Strategic Studies Quarterly, 5*(2), 3–12.

Bendrath, R. (2003). The American cyber-angst and the real world–Any link? In Latham, R. (Ed.), *Bombs and bandwidth: The emerging relationship between information technology and security* (pp. 49–73). New York, NY: The Free Press.

Brito, J., & Watkins, T. (2011). Loving the cyber bomb? The dangers of threat inflation in cybersecurity policy. *Mercatus Center Working Paper No. 11-24* April.

Conway, M. (2008). Media, fear and the hyperreal: The construction of cyberterrorism as the ultimate threat to critical infrastructures. In Dunn Cavelty, M., & Kristensen, K. S. (Eds.), *Securing the 'homeland': Critical infrastructure, risk and (in)security* (pp. 109–129). London, UK: Routledge.

Department of Defense. (2011). *Department of Defense strategy for operating in cyberspace.* Washington, DC: Department of Defense.

Dunn Cavelty, M. (2008). *Cyber-security and threat politics: US efforts to secure the information age.* New York, NY: Routledge.

Langevin, R. J. R. (2008). *Securing cyberspace for the 44th presidency.* Washington, DC: Center for Strategic and International Studies.

Lawson, S. (2011). Beyond cyber-doom: Cyberattack scenarios and the evidence of history. *Mercatus Center Working Paper, No. 10-77.*

Lewis, J. A. (2011). *Thresholds for cyberwarfare. IEEE Security and Privacy, 99.* PrePrint.

Marsh, R. T. (1997). *Critical foundations: Protecting America's infrastructures: The report of the president's commission on critical infrastructure protection.* Washington, DC: The White House.

Nye, D. E. (2010). *When the lights went out: A history of blackouts in America.* Cambridge, MA: MIT Press.

Sommer, P., & Brown, I. (2011). *Reducing systemic cybersecurity risk.* Paris, France: OECD.

The White House. (2009). *Cyberspace policy review: Assuring a resilient information and communications infrastructure.* Washington, DC: The White House.

The White House. (2011). *International strategy for cyberspace: Prosperity, security, and openness in a networked world.* Washington, DC: The White House.

KEY TERMS AND DEFINITIONS

Diagnostic Framing: In relation to securitization, diagnostic framing refers to those activities that diagnose the threat to be addressed. Diagnosis involves assessing the significance and harmfulness of the threat.

Harmfulness: The issue in policy debate and argumentation that addresses the degree of danger posed by a problem to be solved. Priority is given to those problems with the potential to cause loss of human life or human suffering.

Motivational Framing: In relation to securitization, motivational framing refers to those rhetorical and argumentative tactics used as a call to action, to motivate the public and policymakers to take action in response to the diagnosed threat. Motivational framing often relies upon appeals to emotion or ideology—e.g. fear, patriotism, etc.

Prognostic Framing: In relation to securitization, prognostic framing refers to proposing responses to the diagnosed threat. These responses are usually in the form of "extraordinary measures" that lie outside the normal functioning of democratic politics and often involve actions by intelligence or military organizations.

Securitization: The process in political discourse of "constructing"—i.e. identifying, specifying, and responding to—security threats.

Significance: The issue in policy debate and argumentation that addresses the prevalence, scope, or extent of a problem to be solved.

Threat Object: In the process of securitization, the threat object is that which is threatened—e.g. territorial integrity, political sovereignty, critical infrastructures, etc.

Threat Subject: In the process of securitization, the threat subject is that which is threatening—e.g. foreign states, terrorist organizations, etc.

Chapter 8

Patching our Critical Infrastructure:
Towards an Efficient Patch and Update Management for Industrial Control Systems

Konstantin Knorr
Trier University of Applied Sciences, Germany

ABSTRACT

Worm epidemics such as Stuxnet and Conficker have raised great interest in the public and media lately and stressed the question of how our critical infrastructure can be protected against such attacks. Besides reactive measures like incident response, pro-active counter measures are required. Patch management is such an essential pro-active measure for the secure operation of our critical infrastructure. It is an indispensable activity which is required in many standards. This chapter focuses on patch and update management for industrial control systems that are part of our critical infrastructure. Standards for the automation of patch management and selected operational security standards are discussed in the context of patch management. The main contribution of the chapter is the definition and description of a standard conform patch management process for industrial control systems with special focus on the interaction between operator and vendor of such systems.

INTRODUCTION

The security of industrial control systems (ICSs) has received considerable attention over several years e.g. by Knapp (2011), Stouffer, Falco, & Scarfone (2011) and Weiss (2011). This can be traced back to an increased awareness for this topic and several technological trends for ICSs. The National Vulnerability Database (http://www.nvd.gov) currently stores ~50.000 vulnerabilities. Even though many of these vulnerabilities cannot directly be applied to ICSs, they have to be taken seriously for ICSs due to the following ICS trends:

DOI: 10.4018/978-1-4666-2659-1.ch008

Copyright © 2013, IGI Global. Copying or distributing in print or electronic forms without written permission of IGI Global is prohibited.

- ICSs increasingly use and consist of standard third party software like Windows operating systems and Apache web server often due to cost pressure and customer requirements.
- ICSs increasingly use standard communication protocols like TCP/IP, public communication networks like the Internet, and wireless technologies often also due to cost saving and customer requirements.

These trends lead to a multiplication of the attack surface in comparison to former ICSs. Hacking know-how of such standard software and protocols is readily available and sets ICSs in the focus of attackers who have previously focussed rather on standard IT systems. Malware like Stuxnet clearly indicates that attackers are already taking advantage of the changing environment. The US Computer Emergency Response Team (CERT) reacted to the increasing threats to ICSs by creating the Control System Security Program (cf. http://www.us-cert.gov/control_systems/). Within the program 100 control system advisories and reports were published from January 1st to October 18th 2011. For the entire year 2010 only 36 advisories and reports have been published which clearly indicates the increased attention ICS vulnerabilities have been getting lately.

The following timeline of security events for ICSs illustrates the growing relevancy and importance of patch management for ICSs:

- In 2003 the Slammer worm attacked a nuclear power plant in Ohio and blocked a safety monitoring system for several hours, cf. Poulsen (2003). Malware like Slammer infects unpatched systems. Patching is therefore one of the most important measures to protect an ICS against malware.
- In 2006 a remotely exploitable buffer overflow in the LiveData Inter-Control Center Communications Protocol (ICCP) implementation was found and publically announced. ICCP is an example of a protocol

used between ICSs and stresses the importance of patching protocol implementations, as a single malformed packet could crash the ICS's communication servers, cf. US CERT (2006) for more information.
- Krebs (2008) reports how a software update caused an emergency shutdown of a nuclear power plant in Georgia. Note that in contrast to the incident described by Poulsen (2003) here the installation of the patch caused the problems, while in Ohio the Slammer worm was able to penetrate the system because security patches were not applied.
- Stuxnet has given the patch management for ICSs a major push. Even though Stuxnet used several Windows zero-day-exploits for which patches have not been available at the time of the first break out, Stuxnet nicely illustrates the necessity of patching and protecting ICSs and the timely reaction to security alters. Falliere, Murchu, & Chien (2011) provide more details on Stuxnet.

The above events clearly demonstrate the necessity to develop patch management practises suitable for ICS environments. The fundamental challenge is to find a balance between fixing exploitable security holes by applying patches on the one hand, and guaranteeing the system's availability which is challenged by system downtimes caused by the installation of patches and malfunctioning patches on the other hand.

The fundamental approach required to systematically handle vulnerabilities and corresponding exploits is to tackle vulnerabilities in a process oriented way. The generic process followed in this chapter is depicted in Figure 1. The main phases of the process are:

- **Security Monitoring:** Systematically collect information about new or updated vulnerabilities.

Figure 1. Generic Patch Management Process for ICS Operators. Grey arrows indicate the information and process flow and continuous activities. White arrows indicate read/write access to the knowledge base.

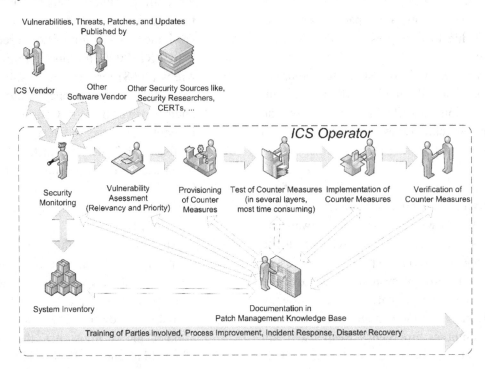

- **Vulnerability Assessment:** Is the vulnerability relevant for the ICS? If yes, what is its criticality? How fast does the patch need to be installed?
- **Provisioning of Counter Measures:** Which counter measures like patches of workarounds are available? Where can they be obtained?
- **Test of Counter Measures:** As availability is paramount for ICSs, testing counter measures is often the most time consuming part of the process.
- **Implementation of Counter Measures:** e.g. Installation of the patch.
- **Verification of Counter Measures:** Verify if the implemented counter measures really fix the underlying vulnerability.

The process and its phases will be described and discussed in detail the process part of this chapter. In order to do so prior discussion of patch management and ICS background information is needed.

The remainder of the chapter has the following structure: In the background part of this chapter these issues are discussed:

- **Basics of Patch Management:** Patch management and related terms like vulnerability and update will be defined. Patch management statistics, the differences in patching open and closed software, different vulnerability disclosure models, and patch delivery strategies are also discussed.
- **Basics of ICSs:** Definitions of ICSs will be given; the architecture of ICSs and the roles of vendor and operator are discussed.
- **Recommended Standards for the Automation of Patch Management:** The standards CVE, CPE, and CVSS allow automating the handling of vulnerabilities and patches. The standards, their advantages, and automation potential will be described.

The security differences between traditional IT environments and ICSs will be analysed. The main differences can be traced back among others to the higher availability requirements of ICSs. Additionally, risk evaluation and testing prior to installing patches in productive ICSs is much more challenging and important. This concludes the background part of the chapter.

Readers familiar with this background information can directly refer to the following part which presents the main contribution of the chapter. It is called "Patch Management of Industrial Control Systems" and comprises the following sections:

- **Security Standards and Regulations:** Many security standards have adopted patch management requirements and many operators of ICSs are struggling to fulfil them. Most information security standards focusing on the secure operation of information systems require adequate patch management, unfortunately without giving details about the implementation e.g. ISO/IEC 27002. Standards specific for ICSs addressing patch management have been published by the North American Electric Reliability Corporation (2010) and International Instrument Users' Association (2010). Standards for operators and vendors of ICSs will be listed and typical patch management requirements will be discussed.
- **Related Work:** Existing approaches for patching ICSs are described and compared (cf. Table 4).
- **Generic Patch Management Process for ICSs:** A process based approach (cf. Figure 1) is suggested which includes not only the operator but also ICS vendors, vendors of other 3rd party software, open source projects, and vulnerability intelligence groups such as CERTs. The process, its prerequisites, phases, and advantages will be de-

scribed in detail following the flow of the process.
- **Interaction between ICS Operator and Vendor:** The interaction between ICS operator and vendor is discussed based on the process description (cf. Figure 4).
- **Combining ICS and IT System Patch Management:** The combination of patch management for ICS and IT systems promises efficiency and cost saving. Therefore, the potential and possible pitfalls of this combination are analysed based on the process description.

Finally, the section "Future Research Directions" gives an outlook on future work areas regarding patch management of ICSs. A concluding section summarizes the most important parts and aspects of the book chapter.

BACKGROUND

The following part provides background information on patch management and ICSs. This background information is necessary for the understanding of the later process part.

Patch Management Basics

In order to give a definition and explain how patch management is understood in this chapter, it is necessary to define terms like vulnerability, patch, update, and exploit.

Basic Definitions

Shirey (2000) defines a *vulnerability* as "a flaw or weakness in a system's design, implementation, or operation and management that could be exploited to violate the system's security policy". To clearly distinguish the term vulnerability from other uses it is often called security vulnerability.

Typical examples for vulnerabilities are weak passwords, software bugs like buffer overflows, or the mis-configuration of a web server.

Mell, Bergeron, & Henning (2005) define a *patch* as an additional piece of code developed to address a problem in an existing piece of software. The problem does not necessarily need to be a security problem. To better express the specific focus on security, the term "security patch" is used. A security patch is a patch that addresses a security problem, often a vulnerability. An example is a fix for a buffer overflow in a protocol stack. Note that typically software vendors do not use the terms defined above but create their own wording. Instead of security patches terms like fixes, hotfixes, or security updates are used.

Unfortunately, often security and other patches (like functional updates) are combined. Prominent examples are the Microsoft Service Packs. These Service Packs typically have the size of several hundred MBytes and fix hundreds of security vulnerabilities but additionally add new functionality to the Windows systems.

An *exploit* is defined as a piece of software or data that makes use of a vulnerability to perform an attack. Examples of exploits are code elements that perform SQL injection, privilege escalation, or remote code execution on a specific target system. Often exploits can be easily found readily prepared on the Internet and not much expertise is necessary to use and to customize them for specific targets. Therefore, issuers of patches typically do not provide too much technical details about the underlying vulnerability to complicate reverse engineering and subsequent creation of an exploit by attackers.

What is the interrelation between vulnerabilities, exploits, and patches? Malware like Trojan horses, computer viruses, and worms preferably infect unpatched systems. Once an exploit for a vulnerability is publically available and the corresponding patch is not available or has not been deployed, it is sometimes even remotely possible for malware to systematically exploit the vulner-

ability. Many notorious worms have exploited vulnerabilities for which patches have been available for months. Especially dangerous are exploits, for which no patch is available. These exploits are called zero-day-exploits. Stuxnet lately exploited several Windows zero-day-exploits (cf. Falliere, Murchu, & Chien, 2011).

Patch management is the process of using a strategy of what patches should be applied to which systems at a specified time. Patch management requires a process-oriented approach including the clear definition of corresponding responsibilities and a precise and up-to-date inventory of the software, its configuration and patch level on all machines. This nicely illustrates the required intertwining of technical, organizational, and process oriented mechanisms to enable effective patch management. We will come back to the process issues in the process part below.

Patch Management Statistics

The following selected statistics further motivate the importance of patch management:

- According to the National Vulnerability Database (http://nvd.nist.gov/) the number of vulnerabilities started with several hundred per year in the 90's and increased to a value regularly larger than 4.000 per year since 2005.
- Secunia (2010) published between 3.000 and 4.000 advisories per year in the last five years. Less than 2% of all personal computers have all relevant security patches and updates installed (Secunia 2010). Most computers are therefore not sufficiently patched.
- The Independent Oracle Users Group (2009) states that 30% of all Oracle database systems apply a newly announced patch within three months after the announcement. 25% of all database systems require three to six months. This means

that 45% of all database systems are patched either more than six months after the initial announcement or not at all (11% of the systems).

- Unpatched and unprotected Windows systems will be infected by malware only minutes after directly connected to the Internet.

Open vs. Closed Source Software

Software can be classified into two classes by the availability of its source code: (1) closed source/commercial (e.g. Microsoft products) and (2) open source (e.g. Apache web server). This differentiation has impact on patching the software:

- With commercial software the vendor is often bound to deliver patches within a given time frame to its customers. Such patch delivery agreements are nowadays found in many ICS service contracts and standards (cf. International Instrument Users' Association (2010)). This is not possible for open source software as open source developers often work on a voluntary basis and are neither bound to service level agreements nor to contracts with customers. However, several companies offer patch management support for source software under a commercial license.
- Regarding the patch release intervals, some major commercial software products stick to regular patch releases (e.g. every second Tuesday) while most open source projects do not release patches but generate new software releases that fix security vulnerabilities irregularly and driven by demand.
- The number of vulnerabilities in open and closed source software cannot easily be compared as it depends on many factors including the distribution of the software, the type of target system (client or server) and the expertise and number of users.

- Arora et al. (2004) empirically showed, that open source software vendors patch faster than closed source vendors, and large vendors are more responsive to vulnerabilities disclosed in their products.
- The major similarity is that vulnerabilities appear in open and closed software. Today's ICSs typically consist of software of both worlds. Understandably, patches and patch management are required in both worlds. The patch management process described later works in both worlds. For the sake of simplicity, for the remainder of this chapter the notion "(software) vendor" will be used for open and closed software. When necessary, the differentiation will be made.

For more information on the differences of patching open and closed source software see Schryen (2009).

Vulnerability Lifecycles

A further question to be discussed is how to communicate a vulnerability identified in software to the vendor:

- Following the responsible disclosure model full vulnerabilities details are initially exclusively disclosed to the affected vendor. All stakeholders agree on a period of time to wait before publishing the details. This gives the vendor enough time to verify, test, and patch the vulnerability and announce and distribute the patch.
- The full disclosure paradigm requires that full details of a security vulnerability are disclosed to the public, including details of the vulnerability and how to detect and exploit it. The theory behind full disclosure is that releasing vulnerability information immediately results in quicker fixes and

better security. Contrary, exploits and malware will be readily available.

- Non-disclosure means that a vulnerability and corresponding exploit is kept secret and used possibly with criminal intent when needed. Often, these exploits are zero days and are traded in the underground economy.

Figure 2 shows these three disclosure models and possible corresponding vulnerability lifecycles. Note that the time frame available for the vendor to produce and test a patch differs as well as the "zero day window" which is the time frame an exploitable vulnerability exists without patch.

In spite of the danger of a worm epidemic, full disclosure has its legitimacy. This is because in the past several software vendors – especially in the ICS sector – have been ignorant to reported vulnerabilities or reluctant to produce a patch. As a compromise a responsible disclosure approach with a timer and the threatening of full disclosure after the time-out of the timer is often used by vulnerability researchers.

Though a patch is meant to fix problems, sometimes poorly designed patches or update procedures can introduce new problems as the example described by Krebs (2008) shows. This raises the interesting question when is the best time to apply a patch. Cf. Beattie et al. (2002) for more information on this question. Vulnerability lifecycles specific for ICSs have lately received some attention e.g. by Miyachi et al. (2010, August) and Zhu et al. (2011, April).

Patch Delivery Strategies

Many software vendors, especially those with larger numbers of patches published, nowadays make use of regular patch intervals. This allows for better planning and systematically organizing the application of the patches and has been widely accepted in the community. Unfortunately, the dates for publication are not synchronized over the vendors. The following list gives a comparison of patching strategies of selected software vendors:

- Microsoft publishes security patches once a month, more precisely every second Tuesday. Patches are freely available.
- Oracle follows a three-monthly patch policy on the first Wednesday in January,

Figure 2. Different vulnerability disclosure models. The thick circles represent the vulnerability lifecycles; the inner thin arrows indicate the time periods available for the vendor to produce a patch; the outer dashed arrows show the "zero day windows".

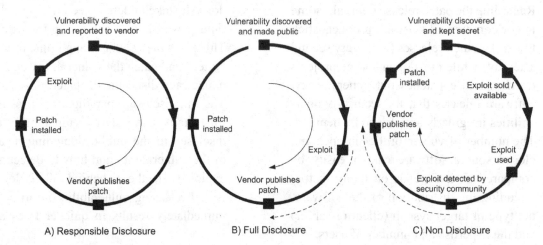

April, July, and October. Patches are not freely available.

- Cisco publishes security updates for the Cisco IOS every six months. The updates are only available for registered customers.
- Adobe uses a three month interval to publish freely available patches and updates.
- Most other vendors publish patches or updates irregularly upon necessity. Examples include many open source projects like Apache and MySQL.

Note that in all patching strategies described above, out-of-band or emergency patches are also possible.

Many vendors and open source projects do not use patches at all. They distribute so-called updates of their software which fix security problems of earlier software versions and also include additional functionality. A prominent example is the Apache web server. On the one hand the practice of combining security with functional fixes/updates complicates reverse engineering for potential attackers. On the other hand this practice tremendously complicates testing, since a new test plan and test cases need to be defined for the additional functionality in comparison to just testing the security patch. For the remainder of this chapter the term "patch" will be associated with security patch and security update if not otherwise stated.

ICS Basics

Stouffer, Falco, & Scarfone (2011, p. 2-1) give the following definition of an ICS:

Industrial control system (ICS) is a general term that encompasses several types of control systems, including supervisory control and data acquisition (SCADA) systems, distributed control systems (DCS), and other control system configurations such as skid-mounted Programmable Logic Controllers (PLC) often found in the industrial sectors and critical infrastructures. ICS are typi-cally used in industries such as electrical, water and wastewater, oil and natural gas, chemical, transportation, pharmaceutical, pulp and paper, food and beverage, and discrete manufacturing (e.g., automotive, aerospace, and durable goods).

The Department of Homeland Security (2009, p. iii) explains the functionality of an ICS as follows:

Simply stated, a control system gathers information and then performs a function based on established parameters and/or information it received. For example, a control system might gather information pertaining to a leak in a pipeline. The system would then transfer the information back to a central site alerting a control station that the leak has occurred, carrying out necessary analysis and control such as determining if the leak is impacting operations and displaying the information in a logical and organized fashion. In this example, shutting down the pipeline is one of the functions that the control system could perform if a leak is detected.

ICS Roles: Vendor and Operator

In this chapter two different roles in the context of ICSs will be differentiated: (1) ICS vendor and (2) ICS operator. Sample vendors of ICSs include Siemens, General Electric, and Honeywell. Sample operators are energy producers, municipal utilities, and large transportation companies. In real life the situation is often more complex. The vendor does not need to be the manufacturer of the ICS. Installation of and service for the ICS may be done by system integrators and other third party companies. The operator and owner of the ICS can also differ. An ICS can consist of many different parts which are bought from different vendors. Operator and vendor could even be the same party.

However, for the sake of simplicity these two roles will be used. The vendor produces and sells the ICS. The operator buys the system from the vendor. The vendor installs the system and provides service for a defined time frame all of which is regulated in a service contract. The handover of the ICS is done in several steps including excessive testing. These tests are e.g. called factory acceptance test and site acceptance tests.

Architecture of an ICS

SCADA system and network architectures often comprise three or more layers:

- Control System
- Substations
- Field Devices

The names of the layers depend on the industry. The names given above stem from the energy distribution industry.

Communication between these layers utilizes varying protocols and technologies ranging from token ring, bus systems, and wireless technologies to fibre optics. The network towards the substations usually makes use of IP. Lots of different network technologies are deployed. Therefore in Figure 3 the generic term "transfer network" is used. This could be a publically accessible wide area network like the Internet, company owned underground cable network on the company's premises, or even using GSM or UMTS networks. Depending on the technologies used the attack surface and security protection mechanisms will vary.

The communication protocols used include serial and proprietary protocols and with growing importance of TCP/IP and HTTP. Control systems are typically nowadays also connected to the operator's company intranet and other ICSs. A firewall separates these networks. The ICS comprises an own internal network whose communication between the ICS nodes is typically based on IP on the network layer and HTTP plus many other protocols on the application layer.

Today's ICSs typically comprise several clients and servers which deploy up to one hundred different open source and commercial software components like Microsoft Windows, Oracle databases, and Apache web servers. Typically a layered software approach is followed on the servers:

- Application Code: Web applications and web services are gaining importance.
- Additional required software like protocols stacks and web servers like Apache and Microsoft's IIS.
- Middleware
- Databases such as Oracle and MySQL
- Operating systems such as Sun Solaris, Linux, BSD Unix, and Microsoft Windows.

The vendor's main software contribution lies (1) in the application code which realizes e.g. control, emergency, and forecast functionality and (2) in ICS specific protocol implementations. Note that the functionality and protocols are dependent on the supported industries. The re-use of existing standard software is an important design pattern for ICSs in order to focus development efforts on the industry specifics like specialized algorithms or protocols. Additionally, the training effort for the operator's staff is reduced by using standard graphical user interfaces e.g. provided by Microsoft's Windows operating systems and the Internet Explorer. Clients are often based on standard functionality, thin/web and rich client being the standard.

Lots of different software license models are used simultaneously in an ICS. Especially with open source software or unsupported software it is often difficult for the ICS vendor to guarantee the operator of the ICS the availability of a security patch or workaround within a defined time frame.

Patch management for ICSs therefore includes security patches and updates for:

- The ICS vendor's software.
- Software of other vendors and open source software.
- Software developed by the ICS operator (if the contracts between ICS operator and vendor allow for such adaption).

Figure 3. Generic architecture of a SCADA system and network

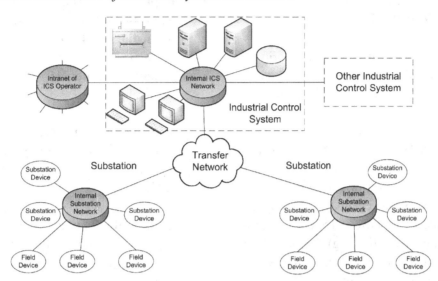

Security updates and patches in protocol implementations are of special relevancy, especially if the protocols are externally accessible. Several attacks on unsecure protocol implementations have been found in the past, cf. US CERT (2006), and their number is increasing.

Weiss (2011) and Stouffer, Falco, & Scarfone (2011) provide additional information about ICSs.

Recommended Standards for the Automation of Patch Management

Due to the large number of patches and updates for ICSs, it is necessary to automate the handling of patches and vulnerabilities as much as possible. This section introduces several standards which can be used for this purpose. While other standards have been proposed, the three discussed below show the greatest potential for supporting the patch management of ICSs.

Common Vulnerability Enumeration (CVE)

CVE was launched in 1999 by the Mitre Corporation when information security tools, researchers, and publications used their own databases with their own names for security vulnerabilities. This made comparisons difficult and additionally led to confusion and undetected redundancy. CVE solves these problems by assigning a unique standardized identifier to a vulnerability which is nowadays globally accepted in the community. A typical CVE identifier has the following form:

CVE-Year-Number, e.g.
CVE-2011-1345

The CVE editorial board checks vulnerability candidates and assigns the numbers. The corresponding CVE database with currently ~ 50.000 CVE entries can be searched at the National Vulnerability Database at http://web.nvd.nist. gov. CVE is the de facto industry standard for referencing vulnerabilities. Several thousand CVE entries are generated each year. For more information see http://cve.mitre.org/

Note that software vendors and open source projects still use additional proprietary identifiers for their vulnerabilities but include the corresponding CVE identifiers in the vulnerability description. For instance the Microsoft security advisory 2588513 deals with CVE-2011-3389. Also, many CVE entries can be covered by a single patch.

Common Vulnerability Scoring System (CVSS)

Issuers of patches typically assign a priority to the patch. In its simplest form a "high", "medium", and "low" ranking is used. High priority patches should be applied faster than low priority patches. Issuers of patches tend to create their own ranking. CVSS proposed by Mell, Scarfone, & Romanosky (2003) provides a homogeneous and standardized way to prioritize vulnerabilities and patches. CVSS was created in 2006 by the Forum of Incident Response and Security Teams (FIRST, cf. http://www.first.org). Before CVSS no consistent vulnerability scoring system was in place. The score is equivalent to the priority of a vulnerability. Each source used its proprietary scoring system (e.g. using the scale high, medium, low). This made comparisons difficult and also yielded contradictions. In contrast CVSS maps the priority of a vulnerability to the scale from 0 to 10.

CVSS uses the following metrics and sub-metrics to calculate the final CVSS score of a vulnerability. Note that the standard defines separate scales und corresponding numerical values for each of the metrics and sub-metrics.

The Base Metric represents the basic characteristics of a vulnerability that do not change over time and environment and comprises the following sub-metrics:

- **Access Vector:** Can the vulnerability be exploited from remote or only locally on the system?
- **Access Complexity:** Is prior authentication required to exploit the vulnerability?
- **Authentication:** How often does an attacker need to authenticate?
- Confidentiality, integrity, and availability impact of the vulnerability.

The Temporal Metric represents the characteristics of a vulnerability that change over time but not among environments and comprises the following sub-metrics:

- **Exploitability:** Is an exploit available and which maturity does this exploit have?
- **Remediation Level:** Is a (temporary) patch available or not?
- **Report Confidence:** Who reported the vulnerability?

The Environmental Metric represents the characteristics of a vulnerability that are unique to an environment and comprises the following sub-metrics:

- **Collateral Damage Potential:** which measures the potential for loss of life or physical assets through damage or theft, and the loss of productivity or revenue.
- **Target Distribution:** How many exploitable systems are in the environment?
- Confidentiality, integrity, availability impact of the vulnerability in the environment.

The final score lies between 0 (lowest priority) and 10 (highest priority) typically given with one position after the decimal point. Note that with appropriate security mechanisms in the environment, the score can be reduced to zero, even if the base and temporal score is high. The details of the calculation behind the scores can be found in Mell, Scarfone, & Romanosky (2003). Note that the base and temporal metric can be calculated by the software vendor or other security intelligence groups, while the environmental metric and subsequent final CVSS score can only be calculated with detailed knowledge of the corresponding target environment.

Common Platform Enumeration (CPE)

What misses in the two standards introduced so far is a standardized and formalized way to automatically map a vulnerability to a given software and hardware inventory. CPE fills this gap by providing a structured naming scheme for information technology systems, platforms, and packages. CPE includes a formal name format, a language for describing complex platforms, a method for checking names against a system, a description format for binding text and tests to a name, and a dictionary with many software and hardware components described in the CPE naming schema. The structured CPE naming schema is as follows:

```
cpe:/ {part}: {vendor}: {product}:
{version}: {update}: {edition}: {lan-
guage}
```

Examples including operating system (part = "o"), application (part = "a"), and hardware (Part = "h") are:

- cpe:/o:microsoft:windows_vista::sp1:x64
- cpe:/a:apache:httpd:2.0.52
- cpe:/a:adobe:reader:8
- cpe:/h:cisco:router:3825

Buttner & Ziring (2009) give further detailed information about CPE.

Summary of the Standards for the Automation of Patch Management

Neither CVE, nor CVSS, nor CPE has been specifically designed for ICSs. However, ICSs use a large number of different software products. Due to the large number of potential vulnerabilities and subsequently patches in these software products standardization and automation of the patch and vulnerability handling is necessary. CVE, CVSS, and CPE allow for automating the vulnerability and patch handling. How to incorporate them into the patch management process is discussed below. While CVE is broadly accepted, CVSS is used in several advisories, CPE only in few. However, with an increase in the number of vulnerabilities a further increase in deployment of these standards is expected. Table 1 gives a summary.

An additional measure to automate patch handling is the use of patch management tools and automatic update tools. Many operating systems and applications provide corresponding tool support. The Centre for the Protection of National Infrastructure (2006) and Mell, Bergeron, & Henning (2005) provide comprehensive tool lists and recommendations concerning these tools for different platforms and operating systems.

Security Differences of Standard IT and ICSs

The security differences of IT systems and ICSs are of great importance for this chapter. The distinction has been extensively analysed e.g. by Stouffer, Falco, & Scarfone (2011, pp. 3-3 – 3-4). Table 2 lists important criteria to distinguish IT system security from ICS security. Note that these are generic differences which are true for general IT systems and ICSs but can be wrong for specific systems.

From Table 2 differences for the patch management of IT systems and ICSs can be derived:

- Due to the long life time of ICSs, the availability of patches cannot be guaranteed by the vendor. Standards like the International Instrument Users' Association (2010) and the Department of Homeland Security (2009) suggest including this issue in the contracts between vendors and operators. If patches for older, unsupported software are not available any more, the source code can be used and analysed to code corresponding security fixes. If the source code is not available, suitable workarounds need to be identified.

- The spatial extension of many ICSs further complicates the distribution and installation of patches. Many ICSs do not provide remote access for the installation of patch-

Table 1. Summary of standards for the automation of vulnerability handling

	CVE	CVSS	CPE
Year of creation	1999	2006	2007
Created by/maintained by	Mitre Corporation, Nation Vulnerability Database	Forum of Incident Response and Security Teams	Mitre Corporation
Motivation behind standard	Provide consistent identification for vulnerabilities	Provide standard way of defining and calculating priorities for vulnerabilities	Provide standard and formalized way of giving software and hardware information
Current deployment level	High	Medium	Low

es while extending over many sites, with a large number of devices to patch at each site. In this case the installation needs to be done on site which increases the cost of patch management.

- Due to the different educational background of ICS personal, patch management techniques need to be trained in ICSs.
- The primary concern about availability in ICSs is the major difference to IT systems concerning patch management. Unfortunately, patching requires a certain downtime (e.g. reboots of the system) or decrease in performance on most systems. This is not acceptable in many ICS settings. Some industrial sectors require 99.999% or greater ICS uptime (Tom, Christiansen, & Berrett, 2008, p. 2) which stands in fundamental contrast to installing patches. Redundant system design helps but dramatically increases the costs.
- The heterogeneous communication protocols used in ICSs stress the need to include these protocol implementations in the patch management process. Especially remotely exploitable vulnerabilities need to be addressed in a timely manner. The communication network within the ICS also has extremely high availability requirements which are especially difficult to fulfil when the network infrastructure needs to be patched.

- Tom, Christiansen, & Berrett (2008) list the following additional patch management issues that differ between IT systems and ICSs:
  - **Slower Patch Evolution:** ICS specific vulnerabilities are not fully understood or widely known and funds and resources may not be available to resolve known vulnerabilities.
  - **Reliable Patch Information:** Only few security intelligence sources are available for ICS specific vulnerability information.
  - **Disclosure of Vulnerabilities:** ICS vendors do not have much experience with responsible disclose and patch and vulnerability dissemination.
- These specifics have to be taken into account when addressing patch management for ICSs as will be done the process part of this chapter.

Patch Management of Industrial Control Systems

The fundamental approach described in this part is to leverage the potential of existing patch management related standards in a process oriented approach to automate and streamline patch management for ICSs. Only a process oriented approach guarantees (1) to systematically address vulnerabilities, (2) to comply with relevant standards, (3) to be able to prove the handling of

Table 2. Generic security differences of IT systems and ICSs partially based on Stouffer, Falco, & Scarfone (2011)

	Information technology systems	Industrial control systems
Lifetime of the system in years	Few years	Up to 20 years
Spatial extension of the system	Manageable	Can get very large e.g. in case of energy distribution or oil & gas pipelines
IT know-how of typical user	Basic knowledge can typically be assumed	Users often have different educational background e.g. mechanical or engineering approach rather than IT
Order of classical security objectives	1. Confidentiality 2. Integrity 3. Availability	1. Safety 2. Availability 3. Integrity 4. Confidentiality
Communication technologies used	Predominately TCP/IP	Still quite heterogeneous. Usage of TCP/IP is increasing.

vulnerabilities by providing the corresponding documentation, and (4) cost efficiency due to division of work.

This is done in the following sections: Security standards and regulations relevant for patch management and ICSs will be discussed first. Then, the "Related Work" section describes other patch management plans and processes. The main contribution follows in the next section which describes the generic patch management process for ICSs (cf. Figure 1) and its phases in detail. The last two sections discuss the interaction between ICS vendor and operator and the combination of jointly patching ICSs and IT systems based on the process defined.

Security Standards and Regulations

Many security standards have identified and mandated patch management as an important cyber security building stone. Especially for the secure operation of an ICS patch management is of utmost importance. Prior to introducing a patch management process for an ICS, it is recommended to review the relevant standards. This is done in this subsection.

Bühler et al. (2011) compare general (not ICS related) standards concerning patch management and identify common „building stones" like the

definition of responsibilities, requirements to perform documentation of patch management related activities, the need of continuous monitoring for new vulnerabilities, and an emergency concept for critical patches. A detailed analysis of patch management specifically in ICS related standards is missing. Table 3 proposes a first step in this direction by systematically comparing selected relevant ICS and patch management related security publications.

- **NERC CIP** is the only regulation. Compliance with the requirements is strictly monitored. Monetary penalties are due if requirements are not met by the operator.
- **Regional Origin:** Security related publications for ICSs are nowadays published in many countries. Table 3 only lists a small selection. Historically, the United States often started to publish ICS related security publications and still play a dominant role.
- **Vendor or Operator Oriented:** The documents can be distinguished whether they address vendors or operators. The vendor oriented documents are often used in tenders and in the further procurement process to systematically incorporate security requirements. The requirements in the

Table 3. Selected patch management and ICS related publications and their classification

Abbreviation/reference to document	Type: S(tandard) Reg(ulation) or Rec(ommodation)	Addressing the O(perator) or V(endor)	Country of origin (I = International)	Industry	Number of pages	Parts of the document specific for patch management
American Petroleum Institute (2005)	Rec	O	US	Oil & gas	58	7.2.8 Network Security 7.2.9 Systems Development 7.2.11 Viruses and other Malicious Code
German Association of Energy and Water Industries (2005)	Rec	V	D	Energy	33	2.1 General Requirements and Housekeeping 2.2.1 System Hardening 2.3.1.1 Deployed Communication Technologies and Network Protocols 2.5.3 Secure Development, Test- and Staging Systems, Integrity Checks 2.5.4 Secure Update and Maintenance Processes 2.5.5 Configuration and Change Management, Rollback
Cyber Security Procurement Language for Control Systems, Department of Homeland Security (2009)	Rec	V	US	ICS, general	145	2.6 Installing Operating Systems, Applications, and Third-Party Software Updates 6.1 Notification and Documentation from Vendor 6.2 Problem Reporting
International Instrument Users' Association (2010)	Rec	V	F, NL, UK	Production	52	Process area 06: Implement patch management
ISO/IEC 27002:2005, International Organization for Standardization (2005)	S	O	I	General	128	12.4 Security of system files 12.5 Security in development and support processes 12.6 Technical Vulnerability Management
NERC CIP, North American Electric Reliability Corporation (2010)	Reg	O	US	Energy	~90	CIP-007-4 R3

documents are readily prepared to include them in tenders. E.g. the International Instrument Users' Association (2010) uses the different security maturity levels gold, silver, and bronze for their requirements. The operator oriented documents have the common goal to incorporate patch management in the daily business of an ICS. Note that the operator oriented publications often stay on a management level, whereas the vendor oriented documents provide technical details.

- **Industry:** Many SCADA industry bodies nowadays publish ICS related security publications. Specific industries like the energy distribution and oil & gas industry are especially affected by cyber security threats due to the large spatial extension of their systems. Table 3 only gives a small selection.

- **ISO/IEC 27002:2005** is not ICS specific. It has nevertheless been included in Table 3 as being the oldest and internationally most renowned best security practice collection including patch management. Comparing other publications like NERC CIP with ISO/IEC 27002:2005 shows major parallels e.g. concerning the structure and the requirements.

To give an example for ICS specific patch management requirements, the North American Electric Reliability Corporation (2010) addresses patch management in its standard CIP-007-4 in requirement 3:

R3. Security Patch Management —The Responsible Entity, either separately or as a component of the documented configuration management process specified in CIP-003-4 Requirement R6, shall establish, document and implement a security patch management program for tracking, evaluating, testing, and installing applicable cyber security software patches for all Cyber Assets within the Electronic Security Perimeter(s).

R3.1. The Responsible Entity shall document the assessment of security patches and security upgrades for applicability within thirty calendar days of availability of the patches or upgrades.

R3.2. The Responsible Entity shall document the implementation of security patches. In any case where the patch is not installed, the Responsible Entity shall document compensating measure(s) applied to mitigate risk exposure.

Another example has been published by the International Instrument Users' Association (2010). The implementation of patch management is listed as a separate process area. The following best practises and sample requirements are given:

- **Policy Documentation:** The vendor shall provide documentation describing the software patching policy.
- **Patch Qualification:** If a security patch is considered not relevant, the reason shall be provided.
- **Provide Patch List:** The vendor shall provide secure access to all patches.

- **Prompt Patch Notification:** The vendor shall inform the operator within 30 days after the release about the relevancy of a patch.
- **Audit Tools:** The vendor shall provide tools to audit the current patch status.
- **Patching Documentation:** The vendor shall describe roll-out procedures for patches.

The problem with these standards is that they fail to give precise advice on how to fulfil the patch management requirements. This objective is the focus of the next section by giving recommendations on how to design and implement an efficient patch management process for ICSs.

Related Work

Patch management processes for ICSs have not been extensively covered in the literature with the notable exception of Tom, Christiansen, & Berrett (2008) and the Electricity Sector Information Sharing and Analysis Center (2005). General patch management processes have received greater coverage e.g. by the Centre for the Protection of National Infrastructure (2006) and NIST SP 800-40 (Mell, Bergeron, & Henning, 2005). Table 4 compares these four publications. The definition and introduction of a patch management process is often also called a patch management program. All documents listed in Table 4 address this topic. Note that all publications propose a process oriented approach and additionally stress the importance of organizational topics.

The Electricity Sector Information Sharing and Analysis Center (2005) states that a comprehensive patch management program requires the following topics:

- Control system asset inventory
- Vulnerability notification

Table 4. Categorization of selected publication which address the introduction of a patch management process

Abbreviation and reference to document	Number of pages	Specific for ICSs	Comments
Centre for the Protection of National Infrastructure (2006)	41	No	Focuses on process and metrics. Also lists patch management tools.
Electricity Sector Information Sharing and Analysis Center (2005)	6	Yes	Provides patch management guidelines specific for the energy sector following a process with four phases.
NIST SP 800-40, Mell, Bergeron, & Henning (2005)	75	No	Focuses on organizing patch management by giving eleven tasks and provides vulnerability metrics.
Tom, Christiansen, & Berrett (2008)	29	Yes	Focuses on plans for a patch management program and provides a metric of the patching analysis.

- **Risk Assessment:** This includes the assessment if a patch is relevant for a particular system.
- **Implementation, Documentation, and Testing:** This includes testing for patch implementation without undesirable effects, proper installation, post-implementation system observation, and validation.

Tom, Christiansen, & Berrett (2008) give the following building blocks of a good patch management program:

- Configuration management program
- Patch management plan
- Backup/archive plan
- Patch testing
- Incident response plan
- Disaster recovery plan
- Unit patching operations

The Centre for the Protection of National Infrastructure (2006) differentiates the following process phases:

- **Assessment and Inventory:** What software components comprise the operational environment and what security threats and vulnerabilities exist?

- **Patch Identification:** Includes the discovery of patches and updates, the relevancy determination, and the provision and verification of the patches.
- **Evaluation, Planning, and Testing:** Decide on the priority of the patch, determine the appropriate response, plan the release of patch, build and test the release.
- **Deployment:** This includes the planning of the patch, the writing of a release plan, and the deployment preparation and execution.

Patch management according to NIST SP 800-40 (Mell, Bergeron, & Henning, 2005) recommends the creation of Patch and Vulnerability Group (PVG) as a starter. The main focus of the publication lies in defining the duties of this group which are:

- Create an inventory of the organization's IT resources to identify the hardware equipment, operating systems, and software applications that are used within the organization.
- Monitor security sources for vulnerability announcements, patch and non-patch methods of remediation, and emerging threats that match up with the software within the system inventory.

- Prioritize the order in which the organization addresses the remediation of vulnerabilities, based on analysis of risks to systems.
- Create a database of remediation methods that need to be applied within the organization.
- Conduct the testing of patches and non-patch remediation methods on IT devices that use standardized configurations.
- Oversee the vulnerability remediation process in the organization.
- Distribute vulnerability and remediation information to local administrators.
- Perform automated deployment of patches to IT devices using enterprise patch management tools.
- Configure automatic updates of applications whenever possible and appropriate.
- Verify vulnerability remediation through network and host vulnerability scanning.
- Train administrators on how to apply vulnerability remediation.

Generic Patch Management Process for ICSs

A description of a generic patch management process for ICSs is given in this subsection with special focus on the incorporation of CVE, CPE, and CVSS following a generic process model derived from the last subsection. Figure 1 illustrates the generic patch management process for ICS operators. The individual steps and phases of the process will now be described. The description will be divided into (1) the preparatory activities, (2) the individual phases of the process, and (3) the supporting activities.

Preparatory Activities

The first and most important task is the creation of the necessary organizational structures, especially the provisioning of personnel. Patch management requires an interdisciplinary team consisting of personnel from IT, IT security, process engineering, operations, and senior management. The core team responsible for most activities in the following process will be called Patch and Vulnerability Group (PVG) as proposed by Tom, Christiansen, & Berrett (2008). Additional tasks of the PVG can include incident response (e.g. in case of a hacking incident) or disaster recovery (e.g. in the case of a malware epidemic). Many ICSs are currently rarely patched or totally refrain from patching. An argument often heard is that no financing is available. To gain an understanding of the number of vulnerabilities and patches, the number and priority of patches for a specific ICS can be monitored over an appropriate time frame (e.g. three months). These numbers can then be extrapolated to request financing for the corresponding patch management project and personnel.

A system inventory of software, hardware, networks, their cross references, and their configuration needs to be created and maintained. This system inventory should include the operating system types and versions, application names and versions, middleware names and versions, legacy status of the software (Are patches still available?), computer roles (server or client), network architecture including connectivity, installed and missing patches, installed security measures, and available source code. Note that the system inventory needs regular updates, backups and has to be protected against unauthorized access. Tom, Christiansen, & Berrett (2008) call these activities "configuration management" and provide further details.

A Patch Management Knowledge Base needs to be created and installed to contain all patch management related information created during and needed for the process execution. Authentication and access rights for all parties involved need to be defined and enforced, as confidential information is contained in the knowledge base like open vulnerabilities of the ICS.

Phases of the Patch Management Process for ICSs

The generic process proposed consists of the following phases which are depicted in Figure 1:

- Security monitoring
- Vulnerability assessment
- Provisioning of counter measures
- Test of counter measures
- Implementation of counter measures
- Verification of counter measures

The *security monitoring* is optimally carried out centrally for the entire ICS by the PVG. This is more efficient and provides a better coverage than letting the local systems administrators do the monitoring. Relevant sources for vulnerability information include:

- The ICS vendor
- Other software vendors
- Security advisories of open source projects
- Other sources for vulnerabilities and patches like CERTs, independent security web sites, and security researchers

The sources can be accessed over several channels such us electronic mail, web sites, and RSS feeds. Note that security monitoring can be very time consuming due to the large number of vulnerabilities. To automate the handling of potential vulnerabilities, a consistent and automated way to filter security notifications according to the system inventory is needed. CPE is recommended here. The National Vulnerability Database (http://nvd.nist.gov/) is already providing CPE entries with their security notifications. CVE is of importance to guarantee a unique mapping of vulnerabilities in the system inventory to the knowledge base and to the security notifications received. Redundancy can thereby be avoided.

The *vulnerability assessment phase* is the next phase in the process and is also carried out by the PVG. The main objective is to check the relevancy of the vulnerability or patch. If based on the information contained in the system inventory, the PVG concludes that the vulnerability is not relevant, then the process for this vulnerability ends by documenting this decision in the knowledge base. It should be the goal to find appropriate counter measures to reduce the necessity for patches as much as possible because this allows for an enormous time and resource saving. Suitable counter measures are e.g. compartmentalization of the network, uninstalling all unneeded software, applying defence in depth, and hardening the entire system.

CVSS is recommended to decide on the patch relevancy. The base and temporal CVSS score is available from the sources in the previous phase. The environmental score needs to the calculated based on the information in the system inventory and knowledge base. If the environmental and subsequently the final CVSS score falls under a predefined threshold, the patch is classified as not relevant. The CVSS score can also the used to set deployment timelines for patches, e.g. vulnerability with CVSS scores between 4.0 and 6.0 must be fixed within 30 days.

If the patch is deemed relevant, the next phase is the *provisioning phase*. The patches could stem from the ICS vendor, other software vendors, open source projects, and other sources. Note that e.g. for a patch of the operating system it is often necessary and required by contract to wait for the official ICS vendor statement on how to proceed rather than downloading and installing the patch directly from the vendor of the operating system. In all cases the integrity and authenticity of the patch needs to be controlled by suitable measures (e.g. digital signatures). Otherwise manipulated patches could e.g. infect the ICS with malware. If no patch is available, a suitable workaround needs to be found. The workaround must fit to the local environment and could e.g. encompass temporary physical isolation of system parts or "air gapping" of network connections. Also, suitable verification methods for successful application of patch and workaround need be defined for the later verification phase. The patches, workarounds, and verification methods should be stored and documented in the knowledge base.

The next phase is the *test phase* and is carried out by the PVG or by the testing department. Testing is the most time-consuming part of patch management. Microsoft (2010, p. 12) uses 40% to 80% of its security update development time for testing. Rather than directly testing the patch on many different systems, a layered approach is recommended e.g. central testing, utility testing, and site testing. Redundant test systems which resemble the productive system as closely as possible are recommended. It is understood that this is a major cost driver. But the quality of the testing will increase with greater resemblance of the testing and operational system. The testing results including the test cases, test plan, release plan, deployment preparations, recommendations for update timeline, number of reboots, etc. should be documented in the knowledge base.

The main objective of the *implementation phase* is to install the patch or to implement the counter measure on the productive systems. This is a very delicate phase as downtimes of the ICS are often required and any malfunctioning will further prolong the downtime. The recommendations of the previous test phase should therefore be followed carefully. Physical redundancy of the system is useful: in this case the servers can be patched one after the other. The actual installation is carried out by the local system administrator. The result should be documented in the knowledge base.

In the *verification phase* installation of the patch or implementation of the counter measure will be verified by the PVG. The verification methods documented during the provisioning phase in the knowledge base will be used. The result of the verification will also be documented in the knowledge base. Unsuccessful verification will cause the process to restart.

Supporting activities in the patch management process include the following:

- Documentation of all patch management related activities in the Patch Management Knowledge Base. This includes all the information mentioned above in the description of the process phases and the process description. Note that especially the documented decision why not installing a patch is required by many standards e.g. by the North American Electric Reliability Corporation (2010).
- Training of Parties Involved: Especially when introducing a patch management program, the training of all parties involved is important. It is recommended that the training is organised and partially held by the PVG and that the training is tailored for different target audiences like management, local administrators, or testing department.
- Tom, Christiansen, & Berrett (2008) recommend establishing an archive. This archive should be created and/or updated prior to any patching activities and provides a last, "good" snapshot of the production system. The plan should describe details about the frequency and process of the backup, verification procedures, retention period, and physical storage.
- Further supporting activities include continuous process improvement, incident response, and disaster recovery related to patch management.

Interaction Between ICS Operator and Vendor

Typically ICS vendor and operator stand in a trust relationship which is an important prerequisite when it comes to handling vulnerability information of operational ICSs. These two parties are heavily interconnected also through service contracts, trainings, and during incident response and disaster recovery. The interaction between operator and vendor when it comes to patch management has been analysed by Knorr (2006, March and 2009, September) and Rohrmair & Knorr (2007). The mutual dependencies regarding patch management are depicted in Figure 4.

The typical vulnerability information flow will be as follows: A software vendor or open source project announces a vulnerability in one of its software products and proposes a patch. This information will be received by the ICS vendor. In case of publically available patch information the ICS operator can receive the notification at the same time. Now, the ICS vendor needs to check the relevancy and subsequently the priority of patch. Within the ICS vendor a similar approach as described in the generic patch management process for the operator will be followed. A central security group performs the security monitoring and notifies the ICS product development and subsequently the product test group about the vulnerability. The final release to the operator will be done by the service department which could e.g. deliver the necessary patch over an information system jointly used by ICS vendor and operator.

As testing can take a long time, an advance notification about the vulnerability and current testing status should be sent to the operator, especially for high priority patches. Again, CVE, CPE, and CVSS help to automate this process. The operator can also directly request information about a specific vulnerability from the ICS vendor. This is indicated by the double-headed arrow in Figure 4.

A similar information flow can be observed if the vulnerability is reported by other vulnerability sources such as CERTs or security researchers. In case no patch is available, the ICS vendor proposes suitable workarounds and informs the operator.

In case a security vulnerability is discovered by the ICS vendor in his product or if the operator detects a vulnerability in the ICS, this is usually handled and solved confidentially between the two parties.

An alternative approach for the operator is to outsource parts or the entire patch management process to the ICS vendor. Many vendors offer such services. The details are regulated in corresponding service contracts. Many contracts exclusively allow the vendor to install patches and updates on the ICS, otherwise the warranty is broken. Note that the vulnerability information flow described here and in Figure 4 nicely interfaces with the generic process depicted in Figure 1.

Combining ICS and IT System Patch Management

Most companies running ICSs have the ICS connected to their office networks and intranet. The interfacing between ICS and such "standard" IT systems (ITSs) is depicted in Figure 3. Treating ICS and ITS vulnerabilities together is highly desirable for the sake of cost saving and efficiency. The generic process depicted in Figure 1 and described above can be extended to also include ITSs. The major differences between ICSs and ITSs have been described above (cf. Table 2) and yield the following aspects that need to be addressed when combining patch management of ICSs and ITSs:

- Personnel: Many operators strictly separate staff and responsibilities for their ITS and ICS. Therefore, the organization of PVG needs to reflect these conditions e.g. by forming ICS and ITS sub-teams that exchange their knowledge over a common knowledge base.
- Security monitoring needs to be extended to also include vulnerabilities relevant for the IT systems. This requires the system

Figure 4. Vulnerability information flow between ICS vendor and operator

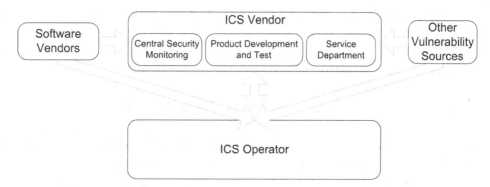

inventory either to be split in two parts or to generate two distinct system inventories with the need to interface the two inventories. The same considerations apply to the patch management knowledge base.

- The vulnerability assessment for a vulnerability relevant for both worlds can be different for ICS and ITS. This can nicely be addressed by different CVSS scores for the same CVE number. For ICSs, often the availability requirements will be higher than for the ITS.
- Counter measures may differ. For the ITS it might be acceptable to automatically download the required patch from the original software vendor while for the ICS a corresponding patch release by the ICS vendor is required (cf. Figure 4). For the ICS a change of configuration could be required while at the same time the update to a new software version might the done for the ITS. This requires also different verification techniques for the counter measures.
- Due to the high availability requirements the testing effort for the ICS can be much higher than for the ITS.

FUTURE RESEARCH DIRECTIONS

Future research directions encompass but are not limited to the following issues:

- Fast patching or emergency patching is one of the big open challenges concerning patch management for ICSs. In case of high priority patches e.g. after the outbreak of a malware epidemic it might be necessary to speed up the entire patching process to several hours. This fundamentally collides with the time needed to do a thorough testing of the patch or workaround by the ICS vendor and operator. Testing is the most time consuming activity in the patch process. In case of emergency patches this time is not available. Possibly suitable workarounds can be identified fast enough. But also workarounds need testing.
- An additional challenge lies in legacy systems with no patch support (e.g. a discontinued open source project) or software from companies that have gone bankrupt. In newer contracts between ICS vendor and operator it is often required to deposit source code e.g. at a trusted third party to counter this problem. This is called "source code escrow" by the German Association of Energy and Water Industries (2005, p. 28). But even then it is challenging and

time consuming to work through the code and produce adequate patches. A possible solution is to strengthen the resilience of legacy systems by adding protective network devices to legacy systems. These protective devices could scan incoming network traffic and perform intrusion detection and prevention.

- This chapter addressed patch management for ICSs. The SCADA system and network architecture presented in Figure 3 consists of several layers with the ICS being the top layer. Patch management for the lower layers (e.g. substations and field devices) could require different approaches due to different characteristics of these levels like remote accessibility, amount of embedded devices, patch availability, and amount of legacy software.

- The CPE dictionary (http://cpe.mitre.org) already includes first ICS components. It should be extended to include more ICS specific hardware and software. This is highly required in order to use CPE to describe the system inventory.

- CVE is readily used in ICSs. The potential of combing CVE, CVSS, and CPE to automate patch handling in ICSs should be analysed in a productive environment, e.g. by conducting appropriate field trials.

- The Common Configuration Enumeration (CCE, cf. http://cce.mitre.org/) has been proposed by the Mitre Corporation to standardize system configurations. Especially for the system inventory of the generic patch management process described, CCE could prove helpful in supporting an automated decision if a given patch is relevant for the current configuration of the ICS.

- Several vulnerability advisory formats have been proposed e.g. by Bourgeois et al. (2004). However, they lack the support of the CPE, CVSS, and CCE standards that are needed to automate vulnerability handling.

CONCLUSION

This chapter discussed patch management challenges for ICSs and proposed several solutions. The major differences to patching traditional IT systems are the higher availability requirements of ICSs, the longer lifetime of ICSs, the possibility of unsupported software components, and missing remote update functionality. The fundamental challenge is to apply the necessary security patches and updates in a timely manner and to guarantee at the same time the availability and reliability of the system. The proposed solution is a process oriented approach in close cooperation between vendors and operators.

The automation of patch management which is highly required due to the large number of patches for ICSs can be fostered by utilizing the three standards CVE, CPE, and CVSS. While CPE is still in its infancy and is not broadly used, CVSS is increasingly used by vendors and researchers. Finally, CVE is the accepted standard for the unique identification of vulnerabilities.

For ICS operators who are currently not following strict regulations like NERC CIP it is helpful to have an overview of which requirements are included in typical standards and regulations concerning patch management. Table 3 and Table 4 and the corresponding subsections provide this information. One important lesson is that all relevant publications strictly differentiate between monitoring for vulnerabilities and the actual installation of patches. By reducing the attack surface of an ICS, here it may very well be possible to reduce the number of patches that need to be installed.

The major recommendation for operators of ICSs is to organize their patch management in a process oriented way. The corresponding section gives a generic description of such a process and stresses the importance of a close interaction between operator and vendors of the ICS and to automate the vulnerability handling as much as possible e.g. by using standards like CVE, CPE, and CVSS.

The vendor systematically monitors its ICS for vulnerabilities and notifies the operator in case of relevant vulnerabilities. The vulnerabilities are then analysed by the operator. Their relevancy and priority is defined following a vulnerability analysis. If no patch is available, a suitable workaround is proposed. A patch requires thorough testing and validation in the system test. The information about patch or workaround is then communicated towards the party responsible for the implementation. It is recommended to test the patches in a suitable test system at the utility prior to installing them on the productive system. Note that as the reliability and availability of the ICS is so important, testing is required at various stages during this process. This process, especially the interfaces and responsibilities should be mutually agreed upon between vendor and operator. Patch management can also be done by a vendor's service team, possibly remotely in a cost-efficient manner.

REFERENCES

American Petroleum Institute. (2005). *Security guidelines for the petroleum industry*, 3rd ed. Retrieved October 15, 2011, from http://new.api.org/policy/otherissues/upload/Security.pdf

Arora, A., Krishnan, R., Nandkumar, A., Telang, R., & Yang, Y. (2004). *Impact of vulnerability disclosure and patch availability - An empirical analysis*. Paper presented at the Third Workshop on the Economics of Information Security, 2004, Minneapolis, MN.

Beattie, S., Arnold, S., Cowan, C., Wagle, P., Wright, C., & Shostack, A. (2002). *Timing the application of security patches for optimal uptime*. Paper presented at the Sixteenth Systems Administration Conference, Berkeley, CA.

Bourgeois, P., Conesa, O., Grobauer, B., & Price, G. (2004). *EISPP common advisory format description*, version 2.0. Retrieved February 7, 2012, from http://www.cert-verbund.de/daf/documentation/eispp_v20.pdf

Bühler, B., Rohrmair, G., Ifland, M., Lode, N., & Lukas, K. (2011). Ein standardkonformer Patch Management Prozess. In Schartner, P., & Taeger, J. (Eds.), *DACH security 2011* (pp. 248–258).

Bundesamt für Sicherheit in der Informationstechnik. (2008). *IT-Grundschutz methodology*. BSI-Standard 100-2. Retrieved October 21, 2011, from https://www.bsi.bund.de/SharedDocs/Downloads/EN/BSI/Publications/BSIStandards/standard_100-2_e_pdf.pdf?__blob=publicationFile

Buttner, A., & Ziring, N. (2009). *Common platform enumeration (CPE) – Specification*, version 2.2. Retrieved October 20, 2011, from http://cpe.mitre.org/files/cpe-specification_2.2.pdf

Centre for the Protection of National Infrastructure. (2006). *Good practice guide patch management*. Retrieved October 15, 2011, from http://www.cpni.gov.uk/Documents/Publications/2006/2006029-GPG_Patch_management.pdf

Department of Homeland Security. (2009). Cyber security procurement language for control systems. Retrieved October 16, 2011, from http://www.us-cert.gov/control_systems/pdf/FINAL-Procurement_Language_Rev4_100809.pdf

Electricity Sector Information Sharing and Analysis Center. (2005). *Security guidelines for the electricity sector: Patch management for control systems.* Retrieved October 15, 2011, from http://www.esisac.com/Public%20Library/Documents/Security%20Guidelines%20for%20the%20Electricity%20Sector/Patch%20Management%20for%20Control%20Systems,%20Version%201.0.pdf

Falliere, N., Murchu, L., & Chien, E. (2011). *W32. Stuxnet dossier,* Version 1.4. Retrieved October 17, 2011, from http://www.symantec.com/content/en/us/enterprise/media/security_response/whitepapers/w32_stuxnet_dossier.pdf

German Association of Energy and Water Industries. (2005). Requirements for secure control and telecommunication systems, Version 1.0. Retrieved October 17, 2011, from http://www.vdew.net/bdew.nsf/id/52929DBC7CEEED1EC125766C000588AD/$file/Whitepaper_Secure_Systems_Vedis_1.0final.pdf

Independent Oracle Users Group. (2009). *Security patching practices by Oracle customers.* Retrieved October 17, 2011, from http:/ioug.itgonvergence.com

International Instrument Users' Association. (2010). *Process control domain: Security requirements for vendors,* Version 2.0, Report: M 2784-X-10. Retrieved October 17, 2011, from http://www.wib.nl/download.html

International Organization for Standardization. (2005). *ISO/IEC 27002:2005. Information technology - Security techniques - Code of practice for information security management.*

Knapp, E. D. (2011). *Industrial network security: Securing critical infrastructure networks for smart grid, SCADA, and other industrial control systems.* Syngress Media.

Knorr, K. (2006, September). *Security monitoring for siemens products.* Paper presented at the 19th Task Force of Computer Security Incident Response Teams Meeting, Espoo, Finland.

Knorr, K. (2009, March). *Product vulnerability management - The Siemens CERT perspective.* Paper presented at the Workshop on the EU policy dimension of vulnerability management and disclosure process, Brussels.

Krebs, B. (2008, June 5). Cyber incident blamed for nuclear power plant shutdown. *Washington Post Online.* Retrieved October 17, 2011, from http://www.washingtonpost.com/wp-dyn/content/article/2008/06/05/AR2008060501958.html

Mell, P., Bergeron, T., & Henning, D. (2005). *Creating a patch and vulnerability management program.* NIST Special Publication 800-40 v2.0. Retrieved October 15, 2011, from http://csrc.nist.gov/publications/nistpubs/800-40-Ver2/SP800-40v2.pdf

Mell, P., Scarfone, K., & Romanosky, S. (2003). *A complete guide to the common vulnerability scoring system,* Version 2.0. Retrieved October 14, 2011, from http://www.first.org/cvss/cvss-guide.pdf

Microsoft. (2010). *Software vulnerability management at Microsoft.* Retrieved October 17, 2011, from http://www.microsoft.com/download/en/details.aspx?id=4372

Miyachi, T., Narita, H., Oguma, N., & Furuta, H. (2010, August). Consideration on vulnerability handling for control systems. *Proceedings of the SICE Annual Conference,* (pp. 1200–1203). Taipei.

North American Electric Reliability Corporation. (2010). *Critical infrastructure protection standards.* Retrieved October 17, 2011, from http://www.nerc.com/page.php?cid=2%7C20

Poulsen, K. (2003). *Slammer worm crashed Ohio nuke plant network*. Retrieved October 13, 2011, from http://www.securityfocus.com/news/6767

Rohrmair, G., & Knorr, K. (2007). Patch Management aus Sicht eines Herstellers. In Schartner, P. (Ed.), *DACH Security 2007* (pp. 248–258).

Schryen, G. (2009). *A comprehensive and comparative analysis of the patching behaviour of open source and closed source software vendors*. Paper presented at the Fifth International Conference on IT Security Incident Management and IT Forensics, Retrieved February 6, 2012, from http://www.icsi.berkeley.edu/pubs/networking/comprehensiveand09.pdf

Secunia. (2010). *Secunia half year report 2010*. Retrieved October 17, 2011, from http://secunia.com/gfx/pdf/Secunia_Half_Year_Report_2010.pdf

Shirey, R. (2000). *Internet security glossary*. Request for Comment 2828. Retrieved October 16, 2011, from, http://www.ietf.org/rfc/rfc2828.txt

Stouffer, K., Falco, J., & Scarfone, K. (2011). *Guide to industrial control systems (ICS) security*. NIST Special Publication 800-42. Retrieved October 15, 2011, from http://csrc.nist.gov/publications/nistpubs/800-82/SP800-82-final.pdf

Tom, S., Christiansen, D., & Berrett, D. (2008). *Recommended practice for patch management of control systems*. Retrieved October 14, 2011, from http://www.us-cert.gov/control_systems/practices/documents/PatchManagementRecommendedPractice_Final.pdf

US CERT. (2006). *Vulnerability note VU#190617: LiveData ICCP server heap buffer overflow vulnerability*. Retrieved February 7, 2012, from http://www.kb.cert.org/vuls/id/190617

Weiss, J. W. (2010). *Protecting industrial control systems from electronic threats*. Transatlantic Publishers.

Zhu, Q., McQueen, M., Rieger, C., & Basar, T. (2011, April). *Management of control system information security: Control system patch management*. Paper presented at the Workshop on Foundations of Dependable and Secure Cyber-Physical Systems, Chicago, Illinois.

ADDITIONAL READING

Arora, A., & Telang, R. (2005). Economics of software vulnerability disclosure. *IEEE Security & Privacy*, Jan-Feb 2005, 20-25.

Cavusoglu, H., & Zhang, J. (2006, June). *Economics of security patch management*. Paper presented at the 5th Workshop in the Economics of Information Security, University of Cambridge, England.

Chan, J. (2004). *Essentials of patch management policy and practice*. Retrieved October 27, 2011, from http://www.patchmanagement.org/pmessentials.asp

Department of Energy. (2003). *21 steps to improve cyber security of SCADA networks*. Retrieved October 27, 2011, from http://energy.gov/sites/prod/files/oeprod/DocumentsandMedia/21_Steps_-_SCADA.pdf

Fink, R., Spencer, D., & Wells, R. (2006). *Lessons learnt from cyber security assessments of SCADA and energy management systems*. Retrieved October 31st, 2011, from http://www.inl.gov/scada/publications/d/nstb_lessons_learned_from_cyber_security_assessments.pdf

Gerace, T., & Cavusoglu, H. (2009). The critical elements of the patch management process. *Communications of the ACM, 8*(52).

Grobauer, B. (2005, June). *CVE, CME, ...CMSI? Standardising system information*. Paper presented at the 17th Annual the Forum of Incident Response and Security Teams (FIRST) Conference, Singapore.

Internet Security Systems, I. B. M. (2007). *A strategic approach to protecting SCADA and process control systems.* Retrieved October 27, 2011, from http://www.iss.net/documents/white-papers/SCADA.pdf

Mann, D. (2008). *An introduction to the common configuration enumeration,* Version: 1.7. Retrieved October 31st, 2011, from http://cce.mitre.org/documents/Introduction_to_CCE_White_Paper_July_2008.pdf

McQueen, M., Boyer, W., McQueen, T., & McBride, S. (2010). *Empirical estimates of 0Day vulnerabilities in control systems.* Paper presented at the SCADA Security Scientific Symposium (S4), Miami, FL.

National Vulnerability Database. (2011). Retrieved October 27, 2011, from http://nvd.nist.gov

Ozment, A. (2007, October). *Improving vulnerability discovery models.* Paper presented at the ACM Workshop on Quality of Protection, Alexandria, Virginia.

Ruest, N. (2004). *A practical guide for patch testing.* Retrieved October 27, 2011, from http://www2.wise.com/Library/Patch_Whitepaper.pdf

Sihvonen, H., & Jäntti, M. (2010). *Improving release and patch management processes: An empirical case study on process challenges.* Paper presented at the 5th International Conference on Software Engineering Advances, 2010.

Stamp, J., Campbell, P., DePoy, J., Dillinger, J., & Young, W. (2008). *Sustainable security for infrastructure SCADA.* White Paper, Sandia National Laboratory. Retrieved October 27, 2011, from http://www.tswg.gov/subgroups/ps/infrastructure-protection/documents/SustainableSecurity.pdf

KEY TERMS AND DEFINITIONS

CERT (Computer Emergency Response Team): Team of security professionals which deals among other topics with vulnerability research, vulnerability coordination, and patch testing. CERTs publish security advisories which include patch recommendations and technical workarounds for vulnerabilities.

Exploit: Piece of software or data that makes use of a vulnerability to perform an attack.

Industrial Control System (ICS): An ICS is a system controlling information systems and networks of our critical infrastructure industries like manufacturing, dams, water, energy, and transportation. The ICS is the top layer of a multi layered architecture and typically manned.

Patch: Additional piece of code developed to address a problem in an existing piece of software. A security patch typically fixes a vulnerability.

Patch Management: The process of using a strategy and plan of what patches should be applied to which systems at a specified time.

Update: New version of software which provides security fixes and functional updates.

Vulnerability: A bug, flaw, weakness, or exposure of an application, system, device, or service that could lead to a failure of confidentiality, integrity, or availability.

Zero-Day-Exploit: Exploit that attacks a vulnerability which is known only to few and for which therefore no vendor patch or workaround is available.

Chapter 9
ICS Software Protection

Peter H. Jenney
Security Innovation, USA

ABSTRACT

Industrial Control System (ICS) cyber security is weak and exploitable. As evidenced by STUXNET's attack on the Iranian Natanz[1] nuclear facility in 2010 and others since global critical infrastructure is in danger of cyber attack. The problem stems from the growth of industrial management systems over three distinct generations that moved process management systems from manual to fully networked controls and sensors. In many cases the transition has been poorly managed and proper IT management techniques were not employed. In others, the software and hardware systems are so fragile that any change or unexpected access can crash or otherwise render them useless. These instabilities, both caused by poor management and weak equipment open large security holes that allow hackers to exploit critical systems with potentially disastrous results. For example, a petroleum distillery could be made to vent and burn excess gas at a time where it could potentially destroy the facility or perhaps take down entire electrical grids, inconveniencing and possibly causing significant harm.

INTRODUCTION

The approach to solving the cyber security problem is to apply common IT best practices to the current ICS space and address the network and application security problems in a manner similar to that being taken by the rest of the IT industry, both commercial and military—lockdown. The application of a solution requires techniques not common to the normal IT space, specifically, industrial control systems cannot be shut down for any length of time as doing so would "break" the processing flow and potentially cause damage to that being manufactured/processed/controlled or carry an unacceptable effect on profitability. For example an oil pipeline cannot be out of service for very long before it starts to cause underflows throughout systems, and similarly, a train track switching system cannot be taken offline for and expect to transport the required daily loads.

DOI: 10.4018/978-1-4666-2659-1.ch009

Copyright © 2013, IGI Global. Copying or distributing in print or electronic forms without written permission of IGI Global is prohibited.

The key to the solution is to implement a process that allows a lockdown with minimal impact to executing processes for locking down control systems using best "least privilege" IT practices, implementing virtual machines, sophisticated white listing and finally enclosing them in a secure subnet where data can only flow outwards, provides a stable and secure environment for processes can execute without fear of attack or requiring systems to be changed enough to cause unexpected failures.

Industrial control systems (ICS) provide the critical infrastructure required by nations to support their populations and economies, and to do so in a safe manner. The computing systems responsible for managing critical processes however are extremely weak from a cybersecurity perspective. ICS networks have historically relied on a common *defense in depth* component called *Security Through Obscurity*[2] meaning that if the hackers didn't know they were there, they wouldn't be attacked[3]. The explicit belief is a carryover from the early days of control system technology were manual or simple electronic switching systems were enclosed in "secure" facilities with no connection to the outside world. Current control system technology relies on newer, cheaper commercial off the shelf (COTS) equipment and the transition from closed, isolated systems to open, Internet connected systems left unforeseen gaps in the perimeter, leaving them open to attack. The U.S. Industrial Control System Cyber Event Response Team (ICS-CERT)[4] and many other organizations around the world have been working the past several years to raise ICS cyber security awareness, but it wasn't until recently that the industry and public learned there was a problem. The trigger event was the discovery of STUXNET in mid 2010. STUXNET is a weaponized computer worm that was specifically targeted at the Iranian nuclear power industry. What it did was to take over certain *supervisory control and data acquisition* (SCADA) systems that were responsible for managing specific *programmable logic*

controllers (PLC) that ran specific devices, in this case industrial centrifuges used in the production of nuclear fuel, and attempted to destroy them and cripple the Iranian program. While STUXNET did manage to attack the Natanz nuclear facility, it failed to do the necessary damage. Regardless, STUXNET provided the world's general public with two critical pieces of information:

1. Industrial Control Systems such as uranium enrichment facilities were vulnerable to attack.
2. People are out there attacking the infrastructure.

From a cybersecurity professional standpoint STUXNET told of many other things including:

1. There are serious threats to global critical infrastructure that have been and are being exploited.
2. Someone is willing to spend an enormous amount of money to create extremely sophisticated malware to exploit ICS.
3. STUXNET provides a solid template for a weaponized worm that can be copied by the general cyber hacking community.
4. There are several other similar examples[5] in the wild that have been discovered though we don't know what we don't know and new malware can be lurking anywhere poised to attack.

The situation is frightening and makes the protection of the global critical infrastructure an extremely high priority for all, however the problem is not an easy one to solve as the state of ICS networks and SCADA systems is extremely poor and needs to be upgraded to withstand cyber attacks of all forms.

Addressing weakness in ICS is a difficult problem. ICS, or just "control systems" as used throughout this chapter, have evolved over time from manual management where a workman would, for example, turn a valve on a predefined schedule to allow oil in a single pipeline, all the way to a complicate modern SCADA *human machine interface* (HMI) workstation that controls flow of several long-range pipelines using innumerable valves and sensors. The complexity is immense and the machinery comes from several generations. For example, there are still manual valves in factories, there are hard-wired *direct control systems* (DCS) using serial or network connections to controllers and modem banks using old communication protocols, and there are modern TCP/IP systems that control *local area network* (LAN) and Internet connected devices—and they typically all coexist in a single facility. Add to this that the priorities of the ICS and IT management teams are quite different (Table 1[6]) and the problem further compounds.

The differing priorities and diversity of devices provides multiple entry points to the network presents a large attack surface with multiple attack vectors that can and will be exploited by malicious hackers. The challenge facing the ICS space is locking down the attack surface, specifically closing all attack vectors, and doing so without interrupting or breaking the critical processes managed by the network. There is another critical factor that must be addressed for complete cyber security. One which was ranked the highest in the 2011 Ponemon Institute survey "State of IT Security: Study of Utilities and Energy Companies" to the question "What is the biggest threat to your SCADA network?"

Negligent Users

Negligent users, or to be fair, mostly uninformed, untrained and/or clueless users represent a huge attack vector due solely to their access to the Internet, which is a cesspit of malware that without proper controls can invade ICS and Enterprise networks alike and be the root cause of failure in the planets critical infrastructure.

This chapter introduces process for locking down a typical facility that uses networked industrial controls and has a parallel network for managing the facility and the business. The process takes into account the following key items:

1. Protection of ICS assets at all points in the process.
2. Mitigation of the "negligent user" as a primary attack vector.
3. Structuring a network architecture that allows generational controllers to coexist and function properly.
4. Providing a platform for managed growth while maintaining absolute security for control systems.

The key technologies that are introduced are common to existing IT management best practices and include the use of Virtual Machines (VM), system whitelisting, least privilege account management, system policy management and the creation of a network topology where individual control systems are securely segmented from other networks and safe from penetration by hackers or other cyberthreats.

Table 1. ICS/IT network differences

Category	IT Implementation	ICS Implementation
Security Priorities	1) Confidentiality 2) Integrity 3) Availability	1) Availability 2) Integrity 3) Confidentiality
Performance Requirements	• Non-real time • Consistent response	• Real time • Response is time critical
Component Lifetime	3-5 Years	10 – 20 years

BACKGROUND

Industrial control systems (ICS) or just "control systems" includes *supervisory control and data acquisition* (SCADA), *process control systems* (PCS), *distributed control systems* (DCS) and any other control systems specific to any of the critical infrastructure industry sectors.

The field is diverse and draws on many technologies that are derived from strictly hardware-based systems, hardware with controller specific programming languages on up to full operating systems and user applications. Much of the equipment may come from any of the three generations of electronic SCADA systems described as Monolithic, Distributed and Networked. *Monolithic* systems were the first generation and were both mainframe based and relied on serial connections or other direct connections to manage control devices and sensors. There was no connectivity to other systems and their operation required the presence of an operator and that they be co-located with the systems they managed. *Distributed* Systems are tightly coupled networked systems that break up the tasks of monolithic systems and allow for the use of cheaper controllers and improved performance. *Networked* systems are loosely coupled systems that use more generic hardware and protocols to do something similar to distributed systems and may use wireless and other more modern technology in its implementation. While there are few monolithic systems in operation today, many distributed/networked systems are in use. These distributed systems are the basis of the cybersecurity issues that plague ICS networks as they bring with them all of the security issues of normal networks, but few of the basic IT best practices normally employed in the enterprise space such as sub-netting and least privilege accounts.

As the technology in play is relatively generic it makes sense that most of the control systems used today are based on either Microsoft® Windows™ or Linux and employ normal *commercial off the*

shelf (COTS) software and frameworks such as Microsoft .NET and Java. Device controllers and sensors on the other hand such as *remote terminal units* (RTU), *programmable logic controllers* (PLC), *intelligent electronic devices* (IED) may instead use other specialized O/S types including VxWorks, QNX, Windows Embedded (CE, XPe, 7), RT Linux or even something home grown.

The quality of "modern" control systems in many cases is quite poor, much of which is attributed to the stability and security of the operating systems. In many cases this may be the case and in others it's the fault of the systems managers and the resistance to change things for fear of breaking them, perhaps by introducing a software patch that causes them to stop working correctly. In many cases the fault lies in the quality of the SCADA software itself, Siemens WinCC being the primary example. In WinCC the passwords for the SCADA Historian databases had to be the default password[7] or the system would not work. This and several other core tenets of secure software development with the result being a collection of SCADA software components with several open and exploitable attack vectors. Siemens is by no means the only organization in the software space to have written insecure software, they are the most famous in the SCADA environment currently, hence an easy target.

Network Security (NetSec)

Typically an organization will have two networks in a facility, one to run the business, the Enterprise network, and one to run the control systems, the ICS network. An ICS network should be completely isolated from the Enterprise network so that nothing from the Enterprise can cross over into the control system and potentially damage controllers or systems. For example, malware that finds its way onto the Enterprise network through a browser has no direct or indirect route between the two network segments, thereby mitigating the threat to the control network. The example in Figure 1 shows the firewalls that need to be in place to lock down the routes. The firewalls are configured to only allow specific traffic from predefined place to place and there is a data diode [a channel that only allows data traffic in a single direction] in place to enable traffic from the control system side to the enterprise side, which will typically be required for regulatory or reporting requirements. One-way data flow in this manner is appropriate, however the reverse is never allowed.

If all networks were set up in this manner then there would be far fewer problems to deal with however it's rarely the case. Most networks, regardless of function, are organically grown using parts from different generations and vendors with different functions and no real implementation plan other than "get it on the system and make it work." In reality, a typical installation is sketchy and provides several places where data can cross over from network to network unimpeded and can be used by malware or hackers to make their way to key control systems. Figure 2 outlines some points of contact that are commonly found, for example, wireless access points that bridge network segments and no firewalls between network segments.

Threats

Regardless of vendor or technology type, it's generally accepted that ICS network cybersecurity is weak and vulnerable to attack. There are hundreds of examples published by various global governmental and non-governmental organizations such as *ICS-CERT*[8] that describe severe and not so severe attacks ranging from the release of sewage into an Australian resort community[1] to the STUXNET attack on the Iranian nuclear facilities. The question is how are ICS networks vulnerable and what can be done to quickly lock them down.

Cyber attacks are similar to any attack on a fortified facility. The idea is to breach the outer defenses to gain access to the inner realm where there are assets to attack and rob. In a castle the outer perimeter is the moat and the outer wall, the inner realm is the courtyard and the assets are the armory, granary, stables and the inner castle. On a network the outer defenses are the firewall facing the Internet, the inner realm is the local area network (LAN) and the assets are the workstations and servers on the LAN. Referring back to Figure 2, the assets are things like the HMI, Configura-

Figure 1. Well-partitioned ICS/Enterprise network

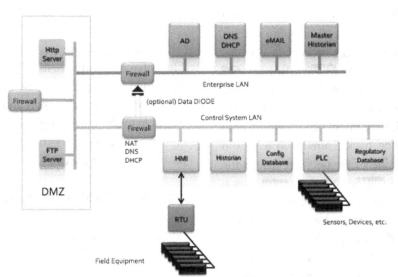

Figure 2. Typical ICS network connectivity

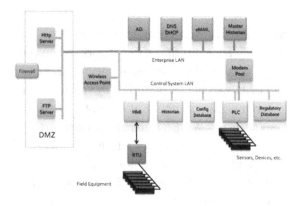

tion Database and Active Directory (AD) server. Simple tactics that provide entrée to a network are described in Table 2.

Each of these attack vectors are quite common. In each case, exploiting the vector allows either a hacker or malware onto the network, likely with privileges high enough to access critical systems on the control system network. This threat outline provides a decent framework for understanding the exploitable vulnerabilities in a typical ICS network, but to make things a little clearer, consider the following two scenarios – *a walk in the park* and *a shopping spree*.

Scenario One: A Walk in the Park

A man in a trench coat strolls through a parking lot of a petroleum refinery one-morning scattering colorful memory sticks around in obvious and tempting places. Later, as the office empties for the lunch hour, employees find the sticks and put them in their pocket—there's nothing like free memory and there might be something cool on it to boot. Once back from lunch a person on the corporate side of the network inserts the stick into his workstation and sees nothing on it but a gigabyte of free space—sweet! Behind the scenes what actually occurred was a clever piece of malware loaded itself onto the system, erased the memory stick behind it and started snooping around the network looking for SCADA Human

Machine Interfaces (HMI) and Master Terminal Units (MTU). Once finding an appropriate system it installed itself as a root kit, making it invisible to normal operating system tools, and sets itself up as a man in the middle, intercepting all commands from the HMI software and replacing it with its own, and providing responses to the HMI software that makes it believe everything is normal. This network is compromised and completely open to the attacker! The protections normally in place, specifically *Air Gap* and *anti-malware* software should have protected the industrial control side, but it didn't.

Mr. Sean McGurk, the Director of National Cybersecurity and Communications Integration Center (NCCIC) at the Department of Homeland Security put it best:

In our experience in conducting hundreds of vulnerability assessments in the private sector, in no case have we ever found the operations network, the SCADA system or energy management system separated from the enterprise network. On average, we see 11 direct connections between those networks. In some extreme cases, we have identified up to 250 connections between the actual producing network and the enterprise network.[9] --The Subcommittee on National Security, Homeland Defense, and Foreign Operations May 25, 2011 hearing. 58:30 -- 59:00

The air gap didn't exist. It hardly ever does. The anti-virus software didn't catch the malware either and it's supposed to be the best available, but this code was new, smart and polymorphic. It was able to change the way it looks in memory, its signature, fooling the anti-malware and slipping past to do its dirty work.

Scenario Two: A Shopping Spree

A young lady sitting at the console running the HMI software on the SCADA network is a bit bored. With nothing else to do she opens a browser and

Table 2. Sample attack vectors

Attack Type	Attack Vector
Social Engineering	1. Browser based malware 2. Outside hardware based malware 3. Phishing
Perimeter Breach	1. Unused open ports 2. Default passwords (VPN, Login, RDP,...) 3. Unstable DMZ machines 4. Open modem pools 5. Misconfigured firewalls

surfs out to a site that sells inexpensive knockoff shoes. There are banners and videos galore showing off the latest in faux fashion and she clicks on one that says "Sneak a peek at what's coming" and a PDF catalog opens up. She pages through the document for a while, finally closing her browser when she's done. Behind the scenes, the second that the Adobe Reader software loaded the PDF, code embedded in the PDF exploited the reader and loaded its own code onto the system and started to run. Seeing that the it was actually on an HMI it set itself up as a root kitted man in the middle and takes over the SCADA network. The anti-malware that was supposed to stop this from happening didn't catch it because the code rewrote itself as it was loading and came out looking like nothing that the anti-malware recognized, giving the virus free rein on the system. That malware not only controls the HMI it installed itself in, but also now has access to the internet to call out and freely download what ever it wants, such as a controller attack module, and it has adequate privileges, because its installed on a control system, to access and infect any other workstation or controller on the network.

In a recent [2011] survey by the Ponemon Institute it was found that 96% of the organizations interviewed in the utilities and energy sectors believed both that SCADA security is their largest problem and that it is the hardest to address. Of those interviewed, 43% identified the largest security threats to their systems were "Negligent Users" and 40% identified "Insecure Web Applications."[10]

The ICS Context

There's nothing special about either of these attacks, they are simple social engineering techniques and are extremely effective. They happen every day all over the world to millions of people. The problem is that the malware is infecting critical infrastructure (CI) and, if specifically targeted can do real damage.

Measuring the effect on an attack against critical infrastructure requires a paradigm shift. We can't measure the cost of such an attack in the way we would an attack on a bank for example. With a bank we're looking at theft of credit cards and it's easy to measure how much is spent using those stolen cards and how much it costs to turn them off and replace them for their customers.

In an ICS environment we need to measure damage in terms of *loss of life, cost of recovery, environmental impact and global/regional economic impact.* Attacks against ICS facilities are aimed at "soft targets" such as hydroelectric dams, electrical distribution power stations and transmission towers, chemical manufacturing, petroleum refining and fuel transport, irrigation systems, large-scale HVAC systems, the nuclear industry—and other things that have the possibility of going boom and are controlled using software.

The type of attack that can be easily executed, the nature of the targets and the potentially disastrous result of exploit makes it imperative to lock down as much of the attack surface as possible and deny attackers access to vulnerabilities they can exploit and damage systems. This chapter is focused on isolating critical attack vectors, beginning at the application level and expanding out to the network perimeter, and applying mitigation techniques that reduce the attack surface to near zero exploitable vectors.

Secure Separation of Duties

ICS networks used to manage processes and Enterprise networks used to manage business are supposed to be physically separated and have their own perimeter defenses. The operating principle is that the separation protects the control systems from any damage from an attack on the enterprise network and vice versa. In reality, it is highly unlikely that such a separation exists. There are too many shared systems such as email, management dashboards, VoIP Soft PBX telephone and video monitoring systems that provide hard paths between networks and breaking the air gap. From a network management standpoint there are perimeter issues that come into play, for example a help desk application that's needed by both networks is placed in the DMZ so that it can be accessed by both internal networks and remote sites. Another example might be an FTP server in the DMZ used by the control system to push regulatory data for collection by an appropriate agent. While this should be set up as a one way/outbound only connection, it is simple to make the mistake of installing a bi-directional firewall rule, perhaps to allow the regulatory agency to drop off information for pick up by the control system operators (See Figure 3).

A secure ICS network is one where the critical processes remain active and that the controllers and management systems are not compromised. The job of locking down a network is huge and there are too many moving parts to consider all at once. When presented with a security problem of this magnitude there are two directions one can take: perimeter in or control system out.

The perimeter in approach involves the redesign of the network infrastructure so that breaking through the firewalls from the outer perimeter/DMZ or other vector is impossible, thereby protecting the critical processes. The control system out approach locks down the computers and devices that comprise the control system and makes sure that the software on the systems is untouchable and that users cannot make stupid mistakes that allow attackers to plant malware on control systems. Both approaches have their benefits and drawbacks, however they are both just starting points and the organization will end

up doing both ends and everything in the middle, so the decision is which is a greater exposure and which can be implemented quickly enough and is strong enough to protect critical systems while the rest of the infrastructure is being configured. In almost all cases, since it's the control software and its users that are a) the primary target of the attacker and b) the largest general attack surface, it makes sense to use the control system out method and protect the workstations and system from malware and negligent users.

The rest of this chapter is dedicated to identifying hardening opportunities and applying appropriate technology, policies and configurations to the problems and establish a baseline for complete hardening of the control system network.

ADDRESSING THE PROBLEM SPACE

The social engineering examples above illustrate a simple method of attack that takes advantage of both human nature and technical ignorance. Defending against such a broad vector is very difficult, and yet it is just one vector of many that hackers may use to penetrate and take over a network.

Figure 3. A simple proper parallel network configuration

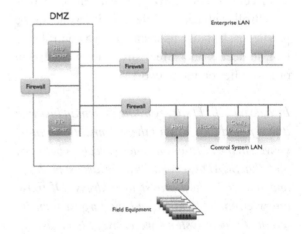

Penetrating networks is a process of discovery where the key items are mistakes made in the networks implementation such as finding an Internet facing workstation or device that still has the default administrator username and passwords active, thus providing a simple vector to take over the control system or compromise the network with malware. Other attacks are much more complicated, involving techniques that exploit buffer overflow vulnerabilities that allow attackers to execute arbitrary code on systems and take them over with administrative privileges. Whatever vector they exploit, the target is the same, control system software and hardware.

Once the attacker has taken over a control system, s/he has several options to employ depending on their goal. If the goal is to destroy the system they can just put the device into an operating state that causes the control system to destroy itself and the mechanisms it manages. If the goal is to take over the network and use it for evil: industrial espionage, terrorist weapons, propagation to other systems or something equally as bad, then the attacker will likely try a *Man in the Middle (MitM)* attack that will give them long term and absolute control over the control system.

The Man in the Middle

A MitM attack installs a piece of software between the control system and the devices or processes it controls, and makes it appear to both the device and the controller that things are operating normally, while the MitM is actually making bad things happen.

Take for example the Human Machine Interface (HMI) in SCADA. The malware embeds itself in the system, probably as a root kit, making it completely invisible to the users, operating system and control software, and potentially egress through the network firewall and establish communications with the attackers platform. Once appropriately ensconced, the malware would intercept every HMI command and return an appropriate value

that indicates the command was executed successfully. The malware, having fooled the HMI software is now free to do what ever it likes and send whatever commands it wants to the devices being controlled, effectively replacing the HMI completely and able to do whatever nasty things the attacker defined for it.

Security mechanisms including passwords, MAC address resolution and any other host based security protections are completely useless as the man in the middle software has control of all the I/O and can just intercept any streams and extract any information it needs, hence it never needs to do any heavy lifting such as password cracking; it's all taken care of and the malware is in complete control.

A man in the middle attack can be devastating and once installed the only way to clear it out is likely to turf the control system and restore from an earlier backup, and hope that the backup isn't itself infected (See Figure 4).

Protection

As described earlier, control system software typically requires a very specific environment in which to run and any changes, such as closing ports that the software relies on or even pinging the wrong port, can quickly bring down a complete system. For this reason, control system administrators are hesitant to introduce any change such as patching or upgrading software for fear that it will cause an outage. A specific example of this is the Microsoft® Windows XP/SP2[11] upgrade. XP/SP2 was a massive update released by Microsoft to address the security vulnerabilities in the earlier versions. They were under terrific pressure by industry and government to fix the security problems and they did so by adding features such as Data Execution Prevention (DEP), support for the NX[12] (Never Execute) bit, the Security Center which provided Software Restriction Policies, a new and improved version of the local firewall and the removal of things like raw socket support. Overall the patch

Figure 4. Man in the middle attack structure

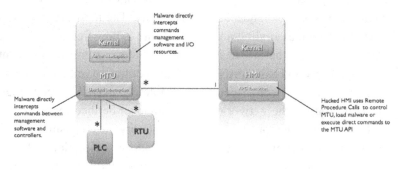

achieved the goal of making XP more secure, however caused more than a few problems for upgraders in all industry sectors which resulted in slower uptake than would be expected given the demand for it.

Improving security means changes to the way things are configured and operate in order to reduce its attack surface and eliminate vulnerabilities that could be exploitable attack vectors. The XP/SP2 attack surface reduction, which was a dramatic improvement to the operating system unfortunately, rendered hundreds of software applications inoperable, with some being unrecoverable regardless of configuration changes. This is the case in much of the control system space and is one reason why we see so many vulnerable, unpatched machines in facilities.

There are several approaches to the problems and just as many objections to the solutions, for example Table 3 which highlights some typical ones:

Solutions to Consider

Organizations that are serious about securing their systems have to step up and make the required changes regardless of the level of effort; however the strategy does not have to be complicated. Here's what's known generally about the ICS environment:

1. Network users unaware of dangers or simply negligent in their system usage may undermine security. Users are allowed to have unmanaged applications on their systems such as Internet browsers, PDF readers and email, all of which are vectors for phishing and other click and run attacks.

2. Security may be undermined due to poorly protected machines that may not be running proper malware protection systems or improperly configured access control and/ or authentication mechanisms.

3. Security may be undermined by the use of antiquated or poorly maintained equipment. For example the XP/SP2 patch broke a large number of applications because of the default port lockdown that in turn broke control software dependent on those ports. The amount of time required to understand the changes and adjust for them is considered excessive in a production environment, hence its deferred or ignored.

4. Security may be undermined because the attack surface of a typical industrial control system (ICS) is large and situational awareness is poor. For example, the combination of ineffective DMZ configurations, firewall rules, poor intrusion detection and intrusion prevention systems (IDS/IPS) make it difficult to keep attackers out.

Table 3. Objections

Option	Solution	Implementation	Objection
System Upgrade	Replace control system hardware and software with secure systems	Purchase new hardware and control software, burn it in and then replace the existing system	The new software may work differently and/or not support the existing controllers. Equipment purchase and training may be prohibitively expensive
Install Anti-Virus	Add an antivirus package to the HMI or Control Station	Purchase Antivirus tool and subscription, install and execute	The processing overhead may be too high for the machine its installed on The AV may not support the level op operating system installed on the control machine There would need to be a port opened in the firewall to get updates to the AV database
Apply Security Policies	Use embedded security policy support	Define and apply specific security policies to the systems and control access to them	The policy management software may not be available at the patch level of the systems
Install Virtual Machines	Replace existing stand alone systems with VM	Move existing management system image into a VM and move the VM to heavy duty secure iron	Putting the control software into a VM does not make it less vulnerable
Segment the network	Break the network into subnets/unflatten	Create specific subnets for process controllers and control software making it more difficult for hackers to locate and exploit systems	Changing the IP addresses may crash the entire system due to explicit dependencies Adding routers increases the network attack surface and may be exploitable It won't protect against negligent users It may degrade usability unacceptably – this is probably why the network wasn't segmented in the first place.
Encrypt I/O Traffic	Implement SSH/SSL/some other standardized security protocol for over the wire communications	Configure all the control systems and controllers to use encrypted communications to block network sniffers	Some controllers don't support encrypted communications Different portions of the control systems use software with different encryption mechanisms and are not compatible Encrypting I/O may cause the system to crash if a machine that doesn't supported is used (e.g. a machine on the network that nobody remembers)
Implement Authentication	Implement appropriate authentication and authorization for all system components	Change all default passwords and implement strict machine to machine/user to machine authentication and authorization based on roles and implement the rule of "least privilege"	Some machines will crash the entire system if the default password is changed Implementing authorization and authentication would require the addition of a management system Negligent users would just write their passwords on their office whiteboard For systems in which the users are distributed, user management can be difficult and failure to add or remove user permissions in a timely manner can lead to breaches or system failures.

5. Security may be undermined because management prioritizes production and regulation over security, where *availability* trumps *confidentiality*, creating a potentially insecure environment.

There are several other considerations including improper use of authentication and authorization mechanisms such as leaving default passwords on databases[13] or workstations, failing to encrypt network I/O traffic, failing to password protect remote procedure call (RPC) interfaces and many other all too common IT management failures. The key point is that the perimeter defenses are weak and allows hackers easy access to control software that is virtually unprotected, and is therefore an uncontested attack vector to allowing access to entire industrial control systems with minimal effort. Protecting control system networks requires a defense in depth strategy that involves the application of some specialized software and a lot of basic network configuration common sense.

Phase I – Protect the Weak Workstation

The ultimate target of an attack is the control workstation, specifically the HMI, master terminal units (MTU), master control stations (MCS), and Data Historians (DH). These are the systems that have access to all the important bits including RTUs, PLCs, IEDs, Process Control Rules and Data. Should these systems be significantly hardened, the attack surface is dramatically reduced, changing the game from a simple software attack vector to a physical attack vector. Techniques such as attack surface reduction and system whitelisting are key to success in the hardening process and, properly configured a system can be very resistant to attack, therefore blocking the attackers path to other critical devices and/or systems (See Figure 5).

Similar approaches have been applied to web facing systems to protect support infrastructure, specifically Web Application Firewalls (WAF). These systems are good Band-Aids that can be applied to protect weak systems while the actual software is being hardened and finally redeployed obviating the need for the bolt on WAF protection. With web applications it's a useful approach, but it doesn't work well with workstations, embedded systems or other PCs. What does work is *whitelisting* the systems, constraining them to only run a predefined, trusted set of applications and nothing else. Doing this means that malware brought onto the system by a click on a browser or email link

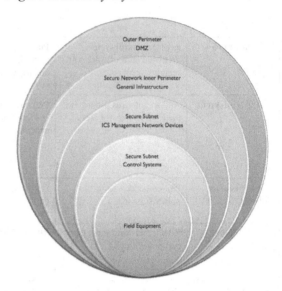

Figure 5. Security layers

won't run, arbitrary code loaded from a remote buffer overflow exploit won't run, in fact, nothing that hasn't been explicitly authorized to execute, can run making it impossible for malware to get a foothold. Most IT folks don't think highly of whitelisting because it limits the flexibility of systems and users gripe about it to no end. It's understandable in a general computing environment where change is a daily thing and flexibility is needed, but in a control system whose sole purpose is to manage critical infrastructure and processes, there's no logical reason why anything should need to change, hence a whitelisting strategy makes real sense (See Figure 6).

The advantages to the whitelisting approach are clear. If there are no attack vectors to exploit, there's no way that a man in the middle system can be installed, which then protects all the downstream devices. That goes a long way to protecting the entire ICS; SCADA software and otherwise. Unlike the WAF, which is considered a bit of a Band-Aid™, the whitelist protection is a core portion of the overall solution rather than an intermediate solution used while the organization fixes their vulnerable applications or the network is reconfigured.

There are several issues with whitelisting that need to be addressed before it can be completely trusted in a production environment. Specifically:

1. Care must be taken not to whitelist malware, defeating the purpose of installing the system in the first place.
2. Systems should not rely on a centralized database of "Known Safe" application signatures or other ID mechanisms. Someone *will* figure out how to spoof a signature and get malware on the system eventually.
3. The problem of malware propagation from system to system must be managed and make sure that whitelisted applications are tied directly to the machine they're supposed to run on.
4. There must be a mechanism for safely applying needed updates to vendor applications and operating systems as needed without requiring a round trip across the Internet.
5. The malware protection system must be able to stop zero day attacks and self rewriting/ polymorphic code that may be hidden in trusted applications.
6. One must be sure that the protection system is capable of stopping an attack borne from a chip containing malware on the system motherboard (supply chain attack).

In the meantime while researchers are perfecting software whitelisting systems, the responsibility falls to the IT manager who must take the following steps to prepare and harden systems prior to installing an antimalware system:

1. Execute a complete virus scan using a reliable scanner that will run on the machine, regardless of age or patch level of the operating system. Ensure that the tool used is capable of locating rootkits, kernel based things, and other "intermittent" malware that pops up occasionally to look around for targets of opportunity but is otherwise benign.
2. Engage in a complete attack surface reduction exercise that includes the following activities:
    a. Reducing the number of running applications to the absolute minimum required by the system to operate. The more code running on a system the larger the attack surface, so getting rid of unnecessary processes and files reduces opportunities. An example is the most widely used portable document file (PDF) Reader which when launched loads hundreds of dynamic link libraries (DLL) for things like native language support. Instead of loading just the current localization it loads the support files for all of the languages it supports making it a target rich environment for hackers.
    b. Reduce the number of authorized users to the minimum required to run the system. The fewer users that have access to the system the fewer opportunities hackers have to execute password attacks (dictionary attacks, crack attacks etc.) and further reducing the attack surface.
    c. Set up the authentication and authorization policies on the system to provide the lowest privilege levels possible for all objects and allow the station to run. This way even if an application vulnerability is successfully exploited, the highest permission level the attacker can get is too low to do any real reconnaissance or damage.
    d. Locate and change any default username/passwords (cisco/cisco) on the system and change them to secure, unique passwords; and ensuring that the change doesn't affect any other dependent systems or systems it depends on.

Figure 6. Block attacks upstream to protect weak devices

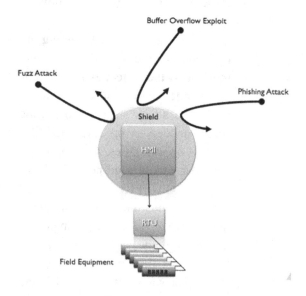

e. Reduce the number of open ports to the absolute minimum required by the devices the system manages. Any unnecessary and unused open port is an attack vector. Ports that are open and in use are safer because the port can only be used by a single process at a time.

f. Patch the remaining applications and operating system to the highest level possible without "breaking" any vendor software.

g. Ensure that all network I/O is encrypted where possible. Implementing IPSec or other point-to-point encryption will greatly hinder an attackers ability to leverage data flowing across the network for exploits.

3. Document the configuration of the machine completely and attach it to the system in such a way as to be visible and not easily removed.

4. Erase critical information from whiteboards, locate and destroy usernames and passwords written on slips of paper and left in drawers etc.

5. Train staff in Network, Information, Application and General Security Awareness.

If you close your eyes and listen very carefully, you should be able to hear the screams of ICS network managers all over the world... They're saying *"That will take forever and I can't take the machines offline long enough to do all of that and keep on schedule—it's impossible!!!"* Well they're right, it will take a long time but it will be worth it. This is a good time to segue into leveraging some well-vetted modern software technology to allow them to do the needed work and not take the systems offline for any significant amount of time. That would be virtual machines (VM).

Virtual Machine Usage

Leveraging VMs is a simple way to work on live systems while not interrupting any running processes, one just duplicates the running control system in a VM and do all the work there, and then rotate the VM into position to take over for the original "live" system. In addition to allowing access to the critical software offline, it also provides an opportunity to upgrade the underlying hardware, potentially improving performance, stability and general security.

The first step is taking a virtual image of the workstation and using it as the system to lock down, thus allowing IT staff to do all the work without halting any critical processes for any longer than it takes to suck the original system image into a VM. Once the required attack surface work is done in the VM the decision needs to be made whether to drop the new VM on top of the old hardware, which can now be brought up to spec without concerns about damaging the system, or put it on a brand new host running nothing but a secure native hypervisor[14] as shown in Figure 7 - The "Portable" HMI. In either case, the control system is offline for a minimum amount of time and is now not only secured, but flexible enough to be moved around to different hardware platforms.

Additional benefits to this approach are:

1. Immunity from host hardware failure. If the physical machine fails the VM can be quickly moved to another machine and minimize any downtime.
2. The primary VM can be quickly cloned and the clone used to do all updates and system testing to ensure no breakage occurs, and then be swapped back in as the primary. The original primary held as an emergency backup in case something does go wrong with the new one.
3. Performance gains from new hardware could improve the performance of the overall processing system and improve reliability from advances in system architecture and resilience by the use of technologies such as DELL's DDPE[15], Trusted Platform Modules (TPM)[16] or other built in security technologies from Intel and other vendors.
4. If a VM is successfully attacked, it can quickly be taken offline, sandboxed and replaced by a backup VM. The sandboxed VM can then be forensically analyzed and the vulnerability discovered and addressed in the new running VM.

One thing to note while using virtual machines is that the thought is that since they're VMs, one can stack a few of them, each doing different jobs, on a single hardware platform and save a few bucks. This is a false economy because if the hardware breaks, instead of having one control system go down, lots of them go down at the same time. It's better to be safe than sorry in an ICS environment and keep the systems separate, one VM per computer, and one backup computer and one backup VM ready to swap in at a moments notice in case of failure.

Subnet Lockdown

The final phase of the control system lockdown is to put all the systems and devices onto a secure, firewalled subnet that will isolate them from the rest of the ICS network. This may be done immediately after the control systems are finished being configured, or prior to beginning the configuration. As with all changes, care must be taken to understand the dependency relationships between systems and ensure that access to devices that do not belong on the subnet are severed or the device, or a proxy device is brought onto the subnet.

Sub-netting the control systems addresses some weaknesses inherent in some of the systems software, for example, if someone does a port scan using a tool like NMAP, it might cause the control system to restart or crash an embedded device, so pains should be taken to make sure that access to the control systems is strictly controlled. Putting all the systems on a secure, access-controlled subnet raises another barrier to attackers and helps to further protect weak ICS software and hardware. This protection becomes stronger if the ICS subnet firewall is configured to allow outbound traffic only; however if there has to be any inbound traffic, firewall rules for the subnet should be considered as follows:

1. What users must have access and why?
2. What systems must to have access and why?
3. What IT Services need to be provided (DNS, AD, NTP, syslog) and why?

If there is an absolute requirement to allow ingress to the subnet implement both hosts and network firewalls with:

1. "Trusted paths" to users
2. "Trusted channels" to other devices
3. Use the golden rule: *That which is not specifically allowed is denied*[17]

Figure 7. The "portable" HMI

Implementation is best begun with a clean firewall that will eliminate any problems with legacy rules and other long forgotten and undocumented configuration items. Assuming that the sub-netting activity is new, transitioning from a flat network topology, then the use of a clear firewall is an absolute requirement.

The perfect configuration is one where there are no inbound connections to the subnet, just outbound connections for providing situational awareness and regulatory information flow. In this configuration all interaction with the devices would need to occur on devices within the subnet, thus eliminating any network based intrusion possibility but maintaining key data flows required for situational awareness, regulatory flows and emergency alarms etcetera.

With a blank slate *whitelisting* trusted users and channels is simple and the rule-set can easily be kept to a minimum and grown as needed. During the rule development exercise careful attention must be paid to the source devices, making sure that there are no inbound connections allowed from the DMZ, other Internet facing devices and if possible, from the enterprise network.

Once the subnet is securely configured and all the necessary devices and systems are proven to be working properly, the process of securing the rest of the network can begin, one defense level at a time out to the main ICS network and beyond.

Wireless Networking

Using wireless on the control network should be avoided if possible however if they are required for things like drive-by analysis by management laptops, portable HMI devices or the like, ensure that a) they are secured using *WPA2 at a minimum*, b) they are locked into the control system subnet only and c) SSID broadcast, and ICMP are off. One open WAP running WEP[18], or heaven forbid no security, can defeat all of the protection offered by the subnet and provide instant access to other computers, smartphones, tablets and whatever other wireless devices happen to be around!

Network Attached PLC/RTU

Until now the primary topic has been controllers directly attached terminal units or control stations, which in the global sense are straightforward to secure. Many controllers may be directly attached to the network using plug in Ethernet modules and use TCP/IP, UDP/IP, ICCP, OPC or Modbus TCP. The devices themselves may be running full operating systems such as VxWorks, RT Linux Windows Embedded or they may be bare metal with just enough control logic to extract protocol payloads (DNP3/MODBUS) to manage onboard control logic (See Figure 8).

Securing these controllers requires the same type of protection as the control stations with devices attached but due to the diversity of configurations. The immediate solution must be a "One Size Fits All" approach that isolates the subnet with the controllers using the same rigid firewall as described earlier, though the number of *trusted paths and channels* to the devices will be minimal, limited to the control stations that manage them, or preferably none and all management is done within the subnet. Additionally the application attack surface should be analyzed and locked down in the same manner as the control stations, for example, many PLCs use home built HTTP and SMTP servers[19] that are clear attack vectors and need to be tightly managed, accomplished by specifically configuring them to communicate only with devices on the secure subnet they're connected too, which may then be passed upstream by a secure connection to higher level systems such as HMIs and Master Historians (See Figure 9).

There are a few other key items that should be considered when locking down control system and device networks. Many of them will seem to be taking steps back in time and making things more difficult, however they do increase the control IT has over the environment. Here's the list:

1. **Assign Static TCP/IP Addresses:** Using DHCP for assigning addresses in a general networking environment is acceptable and simplifies the management of devices the flit on and off the network. In a control system subnet, consistency is the key. Assign a static IP to each device and document it thoroughly including the TCP/IP address, MAC address, O/S, Date of Service, Duty/ Maintenance Cycle and connection type (hardwire or wireless).

2. **Use Subnet Local DNS:** Each subnet should do its own name resolution and not rely on a network wide system.

3. **Block ICMP Requests:** The subnet firewall should block all mechanisms that can be used for reconnaissance.

4. **Restrict Broadcast Capabilities to the Subnet:** Limit UDP broadcasts to the subnet only, further isolating the subnet.

5. **Connect Routers and Firewalls to the Outside using IPSec:** Encrypting traffic on the subnet may not be possible as network attached PLC and RTU operating systems might not support it, however there's no reason that communications going out of the subnet or coming to the subnet cannot be encrypted, and lock down a clear attack vector.

6. **Enable Outgoing Process, Syslog and Event Data:** The data needed by IT, process control et al must be fed a continuous stream of data from the subnet to maintain situational awareness and reporting compliance.

Note that the items specified here describe much of the functionality provided by a vLAN and that is intentional. The operating assumption is that the ICS is built using older equipment that once put in place, isn't touched very much. Firewalls and routers that are already on site can likely be configured effectively to provide high levels of security. If the routers on the site can support vLAN or the organization will purchase new equipment to support the security enablement exercise, then it would make sense to consider it.

SITUATIONAL AWARENESS

Knowing the base and current state of the network is critical to preventing cyberattacks.

Properly configuring the network is key to hardening against attack, but there's always the possibility that something could change on the network and that the change could open a gap in the perimeter that can allow an attacker through. There's always the chance that an employee may turn out to be a spy and hack away from the inside. Mitigating this risk is a matter of *constant monitoring* to establish situational awareness and *active management* of all network components and traffic. Data feeding a proper system will include log files, event management systems, network management systems, traffic analyzers, intrusion detection systems and other key sources, all of which is correlated and analyzed for known malicious patterns and unknown/previously unseen behavior on the wire and/or devices that could potentially be malicious (See Figure 10).

Good situational awareness not only allows the mitigation of threats to networks and systems but also general security management. Many events that end up in logs result from changes to equipment that could lead to vulnerabilities. Users manually changing security policies or setting up personal wireless access points are good examples of simple changes to networks that network managers must be quickly aware of so they can mitigate any vulnerabilities Failing equipment that force traffic rerouting such as a failover to an old, less secure modem bank is another class of problem that has to be quickly managed. Many other examples can be called out though the point is the same—effective security management requires complete awareness of network components and user activities.

Summary

Industrial control system networks are very different from standard IT networks. The manifold challenges faced in the ICS space include dealing with older, less reliable equipment and software that needs to be completely protected so the processes it manages run uninterrupted. Unlike IT networks, ICS network equipment can rarely just be rebooted to solve a pesky problem or a wireless access point added to replace and aging physical switch. ICS networks also suffer from organic growth. As computing and control equipment gets cheaper and organizations trend to purchasing commercial off the shelf equipment and installing it without a clear security plan, opening further vulnerabilities.

Measuring impact of cyber attacks in the ICS space is also very different from that in normal IT. Attacks in IT are generally about loss of money and information and are ranked based on how much. ICS attacks are measured in terms of loss of life, environmental impact, recovery duration and productivity. Very different metrics and considerably more critical than losing a few credit card numbers.

The techniques described in this chapter allow ICS network managers to lock down control systems using common IT best practices to address key security deficiencies. The defense in depth architecture focuses on the core process and works outward to the perimeter, adding levels of security at every stage, making the system secure. The techniques leverage age-old isolation, unidirectional data and control flow, equipment level configuration and virtualization that may be applied incrementally, thereby reducing the magnitude of change and any issues that may arise from doing too much, too quickly.

The techniques also bridge the gap between enterprise IT managers and ICS network managers and provides them with a common vernacular and sets of security management goals that are critical to halting propagation of attacks on the IT network to the ICS network in such a way as to protect the control systems and not require the cutting of cables to establish a physical air-gap.

Cyber security is a dynamic field that changes very rapidly. Attackers are working every minute to find new ways to breach security and other threats such as quantum computers that can crack widely used public key protocols in seconds, portable devices such as phones and tablets that are easily turned into attack platforms and unwittingly brought onto the network by uninformed or negligent users who are the targets of social engineering.

Application of the security techniques described in this chapter will make resilient networks and provide a solid basis for protecting our global

Figure 8. Simple subnet structure and data flow

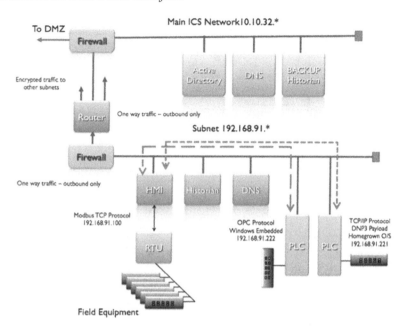

critical infrastructure; but cyberspace is a dangerous place and as such managers need to be ever vigilant in the protection of systems, staff and ultimately, the process.

FUTURE RESEARCH DIRECTIONS

Aspects of cyber security cross many disciplines and provide rich avenues of exploration. We've seen that cyber attacks cross boundaries of human nature, hardware vulnerability, software vulnerability, system design and many other hard and soft areas. Much of the challenge is in the area of trust; can a controller trust that the commands it receives are legitimate? Can the control system trust that the operator of the system is issuing proper commands to the control system network? Is the cryptography used to protect communications between devices unbroken and trustworthy? These things and more are critical to the security of not only control system networks, but networks of all types and uses—each of which is critical to operations in their particular sectors.

Social Engineering Awareness and Training Systems

Social engineering is one of the hacker's most powerful tools. If a person can be convinced to hand over a password to a network and s/he can gain physical access it may be game over for the ICS. Social engineering is a broad category and encompasses phishing, tailgating, online chatting, social networking and a host of other venues and the information that can be gained is enormous.

All the time and expense put into securing networks and software are useless against someone who charmed the admin password out of someone who works in processing facility after hours in a bar. With this in mind, serious consideration needs to be paid to the topic of Security awareness and the effects of social engineering. Simple things like not writing your access codes on the back of your magnetic key card to making sure that your briefcase or pocketbook is always closed when you're not actually using anything in it are big issues that employees, particularly those working in critical infrastructure, must be aware of. The

Figure 9. Sample segmented ICS network

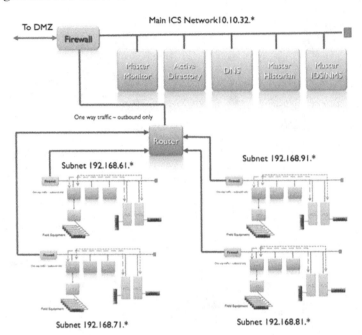

fact is that there are people constantly attacking from all angles, whether it's from a social or cyber standpoint it makes no difference, knowledge is power, defensive power in an age where we need it.

Portable Device Attestation

Man in the middle attacks are the most destructive types of attack in ICS/SCADA and need to be addressed as a separate class of protection for control station TCP/IP based controllers. In section I we discussed the mechanism for tightly locking down control stations and isolating them from attack, presumably making them safe and secure. The nature of the hacker mindset does not allow them to stop trying, particularly when it comes to terrorism or industrial espionage. It is altogether possible that over time someone will discover a chink in some piece of software and exploit it to get around our protections, but more likely, some insider will infiltrate a facility and turn off the control system protections, and install the man in the middle, white list it and then put everything back the way it was found.

A successful man in the middle system is typically installed as a *root kit*[20] and is extremely difficult to find. In order to protect the control systems there needs to be a way to uniquely identify each actor (system, device, …) and should any

Figure 10. Simple intrusion detection

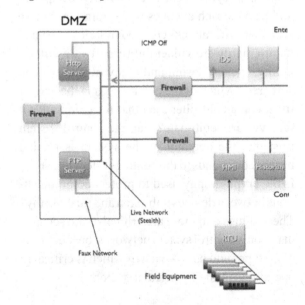

other device receive a command, it should be able to execute it with confidence that its source is legitimate.

There are several paths one can take to implement a system but the *model* has already been defined by the Trusted Computing Module (TCM)[21], a chip that ships on most all laptop and recently, server and workstation hardware. TPMs provide several unique functions for system protection, but the two most interesting at this point are measurement and attestation.

Post Quantum Cryptography

Modern cryptographic systems are rapidly becoming obsolete both through the application of brute force mathematics as in the case of the RSA 768 bit GSM[22] crack, and by the imminent availability of Quantum Computers as witnessed by Google using a D-Wave adiabatic quantum effect computing machine for image searching and matching, the announcement by NIST of a working 2 qubit quantum computer and the application of that quantum computer to calculate the precise energy of molecular hydrogen by a coordinated research team including Harvard University in Cambridge, MA and the University of Queensland in Brisbane, Australia. The events in the cryptography space and the speed at which they are occurring is a clear indication of the need for rapid change in how we protect information, be it at rest or in motion, and cease relying on what is in effect antique [in terms of internet time] technology for that protection.

Platform Integrity

The TPM using the TSS[23] and BIOS combine to provide a "Root of Trust" and uses a set of platform configuration registers (PCR) to store metrics collected by the TPM describing the configuration of the host; and allows the TPM to test for configuration differences between system boots. Should the metrics change between boots the system is assumed compromised and therefore

untrusted. If there is a table available to all actors on the network that can be consulted to verify the identity of each actor and its trustworthiness, each system can require attestation data and validate each actor before accepting commands.

In concept this simple attestation mechanism would do the trick, however in and ICS environment its full of holes, specifically:

1. Control systems are not typically rebooted regularly so the platform integrity check function would not be accurate if the system was changed and not rebooted
2. Most older workstations do not have TPM chips installed so coverage on an ICS network could be inconsistent
3. PLCs, RTUs, IEDs etcetera may not be embedded PC based and not have TPMs or software support
4. If an attacker has managed to crack into a machine s/he may be able to alter attestation table to match the new configuration

In general, it's a problem of homogeny and not easily solved by relying on the presence of any specific hardware. A simpler solution would be to implement similar functionality in software and execute periodic self-analyses of the platform and running software, and use that to generate a unique value that can then be used as an attestation value. The advantage to this path is that unexpected changes to the system could be quickly identified and reported to network management, who can then take immediate action to mitigate the issue such as moving in the last known good VM, if it is a control station.

This path, being pure software, opens to possibility of implementing versions on intelligent controllers running full operating systems such as RT Linux, VxWorks and QNX, and extend the reach of the attestation system further into the field and provide an alerting system that could be leveraged by network managers.

CONCLUSION

In many cases SCADA systems are built from older technology and it's a concern. Newer, more secure equipment is available but it's difficult for organizations to adopt it. The resistance to change is not one of stubbornness or lack of desire, but one of keeping the sometimes antique and nearly unmanaged infrastructure running by not breaking anything.

It is possible that through the application of sophisticated new system whitelisting technologies and virtualization that it is possible to lock down critical systems tightly enough to allow critical infrastructure managers to step back and breath without the constant fear of breach and catastrophe. Given this breathing room it will be possible to go back and apply secure network topology restructuring and the time needed to properly configure and lock down the ICS/SCADA hosts, devices and networks, including creating a resilient perimeter, a clear, unambiguous air gap between process control and business networks—and finally say goodbye to security through obscurity and hello to the modern resilience needed to protect our global critical infrastructure.

REFERENCES

Anderson, R. (2001). *Security engineering: A guide to building dependable systems*. Wiley & Sons, Inc.

Howard, M., & LeBlanc, D. (2003). *Writing secure code*. Microsoft Press.

Oriyano, S. P., & Gregg, M. (2011). *Hacker techniques, tools and incident handling*. Jones and Bartlett Learning.

Perlner, R. A., & Cooper, D. A. (2010). *Quantum resistant public key cryptography: A survey*. National Institute of Standards and Technology.

Shaw, W. T. (2006). *Cyber security for SCADA systems*. PennWell Corp.

Spellman, R., & Stoudt, M. L. (2011). *Nuclear infrastructure protection and homeland security*. Rowman & Littlefield.

Stevens, W. R. (2005). *TCP/IP illustrated: The protocols*. Addison Wesley.

Swiderski, F., & Snyder, W. (2004). *Treat modeling*. Microsoft Press.

Tsang, R. (2008). *Cyberthreats, vulnerabilities and attacks on SCADA networks*. Berkley University.

Weiss, J. (2010). *Protecting industrial control systems from electronic threats*. Momentum Press, LLC.

Young, S., & Aisle, D. (2002). *The hackers handbook: The strategy behind breaking into and defending networks*. Auerbach Publications.

KEY TERMS AND DEFINITIONS

Cybersecurity: A generalized term used to describe resilience in computers and other intelligent electronic devices that comprise the systems we use to manage information, control systems, defense systems and other critical infrastructure.

Firewall: An intelligent electronic device used to manage communications flow from one network to another or from one system to another. Firewalls are configurable using rules and physical connections and are meant to protect networks and other systems from malicious software.

Human Machine Interface (HMI): A specific computer or collection of computers used to manage devices and processes in a SCADA environment on an Industrial Control System network.

IPSec: A protocol suite for securing communications between systems by authenticating and encrypting IP Packets. The practice makes the use of "Packet Sniffers," which are software or devices that analyze IP traffic on the wire and used to attack networks, impossible unless the attacker has the appropriate credentials to decode the traffic.

Malware: Software developed to compromise computers, networks and other intelligent electronic devices typically with the intention of causing damage, stealing information or just being a nuisance.

Subnet: A section of a network isolated by the use of a different IP address and bordered by an electronic switch, router or firewall that require special rules to allow communications between networks and subnets. The intention of a subnet is to isolate network segments from one another for reasons ranging from system management, heterogeneous processing isolation to cybersecurity.

Virtual Machine (VM): A software version of a complete physical computer or intelligent electronic device that behaves exactly as a physical device but is mobile, able to move from one physical machine to another or to share a physical machine with other virtual machines. Virtual machines are implemented as Hypervisors where the VMs reside on a bare metal machine with no underlying operating system, or hosted where the virtual machines reside on a software platform running on top of an operating system.

WPA2: A strong authentication and encryption system to secure communications between network equipment and Wireless Access Points (WAP) used to interface with physical networks.

ENDNOTES

1   http://www.globalsecurity.org/wmd/world/iran/natanz.htm

2   Def: http://en.wikipedia.org/wiki/Security_through_obscurity

3   http://www.cybersecurityuae.com/latest-news/news1/

4   http://www.us-cert.gov/control_systems/ics-cert/

5   http://www.securityincidents.org/

6   Industrial control systems: UNIFIED APPROACH for improving cybersecurity - ICSJWG 13-Apr-2012

7   http://www.langner.com/en/2010/11/14/stuxnet-attacker-profiling/

8   http://www.us-cert.gov/

9   Source: The Subcommittee on National Security, Homeland Defense, and Foreign Operations May 25, 2011 hearing. 58:30 -- 59:00

10   Source: 2011 Ponemon Institute survey "State of IT Security: Study of Utilities and Energy Companies"

11   "How to obtain the latest Windows XP service pack". March 26, 2007. Archived from the original on March 13, 2011. Retrieved September 21, 2007.

12   http://en.wikipedia.org/wiki/NX_bit

13   http://osvdb.org/66441

14   http://en.wikipedia.org/wiki/Hypervisor

15   http://www.dell.com/us/business/p/ddpe-enterprise-edition/pd

16   http://www.trustedcomputinggroup.org/resources/trusted_platform_module_tpm_summary

17   Network Perimeter Security: Building Defense In-Depth□, Rigs, Cliff CRC Press, Oct 27, 2003

18   http://www.computerworld.com/s/article/9015559/Don_t_use_WEP_for_Wi_Fi_security_researchers_say

19   http://www.automationdirect.com/static/specs/h0ecomx.pdf

20   http://en.wikipedia.org/wiki/Root_kit

21   http://en.wikipedia.org/wiki/Trusted_Platform_Module

22   http://www.bit-tech.net/news/bits/2010/01/13/researchers-crack-768-bit-rsa/1

23   http://securityinnovation.com/products/trusted-computing/

Chapter 10
A Community–Oriented Approach to CIIP in Developing Countries

Ian Ellefsen
University of Johannesburg, South Africa

Sebastiaan von Solms
University of Johannesburg, South Africa

ABSTRACT

Developing countries are fast becoming players in an increasingly interconnected world. Many developing countries are making use of technological solutions to address unique challenges. However, in many cases, this growth is not accompanied with the development of appropriate information infrastructure protection structures. As technological solutions are deployed in developing countries, there will be a large number of new users gaining access to Internet-based systems. In many cases, these new users might lack the skills necessary to identify computer security threats. Inadequate cyber security measures can increase the risk and impact of cyber attacks. The development of internal structures to address Critical Information Infrastructure Protection (CIIP) is dependent on the environment in which it will be deployed. Therefore, traditional CIIP structures might not adequately address the technological challenges found in developing countries. In this chapter, the authors aim to address the development of CIIP structures in developing regions by elaborating on the set of unique challenges that exist. Furthermore, they aim to present a community-oriented structure aimed at providing CIIP, in what they refer to as a "bottom-up" manner. The larger aim of CIIP structures in developing regions is to support the future development and deployment of cyber security mechanisms and to allow developing countries to play a trusted role in global cyber security efforts.

DOI: 10.4018/978-1-4666-2659-1.ch010

Copyright © 2013, IGI Global. Copying or distributing in print or electronic forms without written permission of IGI Global is prohibited.

INTRODUCTION

The developing world is experiencing unprecedented growth of broadband and communication technologies. The interconnectivity provided by these new technologies allows developing countries to interact on an international level. In many cases, the driving force behind the development of interconnecting technologies is in improved service delivery. The newfound level of interconnection allows many new users to become part of a growing global community.

The development of new interconnecting technologies can have the desired effect of improving the delivery of services, such as Governmental Services or Financial Services. However, it can also dramatically increase the number of global Internet users and Internet-enabled devices. These new users might not have been equipped with the skills to identify and manage many of the cyber threats that are prevalent on the Internet. Furthermore, it could be the case that systems that are connected to the Internet are without adequate cyber protection measures in place; this increases the potential for these systems to become infected with various forms of malware.

The global nature of the Internet compounds the above problem where unprotected systems can be affected by cyber attacks, and this can have global implications. With millions of new users, the potential threat to existing systems increases dramatically. In recent years, the impact of malware on critical system and SCADA devices has taken centre stage, and therefore the potential threat to global critical systems cannot be overlooked.

The impact of cyber attacks on existing systems is well understood, and as such, many countries create internal protection structures to identify and respond to threats and vulnerabilities. The development of Critical Information Infrastructure Protection (CIIP) structures, such as Computer Security Incident Response Teams (CSIRTs) is a well-established platform managing these threats. To combat the potential impact of cyber attacks on critical systems, developing countries should implement equivalent CIIP structures to address their growing cyber security needs.

However, this is easier said than done. In many cases the situation on the ground does not provide for an environment where a traditional CIIP structure could be developed directly. This is due to the development of CIIP structures being highly coupled to the environment where they will be deployed. Alternatively, the development of a traditional CIIP structures is limited by a number of political, legal, or social factors. To address these concerns, in this chapter we aim to discuss the development of community-oriented CIIP structures that are suitable for deployment within developing countries.

In a traditional environment, CIIP is provided in a "top-down" manner, with protection mechanism driven from a national or governmental level. Structures of this form are particularly sensitive to political and legal fluctuations. However, an alternative approach is to provide CIIP in a "bottom-up" manner. This approach relies on the development of community-oriented structures, where CIIP is driven in a less formal manner. Community-oriented structures provide a potential solution to the development of effective CIIP structures within developing countries.

Throughout this chapter we will discuss developing countries in the content of the African Continent. This is done to provide context to the content of this chapter. The status of "developing country" is very difficult to define, and often controversial in nature. For the sake of facilitating the discussion in this chapter we will consider "developing countries" to refer to countries listed as list as have a "developing economy" by the International Monitory Fund (IMF) as of April 2012 (IMF, 2012). In the following section we will outline the objectives of this chapter.

Objectives

In this chapter we will address the development of Critical Information Infrastructure Protection (CIIP) structures that can be deployed in developing countries and to elaborate on the necessity to develop appropriate CIIP structures. It is the objective of this chapter to identify the reasons for the creation of such a structure as it applies to the developing world, and to elaborate on the rationale for the development of such structures.

The further objective of this chapter is to discuss the development of a community-oriented CIIP structures that can be deployed in developing countries. We will address these objectives by presenting background into the development of information infrastructure within developing countries. We will then go on to discuss a number of risk factors that can influence the development of effective protection structures in a developing country. We will then go on to discuss the potential threats to existing systems, this discussion is not limited to purely a developing world context, but is discussed in terms of a wider global impact.

We will go on to discuss the development of CIIP structures within developing countries. To this end, we will provide a number of limitations of existing models within the framework of a developing country. To extend upon this discussion, we will elaborate the requirements for developing countries with respect to an effective CIIP structure. To set the stage for the sections to follow later in this chapter, we will then provide a comparison of "top-down" and "bottom-up" CIIP structures.

We will go on in the final part of this chapter to discuss a community-oriented structure that can be used to realise a CIIP structure created in a "bottom-up" manner. In these latter sections, we will highlight the basic construction, organisation, and relationship of these community-oriented structures and their associated community. In the

following section we will elaborate on the required background that will aid in the understanding of the later sections.

BACKGROUND

Developing countries are fast becoming partners in international communication due to the level of technical grow experienced in these regions. Interconnection comes in the form of high bandwidth information infrastructures that are deployed throughout these regions. New information infrastructures provide these countries with much needed interconnectivity to allow them to effectively operate on the world stage. The development of information infrastructure can however introduce the potential for many new global cyber threats. In this section we will elaborate on various aspects relating to the development of information infrastructure in developing countries.

Challenges of Expanding Infrastructure

The expanding use of information infrastructures is essential for the growth of developing regions, and furthermore, these regions cannot compete on a global level if they do not have access to these infrastructures. Historically, the African Continent has been the poorest in terms of available information infrastructures (Heacock, 2009). However, this situation is now changing, with many new telecommunication links being established throughout the African Continent (Song, 2011). These new telecommunication links provide these regions with opportunities to improve the provision services and to experience growth in related areas (Ellefsen & von Solms, 2010b).

The task of providing interconnection to these developing regions is a complex logistical task. As is seen in Figure 1, the size of the African

Figure 1. Illustrating the size of the African continent. (Adapted from (Kruze, 2010). Image released by the original author into the Public Domain – http://edge.org/documents/Edge-Serpentine-MapsGallery/high-res/Krause.pdf).

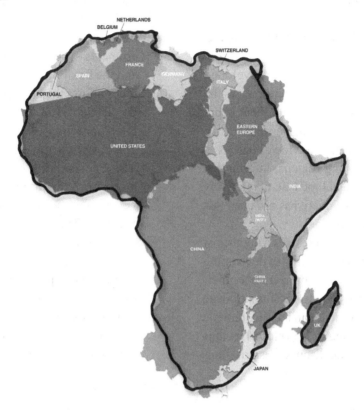

Continent is often underestimated, and this size often has an impact on the ability of countries in these regions to introduce new information infrastructures (Krause, 2010).

The geographic size of many developing regions implies that the use of information infrastructures to connect critical systems is commonplace. Administration of large critical systems would be complicated if a level of interconnection was not introduced. Nevertheless, the expanding use of information infrastructures in developing countries has the potential to improve the ability of these regions to interact on a global level.

Expanding infrastructures does not only influence traditional fixed-line technologies. The use of cellular telephones in developing regions is among the highest in the world, with as many as 75% of all mobile telephones being used in the developing world (Cisco, 2009). As such, a related field of growth is that of wireless Internet-technologies. Using traditional fixed-line methods to interconnect users is often too costly for many countries. Wireless technologies can be used to provide interconnection for a large number of users at a fraction of the cost of traditional means (International Telecommunication Union, 2010). For example, the number of mobile banking users in developing countries is fast outpacing the use of traditional banking services (Mansfield, 2011).

In some cases, the use of wireless technologies is also used to provide interconnection for critical control system, however wireless interconnection of systems can have its own associated risks, such as with the attack on the Maroochy Water Services infrastructure in Australia (Abrams & Weiss, 2008). Furthermore, there are a number of potential risks associated with the development of information infrastructures. In the following section we will investigate a number of potential risks.

Risk Factors in the Developing World

Information infrastructures in the developed world have been built gradually over time. As the Internet has grown, the infrastructure that is put in place to protect these regions has also grown to meet the required demand. However, this is not the case in developing regions, information infrastructures have developed at a relatively quicker rate, and as such, there has not been this extended development period.

This accelerated growth presents a number of problems that impact on the ability of developing regions to effectively provide protection for their interconnected systems. These problems introduce a number of risk factors that can have a dramatic impact on both developing and developed regions alike. We will outline and discuss these risk factors below.

- **Short Development Times:** Many developing regions are faced with having to integrate information infrastructures in a very short timeframe. In developed regions, information infrastructures, and associated technologies have been developed over an extended period. This developmental period has allowed protection mechanisms to develop alongside the development of information infrastructures. Furthermore, the use of information infrastructures in the development of control systems for critical systems has also developed over time. However, in developing regions the use of technologies to provide interconnection is being applied at a much faster rate, this could allow vulnerabilities and oversights to be built into new interconnected systems.

- **A Drive to Interconnect Systems:** Developing regions must continually attempt to provision services. Basic services such as water, sanitation, or electricity, are often high on the agenda of many of governments. The interconnection of systems and the flexibility that interconnection provides allows the provision of services to be accelerated. However, this drive to provide interconnection of systems can introduce potential vulnerabilities.

- **The Provisioning of Services:** A further mechanism to provision services in developing regions is to adopt Electronic Services. The efficiency of many governmental services, such as taxation, the issuing of licenses, and electricity distribution can be supplemented through the use of Electronic Services. Services provided in this way allow developing countries to provide a high-level of service without having to commit and maintain a large human workforce. However, in most cases, the platforms used to provision Electronic Services are unique to the agency or division that commissioned it. This can create a high level of interdependency and islands of information due to the fragmentation of data. Furthermore, if security is not considered as a primary design goal, these systems could become vulnerable to cyber attacks.

- **A Lack of Computer Literacy:** Literacy levels in developing regions are lower when compared to developed regions (Wikipedia, 2012a). In some cases, a large percentage of the population does not have basic literacy skills. It follows that levels of computer literacy in developing countries is even lower. This stems from the lack of access to computer devices on a grass roots level. Many would consider computer literacy a bare minimum for people entering the work place, and in order to become internationally competitive, developing countries must take steps to improve computer literacy. However, computer literacy alone is not sufficient, it follows that levels of computer security literacy are also lower in many developing regions. Many individuals do not understand the nature of computer security and the importance of computer security as it relates to computer systems. As systems are developed, levels of computer security literacy must be improved to minimise the risk of cyber attack.

- **Outdated Legislation:** In many cases, current legislation and policy in developing regions does not adequately address new technological growth. To address this, changes in legislation may have to be made. However, this process is often lengthy and time consuming. Effective legislation is a key component of any protection structure in a country, as it provides protection structures with legitimacy and an ability to operate effectively. Laws that specifically address computer security, the application of computer-related technologies, and the provisioning of electronic services are essential to allow developing countries to operate on the international stage.

- **The Development of Parallel Technologies:** The development of information infrastructures is often coupled with the development of related technologies. These technologies will enable services to be brought to individuals, or areas, that might not have previously had access to them. For instance, the development of wireless and cellular technologies in the developing world is much better placed to provide Internet connectivity than fixed-line alternatives. However, the growth of alternate technologies also introduces other risk factors and other challenges that must be addressed. In many cases, the de-

velopment of alternate technologies is the only viable method of providing interconnectivity to a large number of users.

- **A Lack of Understanding of Modern Threats:** The development of information infrastructures introduces a number of new threats to users that have not experienced such challenges before (Cisco, 2009). A lack of understanding can have a major impact on global systems if malware is allowed to flourish in unprotected and unmonitored environments.

A number of risk factors can be identified through the development of information infrastructure in developing regions. These risk factors have a global impact, not only on other international users, but also on other systems connected to the Internet. In many cases the provisioning of services overshadows the application of effective security mechanisms. The aim when deploying and creating systems in developing countries should be to mitigate the aforementioned risk factors while still providing an adequate level of service.

The risk factors mentioned above should not impede the development of information infrastructures in developing countries, as they are essential for achieving long-term sustainability in these regions. Nevertheless, these risk factors do present a challenge to existing systems in both the developing and developed world. In the following section we will outline potential threats to existing systems.

Threats to Existing Systems

As discussed in the previous sections, the development of information infrastructures in developing regions can introduce many potential benefits. However, there are various threats that can also be introduced. These threats are not limited to particular regions and have the potential to affect systems on a global level. The expanding use of information infrastructures and the associated risks can be summarised by the following statement:

IT experts estimate an 80% infection rate on all PCs continent - wide (in Africa), including government computers. It is the cyber equivalent of a pandemic. Few can afford to pay for anti-virus software...

Now, with the arrival of broadband services delivered via undersea cables, there will be a massive, target-rich environment of almost 100 million computers available for botnet herders to add infected hosts to their computer armies. (Carr, 2011)

A side effect of unmonitored technological growth has the potential to impact global systems. Consider Africa with an estimated population of 1 billion in the year 2010 (United Nations, 2011), the potential size of the user base created by expanding information infrastructures could expand the potential size of the user pool for botnet operators (as outlined by the above statement). This effect is not limited to developing regions. If a control system is compromised in the developing world, it can have a direct impact on other countries. This can be illustrated by the Distributed Denial of Service (DDoS) attacks that were targeted against Georgia. When compromised Georgian systems were relocated to servers based in the United States, a number of U.S. based systems felt the effects of this DDoS attack (Korns & Kastenberg, 2008).

To further illustrate this point, consider nuclear control systems located in the developing world falling prey to another Stuxnet-type worm. In regions where there might not be the required cyber security skills available to adequately monitor and react to computer security incidents, the result could have devastating worldwide consequences. Although there are a few projects in place to address this possibility, the global response mechanism is far from adequate. The threats discussed above are compounded by the development of parallel technologies; consider the following statement relating to the deployment of wireless telephones in developing regions.

...By the end of 2010, there will be an estimated 5.3 billion mobile cellular subscriptions worldwide ...Access to mobile networks is now available to 90% of the world population and 80% of the population living in rural areas. (International Telecommunication Union, 2010)

The growth of these alternate technologies, such as the growth of mobile devices allows consumers to have access to technology and services that they would not previously have had access to. Governments and companies are able to leverage these alternate technologies to provide services that are more effective to many new users. Wireless technologies allow more uses to be connected at a much greater rate than when compared to fixed line alternatives. However, the impact of this is that users are more mobile than they previously were, while still having access to high-speed Internet access. As is illustrated by the following statement, the use of these alternate technologies will have a significant impact on both users and systems.

...And as more individuals worldwide gain Internet access through mobile phones (because, in many parts of the world, it's faster than waiting on the availability of broadband), expect cybercrime techniques that have gone out of fashion to re-emerge in many developing countries. (Cisco, 2009)

The introduction of new, unaware users could create the potential for new forms of malware and cyber threats to emerge. This has the potential to allow events such as the Stuxnet worm to be a normal situation instead of the exception.

Case Study

The Stuxnet worm was designed to target SCADA devices. The Stuxnet worm delivered a payload that affected the control devices that are found in many different control systems (Symantec, 2011). This payload allowed a third party to take control of the infected systems by injecting their own commands.

The Stuxnet worm was designed to target Microsoft Windows machines that were running the SIMATIC Step 7 control software. Once the control system had been infected, it contacts a command and control server that relays commands from the remote attacker. (Matrosov, Rodionov, Harley, & Malcho, 2011; Symantec, 2011).

The infection rate of the Stuxnet worm varied between different regions, however Iran accounted for 52% of global infections (Matrosov et al., 2011). It is speculated that the initial infection could have been through the use of an infected USB device; however there is the possibility that other methods of infection were used.

Although the effect of the Stuxnet worm was limited, it highlights the vulnerability of many worldwide control systems. Had the third party chosen to exercise their control over the infected control systems, it could have caused worldwide disruptions. The complexity of the Stuxnet worm, and the potential effect that could have caused to control systems provides an illustration of the potential form of future cyber attacks (Symantec, 2011). A similar example is that of the Flame malware which was detected in May 2012 and reportedly infected Windows computer systems in the Middle East with smaller infection rates around the world (Wikipedia, 2012b).

Consider the risk factors associated with developing regions discussed in the previous section, and the potential threat of future cyber attacks to control systems, the following question should be asked: how would the developing world be able to address these challenges while still supporting the development of information infrastructures?

This question, although simple in nature, does not only impact on developing regions but has worldwide implications.

The potential threat to existing systems posed by the development of information infrastructures in the developing world cannot be overlooked. An effective solution is for developing regions to invest in the development of CIIP structures. However, as discussed in the sections above, there are many challenges impacting on the creation of such structures. In the following section we will further investigate the creation of CIIP structures within developing countries.

DEVELOPING WORLD INFORMATION INFRASTRUCTURE PROTECTION

The developing world has a number of unique requirements with respect to Critical Information Infrastructure Protection. These requirements stem from the challenges discussed in the previous section. The protection of computer systems is dependent on the effective management of computer security incidents. Incidents in this context refer to the effects of computer security threats, such as malware, virus, Trojan horses, worms, hacking attempts, and so on. Such threats are well known for there ability to spread rapidly and damage computer-based systems. A common platform for managing threats on a national level is to implement a Computer Security Incident Response Team (CSIRT) structure. A CSIRT (or similar) structure is responsible for providing computer security related services, and to manage computer security incidents (Killcrece, 2004; West-Brown et al., 2003). In the context of this chapter, we refer to a CSIRT to mean a centralised computer security structure that would normally be mandated and directed from a governmental level. The definition and construction of a cyber security structure of this nature is usually discussed in the context of the environment in which it is constructed and can go by many different names. For the sake of this discussion we will elaborate on a generic structure of this type as outlined in Figure 2.

A generalised CSIRT structure consists of various levels; at the core is a national coordinating level that is responsible for a national cyber security protection effort. Normally, a number of smaller regional structures are used to manage computer security incidents for a particular region or sector. Finally, there are a number of complementary computer security structures that provide computer security protection for specialised groups (West-Brown et al., 2003; Ellefsen & von Solms, 2010c).

Each of these layers in a CSIRT structure can be implemented in a number of different ways, and it depends on the needs of the country that is deploying such a structure. A CSIRT can provide a number of different services to its constituency; these services can either be reactive or proactive in nature (West-Brown et al., 2003).

Reactive services are those that are provided in response to a computer security threat or incident. Proactive services are those designed to prevent or protect against computer security threats. These services are provided with the aim of building a comprehensive infrastructure for coordinating the response to computer security threats (Killcrece, 2004).

Furthermore, a CSIRT structure maintains links with international peers. Cooperative international partnerships allow many CSIRT structures around the world to coordinate global computer security incidents. It is rare that a computer security threat (such as a virus infection) is limited to a single country, or a single network. The nature of modern computer systems implies that malware can spread rapidly between international networks. The role of international cooperation is therefore an important aspect of a CSIRT, as information can be shared and distributed quickly within an international network of CSIRTs to aid in the resolution of incidents.

Figure 2. Illustrating a generalised CSIRT structure. (Adapted from Ellefsen, von Solms (2010c))

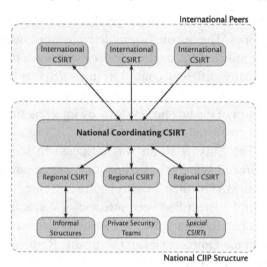

Consider the following contrived scenario to highlight the role of a CSIRT structure with regards to Critical Information Infrastructure Protection. A company that generates electric power has a number of power stations forming a national power distribution grid. To allow for efficient management of power generation, each power station is connected to a central monitoring point from which they can be remotely adjusted. As in the case of the Stuxnet worm, consider that the control systems at one of the power stations becomes infected by malware, causing a remote attacker to gain access to the control systems, and feed incorrect monitoring information back to the control point. Consider then, that a technician at the control centre notices that there is some problem, and notifies an internal security team. If the security team is not able to resolve the problem, the CSIRT could be notified. The CSIRT could then use its expertise, contacts, and international partnerships to aid in the resolution of the threat.

Now, consider the situation if a CSIRT did not exist, once all the internal avenues have been exhausted, the problem may go unresolved. This could allow the malware to spread, to infect other control systems, and could cause irreparable damage both on a national and global level.

CSIRTs provide a platform for managing computer security threats to many control systems. However, it is often the case the there is no CSIRT structure in developing countries, in the following section we will elaborate on a number of limitations for the creation of a traditional CSIRT structure in developing regions.

Developing World Limitations

CSIRT structures are an effective mechanism to provide CIIP in many countries around the world, however there are challenges that limit the development of these structures in the developing world. These challenges range from political influences to various social challenges, and it is often the case that the creation of effective CIIP structures is not a priority. In this section we will investigate a number of these challenges, namely, computer literacy, security awareness, legal frameworks and skill shortages. Many of these challenges are related to the risk factors discussed above. However, they play a dual role of increasing risk and limiting CIIP development.

Firstly, computer literacy is a primary challenge to the creation of effective CIIP structures. As discussed above, computer literacy is considered a requirement for individuals to compete internationally (Tucker, 2003). However, the idea of computer literacy can be extended to include computer security literacy. A key component of this is the understanding of how threats can affect computer security, and therefore is essential to ensure the security of a system as a whole. In the developing world, both enabling computer literacy and ensuring computer security literacy is a primary challenge.

Secondly, providing computer security awareness training is a further challenge. This concept is closely related to computer security literacy, however it extends to provide coverage of concepts such as password management, web usage, the importance of data backups, and incident response mechanisms (Wilson & Hash, 2003). A human operator is often the first line of defence against computer security threats, and giving users the ability to identify threats is a key component of the development of any protection mechanism.

Thirdly, many developing regions have ineffective policies and legislation relating to cyber and computer security, or the protection of data (Ellefsen & von Solms, 2010b). Legislation underpins any national computer security structure, as it defines the framework and the operational environment in which the structure will operate. Without the appropriate legislation, a computer security structure would operate with one hand tied behind its back. Nevertheless, some developing countries have legislation relating to computer security. India and South Africa are two examples of such countries. The Electronic Communications and Transactions (ECT) Act (South African Government, 2002) in South Africa and the Information Technology Act (Indian Government, 2000) in India, both provide legislation relating to issues such as spam, hacking and IT regulation. However, efforts must be made to introduce effective legislation in other developing countries. In the following section we will elaborate on these challenges outlined above and discuss the various requirements for CIIP in developing countries.

Developing World Requirements

In order to create an effective CIIP structure in a developing country a number of aims must be met. These aims are outlined below to address the challenges expressed in the previous section. The aims listed below are discussed in a generic manner. Each country that implements a CIIP structure will have unique aims for CIIP that they will require.

1. **Ongoing Technical Developments:** This aim addresses the rate of technological development in various developing regions. As discussed above, the accelerated rate of technological development in developing regions must be taken into consideration when implementing a CIIP structure. Developed

countries have created and evolved CIIP structures since the early days of the Internet. However, developing regions are not able to manage their information infrastructure in this way. In essence, they will have to "hit the ground running".

2. **Public, Private, and International Partnership:** This aim addresses the integration of existing internal and international CIIP structures. In many multinational organisations there will exist computer security teams that maintain internal information infrastructures. Likewise, many developed regions have existing CIIP structures in place. A new CIIP structure in a developing country can utilise the pre-existing expertise to enable them to deploy their structures at an accelerated rate.

3. **A Holistic Approach:** This aim addresses all levels of society to create a CIIP structure that is able to effectively protect against new and emerging cyber threats. In the past, propagation of Internet technologies has occurred over a number of years. However, in developing regions, many new users are getting access to Internet services in a very short space of time. This increases the risk of cyber threats impacting on this new user base. To address this, a CIIP structure should be generic in nature and be able to services all levels of society in a holistic manner.

4. **Support from International Peers:** This aim leverages the lessons learned by international partners to supplement the growth of a local CIIP structure. As with building international partnerships, having support of international peers will also aid in the development of effective CIIP structures. This aim ensures that a new CIIP structures have the best chance to succeed.

5. **Building Capacity:** This aim focuses on growing local skills to reduce the dependence on acquiring international skills. As discussed above, developing regions might not have the available skills to form a CIIP

structure. By ensuring that a CIIP structure is able to grow and support its own skill set, it will be able to reduce its dependence on acquiring outside skills.

6. **Future-Proof Construction:** This aim addresses the ability to create a structure that is flexible and able to respond to unknown future threats. The future state and construction of the Internet is unknown. The role of new interconnecting technologies and new methods of communication create a dynamic environment. Furthermore, the threats of tomorrow are unknown, therefore a CIIP structure should be able to adapt to this dynamic environment to ensure that new threats are successfully managed.

To address these aims, the various possible high-level models for CIIP structures should be defined. In the following section we will contrast top-down with bottom-up CIIP structures.

Top-Down Structures

To elaborate on an effective approach for CIIP in developing regions, it is important to understand the current scope of protection provided by a generic CSIRT. The actual level of coverage of a CSIRT is dependent on its operational environment, however in this section we will focus on a generalised CSIRT structure.

In general, CSIRT services are applied from the top-down, driven at a governmental level and then applied to lower levels of society. The primary areas of operation of a CSIRT are Government, Large Industry and Large Academic Institutions (such as large research institutions). These levels cover a range of the industries that drive a country's economy.

The coverage of a CSIRT is illustrated in Figure 3, where the direct protection of industry groups is indicated. The industry groups that have direct protection applied through a CSIRT structure are described and discussed below.

- **Government:** This level will include all operational areas within a government, this includes entities such as governmental departments and military structures. Generally, governments consist of a vast number of civil servants with a large number of computers, and as such individual government departments may employ the use of private security teams to manage their internal information infrastructure. Due to the critical role governmental departments play in the operation of a country they will generally fall under the direct coordination of a CSIRT.

- **Large Industry:** This level comprises all large industry players within a country. Such industries could constitute large public or private companies, or multinational organisations. These organisations will have a large number of employees and a large number of computers. An example of such organisations could include financial institutions. These industries will have a direct impact on the infrastructure of a country. These companies will often employ their own computer security teams to manage their internal infrastructure, and will be responsible for mitigating any threats to their networks. However, these companies will be under the coordination of a CSIRT structure that will be responsible for coordinating any national level risks.

- **Large Academic Institutions:** This level will include large academic and research institutions within a country. These institutions will generally have access to a large number of computers and a large number of personnel. Furthermore, these institutions are likely to have large internal networks that will be protected by an internal security team.

Each of the above mentioned levels would be characterised by a complex internal structure that is supplemented by a complex internal network.

Figure 3. Illustrating the coverage of a typical CSIRT. The focus of the CSIRT will be to provide incident response services for these types of industry. Indirect protection applied to smaller industries is highlighted. (Own Composition)

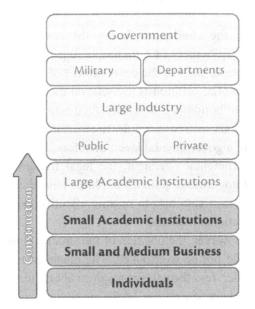

They will also exhibit a high number of users with a fairly large amount of exposure should their systems be compromised. As such they generally have internal protection structures in place, these structures will have direct interaction with a national CSIRT in order to coordinate any incident that occurs.

The aforementioned situation is not always the case; it does depend on the unique construction and deployment of a CIIP structure. However, this generic situation can be applied to many operational CSIRTs. Smaller players do not get the same level of protection from the national CSIRT when compared to a larger player. Any protection that is offered is done so in an indirect manner, services are provided through indirect channels rather than to smaller stakeholders directly. In the context of a developing country the challenges that are faced in creating an effective CIIP solution are largely due to the unique risk factors that exist in these countries (Ellefsen & von Solms, 2010b). To provide a contrasting structure, consider a

CIIP structure created from the bottom-up. In the following section we will explore the concept of a bottom-up CIIP structure.

Bottom-Up Structures

With the challenges facing the construction and deployment of a traditional top-down CIIP structure, such as the development of a CSIRT, a potential solution is to focus on the construction of bottom-up structures. As discussed in the previous section, a top-down structure is driven from a governmental level; therefore, it requires governmental oversight, the legal frameworks and governance policies in place. This allows a top-down structure to operate effectively in its operational mandate.

However, the position of the smaller entities should not be overlooked. The management of smaller, less formal, groups does not require the same legal foundation. Furthermore, these smaller groups are often less encumbered by political factors. Take, for instance, a small business with a single owner and a number of employees. Any decision made with respect to the business is made by the owner and executed by the employees. In a traditional structure, a small business would not have access to a large CIIP structure, and may not have access to the services that a CIIP structure would offer. Consider computer security risks managed by a small business; in many cases there will not be computer security knowledge and skills available to manage threats effectively. This would make the business vulnerable to a number of forms of cyber attack. Furthermore, in many cases, computer security threats would be managed in a retroactive manner. This creates a potentially volatile situation where computer security threats could propagate.

The scenario described above would benefit from the services offered by some type of CIIP structure. A bottom-up CIIP structure could be designed to fulfil the computer security needs of smaller businesses and individuals. Furthermore, a "bottom-up" CIIP structure could be engineered to provide focused computer security support that is executed in a loosely-coupled manner by reducing the dependence on external structures.

Such a structure would offer a number of benefits for deployment in a developing country where there is no existing CIIP structure, or an immature CIIP structure in place. It is important to note that the development of a bottom-up structure should not be dependent on a pre-existing top-down CIIP structure. Ideally, a bottom-up structure should be self-sufficient, and able to provide moderate computer security support. Furthermore, the existence of a bottom-up CIIP structure will not compensate for a top-down CIIP structure. A bottom-up structure could be used to establish the foundation for a larger top-down structure to create a holistic CIIP solution. Figure 4 illustrates the types of industries that would benefit from the introduction of a bottom-up CIIP structure.

In the following section we will expand upon the concept of a bottom-up CIIP structure by describing a model that could be used to realise it.

COMMUNITY-ORIENTED SECURITY, ADVISORY, AND WARNING

The realisation of a bottom-up structure that is applicable for deployment in developing regions should be designed such that it can address the unique challenges faced by these countries. A potential model that could realise the bottom-up construction for CIIP in developing regions is the creation of a number of community-oriented teams.

It is important to define the idea of a "community" in the context of a CIIP structure, this will aid in elaborating on the construction of a community-oriented structure. A CSIRT provides computer security services to a constituency that is formed of all the industries, groups, businesses, and departments that consume the services provided by the CSIRT. The composition of a constituency is dictated by the overall mandate of the CSIRT. An analogous concept is that of a community, however it applies to a bottom-up CIIP structure. The primary difference between a constituency and a community is that a community has a defined relationship between the members. In the case of a bottom-up structure, the community could be formed from small businesses, small academic institutions, or individuals. These types of community members are characterised as have a dependence on computer-based systems and limited knowledge concerning computer security threats. This section aims to outline the potential construction of a "bottom-up community-oriented" CIIP structure, however as with any CIIP structure, the actual implementation will be dependent on the requirements of the environment in which it will be deployed.

There are CIIP structures in existence that employ this concept of a community. One such example is that of a Warning, Advice, and Reporting Point (WARP) (Askwith, 2006). A WARP operates within a community of members to provide a platform for computer security. WARPs generally exist as complementary structures to a larger top-down CIIP structure, acting as a bridge between a CSIRT and the community, and as such a WARP does not generally exist separate from a larger CIIP structure (Harrison & Townsend, 2008).

This concept of a community can be extended and used as a basis for a bottom-up CIIP structure that can be deployed within a developing world context. Furthermore, to add substance to a loosely coupled CIIP structure, the collective knowledge of the community can be harnessed to address and resolve computer security threats. A model that can utilise this concept of a community to provide computer security incident services is that of a Community-oriented Security, Advisory and Warning (C-SAW) Team.

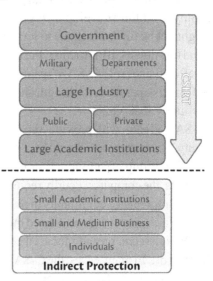

Figure 4. Illustrating the coverage of a bottom-up CIIP structure. The primary focus is on smaller entities where traditional CIIP structures would be ineffective. (Own Composition)

Basic Construction

To effectively realise the bottom-up construction of a CIIP structure, a C-SAW Team should be constructed with the following design goals in mind. These design goals will allow a C-SAW Team to operate within a community, and function apart from a larger CIIP structure. These goals are:

1. It must be cost effective.
2. It must be community oriented.
3. It should service a moderate to large number of community members.
4. There should be communications links with other C-SAW Teams.
5. Information exchange and openness between community members should be encouraged.
6. It should provide filtered computer security information.
7. It should be loosely coupled.
8. It should expand its service offering over time.

These design goals allow a C-SAW Team to operate within an identified community, and provide tailored services for the identified community. The cost-effective nature of a C-SAW Team enables it to be deployed within a developing region, where there might not be funds available to implement a traditional top-down CIIP structure. Furthermore, the cost-effectiveness of a C-SAW Team should be derived from its operation, its design, and thought the community it serves.

A C-SAW Team will provide services to a community. The community should be constructed from a related group of individuals or industries. In many cases, the computer security requirements will be similar for related community members. By constructing a community from related members, the C-SAW Team can provide focused computer security support. In many cases, the C-SAW Team itself will be formed directly from personnel within the community; therefore having related interests would be of benefit.

The services that a C-SAW Team provides would be supplemented by community knowledge. The community will be actively involved in the services that a C-SAW Team would provide. As such, there must be a balance between the size of the community and the services that a C-SAW Team offers. If the community is too large, then it will become difficult for a C-SAW Team to manage. If the community is too small, the scope of the services that the C-SAW Team provides will be limited.

An effective C-SAW structure will be built up from a number of C-SAW Teams, with each team providing services to their community. However, in many cases there will be crosscutting concerns that will require that information be exchanged between various communities. Allowing information to be exchanged openly, computer security threats in communities can be identified and resolved. To this end, a C-SAW Team should also have a number of goals with respect to its operational environment. A C-SAW Team should meet the following environmental goals:

- **Autonomous:** A C-SAW Team should be able to operate on its own, independent from any larger CIIP structure. This extends the operational flexibility of a C-SAW Team and reduces it dependence on external structures, while still allowing it to provide services to its community. In countries where a top-down CIIP structure is not available, this goal is an essential component of a C-SAW Team.

- **Geographic and Domain Independent:** The community and service area of a C-SAW Team should be well understood and rigidly defined. Geographic independence can be used to ensure that C-SAW Teams do not provide services to overlapping communities. Domain Independence can used to ensure that more than one C-SAW Team does not serve two communities.

- **Openness:** The community members, the C-SAW Team, and other external parties should be able to communicate in an open manner, within reason. This is not to imply that trade secrets or operational details of the community member should be disclosed, only that security concerns are discussed openly.

A C-SAW Team should provide filtered computer security information to its community members. Due to the relationship between a C-SAW Team and its community, information concerning relevant computer security threats can be identified and delivered. This will prevent unneeded or unnecessary information being relayed to the community members. Providing filtered information is the most basic service type that a C-SAW Team could provide. Over time, a team should strive to improve the types of services that would be provided to a community.

Organisation

A C-SAW structure is not built up of a single C-SAW Team. In the previous section we outlined the role and basic construction of a C-SAW Team. However, a single C-SAW Team will not be able to act as a complete CIIP structure. To provide complete protection for various different communities, a number of C-SAW Teams will need to be created and deployed.

To facilitate this approach, it becomes useful to organise communities into various operational domains. As discussed in the previous section, a community is created from a group of related members; ideally these members will operate within a specific operational domain. C-SAW Teams can be created within these operational domains and be used to build up a net of protection (Ellefsen & von Solms, 2010a).

Furthermore, due to the construction of a C-SAW structure, there will be a level of inter-domain communication between various different C-SAW Teams. A key component of developing an effective bottom-up CIIP structure is the ability to provide effective communication mechanisms between all the stakeholders. C-SAW Teams must therefore be able to communicate with each other. This allows them to expand the pool of available knowledge and to aid in the resolution and identification of threats. Furthermore, it allows C-SAW Teams that do not have the same level of expertise to benefit from the knowledge of other C-SAW Teams in other operational domains.

Although communities are created to allow C-SAW Teams to provide focused computer security services, many computer security concerns are universal. This further highlights the benefit of creating a structure in which communication is provided as a key component.

Figure 5 illustrates where a C-SAW Structure would be positioned relative to a larger national CIIP structure. This illustration is provided to highlight the role that a collection of C-SAW Teams would play in a larger national structure. However, the design and implementation of the C-SAW Teams should be such that it is not dependant on the existence of a larger CIIP structure (to satisfy the autonomy goal). Nevertheless, the benefit of integrating a larger top-down structure and a bottom-up structure cannot be ignored.

Developing countries would benefit from the deployment of C-SAW Teams to provide the necessary support at a grass roots level. The loosely-coupled nature of their design, the ability of the teams to provide active computer security support, and the integration of community members allows a C-SAW Team to build a firm platform for CIIP. Furthermore, the loosely-coupled nature of a C-SAW structure aids in its deployment, as both the top-down and bottom-up components of the CIIP structure can develop independently, with the C-SAW Teams providing a necessary stop gap in the period where a larger CIIP structure is becoming operational. In the following section we will provide an example scenario to which a C-SAW Team could be applied.

Example

Consider the following, non-exhaustive, characteristics that might describe a number of schools in a city region and the computer infrastructure supporting them:

1. There are a number of communal computers.
2. There is limited computer security expertise.
3. Educators and learners will use the computers.
4. Maintenance of the computer facilities will be designated to an individual or small group.

It would be the case in many of these schools that there are limited funds available for computing resources or computer maintenance. In many cases, there will be a single individual that would be tasked with maintaining the computer systems. With limited funds and skills available, it is possible for computer systems in this environment to be heavily effected by malware.

Schools in a similar geographic area might have the same characteristics and concerns. In order to pool their available computer security skills, they could form a C-SAW Team. To act as a point of contact regarding computer security related issues.

Once the C-SAW Team has been established other schools could become part of the programme this would increase the available body of skills, and the effectiveness of the C-SAW Team. In the following section we will discuss a number of services that a C-SAW Team would provide. This will allow us to define the context in which a C-SAW Team would operate.

SERVICES

The services that a C-SAW Team would provide will be dependent on the community that it services. However the services themselves would fall into two distinct categories. Normally, services provided by a CIIP structure are classed as either reactive or proactive (West-Brown et al., 2003), and the services provide by a C-SAW Team are no different. That is not to say that these services discussed in this section are the only services that could be provided, they are given as examples of the type of services and the scope of service provision that is possible.

In general, a CIIP structure must provide some level of Incident Response (Brownlee & Guttman, 1998) and a C-SAW Team should provide a similar service to its community. However, the form of this service need not be as comprehensive as that provided by a CSIRT, however it should provide some mechanism for a community member to report and receive support for a computer security incident. This type of service would be classed as a reactive service, as it is provided in reaction to a particular computer security event.

A further possible service that a C-SAW Team could provide is a form of vulnerability management (Ellefsen & von Solms, 2010c). As discussed above, a C-SAW Team operates within a particular community, and the community will have related computer security needs. Vulnerability management could take the form of providing proactive Security Warnings concerning potential computer security threats. In many cases, community members would not have the expertise to identify threats to their systems and as such, a C-SAW Team could provide filtered reactive information based on the particular internal configuration of its various community members. To provide insight and to elaborate on the various types of services a C-SAW Team could provide, in the following section we will discuss two such services in more detail.

Community-Driven Incident Response

The Community-driven Incident Response service forms the core service that a C-SAW Team provides to its community. If a community member detects a computer security threat, the C-SAW Team can be notified to aid in the resolution of the threat. There are various stages that a C-SAW Team would have to go through to resolve the computer security incident. A key aspect of the incident response service is the ability of the C-SAW Team to utilise the collective knowledge of the community to aid in the resolution process.

Figure 6 illustrates such a resolution process that can be used by a C-SAW Team to provide an incident response service. The following process would be followed when a threat is detected; firstly a community member would detect some threat to their internal systems. The C-SAW Team is notified and goes through a process of identifying, evaluating, and resolving the threat.

Once the C-SAW Team has received notification of the threat, it must be identified and qualified. There is a possibility that a similar threat has been seen before, in which case the C-SAW Team can provide support directly. If the threat is unknown, or cannot be managed by the C-SAW Team then a solicitation phase would follow. During the solicitation phase information is ob-

Figure 5. Illustrating where a C-SAW structure would be placed if a larger CIIP structure existed (Own Composition)

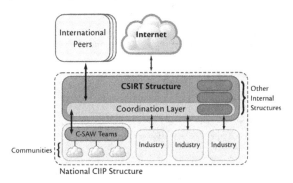

tained from other community members (in the same domain), other C-SAW Teams, or a larger CIIP structure. The scope of the solicitation process would depend on the complexity of the threat.

The level at which other members of the community are involved in the resolution process would depend on the size of the C-SAW Team and the collective ability of the community. In the case where there is not the required expertise available in the direct community, other C-SAW Teams could be contacted for assistance. Once the identification and solicitation phases have been completed, the C-SAW would be in a position to resolve the threat. This would involve either pro-

viding support directly to the original community member, or to co-opt other community members to provide additional support.

Once the threat has been resolved, the details of the threat should be recorded to aid in future incident response. To provide a comprehensive service to the community members, issuing reactive advice would form part of the services offered by a C-SAW Team. In the following section, the ability of a C-SAW Team to provide advice to community members in response to queries is discussed.

Computer Security Advice

A C-SAW Team provides reactive advice to a specific community member in response to a direct request for information. For instance, if a community member is experiencing a computer security issue that is out of its direct expertise, it should be able to obtain further information from the C-SAW Team. Figure 7 illustrates how a community member can request information from the C-SAW Team. The C-SAW Team would then solicit the required information and respond to the community member. The C-SAW Team can solicit this information either from an internal knowledge base or from various other sources.

Figure 6. Illustrating the incident response process for a community member and their associated C-SAW Team (Own Composition)

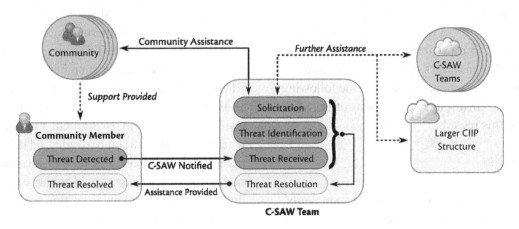

Figure 7. Illustrating a community member obtaining advice. The advice is classed as reactive because of the community member's request for information. (Own Composition)

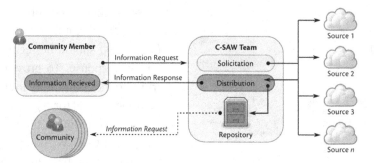

Typical sources would consist of other community members, C-SAW Teams in different domains, a larger CIIP structure, or any other relevant information source (such as a software vendor).

Allowing community members to ask for information directly allows a C-SAW Team to build up a knowledge base of relevant information. Community members in the same domain will experience similar problems; therefore by creating a domain specific knowledge base, it allows the C-SAW Team to address the needs of its community. This knowledge base does not have to be housed in the C-SAW Team itself, but could be a central point that is shared among many C-SAW Teams.

The services discussed above can be categorised as reactive as the community member initiates the service. However, these services could be supplemented with proactive services, where the C-SAW Team provides information to community members without a direct request. The operation of a C-SAW Team does not need to be constrained to a particular country; the loosely coupled design allows such a structure to operate across international borders. In the following section we will discuss the flexibility of a C-SAW Team in this regard.

Flexibility

The design and implementation of a community-based structure is not limited to only a national setting. In the previous sections, we have consid-

ered a structure that is created within the national framework of a country. However, the use of a community-based structure only requires a community in order to function. Therefore it is a possible to create a C-SAW Team to operate within an international community, such as between Multinational Organisations.

Consider SCADA systems created with similar control system hardware and software. Control systems of this nature might be implemented in various countries around the world, controlling a diverse number of systems. The operators of these systems could be arranged into a community and have the benefits of a community structure available to them. Consider if a generic vulnerability were detected within such an international community, the other community members could be informed and any further potential vulnerabilities could be identified and managed.

This ability of a C-SAW Team to manage its associated community stems from its loosely-coupled design. It is important to stress that the flexibility of a C-SAW Team is driven by the nature of the community members. In the case where a community requires a high-level of legal or governmental oversight, the flexibility of the resulting system will be limited. Furthermore, where a top-down structure would find it difficult to operate in this manner, a bottom-up structure, such as a C-SAW Team, would not have the same limitations. In the following section we will present our conclusions to this chapter.

CONCLUSION

The development of CIIP structures is an important aspect of the development of information infrastructures in developing countries. Developing countries are experiencing growth in in many areas. Countries are leveraging new technologies to provide more effective services. However, with the development of Internet technologies also comes with the threat of cyber attack. Many new users and systems are being exposed to cyber threats that could have impact systems on a global level.

The development of CIIP structures can be used to combat the threats that cyber attacks would have on developing countries. However, the development of traditional CIIP structures in these regions is impacted by a number of political, legal and social challenges.

In this chapter we investigated the requirements for the creation of a CIIP structure in developing regions. We provided a discussion of the various challenges and developmental risks that will have an impact on the development of CIIP structures in these regions. We then went on to discuss a community-oriented CIIP structure, where the management of cyber threats is driven in a bottom-up manner within a specific community. Such a structure is not susceptible to the same challenges that a traditional CIIP structure would experience in a developing country. Furthermore, the development of a community-based CIIP structure can be used to provide an effective platform for the future development of a top-down CIIP structure.

The creation of CIIP structures in developing regions is a vital component for the future of Internet-based systems. Developing countries are in a position where they must create effective CIIP structure in order to secure their critical systems, to protect their national critical infrastructure, and to create awareness to support Internet users.

REFERENCES

Abrams, M., & Weiss, J. (2008, July). *Malicious control system cyber security attack case study – Maroochy water services, Australia.* Retrieved from http://csrc.nist.gov/groups/SMA/fisma/ics/documents/Maroochy-Water-Services-Case-Study_report.pdf

Askwith, B. (2006, May). *WARP case study - Experience setting up a WARP.* Retrieved from http://www.warp.gov.uk/Index/indexarticles.htm

Brownlee, N., & Guttman, E. (1998, June). *RFC2350: Expectations for computer security incident response.* RFC. Retrieved from http://www.ietf.org/rfc/rfc2350.txt

Carr, J. (2011). *Inside cyber warfare: Mapping the cyber underworld* (2nd ed.). O'Reilly Media.

Cisco. (2009). *Cisco 2009 annual security report* (Tech. Rep.). Cisco Systems Inc. Retrieved from http://www.cisco.com/en/US/prod/vpndevc/annual_security_report.html

Ellefsen, I., & von Solms, S. (2010a). The community-oriented computer security, advisory and warning team. In *IST-Africa 2010 Conference Proceedings.* IIMC International Information Management Corporation.

Ellefsen, I., & von Solms, S. (2010b). Critical information infrastructure protection in the developing world. In Moore, T., & Shenoi, S. (Eds.), *Critical Infrastructure Protection IV* (Vol. 342, pp. 29–40). Boston, MA: Springer. Retrieved from. doi:10.1007/978-3-642-16806-2_3

Ellefsen, I., & von Solms, S. (2010c). C-SAW: Critical information infrastructure protection through simplification. In *What Kind of Information Society? Governance, Virtuality, Surveillance, Sustainability, Resilience* (Vol. 328, pp. 315–325). Boston, MA: Springer. Retrieved from. doi:10.1007/978-3-642-15479-9_30

Harrison, J., & Townsend, K. (2008, December). An update on WARPs. *ENISA Quarterly Review, 4*(4), 13-14. Retrieved from http://www.warp.gov.uk/downloads/enisa_quarterly_12_08.pdf

Heacock, R. (2009). *Internet filtering in sub-Saharan Africa* (Tech. Rep.). OpenNet Initiative. Retrieved from http://opennet.net/sites/opennet.net/files/ONI_SSAfrica_2009.pdf

Indian Government. (2000, October). *Information technology act, 21 of 2000.* Retrieved from http://www.mit.gov.in/content/view-it-act-2000

International Monetary Fund (IMF). (2012, April). *World economic outlook report.* Retrieved from http://www.imf.org/external/pubs/ft/weo/2012/01/pdf/text.pdf

International Telecommunication Union. (2010, November). *Facts and figures 2010.* Retrieved from www.itu.int/ITU-D/ict/material/FactsFigures2010.pdf

Killcrece, G. (2004, August). *Steps for creating national CSIRTs.* Retrieved from www.cert.org/archive/pdf/NationalCSIRTs.pdf

Korns, S., & Kastenberg, J. (2008). Georgia's cyber left hook. *Parameters, 38,* 60–76. Retrieved from http://www.carlisle.army.mil/usawc/Parameters/08winter/korns.pdf

Krause, K. (2010). *The true size of Africa.* Retrieved from http://edge.org/documents/Edge-Serpentine-MapsGallery/high-res/Krause.pdf

Mansfield, I. (2011, May). *Mobile banking surges as emerging markets embrace mobile finance.* Retrieved from www.cellular-news.com/story/49148.php

Matrosov, A., Rodionov, E., Harley, D., & Malcho, J. (2011, January). *Stuxnet under the microscope.* Retrieved from http://www.eset.com/us/resources/white-papers/Stuxnet_Under_the_Microscope.pdf

Song, S. (2011, October). *African undersea cables.* Retrieved from http://manypossibilities.net/african-undersea-cables

South African Government. (2002, August). *Electronic communications and transactions act, 25 of 2002.* Retrieved from http://www.acts.co.za/ect_act/

Symantec. (2011, February). *W32.Stuxnet dossier.* Retrieved from http://www.symantec.com/content/en/us/enterprise/media/security_response/whitepapers/w32_stuxnet_dossier.pdf

Tucker, A. (2003, October). *A model curriculum for K–12 computer science: Final report of the ACM K–12 task force curriculum committee.* Retrieved from http://csta.acm.org/Curriculum/sub/CurrFiles/K-12ModelCurr2ndEd.pdf

United Nations. (2011, October). *World population prospects: The 2010 revision.* Retrieved from http://esa.un.org/unpd/wpp/index.htm

West-Brown, M., Stikvoort, D., Kossakowski, K., Killcrece, G., Ruefle, R., & Zajicek, M. (2003, April). *Handbook for computer security response teams* (CSIRTs) (2nd ed., (pp. 15213-3890). Retrieved from http://www.cert.org/archive/pdf/csirt-handbook.pdf

Wikipedia. (2012a, July 20). List of countries by literacy rate. In *Wikipedia, The Free Encyclopedia.* Retrieved July 21, 2012, from http://en.wikipedia.org/w/index.php?title=List_of_countries_by_literacy_rate&oldid=503242769

Wikipedia. (2012b, July 20). Flame (malware). In *Wikipedia, The Free Encyclopedia.* Retrieved 14:14, July 21, 2012, from http://en.wikipedia.org/w/index.php?title=Flame_(malware)&oldid=503359927

Wilson, M., & Hash, J. (2003, October). *Building an information technology security awareness and training program.* Retrieved from http://csrc.nist.gov/publications/nistpubs/800-50/NIST-SP800-50.pdf

KEY TERMS AND DEFINITIONS

Bottom-Up Construction: The creation of a CIIP structure that is driven from a community-level, where the services provided by such a structure are provisioned from within a community setting.

Community: A community is analogous to that of a constituency in a traditional CIIP structure, however, a community is more closely related than a constituency. A community of members forms the basis for Community-oriented CIIP structures.

Community-Oriented Critical Information Infrastructure Protection: Methods and mechanisms used to provide CIIP where the primary focus is on a related community of members rather than a collection of constituents.

Community-Oriented Security, Advisory, and Warning (C-SAW) Team: A model for providing Community-oriented CIIP that is created from a community of members. Alternate structures which provide a similar function is that of a Warning, Advice, and Reporting Point (WARP).

Critical Information Infrastructure Protection (CIIP): Measures and mechanisms that are put into place to protect critical information infrastructures from threats and vulnerabilities that could in turn affect critical systems.

Incident Response: The mechanisms that are put in place to respond to, and manage, threats against a particular system.

Top-Down Construction: The creation of a CIIP structure in the traditional sense, where services are driven in a "top-down" manner (i.e. from a Governmental level).

Chapter 11
Designing a Security Audit Plan for a Critical Information Infrastructure (CII)

Eduardo E. Gelbstein
Webster University, Geneva, Switzerland

ABSTRACT

Critical Information Infrastructure Infrastructures (CII) have been recognized as potential targets for cyber-attacks since the late 1990s and many have already been successfully attacked since then. The attacks that took place on September 11, 2001 have increased the concerns of the impact such attacks could have and many governments, professional bodies, and vendors have put in place advisory and coordination mechanisms to share and encourage such good practices. Critical infrastructures are monitored and controlled by information systems, and this makes it increasingly difficult to distinguish a Critical Infrastructure from a Critical Information Infrastructure. It is also acknowledged that such information systems are complex, interdependent, and convergent as they share components that use a small number of products and standards. All of these systems and the products with which they are built are known to have known and unknown vulnerabilities that could be exploited by attackers.

SCENE SETTING

CIIs usually have three categories of information systems and data: Enterprise systems, mostly commercially supplied, Line of Business systems, mostly one-of-a-kind tailor made systems and Systems Control and Data Acquisition (SCADA) facilities, many of which are implemented using commodity technologies and, perhaps more significantly not managed by the I.T. function and therefore likely to address security differently.

There are several sets of standards and good practices that are regularly updated and improved as experience is gained by both attackers and defenders. There are complemented by numerous books, journals and websites. In parallel with this,

DOI: 10.4018/978-1-4666-2659-1.ch011

Copyright © 2013, IGI Global. Copying or distributing in print or electronic forms without written permission of IGI Global is prohibited.

the skills of those intent on cyber attacks and the sophistication of the tools they use, continues to evolve and this paper suggests that attackers are engaged in an asymmetrical war of attrition against the defenders.

Cyber attacks are non-random – they are almost always targeted. This makes them unpredictable and cannot be excluded just because they may be believed to be unlikely. On the contrary, it should be taken for granted that such an attack will happen and succeed.

The timing, source and motivation of an attack should be treated as known unknowns and the source may remain unknown even after the event. Good intelligence and strong incident response capabilities are essential components of security management.

The security performance of a CII can be assessed by a) looking at its incident history, b) a self-assessment of its risks and mitigation actions c) by a specialized audit and d) by penetration tests (also called Ethical Hacking).

This chapter concentrates on how to design the scope of a security audit so that the audit can be conducted in a reasonable time and deliver valuable and actionable recommendations by focusing on a structured approach to auditing security management domains in line with the most recent set of good practices.

The appendices a list of references that complements the footnotes in the text and the literature review in Section 2 as well as a list of reputable sources of guidelines online. A third appendix consists of a list of questions designed to facilitate the formulation of the scope of audit.

1. CONTEXT: CIIS IN 2012

There are many ways to define what is a Critical Information Infrastructure (CII). For example the European Network and Information Security Agency (ENISA)[1], part of the European Union, states that a CII are:

Those interconnected systems and networks, the disruption or destruction of which would have a serious impact on the health, safety, security, or economic well-being of citizens, or on the effective functioning of government or the economy.

For the purpose of this paper, the specific and essential characteristics of a CII are that:

- It operates 7 days a week, 24 hours a day AND
- Their operations require information systems and networks, sensors and other mechanisms for data acquisition.
- CIIs frequently are required to operate physical devices ranging from cash dispensers (ATM) to motors (such as to switch a railroad track) and robotic systems (for example in manufacturing).
- It is part of a supply chain – failure to operate propagates to other entities that may also be CIIs.

This definition applies to many areas of activity. To list just a few, they include utilities (electricity, gas, water), transportation (air traffic control, airport operations, railways), all continuous manufacturing (oil refineries, glass and paper processing), defense and law enforcement (army, air force, police), banking (ATM networks and online), telecommunications (fixed line and mobile telephony, internet service providers) and many more.

Around the mid 1990s, before the Internet and the World Wide Web became established, all these critical infrastructures were confronted with the rollover of the date management in computer systems from 1999 to 2000, the so called Y2K problem.

While these days many consider that this was an artificial crisis and that the problem was hyped beyond its potential impact, much effort and investment around the world went into addressing it. This required all organizations, particularly CIIs to fully understand what IT systems they had and the extent of their exposure to the Y2K problem. In the event, there was no disruption.

Much has changed in the last 10 years. Y2K was a well-defined problem with known solutions. Was it a security issue? Yes, because *availability* was at the core of this issue. By the time of Y2K, information security practices had expanded to be also concerned with *confidentiality*. At that time the implementation of firewalls had become an additional task for the IT department.

Some of the components that made Y2K a challenge may still be there, particularly in the areas of configuration management and software documentation, particularly for systems specifically designed for a business activity.

The situation today should be regarded as more challenging than Y2K: global connectivity based on a protocol not designed to be secure (the Internet Protocol IP V.4), technology solutions based on a relatively small number of platforms with known (and unknown) vulnerabilities (e.g. Windows-Intel and Open Source products such as Apache and Linux), mobile platforms and access to sensitive data through wireless networks of unknown (or no) security such as public Wi-Fi, all of which are targets for attackers of all kinds, from the enthusiastic teenage hacker to state-sponsored professionals.

2. REVIEW OF SIGNIFICANT CII SECURITY EVENTS IN THE LAST FEW YEARS

By there very nature, CIIs are potential targets for an attack (electronic or other). When the author was working for the British Railways, the protection of critical information systems was focused on physical access controls. At that time, London and other major cities in the UK were the target of bombs and incendiary devices by

the Irish Revolutionary Army. Railway stations and signalboxes (traffic control centres) were the targets of many such attacks.

One of the many critical systems, running in a data centre protected by a joint team of the Ministry of Defense and the British Transport Police was used to track in real time all train movements in the UK, including the transport of nuclear waste for reprocessing, the Royal train, military transports as well as providing current information about the travel arrangements of senior government figures and other VIPs.

Logical security was based on providing access to the system on the basis of "need to know" and "least privilege". There were also strict change control procedures and extensive pre-production testing for all changes to this and other critical systems. At that time, the network linking to this system was private and used proprietary protocols.

Management was aware that a successful logical attack on this network would require the participation of an insider with detailed knowledge of its architecture. The few people who met this profile were trusted individuals and treated as such.

The situation today is very different and numerous successful cyber-attacks around the world over the last few years confirm this.

Attacks on *availability* through Distributed Denial of Service (DDOS) attacks are commonplace and relatively frequent. These primarily target the availability of servers connected to the Internet and can be effective in shutting down many services for several days. Two examples of such attacks are those in Estonia in 2007[2] and the many attacks launched by a group calling themselves Anonymous are briefly discussed below:

Estonia

At the end of April 2007, the country became the target of a series of Denial of Service attacks targeting the websites of several Estonian organizations, including banks, newspapers, ministries and it's parliament. This had considerable impact on the general public, as at the time, Estonia was one of the leaders in providing Internet connectivity to its citizens and an advanced implementer of e-government. The attacks followed a dispute with Russia about the relocation of a Soviet-era statue but nobody has claimed responsibility for them.

Shortly after these attacks Estonia urged its allies in the European Union and NATO to take firm action against a new mode of warfare. This led to the establishment, in May 2008, of the NATO Cooperative Cyber Defence Centre of Excellence[3], located in Tallinn, Estonia.

Its sponsoring nations are Estonia, Latvia, Lithuania, Germany, Hungary, Italy, Poland, Slovakia, Spain, the Netherlands and USA and has the status of an international military organization.

On 24 January 2008, Dmitri Galushkevich, a 20 year old ethnic Russian student living in Tallinn, was found guilty[4] of participating in the attacks. He was fined 17,500 kroons (approximately US$1,600) for attacking the website of a political party.

Anonymous

Their activities began in 2003. Anonymous describes itself as a group without leadership, no ranking and many means of communications. The group can be joined simply by wishing to do so. People from all over the world have done so.

Amongst their numerous and well publicized exploits, in December 2011 Anonymous launched attacks under the codename *Operation Avenge Assange* in retaliation for perceived anti-WikiLeaks behavior. Its targets included Amazon, PayPal, MasterCard, Visa and the Swiss Postal bank. These attacks succeeded in shutting down the websites of both MasterCard and Visa.

Numerous arrests for alleged involvement in these attacks were made in several countries. All the detailed people were young – some as young as

16. In an article in the Wall Street Journal[5] it was stated that Federal law-enforcement officials say they are concerned about cyber-retaliation against agents and prosecutors and included the statement that *"The forces out there are very, very good at moving very, very fast to make it unpleasant."*

Attacks on *confidentiality* – ranging from unauthorized disclosures to the theft of intellectual property and other forms of spying – are perhaps the best known and possibly the oldest form of information security threat.

The notorious Wikileaks incident of November 2010 (also known as Cablegate) when a collection of over 250,000 sensitive diplomatic communications was disclosed to the press will not be discussed in this Chapter as this did not occur as a result of a cyber-attack.

The alleged source for this disclosure was a U.S. soldier, Bradley Manning, who held the required access credentials and authorizations to access this information, and proceeded to copy sensitive information to a disk which was subsequently passed onto the Wikileaks organization. The legal issues surrounding this event remain, to this date, complex and unresolved.

The insider with access, knowledge, motivation and opportunity remains, in the whole field of security, the weakest link and the hardest to identify and manage.

The nature of these attacks has changed in 2011 with the emergence of sophisticated malicious software specifically designed to conduct cyber espionage. Researchers at Kaspersky Labs, a Russian cyber-security company, have identified various forms of such software (these were named Duqu, Flame and more recently Gauss). Their primary target were banks in Lebanon and other countries in the Middle East. The discovery of Gauss was part of work initiated by the International Telecommunications Union, a U.N. Agency in Geneva in support of their Cyber Peace[6] initiative.

An analysis of Flame and Gauss revealed that it targets computers running the Windows operating system and is designed to steal information. In addition, it appears to include a payload of unknown purpose but it is thought that it could be destructive against critical infrastructures. The sophistication of this malware suggests that such software was likely to be state sponsored but, so far, no government has ever admitted to being involved in such activities.

Kaspersky Labs has invited the assistance of cryptographers to support their efforts to break the encryption of the Gauss malware. In a press article[7] published in August 2012 Vitaly Kalmuk, a senior officer at Kaspersy Labs, urged the United Nations to "wake up to the threats because disaster may happen any day". In May 2012, in his keynote speech to CEBIT 2012 Australia, Eugene Kaspersky, CEO of the company, said that[8] cyber weapons were "a thousand times cheaper" to develop than conventional bombs or missiles, and as such, were even more dangerous.

Attacks on data *integrity*[9], also known as semantic attacks, have also been known for some time, particularly as they were focused on fraud. The largest such events (Barings Bank (1995), Societé Generale (2008), UBS London (2011), will not be discussed in this chapter as they only apply to the banking sector and carried out by insiders. However, there were confirmed reports that in 2010 a successful attack was launched on Iran's uranium enrichment facilities in Iran through malicious software named Stuxnet[10].

This was designed to damage the centrifuges while, at the same time, displaying normal operating conditions to the controllers. This malicious software was introduced even though these facilities are not connected to the Internet. It is widely believed that the malware was introduced into the control systems using a USB flash memory device with the participation of an insider with the required access controls and authorities.

Nobody has, so far, claimed responsibility for this – there has been speculation that governments were involved - and Iran's reaction to this event was surprisingly muted.

The alleged or suspected involvement of governments in the development of sophisticated malicious software, directly or by sponsoring others with the necessary skills, is a matter for concern as it broadens the scope of a hypothetical conflict beyond the domains currently covered by the Laws of Armed Conflict and other international treaties and conventions to areas that could have a major impact on civilian populations.

None of the international treaties found during the preparation of this article covers information warfare or the use of computers. The most recent treaty to enter into force in 2010 was on cluster munitions. Non-State actors, regardless of the label attached to them (criminals, terrorists, activists, freedom fighters, etc.) ignore such treaties and conventions anyway.

While lawyers, diplomats and international organizations debate whether software can be used as a weapon and on definitions on cyber-war and cyber-terrorism, senior members of the United States of America military made two notable statements in 2011:

In May, General K. Chilton[11], U.S. Military Strategic Command said that: "In the event of a cyber-attack, the Laws of Armed Conflict will apply" and in October, General R. Kehler, from the same organization said that: "... there is a need to define Rules of Engagement for Offensive Computer Warfare". To be noted that the latest edition of the Dictionary of the International Law of Armed Conflict[12] was published in 1992 and makes no reference to computers.

Therefore, as attrition through cyber-attacks progresses from independent hackers to hacktivists (such as Anonymous), organized crime, military and terrorist players, there is a good case for providing assurances of the measures taken to protect a CII from a cyber-attack is becoming stronger. This chapter focuses on independent audits as a component for providing such assurances.

Other approaches for demonstrating due diligence in the implementation and management of information security include the collection and analysis of appropriate metrics, self-assessments of vulnerabilities, threats and risk and penetration tests.

3. BRIEF REVIEW OF RELATED LITERATURE

Much has been published on the subject of the protection of information systems used in critical infrastructures as well as critical information infrastructures. It is becoming increasingly difficult to distinguish between them as computer systems and networks have become ubiquitous and play a vital role in their activities.

Appendix 1 contains a list of the main references used by the author to support this Chapter and they consist of a mix of government publications, books and articles in academic and professional journals. Few of the latter have been included as many such articles are vendor-sponsored and are used to advocate specific products and, besides, not always subject to peer-review. The references listed in this Appendix represent the author's interests and knowledge. The list is nowhere near comprehensive as there are hundreds of articles on related topics published every year.

Appendix 2 contains a selected (and selective) summary of online sources representing the state of the art. It is limited to government sources and professional bodies independent from vendors and consulting companies. As with the literature, this selection is considered by the author to consist of sites that can be considered as trustworthy and unbiased (and are the proverbial tip of the iceberg).

While publications on the protection of critical infrastructure go back to the mid 1990s, few of them will be discussed as the nature of technologies, computer programs, networks and operat-

ing practices have changed considerably in the intervening period and so has the nature of the threats and attack techniques.

Two government publications deserve to be mentioned for their historical interest, as they were prescient: "Australia's Vulnerability to Information Attacks" (Cobb, 1977) and "Critical Foundations", (US Government Printing Office, 1977). Most of their content should now be considered as having been overtaken by events and more recent publications.

The list in Appendix 1 begins with the most recent publications. The most recent is a report (in French) commissioned by the French Senate (J-M Bockel, 2012) which includes a critical review of the current status of CII protection and makes a case for the further strengthening of international cooperation, making a priority of the protection of national critical infrastructures and providing appropriate resources to the French national Agency for the protection of information systems, the Agence Nationale de la Securité des Systèmes d'Information[13] (ANSSI).

A second highly informative and detailed reference is the report "Cybersecurity Guidance Is Available But More Can Be Done To Promote Its Use", (US GAO, 2011). This report includes detailed cyber security guidance by sector of activity. Its Table 1 provides a summary of the various types of cyber-exploits currently used to target CIIs.

The publication in January 2011 of "The Quest for Cyber Peace", by the Secretary General of the International Telecommunications Union and the permanent monitoring panel on Information Security of the World Federation of Scientists, recognizes that:

Military leaders around the world are announcing cyber-commands with capabilities to attack, defend and exploit networks" and that "we are approaching a dangerous precipice at which time the dark side of the internet may overshadow the enormous benefits of ICT and upset the world order.

This publication advocates the creation by the international community of a cyber code of conduct equivalent to a non-proliferation treaty.

The book "Cyberwar" by Richard Clarke, sometimes referred to as a former "cyber-terrorism czar" as an employee of the US State Department covers the subject from a non-technical and non-military perspective, which makes the book readable. It's critics however described as simplistic. Richard Clarke is amongst those who consider that cyber warfare has already started and that Stuxnet was the first acknowledged cyber weapon.

The most substantial part of the reviewed literature consists on "how to" guidelines. The publications dedicated to the management of Systems Control and Data Acquisition Systems (SCADA) are particularly relevant to practitioners but assumed to be of limited interest (or comprehensibility) to decision makers.

4. SECURITY ANATOMY OF A CII

Many people, and even organizations, seem to be unaware of the differences between Information *Technology* security and Information security and that enterprise security is a superset within which they belong, as shown in Figure 1.

Information Technology Security is the responsibility of service providers consisting of a mix of resources internal to the organization and 3rd party service providers such as outsourcers, telecommunications and Internet Service Providers, vendors and, more recently cloud services.

Information security requires clear ownership of information assets and accountability for their classification (e.g. from public to secret), the authorization of access provision and definition of privileges, i.e. what authorized people can access and what they can do with it (ranging from "read only" to "create"). Good information security practices also require systems and data owners to conduct Business Impact Analyses, develop, maintain and test appropriate contingency and business continuity plans and ensure data integrity.

Figure 1. Security layers in a CII

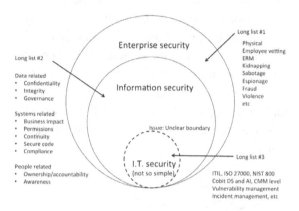

Those responsible for information security should also take steps to raise awareness of its importance amongst all parties who have access to data and information systems. It is the author's contention that the boundary between information technology security and information security is often unclear and that data and system owners may not give adequate priority to their responsibilities in this respect.

In most CIIs the situation is more complex still. Figure 2 maps the main components of their I.T. architecture. Generic systems, such as Enterprise Resource Planning (ERP), Customer Relationship Management (CRM), Electronic Content Management (ECM), etc., are usually commercial products, sometimes customized to reflect preferred practices. Accountability for the security of their programming code is entirely with the vendor, although the terms of the software license may say that the vendor is not liable for any malfunction. Besides, unless it is an Open Source product, vendors do not disclose details of their software.

CIIs however, have made important investments in "Line of Business Systems". These have four characteristics in common:

1. They are usually One-Of-A-Kind – specifically designed for (or by) an individual company or organization,

Figure 2. Components of a CII's security architecture

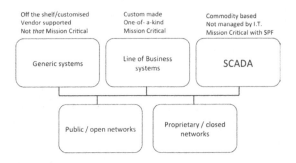

2. Examples are: An airline (or hotel) Yield Management system, the control systems for robotic assembly lines, or those in a refinery, etc.

3. The intellectual property of the software used in these systems is carefully guarded and expertise tends to be limited to a small number of people.

4. They are Mission Critical – failure to operate correctly has immediate impact and, if they cannot be restored to normal operation fast enough, could have catastrophic consequences for the business.

The Y2K problem mentioned earlier required a major review of such systems documentation and, where appropriate corrective actions. However, this was 15 years ago and many new systems have since been developed and put into service. It is conceivable that many of these One-Of-A-Kind systems may have unknown vulnerabilities as software is never perfect and hidden or undocumented features such as back doors introduced by designers for ease of future access are not uncommon. With the growth of outsourcing and offshoring of such systems, there additional risks of them containing a Logical Bomb, software that can stop the system's operations controlled by a member of the design team, usually used to extort payment, or a Kill Switch, a similar concept but introduced by a manufacturer to disrupt the target in a cyber-war situation.

There have been several articles in the serious press speculating about the possibility of such a Kill Switch. A recent article in the Economist[14] specifically discusses telecommunications equipment manufactured in China. Whether this is suspicion, fantasy, paranoia or fact is impossible to tell. While such systems are extensively examined and tested their complexity and sophistication ensures that such studies cannot ever be complete.

The third category of information systems and technology are collectively referred to as SCADA: Systems Control and Data Acquisition. These are the primary component of any automation of physical processes and have been in use for 50 years or more. As such, they are designed to operate in a hostile physical environment, use standard components, including stripped down personal computers, with an emphasis on reliability.

However, their design and operation does not always follow the practices, or address the concerns, of information technology security practitioners notably data protection, single points of failure, change management and access controls, encryption and their implementation and operation may not follow what are considered to be good information security practices.

In practice, their procurement, installation and operational management is totally separate from I.T. and Information security in the organization. The proprietary networks used in many SCADA installations are simple, low speed and unencrypted. In addition, such networks are sometimes reasonably accessible and, as the price of copper has risen, they have been the target of thieves. The result is always significant disruption as has been the case for railroad operations in many countries, including the UK and France.

This fragmentation of security practices has the potential to create problems within an organization. These include a lack of a cohesive approach to the protection of information assets, such as the adoption of consistent practices and standards, and a lack of dialogue between the respective parties with the consequent loss of knowledge and shared experiences.

5. BRIEF REVIEW OF INFORMATION SECURITY STANDARDS AND GOOD PRACTICES

This chapter will not explore in any detail the many sources for best practices and standards other than to highlight the challenges of selecting those that best fit the culture and practices of an organization and then finding the time to study, understand and implement them as these are substantial tasks and time is in short supply.

Best practices and standards for practitioners (which may also be used by auditors) include:

- COBIT 5 for Information Security
- The International Security Forum Standard of Good Practice The ISO 27000 series issued by the International Standards Organization
- The NIST SP 800 series issued by the United States National Institute for Science and Technology (in the public domain)
- The Information Technology Infrastructure Library (ITIL)
- The Software Engineering Body of Knowledge (SWEBOK)
- The Data Management Body of Knowledge (DMBOK)
- The Risk IT Framework issued by ISACA
- The Information Technology Assurance Framework (ITAF) issued by ISACA

Of these, *COBIT5* (Control Objectives for Information Technology) *for Information Security* deserves a special mention because not only it was published in June 2012 and can be considered the most up to date set of guidelines and practices, but also because it was developed jointly with two other key organizations: the Information Security Forum[15] (ISF) and the International Information Systems Security Certification Consortium[16] (ISC2).

The Control Objectives for Information Technology (COBIT) – is the parent publication of the volume dedicated to information security.

First issued as a tool for auditors in 1990 by the Information Technology Governance Institute (ITGI) and the Information Systems Audit and Control Association (ISACA), it underwent several revisions and has been translated into several languages.

Its evolution from Version 1 to the latest Version 5 has transformed it into a holistic framework that maps against many other standards and good practices that covers governance, planning and organization, acquisition and implementation, delivery and support and finally, monitoring and evaluation.

COBIT 5 for Information Security is structured in 37 processes and 219 practices. Each practice is complemented with metrics (both lagging and leading indicators) and can be attributed a capability maturity level. This tool is well suited to support self-assessments as well as audits.

Audit guidelines include:

- The Global Technology Audit Guidelines (GTAG) issued by the Institute of Internal Auditors which include GTAG 15 "Information Security Governance"
- The collection of auditing standards and guidelines for information security[17,18] published by the Information Systems Audit and Control Association (ISACA)

While adopting such best practices, standards and guidelines is not mandatory they do provide frameworks that are widely used that are superior to improvising or, worse, learning by experience (described in the strip of paper in a fortune cookie as "the best teacher and also the most expensive".)

On the other hand, the collection of documents mentioned above represents a very large stack of paper once printed and that is only the first step – they need to be studied, understood and applied by people who would normally be so busy doing their job that they would not be able to find the time to do so.

6. ASSESSING SECURITY PERFORMANCE

In a lecture given in 1893 to the UK Institute of Civil Engineers, William Thompson (Lord Kelvin) said "If you can measure that of which you speak and can express it by a number, you know something of your subject; but if you cannot measure it, your knowledge is meager and unsatisfactory." This is often simplified to "you cannot manage what you do not measure". Lord Kelvin was right (and the (over) simplification is misleading).

This does not make it easy to find metrics that are meaningful in business terms for information security. (COBIT5, NIST SP800 and ISO 27000 publications suggest lists of possible metrics). Such metrics fall in three categories:

A. Key Indicators

Key Performance Indicators (KPIs)

These can include a wide range of items such as for example:

- Incident history
- Number of attempted intrusions detected
- Number of successful intrusion detected
- Number of orphaned accounts for access to sensitive information or critical systems
- Time required to close a reported security incident (by incident)
- Total downtime (per critical system) in the period reported
- Availability (excluding planned service interruptions) over a defined period of time

Plus points for these metrics are: They are related to verifiable facts, the data is traceable and allows analysis for trends, correlations and other statistics.

The Minus points are that these are lagging indicators unsuitable to predict future performance. Given that cyber attacks are carried out through deliberate human actions and exploit unknown

unknowns (as is the case in zero day exploits) the laws of statistics based on randomness do not apply.

Key Risk Indicators (KRIs)

These can also be numerous and cover a wide range to subjects, for example:

- Number of information security policies not review or updated for more than X months (e.g. 24)
- Number of information security processes or activities carried out by a single individual for whom there is no immediate backup or replacement
- Number of unfilled positions in the security organization
- Number of "near misses" in information security activities where no incident occurred but could have done so
- Number of related audit recommendations that have not been implemented
- Number of high impact items in the Risk Register where mitigation activities have not been completed

The Plus points for these metrics is that they are leading indicators and focus on specific problems or actions to be taken.

The Minus points are that such actions may require diverting resources from other activities.

B. Risk and Performance Self-Assessments

Self-assessments have the advantage that they have clearly identifiable ownership, should be a routine part of management's responsibilities and conducted regularly. As a routine activity, it should also be relatively simple to conduct.

Good practices for risk assessment are based on the use of a generally accepted framework such as NIST SP800-30[19], the ISACA Risk IT Framework[20] or the proprietary but widely applied

VERIS[21] Framework (or their equivalents) to focus on Business Impact and Vulnerability Assessment. The results include a Risk Register with defined action plans to mitigate those considered to be those with highest impact.

The main Minus points of self-assessments is that other than quantifiable Key Performance and Key Risk Indicators, they could be subjective and, often, optimistic to the degree than some practitioners may see themselves as "best in class" without tangible proof that this is the case. The truth is that the author has, during several audits and at conferences, come across such individuals.

Those readers with a specific interest in the effectiveness of Risk Assessment and Management practices may consider studying the 2009 book "The Failure of Risk Management: Why It's Broken and How to Fix It" by Douglas W. Hubbard. The essence of the book is that basic analysis methods are often misapplied and goes on to shows how some of the most popular "risk management" methods are no better than astrology (Hubbard's words). A more detailed discussion of this book falls outside the scope of this Chapter.

The non-random nature of cyber-attacks targeting a CII support Nassim Taleb's views in The Black Swan that past performance is not a good predictor of future performance. Hence, metrics, particularly leading indicators, are necessary but not sufficient. The same is true for risk assessments.

C. Penetration Tests (Ethical Hacking)

A substantial topic in its own right, such tests are no different from the actions of attackers except that they are conducted with the explicit consent of management. They differ fundamentally from audits in many ways, in particular:

They may be carried out without the knowledge or participation of the information security practitioner, thus replicating the conditions of a real external attack. The focus is the identification and exploit of vulnerabilities that may be unknown to the practitioner.

Audits are announced, the target entity is consulted on the scope and timing of the audit. The practitioners' participation is essential. Any vulnerabilities found during the audit are reported and may be the subject of specific recommendations that the practitioners may or may not accept and implement.

The Plus points for penetration tests is that they can come closest to the circumstances of a real attack (depending on the skills of the team and time available to them to break into the target systems)

The Minus points for such tests are that they are invariably time-limited, mostly to contain costs and limit disruption to operations. External attackers are not subject to such constraints and may continue to try for as long as it takes. Another issue to consider is that the ethical hacking team will end such tests with very detailed knowledge of the security arrangements and adequate Non Disclosure agreements need to be in place.

8. AUDITING THE GOVERNANCE AND MANAGEMENT OF INFORMATION SECURITY AT A CII

The potential scope of an information security audit is huge – ISO 27002[22] (Code of Practice for the Management of Information Security) has 127 main controls and over 500 detailed controls.

The previously mentioned COBIT5 for Information Security covers 37 processes and 192 practices in five domains. Each process's practices are defined with a set of high level controls and metrics consisting of leading and lagging indicators. COBIT also allows for the evaluation of the maturity of each process using the principles of the Capability Maturity Model[23] (CMM).

Without careful planning, a security audit could in fact become a hindrance rather than a help as it would take too much time to the point that many other I.T. activities such as applications controls, data governance, outsourcing and off-shoring arrangements could not be audited. Besides it would also occupy the information security practitioners to the extent they would be unable to do the work expected of them while the audit progresses.

One way to approach audit planning would be to focus on the management of information security and consider it as a kind of "Olympic games" consisting of hurdle events and endurance events. At such games no medals are awarded.

Hurdle Events

These are primarily associated with the governance of information security and require senior management participation and, ideally, commitment. Such events typically include activities that occur sporadically and without which information security cannot be implemented or maintained. Examples are:

- Enterprise strategy for information security
- Building enterprise awareness of the role of information security
- Enterprise contingency planning, disaster recovery and business continuity
- Business case for investments and operational expenditures
- Budgets and funding
- Policies and compliance
- Reviewing the status of the risk register
- Reviewing the status of relevant audit recommendations
- … etc.

Endurance Events

These are operational activities that are performed on a day-to-day basis and require a combination of people, process and technology. Examples are:

- Identity and access management
- Vulnerability assessments
- Security intelligence gathering
- Information Security Risk Management
- Incident detection
- Incident management
- Emergency response
- … etc.

The section that follows proposes a small number of domains that would give the greatest value if and when audited.

Given the many differences that exist between security needs and how these are met by individual organizations, the reader may have a different view of what the domains should be. This chapter advocates that creating a short list of domains to audit should be the starting point for establishing the scope of a realistic and useful audit.

Decisions on the final scope will be influenced by any audit history of the organization and security related topics.

9. NARROWING THE SCOPE OF AUDIT AT A CII

This Section reflects the author's experience of working in CII's as well as auditing them. Appendix 3 lists 30 questions (and their rationale) that can be used to support the definition of the scope of audit as they build a multidimensional picture of the current status of the governance and management of information security.

The scope of audit should normally be discussed and agreed with senior management, the parties to be audited and, if appropriate, the Audit

Committee of the organization. At this point, senior management and the Director of Internal Audit are in a position to assess whether the internal audit organization has the resources and skills to carry it out or if there is a need to engage qualified and experienced auditors from a specialized company.

This section focuses on five domains as candidates for high-level audits – as distinct from a detailed audit of, for example, application controls. These audits should be seen as complementing other related activities outside the scope of internal audit such as ethical hacking (penetration tests) or investigations (digital forensics and legal proceedings).

These domains have been selected to reflect the author's experience in the management and, subsequently, the auditing of information systems and technologies as well as their security.

- Information Security Governance
- Information Security activities outside the I.T. function
- Information Security activities within the I.T. function
- Personnel security in the enterprise
- Security awareness and communications

Information Security Governance (ISG)

Guidelines for the conduct of ISG by senior management were published by ISACA[24] in 2006 and specific audit guidelines were subsequently issued by the Institute of Internal Auditors published in 2010 GTAG 15, Information Security Governance Practice Guide[25]. An article by this author[26] discussed the factors that make the difference between effective information security governance and failure.

An ISG audit should determine whether accountabilities for information security governance are clearly defined and carried out systematically. The audit should also determine the completeness, quality and timeliness of the inputs to the governance process that should include, as a minimum:

- Status of (and changes to) high impact items in the Risk Register
- Status of open past audit recommendations relating to information security
- Changes to the enterprise's Business Impact Analysis
- Key Performance and Risk Indicators that fell outside acceptable targets in the reporting period
- Security intelligence
- Regulatory and legal compliance issues
- Review of significant security incidents in the reporting period.

An ISG audit should also determine the completeness, quality and timeliness of the outputs of the governance process, in particular:

- Enterprise Information Security strategy, its updates and dissemination for action
- Security policies (formally approved and disseminated, awaiting approval, policy gaps)
- Extent to which such policies are enforced by systems and assurance of compliance with such policies where such enforcement is not possible or not practiced
- Accountabilities for information security, including core systems, line of business systems, SCADA and networks
- Resource allocation, including budgets
- Executive reporting (to the Board, to the Audit Committee, to other stakeholders, etc.)

While resource allocation is the responsibility of senior managers, organizations in the private and public sectors are continually under pressure to contain costs. Given that the business case (or return on security investments) is a subject where there is more debate than agreement any recommendations concerning resources need to be adequately justified.

Information Security Activities outside the I.T. Function

Several activities impacting information security are carried out outside the I.T. function regardless of whether the latter is internal or outsourced. These fall in two distinct categories:

Applying to all organizations:

- Data governance, in particular data classification and the assurance of data quality and integrity
- The assignment of access to data and information systems as well as the definition of privileges and segregation of duties requirements
- For information systems designed and maintained in-house (including spreadsheets), change management and quality assurance

Applying to organizations with process control relying on systems and networks (SCADA).

These may be implemented, managed and operated by other departments (e.g. Production) or, as if frequently the case by parties external to the enterprise, often the vendors of such systems. The key activities that define how effective information security is, are the same as those in C. below.

The auditors' opinions and appropriate recommendations should reflect their findings.

Information Technology Security Activities

Regardless of who performs these activities (i.e. in-house or any form of third party service) a small number of activities make a significant difference to information security. In the author's opinion the most important of these are:

- Vulnerability management
- Change management (including patch management)
- Configuration management

- Incident response
- Management of Privileged Users (systems and network administrators, etc.)
- Security intelligence

It is possible that the I.T. security activities have been designed and implemented to meet the requirements of an established standard, such as ISO 27001, "Security techniques – Information Security Management Systems (ISMS)" issued in 2005. This standard supports and independent certification process that must be conducted by an accredited registrar (also called certification body or registration body, sometimes simply "registrar".).

While this is a valuable complement to the management of information security it should be noted that it is possible to obtain such certification for just a specific component of the I.T. infrastructure rather than for the full portfolio of systems, databases, networks and other infrastructure.

If the component(s) for which certification has been obtained are limited in scope such certifications may only provide a false sense of "security". The auditors should determine the scope covered by such certification and assess its relevance to the organization as a whole.

The auditors' opinions and appropriate recommendations should reflect their findings.

Personnel Security in the Enterprise

Auditors should assess the extent to which due diligence is exercised at the recruitment stage to validate candidates' backgrounds and references, and where the organization's security strategy so requires, at other times (e.g. prior to a change in accountabilities/promotion).

The same applies to the issue of credentials and the provisioning of access controls to sensitive areas. The auditors should also examine the life-cycle management process for maintaining these up to date with changes of assignments, prolonged absences and when leaving the organization.

The auditors should review whether the information security policies describe the actions to be taken in the event of non-compliance resulting in a security breach.

Security Awareness and Communications

Critical Information Infrastructures are, by their very nature, expected to develop security awareness amongst its workforce, be they employees, partners or contractors. The same is true for information security policies and other briefings.

An audit of this domain should examine the completeness of the policy portfolio, the measures taken to validate that the workforce has seen, understood and agreed to comply with these policies as well as the measures to monitor compliance.

In situations where information security is considered a high priority, the auditors should review the measures taken to build awareness – training programs, communication campaigns, issuance of security awareness certificates (a "security driving license") as a prerequisite for access to sensitive systems and data.

10. AUDIT REPORTING

An effective audit report should contain information that is new to the organization as there is little point in telling the auditees and senior management things they already know. The report's recommendations should be implementable and deliver genuine benefits.

The auditors, as is established practice, should hold an Exit conference with the auditees and discuss their response to points raised in the report, including them, as appropriate in the draft audit report. Adequate time should be provided to the auditees and senior management to formally comment on the draft report, hold additional discussions and amend the report as necessary so that it can be issued as a final report.

The final report and its associated Executive Summary (or Management Letter) should be issued as soon as practicable after the completion of the audit. Its distribution should be agreed with senior management at the time of defining the scope of the audit.

In practice, the value of the audit will ultimately depend on the inputs provided, the knowledge and experience of the auditors and the actions taken on the recommendations. It should be recognized that however good the intention and execution, an audit is based on a sample over a relatively short period of time and may have missed important items.

As stated in The Black Swan, "no evidence of a problem" is fundamentally different to "evidence that there is no problem".

11. DISCUSSION: ASSUMPTIONS MADE IN THE PREPARATION OF THIS CHAPTER

These assumptions are as follows:

Critical Information Infrastructures are a potential target for a multitude of attackers, including individual hackers, industrial spies, assorted state and non-state actors including hostile military outfits.

Organized crime cannot be left out even though their primary target is money because of the possibility they may act as mercenaries and make their knowledge and experience of cyber-attacks to other parties.

Those carrying out cyber-attacks should be assumed to be at least as knowledgeable, if not more so, than the professionals protecting the organization and have little or nothing to lose by launching an attack – in fact even an unsuccessful attack provides them with valuable knowledge about the organization's defenses.

Information threats change rapidly and are driven by innovative technology with inbuilt vulnerabilities. Many of these technologies become "objects of desire" and will be adopted by the workforce whether the organization likes it or not and sooner or later will displace or replace corporate end user technologies. (This has already happened with personal choices for home computing, smart phones and tablets).

The most commonly used techniques to assess how effective security is are the collection of metrics such as Key Performance Indicators and Key Risk Indicators and self-assessments. The first are lagging indicators and, as such, not a robust way to predict future performance as the threats and vulnerabilities change all the time. Self-assessments risk being incomplete and optimistic.

Certification for compliance with a standard such as ISO 27001 may give a false sense of security, as it is possible to obtain such certification for a specific part of the I.T. infrastructure and thus not be representative of the Information Security Management System of the whole organization.

Independent assurance in the form of a competent audit is a valuable complement to the measures taken by the organization to maintain an appropriate level of information security.

12. CONCLUSION

Will a Cyber-Attack on a CII Happen?

While with the possible exception of the Stuxnet attack on the Iranian uranium enrichment facilities in 2010 there the speculation about the possibility of a successful cyber-attack on a CII is more extensive that the history of such attacks.

However, as Taleb argues in the book "The Black Swan", the fact that something, however unlikely, has not happened does not mean that it cannot happen at some future and unpredictable time. The author is inclined to join the pessimists and assume such attacks will take place.

The role of an insider with knowledge, motivation and opportunity to participate or initiate such an attack should not be underestimated. Anticipating and identifying a potential attacker within the organization is a matter of luck.

Justifying Information Security Expenditures

Caution practiced in the midst of uncertainty (the Precautionary Principle) may be an appropriate strategy in situations where risk aversion is justified by the impact of such an event.

Such a strategy however is incompatible with the requirement to present plausible financial justifications for expenditures (investments and operational) in information security that, in practice, cannot be more than creative accounting. These expenditures may be estimated reasonably well while the multi-dimensional and longer-term costs of an event cannot be even roughly guessed.

It is however for each organization facing such decisions to select the decision criteria that best fits its culture and governance framework. The debate amongst information security professionals of the value of Return on Security Investment (ROSI) calculations continues to be inconclusive.

Legislation and Treaties

The assumption that there will be a coordinated international effort towards a cyber code of conduct and/or treaties on the use of cyber weapons comparable to the Laws of Armed Conflict is, in the author's view and experience, optimistic.

Such international efforts take a long time to come to fruition and then, some countries choose not to sign or ratify the outcome. This has been the case with the United Nations Convention on the Law of the Seas (LOAS), ratified by 162 Countries but not by the United States of America.

Another example is the nuclear Non-Proliferation Treaty for Nuclear Weapons that entered into force in 1970 but has not been signed by countries that have demonstrated nuclear weapons capabilities, notably India and Pakistan. Israel, which is believed to also have such capabilities, has also not signed it. North Korea did sign the treaty but not complied with it.

In the field of cyber security, the Council of Europe Convention on Cyber Crime became available for signature in 2001 and entered into force in 2004. Although available to signature to all countries, it has only been ratified by 30 so far. A further 16 have signed but not yet ratified it.

It may be good to remember that that the United Nations has 193 Member States. And the number of countries participating at the London 2012 Olympics was 205.

REFERENCES

Bosch, O. (2002). *Cyber-terrorism and private sector efforts for information infrastructure protection*. International Institute for Strategic Studies.

Bosch, O. (2012). Critical information infrastructure and cyber-terrorism. In Reich, P., & Gelbstein, E. (Eds.), *Cyberwar, cyberterrorism and internet immobilization*. Hershey, PA: IGI Global.

Cavelty, M. D. (2008). *Securing the homeland: Critical infrastructure, risk, and (in)security*. Hampshire, UK: Routledge.

Clarke, R. (2010). *Cyberwar: The next threat to national security and what to do about it*. Ecce Books.

Cobb, A. (1997). *Australia's vulnerability to information attacks*. Australian Strategic and Defense Studies Centre.

European Court of Auditors and INTOSAI. (2012). *Audit of disaster preparedness*, Draft ISSAI SSXX. Retrieved from http://eca.europa. eu/portal/page/portal/intosai-aada/meetings/- SixthmeetingoftheINTOSAIWorkingGroup/Microsoft%20Word%20-%20Draft%20ISSAI%20 on%20Disaster%20Preparedness%205.pdf)

Farwell, J. P. (2011). Stuxnet and the future of cyber-war. *Survival Journal, 53*(1), 23-40. Retrieved from http://www.tandfonline.com/doi/ab s/10.1080/00396338.2011.555586

Gelbstein, E., & Kamal, A. (2002). *Information insecurity*. New York, NY: United Nations ITC Task Force.

Hammerli, B., & Renda, A. (2010). *Protecting critical infrastructure in the EU*. Task Force Report. Brussels, Belgium: Centre for European Policy Studies. Retrieved from http://www.ceps. eu/ceps/download/4061

Hubbard, D. W. (2009). *The failure of risk management and what to do about it*. Hoboken, NJ: Wiley.

Luijf, E. (2003). *Critical information infrastructure in the Netherlands*. The Netherlands: TNO Physics and Electronics Laboratory.

National Institute of Standards and Technology. (2009). *Recommended security controls for federal information systems and organizations*. NIST SP800-53, Revision 3. Retrieved from http:// crsc.nist.gov

Nickolov, N. (2005). Critical information infrastructure protection: Analysis, evaluation and expectations. *Information & Security, 17*, 105–119.

Saadwi, T., & Jordan, L., Jr., (Eds.). (2011). *Cyber infrastructure protection*. Retrieved from http:// www.strategicstudiesinstitute.army.mil/pdffiles/ PUB1067.pdf

Senator Jean-Marie Bockel. (2012). *Rapport d'information on cyber defense*. Retrieved from http://www.senat.fr/notice-rapport/2011/r11-681- notice.html

Stamp, J. (2003). *Common vulnerabilities in critical infrastructure control systems*. Albuquerque, NM: Sandia National Laboratories.

Suter, M. (2007). *A generic national framework for critical information infrastructure protection*. Centre for Security Studies, Zurich University, Prepared for the World Summit on the Information Society and the International Telecommunications Union. Retrieved from http://www.itu.int/ ITU-D/cyb/cybersecurity/docs/generic-national- framework-for-ciip.pdf

Taleb, N. (2010). *The black swan* (2nd ed.). New York, NY: Random House.

Touré, A., et al. (2011). *The quest for cyberpeace*. International Telecommunications Union. Retrieved from http://www.itu.int/pub/S-GEN-WFS.01-1-2011

UK Centre for the Protection of National Infrastructure. (2010). *Good practice guide: Cyber security assessments of industrial control systems*. CPNI.

UK Centre for the Protection of National Infrastructure. (2010). *Good practice guide: Guide 2 – Implement secure architecture*. CPNI.

UK Centre for the Protection of National Infrastructure. (2010). *Good practice guide: Guide 3 – Establish response capability*. CPNI.

UK Centre for the Protection of National Infrastructure. (2010). *Good practice guide: Guide 4 – Improve awareness and skills*. CPNI.

UK Centre for the Protection of National Infrastructure. (2010). *Good practice guide: Guide 5 – Manage 3rd party risk*. CPNI.

UK Centre for the Protection of National Infrastructure. (2010). *Good practice guide: Process control and SCADA security*. CPNI.

UK Centre for the Protection of National Infrastructure. (2010). *Protecting against terrorism* (3rd ed.). CPNI.

U.S. Government Accountability Office. (2011). *Cybersecurity guidance is available but more can be done to promote its use*. GAO 12-92. Retrieved from http://www.gao.gov/assets/590/587529.pdf

US Government Printing Office. (1997). *Critical foundations*. (Report 040-000-0699-1).

Verissimo, P., et al. (2006). *The CRUTIAL reference critical information infrastructure architecture: A blueprint*. Retrieved from http://homepages.gsd.inesc-id.pt/~mpc/pubs/04_Verissimo.pdf

KEY TERMS AND DEFINITIONS

Audit: An independent and objective evaluation of a process or system usually following guidelines issued by a professional body such as the Institute of Internal Audit or the Information Systems Audit and Control Association.

Availability: One of the three essential components of information security, it measures the ability of an information system or service to perform its function when required.

Confidentiality: The second of the three essential components of information security, it is the requirement that information is appropriately protected so that it is accessible only to those authorized to have access to it.

Ethical Hacking: The collection of activities, tools and methods that experts may use to break into computer systems, networks and data with the consent of management with the purpose of identifying vulnerabilities in the protection of said systems, networks and data.

Governance: The mechanisms an organization uses to ensure that stakeholders follow established policies and processes. Governance supports oversight and accountability.

Integrity: The third of the three essential components of information security, it is the requirement that information is appropriately protected so that it can only be modified (created, changed, deleted, etc.) only by those authorized to have access to it and the required level of rights.

SCADA: Abbreviation of Systems Control and Data Acquisition, it is the collective name for those devices and networks an enterprise uses for these purposes.

ENDNOTES

[1] www.enisa.europa.eu (located in Heraklion, Greece)

2   Hackers Take Down the Most Wired Country in Europe, Wired Magazine, 15 September 2007

3   www.ccdcoe.org

4   http://news.bbc.co.uk/2/hi/technology/7208511.stm

5   http://online.wsj.com/article/SB10001424 05297020336350457718536423041 7098. html

6   *"The quest for cyber peace"*, by Dr. H. Touré and the Permanent Monitoring Panel on Information Security, World Federation of Scientists

7   http://www.guardian.co.uk/technology/2012/aug/09/cyber-espionage-state-sponsored-lebanon

8   http://www.techweekeurope.co.uk/news/kaspersky-warns-about-cyber-weapons-79136

9   Data integrity – information security's poor relation, by Eduardo Gelbstein, ISACA Journal, volume 11, issue 6, November 2011

10   Stuxnet and the future of cyberwar, James P. Farrell and Rahal Rohozinski, Survival, 28 January 2011

11   http://www.nytimes.com/2011/06/01/us/politics/01cyber.html

12   Dictionary of the International Law of Armed Conflict, by Pietro Verri, 1992, International Committee of the Red Cross, Geneva

13   www.ssi.gouv.fr

14   The Company that Spooked the West, The Economist, 4 April 2012, http://www.economist.com/node/21559929

15   www.securityforum.org

16   www.isc2.org

17   Guidance for Best Practices in Information Security and IT Audit, ISACA, November 2009

18   IT Standards, Guidelines and Tools and Techniques for Audit and Assurance and Control Professionals, ISACA, August 2010

19   NIST SP800-30, Revision 1, September 2011, Guide for Conducting Risk Assessments (http://csrc.nist.gov/publications/drafts/800-30-rev1/SP800-30-Rev1-ipd.pdf).

20   ISACA Risk IT Framework, http://www.isaca.org/Knowledge-Center/Research/ResearchDeliverables/Pages/The-Risk-IT-Framework.aspx

21   Verizon Enterprise Risk and Incident Sharing Metrics Framework, 2012 http://www.verizonbusiness.com/resources/whitepapers/wp_verizon-incident-sharing-metrics-framework_en_xg.pdf and https://verisframework.wiki.zoho.com/sitemap.zhtml

22   ISO 27002 "Code of Practice for the Management of Information Security", 2005, International Standards Organization.

23   Capability Maturity Model, The Open Directory http://www.dmoz.org/Computers/Programming/Methodologies/Capability_Maturity_Model/

24   Information Security Governance: Guidance for Boards of Directors and Executive Management, 2nd edition, 2006, ISACA (www.isaca.org)

25   GTAG 15, obtainable from the Institute of Internal Auditors (www.theiia.org)

26   Strengthening Information Security Governance, by E. Gelbstein, ISACA Journal, Volume 12, Issue 2, March 2012

APPENDIX 1: ONLINE RESOURCES RELATING TO THE PROTECTION AND AUDIT OF CRITICAL INFORMATION INFRASTRUCTURES

This list is primary focused on the resources provided by Governments and professional bodies and does not include links to either vendors or consultancy organizations. Personal and corporate blogs have also been omitted even when their owners are reputable companies and recognized information security "gurus".

Critical Infrastructure Protection

United States (Sample – More Entities Can be Found Using a Search Engine)

Department of Homeland Security – www.dhs.gov/critical-infrastructure
North American Electricity Reliability Corporation - www.nerc.com/page.php?cid=6%7C69

Other (Sample of Various Countries with Websites Including Pages in English)

The European Network and Information Security Agency (ENISA) – www.enisa.europa.eu
The UK Centre for the Protection of National Infrastructure (CPNI) – www.cpni.gov.uk
German Federal Office for Information Security (BSI) – (English version) – www.bsi.bund.de
Swiss Programme for Critical Infrastructure Protection - http://www.bevoelkerungsschutz.admin.ch/
    internet/bs/en/home/themen/ski.html
The Australian Trusted Information Sharing Network for Critical Infrastructure Resilience – www.tisn.
    gov.au
The Spanish Centre for the Protection of Critical Infrastructure – www.cnpic-es.es/en/index.html

Business Continuity Management

The Business Continuity Management Institute Wiki - www.bcmpedia.org/wiki/Business_Continu-
    ity_Management_(BCM)
The Business Continuity Institute – www.thebci.org

Audit Related Institutions

The Institute of Internal Audit – www.theiia.org (some publications can be purchased, otherwise mem-
    bership required)
Information Systems Audit and Control Association – www.isaca.org (some publications are freely
    available, others can be purchased, otherwise membership required)
International Organisation of Supreme Audit Institutions (INTOSAI) – www.intosai.org
European Court of Auditors – www.eca.europa.eu

Most countries in the world have a National Audit Office and related websites – for example:

USA: General Accountability Office - www.gao.org - most publications available for download
UK: National Audit Office – www.nao.org - most publications available for download
Australia: Australian National Audit Office – www.anao.gov.au

APPENDIX 2: INFORMATION REQUIREMENTS TO DEFINE THE SCOPE OF AN INFORMATION SECURITY AUDIT

Given that the audit universe related to an information security audit is vast, answers to the questions below should help to narrow down the topics that would result in a valuable report.

Background Information and Recent History

1. What does the audit history (of e.g. the last three years) say about information security?
2. Are there any high priority recommendations made in the past 3 years that have not been implemented and re-audited? If so, which and why have these not been implemented?
3. Has the organization being audited been the target (successfully or not) of a cyber-attack (assuming they know (e.g. Shady Rat or High Roller))?
4. Have there been instances of a deliberate internal act resulting in an information security incident (data leakage, data corruption or theft, fraud,, unauthorized modifications, sabotage)?
5. Has ethical hacking been performed by a vendor-independent specialist?
6. Were the I.T. Auditors invited to participate and/or observe?
7. What were the findings and recommendations?
8. Is the organization actively involved with the national Critical Infrastructure Protection initiative? If not, why not?

Rationale and Discussion

An audit needs to have a well-defined starting point or baseline. Without it too much time will be spent trying to understand the current situation with the risk that some critical questions will be missed.

Answers to these questions should be sought from the Chief Information Security Officer and from the Chairman of the ICT Steering Committee or equivalent, or, ideally, the Chairman of the Information Security Governance body. In addition it would be desirable to get answers to these questions from the Chief Operating Officer and/or Chief Executive Officer and the Chairman of the Audit Committee.

A lack of informed answers to any of the above questions should be taken as a warning sign that the management of information security may need strengthening.

Information Security Governance

9. Are Information Technology Governance and Information Security Governance formally addressed by the organization?
10. How frequently are security governance topics discussed, who participates in the discussion and decision making process?
11. When were risk assessments and their related BIA and risk mitigation measures last review and updated?
12. When were the I.T. Strategy and/or an Information Security strategy and Security Policies Portfolio last reviewed and what progress has been made in implementing them?
13. To what extent are any of the established governance standards and best practices known to the organization, adopted and applied in practice?
14. Do information security practitioners assess Governance as being effective in supporting their activities and if not, why not?
15. Is the organizational culture such that it leads a visible part of its workforce (e.g. 50% or more) to become disengaged? How is this determined and by whom? What is done about it?
16. What information on security incidents information is collected?
17. Are the collection methods and processes compliant with legislation and regulations (e.g. seizure, chain of custody, forensic analyses)
18. What is reported and to whom?
19. Are such reports considered useful?

Rationale and Discussion

The questions in this section aim to identify the extent to which key governance issues are addressed. Without good answers to these points, information security practitioners have little choice but to work on the basis of a self-assumed "best effort" without clear guidance from the Business. This makes them vulnerable to becoming the target of blame when things go wrong (as they do.)

Accountabilities, Coordination, and Operational Performance

20. What is the extent of coordination of security measures for the following categories of systems: Commercially procured "enterprise systems", Custom developed Line of Business systems and SCADA) and also Networks (public (e.g. Internet) and private (leased lines, etc.)?
21. Are the architectures of individual components and the lines of accountability for them clearly defined and up-to-date?
22. Other than unknown vulnerabilities such as zero day exploits, are the other areas of concern adequately documented and have action plans to mitigate them been defined?
23. Which sets of standards and/or best practices have been formally adopted and what is their scope of application?
24. How extensive is the scope of implementation of the processes associated with the selected set of standards and/or best practices?
25. How is compliance with the processes defined in the standards/best practices monitored?

26. What is the current maturity level of key processes and is it appropriate for the nature of the activities of the business?

Rationale and Discussion

These questions aim to identify the extent to which clarity in accountabilities and information flows are implemented as well as obtaining information on adopted standards, best practices, frameworks and methodologies and their deployment.

Certification

27. Has the organization already sought and/or achieved certification of compliance with a security-related standard, and if so, when?
28. Has the issue of certification been formally discussed within the organization and, if so, what decision was made?
29. Does the organization formally require that those who have responsibilities for information security acquire and maintain appropriate professional certifications?
30. How many (in number or percentage) of the people with responsibilities for information security possess such a certification?

Rationale and Discussion

Given that most, if not all, certification initiatives are voluntary, this set of questions aims to identify the corporate strategy with regards to certifications and the extent to which these have been pursued.

Assumptions Made during the Preparation of the above List

1. Critical Information Infrastructures are a potential target for a multitude of attackers, including individual hackers, industrial spies, assorted state and, increasingly non-state actors and hostile nations. (Stuxnet, Duqu, Flame, Gauss and other intrusions (e.g. Shady Rat and High Roller)).
2. Organized crime cannot be ignored even though their primary target is thought to be money. It is conceivable they may choose to act as mercenaries and make their knowledge and experience of cyber-attacks to other parties.
3. Those carrying out cyber-attacks are at least as knowledgeable, if not more so, than the professionals protecting the organization. They also have little or nothing to lose by launching an attack – in fact even an unsuccessful attack provides them with valuable knowledge about the organization's defenses while remaining hard or impossible to identify.
4. Information threats change rapidly, driven by innovative technology with inbuilt vulnerabilities (some could even be by design). Many of these technologies become "objects of desire" and are adopted by the workforce whether the organization likes it or not. (This has happened with home computing choices, smart phones and tablets and there is no reason to believe it will change).

5. The most commonly used techniques to assess how effective security is, include: metrics such as Key Performance Indicators and Key Risk Indicators and also self-assessments. The first are lagging indicators and, as such, not a robust way to predict future performance as the threats and vulnerabilities change all the time. Self-assessments risk being incomplete and potentially optimistic.

6. Certification for compliance with a standard such as ISO 27001 may give a false sense of security. Such certification can be obtained for a specific (possibly small) part of the I.T. infrastructure and thus not be representative of the Information Security Management System of the whole organization.

7. Independent assurance in the form of a competent audit is a valuable complement to the measures taken by the organization to maintain an appropriate level of information security.

8. Human factors are rarely considered in security evaluations and assurance programmes.

Chapter 12
Safety and Security in SCADA Systems Must be Improved through Resilience Based Risk Management

Stig O. Johnsen
The Norwegian University of Science and Technology, Norway

ABSTRACT

This chapter describes vulnerabilities related to safety and security in distributed process control systems integrated with information and communication technology (ICT). The author describe key vulnerabilities and how to mitigate these vulnerabilities by current best practices, which have worked in an industrial setting in Norway. Distributed process control systems are denoted as SCADA systems, i.e. supervisory control and data acquisition systems. Increased networking and increased use of ICT impacts the complexity and vulnerability of the SCADA systems. To improve safety and security, there must be a focus on systematic knowledge generation between ICT and process experts and a focus on exploring resilience as a strategy to manage risks and support continuity of operations (resilience seen as the ability to bounce back and sustain operations). Best practices in risk management in this area are to establish policies, improve risk awareness, perform risk assessment in collaboration between ICT and SCADA professionals, focus on segregation of networks, focus on active protection against malicious software, improve reporting and sharing of incidents, and establish and explore disaster/recovery plans. In addition, there should be focus on certification and testing of components in ICT and SCADA systems and improvement of resilience to mitigate uncertainty and complexity.

DOI: 10.4018/978-1-4666-2659-1.ch012

Copyright © 2013, IGI Global. Copying or distributing in print or electronic forms without written permission of IGI Global is prohibited.

1. INTRODUCTION: SAFETY AND SECURITY MUST BE IMPROVED

This chapter consists of the following five parts:

- This introduction, where we have argued that integration of SCADA systems with ICT systems creates new vulnerabilities and uncertainties that must be mitigated through improved risk assessment and improved risk governance.
- Description of a general framework and best practice guidelines that have been implemented in the Norwegian Oil and Gas sector to support risk governance of integration of SCADA and ICT.
- Description of how to assess the use of the framework and the guidelines.
- Documentation of the actual use of the guidelines and how safety and security have been impacted.
- Discussion of the impact of the guidelines and suggested improvements in the future.

Distributed process control systems are a key part of industrial production. In the following we are focusing on process control systems used in the oil and gas industry. SCADA (i.e. supervisory control and data acquisition systems), is used when we describe distributed process control systems, that is systems that monitor and control industrial processes, including safety instrumented systems used to perform emergency shut down or emergency disconnect. Safety and security are key issues in SCADA systems. In the following commentary safety is defined as *"the degree to which accidental harm is prevented, reduced and properly reacted to"* and security is defined as *"the degree to which malicious harm is prevented, reduced and properly reacted to"* (both definitions are taken from Firesmith (2003)). Thus the avoidance of harm is dependent on both safety and security.

Initially, SCADA systems were independent and based on specialized hardware and software. Hardware consisted of networks with remote terminal units (RTU) or by programmable logic controllers (PLC). However, SCADA systems are no longer independent and based on specialized technology, but are increasingly connected to local and public networks and are often based on standardized commercial "off the shelf" technology (COTS). The SCADA systems are increasingly communicating with other ICT systems in real time and communicating with distributed users connected to the different networks. The SCADA systems are consisting of many interrelated systems and interrelated users. It seems that complexity and connectivity is increasing, defining complexity as a system *"consisting of many interrelated parts"*, from Perrow (1999).

Increased connectivity has exposed the SCADA systems to a wide range of security issues, as described by Igure, Laughter and Williams (2006) and Stouffer, Falco and Kent (2008). Key challenges and security issues mentioned by these papers are access controls, monitoring of activities and management policies. If these challenges are not managed, incidents may happen. In a SCADA environment the incidents may impact safety, since the SCADA systems are controlling key industrial processes. A study by the National Transportation Safety Board in 2005, NTSB (2005), scrutinized 13 pipeline mishaps from 1992 to 2004. The study found key issues from the mishaps related to the SCADA systems. In 10 of these accidents, some aspect of the SCADA system contributed to the severity of the accident. However, NTSB didn't perform systematic exploration of the role of SCADA systems in gas line accidents earlier. They started to perform systematic exploration from 2010. Thus there is a need for increased focus on SCADA systems and their role in accidents and support of safety in operations.

Examples of serious incidents from operation of SCADA systems can be found in Stouffer, Falco and Kent (2008), section 3.7. One example mentioned is the Maroochy Shire Sewage Spill, where a disgruntled employee broke into the controls of a sewage treatment system and caused malfunctions that caused 264,000 gallons of raw sewage to be released into nearby rivers and parks. However, many consequences are based on incidents that were unintentional or accidental thus a safety perspective is important.

It seems that SCADA failures, although very unlikely, may have severe impact due to the criticality of the process managed. This may be characterized as a "black swan incident" as described by Taleb (2007), i.e. a catastrophic accident with low probability. Due to the consequences of a "black swan incident", a policy must be established to mitigate and reduce the consequences of these incidents. A risk assessment should help identify the probabilities of an accident, and help to identify mitigating actions to reduce the probability and consequences of an accident/incident. Thus a risk assessment is an important tool to prioritize mitigating actions based on costs and benefits. If a major incident, such as a "black swan incident", can be avoided or reduced, there is an evident pay-back of the effort used to perform a risk assessment of the SCADA systems.

Also, concerns of safety and security have increased recently due to malicious attacks such as Stuxnet described by Symantec (2011) and the "Night Dragon" as described by McAfee (2011). The Stuxnet attack demonstrated the vulnerabilities and hazards of SCADA systems accessed through the ICT infrastructure. The "Night Dragon" attack documented the vulnerabilities of the ICT infrastructures in oil and gas companies and the interest of external actors to get access to key information, such as prospects of oil and gas fields and knowledge of key industrial processes. These external actors may also have taken the next step, and influenced the SCADA systems. These vulnerabilities and the criticality of the SCADA systems must be included in an extended risk assessment, both to mitigate known vulnerabilities

but also to improve the ability of the system to handle deviations outside the boundaries of acceptable behaviour. In addition, all incidents must be reported and shared to improve awareness and knowledge of the key challenges in the industry and among the regulators and authorities.

It has been demonstrated that SCADA systems and components are vulnerable when exposed to ICT generated load, see documentation in Luders (2006). Between 26% and 18% of tested PLC's crashed due to high network loads (Denial of Service – DoS) or due to penetration and vulnerability tests. The components had poor resilience; they halted and had to be "re-booted". These vulnerabilities in SCADA components have also been documented by vendors such as Wurldtech Security, and have become a focus of the ISA Security Compliance Institute. To mitigate these vulnerabilities logging of all load levels should be established, resilience should be improved in the system and barriers should be established to mitigate unwanted load in the network, penetration and other external factors. Resilience is defined as "*the intrinsic ability of a system to adjust its functioning prior to or following changes and disturbances, so that it can sustain operations even after a major mishap or in the presence of continuous stress*", from Hollnagel, Woods and Leveson (2006). This seems to be a key strategy to support continuity of critical parts of the system.

A rupture of a pipeline in Bellingham, Washington Park, happened in 1999. This rupture led to the release of gasoline, see NTSB (2002). The gasoline was ignited; causing an explosion that caused 3 deaths and 8 injuries. The pipeline failure was exacerbated by control systems, i.e. SCADA systems not able to perform control and monitoring functions. As mentioned in the NTSB report "immediately prior to and during the incident, the SCADA system exhibited poor performance that inhibited the pipeline controllers from seeing and reacting to the development of an abnormal pipeline operation". Thus monitoring of load and the ability of the SCADA system to be resilient and continue operation even during unanticipated stress must be included in risk management of the systems.

Even "fail-safe" SCADA systems with watchdog functionality may fail. The failure of a watchdog timer due to common-cause failures is documented in Leveson (1995) chapter 16.5.3.

In the Deepwater Horizon accident, NC (2011), the emergency disconnect system (EDS), a SCADA safety system, did not function when it was activated. An analysis of the performance of the EDS is not possible to perform since the system was destroyed. The cause of the malfunction is not known. Also, there were two drilling systems; the Hitec system and the Sperry Sun system, NC (2011), pp. 110. The Sperry Sun system sent data back to shore in real time, creating a log, allowing personnel to access and monitor data from anywhere with an Internet connection. During an emergency, onshore experts could have explored the Sperry Sun data to increase resilience and avoid accidents in operations, but this was not performed. The drilling crew used the Hitec system, but the data set sank with the rig, leaving only the Sperry Sun subset of the data behind. The Sperry-Sun data was explored in the accident report. Thus, to document the performance of critical systems during an emergency, a log, stored away from the operational site, should be available to be analysed. In addition, the disaster plans should include failures of "fail-safe" systems or emergency systems such as ESD.

As suggested by the above cases and incidents, the integrated SCADA and ICT systems have several vulnerabilities that may impact both safety and security. Thus it is important to establish management policies for safety and security of SCADA/ICT, establish a risk assessment based on latest available knowledge, establish open reporting of incidents, ensure risk awareness, monitor the systems, ensure resilience and provide barriers to both reduce probability and reduce consequence of incidents. This should include logging the performance of the systems

and the establishment of disaster/ recovery plans based on discussing "worst-case" scenarios. In the following discussion we have described how this can be implemented.

2. DESCRIPTION OF A FRAMEWORK TO MANAGE SAFETY AND SECURITY

In the following section, we are describing a framework and guidelines that have been used in practice to manage safety and security in the complex distributed SCADA systems integrated with the ICT systems.

In the oil and gas industry, the SCADA and ICT systems must be accessed both from onshore and offshore. Risks are influenced by this distribution of organization, technology, solutions and teams. This complexity in organizational structure, technology and human factors of systems and teams must be taken into account. Risk assessment and risk management must be performed in an environment of several distributed stakeholders, and human factors issues must be incorporated. Based on developments and the incidents and failures described in the prior section, the complexity and uncertainty in the modern integrated SCADA and ICT environment appears to have increased. When discussing safety and security both complexity induced risk problems and uncertainty induced risk problems must be managed. These challenges have been explored in modern strategies for risk governance such as in Renn (2005), and the suggested framework and approach has been used, i.e. using resilience as a management strategy of complexity and uncertainty. Thus management strategies such as robustness-focused and resilience focused strategies from Renn (2005); must be used when relevant. In addition, key specific technical guidelines related to human factors, safety and security; are mentioned in the following and should be used in risk governance.

2.1 Guidelines and Practice to Improve Safety and Security Differs between SCADA and ICT in General

In Pietre-Cambacedes and Chaudet (2010), a broad survey of safety and security guidelines for SCADA systems can be found. However, only key guidelines relevant to the oil and gas industry are mentioned in the following. SCADA systems manage critical processes impacting health, safety and environment. In the SCADA environment, a main focus has been on safety. The normative safety standard IEC61508 (2010) has often been used, and is a key reference.

Historically, ICT systems manage information, thus in the ICT environment, a main focus has been on information security. The normative security standard ISO27001 (2005) has often been used.

When the SCADA systems and ICT systems are increasingly integrated, safety and security (in the con-text of safety) has been of key interest. Standards and guidelines are being developed to address security in SCADA systems and safety in ICT systems; such as IEC62443 (2008) and guidelines such as found in Stouffer, Falco and Kent (2008). The International Instrument Users' Association (WIB) has also released a comprehensive cyber Security Standard, documenting best practices, ref WIB (2010).

In the Norwegian oil and gas industry, safety and security of the integrated SCADA and ICT systems has been prioritized, and relevant guidelines based on both safety and security are discussed in the next section, such as OLF104 (2006), referenced as OLF104 in the following. In addition, the human factors perspective must be included.

2.2 Two Guidelines Have Been Developed

Two guidelines have been developed to support the focus of safety and security in the oil and gas industry in Norway.

One guideline, see Johnsen et al (2011), has been developed based on a human factors (HF) perspective – to be used when control centers are established, managing the control and safety systems used in operations.

The other guideline, OLF104, has been developed together with the oil industry association based on ISO27001 (2005) and includes safety challenges from SCADA systems, in order to improve company policy and company procedures.

In the following we have described these two guidelines.

Safety and security from the perspective of Human Factors: The management and use of SCADA systems is usually performed in control centers. These centers are usually designed based on human factors, as described in ISO11064 (2000). To ensure safety of operations through SCADA systems, human factors, alarm design and alarm handling are key issues. A verification and validation program of control centers based on ISO11064 (2000), has been established in the Norwegian oil and gas industry. The program has been called CRIOP and is documented in in Johnsen et al (2011). Human factors, alarms and safety and security of SCADA and ICT systems are examined through checklists in the CRIOP program. Key issues of safety and security addressed within CRIOP (with references to actual questions) are: management policies (E11.2), risk assessment (E11), open reporting of incidents (E12), risk awareness (E14), barriers to reduce risks (E11.5), analysis of disaster/recovery plans (E13) and reporting of incidents (E12). (The topics are listed in the same order as the following guideline based on ISO27001). In addition, the CRIOP method suggests a scenario analysis based on breakdown of the SCADA/ICT systems due to loss of communication between the distributed stakeholders or other failures. The CRIOP method has been widely used by the industry, as documented in Aas, Johnsen and Skramstad (2009).

Safety and security from the perspective of technical standard ISO27001: The oil and gas industry association in Norway, OLF, has developed a "best practice" safety and security guideline of integration between SCADA and ICT systems based on ISO27001 (2005). The "best practice" consists of 16 key issues suggested to be of critical importance. The guideline OLF104 has been developed in collaboration between ICT and SCADA professionals. Formal acceptance and compliance of the 16 issues in OLF104 was from 2007-07-01 to 2009-07-01. Key issues in the guideline (with reference to guideline number) are: management policies (1), risk assessment (2), segregation of networks (4), risk awareness (5), disaster/recovery plans (7), active protection against malicious software (13) and reporting of incidents (16). These key issues are similar to the issues in the CRIOP checklist, exploring safety and security of SCADA and ICT systems.

The actual implementation, adherence and suggested improvement of the guidelines, is explored in the next chapter, since these issues may impact safety and security of operation.

3. HOW TO EXAMINE THE PRACTICAL USE OF EXISTING GUIDELINES

In the following we have discussed the actual use of the guidelines; the key actors involved in safety and security; and we have documented the surveys and workshops that have been performed.

3.1 Practice and Use of the Guidelines

The actual use of the guideline OLF104 has been examined. It is assumed that structural modification such as establishing a guideline, will impact the physical and organizational environment, i.e. the procedures and structure in use at the workplace. This is based on theory and empirical results from Lund and Aarø (2004). The proce-

dures and structure in use at the workplace will impact behaviour, and ideally reduce accidents and incidents. Thus the use of the guidelines should be reflected in updated internal procedures, structures and audits; and this has been explored in the following.

In addition, Lund and Aarø (2004) also suggests that when several preventive measures are used in combination to influence social norms and cultural factors, the combined preventive measures are probably more effective. In our case we are trying to influence knowledge and awareness of safety and security issues through action based research, i.e. trying to influence practice by new guidelines followed by reflections and discussions of the effects in a group setting between the involved key stakeholders. According to Baskerville and Pries-Heje (1999): "*The fundamental contention of action research is that a complex social process can be studied best by introducing changes into that process and observing the effects of these changes*". The approach to action research has been based on the cyclical action research described by Susman and Evered (1978). The five phases of action research are 1) Diagnosing (diagnosing the weaknesses and strengths); 2) Action planning (consider alternative future courses of actions); 3) Action taking (implementing actions for solving the problem); 4) Evaluating (study the consequences of the action taken) and 5) Specify learning – the learning between the stakeholders in the action research process.

The practical use and effect of action research has been described by Smith, Jamieson and Winchester (2007), through a description of how information systems security compliance across government agencies were improved by using action research, along with surveys and meetings to reflect and improve on existing practice. Smith, Jamieson and Winchester (2007) discussed the use of ISO standard ISO27001 (2005). Our focus is guideline OLF104 related to safety and security of ICT and SCADA systems, and an action-based approach is described in the following.

3.2 Key Actors Influencing and Being Influenced by Safety and Security Guidelines

The stakeholders involved in developing safety and security guidelines are industry associations, government authority, media, suppliers, operators (oil and gas companies) and professionals from the SCADA and ICT area. These stakeholders have been considered to be collaborators to improve safety and security based on knowledge sharing.

3.3 Surveys and Workshops that Have Been Performed from Different Perspectives

A question-based survey has been performed focusing on safety and security of SCADA and ICT systems, distributed to 46 offshore installations. Six in-depth expert meetings to explore findings from the question-based survey were arranged. Summaries of some findings are documented in Hauge, Johnsen and Onshus (2009). The findings are based on collaboration between operators, suppliers and authorities.

Verification and validation related to safety and security of SCADA and ICT systems used offshore has been performed in 2009 and 2010 at five different installations, involving groups from between 2 and 8 participants from different areas of expertise. The CRIOP checklists were explored, in addition to conducting scenario discussions. In the scenario discussions, a hazard and operability study (HAZOP) was used to explore relevant scenarios in a distributed setting. The guideline OLF104 was discussed. The group discussions were based on participation and involvement from different groups, and management. Vulnerabilities, issues and mitigating actions were discussed and prioritized in collaboration. Thus the findings are based on identified and prioritized issues from operators, suppliers and workforce.

In addition, a survey of relevant audits from the authorities in Norway, the Petroleum Safety Authority (PSA) has been performed in 2010. The survey was performed in order to identify audits that have focused on OLF104. Two audits were performed in 2010 by PSA, exploring OLF104. The issues prioritized by PSA have been documented.

4. THE USE OF THE GUIDELINES AND IMPACT ON SAFETY AND SECURITY

In the following we have documented how the guidelines have impacted safety and security guidelines; and impacted the key stakeholders in the Norwegian Oil and Gas industry. Key stakeholders are the authorities, PSA, and major oil and gas operators such as Statoil.

4.1 Impact of the Guidelines

In the following we have assessed adherence to the following six selected issues from the 16 points in OLF104: management policies (1), risk assessment (2), segregation of networks (4), risk awareness (5), disaster/recovery plans (7), active protection against malicious software (13) and reporting of incidents (16).

Management Policies Have Been Established

In Hauge, Johnsen and Onshus (2009), it was pointed out that information security policies for process control, safety and support of ICT systems were missing. During several audits and verifications in 2010, the need for relevant policies were explored at several installations and discussed by the authorities, see PSA (2010) and PSA (2010b). It was found that company policies had been established, an example was a company policy such as TR1658 (2009), by the large oil and gas company Statoil, see PSA (2010b). However, the knowledge and use of the policies had not been fully implemented at all places and in all relevant procedures. Thus there is a need to raise awareness of policies and implement the policies in work procedures and awareness education.

Risk Assessments Are Mandatory

When new solutions are discussed, risk assessment shall be performed as agreed in OLF104 and internal guidelines. However, some risk assessments for new solutions are not exploring incidents in a distributed environment, such as loss of communication between different distributed installations. The risk assessments should explore technical, organizational and human factor issues and should explore issues related to integration of SCADA/ICT and the stability and quality of data communication between distributed actors. Thus risk assessments are prioritized, although they could be improved. In a distributed environment, "*loss of communication*", should be explored and highlighted as a defined situation of hazard and accident.

Segregation of Networks is Specified

Internal guidelines specify that network segregation shall be performed. Network segregation may increase complexity, but new technical solutions have been designed to enable simple network segregation. The focus on network segregation may improve resilience, since critical safety functions such as emergency shut down of the SCADA system is segregated and protected from network load or attacks.

Risk Awareness through Education

Training and risk awareness was identified as an area of improvement during audits, ref PSA (2010) and PSA (2010b). The operators have described

their policies, and have made it clear that an ICT security awareness course shall be made available and mandatory for key groups.

Disaster/Recovery Plans Are Mandatory

Guiding documentation clearly states that disaster and recovery plans are a normal part of activities on an installation. As mentioned earlier, disaster and recovery plans related to loss of communication in a distributed environment, could be improved.

Active Protection against Malicious Software

Active protection against malicious software has been specified as key requirements, and has been focused. Protection of Universal Serial Bus (USB) memory sticks, and other portable storage media, was also mentioned as an issue in the audits, ref PSA (2010).

Incidents Shall be Reported

The internal guideline specifies that all incidents should be reported – however the actual "reporting culture" has sometimes not considered ICT and network incidents as important to report as other safety issues. Thus the network and ICT incidents have not always been identified and reported on the same level as other incidents.

4.2 Involvement of Key Stakeholders

Different stakeholders, with varying concerns, have been involved in exploration of safety and security of ICT and SCADA systems. The stakeholders, communicated goals and knowledge influencing safety and security have been suggested in the following list.

- **Industry Association:** The Norwegian Oil and gas industry association (OLF) has been working to establish guidelines through open collaboration and agreement. One of the main goals of OLF is safety: *"the ambition is to be a world leader in the oil and gas industry for health, safety and the working environment"*. In addition, the Norwegian Computer Society (DnD) has been supporting work on safety and security in systems, through an award process, ref DnD (2008), giving OLF a security prize due to the innovative establishment of security guideline OLF104 in the oil and gas industry.

- **Government:** The Petroleum Safety Authority (PSA) has pointed out that the industry may have *"insufficient understanding about the possible safety consequences of undesirable information and communication technology (ICT) incidents"* and they have suggested that awareness should be improved through increased use of risk and vulnerability analyses, ref PSA (2010c). PSA has focused on collaboration with the industry through goal setting, dialogue and audits.

- **Newspapers/Trade Journals:** Newspapers and technical trade journals have focused on potential safety challenges and risks of the use of SCADA technology in the oil and gas industry. One example is the technical journal TU (2009), claiming that the SCADA networks in the oil and gas industry are vulnerable, and production may be impacted. This statement is considered to be without validation and therefore uncertain, but the area has been in focus by the trade journals and newspapers.

- **Suppliers:** Suppliers and vendors have collaborated with OLF to establish the OLF104 guideline and have focused on increasing awareness and guidelines.

- **Operating Companies:** Operators have been proactive to assess vulnerabilities and establishing general guidelines through industry associations such as OLF. The operators have established internal, company specific guidelines, based on OLF104, such as was accomplished by a large Norwegian oil and Gas company – Statoil; that established the guideline TR1658 (2009), and have focused on safety and security on new and old installations when implementing integration of SCADA and ICT systems.

- **Stakeholders and Professional Networks:** Professionals (from ICT and SCADA) have actively been involved in establishing the OLF104 guideline. The interconnectivity between systems and vulnerabilities has not always been known among the SCADA and ICT professionals. The SCADA systems are considered a class of "fail-safe" systems, and it has been a focus on dependability and stability of the SCADA systems – especially the ability to perform a controlled degradation and recovery. It has been uncertain if a SCADA incident could result in a major safety related accident.

The need for guidelines, to focus on safety and security and risk has been regarded as important among these key stakeholders. Thus, these actors have supported the development and exploration of guidelines such as OLF104.

5. DISCUSSION OF THE IMPACT AND FUTURE IMPROVEMENTS

In the following we have described how the industry and authorities have accepted the suggested guidelines. We have described the action research process that has been performed in order to create and share knowledge between the different stakeholders. Lastly, we have described suggested improvements in the guidelines.

5.1 Industry and Regulatory Acceptance

All issues in the OLF104 guideline have entered into force from 2009-07-01. PSA is using and referencing OLF104 in their audits as documented in PSA (2010) and PSA (2010b). One large operator, Statoil, is using the OLF104 in their governing documentation, as documented in TR1658 (2009). TR1658 is used in design, procurement and implementation. OLF guideline 104 has been recognized by the ICT industry in Norway, since OLF was awarded the Rosing award from The Norwegian Computer Society (DnD) in the category ICT-Security in 2008, see DnD (2008).

The guidelines are not fully implemented into procedures and organizational responsibilities yet, but the guidelines have been established. Audits and focus on knowledge creation and sharing should assist in further acceptance of the guidelines.

5.2 Process of Knowledge Sharing and Knowledge Creation

When discussing the process of knowledge sharing and knowledge creation, related to implementation of OLF104, the process has been based on action research and the five steps as mentioned earlier:

1. **Diagnosing:** Diagnosing the weaknesses and strengths, documenting the problem, context and policies.
2. **Action Planning:** Consideration of alternative future courses of actions, based on risk assessment and risk perceptions.
3. **Action Taking:** Implementing actions and mitigating actions for solving the problem;
4. **Evaluating:** Studying the consequences of the action taken, as an example share unwanted incidents and create awareness).
5. **Specify Learning:** The learning between the stakeholders in the action research process i.e. reflect on mitigating actions.

These phases are an iterative process; exploring and sharing knowledge between different actors as knowledge of events and issues are improved. The initial phase has been to define the problem, context and policies. Different knowledge from the different standards in SCADA and ICT has been combined; and differences in focus of safety and security have been explored. The established guidelines can be seen as a result of this combination of knowledge from different areas. There are differences in knowledge between ICT and SCADA professionals, and this is an area of continuous learning and exploration. The next steps have been to discuss and explore risk assessment and risk perceptions by sharing incidents across competencies and implementing OLF104 in the internal practice and guidelines. Due to different organizational and meeting arenas of ICT and SCADA professionals, an important issue is to create and sustain common meeting arenas. Key stakeholders must have the ability to collaborate, to explore and discuss relevant incidents and knowledge. They must be able to share practices to reduce operational risks and establish working practice in interaction with guidelines. This is dependent on organizational issues, if there are different activities in different places, such as onshore or offshore, then the stakeholders must be able to meet to share knowledge. The workshops and discussions performed, have supported this sharing, but this must also be supported by organizational measures and working practice.

Knowledge sharing does vary. There have been examples of missing combination of knowledge between ICT, telecommunication and SCADA teams. At one installation it was not known that common networks were used for ICT, SCADA, radio and telephony applications making the stability of networks more critical. The role of audits, training, organizational meeting arenas and public incident reports are important to improve knowledge sharing.

We have seen challenges of safety and security when exploring knowledge sharing, related to the following issues:

- Fragmentation, the inability to perform combination of necessary knowledge from different competencies into a knowledge system. This may impact risk assessment and thus increase risk to critical processes.
- Learning disability, or a poor ability to create shared mental models and technical know how. This may create poor internal procedures, and differences in risk awareness.
- Individualization, due to poor possibility or ability to observe and imitate behaviour of key collaborators. This may impact safety and security in operation.
- Closed mindedness or a poor ability to share metaphors, analogies or concepts. Sharing may require work rotation across geographical or organizational interfaces.

5.3 Suggested Improvements in the Guidelines

The OLF104 guideline has increased awareness of safety and security. However several strategic and operation issues should be added to the guideline.

Missing Clarity in Strategy, Responsibility, and Work Procedures in a Distributed Control Environment

Work procedures must be adapted based on OLF104. However during audits, new procedures were missing or not adapted, ref PSA (2010). In addition, the background strategies were missing or wanting. A prerequisite should be that the necessary context, strategy and environment are established before the use of OLF 104, especially in a distributed environment. Strategies are a prerequisite to discussing control objectives in the systems. Thus clarity in strategies, responsibilities and work procedures should be mentioned as a prerequisite in OLF104, prior to establishing policies and risk assessments.

Development and Refinement of Guidelines in Collaboration between Key Actors

At present there is insufficient understanding of the safety consequences of SCADA incidents. Incidents must be documented and shared, and awareness should be strengthened through exploration of risk and vulnerability analyses. The involved disciplines (automation/process/SCADA, ICT, instrumentation and telecom) should collaborate to share and create explicit and tacit knowledge. Thus the guidelines should be improved and refined in collaboration. This could be done as a part of adaption, when OLF104 is implemented, and could be suggested in the guidelines.

Proactive Indicators Related to Safety and Security as a Part of Risk Governance

Integration between systems creates complexities and dependencies that may influence safety and security. Many different actors are involved and it could be useful to identify a set of indicators to be explored, such as stability of technical communication, subjective assessment of safety critical communication and subjective assessment of risk among key actors collaborating, ref Johnsen et al (2010). Thus proactive indicators of safety and security should be explored in the guidelines, and should be a part of a resilience based risk assessment and on-going risk governance.

Missing Certification and Testing of Components in ICT and SCADA Environment

SCADA components may fail when they are subjected to high network load. There is need to establish systematic independent certification and testing of the integrated ICT and SCADA systems, to ensure reliable operation. The ISA institute has been developing a certification process, via the ISA Security Compliance Institute, ref ISA

Secure (2010). Vendors have established certification schemes, such as the Wurldtech Achilles certification. Certification, preferably a vendor independent certification, should be required in the guidelines.

Definitions and References to Standards

The OLF104 guideline must assess both safety and security, and these concepts should be clearly defined in the standard. This is explored in Pietre-Cambacedes and Chaudet (2010). Key, relevant safety and security guidelines should be referenced in the standard such as mentioned in the introductory section of this paper.

Resilience to Mitigate Uncertainty and Complexity

Complexity and uncertainty are key issues when discussing safety and security. Resilience is a strategy to improve capability to cope with surprises. A framework of risk governance, as described by Renn (2005), helps to structure this process. An example of operational resilience could be diversity or flexibility. The SCADA/ICT systems are integrated with production equipment. The systems may be destroyed in an accident, making it impossible to analyse data from the accident. Resilience may be improved by storing process data at a remote location, ensuring later analysis and in addition, a remote expert team could explore data to improve safety of operations during stress or dangerous situations. Resilience should be systematically explored in a resilience based risk assessment by establishing proactive indicators of risk and supporting the ability to recover as early as possible.

Mandatory Use of the Guidelines

In Hopkins (2011) there is a discussion of rule-compliance and risk management. Some of the issues that are mentioned in Hopkins (2011) are:

"The need to formulate industry good practice as rules, in order to force laggards into line; the need to formulate rules in order to raise the standards higher; and the need to formulate rules when the consequences of failures are catastrophic."

There are key vulnerabilities in the existing SCADA and ICT systems used in the oil and gas industry, as documented by Hauge, Johnsen and Onshus (2009). Some of the identified vulnerabilities in the integrated SCADA and ICT systems could impact safety of production in the oil and gas industry. Since the consequences of failures of the control systems may be huge, it is recommended that the authorities should improve their regulatory actions in this area and make OLF104 mandatory. In addition, the role of control systems in accidents should be an area of focus and exploration by the authorities.

Summary: Key Future Activities

There is missing documentation and analysis of unwanted SCADA incidents involving integration with ICT. The number of safety critical incidents are low; however near misses should be documented, analysed and shared. The incidents should be analysed to improve safety, security and resilience of the total socio-technical system, including organizational, technical and human factors.

Risk assessment of the integrated SCADA and ICT systems should be explored and validated, especially in a distributed environment, when there is remote support or remote operations between onshore and offshore. Loss of communication, misunderstandings or weak signals must be explored to ensure resilience and to avoid accidents or incidents. There is a need to improve mindfulness during operations in this setting, as described by Butler and Gray (2006). Proactive indicators and a focus on resilience could aid in this. Thus this is an area that should be prioritized by the authorities and industry, in order to avoid incidents and accidents.

In this section there has been a focus on knowledge creation to support collective mindfulness. Knowledge creation, such as knowledge of safety critical issues should be explored across interfaces. Scenario discussions through techniques such as HAZOP could help.

REFERENCES

Aas, A. L., Johnsen, S. O., & Skramstad, T. (2009). Lecture Notes in Computer Science: *Vol. 5775. CRIOP: A human factors verification and validation methodology that works in an industrial setting. Safecomp 2009* (pp. 243–256). Hamburg, Germany.

Ask, R., Røisli, R., Johnsen, S., Line, M., Ueland, A., & Hovland, B. … Losnedahl, T. (2006). *Information security baseline requirements for process control, safety and support ICT systems.* ISBR. Retrieved January 1, 2011, from www.olf. no/no/Publikasjoner/Retningslinjer/Kronologisk/

Baskerville, R., & Pries-Heje, J. (1999). Grounded action research: A method for understanding IT in practice. *Accounting Management and Information Technologies*, 9(1), 1–23. doi:10.1016/ S0959-8022(98)00017-4

Butler, B. S., & Gray, P. H. (2006). Reliability, mindfulness and information systems. *Management Information Systems Quarterly*, 30(2), 211–224.

DnD. (2008. *Rosing ICT-Security award.* Retrieved October 10, 2010, from www.dataforeningen.no/it-sikkerhetsprisen.4796706-160557.html

Firesmith, D. G. (2003). *Common concepts underlying safety, security, and survivability engineering. Technical note CMU/SEI-2003-TN-033.* Carnegie Mellon University.

Hauge, S., Johnsen, S. O., & Onshus, T. (2009). *Uavhengighet av sikkerhetssystemer / Functional independence of safety systems.* Sintef Report. Retrieved January 1, 2011, from www.ptil.no/ nyheter/ny-rapport-om-sikkerhetssystemers-uavhengighet-article7292-24.html

Hollnagel, E., Woods, D., & Leveson, N. (2006). *Resilience engineering.* Ashgate.

Hopkins, A. (2011). Risk-management and rule-compliance: Decision making in hazardous industries. *Safety Science, 49*, 110–120. doi:10.1016/j. ssci.2010.07.014

IEC 61508. (2010). *Functional safety of electrical/electronic/ programmable electronic safety-related systems.*

IEC 62443. (2008). *Security for industrial process measurement and control - Network and system security.*

Igure, V. M., Laughter, S. A., & Williams, R. D. (2006). Security issues in SCADA networks. *Computers & Security, 25*, 498–506. doi:10.1016/j. cose.2006.03.001

IsaSecure. (2010). *International Society for Automation, ISA Security Compliance Institute, North Carolina.* Retrieved January 1, 2011, from www. isasecure.org/

ISO/IEC 27001. (2005). *Information technology -- Security techniques -- Information security management systems.* Requirements, ISO.

ISO 11064. (2000). *Ergonomic design of control centers.*

Johnsen, S. O., Bjørkli, C., Steiro, T., Fartum, H., Haukenes, H., Ramberg, J., & Skriver, J. (2011). *CRIOP – A scenario method for crisis intervention and operability analysis.* SINTEF. Retrieved February 10, 2011, from www.criop.sintef.no

Johnsen, S. O., Okstad, E., Aas, A. L., & Skramstad, T. (2010). *Proactive indicators of risk in remote operations of oil and gas fields.* SPE International Conference on Health, Safety and Environment in Oil and Gas Exploration and Production. DOI 10.2118/126560-MS

Leveson, N. (1995). *Safeware – System safety.* Addison-Wesley.

Luders, S. (2006). CERN tests reveal security flaws with industrial networked devices. *The Industrial Ethernet Book, 35,* 12-23. Retrieved May 12, 2009, from www.iebmedia.com

Lund, J., & Aarø, L. E. (2004). Accident prevention. Presentation of a model placing emphasis on human, structural and cultural factors. *Safety Science, 42*(4), 271–324. doi:10.1016/S0925-7535(03)00045-6

McAfee. (2011). *Global energy cyberattacks - Night Dragon.* Retrieved February 20, 2011, from www.mcafee.com/us/resources/white-papers/wp-global-energy-cyberattacks-night-dragon.pdf

NC. (2011). *The National Commission on the BP Deepwater Horizon oil spill and offshore drilling's final report.* Retrieved February 1, 2011, from www.oilspillcommission.gov

NTSB. (2002). *Pipeline rupture and subsequent fire in Bellingham, Washington, June 10, 1999.* (Pipeline Accident Report NTSB/PAR-02/02). National Transportation Safety Board.

NTSB. (2005). *National Transportation Safety Board safety study – Supervisory control and data acquisition* (SCADA). (Report NTSB/SS-05/02).

Perrow, C. (1999). *Normal accidents: Living with high-risk technologies.* Princeton, NJ: Princeton University Press.

Pietre-Cambacedes, L., & Chaudet, C. (2010). The SEMA referential framework: Avoiding ambiguities in the terms security and safety. *International Journal of Critical Infrastructure Protection, 3,* 55–66. doi:10.1016/j.ijcip.2010.06.003

PSA. (2010a). Audit of BP Norge's follow-up of new work processes within drilling and well activities using information and communication technology (ICT). *PSA Journal,* 2010/1112. Retrieved January 1, 2011, from www.ptil.no/news/audit-of-bp-s-follow-up-of-new-work-processes-article7566-79.html

PSA. (2010b). Audit of Norne 2010. *PSA Journal,* 2010/93. Retrieved January 1, 2011, from www.ptil.no/nyheter/tilsyn-med-beredskap-norne-fpso-article6834-24.html

PSA. (2010c). *Safety system independence.* Retrieved January 1, 2011, from www.ptil.no/news/safety-system-independence-in-focus-article7293-79.html?lang=en_US

Renn, O. (2005). *Risk governance – Towards an integrative approach.* White paper no.1. Geneva, Switzerland: IRGC.

Smith, S., Jamieson, R., & Winchester, D. (2007). An action research program to improve information systems security compliance across government agencies. *Proceedings of the Fortieth Annual Hawaii International Conference on System Sciences,* (p. 99).

Stouffer, K., Falco, J., & Kent, K. (2008). *Guide to supervisory control and data acquisition and industrial control systems security.* NIST Special Publication 800-82, USA.

Susman, G., & Evered, R. (1978). An assessment of the scientific merits of action research. *Administrative Science Quarterly, 23,* 582–603. doi:10.2307/2392581

Symantec. (2011). *W32.Stuxnet dossier.* Retrieved March 1, 2011, from www.symantec.com/content/en/us/enterprise/media/security_response/white-papers/w32_stuxnet_dossier.pdf

TR1658. (2009). *Statoil governing document.* Technical Network and Security of Automation Systems.

Taleb, N. N. (2007). *The black swan, the impact of the highly improbable*. Random.

TU. (2009). *Computer incidents may halt oil and gas production/Dataangrep kan stoppe Olje-Norge*. Retrieved from www.tu.no/it/article193101.ece

WIB. (2010). *Cyber security standard to protect global critical infrastructure*. Press release. Retrieved from www.wib.nl/pressreleasenov2010.html

ADDITIONAL READING

ANSI/ISA-99. 02.01, International Society for Automation. (2009). *Security for industrial automation and control systems: establishing an industrial automation and control systems security program*. Research Triangle Park, NC: ANSI/ISA.

ENISA. (2008). *Measuring information security awareness - Current practices*. Retrieved from http://enisa.europa.eu/doc/pdf/deliverables/enisa_measuring_awareness.pdf

Howard, J. D., & Longstaff, T. A. (1998). *A common language for computer security incidents*. Sandia National Laboratories. [Sandia Report: SAND98-8667] doi:10.2172/751004

HSE. (2006). *Developing process safety indicators*. ISBN 0 7176 6180 6

Robson, L. S., Shannon, H. S., Goldenhar, L. M., & Hale, A. R. (2001). *Guide to evaluating the effectiveness of strategies for preventing work injuries*. Retrieved from http://www.iwh.on.ca/evaluating-safety-programs

Chapter 13

Fortifying Large Scale, Geospatial Networks:
Implications for Supervisory Control and Data Acquisition Systems

Alan T. Murray
Arizona State University, USA

Tony H. Grubesic
Drexel University, USA

ABSTRACT

Large scale, geospatial networks—such as the Internet, the interstate highway system, gas pipelines, and the electrical grid—are integral parts of modern society, facilitating the capability to communicate, transport goods and services between locations, and connect homes and businesses to basic necessities like water and electricity. The associated management and protection of this critical infrastructure is a challenging task because it is often compromised or damaged by natural disasters, human error, or sabotage. Further, the cascading effects associated with disruptions can impact related interdependent infrastructure, such as supervisory control and data acquisition systems (SCADA). In this context, although the protection and/or hardening of network elements can reduce disruptive impacts, the cost to protect all equipment in the system is prohibitive. The purpose of this chapter is to detail an optimization approach for selecting elements on a network to be protected, under budget constraints, in order to maximize system performance if one or more components are damaged or destroyed. Applications results for a large scale, geospatial network are explored and presented, illustrating problem complexities as well as the potential for informed strategic investment decision making. The implications for SCADA systems relying on large scale geospatial networks, including the public Internet, are also discussed.

DOI: 10.4018/978-1-4666-2659-1.ch013

Copyright © 2013, IGI Global. Copying or distributing in print or electronic forms without written permission of IGI Global is prohibited.

INTRODUCTION

Large-scale, geospatial networks are integral parts of modern society, facilitating the capability to communicate, transport goods and services between locations, as well as connecting homes and businesses to basic necessities like water and electricity (Grubesic and Murray, 2006).

Continued and uninterrupted performance of critical infrastructure systems is a top priority for federal, state and local governments, management agencies or service providers in charge of such systems. Unfortunately, service disruptions are inevitable. Everything from intermittent outages in Internet access to power blackouts and routine highway maintenance highlights the difficulties in continued and uninterrupted system performance. Critical infrastructure systems and associated network infrastructures (e.g. electrical grid, gas pipelines and telecommunication systems) are also vulnerable to catastrophic failure, natural disasters and sabotage, all of which disrupt systems in predictable (and sometimes unpredictable) ways.

Of particular importance is the increasing level of interconnectivity between critical infrastructure systems and supervisory control and data acquisition systems (SCADA). Although there are many ways to conceive of, represent and detail the complex interdependencies between these systems, their increasing level of interaction through remotely controlled Internet-based platforms can pose a significant threat to the global economy if they are not secured (Fernandez and Fernandez, 2005). Specifically, although there is a growing emphasis on the cyber security of SCADA systems (Igure et al., 2006), physical threats and destruction of industrial control systems remain the largest threat to critical infrastructure (Oman et al., 2001). Further, it is important to note that physical threats do not always represent a direct attack. Cascading failures (Little, 2002; Grubesic and Murray, 2006), where a disruption in one system triggers the failure of interconnected systems, are relevant when detailing interactions between large scale networks and SCADA systems.

Where critical infrastructure networks are concerned, they are typically composed of components identified as nodes/vertices and arcs/edges (Murray and Grubesic, 2007). Arcs connect pairs of nodes to form a graph. For example, in a telecommunications network, nodes often represent systems for routing data packets on the network and arcs represent the cables physically connecting routers. In a gas pipeline, the systems which control pumping stations can represent a node and the pipelines which transport the liquefied gas represents the arcs. Given the network, there are many ways that a system performs or operates. Commonly considered modes of performance associated with network vulnerability include (Murray 2012): maximum flow through the network (Wollmer 1964; Baran 1964), shortest path between an origin and destination (Harding 1977; Corley and Sha 1982), and connectivity and flow between all origins and destinations (Albert et al. 2000; Myung and Kim 2004; Murray et al., 2007).

Irrespective of the particular network system performance measure being examined, consequences arise when either components (nodes or arcs in a network) are interdicted or damaged in some way.[1] The loss of one, two or more components can result in a measurable decrease in system functionality. Given that components could be rendered inoperable due to failure, natural disasters and/or sabotage, management and oversight of network infrastructure has recognized the importance of protection and hardening of system controls and components, or more generally fortification (see Church et al. 2004; Brown et al. 2006; Sternberg and Lee 2006; Powell 2007; Scaparra and Church 2008a,b; Murray and Grubesic 2012).

The general problem of interest along these lines may be stated as follows:

Identify components in a system to be fortified in order to ensure the most effective operation should interdiction/damage occur, given a limited budget for protection investment.

Again, the crux of this problem is that one cannot afford to fortify the entire system because of the extraordinary costs associated with such an effort. As a result, one must allocate fortification resources to a specific set of components. If the components are located on a network, then a more specific problem statement is possible. If there are m network components (e.g., nodes, arcs), select q of these m components to fortify such that the loss/interdiction of k out of the remaining m-q unprotected components would disrupt network performance the least. This assumes that the cost to protect each component is approximately the same, and that hardening/fortifying a component renders it less vulnerable to loss/interdiction. There are two additional assumptions. First, it is assumed that the cost of fortifying components is roughly equivalent. This is not farfetched, although the local environmental conditions and small variations in network component characteristics would ultimately dictate the actual costs. Regardless, one would be working with a specific, set budget. Second, the likelihood of loss/interdiction is roughly identical for network components. Again, this is a realistic assumption, but variations in natural disaster distribution and a saboteur's knowledge of a system may influence interdiction probabilities. Finally, as noted above, it is implicit that one would know the number of components, k, to be interdicted, though in reality this would be difficult to determine a priori. In this context, the full range of components 1-k could be modeled.

This problem is related to the attacker-defender problems discussed Brown et al. (2006), and more generally interdiction problems, as noted above. Based upon the general problem statement, the problem of interest here is similar to that of Scaparra and Church (2008b), Liberatore et al. (2011) and Murray and Grubesic (2012), though the specific metrics, measures, objectives and intent varies.

Interdiction and damage to network systems is a practical reality. Protection, fortification and/or hardening are clearly important to keep large scale geospatial networks performing and to prevent associated SCADA systems protected from cascading failures should interdiction or damage occur. The complexities of system impacts necessitate informed management decision making. This chapter details an optimization based approach to support critical infrastructure network hardening in the event of interdiction and/or damage, enabling network managers to make strategic investments that will ensure continued system performance to the greatest extent possible. Moreover, rather than taking a small-scale approach for evaluating a single, localized system, we adopt a large-scale geospatial network perspective to both model and evaluate fortification decisions. The implications of fortification decisions for SCADA systems that are interconnected to large geospatial networks are also detailed.

BACKGROUND

SCADA systems, in general, consist of two basic components. The first, *remote control terminal units* (RTUs), are used to collect field data. These can be wired or wireless devices for detecting movement, atmospheric composition (e.g. particulate levels), ambient environmental conditions (e.g. temperature, dew point) or system performance (e.g. flow in a network). Although the physical form of RTU hardware varies between industrial sectors and applications, it is similar to a generic desktop computer. There are circuit boards, processors, cable connectors and electronic control devices that can receive and help execute commands. For example, RTUs are connected back to a master station which displays the acquired data and allows for operators to interact with the system and perform remote control tasks (Daneels and Salter, 1999; Bailey and Wright, 2003). The major advantage of this type of system architecture is that it allows for centralized command and control, where real-time remote feedback allows for the optimization of systemic operation. Bailey and Wright (2003) also note that in addition to SCADA increasing systemic efficiencies, operation costs are reduced and systems are more reliable and safer. While there is some debate on the differences between SCADA and more general process control systems, SCADA is generally associated with geographically dispersed systems, where using direct wire control is impractical or too expensive. As a result, SCADA systems are often connected via telecommunications systems (although not always), including the public Internet, for relaying information and instructions between remote sites and command centers.

Currently, one serious concern with SCADA and critical infrastructure in general is the degree to which systems and their elements are vulnerable to disruption. As noted previously, the failure of critical infrastructure systems and the potential for associated losses (due to interdependencies) of SCADA have significant ramifications for the global economy, national security and the everyday activities enabled by electrical, telecommunication and transportation systems, among others (Grubesic and Matisziw, 2012).

To better illustrate the potential problems associated with the interconnections and interdependencies between large scale critical infrastructure networks and SCADA systems, consider the implications of geomagnetic disruptions. Although rare, and certainly *not* the only type of threat that critical infrastructure systems and SCADA face, the implications of a geomagnetic disruption are representative of what can happen both within and between systems when subjected to stress or interdiction.

Geomagnetic disruptions come in two basic forms. The first is related to solar storms or solar flares (Hutchins and Overbye, 2011) that eject proton and neutron charged plasma toward Earth. Once these particles are absorbed by the Earth's magnetic field, auroral currents are generated in the atmosphere and an opposing direct current is generated by the Earth's surface (ibid). Although there are variations in the intensity of this process which are largely contingent on the size and inten-

sity of the solar flare, these geomagnetic storms can have a significant impact on the operation of electronic devices, including SCADA systems. For example, in March 1989 a large geomagnetic disturbance hit the U.S./Canada border. Within 90 seconds, seven automatic compensating devices (i.e. SCADA) for Hydro Quebec (the second largest utility in North America) failed, generating a province wide blackout (Kappenman et al., 2000). Several additional geomagnetic disturbances were observed during the next 24 hours, nearly crippling the North American electrical grid. In sum, 200 anomalies were reported across the continent during the 1989 storm (NERC, 1989).

A second source of geomagnetic disturbances does not originate naturally in the environment. High Altitude Electromagnetic Pulse (HEMP) is a geomagnetic disruption generated by a nuclear detonation above the Earth's surface. As noted by Glasstone and Dolan (1977), the peak geomagnetic field strength resulting from a HEMP insult is relatively low, but its geographic reach is significant. For example, the electromagnetic fields are large enough to disrupt unprotected computer systems and SCADA equipment over hundreds of miles from the center point of the detonation. As illustrated by Figure 1, if the HEMP had a burst altitude of 120 miles above Kansas City, Missouri, SCADA systems as far away as Salt Lake City, San Antonio, Atlanta and Washington, DC could be impacted.

Of particular interest to this paper are the potential impacts of these disruptions to large-scale telecommunications systems and interconnected SCADA systems. As telecommunications service providers in the United States and abroad continue pushing systems toward a converged network, where voice, data and video are carried on a single system, the implications of systemic disruption grow larger and more significant. For example, because the telecommunications sector makes such heavy use of SCADA (Haimes and Chittester, 2005), it is not surprising that electromagnetic pulse (EMP) disruptions, in whatever

Figure 1. The geographic footprint of a high altitude electromagnetic burst over Kansas City, Missouri

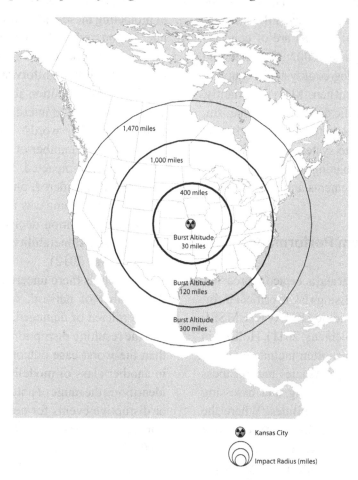

form they are generated (environmental or technological), have the potential to negatively impact telecommunications support during emergencies (i.e. inability to place or receive calls on wireless and wireline networks) and any *interdependent* systems that require telecommunication connections for operation (e.g. banking and finance, space systems, transportation, etc.) (Rinaldi et al., 2001). Further, although many elements in the telecommunication system would be damaged or disrupted after an extreme geomagnetic event, empirical results simulating an EMP attack suggest that damage to communications devices and networks would not be sufficient to curtail higher than normal call volumes on the civilian network (Foster et al., 2008). In fact, this spike

in traffic would likely generate problems with network congestion because the remaining functional elements in the system are likely ill-equipped to handle traffic spikes (Grubesic and Murray, 2006). To reiterate, problems are further compounded by corresponding failures in the electrical grid due to geomagnetic disturbance. While most major telecommunication nodes (e.g. central offices) use a combination of backup generators and batteries to maintain operational continuity during extreme events, 72 hours of backup support is generally the limit in most locations.[2] Thus, extended outages in the electrical grid often produce extended failures in telecommunication systems (Grubesic and Murray, 2006).

In sum, the presence of both known and hidden interactions between critical infrastructure networks and SCADA systems are of concern. Cascading failures (Little, 2002; Grubesic and Murray, 2006) and the degree of systemic coupling (Perrow, 1999) are salient here. More importantly, regardless of the specific disruptive mechanism, the ability to anticipate outcomes or clarify the effects of disruptions to systems under stress is critical for better formulating strategies to fortify and protect network elements and SCADA from failure.

Measuring System Performance

There are several popular and accepted approaches for evaluating and assessing risk in critical infrastructure systems, including OCTAVE (CMSEI, 2012) and CRAMM (Siemens, 2011). Holistic in nature, these approaches often include methods for evaluating asset dependencies and business impacts, as well as identifying and assessing potential threats and vulnerabilities. Where the latter is concerned, scientific literature pertaining to the development and application of approaches that identify the worst case impact on a system are numerous (Murray, 2012). For example, Wollmer (1964) and Baran (1964) both focused on network interdiction approaches that disrupt the maximal flow in a network. Fulkerson and Harding (1977) and Corley and Sha (1982) dealt with increases in shortest path lengths due to network damage. Reviews of this and related work can be found in Wood (1993) and Snyder et al. (2006). Clearly, a range of models exist that account for network component damage, and its impact on aspects of network performance. Any of these associated models enables the identification of a situation where the system is degraded the most. Thus, the basic underlying idea is that particular network components which are most critical to system performance during extreme events and/or disruptions can be identified through mathematical modeling approaches. Once these critical components are determined, one can begin the process of protecting these critical nodes to guard against interdiction and/or damaging events in order to decrease network vulnerability. While this seems like a relatively straightforward and sensible strategy, it relies on intuition about what *may* or *may not* occur relative to interdiction and subsequent damage. In other words, assumptions must be made about the number of network components expected to be impacted. Further, if a range of impacts are considered, one is left to synthesize vulnerability in some way and then make protection and fortification decisions. This is widely known as the vulnerability conundrum (Murray and Grubesic, 2012).

Not only is there uncertainty associated with the number of network components that may be interdicted or damaged, there is a possibility that the resulting disruptions are something other than the worst case outcome. This has resulted in another class of modeling efforts focused on identifying the range of potential interdiction and/or disruptive events for network based systems. For example, Albert et al. (2000), Grubesic et al. (2003) and Matisziw et al. (2009) report simulation approaches designed to find different interdiction combinations. Once identified, events can be viewed in what Church and Scapara (2007a) refer to as a *reliability envelope*, though there are many examples of attempting to place potential vulnerability in such a context (see Baran 1964, Colbourn 1987, Albert et al. 2000, Myung and Kim 2004, Doyle et al. 2005). With a range of vulnerability events, it is then possible to make protection and fortification decisions. Again, while this seems like a relatively intuitive strategy, this is not necessarily an easy or straightforward task.

Again, within the larger spectrum of risk assessment and its tools (e.g. CRAMM), the identification of network infrastructure vulnerabilities is a small, but important facet. Given limitations in using many of the modeling approaches detailed above to support network component fortification in a more comprehensive manner, recent work has focused on the development of explicit approaches that account for fortification and game theoretic behavior. Representative examples include Brown et al. (2006), Church and Scaparra (2007b), Scaparra and Church (2008a,b), Salmeron et al. (2009) and Murray and Grubesic (2012). Of interest here is *connectivity* and *interaction* as these are central to the function and operation of large geospatial networked systems and SCADA.

Infrastructure Component Protection

In order to better understand the nature of the problem faced in fortification planning, let us first review aspects of interdiction and disruption in more specific terms. A *scenario* can be defined as follows:

A scenario is the situation where damage or loss of specific network components has occurred.

Consider the network shown in Figure 2 comprised of 5 nodes and 7 arcs, where interdiction and disruption can only occur through the loss or damage of equipment associated with nodes. Based upon this, Table 1 lists the 31 possible damage scenarios. Each scenario is labeled, 1-31, and the number of components damaged, k, is indicated as well. For example, scenario 14 in Table 1 involves the interdiction of nodes 3 and 5, which means that $k=2$ in this case. Beyond what is detailed in Table 1, we know that each scenario would likely impact system performance in some measurable way, with some scenarios expected to degrade the system more than others.[3] It is precisely this fact that makes fortification of system components an important and challenging strategic planning problem. A *fortified component* is defined as follows:

A fortified (or protected or hardened) component involves some sort of performance upgrade and/or enhanced security, rendering it less vulnerable and possibly immune to interdiction.

The significance of fortified components in a network whose components are vulnerable to interdiction/destruction is that it alters scenarios that are possible. Scaparra and Church (2008b) provide a proof of this observation. Consider then the scenarios identified in Table 1. For example, if node 5 is protected, this means that any scenario involving the interdiction/destruction of equipment located at node 5 is much less likely. Therefore, scenarios 5, 9, 12, 14, 15, 18, 20, 21, 23-25, 27-30 and 31 would likely not occur because of the protection of node 5. Of course, all other scenarios *not* involving node 5 are still possible.

A final observation is made in regard to scenario likelihood. There are two facets of likelihood that are relevant here. One is that because of spatial proximity, local security, historical performance, and other factors, some scenarios could be more probable than others. For example, if critical infrastructure systems and SCADA components located in Region A have a long history of exposure to natural disasters (e.g. flooding), they may be more likely to experience disruptions than those located in Region B, where natural disasters are infrequent. A second facet is that some levels of disruption may be of more likely than others. Specifically, as the number of components interdicted decreases,

Figure 2. Example network

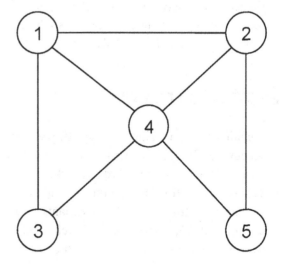

$k{\rightarrow}1$, there are many circumstances where this would reflect a greater chance of occurring. In other words, the disruption of one component is more likely than the disruption of multiple components. This is an important consideration because most critical infrastructure systems operate under budget constraints. This means that only a limited number of the m components can be fortified. Thus, if q components are to be protected, this implies that $q<m$. As the number of components interdicted/damaged increases, $k{\rightarrow}m$, this approaches a situation where no amount of protection will significantly alter system impact. That is, fundamental failure of the system is likely. Therefore, it would be most beneficial to focus on events associated with smaller values of k. For example, for the different levels of interdiction in Table 1, protection makes a lot of sense when $k=1$ for this network, but when k equals 3, 4 or 5, most of the network is destroyed and little relative interaction is possible. Thus, focusing too much emphasis on higher k component scenarios is both expensive and likely misguided.

In the next section, an optimization-based approach for addressing the defender-attacker-user problem is presented in the context of the system performance for a large, geospatial network. In addition to highlighting the complexities associated with the fortification of critical infrastructure and its implications for SCADA, the use of a large-scale geospatial network illustrates the massive number of complications and scenarios inherent to infrastructure fortification planning.

PROTECTION PLANNING

The challenge in modeling this type of problem is accounting for system performance as well as fortification and possible interdiction likelihood. Recent research efforts have turned to multilevel approaches to structure problem variants (e.g., Brown et al. 2006; Scaparra and Church 2008a). However, it is possible to structure an exact approach if all scenarios are identified a priori, with system performance impacts assessed in each case. This is precisely what was proposed for particular problems by Scaparra and Church (2008b), Liberatore et al. (2011) and Murray and Grubesic (2012).

System performance associated with the network could be measured in many ways (Murray 2012). Here we are particularly interested in connectivity and flow between all pairs of network nodes in the system along the lines studied in Myung and Kim (2004), Murray et al. (2007) and Arulselvan et al. (2009), as this is an important facet of networked system operation. Interaction between any two pair of nodes is possible if there is a path along arcs in the network, either directly or through other nodes, connecting the origin and destination nodes.

The proposed approach to vulnerability analysis of a network with a goal to fortify components requires: information about the performance of the system without any disruption, Γ^*; identification of interdiction scenarios l to be considered (including components damaged in each scenario); and, subsequent system performance associated with scenario l, Γ_l. The degradation in system performance can then be measured in a relative way as $a_l = 100\dfrac{\Gamma_l}{\Gamma^*}$. The assumption is that system performance is always greatest when the network is fully functional. Thus, $\Gamma^* \geq \Gamma_l$ for each interdiction scenario l, and therefore $a_l \in \left[0, 100\right]$. Consider the following additional notation:

j = index of network components (nodes and/ or arcs);

l = index of scenarios (total number n);

k = number of network components interdicted/ damaged;

w_k = weight of importance for number of components interdicted k;

Table 1. Disruption scenarios for 5 node network

Scenario	k	Nodes interdicted
1	1	1
2	1	2
3	1	3
4	1	4
5	1	5
6	2	1, 2
7	2	1, 3
8	2	1, 4
9	2	1, 5
10	2	2, 3
11	2	2, 4
12	2	2, 5
13	2	3, 4
14	2	3, 5
15	2	4, 5
16	3	1, 2, 3
17	3	1, 2, 4
18	3	1, 2, 5
19	3	1, 3, 4
20	3	1, 3, 5
21	3	1, 4, 5
22	3	2, 3, 4
23	3	2, 3, 5
24	3	2, 4, 5
25	3	3, 5, 5
26	4	1, 2, 3, 4
27	4	1, 2, 3, 5
28	4	1, 2, 4, 5
29	4	1, 3, 4, 5
30	4	2, 3, 4, 5
31	5	1, 2, 3, 4, 5

a_l = disruption impact of scenario l;

q = number of components to be fortified;

Φ_l = components interdicted in scenario l;

Ω_k = set of scenarios containing exactly k disrupted components;

$$X_j = \begin{cases} 1 & \text{if component } j \text{ is fortified} \\ 0 & \text{otherwise.} \end{cases}$$

$$Y_l = \begin{cases} 1 & \text{if scenario } l \text{ guarded against} \\ 0 & \text{otherwise.} \end{cases}$$

Z_k = total possible disruption guarded against involving k components.

The decision variables address three important aspects of what is involved in fortification planning. First, X_j identifies explicitly which components to fortify. Second, Y_l indicates whether the fortification plan thwarts or guards against scenario l from possible occurrence. In particular, any component fortified that is part of scenario l represents a case where the scenario is thwarted and therefore no longer possible per the fortification proposition. Finally, the decision variables Z_k track the total impact averted for a given number of components disrupted k. Combined with an importance weight w_k, it is possible to give greater importance to the protection of certain levels of possible interdiction and/or damage. A model for network protection planning given the above is:

Maximize

$$\sum_k w_k Z_k \tag{1}$$

Subject to

$$\sum_{l \in \Omega_k} a_l Y_l = Z_k \quad \forall k \tag{2}$$

$$\sum_j X_j = q \tag{3}$$

$$\sum_{j \in \Phi_l} X_j \geq Y_l \quad \forall l \tag{4}$$

$$\begin{aligned} X_j &\in \{0,1\} \quad \forall j \\ Y_l &\in \{0,1\} \quad \forall l \\ Z_k &\geq 0 \quad \forall k \end{aligned} \tag{5}$$

The objective, (1), maximizes the total weighted potential scenario impacts that have been guarded against. Constraints (2) track scenario impacts fortified against by the number of components interdicted. Constraint (3) specifies the number of components to be fortified. Constraints (4) account for whether a scenario has been thwarted based on decisions to fortify components. Integer and non-negativity conditions are established in Constraints (5). This model can be considered a generalization of the maximal covering location problem (MCLP), first introduced in Church and ReVelle (1974) and relied upon in Scaparra and Church (2008b) to solve the interdiction median problem. This model accounts for specific scenario attributes based on the number of components interdicted, k. If $w_k = w_{k'}$ for all k and k', then this model is effectively equivalent to the MCLP.

Some further discussion of this model may be helpful. First, the limited budget feature of the model is reflected in Constraint (3), and assumes that the relative cost of fortification is basically the same for any network component being considered. If this is not the case, it is straightforward to modify this constraint to account for varying costs by component with a specific total monetary budget.

A second issue is the linkage of fortification decisions to the prevention of interdiction scenarios. According to the fortification proposition, any scenario containing component j is rendered impossible. Thus, for a scenario l containing component j there are two cases:

Case A: No components associated with scenario l are fortified. This means that $\sum_{j \in \Phi_l} X_j = 0$, so Constraint (4) becomes $\sum_{j \in \Phi_l} X_j = 0 \geq Y_l$. This then bounds $Y_l = 0$. Referring back to the definition of Y_l, when it equals zero, this indicates that scenario l has not been guarded against. Therefore, scenario l is a possible outcome of an interdiction and/or damage effort.

Case B: One or more components associated with scenario l are fortified. This means that $X_j = 1$ for one or more $j \in \Phi_l$. Constraint (4) in this case gives $\sum_{j \in \Phi_l} X_j \geq 1 \geq Y_l$. Y_l can therefore take on a value of zero or one. Combined with Constraints (2) and the objective (1), the weighted sum of the Y_l variables is being maximized. With positive weights, a_l and w_k, $Y_l = 1$. By definition, $Y_l = 1$ indicates that a scenario has been protected against, or thwarted.

Both cases demonstrate that appropriate linkages between fortification variables and thwarted scenarios are established. Thus, the fortification proposition is correctly and accurately reflected in the model formulation.

A third point regarding the formulation is the establishment of capabilities to favor or weight interdiction levels k differentially. The objective, (1), allows for different importance weights w_k according to any a priori decided upon preference. The total scenario impact thwarted by interdiction level k is defined in Constraints (2). For example, Z_1 accounts for only those scenarios where $k=1$, Z_2 accounts for only those scenarios where $k=2$, etc. If this is related to the scenarios detailed in Table 1, as an example, Z_1 would represent that total scenario impact thwarted in scenarios 1-5, Z_2 accounts for total scenario impact thwarted in scenarios 6-15, etc. Thus, the model enables an analyst to vary the importance of interdiction level impacts, if desired. Though not pursued here due to data limitations, it would be straightforward to account for individual scenario probabilities in Constraints (2).

APPLICATION RESULTS

The optimization approach for assisting in fortification decision making of a large scale geospatial network is applied to a telecommunication system.

The Abilene Internet2 backbone is a high performance fiber-optic telecommunications network comprised of 14 links and 11 nodes (routers), facilitating interaction between research institutions in the United States (Figure 3). Recent studies by Snediker et al. (2008) and Matisziw et al. (2009) have made use of this network for examining infrastructure vulnerability. System performance data consists of observed flow (in bytes) between routers, and each router node serves as both an origin and destination. In total there are 121 interacting origin-destination node pairs (including intra-nodal flow).

Again, interdiction and/or damage scenarios represent situations where network components are rendered inoperable. The fortification of one or more components in a scenario greatly reduces the probability of that scenario from being possible as per the protection proposition. To keep the modeling parameters simple, we assume that once a node is fortified, it cannot be interdicted. To illustrate this point, consider the case of a three node interdiction loss ($k=3$) to the network in Figure 3. There are 165 unique scenarios: {New York, Washington DC, Atlanta}; {New York, Washington DC, Chicago; {New York, Washington DC, Seattle}; {Sunnyvale, Seattle, New York}; etc. If a decision is made to fortify New York, as an example, then none of the scenarios involving New York are vulnerable to interdiction and/or damage. Of course, the remaining three node scenarios are still possible interdiction outcomes, but none that involve New York because it has been fortified in some way. The goal here is to identify the best q nodes to protect, thereby eliminating potential scenarios due to natural disasters (e.g. electromagnetic storms), human error or sabotage.

Consistent with Myung and Kim (2004) and Matisziw et al. (2009), the total flow between all 121 node pairs serves as the maximum interaction possible, Γ^*. The maximum total flow possible for the sample period is 48,728,171,337,750 bytes.

Any interdiction scenario l results in a total system flow, Γ_l, with the property that $\Gamma_l \leq \Gamma^*$. Without loss of generality, this will limit the component interdiction and/or damage to nodes of the network. Given this, and the fact that all nodes have positive intra-nodal flow, any node loss scenario experiences at least some decrease in total system interaction.

Matisziw et al. (2009) generated all possible node interdiction/damage scenarios for the Abilene network. There are 2,047 scenarios in total with partial to complete disruption in nodal interaction. The impacts of a three node loss, $k=3$, are summarized in Figure 4. The worst case disturbance for system performance/interaction when three nodes are interdicted/damaged results in only 19% of flow between origin and destination nodes being possible (or an a_l equal to 81% disruption of total flow possible). The nodes associated with this scenario are Indianapolis, Sunnyvale and Washington, D.C. Ignoring other possible numbers of components interdicted for the moment and assuming we wish to protect three nodes, it might be tempting to select these three components for fortification in order to minimize the impacts of potential interdiction. Again, this type of response fits neatly within the vulnerability conundrum (Murray and Grubesic, 2012). While it would prevent the worst case impact from occurring, Figure 4 shows that there are 27 other scenarios whose system impact is within 10% of the worst case, with 14 of these within 5% and 4 within 1%. And, exploration of these scenarios along the lines suggested in Snediker et al. (2008) highlights that each of the 11 nodes in the network are contained in one or more of the 27 scenarios. This no doubt complicates matters as an increase in total nodal flow interaction of up to 28% (or an a_l equal to 72% disruption of total possible flow) in the best case of these 28 scenarios remains a devastating blow to system performance. Of course, similar situations exist for other nodal loss values, k, which could range from 1 to 11 in this case). One

Figure 3. Major components of the Abilene backbone

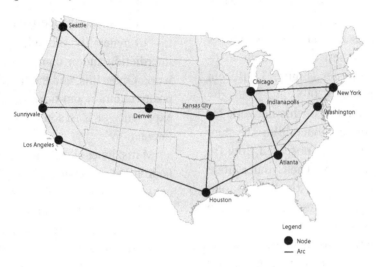

likely would want to consider other numbers of component losses (varying the value of k) as well as fortifying only a limited number of nodes (q) due to budget limitations.

To address this, an analysis, evaluation and modeling system was programmed in Python (ver 2.6.4). The model was structured and subsequently solved using IBM ILOG Cplex (ver. 12.1). All computational processing was done on a Mac Pro with two Quad-Core Intel Xeon processors (3.2 GHz) and 8 GB memory, running Mac OS X 10.5.8.

The model was applied to this network with 11 nodes and 2,047 interdiction scenarios has 2,069 decision variables and 2,059 constraints. A range of weights, w_k, were explored as well as different fortification investment. Select summary results are reported in Table 2, where fortification investment, q (number of nodes to protect), and equivalent importance weightings ($w_1=w_2=w_3=w_4=0.2325$ and $w_5=w_6=\ldots=w_{11}=0.01$) that favor the higher probably, lower number of potentially interdicted/damaged nodes. Processing and solution time is minimal in all cases, with Cplex requiring 3.29 seconds (20,455 iterations and 66 branches) to solve in the worst case using default settings.

There is a certain consistency in the identified fortification plans reported in Table 2 across investment levels q. Washington, D.C. ($q \geq 1$) and New York ($q \geq 2$) are found to be important, as is Atlanta when more than two nodes are to be fortified. The scheme of protecting New York, Washington DC and Atlanta when three nodes ($q=3$) are desired is shown in Figure 5. It seems clear that interaction with and between these East Coast cities is particularly important. Beyond this, these cities tend to be among the larger, most dominant telecommunication hubs in the United States (Grubesic and O'Kelly 2002).

In general terms, a range of weighting values was considered, but it happened to be the case for this network and its associated interaction flow that identified nodes in Table 2 were regularly found to be the best to protect. However, one interesting non-dominated solution when q is equal to four in Table 2 was discovered. In this particular case, a weight of one was used for the two-node interdiction scenarios ($k=2$) and other weights were zero. Effectively this focuses attention only on the two-node interdiction scenarios, in contrast to the weighting of $w_1=w_2=w_3=w_4=0.2325$ and $w_5=w_6=\ldots=w_{11}=0.01$ which considers all possible node interdiction scenarios. What emerges is that Los Angeles (in addition to Washington, D.C., New York and Atlanta) should be fortified rather than Houston. Doing so (protecting Los Angeles) enables 1,519 total two-node interdiction scenario ($k=2$) impact to be thwarted (out of a possible 2,185), whereas the fortification of Houston would provide only 1,516 total impact to be guarded against. Thus, it is possible to do a better job guarding against two-node interdiction scenarios if Los Angeles is fortified. However, if other interdiction scenarios are also considered, then Houston provides greater overall system benefit than would Los Angeles.

Evaluating investment decision making for this telecommunications system is possible through the examination of impacts associated with different levels of investment, q. If all of the potential scenario impacts are summed, $\sum_l a_l$, this total across the 2,047 scenarios is equal to 168,059. If a fortification plan were devised that guarded against all scenarios, then this would be the total system benefit for such a plan. Short of this, a fortification plan guards against only select scenarios, depending on the nodes fortified, and the decision variables Y_l in the model track which scenarios can be thwarted. Given this, it is possible to evaluate the best fortification plan for each level of investment, q. Figure 6 illustrates the level of fortification investment, q, in terms of its overall system benefit:

$$100 * \frac{\sum_l a_l Y_l}{\sum_l a_l} \qquad (6)$$

Note that the numerator in (6) contains the decision variables indicating which scenarios have been eliminated from occurring based on the associated nodal fortification plan. From Figure 6 we see that q equal to one thwarts nearly 55% of potential scenario impacts, and additional fortification of two nodes ($q=2$) gets this up to over 80%, but three fortified nodes ($q=3$) guards against over 91% of the potential scenario impacts. Protection plans involving 5-10 nodes do not enable 100% of potential impacts to be avoided, but come close. For this network, one would in fact have to fortify all eleven nodes to thwart all potential scenarios. However, there is clearly a basis for examining marginal returns on investment in Figure 6, and it may well be that the relatively small percentage gains reflective of $q=4$-11 or $q=5$-11 are not justified. Of course, this would depend on the likelihood of interdiction, the ability to fortify, and the regional and/or global impact of system disruption.

Table 2. Select identified node fortification schemes

q	Weights	Nodes to protect
1	$w_1=w_2=w_3=w_4=0.2325$ & $w_5=w_6=...=w_{11}=0.01$	Washington, D.C.
2	$w_1=w_2=w_3=w_4=0.2325$ & $w_5=w_6=...=w_{11}=0.01$	Washington, D.C.; New York
3	$w_1=w_2=w_3=w_4=0.2325$ & $w_5=w_6=...=w_{11}=0.01$	Washington, D.C.; New York; Atlanta
4	$w_1=w_2=w_3=w_4=0.2325$ & $w_5=w_6=...=w_{11}=0.01$	Washington, D.C.; New York; Atlanta; Houston
4	$w_2=1$ & $w_1=w_3=w_4=w_5=...=w_{11}=0$	Washington, D.C.; New York; Atlanta; Los Angeles

Figure 4. Impact summary of scenarios when three nodes are interdicted

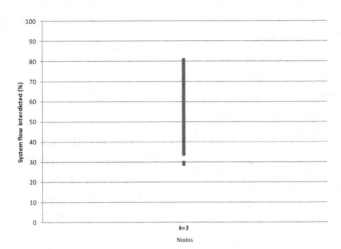

DISCUSSION

It was highlighted previously that many interdiction modeling efforts have focused on identifying system components that if damaged would be most disruptive to the performance of the network. For example, previous work by Matisziw et al. (2009) using the Abilene network found that the worst case three node interdiction would be Washington, D.C., Sunnyvale and Indianapolis. This scenario is the worst case in Figure 4 when k=3, with a_l =81%. In contrast, the interdiction of Washington, D.C., New York and Atlanta would impact only 65% of total system flow (a_l equal to 65%). Of course this is the identified three node (q=3) fortification plan for the network identified in Table 2. What is interesting is that it is not even within 10% of the worst case for a three node interdiction. Moreover, it would not be given a second thought using traditional approaches, yet it proves to be a particularly important strategic fortification scheme. Why is this? Table 3 attempts to provide insight on this issue, summarizing total scenario impact thwarted by interdiction levels k. If New York, Washington, D.C. and Atlanta are fortified, the total scenario impact guarded against is 153,514. This is in contrast to the 151,208 total system impact that Sunnyvale, Washington, D.C. and Indianapolis would thwart if fortified. One can see the breakdown by interdiction level in Table 3, highlighting that the New York, Washington, D.C. and Atlanta combination is able to prevent more scenario impact in the range of k=1-8 and the same amount for k=9-11, resulting in greater scenario aversion. Focusing on fortification across the system for a spectrum of potential interdiction levels is clearly essential. Extreme disruption scenarios, while significant, may not necessarily translate to high priority or advisable fortification schemes.

While perhaps of less significance for the network analyzed here given the dominance of certain nodal interactions, it is more generally the case that elected weighting values could be critical. One might consider developing and applying a probability of occurrence based on scenarios and levels of interdiction. In addition, as an informative mechanism, such a weights based approach is actually referred to as the weighting method in multi-objective optimization (see Cohon 1978) and there exist systematic approaches to finding non-dominated solutions (if they exist) as well as other techniques like the constraint method.

Figure 5. Optimal three node (q=3) network component fortification plan

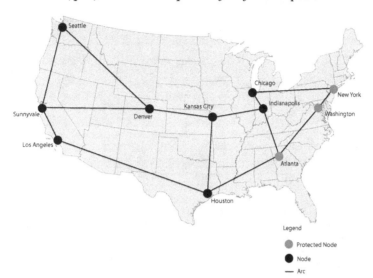

It is also important to note that any system performance approach is possible using the model detailed in this paper. The emphasis in this paper was on total interaction/flow between nodes in the network. There is nothing to prevent one from examining maximal flow, shortest paths, other measures, or variants and extensions (e.g., Wollmer 1964; Baran 1964; Fulkerson and Harding 1977; Corley and Sha 1982; Wood 1993; Israeli and Wood 2002; Church et al. 2004; Lim and Smith 2007). All that is necessary is the ability to identify every scenario to be considered as well as a relative system performance impact for each scenario.

IMPLICATIONS FOR SCADA

Given the methodological framework and results presented in this paper, there are several implications for the operation and continuity of SCADA systems, particularly as they relate to large scale, geospatial network infrastructure. As noted previously, many large scale civil infrastructures are controlled by SCADA over internet protocol (IP) communication networks (Haimes and Chittester, 2005), including the public Internet. This has al-

lowed for infrastructure to operate more efficiently, inexpensively, quickly and across great distances. However, the relationship between SCADA and the public Internet can be an uneasy one. Connections, operations and reliance upon the Internet exposes SCADA systems and their associated infrastructure to denial of service attacks, Internet worms, Trojan horse viruses, human saboteurs, etc (ibid). As a result, it is not surprising that many studies concerned with SCADA continuity focus on cybersecurity issues (Creery, 2005; Igure et al., 2006; Ten et al., 2008). Nevertheless, physical threats that can damage both SCADA and large-scale civil infrastructure systems remain an important consideration (Oman et al., 2001). Again, these threats do not always represent a direct attack. Cascading failures of highly interactive, interconnected and interdependent systems can be the source of many complications when considering SCADA continuity (Rinaldi et al., 2001; Little, 2002). This is not to say that analysts are putting the "cart before the horse" when cybersecurity is emphasized, but it is important to acknowledge the multiplicity of interaction paths within this context of critical infrastructure systems and SCADA failure.

Figure 6. Total scenario impact aversion possible through protection of q nodes

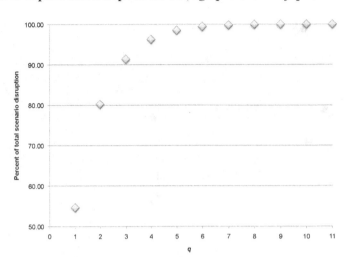

The primary concern for SCADA systems that rely on the public Internet for monitoring and controlling critical infrastructure is that the public Internet is *not* immune to disruption (Murray and Grubesic, 2007). As illustrated in this paper, rmodest interdiction efforts can cause a significant deterioration of Internet infrastructure performance. Although the Abilene backbone modeled in this paper is a relatively simple system, related work on more complex network representations and topologies reinforce the fact that Internet disruptions have complex spatial and temporal footprints (Matisziw et al., 2012). In fact, there are numerous examples that illustrate exactly how sensitive Internet infrastructure can be to interdiction. Case in point, a simple cable cut can disrupt Internet service across a region for several hours (Grove, 2012), or across multiple continents for several days or weeks (Gross, 2008). While these types of disruptions are not common, they are a serious concern for SCADA systems that require a robust and survivable tele-communications platform for monitoring critical infrastructure systems. Put simply, if the public Internet fails, SCADA systems relying upon it cannot function properly. In turn, the infrastructure depending upon SCADA systems for monitoring and feedback are also put at risk for failure (Eusgeld et al., 2011). This type of cascading effect across systems was clearly pronounced in during the Northeast Blackout of 2003 (NERC, 2004), where electrical failures caused outages in water pumps, wastewater pumps, telecommunications systems, transportation, banking, etc. (NERC, 2004; Grubesic and Murray, 2006).

This is not to say, however, that one can simply target fortification resources at Internet components that are ripe with SCADA connections and hope for the best. Although this could certainly help prevent a worst-case scenario, the results detailed in this paper suggest that both known and unknown interaction effects, generated by thousands of unique combinations of infrastructure elements and their associated levels of connectivity (and flow), indicate that a myriad of similarly disastrous failures can occur within and across systems.

Aside from the engineering-related complications of protecting large geospatial networks and SCADA, there are significant political, economic and social priorities at multiple administrative levels (local, regional and national) that dictate how protective resources might be allocated. As noted by Murray and Grubesic (2012), although most

Table 3. Comparison of scenarios thwarted by number of nodes interdicted (k)

k	Protection ($q=3$)	
	Washington, D.C.; New York; Atlanta	Washington, D.C.; Sunnyvale; Indianapolis
1	43	26
2	1250	1143
3	7016	6618
4	19879	19200
5	34214	33575
6	38836	38487
7	29999	29895
8	15708	15695
9	5377	5377
10	1092	1092
11	100	100

government agencies understand the importance of protecting critical infrastructure and key resources, the combination of privately held systems and a historical tendency to pursue a "hands off" regulatory approach creates a policy environment where incentivizing socially responsible levels of protection is difficult. Further, there are fears from the private sector that efforts to disclose the specifics of critical infrastructure operation and associated SCADA systems would lead to more regulation, more expense and less autonomy. As a result, the Critical Infrastructure Information Act (2002), the Homeland Security Act (2002) and the Intelligence Reform and Terrorism Prevention Act (2004) make such information sharing voluntary. In other words, nobody shares a thing.

CONCLUSION

Critical infrastructure is ubiquitous and SCADA plays an important role in remotely controlling, monitoring and helping manage these systems. Because so many daily functions rely on large scale, geospatial networked systems, their protection is an important and challenging task. While these types of infrastructure systems are generally robust to minor, short-term failures, large-scale damage due to natural disasters, human error or sabotage are problematic. Where SCADA is

concerned, the threat matrix is large, ranging from geomagnetic disturbances to failures associated with infrastructure interdependencies. Specifically, for SCADA systems that rely on the public Internet for operation, the Internet's ability to maintain continuity when under attack or duress is critical for infrastructure systems that are reliant on SCADA for management tasks. That said, regardless of the disruptions origin, type or target, the ability to ensure uninterrupted performance of network infrastructure and SCADA systems has become increasingly important for national and global security. Unfortunately, the costs associated with fortifying and protecting all critical components is prohibitive. Therefore, it is incumbent for infrastructure management bodies to develop strategic approaches for identifying network components for protection from damage or destruction that ensure the greatest continued system performance possible.

It is possible undertake SCADA protection planning, particularly for SCADA systems that are reliant upon the public Internet, with the support of an optimization model. The model was applied to a telecommunications network to examine node protection in terms of total system flow between node pairs in the network. The application results highlighted the complexities of the planning and management problem in terms of interdiction impact as well as levels of protection investment.

Interestingly, scenarios imparting the most impact on a system are not necessarily the most effective for decreasing vulnerability across the entire spectrum of potential scenarios. Beyond this, the model enables one to quantify the marginal return relative to potential scenarios thwarted and different levels of protection investment. While this is a relatively small piece of the overall critical infrastructure assurance puzzle, network infrastructure fortification planning can greatly benefit from modeling, especially approaches that can integrate thousands and millions of potential interdiction scenarios in a manner that allows for prioritization and investment by system operators.

The application demonstrated that the approach was feasible, requiring little computational effort, either in identifying scenarios, deriving system performance or optimally solving the resulting fortification planning problems. However, computational limitations would no doubt be encountered with larger networks. Continued research on multilevel methods to address associated protection planning problems is essential, as integrated approaches would characteristically avoid the need for complete enumeration of scenarios.

ACKNOWLEDGMENT

This material is based upon work supported by the National Science Foundation under Grants No. 0908030 and 0718091. Any opinions, findings, and conclusions or recommendations expressed in this material are those of the author(s) and do not necessarily reflect the views of the National Science Foundation. Portions of this work are also supported by the National Academies Keck Futures Initiative Complex Systems grant CS05.

REFERENCES

Albert, R., Jeong, H., & Barabasi, A. L. (2000). Error and attack tolerance of complex networks. *Nature, 406*, 378–382. doi:10.1038/35019019

Arulselvan, A., Commander, C. W., Elefteriadou, L., & Pardalos, P. M. (2009). Detecting critical nodes in sparse graphs. *Computers & Operations Research, 36*, 2193–2200. doi:10.1016/j.cor.2008.08.016

Bailey, D., & Wright, E. (2003). *Practical SCADA for industry*. Burlington, MA: Newnes.

Baran, P. (1964). On distributed communications networks. *IEEE Transactions on Communications Systems, 12*, 1–9. doi:10.1109/TCOM.1964.1088883

Berman, O., & Krass, D. (2002). The generalized maximal covering location problem. *Computers & Operations Research, 29*, 563–591. doi:10.1016/S0305-0548(01)00079-X

Brown, G., Garlyle, M., Salmeron, J., & Wood, K. (2006). Defending critical infrastructure. *Interfaces, 36*, 530–544. doi:10.1287/inte.1060.0252

Carnegie Mellon Software Engineering Institute (CMSEI). (2012). *OCTAVE method*. Retrieved from http://www.cert.org/octave/octavemethod.html

Church, R. L., & ReVelle, C. (1974). The maximal covering location problem. *Papers/Regional Science Association. Regional Science Association. Meeting, 32*, 101–118. doi:10.1007/BF01942293

Church, R. L., & Scaparra, M. P. (2007a). Analysis of facility systems' reliability withn subject to attach or a natural disaster. In Murray, A., & Grubesic, T. (Eds.), *Reliability and vulnerability in critical infrastructure: A quantitative geographic perspective* (pp. 221–241). Heidelberg, Germany: Springer.

Church, R. L., & Scaparra, M. P. (2007b). Protecting critical assets: The r-interdiction median problem with fortification. *Geographical Analysis, 39,* 129–146. doi:10.1111/j.1538-4632.2007.00698.x

Church, R. L., Scaparra, M. P., & Middleton, R. S. (2004). Identifying critical infrastructure: The median and covering facility interdiction problems. *Annals of the Association of American Geographers. Association of American Geographers, 94,* 491–502. doi:10.1111/j.1467-8306.2004.00410.x

Cohon, J. (1978). *Multi-objective programming and planning.* New York, NY: Academic Press.

Colbourn, C. J. (1987). *The combinatorics of network reliability.* New York, NY: Oxford University Press.

Corley, H. W., & Sha, D. Y. (1982). Most vital links and nodes in weighted networks. *Operations Research Letters, 1,* 157–160. doi:10.1016/0167-6377(82)90020-7

Creery, A. (2005). *Industrial cybersecurity for power system and SCADA networks.* 52nd Annual Petroleum and Chemical Industry Conference. Retrieved from http://ieeexplore.ieee.org/xpls/abs_all.jsp?arnumber=1524567

Critical Infrastructure Information Act. (2002). Retrieved from http://www.dhs.gov/xlibrary/assets/CII_Act.pdf

Daneels, A., & Salter, W. (1999). What is SCADA? *International Conference on Accelerator and Large Experimental Physics Control Systems,* (pp. 339-343).

Doyle, J. C., Alderson, D. L., Li, L., Low, S., Roughan, M., & Shalunov, S. … Willinger, W. (2005). The "robust yet fragile" nature of the Internet. *Proceedings of the National Academy of Sciences, 102,* 14497-14502.

Fernandez, J. D., & Fernandez, A. E. (2005). SCADA system: vulnerabilities and remediation. *Journal of Computing Sciences in Colleges, 20,* 160–168.

Fischhoff, B., Slovic, P., & Lichtenstein, S. (1978). Fault trees: Sensitivity of estimated failure probabilities to problem representation. *Journal of Experimental Psychology. Human Perception and Performance, 4*(2), 330–344. doi:10.1037/0096-1523.4.2.330

Foster, J. S., Jr., Gjelde, E., Graham, W. R., Hermann, R. J., Kluepfel, H. M., & Lawson, R. L. … Woodard, J. B. (April 2008*). Report of the commission to assess the threat to the United States from electromagnetic pulse (EMP) attack.* Retrieved from http://www.empcommission.org/

Fulkerson, D. R., & Harding, G. C. (1977). Maximizing the minimum source-sink path subject to a budget constraint. *Mathematical Programming, 13,* 116–118. doi:10.1007/BF01584329

Glasstone, S., & Dolan, P. J. (1977). *The effects of nuclear weapons* (3rd ed.). Washington, DC: U.S. Government Printing Office. doi:10.2172/6852629

Gross, T. (2008). Internet failure hits two continents, and may last two weeks. *National Review.* Retrieved from http://tinyurl.com/87tuus2

Grove, C. (2012, February 29). Cut cable halts service to thousands of GCI customers. *Anchorage Daily News.* Retrieved from http://tinyurl.com/7yurj7f

Grubesic, T. H., & Matisziw, T. C. (2012). A typological framework for categorizing infrastructure vulnerability. *GeoJournal,* online before print. DOI: 10.1007/s10708-011-9411-0

Grubesic, T. H., & Murray, A. T. (2006). Vital nodes, interconnected infrastructures and the geographies of network survivability. *Annals of the Association of American Geographers. Association of American Geographers, 96*(1), 64–83. doi:10.1111/j.1467-8306.2006.00499.x

Grubesic, T. H., & O'Kelly, M. E. (2002). Using points of presence to measure city accessibility to the commercial internet. *The Professional Geographer, 54,* 259–278. doi:10.1111/0033-0124.00330

Grubesic, T. H., O'Kelly, M. E., & Murray, A. T. (2003). A geographic perspective on commercial Internet survivability. *Telematics and Informatics, 20,* 51–69. doi:10.1016/S0736-5853(02)00003-5

Haimes, Y. Y., & Chittester, C. G. (2005). A roadmap for quantifying the efficacy of risk management of information security and interdependent SCADA systems. *Journal of Homeland Security and Emergency Management, 2*(2), 12. doi:10.2202/1547-7355.1117

Homeland Security Act. (2002). Washington, DC.

Hutchins, T. R., & Overbye, T. J. (2011). *The effect of geomagnetic disturbances on the electric grid and appropriate mitigation strategies.* North American Power Symposium (NAPS), 2011.

Igure, V. M., Laughter, S. A., & Williams, R. D. (2006). Security issues in SCADA networks. *Computers & Security, 25*(7), 498–506. doi:10.1016/j.cose.2006.03.001

Intelligence Reform and Terrorism Prevention Act. (2004). House of Representatives. Washington, DC.

Israeli, E., & Wood, R. K. (2002). Shortest-path network interdiction. *Networks, 40,* 97–111. doi:10.1002/net.10039

Kappenman, J. G., Radasky, W. A., Gilbert, J. L., & Erinmez, I. A. (2000). Advanced geomagnetic storm forecasting: A risk management tool for electric power system operations. *IEEE Transactions on Plasma Science, 28,* 2114–2121. doi:10.1109/27.902238

Lim, C., & Smith, J. C. (2007). Algorithms for discrete and continuous multicommodity flow network interdiction problems. *IIE Transactions, 39,* 15–26. doi:10.1080/07408170600729192

Matisziw, T. C., Grubesic, T. H., & Guo, J. (2012). (in press). Robustness elasticity in complex networks. *PLoS ONE.* doi:10.1371/journal.pone.0039788

Matisziw, T. C., Murray, A. T., & Grubesic, T. H. (2009). Exploring the vulnerability of network infrastructure to interdiction. *The Annals of Regional Science, 43,* 307–321. doi:10.1007/s00168-008-0235-x

Murray, A. T. (2012). An overview of network vulnerability modeling approaches. *GeoJournal.* doi:doi:10.1007/s10708-011-9414-z

Murray, A. T., & Grubesic, T. H. (Eds.). (2007). *Critical infrastructure: Reliability and vulnerability.* Heidelberg, Germany: Springer.

Murray, A. T., & Grubesic, T. H. (2012). Critical infrastructure protection: The vulnerability conundrum. *Telematics and Informatics, 29,* 56–65. doi:10.1016/j.tele.2011.05.001

Murray, A. T., Matisziw, T. C., & Grubesic, T. H. (2007). Critical network infrastructure analysis: interdiction and system flow. *Journal of Geographical Systems, 9,* 103–117. doi:10.1007/s10109-006-0039-4

Myung, Y. S., & Kim, H. J. (2004). A cutting plane algorithm for computing k-edge survivability of a network. *European Journal of Operational Research, 156,* 579–589. doi:10.1016/S0377-2217(03)00135-8

North American Electric Reliability Corporation (NERC). (1989). *The 1989 system disturbances.* NERC Disturbance Analysis Working Group.

North American Electric Reliability Corporation (NERC). (2004). *Final report on the August 14, 2003 blackout in the United States and Canada: Causes and recommendations.* Retrieved from http://www.nerc.com/filez/blackout.html

Oman, P., Roberts, J., & Schweitzer, E. (2001). *Obstacles to self-healing reliable complex control systems.* Fourth Information Survivability Workshop: Impediments to Achieving Survivable Systems. Retrieved December 6, 2011, from http://tinyurl.com/4x4wf33

Powell, R. (2007). Defending against terrorist attacks with limited resources. *The American Political Science Review, 101,* 527–541. doi:10.1017/S0003055407070244

Rinaldi, S. M., Peerenboom, J. P., & Kelly, T. K. (2001). Identifying, understanding and analyzing critical infrastructure interdependencies. *IEEE Control Systems Magazine,* (December): 11–25. doi:10.1109/37.969131

Salmeron, J., Wood, K., & Baldick, R. (2009). Worst-case interdiction analysis of large-scale electric power grids. *IEEE Transactions on Power Systems, 24,* 96–104. doi:10.1109/TP-WRS.2008.2004825

Scaparra, M. P., & Church, R. L. (2008a). A bilevel mixed-integer program for critical infrastructure protection planning. *Computers & Operations Research, 35,* 1905–1923. doi:10.1016/j.cor.2006.09.019

Scaparra, M. P., & Church, R. L. (2008b). An exact solution approach for the interdiction median problem with fortification. *European Journal of Operational Research, 189,* 76–92. doi:10.1016/j.ejor.2007.05.027

Schneier, B. (1999). *Attack trees: Modeling security threats.* Dr. Dobb's Journal.

Snediker, D., Murray, A. T., & Matisziw, T. C. (2008). Decision support for network disruption mitigation. *Decision Support Systems, 44,* 954–969. doi:10.1016/j.dss.2007.11.003

Snyder, L. V., Scaparra, M. P., Daskin, M. S., & Church, R. L. (2006). Planning for disruptions in supply chain networks. *INFORMS Tutorials in Operations Research,* 234-257.

Sternberg, E., & Lee, G. C. (2006). Meeting the challenge of facility protection for homeland security. *Journal of Homeland Security and Emergency Management, 3*(1), 11. doi:10.2202/1547-7355.1153

Ten, C.-W., Liu, C.-C., & Manimaran, G. (2008). Vulnerability assessment of cybersecurity for SCADA systems. *IEEE Transactions on Power Systems, 23*(4), 1836–1846. doi:10.1109/TP-WRS.2008.2002298

Wollmer, R. (1964). Removing arcs from a network. *Operations Research, 12,* 934–940. doi:10.1287/opre.12.6.934

Wood, R. K. (1993). Deterministic network interdiction. *Mathematical and Computer Modelling, 17,* 1–18. doi:10.1016/0895-7177(93)90236-R

ADDITIONAL READING

Albuquereque, C., Vickers, B. J., & Suda, T. S. (2004). Network border patrol: Preventing congestion collapse and promoting fairness in the Internet. *IEEE/ACM Transactions on Networking, 12*(1), 173–186. doi:10.1109/TNET.2003.820248

Alderson, D. L., & Doyle, J. C. (2010). Contrasting views of complexity and their implications for network-centric infrastructures. *IEEE Transactions on Systems, Man, and Cybernetics. Part A, Systems and Humans, 40*(4), 839–852. doi:10.1109/TSMCA.2010.2048027

Bell, M. G. H. (2000). A game theory approach to measuring the performance reliability of transport networks. *Transportation Research Part B: Methodological, 34*, 533–545. doi:10.1016/S0191-2615(99)00042-9

Campbell, A. M., & Jones, P. C. (2011). Prepositioning supplies in preparation for disasters. *European Journal of Operational Research, 209*(2), 156–165. doi:10.1016/j.ejor.2010.08.029

Carlson, J. M., & Doyle, J. C. (2007). Complexity and robustness. *Proceedings of the National Academy of Sciences of the United States of America, 99*, 2538–2545. doi:10.1073/pnas.012582499

Cormican, K. J., Morton, D. P., & Wood, K. R. (1998). Stochastic network interdiction. *Operations Research, 46*(2), 184–197. doi:10.1287/opre.46.2.184

Doyle, J. C., Alderson, D., Li, L., Low, S., Roughan, M., & Shalunov, S. … Willinger, W. (2005). The 'robust yet fragile' nature of the Internet. *Proceedings of the National Academies of Science, 102*(41), 14497-14502.

Grubesic, T. H., Matisziw, T. C., Murray, A. T., & Snedicker, D. (2008). Comparative approaches for assessing network vulnerability. *International Regional Science Review, 31*(1), 88–112. doi:10.1177/0160017607308679

Grubesic, T. H., & Murray, A. T. (2005). Spatial-historical landscapes of telecommunication network survivability. *Telecommunications Policy, 29*(11), 801–820. doi:10.1016/j.telpol.2005.06.011

Haimes, Y. Y. (2002). Strategic responses to risks of terrorism to water resources. *Journal of Water Resources Planning and Management, 128*, 383. doi:10.1061/(ASCE)0733-9496(2002)128:6(383)

Hodgson, M. J., Rosing, K. E., & Zhang, J. (1996). Locating vehicle inspection stations to protect a transportation network. *Geographical Analysis, 28*, 299–314. doi:10.1111/j.1538-4632.1996.tb00937.x

Johansson, J., & Hassel, H. (2010). An approach for modeling interdependent infrastructures in the context of vulnerability analysis. *Reliability Engineering & System Safety, 95*(12), 1335–1344. doi:10.1016/j.ress.2010.06.010

Keeney, M. (2005). *Computer system sabotage in critical infrastructure sectors*. Washington, DC: U.S. Secret Service and CERT Coordination Center/SEA.

Lewis, T. G. (2006). *Critical infrastructure protection in homeland security*. New York, NY: Wiley. doi:10.1002/0471789542

Magnanti, L. T., & Wong, R. T. (1984). Network design and transportation planning: Models and algorithms. *Transportation Science, 18*(1), 1–55. doi:10.1287/trsc.18.1.1

McDaniels, T., Chang, S., Peterson, K., Mikawoz, J., & Reed, D. (2007). Empirical framework for characterizing infrastructure failure interdependencies. *Journal of Infrastructure Systems, 13*(3), 175–184. doi:10.1061/(ASCE)1076-0342(2007)13:3(175)

Murray, A. T., Matisziw, T. C., & Grubesic, T. H. (2008). A methodological overview of network vulnerability analysis. *Growth and Change, 39*(4), 573–592. doi:10.1111/j.1468-2257.2008.00447.x

Pederson, P., Dudenhoeffer, D., Hartley, S., & Permann, M. (2006). *Critical infrastructure interdependency modeling: A survey of U.S. and international research*. Idaho National Laboratory. Retrieved from http://tinyurl.com/6fzweo.

Peterson, S. K., & Church, R. L. (2008). A framework for modeling rail transport vulnerability. *Growth and Change*, *39*(4), 617–641. doi:10.1111/j.1468-2257.2008.00449.x

Qiao, J., Jeong, D., Lawley, M., Richard, J. P., Abraham, D. M., & Yih, Y. (2007). Allocating security resources to a water supply network. *IIE Transactions*, *39*, 95–109. doi:10.1080/07408170600865400

Ratliff, H. D., Sicilia, G. T., & Lubore, S. H. (1975). Finding the *n* most vital links in flow networks. *Management Science*, *2*, 531–539. doi:10.1287/mnsc.21.5.531

Rinaldi, S. M., Peerenboom, J. P., & Kelly, T. K. (2001). Identifying, understanding and analyzing critical infrastructure interdependencies. *IEEE Control Systems Magazine*, (December): 11–25. doi:10.1109/37.969131

Salmeron, J., Wood, K., & Baldick, R. (2004). Analysis of electric grid security under terrorist threat. *IEEE Transactions on Power Systems*, *19*, 905–912. doi:10.1109/TPWRS.2004.825888

Siemens. (2011). *CRAMM*. Retrieved from http://www.cramm.com/capabilities/risk.htm

Snyder, L. V., Scaparra, M. P., Daskin, M. S., & Church, R. L. (2006). *Planning for disruptions in supply chain networks*. Tutorials in Operations Research.

Willinger, W., Alderson, D., & Doyle, J. C. (2009). Mathematics and the Internet: A source of enormous confusion and great potential. *Notices of the American Mathematical Society*, *56*(5), 586–599.

KEY TERMS AND DEFINITIONS

Abilene: A high performance backbone network that is now known as the Internet2 Network.

Arc: A segment of a differentiable curve.

Critical Infrastructure: Assets and systems that are essential for societal and economic function, including the electrical grid, gas transport and distribution, transportation systems, public health facilities, financial services, water supply, etc.

Fortify: To strengthen and secure.

Interdict: To destroy, damage or cut off.

Node: A point that terminates an arc or comprises the intersection of two or more arcs.

Vulnerability: Susceptibility to injury or attack.

ENDNOTES

[1] Interdiction is generally recognized as destroying/damaging/disabling infrastructure by an enemy with the intent cause harm or disruption (see Wood 1993; Israeli and Wood 2002; Salmeron et al. 2009). In addition to interdiction and damage a system may also be disrupted due to congestion. Here we are focusing on issues of network component failure or loss (damage and interdiction), so congestion issues will not be considered.

[2] Central offices (COs) are typically large, windowless, concrete buildings that house telecommunications equipment for local providers. Most often, these are locations where subscriber lines are joined to switching equipment for connecting subscribers together. COs can also serve as locations where several infrastructure providers connect to a larger network, such as a transcontinental fiber-optic backbone (Newton, 2002).

[3] In many ways this type of evaluation is related to attack trees (Schneier, 1999) and fault tree analysis (Fischhoff et al., 1978)

Chapter 14
Information Sharing for CIP:
Between Policy, Theory, and Practice

Neil Robinson
RAND Europe, UK

ABSTRACT

This chapter describes and contrasts policy, economic theory, and insights concerning the establishment and operation of Information Exchanges (IE). In the context of this chapter, IEs are specific mechanisms meant to stimulate the exchange and sharing (aside from pure disclosure) of a range of confidential information relating to security between owner-operators of critical infrastructure. Information shared in IEs may be of varying types but is reported to generally be of a non-technical nature. In the Supervisory Control and Data Acquisition (SCADA) community, a number of nations have established IEs; for example, European SCADA and control systems exchange has been operating since 2005. The chapter primarily considers these issues through the perspective of efforts to address the security of the Critical Information Infrastructures (CII). Despite IEs being seen by policy-makers as important to tackle CIP issues, limited empirical operational evidence exists to suggest that IEs constitute a useful mechanism to successfully overcome the economic incentives governing the disclosure of information. The chapter concludes by identifying opportunities to further explore the disparities and reasons for the indicative disjuncture between economic theory, policy, and practice. The chapter is thus aimed primarily at managers, policy-makers, and non-technical personnel considering participation in an IE.

INTRODUCTION

The vulnerability of critical infrastructures to various types of physical and cyber incidents remains high on the policy agenda, especially after the headlines generated by the appearance of Stuxnet (Bellovin; 2010). There is increasing interest in the security of critical infrastructures, driven by a number of related developments.

Firstly, margins of profit for infrastructure operators in the increasingly globalised economy have led to those firms owning or operating criti-

DOI: 10.4018/978-1-4666-2659-1.ch014

Copyright © 2013, IGI Global. Copying or distributing in print or electronic forms without written permission of IGI Global is prohibited.

cal infrastructures to seek more and more ways to cut costs, often at the expense of security. This, in conjunction with the now pervasive presence of the Internet in all walks of life, has resulted in firms owning or operating critical infrastructure evaluating the use of public networks as a route to deploying some aspects of their control systems.

Secondly, the increasing confluence of connectivity between operational systems that link to PCS with business information systems (used for billing, revenue management and other back office operations) has meant that the potential for damage increases significantly (Riptech; 2001). It is received wisdom that attack dynamics are changing. Although extensive research into those that developed Stuxnet indicated that this took a team of 4-6 people server months to prepare, the increasing proliferation of easy to use, accessible tools on the criminal underground also drives the increased risk to Critical Infrastructures. Concern over the increasing use of Commercial Off the Shelf Technology (COTS) and the connection of SCADA systems to other potentially more insecure networks would appear to be supported by recent evidence concerning the expectations of infrastructure owner operators to link up elements of their infrastructure:

The key observation to report again this year is that links from/to control center-based systems are substantial, and indeed appear to be continuing to increase from what was once a completely closed control center-based system. (Newton-Evans, Market Trends Digest, 2008, p4)

Thirdly, and perhaps most importantly for the subject of this chapter, unlike historical consideration of infrastructure risk, it is widely regarded that the majority of such infrastructure is owned and or operated by the private sector (Assaf; 2008) although there has been criticism of the provenance of specific percentages used as received wisdom (Bellavita; 2009). Nonetheless, the need to obtain private sector involvement in securing these networks has been noted in various forms of declaratory policy including for example the US White House 60 day Cybersecurity Policy Review. This concluded that the private sector "designs, builds, owns and operates most of the network infrastructures that support government and private users alike" (White House; 2009).

Technical estimations of the threat and risk posed to these infrastructures vary. For example, following disclosure of news of a specific vulnerability, security expert Bruce Schneier indicated that vulnerabilities in SCADA security were an important concern (Schneier; 2007). Shapiro et al (2011) conducted an assessment of the vulnerability of SCADA devices whilst in Rosslin and Choi (2009) the vulnerabilities of SCADA control systems are further explored. Security researchers and experts agree that conceptions concerning the standalone nature of SCADA systems, the high security applied to such systems and the bespoke character of software used to run SCADA are largely false (Rosslin and Choi; 2009 and Riptech; 2001).

Nonetheless, the private sector faces a dilemma in addressing cyber-security with respect to these contextual factors, namely that they must understand how a wide range of imperatives (especially financial) drive security and the possibilities to mitigate security risks in an increasingly diverse operational environment. These financial drivers interact with other pressures that add to the complexity of making security investment decisions. For owner-operators of Critical Infrastructure, one of the main factors stems from government, who may be concerned that the security of infrastructure whose failure might have serious national implications, is put at risk by the private sector ignoring security. Although the concerns relating to regulation apply to those strategically important owner-operators of Critical Infrastructure, the complexity of applying security cost benefit trade-offs applies more broadly to a range of security issues.

Sharing of Information

It is received wisdom that in order to successfully address these and other types of risks to critical infrastructures, it is useful to share information. Such information might include a wide variety of relevant data such as threats, risks, trends and best practices for resolution (General Accounting Office; 2004). For the purposes of this chapter we differentiate between disclosure (an implied one-way transmission of information) with sharing (a two way exchange of information). Numerous mechanisms exist such as the 2009 Common Vulnerability Exposure (CVE) taxonomy (Mitre; 2009) for classification of vulnerabilities; the 2007 Common Vulnerability Scoring System (CVSS) (Forum of Incident Response Teams; 2007) for scoring of the severity of vulnerabilities and the Incident Object Description Exchange Framework (IODEF) for exchange of incident data (Danyliw et al; 2007).

Types of Information Sharing

The disclosure and sharing of cyber-security information takes many forms. This may include:

- The disclosure of threat data between the authorities (e.g. Law Enforcement or intelligence agencies) with owner-operators of critical infrastructure;
- Disclosure of vulnerabilities in a specific product – either as part of a responsible disclosure programme, via a vendor initiated alerting system or openly[1] via services such as Bugtraq;
- The exchange of information such as Internet Protocol (IP) addresses, traffic data or other telemetry between Computer Emergency Response Teams (CERTs) in order to remediate incidents;
- The disclosure of various types of security information that may be required by law or regulation such as, in breach notification laws (e.g. the state level Data Breach

Notification legislation in the United States, or, in Europe, the security breach reporting mechanisms applying to operators of publicly available communications established as part of European regulations applying to telecommunications operators).

Exchange of Cyber-Security Information between Peers

The sharing of some types of information between peers is commonly understood to be useful for two reasons: firms are able to learn from each other's mistakes to improve their own levels of cyber-security and secondly if the government can access such information then it provides a 'window' into the level of security of critical infrastructures, further informing long term policy intervention (Dependability Development Support Initiative; 2002).

Within the organization, reliance upon other information sources for security information (especially from peers operating in the same sector) may be seen as a useful way to triangulate understanding and attractive especially regarding the application of mitigation measures and best practice on the basis that if something was reportedly successful for one organization then there is the possibility that it might also be the case for others. Such activities can be useful in both the current and future efforts: firstly by allowing the organization to reduce vulnerabilities on deployed systems and secondly by highlighting to the recipient that risks could be avoided in the future by not implementing a specific technology that another party has reported problems with.

However, public and private sector organisations playing a role are conflicted by widely differing agendas. Governments must work with broader economic or national security objectives in mind whilst it is generally understood that firms are generally (if they are acting as rational economic agents) trying to act the interests of profit, beholden to shareholder value.

Assaf comments that this may be seen in the different models adopted by both the private sector stakeholders (who operate a business continuity based model, based on economic drivers) and state organizations responsible for Critical Infrastructure Protection who adopt a national security model (based on priorities for security and safety) (Assaf, D. 2008). In economic terms, this is the difference between social welfare (national security) and private welfare (profit; shareholder value) and is central to any understanding about information sharing in critical infrastructures – since a majority of critical infrastructures are privately owned having security features and characteristics determined by the maximization of private welfare, the imposition of mechanisms upon them to do things in the interests of social welfare (security, resilience, other forms of public good) contradicts with such mechanisms. Understanding what form of good is at stake and is trying to be maximized is the key to unpicking the different barriers to information sharing. Security measures in critical infrastructure operators are applied on the basis that these measures are an important component in the production of critical infrastructure goods and services. From a national security perspective where security is a classic example of a public good (Trebilcock et al; 2003), a different set of economic drivers exist (Assaf; 2008).

It is within this rationale that government intervenes by attempting to create regulations to encourage information sharing. These may include the aforementioned breach disclosure mechanisms or others, like the recently announced Securities and Exchange Commission obligations for the disclosure of cyber-security risks and incidents (Securities and Exchange Commission; 2011). It is hoped that the threat of disclosure of adverse information concerning the firm's security practices affecting their valuation encourages firms to spend on security. The assumption that the costs of implementing a security programme would be dwarfed by the possible costs of damage to the firm's reputation and thus market valuation. A similar argument is advanced concerning breaches of personal data and is currently being considered by regulators in Europe (European Commission; 2012).

A range of sources illustrate the importance of sharing information both between peers but also between commercial actors and the public sector. Many official sources of guidance recommend the sharing of various types of information in order to 'raise the bar' of security and resilience of critical infrastructures. For example, the guidelines for Telecommunications resilience published by the UK's Centre for the Protection of the National Infrastructure (CPNI) indicate that sharing of information is an important aspect of dealing with the challenges facing resilience of information infrastructures (Centre for the Protection of the National Infrastructure; 2006). In 2009 the revised US National Infrastructure Protection Plan also noted that its effective implementation is predicated upon:

...the degree to which government and private sector partners engage in effective, multi-directional information sharing (Department for Homeland Security, 2009, National Infrastructure Protection Plan; 2009 p. 56)

In 2009 the Crisis Resource Network noted that:

New risks such as a breakdown of critical infrastructures, cyber-attacks, and international terrorism blur the boundaries between the public and private sectors and thus cannot be handled via traditional hierarchical top down approaches (Crisis Resource Network, 2009: p. 3)

European Policy Support toward Information Sharing

Within Europe, there is increasing policy impetus for the development of information sharing. For example the Communication on Critical Information Infrastructure Protection (CIIP) (COM 163):

Achievements and next steps: towards global cyber-security" of the European Commission in 2010 highlights the need to work on information exchange. Actions to progress EU level information exchange were articulated in the context of the need to take 'shared responsibility' for security. This was backed up by political agreement reached by EU Member States at a European Council meeting in Balatonfüred in April 2011 which invited stakeholders (i.e. the EU institutions, Member State governments and private industry) to participate in PPPs for the development of resilient and secure networks and reinforce multi-stakeholder dialogue and understanding. The European Network Information Security Agency (ENISA) has also been at the forefront of promoting information sharing activities under various initiatives (European Network Information Security Agency; 2010, 2011a, 2011b).

Private sector infrastructure providers thus find themselves on the horns of a dilemma – they must invest optimally in security efforts to maintain their economic viability but must also be cognizant of their role in the critical infrastructure. As owner operators of parts of the CI they may be subject to pressure or interest from governments, who are concerned with the broader context of the national implications of poor security. The unwillingness of firms to invest in security to a suitable level as required by the public sector leads to market failure, requiring public policy intervention. To support such interventions, information sharing via trusted closed networks or communities is seen as one increasingly viable approach.

The Key Dilemma

The considerable uncertainties that remain with the IE concept, coupled with the significant economic issues, point to the existence of a central problem: does the private sector nature of participants of IEs mean that no information is shared (thus requiring government intervention to create a common platform) or is there little of worth to

be shared in the first place (participants view that they stand to gain very little) because, relatively speaking to other concerns, the problem is not significant enough to require them to engage in this kind of activity.

Structure of the Remainder of the Chapter

The remainder of this chapter is structured in the following way. After a short background on a specific type of information sharing mechanism called Information Exchanges (IEs) we turn to a description of the popularity of specific examples of this mechanism where different types of cyber-security information may be shared between competitors. We then discuss some of the most economic factors that may affect if and how an organization participates in such mechanisms. These include:

- Externalities (accounting for the wider positive and negative implications of information sharing)
- Free-riding (benefiting from others disclosing information but not contributing)
- Misaligned incentives (reputational damage, the structure of the market)
- The way individuals make choices (behaviour and psychology)

In the next section we consider the gaps between policy efforts and economic rationale. We then report on solutions and recommendations, discussing ways to mitigate some of the adverse implications, followed by suggesting some future directions as to how IEs can contribute to improved security within the organization. Throughout the chapter we refer specifically to information sharing (implying a bi-directional flow of information) as compared to disclosure (implying a one-way or broadcast transmission of information)

BACKGROUND

The nature of information sharing mechanisms varies widely across critical infrastructure domains. For the purposes of this Chapter, we define information exchange as the exchange of different types of information (see below) pertaining to CI security risks between both peer competitors and the public and private sectors. Although other types of information exchange e.g. software disclosure vulnerabilities or the sharing of incident data between CERTs share many similar concerns (European Network Information Security Agency; 2010, 2011b) as we will see when we consider economic aspects of sharing, these are not considered in detail in this Chapter.

Whilst there are differences between these different partnerships and those operating in other countries, in this report we use the term 'Information Exchange' (IE) to refer to those information sharing mechanisms which primarily involve commercial peers but also the public sector in some form (either as mere facilitators of the platform or via taking a more direct role).

It is also instructive to consider the definitional differences in the use of the term Public Private Partnership. Outside of the CIP and cybersecurity field, this term has a different connotation, involving financial mechanisms to allow the transfer of financial risk from the public sector to the private sector. It is nowadays seen in complex capital intensive projects or where the public sector tries to incentivize the private sector to share some kind of financial risk or burden associated with investment for broader public goods.

What Information is Being Shared?

According to various publicly available sources, information exchanges often host discussions about 'incidents and best or good practices' for mitigation. For example, the UK Centre for the Protection of the National Infrastructure (CPNI) indicated in 2009 that a variety of information

is shared including: risks and mitigation; security incident and vulnerability information and confidential incident and vulnerability reporting (between private sector participants) as well as public sector good practices and incident and vulnerability alerts (Powell; 2010).

In the Netherlands, reports describe the sharing of lessons learned via fact sheets, exchanges during meetings and presentations. By reviewing the scope of its Information Dissemination document (based on the Traffic Light Protocol), it is possible to discern some idea of what else might be shared:

- **Red**: Ongoing incidents, information with potential PI damage, information form secret services;
- **Yellow:** Information meant/permitted for further distribution by the participant (which is nonetheless confidential and anonmyised);
- **Green/White:** No restriction on onward disclosure.

This suggests at least within this example that provision is made for the discussion of live 'ongoing incident data' (Zielstra and Hafkamp; 2010).

Policy research carried out in 2009 by the European Network and Information Security Agency (ENISA; 2009) identified a range of types of information which have been reportedly shared by IEs in different countries including the UK, Netherlands and Germany. Some of the reported types of information being shared in IEs include:

Experience on threats, attacks countermeasures (lessons learned); Advisory support to implement protective measures; Alerting service; Analysis of threats, impacts, risks and vulnerabilities; Information on contingency planning; Security advisories and best practices; Peer good practice; Discussions around recent trends and developments.(ENISA Good Practice Guide on Setting up a Network Security Information Exchange 2009, p 27)

The reported nature of information disclosed in such platforms defined above includes incident data, remediation and best practices. Although this is somewhat of an unknown quantity (due to the closed nature of these platforms) some reasonable assumptions concerning the types of information shared may be made. Firstly, it may reasonable to consider that information shared is not detailed technical data on events e.g. Internet Protocol (IP) addresses of attackers or Common Vulnerability Exploitation (CVE) data concerning the vulnerabilities exploited. This is because of two reasons – firstly, the declaratory policy of IEs is that managerial personnel are present and secondly the periodic nature of IEs would not fit with the real-time nature of such data exchange. Furthermore (and perhaps more importantly), the presence of mature and extensive peer networks of other organizations (chiefly Computer Emergency Response Teams, composed of technical specialists) charged with dealing with real-time, highly sensitive data on incidents already exists.

Why Share Information?

There are varying views as to why it is necessary or useful to share information. A number of overriding concerns spring to mind, which relate to the types of information being shared described above. Recall that there is still some ambiguity about the exact types of information shared. However it seems safe to assume that generalized best practice or lessons learnt are in the main, the most obvious thing to be shared in such exchanges.

In the late 2000s, the EU funded Dependability Development Support Initiative (DDSI) conducted research which articulated the value of information sharing for three main types of actor: 1) governments as they could better formulate policy if they understood the extent of maturity of different elements of the information infrastructure and thereby identify whether policy intervention (e.g. via legislation) is necessary; 2) industry could benefit from the information as necessary for risk management purposes and finally 3) citizens might benefit from such information to take appropriate preventative measures to protect themselves (Dependability Development Support Initiative; 2002).

The US National Infrastructure Advisory Council (NIAC) reported that information sharing was of value in a number of critical infrastructure related case studies including the August 2003 Blackout in the North-Eastern United States, the July 2004 Financial Services Threat Alert; the bombings in London in july 2005 and, later that year, the October 2005 threat alert on the New York public transportation system (National Infrastructure Advisory Council; 2006).

Information sharing has also been reported as beneficial when a vulnerability concerning poisoning of the Domain Name System (DNS) was published in July 2008. In this instance, Information Sharing and Analysis Centers in the United States alerted each other and shared information including mitigation strategies. A joint bulletin was subsequently prepared by the IT, Communications and FS-ISACs (Information Sharing and Analysis Centre Council; 2009)

The UK has also articulated that the sharing of information is necessary because of the aforementioned high levels of ownership of critical infrastructures by the private sector and a view that regulation (i.e. forcing disclosure of certain information) is a 'blunt instrument'. Furthermore, there is an added value for all as information exchange permits others to benefit from the experience of those who have had firsthand experience of incidents (for example). However, as we shall see this may paradoxically result in sub-optimal sharing.

Another way to consider this sharing is in helping organizations to avoid losses. The homogeneity of ICT products in both SCADA and other areas means that vulnerabilities have the potential for wide effects. For example, according to UBS Research, in 2010, just one company (Cisco Systems) accounted a 67 per cent market share of core, edge routing and network switching (Channelnomics; 2010) products. Similarly, in the SCADA domain a small number of firms (e.g. ABB and Siemens AG) dominate the SCADA control systems marketplace. Market research firm Gartner indicated in 2011 that Microsoft held nearly 78.6% of market share in the overall O/S market place (Gartner; 2011). The domination of software or system monocultures means that sharing modus operandi where attackers have exploited problems in software or hardware may help those who have not yet been affected but may be exposed to the same vulnerabilities – a defensive local rationale. Whilst it is hard to ignore this as being un-justifiable, it also could constitute the duplication of the work of Product Computer Security Incident Response Teams (PCSIRTs) whose sole job it is to alert users of products and service to security problems and support remediation.

Secondly, there is an intelligence rationale that knowing patterns of abuse of specific vulnerabilities allows the better allocation of resources (at both the enterprise and social level). This can apply to both private and public sector. In economic terms this can result in a more social welfare since firms have a better handle on what where vulnerabilities occur, the modus operandi of attackers. Governments can also benefit – both from an intelligence perspective (e.g. by having a better understanding of patterns of attackers so as to deploy various forms of countermeasure or, depending upon the severity and perceived motivation, response) and also from a more long term perspective (e.g. if a specific sector or technology is found to be constantly exploited then governments could identify possible policy initiatives to try to close such loopholes.

Further limited published anecdotal evidence alluding to the benefits of information sharing can be found in Goode and Lacey (2009) which provide empirical evidence as to benefits of information exchange in a telecommunications provider in the Asia Pacific Region. ENISA (2010) reported a prioritized list of benefits of information sharing described by information exchange practitioners in various types of IE across Europe in 2010.

EXISTING INFORMATION SHARING MECHANISMS

Many countries have established sector-specific information sharing partnerships between the government and the private sector. We present summary analysis of some selected examples below as a way to highlight approaches to facilitating information exchange as a way to overcome the economic issues outlined above. It must be noted that the notion of information exchange is in and of itself subject to varying differences in interpretation. Information exchange is driven by the cultural, historical and regulatory context of how the private sector is viewed in a particular country. It is naïve to consider that just because a model works in one jurisdiction it would transfer easily to another.

The Centre for the Protection of National Infrastructure (CPNI) in the United Kingdom has been pro-active in the development of a number of different information sharing models in the UK. CPNI has also been driving the development of the IE as a PPP model across Europe to facilitate sharing of information relating to a range of critical infrastructure threats. CPNI's work on information exchange includes facilitating sector based Information Exchanges, (IE), of which there are now a number and which are loosely based on a model originating in the United States, the Network Security Information Exchange (NSIE).

The IE model is based on participation by a trusted group of industry and government representatives (such as CPNI itself, but also law enforcement and intelligence agencies) aiming to discuss security incidents and vulnerabilities. There are rules of membership and although there is no cost associated with participation there is a limit to the number of members per organization and members cannot delegate their participation beyond the prime and deputy representatives. Members are elected by the group as a whole. Chairs and co-chairs of the IE are taken from both the private and public sector although CPNI takes a co-ordination and hosting role (providing the physical facilities for face to face meetings). Meetings can be supported by email and extranet based exchange. Finally, information exchange is governed by the increasingly popular 'traffic light protocol' (TLP).

UK: Network Security Information Exchange

In 2003 CPNI established the UKNSIE which is charged with sharing sensitive information in the information and communications technologies sector. It is perhaps (alongside the FI-ISAC) one of the model IEs. Participating companies include incumbents and new market entrants as well as traditional fixed line and mobile operators, and those providing Internet Protocol (IP) services. Coverage extends to 80% of the UK telecommunications market. CPNI acts as the facilitator of the NSIE, providing meeting space and administrative support for the physical meetings. NSIE working groups have prepared guidance and best practice on resilient telecommunications and the guidance on deployment and use of Border Gateway Protocol (BGP). As of June 2009 it was reported that there were 12 exchanges involving 220 companies across a broad range of sectors including one dedicated to SCADA. The pharmaceutical IE, for example includes 12 representatives from 7 companies, the defence IE has 32 representatives from 17 different companies and 54 representatives from 34 different companies in the financial services sector (Powell, 2010).

Netherlands: National Infrastructure against Cybercrime

The Dutch National Infrastructure against Cybercrime (NICC) is a cross-sector group which meets bi-monthly in a face-to-face setting (National Infrastructure Against Cybercrime; 2010). This established a set of initiatives including sector wide benchmarking, awareness raising about process control security, development of good practices and the sharing of incident information. There are 8 meetings a year with open and closed sessions. Each member is allowed two participants who must be senior security/fraud experts. The NICC guidelines are based on a proven effort, non disclosure agreement between parties to information and the use of the Traffic Light Protocol, an information control model that has been popularised for use in such situations. The NICC has build ISACs based on the CPNI IE model (and not the subscription based US ISAC model, described below). Sectoral and thematic ISACs have been set up by the NICC in a variety of areas, covering telecoms, banking, Schiphol airport, rail, energy and SCADA systems. Although each ISAC is composed of peers four government agencies also participate: the AVDI (Dutch Intelligence Agency) KLPD (Dutch Criminal Intelligence Bureau); GOVCERT (the Dutch government CERT) and NICC itself. The NICC acts as a neutral facilitator. Information circulated in these ISACs may, with the permission of the participants, be shared by governmental authorities to other ISACs in the so called 'flower petal' model, or to other entities. The ISAC is governed by confidentiality rules and named individuals must participate (in order to build trust). Like the IE model, the participant provides the chair (President, in this case) and the agenda (Zielstra and Hafkampl 2010). With a specific focus on SCADA systems, in 2010 the NICC established the Process Control Security Roadmap which aims to improve and integrate existing efforts. An important facet of this is sharing of information with all participants and information exchange. Like the CPNI supported IEs, the NICC has an ISAC dedicated to SCADA.

Germany: Up-KRITIS

The German Up-KRITIS effort is run by the Bundesamt für Sicherheit in der Informationstechnik (BSI – Federal Office for Information Security) and is a broad group mechanism utilising Single Points of Contact (SPoC) per sector. Voluntary information exchange (aside from that required under the German Telecommunications Act) stems from the 2007 CIP implementation plan which had as its target the protection of the German Critical IT infrastructures. Under this plan, four working groups were established, including one covering crisis response and management. This last working group created a SPoC for the Communication infrastructure – a single representative company aimed at providing the interface between the BSI and the sector. The SPoC model works that each sector appoints a single representative to interact with Unit 121 (the BSI's IT situation centre). As of 2011 there were SPoCs established in 5 other sectors aside from communications infrastructure. Information exchange is governed by confidentiality agreements and disseminates three types of output: information, warnings and alarms. The Information exchange element uses the TLP and as of 2009 it was understood that the BSI were working on an updated information exchange policy (known as an "Extended TLP") (Hendricke; 2011).

Europe: E-SCSIE

At the European level the EU-SCADA and Control Systems Information Exchange (E-SCSIE) has existed since 2005. According to publicly available data up until 2006 there had been five meetings held (Institute for the Protection and Security of the Citizen; 2006). E-SCSIE is aimed at collaboration on a range of common issues and includes as its members European industry, government and research community. The group has issued papers and helped to inspire its individual members to improve SCADA/CS security within their own systems or countries. The aims of the group (which is described as being an Institutional Network) are to define a European exchange system for security related information about SCADA and control systems; to share information using the TLP method, to cultivate a network across the relevant government, industrial and research communities in order to establish a basis for a pan European system for the exchange of security related information concerning SCADA and control systems. Membership is reportedly drawn from each European country with government and industry representatives being sourced from the countries own SCADA IE. Membership is decided through 'discussion and agreement' between participants and members are encouraged not to attend just in order to obtain information without providing any themselves. The types of information shared at the E-SCSIE includes event reports of incidents, warnings about vulnerabilities, reporting advice and exchange experience on good practice to mitigate SCADA and control system security issues.

Europe: Information Exchanges

The IE model, although first originating in the United States, has thus appeared to gain significant traction in Europe and is being further popularised through the work of the European Network and Information Security Agency (ENISA) and the European Public Private Partnership for Resilience (EP3R). The work of the EP3R should be seen in the context of EU level policy initiatives on CIIP, outlined above which are increasingly advocating information sharing as an important tool in European CIIP efforts. The EP3R was established in June 2010 (European Commission;

2010) by the European Commission following the publication of policy documents on CIIP and an accompanying Action Plan (European Commission; 2009). This policy statement has a number of objectives one of which is to share information and stock-taking/exchange of good practice and policy between public and private sector players. In this way it might be through of as almost a 'Pan European IE (although uncertainty exists about whether the same types of risk and mitigation information is shared). There are around 50-60 regular participants at the EP3R meetings who come from a mix of government, providers (hardware and software manufacturers) and other industry. Since its establishment there have been six meetings and three working groups have been established.

Switzerland: MELANI

The Swiss Reporting and Analysis Centre for Information Assurance (MELANI) is an organisation which comprises a number of different sector groups and which organises workshops and exercises on a frequent basis. MELANI works with a closed constituency of critical infrastructure sectors, as articulated in the Swiss Constitution which sets out constitutional responsibility that the government and the private sector must work together in a public private partnership. MELANI is organised according to an organisation of 8 people who work on a variety of reporting and analysis activities. In addition to running exercises and workshops, MELANI conducts analysis providing situation reports, factsheets and alerts to constituency. The closed constituency of Critical Infrastructure operators works with the Federal Office of Police; the Swiss Governmental CERT and a Federal Strategy Unit for IT. As of March 2010 it included 213 individuals across 9 sectors from 83 different companies. The sectors include telecommunications; finance (accounting for a large proportion of the companies participating) and energy (Klaus; 2010).

United States: ISACs

In the United States, similar sentiments concerning the importance of information exchange between public and private sectors have been echoed since the 1998 Presidential Commission on Critical Infrastructure Protection (President's Commission on Critical Infrastructure Protection; 1997), which established a number of Information Sharing and Analysis Centre (ISAC) for different infrastructures. This approach which may be likened to a private sector intelligence agency (since it creates and disseminates products to a subscribing customer base). PDD 63 (the policy document which took forward the recommendations of the PCCIP) urged industry leaders to create ISACs as part of the then US national security policy (The White House; 1998). A financial services ISAC (FS-ISAC) was the first to be set up, followed by the IT-ISAC which was founded in January 2001 by nineteen prominent Information Technology firms. An ISAC is a method to facilitate information sharing amongst members of a particular sector and between the sector and the government (Wentworth; 2000). PDD-63 established that the actual design of an ISAC would be determined by the private sector with the view that ISACs would play a role to gather, analyse, appropriately sanitize and disseminate private sector information to both industry and the National Infrastructure Protection Center (NIPC).

The ISAC thus acts like a central repository of security related information. The objective of the ISAC (like many information sharing schemes) is to increase security of participants. Companies participating share information on a voluntary basis which is anonmyised for the benefit of the rest of the participants. An important distinction between an ISAC and an IE is that ISACs perform more of an analytical function to allow participants to understand the implications of the information being shared. It should be noted that this type of ISACs (unlike the federal, state and local government ISACs created under Homeland Security Presidential Decision Directive 7: Critical Infrastructure Identification, Prioritization and Protection (HSPD-7) is composed of purely private sector players (The White House; 2006).

Since then there have been a number of ISACs developed under both models (private sector and between similar types of non commercial organizations) including ISACs for state government (MS-ISAC); first responders (ER-ISAC) and research communities (REN-ISAC).

In 2009, the US White House 60 day Cybersecurity Policy Review argued that since responsibility for security and reliability of cyberspace is shared between industry and governments these two should work more closely together by…engaging in enterprise information sharing. Furthermore the policy review concluded that "…businesses need effective means to share detection methods; information about breaches and attack methods, remediation techniques and forensic capabilities with each other and the Federal Government."

United States: DIB Pilot

A contemporary illustrative example of recent effort in the defence sector (as one of the recognised critical infrastructures) comes from the United States. In late 2011 the US Department of Defense announced the Defense Industrial Base Cyber Security/Information Assurance information sharing program (informally known as the 'Cyber Pilot') to enable information sharing between the DoD and industry partners. This came after a series of high profile cyber attacks against key US defense contractors including Boeing, Lockheed Martin and Raytheon (Computerworld; 2010). In the Cyber Pilot model (which has some of the hallmarks of an information exchange as described above, albeit from government to industry rather than between industry facilitated by government) the DoD provides best practices, threat information and management support (mentoring) to the

private sector members of the Defense Industrial Base (DIB). Companies are asked in return to report incidents via a Collaborative Information Sharing Environment located in the DoD Cyber Crime Centre (DC3). Depending on the situation, DoD then works with the firm to conduct damage assessment to evaluate the potential intelligence the adversary may have obtained and the impact on US national security and economic interests (Department of Defense; 2011).

Australia: TISN

Further afield, the Australian Trusted Information Sharing Network (TISN) provides another case in point. The TISN is made up of seven sector groups covering those infrastructures deemed to be critical by the Australian government (e.g. oil and gas, telecommunications, finance). These are overseen by the Critical Infrastructure Advisory Council which reports to political authority. Each sector group shares information on threats and vulnerabilities and collaborates on appropriate measures to mitigate risks. Crucially, an Australian government agency provides support. This agency is usually that which has regulatory authority over the sector (for example, the Department of Broadband, Communications and the Digital Economy for telecommunications) (TISN; 2011a). TISN information exchange is governed by a deed of confidentially to which members can sign up. The objective of this is to support businesses in meeting the twin (and arguably competing) information disclosure obligations to the market (via reporting anything which may have a material effect on their share price) and contributing information about security vulnerabilities as part of government supported efforts to protect Critical Infrastructure. The Deed provides a limitation of liability on confidential information shared in the TISN. The recipient of information is party to the Deed. The Deed is aimed at assisting signatories in sharing information about vulnerabilities without activating their Continuous Disclosure Obligations (CDOs) under the 2001 Corporations Act and Listing Rules of the Australian Stock Exchange. This is because vulnerability information may be considered as 'price-sensitive' (i.e. likely to have a material effect on its share price) and therefore the non disclosure of such information would constitute a breach of the rules allowing companies to be publicly listed (TISN; 2011b).

It is also useful to consider cultural characteristics of this particular form of Information Exchange. The examples cited above stem from publicly available information and they follow a particular model that is based on a view that the market is the place to solve these concerns and the necessity of 'light touch' regulation. Other examples exist such as the Spanish Groupo Trabalho Securidad (European Network and Information Security Agency; 2010) which work without government intervention. Therefore IE (as is becoming popularized) remains private sector driven with limited involvement from government (merely just facilitating the exchange). Indeed, governments are very wary to intervene further for fear of chilling such exchanges, thus rendering difficult more detailed insight about just how (in) secure critical infrastructures might be. This paradox can be articulated in economic terms: governments have social welfare (protection of critical infrastructure) in mind whereas firms, being rational economic agents, have private welfare (profits) as a primary objective. The incentives acting upon the private sector to invest enough to provide social welfare are widely regarded to be misaligned, leading to market failure (the lack of adequately protected critical infrastructure) requiring government intervention. We now turn to detailed description of these misaligned incentives to illustrate the economic factors affecting private sector participation in those types of information exchange described above.

ECONOMIC DRIVERS AFFECTING PARTICIPATION IN INFORMATION SHARING

Issues, Controversies, Problems

As has been shown, the private sector is at the centre piece of many information exchange efforts relating to Critical Infrastructure. For example, the UK's CPNI noted that the private sector forms the primary membership of IEs, setting the direction, bringing knowledge of good practice and an understanding of operational parameters surrounding mitigation measures (Powell; 2010). Nonetheless, the presence of peer competitors in IE gives rise to the perception of a number of potentially intractable issues concerning what would motivate private sector firms to disclose vulnerabilities to peers (Techtarget; 2001). Such issues stem from the differences between firstly what economic theory indicates drives sharing between peer firms compared to the structure and reported practice in PPP type IE mechanisms described above. Familiarity of the economics behind sharing in this regard is critical, since (assuming classical neo-economic understanding of firm behavior) this may be assumed to be what primarily governs the participation of private sector players either to join an IE or to contribute information. However, as we shall see this may not always be the case.

Theoretical understanding concerning information exchange between peer competitors suggests that information would be shared only when the benefits outweigh the costs.

Gordon et al, (2003) show that when two firms coordinate by sharing information, it is possible to achieve the same level of security prior to information sharing but a lower cost. This results in an increase in total welfare (improved general levels of security). Nonetheless, two main arguments are often identified which can serve to misalign incentives concerning how individuals (acting as rational economic agents) act in groups. The two avenues often used to explain the misalignment of incentives are externalities and free-riding.

With externalities, the participant only takes into account the direct benefit of sharing some information and not the wider social benefits that might accrue to the group. Pragmatically, this may be described as the 'whats in it for me?' factor. Since there might be no benefit perceived by the firm in sharing information about the mitigation of a risk already accomplished, the act of sharing might thus be undervalued (Hahn and Lyne-Farrar; 2006). This reduces social welfare because the rest of the community (the other peers) cannot benefit from the information. Furthermore, the participant might not be incited to putting effort into collecting and producing the information if the benefit to all who would be able to use the information were taken into account (Aviram & Tor; 2004). For example, there might be minor technical details or aspects of the mitigation process that the originator left out when preparing something to be disclosed, but which other members might find useful. Members of an IE thus are already pre-disposed to under invest information sharing compared with the socially optimal amount which governments would prefer. Although theoretical literature from other cybersecurity domains which share this quality of 'information asymmetry) points out that many are already reportedly spending extensively on cybersecurity (for example with respect to software vulnerabilities). Solving this may require subsidies to encourage participants to internalize the benefits of information sharing. However subsidization of IE participation is not present in any of the IE discussed so far. Other approaches might be in the form of some limitation on liability (Aviram; 2004). which is seen in the TISN Deed of Confidentiality.

Free-riders are a related economic character of information exchange pertinent to this discussion and stem from the question of misaligned economic incentives. With free-riding an IE participant may decide to under-invest in infor-

mation sharing in the hopes of obtaining useful information from others. This incentive may be strong given perceptions about the expected reputational damage that publication of cybersecurity vulnerabilities may cause.

Free-riding occurs because of the unique properties of information. Although it is non-exclusive (once shared it can be reproduced at no or little cost compared to the costs of producing it) it is excludable: information may also be hoarded and retained (Aviram and Tor; 2004). Free riding may be seen in the classic Prisoners Dilemma model used to explain non co-operative behavior of firms. In the Prisoners Dilemma as applied to information exchange, if others provide a participant with information then the participant would be better off receiving the information but expending no costs in reciprocating. However, if his perception that everyone else (making the same calculation) would fail to share information then he would still be better off not sharing information. Thus, all parties shirk, and no information is shared (Aviram; 2004).

Aviram (2004) also identifies games of 'stag-hunt' and 'chicken' as possible scenarios that may play in the participants rational choice (to share or not) depending on how interconnected the participants are. These scenarios play out as an economic operator evaluates the likely implication of investing in information sharing or free-riding by trying to benefit from information that others may provide. In the 'stag hunt' if a participant cannot dis-associate himself from a network which derives its strength from the weakest link (Kunreuther & Heal; 2003). and which might be subject to exploitation such as might be if the vulnerability was made public, then the participant is incited to invest no more than the amount he believes is invested by the least protected participant To do so would not be economically viable, since a possible attacker would target the least protected firm to reach the more protected firm. In the game of chicken, the firm that first reveals its vulnerability is ridiculed.

A participant to an IE influenced by this might thus not share information (since to do so would invite ridicule and possible reputational damage from peers). It can be seen that a participant might be motivated by the stag hunt scenario if they were concerned about the onward disclosure of information whereas the game of chicken applies initially in respect of loss of face in front of peers.

Free-riding is characterized as a potential outcome of a rational decision to maximize benefits (learn as much as possible from an IE in terms of information that the participant could take away and use to improve security practices) and minimize costs - either spend as little as possible in collecting and producing information to share with others or alternatively avoid possible reputational risk arising from the sharing of information that the firm has vulnerabilities. This last rationale would cause the firm, if it was acting rationally to play the chicken game. Concern over exploitation of a vulnerability by a possible malicious actor (which might be possible were information shared more widely than the IE) would also lead the firm not to share since it would be operating under the 'stag hunt' game and worried that it would be targeted and incur costs as a result of damage caused by exploitation of a vulnerability.

From a psychological perspective, however, data from a survey of individuals who consume but not contribute information in chat rooms or discussion forums suggest that there might be other explanations: chiefly fear of ridicule or mocking of comments by other, more knowledgeable participants (Preece, et al; 2004).

Other economic misaligned incentives arise from the competitive status of participants – that they could engage in degradation by withholding information from a competitor to give the themselves some kind of competitive edge over rivals. Degradation is likely in network industries such as energy, transportation and telecommunications where there is an incumbent able to influence the market or where differentiated firms have some idiosyncratic advantages and disadvantages over their rivals (resulting in a firm trying to identify as many different opportunities as possible to seek relative advantage). Likewise, once information is shared, competitors might equally benefit from it which would result in tougher marketplace overall. This would result in significant hidden costs. Thus, if the expectations that the hidden costs of having to compete in a more competitive market arising because of the disclosure of some information is more than the costs of producing that information, then the firm will be incited to withhold information (Aviram and Tor; 2004). Much of this logic assumes cornering misaligned incentives arising from competitive markets assumes a link between vulnerabilities and competitive advantage: something that is still being grappled with by many economists.

Still more misaligned incentives arise from perception of reputational damage (linked to the question of chicken and prisoners dilemma indicated above). Particularly for those firms operating as critical infrastructures, their reputation might be considered as especially important. Indeed, recent experience is insightful in the way that poor reputation (either at the firm level or more recently at the national level) affects banking and financial services and the broader economy. In the financial sector the absence of trust could easily lead to spreading contagion. Security researchers have indicated that disclosing information about an attack or vulnerability risks damage to consumer trust and reputation with investors (Camp 2006).

The cost of participation in information exchanges might also play a role. These costs might be direct or indirect in nature, ranging from staff time to attend meetings, through to the lost opportunity cost of participation and contribution (for example the lost possible work that could have been done whilst a representative was collecting or preparing information for or physically attending a meeting). Membership fees (common in the US ISAC model) are another example of a direct cost (United States General Accounting Office, 2001: 2).

Finally, and perhaps most importantly decision-making about rational security investments may play a role. This has been termed by security researchers a 'hard' problem (Anderson; 2001).

Rue et al (Rue et al; 2007) identify a number of different models proposed by security researchers to help decisions makers allocation resources to cybersecurity. These include macro-economic input/output models evaluating the sensitivity of the US economic to cyber attack in particular sectors; econometric techniques; return on security investment analysis; characterization of real world decision-making; heuristic models which rank costs, benefits and risks of different strategies; risk management frameworks and methods from game theory. There is certainly more than enough models proposed to help organizations to conduct cost/benefit or return on investment analysis to consider security investments. Despite the presence of these, however, they have come in for criticism as being inappropriate for use in the real world (which perhaps may go to explain why firms continue to make poor decisions concerning security).

This may be a double edged sword: if the firm poorly understands the cost benefit trade-off of participation in an IE then it may just as easily decide not to participate (on the basis of the perceived direct and indirect costs outweigh any expected benefits) as to participate, if, in the absence of its own information, it believes the possible benefits of participation as reported either by peers, government trade press or research.

A number of researchers have pointed to the poor decision-making of firms concerning investment in security.[2] Rowe and Gallaher note that:

Rarely does an organization undertake a sophisticated or even semi-sophisticated financial analysis (i.e., cost-benefit or rate-of-return analysis) prior to making the investment or deciding on the level of investment that is needed... (Rowe and Gallaher; 2006: p)

Dynes et al (Dynes et al; 2008) comment that from a qualitative study of cyber-security investment in three CI sectors, a wide variety of approaches were taken, some not at all systematic. They report that in general different approaches are taken based on three paradigms – a reactive approach termed the 'sore thumb' paradigm; an approach with a certain degree of implied risk management approach and finally an approach where information security efforts are inseparable from business strategy (Dynes et al; 2008).

Payne et al (1993) describe the difficulty that experts have in decision-making where it is necessary to consider multiple variables simultaneously (as might be the case with security investment decisions such as whether to assume the costs of participating in an IE).

The United States General Accounting Office noted in 2004 that the absence of useful data about the benefits of information sharing (as an example of a cybersecurity decision) are:

...often difficult to discern, while the risks and costs of sharing are direct and foreseeable (United States General Accounting Office, 2004: p. 33)

Shiu et al. observed the impact of economic framing and system modeling on experienced decision-makers concerning security investment decisions (Shiu et al; 2011). This found that even experienced decision-makers favored information that confirmed an initial viewpoint (known as confirmation bias) about the right security measures to take in response to a particular problem, before further inventions.

Researchers propose that decision-makers are automatically predisposed to avoid decisions that have more uncertain outcomes. This ambiguity aversion is based on decision-makers preferences for options with more certain outcomes. For example Aviram and Tor conclude that

...rivals may choose to sacrifice a measure of expected value to avoid the ambiguous course of action of a novel information sharing agreement (Aviram and Tor 2004 p. 263).

This uncertainty and complexity in weighing up current costs versus uncertain expected future benefit can also be explored through the prism of 'behavioral economics' an emergent field of research which considers the role that irrational but consistent behaviour plays in human decision-making (Kahnmann and Tvserky; 1979). In particular Thaler and Sunstein explore the behavior of hyperbolic discounting (Thaler & Sunstein, 2006). This may play a role in information exchange. IE participants might be dis-incentivised to participate or contribute on the basis that long term uncertainty about a negative or positive outcome is outweighed in their decision-making over short term certainty about the costs of participation.

Ironically, returning to the aspects of market failure described in the free-rider problem, this aversion to sharing could be self-perpetuating since without such information it is less likely that a better assessment about the true costs of security vulnerabilities or risks could be undertaken. Again, building upon understanding from the field of behavioural economics, there might be a status quo bias which would operate against information sharing unless the benefits were obvious and large.

The economic concerns presented above are just one element concerning understanding the effectiveness of information exchange mechanisms. However, given the aforementioned primarily private sector character of IE, they may be considered as somewhat pre-eminent. Nonetheless, in an operational context, Lines (2008) also identifies other concerns to information sharing including legal and contractual concerns, trust and sociological or physiological reasons. Establishing the initial handshake of 'trust (a watchword in many of those running IEs) is complex. For example,

CPNI noted that it takes 2 years to develop a trusted network of participation. It may be argued that some IE have been successful because of pre-existing relationships or networks (for example, membership of trade or industry organizations).

Yet other theoretical factors concern legal regulatory or contractual obligations. For example there may be national security restrictions placed on some information distributed in an IE, or participants may be uncertain as to whether disclosing information that may come from downstream partners could expose them to liability that they themselves have been asked to keep confidential. Suppliers may have established non disclosure agreements (NDAs) by which an originator wishing to share information must abide. On the legal side, there may be concerns over Freedom of Information (FoI) legislation or whether information sharing would undermine data protection obligations of the originator. This last aspect is seen as particularly important in the context of the detailed cross border exchange of incident data between CERTS in Europe (European Network and Information Security Agency; 2011b). As has been shown although such personal data (in the form of IP addresses) is more the preserve of CERTs that have a different role to IE, the sheer variety and flexibility of the types of information reported as being shared means that this could become an issue. Other legal factors include: perception of a group of peers sharing information in a closed community might be considered a form of cartel behavior; that sharing of information might cause government organizations to activate obligations to report on the basis of requirements in heavily regulated industries such as finance and telecoms or finally, that participants would be accused of having privileged access to government information, leaving the government open to accusations of distorting the market.

As has been shown there is extensive effort underway by governments to establish and build upon information sharing mechanisms, despite the existence of a number of important factors which could inhibit sharing. Economic considerations in particular, may play an important role, given the private sector ownership of much of the critical infrastructure and the requirement for their participation in such mechanisms. This theoretical economic base suggests that there are a range of drivers acting upon commercial organizations not to participate, appears to be at odds with these efforts. This raises a question as to whether those creating or establishing information exchanges have successfully overcome these barriers, particularly though the use of different mechanisms (e.g. non disclosure agreements or confidentiality mechanisms such as the traffic light protocol). Certainly the attention given to IEs (in Europe at least) would seem to suggest this is indeed the case. There has been little empirical research on how these identified factors play out in reality. Anecdotal empirical data from a 2010 study of those involved in IEs seems to suggest a divergence between such hypotheses and operational reality (European Network and Information Security Agency; 2010). Here, participants reported that the economic barriers indicated above were largely less important, in their experience, than the quality of information and the effective running of the IE.

This raises the possibility of the existence of a gap between the economic theory governing of information exchange and what actually happens in practice. For example, in general IEs are free to join - they do not require participants to pay a subscription or fee (although the US ISAC model does have this in place). The payment of a fee is regarded in the theoretical literature as a possible solution to incite sharing because it would negate any benefits obtained by the firm through taking competitive advantage of information obtained through participation. Similarly there is little evidence of subsidy in the IE models (although as we have seen the Australian example does have a statute of limitation of liability).

The Gap between Policy Efforts and Economic Rationale

There are three speculative possible explanations for this gap which may be proposed.

Firstly, that the economic factors outlined above operate as theory suggests and that information which is highly sensitive and which would raise the concern of senior decision-makers in the firm (who might be expected to be more driven by some of the economic arguments described above) remains undisclosed. That is to say, contrary to the views of participants there is a difference between the perceived value of participation versus that which might accrue to the bottom line in direct, actionable information. Although limited anecdotal evidence exists as to the usefulness of IE as reported above, it is still hard to measure (as with many other forms of physical and cyber security initiative) the relative benefits of one measure over another.

A second possible explanation reinforces the discussion concerning the poor decision-making abilities of firms regarding security investment decisions. Namely, that despite many exhortations in the last few years that senior decision-makers need to be aware of security risks (Johnson and Goetz; 2007) a gap of understanding remains between the senior decision-makers and the operational security personnel who share such information. If there were clearer and more links and awareness then senior executives (who could expect to be motivated more by rational economic arguments in favor of retaining information, for example) perhaps might not authorize participation and the sharing of such information. On the other hand, this might instead be a consequence of delegation of powers. For example, a security manager might be able to report that risk was averted but it would not be necessary to declare that such remediation was only possible because of acting upon information obtained from an IE.

A third explanation is that perhaps those participating in such exchanges are acting altruistically in spite or with ignorance of corporate priorities aligned with economic interests. Recall that in general, models for participation in IEs revolve around operational or managerial professionals. Indeed, in the UK case for example, there is a separate IE which operates at executive/CEO level (Powell; 2010). Under this assumption, security professionals act out of informed concern that by sharing such information they may avert broader catastrophe. In addition, as experts, they may be operating selfishly in the expectation that at some point in the future they may require the help of others based on their understanding about the prevalence of security risks.

Although further research would be required to clarify which (if any) of these possible explanations made sense, a similar conclusion has been drawn elsewhere. For example, Moore (2010) when arguing for the mandated disclosure of SCADA incident data, suggests that the conflicting reports of widespread intrusions versus low actual reported numbers points to the conclusion that either voluntary information sharing has failed (supporting the argument that economic theory plays a preeminent role) or that there is truly nothing to report. Either way spells bad news for the IE concept. Cutting through the perception and received wisdom about the benefits of IEs, either little of value is disclosed because of economic drivers or they are unnecessary because the levels of incidents are not high enough to properly justify their existence.

Solutions and Recommendations

Instruments to address these concerns (particularly about the untoward onward disclosure of information) have been developed as possible solutions to address the challenges, particularly about externalities. The Traffic Light Protocol in particular is a good example – a method of controlling information by labeling it with a colour depending upon the extent to which the originator is comfortable in onward usage (Stikvoort; 2009). According to this model, red means that information is intended for us 'in the meeting only'; yellow means that the information 'can be disseminated within the recipients organization but no further' and green or white indicates that there are 'no rules' or that public dissemination is permitted. The TLP works on the basis of a trusted 'gentlemen's agreement' but has no legally binding force. Nonetheless it could be considered as a more refined version of the now ubiquitous 'Chatham House rule' (Chatham House; 2011).

The perception about how participation in information sharing may leave companies open to the accusation of forming or participating in a cartel may be solved via the creation of internal company firewalls between senior executive decision-makers and operational staff (which goes against best practice concerning obtaining board engagement in cyber-security efforts). This concern (real or not) that IE participation may be mistaken for cartel participation gives rise to two other interesting paradoxes. Firstly, in order to dissuade regulatory interest, those involved would need to disclose some level of detail about what information is being shared at these trusted, closed groups. This may result in undermining of trust, run contrary to the gentlemen's agreements of codes of conduct of information disclosure and be counter-productive to achieving the stated security benefits of such platforms. Secondly, to avoid or defray accusations of cartel behaviour, firms may view that it is important to set up a firewall between the technical and business involvement in information exchange. This may achieved by ensuring that the participants to such information sharing platforms are front line operators rather than senior business executives. This is because as well as being less knowledgeable, senior executives might be more obviously inclined to seek to make commercial gain from what they learn at an information sharing meeting. The requirement for a firewall is so the firm can be clear that they are not engaging in strategic collusion (and raise the interest of the regulators) with their competitors. However, this could also act as a barrier to improved CIP since in order to properly deal with such risks, boards need to be informed and have visibility of such issues.

Other solutions to some of the economic factors affected above include the provision of explicit operating guidance for the IE in order to try and dissuade and deter 'free-riding'. Such measures include having named participant representatives (since this creates a implicit peer pressure for the representative to contribute) as well as having generalized statements about the importance of contribution. The further prohibition of delegates also may support the mitigation of such economic factors.

Still other approaches include codes of conduct or statutes that limit the liability of the originator of information to be subject to regulatory intervention following the disclosure of information at a meeting with public sector participation. This is particularly important in those sectors which are subject to intense regulatory scrutiny (e.g. telecoms, finance and energy).

There are also a host of other legal issues that may arise. In Europe a chief concern revolves around privacy and data protection obligations. Although this might not be as much of a concern for IEs as compared to CERTs (which, in Europe, are more likely to exchange information accorded specific status as personal data, such as IP addresses), nonetheless, firms must be mindful of some specific legal obligations that they may be beholden to. These may also be particularly nuanced when receiving information from government authorities for example law enforcement or the intelligence agencies. Research suggests these questions are complex, for which there are no simple answers and require careful consideration (ENISA; 2011b).

Finally, perhaps one of the more obvious recommendations, given the seeming lack of reliable evidence as to the efficacy of IEs, is to create publicly available, useful, examples of success stories of case studies where information received through/via an IE has directly contributed to the improvement or mitigation of a security issue. This would serve a range of objectives. It would help demonstrate the utility of IEs as a platform, to those who are as yet uncertain. Secondly, it would help mitigate interest from regulators and others who might be suspicious that the mechanism is a front for cartel behaviour (by demonstrating the real utility of IEs) and finally, it would permit an improved understanding from security practitioners and governments as to whether enough information is being shared and hence what would represent an appropriate level of regulation to address any perceived shortcomings.

FUTURE RESEARCH DIRECTIONS

The three possibilities discussed above concerning how the economic drivers identified affect operational practice merit further consideration. In particular the way in which information obtained from such exchanges is actually disseminated and taken up in the enterprise deserves further investigation. This would shed light on the tricky question of the extent to which senior decision-makers need to know about such forums (and therefore might take an adverse perspective on them) whilst making the business case for participation. In general, obtaining a more in depth understanding of participation in IE from the perspective of a participant would be welcome further research contributions.

At a more general level, consideration of the social and behavioural characteristics of information exchange (e.g. through observed ethnographic study) would also benefit an understanding of the extent to which rational economic drivers play (or do not) into 'live' participation at such events. This is related to a further paradox of the IE model – that to fully demonstrate its benefit would require publication of results which would in turn undermine the trust that practitioners argue is so effective for information sharing in such a model. Furthermore, as with Schrödinger's Cat theorem - the very act of observing the phenomena might in and of itself change the phenomena. Hence participation in an IE to observe its operation might in and of itself affect the operation.

Other research opportunities exist by obtaining common understanding of what information is useful to other participants at an IE. Knowledge of the information requirements between participants might shed further light on how the incentives might be operating in practice. This relates to the question of homogeneity of products and services and the fact that participants might be incited to join on the basis that they share some characteristics with participants (for example, in software or system configuration).

Further research avenues revolve around exploring information exchange where the information is and of itself of business value to participants. This may be the case with those firms such as security service providers whose business model is dependent upon selling information that might usually be obtained in an information exchange. This leads to the open question as to the added value of such firms, if participants also need to attend an information exchange. The use of economic models might allow hypothetical constructs concerning whether there is a degree of market failure with the operation of cybersecurity firms.

Exploration of the role of compliance in stimulating security measures is another possibility. For example under the US Sarbanes Oxley regulatory requirement, there is a cost involved in not implementing security control measures in the form of criminal sanctions for executive decision-makers. This raises the question to what extent are voluntary information sharing methods, such as IEs more efficient than mandated security measures. (Kolfal et al. have also explored this using economic models and find that security

measures applied reactively are less efficient under some circumstances than those applied proactively (Kolfal et al. 2011).

To investigate on the last of the open questions about the difference between policy and economic incentives concerning information exchange in the context of CIP, study of the characteristics of security professionals might illustrate how any cultural, attitudinal or behavioural predispositions play in facilitating information exchange. Such a contribution would also be useful in the context of many public and private sector efforts to 'upskill' security capability since an output of such work would be a list of those characteristics deemed as useful for a cybersecurity professional (e.g. altruism) which could then go into recruitment and skills templates.

CONCLUSION

This Chapter has presented an overview of IE mechanisms and some of the economic factors that may affect sharing of threat, vulnerability and mitigation information. IEs are increasingly popular as an apparently effective tool to help address risks to critical infrastructure such as posed by directed, accidental or natural hazards. There are already several sector and national level IEs dedicated to SCADA domains. IEs usually are based on a model where economic competitors from a sector (e.g. energy, telecommunications) gather together and exchange a variety of information. Although there are different reports of the types of information provided, in general vulnerability and risk data are reported as being shared along with best practices on mitigation and remediation. There is limited anecdotal evidence as to the usefulness of the IE model, however. Cases of an Australian telecommunications provider and the US financial services sector provide some practice evidence of their utility. There are a range of information exchange models being deployed across Europe and further afield based on this model, including ones in the United Kingdom, Netherlands, Germany, Australia as well as the United States. However, for participants who are ultimately driven by economic rationale, there are a number of applicable theories that might affect the success of the IE model. These include: externalities, perception of free riding; competition concerns and the fear of reputational damage. Other non-economic factors might include meeting legal or regulatory obligations concerning either the disclosure of vulnerabilities for those companies that operate in highly regulated sectors or non disclosure agreements signed with downstream service providers. There is limited evidence as to the relevance of these factors in an operational context, however. Qualitative research conducted at the European level suggests that participants were more concerned with the quality of the information as a possible factor undermining information sharing above economic concerns. This brings into focus the question about whether the IE model is able to successfully incite sharing, overcoming strong economic incentives of firms to withhold information. Finally, more extensive data on what works would illuminate the benefits of IE participation (but paradoxically be difficult to obtain given the trusted nature of these groups). If the advertised benefits were unequivocally shown to be materially improving the level of security in the firm (and by extension critical infrastructure) then participation has the potential to become useful for those operating critical infrastructures.

ACKNOWLEDGMENT

Thanks to Scott Algeier for review of manuscript.

REFERENCES

Anderson, R. (2001). Why information security is hard: An economic perspective. In *Proceedings of the 17th Annual Computer Security Applications Conference* (pp. 358-365). Washington, DC: IEEE Computer Society.

Assaf, D. (2008). Models of critical information infrastructure protection. In Shenoi, S., & Goetz, E. (Eds.), *International Journal of Critical Infrastructure Protection* (*Vol. 1*, pp. 6–14). Boston, MA: Springer.

Aviram, A. (2004). Network responses to network threats: The evolution into private security associations. *Florida State University College of Law Working Paper, (115)*.

Aviram, A., & Tor, A. (2004). Overcoming Impediments to Information Sharing. *Alabama Law Review, 55*(2), 231–280.

Bellavita, C. (2009) 85% of what you know about critical infrastructure is probably wrong. *Homeland Security Watch*. Retrieved January 1, 2012, from http://www.hlswatch.com/2009/03/16/85-percent-is-wrong/

Bellovin, S. (2010). *Stuxnet: The first weaponized software?* Steve Bellovin's blog. Retrieved January 1 2012, from http://www.cs.columbia.edu/~smb/blog//2010-09-27.html

Brown, I., & Sommer, P. (2010). *Reducing systemic cybersecurity risk*. Organisation for Economic Co-operation and Development (OECD) Multidisciplinary Issues; International Futures Programme on Future Global Shocks, Paris, France: Organisation for Economic Co-operation and Development Camp, L. J. (2006). The state of economics of information security. *I/S. Journal of Law and Policy, 2*(2), 189–205.

Cardenas, A. A., Amin, S., Lin, Z., Huang, Y., Huang, C., & Sastry, S. (2011). Attacks against process control systems: risk assessment, detection, and response. In *Proceedings of the 6th ACM Symposium on Information, Computer and Communications Security* (pp. 355-366). New York, NY: Association for Computing Machinery.

Centre for the Protection of the National Infrastructure. (2006). *Telecommunications resilience good practice guide*. London, UK: Centre for the Protection of the National Infrastructure.

Channelnomics. (2010). *Cisco faces a tough 2011 in switching, routing*. Retrieved January 1, 2012, from http://channelnomics.com/2010/12/22/cisco-faces-a-tough-2011-in-switching-routing/

Chatham House. (2011). *About the Chatham House rule*. London, UK: Chatham House. Retrieved January 1, 2012, from http://www.chathamhouse.org.uk/about/chathamhouserule/

Committee on the Internet Under Crisis Conditions. Learning from September 11. (2003). *The Internet under crisis conditions: Learning from September 11*. Washington, DC: Computer Science and Telecommunications Board: National Research Council; National Academies of Science The National Academies Press.

Computerworld. (2011). *Lockheed Martin acknowledges 'significant' cyberattack*. Retrieved 1 January 2012, from http://www.computerworld.com/s/article/9217126/Lockheed_Martin_acknowledges_significant_cyberattack

Crisis Resource Network. (2009). *Roundtable report: Network governance and the role of public-private partnerships in new risks*. 6th Zurich Roundtable on Comprehensive Risk Analysis and Management. Zurich: Crisis Resource Network.

Danyliw, R., Meijer, J., & Demchenko, Y. (2007). *The incident object description exchange format*. IETF Request for Comments (RFC 5070). Retrieved September 9, 2012, from http://www.ietf.org/rfc/rfc5070.txt

Department of Defense. (2011). *Defence industrial base (DIB) Cyber security/information assurance (CS/IA) programme home – Program description*. Washington, DC: Department of Defense. Retrieved 1 January 2012, from http://dibnet.dod.mil/

Dependability Development Support Initiative. (2002). *Roadmap for warning and information sharing*. Leiden, The Netherlands: RAND Corporation. Retrieved from http://www.ddsi.org/htdocs/Documents/final%20docs/DDSI_D4_WIS_roadmap_f.pdf

Dynes, S., Goetz, E., & Freeman, M. (2008). Cyber security: Are economic incentives adequate? In Shenoi, S., & Goetz, E. (Eds.), *International Journal of Critical Infrastructure Protection* (*Vol. 1*, pp. 15–27). Boston, MA: Springer.

European Commission. (2009). *Communication from the Commission to the European Parliament, the Council, the European Economic and Social Committee and the Committee of the Regions on Critical Information Infrastructure Protection: Protecting Europe from large scale cyber-attacks and disruptions: enhancing preparedness, security and resilience, COM (2009) 149 final*. Brussels, Belgium: European Commission.

European Commission. (2010). *Non-paper on the establishment of a European public private partnership for resilience*. Retrieved 1 January, 2012, from http://ec.europa.eu/information_society/policy/nis/docs/ep3r_workshops/3rd_june2010/2010_06_23_ep3r_nonpaper_v_2_0_final.pdf

European Commission. (2011). *Communication from the Commission to the European Parliament, the Council, the European Economic and Social Committee and the Committee of the Regions on Critical Information Infrastructure Protection: Achievements and next steps: Towards global cyber-security, COM(2011) 163 Final*. Brussels, Belgium: European Commission.

European Commission. (2012). *Proposal for a regulation of the European Parliament and of the Council on the protection of individuals with regards to the processing of personal data and on the free movement of such data (general data protection regulation) COM(2012) 11 final.* Brussels, Belgium: European Commission

European Network and Information Security Agency. (2009). *Good practice guide network security information exchanges.* Heraklion, Greece: ENISA. Retrieved 1 January, 2012, from http://www.enisa.europa.eu/act/res/policies/good-practices-1/information-sharing-exchange/good-practice-guide

European Network and Information Security Agency. (2010). *Incentives and challenges to information sharing.* Heraklion, Greece: ENISA. Retrieved 1 January, 2012, from http://www.enisa.europa.eu/act/res/policies/good-practices-1/information-sharing-exchange/incentives-and-barriers-to-information-sharing?searchterm=Incentives+and

European Network and Information Security Agency. (2011a). *Co-operative models for effective public private partnerships.* Heraklion, Greece: ENISA. Retrieved 1 January, 2012, from http://www.enisa.europa.eu/act/res/other-areas/national-public-private-partnerships-ppps

European Network and Information Security Agency. (2011b). *A flair for sharing - Encouraging information exchange between CERTs.* Heraklion, Greece: ENISA. Retrieved 1 January 2012, from http://www.enisa.europa.eu/act/cert/support/legal-information-sharing/legal-information-sharing-1

Falliere, N., O'Murchu, L., & Chien, E. (2010). *W32.Stuxnet dossier version 1.3.* Mountain View, CA: Symantec.

Forum of Incident Response Teams. (2007). *Common vulnerability scoring system (CVSS); FIRST.* Retrieved September 9, 2012, from http://www.first.org/cvss

Gal-Or, E., & Ghose, A. (2005). The economic incentives for sharing security information. *Information Systems Research, 16*(2). doi:10.1287/isre.1050.0053

Gartner Group. (2011). *Gartner says worldwide operating system software market grew to $30.4 billion in 2010.* Stamford, CT: Retrieved 1 January, 2012, from http://www.gartner.com/it/page.jsp?id=1654914

Ghose, A., Balakrishnan, K., & Ipeirotis, P. (2008, June). *The impact of information disclosure on stock market returns: The Sarbanes-Oxley act and the role of media as an information intermediary.* Seventh Workshop on Economics of Information Security, Hanover, NH.

Goode, S., & Lacey, D. (2009, December). Social embeddedness and sharing security information: Bridging the cost benefit gap. *Proceedings of the 20th Australasian Conference on Information Systems,* Melbourne, NSW.

Gordon, L. A., Loeb, M. P., & Lucyshyn, W. (2003). Sharing information on computer systems security: An economic analysis. *Journal of Accounting and Public Policy, 22*(6), 461–485. doi:10.1016/j.jaccpubpol.2003.09.001

Green, M., Drew, S., Carter, L., & Burnett, D. (2009, January). *Submarine cable network security.* Presentation delivered at the Asia Pacific Economic Forum Workshop on Information Sharing. Retrieved 1 January, 2012, from http://www.iscpc.org/information/Openly%20Published%20Members%20Area%20Items/Submarine_Cable_Network_Security_PDF.pdf

Hahn, R. W., & Layne-Farrar, A. (2006). The law and economics of software security. *Harvard Journal of Law & Public Policy, 30,* 283–354.

Hendricke, U. (2011, July). *Germany's PPP for the protection of CII*. Presentation delivered at the Meeting of the Working Groups of the European Public Private Partnership for Resilience (EP3R) Brussels, 6th July 2011. Retrieved from http://ec.europa.eu/information_society/policy/nis/strategy/activities/ciip/impl_activities/ep3r_06_07_2011/index_en.htm

Hildick-Smith, A. (2005). *Security for critical infrastructure SCADA systems*. SANS Institute.

Information Sharing and Analysis Centre Council. (2009). *The role of information sharing and analysis centres in private/public sector critical infrastructure protection*. New York, NY. Retrieved 1 January, 2012, from http://www.isaccouncil.org

Institute for the Protection and Security of the Citizen. (2006). *European SCADA and control systems information exchange*. Joint Research Centre of the European Commission. Ispra, Italy. Retrieved 1 January, 2012, from http://sta.jrc.ec.europa.eu/index.php/competitive-projects-/21-scni/8-e-scsie

Johnson, M. E., & Goetz, E. (2007). *Embedding information security into the organization. IEEE Security & Privacy, 5(3)*. Los Alamitos, CA: IEEE Computer Society.

Kahneman, D., & Tversky, A. (1979). Prospect theory: An analysis of decision under risk. *Econometrica, 47*(2). doi:10.2307/1914185

Klaus, M. (2010, March). *MELANI: Information exchange –A story of success*. Presentation delivered at ENISA's Workshop on Information Sharing; Amsterdam. Retrieved 1 January, 2012, from http://www.enisa.europa.eu/act/res/workshops-1/2010/information-sharing-workshop/copy_of_agenda-of-the-information-sharing-workshop

Kolfal, B., Patterson, R., & Yeo, L. (2010, June). *Market impact on IT security spending*. Presentation at The Ninth Workshop on the Economics of Information Security Harvard, NH.

Kunreuther, H., & Heal, G. (2003). Interdependent security. *Journal of Risk and Uncertainty, 26*(2-3), 231–249. doi:10.1023/A:1024119208153

Lines, S. (2008, May). *Best practice for sharing threats and warning information between industry and the US government*. Presentation at the CSIIR Workshop Oak Ridge National laboratory, May 13 2008.

Mitre, (2009) *Common vulnerabilities and exposures*. Retrieved 09th September, 2012, from http://cve.mitre.org/

Moore, T. (2010, June). *Policy recommendations for cybersecurity*. Presentation delivered at the Ninth Workshop on the Economics of Information Security, Cambridge, MA (rump session presentation).

National Infrastructure Advisory Council. (2006). *Public-private sector intelligence coordination: Final report and recommendations by the council*. Retrieved 1 January, 2012, from http://www.dhs.gov/xlibrary/assets/niac/niac_icwgreport_july06.pdf

National Infrastructure against Cyber Crime. (2010). *United against cybercrime spring report 2010*. The Hague, The Netherlands. Retrieved 1 January, 2012, from http://www.samentegencybercrime.nl/UserFiles/File/NEW-lentebericht_2010-UK%20DEFINITIEF.pdf

Newton-Evans. (2008). *Market Trends Digest; Executive Summary of Findings From EMS, SCADA, DMS Study*. Ellicott City, MD: Newton Evans Research Company Inc.

Omer, M., Nilchiani, R., & Mostashari, A. (2009). Measuring the resilience of the global internet infrastructure system. In *Proceedings of 3rd Annual IEEE Systems Conference*. Vancouver, BC: IEEE Computer Society

Payne, J. W., Bettman, J. R., & Johnson, E. J. (1993). *The adaptive decision maker*. New York, NY: Cambridge University Press. doi:10.1017/CBO9781139173933

Powell, A. (2010, March). *UK's information sharing national strategy*. Presentation delivered at ENISA's workshop on Information Sharing; Amsterdam. Retrieved 1 January, 2012, from http://www.enisa.europa.eu/act/res/workshops-1/2010/information-sharing-workshop/copy_of_agenda-of-the-information-sharing-workshop

Preece, J., Nonnecke, B., & Andrews, D. (2004). The top five reasons for lurking: improving community experiences for everyone. *Computers in Human Behavior*, *20*(2), 201–223. doi:10.1016/j.chb.2003.10.015

President's Commission on Critical Infrastructure Protection. (1997). *Critical foundations: Protecting America's infrastructures*. Washington, DC: President's Commission on Critical Infrastructure Protection. Retrieved 1 January, 2012, from http://www.ciao.gov/CIAO_Document_Library/PCCIP_Report.pdf

Riptech. (2001). *Understanding SCADA system security vulnerabilities*. Retrieved from http://www.iwar.org.uk/cip/resources/utilities/SCADAWhitepaperfinal1.pdf 2001

Rosslin, J. R., & Choi, M.-K. (2009). Assessment of the vulnerabilities of SCADA, control systems and critical infrastructure systems. *International Journal of Grid and Distributed Computing*, *2*(2).

Rowe, B. R., & Gallaher, M. P. (2006, June). *Private sector cyber security investment strategies: An empirical analysis*. Fifth Workshop on Economics of Information Security, Cambridge, UK.

Rue, R., Pfleeger, S., & Ortiz, D. (2007, June). *A framework for classifying and comparing models of cyber security investment to support policy and decision-making*. Sixth Workshop on Economics of Information Security, Pittsburgh PA.

Schneier, B. (2007) SCADA security hole. *Schneier on Security*. Retrieved 1 January, 2012, from http://www.schneier.com/blog/archives/2007/05/scada_security.html

Securities and Exchange Commission. (2011). *CF disclosure guidance: Topic No. 2* Cybersecurity. Retrieved 09 September, 2012, from http://www.sec.gov/divisions/corpfin/guidance/cfguidance-topic2.htm

Shapiro, R., Bratus, S., & Smith, S. (2011, March). *Assessing the vulnerability of SCADA devices*. Paper Presented at the Fifth Annual IFIP Working Group 11.10 International Conference on Critical Infrastructure Protection, Hanover, NH.

Shiu, S., Baldwin, A., Beres, Y., Duggan, G. B., Casassa Mont, M., Johnson, H., & Middup, C. (2011, June). *Economic methods and decision making by security professionals*. Tenth Workshop on the Economics of Information Security, George Mason University, NH.

Slay, J., & Miller, M. (2007). Lessons learned from the Maroochy water breach. In Shenoi, S., & Goetz, E. (Eds.), *International Journal of Critical Infrastructure Protection* (*Vol. 1*, pp. 73–82). Boston, MA: Springer. doi:10.1007/978-0-387-75462-8_6

Stikvoort, D. (2009). *Trusted introducer information sharing traffic light protocol (ISTLP)*. NISCC (UK). Retrieved 1 January, 2012, from https://www.trusted-introducer.org/links/ISTLP-v1.1-approved.pdf

Tech-Exclusive. (2010). India faces disrupted internet service due to undersea cable issue. *Tech-Exclusive*. Retrieved 1 January, 2012, from http://www.tech-exclusive.com/india-faces-disrupted-internet-service-due-to-undersea-cable-issue/

Techtarget.com. (2001). *IT-ISAC: A matter of trust*. Retrieved 1 January, 2012, from http://searchsecurity.techtarget.com/news/517824/IT-ISAC-A-matter-of-trust

Thaler, R. H., & Sunstein, C. R. (2008). *Nudge: Improving decisions about health, wealth and happiness*. London, UK: Yale University Press.

The White House. (1998). *Presidential decision directive 63- Fact sheet- Protecting America's Critical Infrastructures: PDD 63*. Retrieved 1 January, 2012, from http://www.pub.whitehouse.gov/uri-res/I2R?urn:pdi://oma.eop.gov.us/1998/5/26/1.text.1

The White House. (2006). *Homeland security presidential decision directive 7: Critical infrastructure identification, prioritization and protection*. (HSPD-7) Washington D.C. Retrieved 1 January, 2012, from http://www.dhs.gov/xabout/laws/gc_1214597989952.shtm#0

The White House. (2009). *60 day cybersecurity policy review: Assuring a trusted and resilient information and communications infrastructure*. Washington, DC. Retrieved 1 January, 2012, from http://www.whitehouse.gov/assets/documents/Cyberspace_Policy_Review_final.pdf

Trebilcock, M., & Iacobucci, E. (2003). Privatisation and accountability. *Harvard Law Review*, *116*(5), 1422–1453. doi:10.2307/1342731

Trusted Information Sharing Network. (2011a). *Trusted information sharing network overview*. Canberra, Australia. Retrieved 1 January, 2012, from http://tisn.gov.au/www/tisn/rwpattach.nsf/VAP/(9A5D88DBA63D32A661E6369859739356)~TISN+Overview+-+Fact+Sheet.PDF/$file/TISN+Overview+-+Fact+Sheet.PDF

Trusted Information Sharing Network. (2011b). *Trusted information sharing network deed of confidentiality fact sheet*. Canberra, Australia. Retrieved 1 January, 2012, from http://www.tisn.gov.au/Documents/TISN+Deed+of+Confidentiality+-+Fact+Sheet.pdf

United States General Accounting Office. (2001). *Information sharing. Practices that can benefit critical infrastructure protection*. Washington, DC: General Accounting Office. Retrieved 1 January, 2012, from http://www.gao.gov/new.items/d0224.pdf

United States General Accounting Office. (2004). *Critical Infrastructure protection. Establishing effective information sharing with infrastructure sectors*. Washington, DC: General Accounting Office. Retrieved 1 January, 2012, from http://www.gao.gov/new.items/d04699t.pdf

Wentworth, F. (2000). *Critical infrastructure protection: Establishing an information sharing and analysis center (ISAC) can be like developing an organizational security policy* Global Information Assurance Certification Paper; SANS Institute. Retrieved 1 January, 2012, from http://www.giac.org/paper/gsec/155/critical-infrastructure-protection-establishing-information-sharing-analysis-center-be/100603

ZDNet. (2010). 2015 the year of cyberwar: Gartner. *ZDNet*. Retrieved 1 January, 2012, from http://www.zdnet.com.au/2015-the-year-of-cyberwar-gartner-339307693.htm

Zielstra, A., & Hafkamp, W. (2010, March). *Dutch cybercrime information exchange: A public private partnership*. Presentation delivered at ENISA's workshop on Information Sharing; Amsterdam. Retrieved 1 January, 2012, from http://www.enisa.europa.eu/act/res/workshops-1/2010/information-sharing-workshop/copy_of_agenda-of-the-information-sharing-workshop

ADDITIONAL READING

Camp, L. J. (n.d.). *Information security economics online resource*. Retrieved 1 January, 2012, from http://infosecon.net/workshop/bibliography.php

The International Federation of Information Processing. (n.d.). *Working Group 11.10 on Critical Infrastructure*. Retrieved 1 January, 2012, from http://www.ifip1110.org/

Workshop on the Economics of Information Security (WEIS) series. (n.d.). Retrieved 1 January, 2012, from: http://weis2011.econinfosec.org/index.html

KEY TERMS AND DEFINITIONS

Critical Infrastructure: Those infrastructures such as energy, finance, telecommunications commonly through of to be critical for economic or social wellbeing.

Efficiency: In this precise context, the situation where investment in security measures is precisely equal to the likely costs of an absence of security.

Incentive: An economic driver or argument informing decision-making.

Information Exchange (IE): A public-private partnership mechanism by which private sector competitors engage in information sharing in a closed forum hosted by the public sector.

Information Sharing: The collaborative exchange of information pertaining to the security of critical infrastructures.

Misaligned Incentive: Where an incentive may differ from that necessary for an efficient market.

PLC: Programmable logic controller.

Public Private Partnership: Joint effort by the private and public sector to achieve some strategic goal.

SCADA: Supervisory control and data acquisition technology used to remotely monitor and manage distributed plcs or other remotely accessible infrastructure nodes.

ENDNOTES

[1] Which have the added complexity that open disclosure policy is simultaneously represents a strong driver for those responsible to find and fix the vulnerability but also makes it easier for an adversary to obtain the vulnerability

[2] e.g. see the WEIS series for papers in this domain

Chapter 15

Intrusion Detection and Resilient Control for SCADA Systems

Bonnie Zhu
University of California at Berkeley, USA

Shankar Sastry
University of California at Berkely, USA

ABSTRACT

Designed without cyber security in mind, most existing Supervisory Control And Data Acquisition (SCADA) systems make it a big challenge to modify the conventional Information Technology (IT) intrusion detection techniques, both to counter the threat of cyber attacks due to their standardization and connectivity to the Internet, and to achieve resilient control without fully retrofitting. The author presents a taxonomy and a set of metrics of SCAD-specific intrusion detection techniques by heightening their possible use in addition to explaining the nuance associated with such task and enumerating Intrusion Detection Systems (IDS) that have been proposed to undertake this endeavor. She identifies the deficits and voids in current research and offers recommendations on which strategies are most likely to succeed, in part through presenting a prototype of her efforts towards this goal. Specifically, she introduces an early anomaly detection and resilient estimation scheme consisting of a robust online recursive algorithm, which is based on the Kalman Filter in a state space model setting. This online window limited Robust Generalized Likelihood Ratio Test (RGLRT) that the author proposes identifies and detects outliers among real-time multidimensional measurements of dynamical systems without any a priori knowledge of the occurrence time or distribution of the outliers. It attains a low detection delay and an optimal stopping time that yields low rates in false alarm and miss detection while maintaining the optimal online estimation performance under normal conditions. The author proposes a set of qualitative and quantitative metric to measure its optimality in the context of cyber-physical systems.

DOI: 10.4018/978-1-4666-2659-1.ch015

Copyright © 2013, IGI Global. Copying or distributing in print or electronic forms without written permission of IGI Global is prohibited.

INTRODUCTION

From the massive espionage malware Flame that steals critical information of the Iranian oil industry and other Mideast energy sector (CrySyS Lab, 2012; Lee, 2012) to the destructive Stuxnet (Falliere & Chien, 2011), one of most sophisticated progress control system malware known to date, the game changer has arrived in the field of cyber-physical security in that the attackers not only know the IT content well enough but also understand the physical consequence to those cyber behaviors. In McAfee's report (Baker, Filipiak, & Timlin, 2011), nearly half of those being surveyed in the electric industry said that they had found Stuxnet on their systems. Stuxnet has targeted Siemens *Supervisory Control And Data Acquisition (SCADA)* systems that are configured to control and monitor specific industrial processes, such as Iranian nuclear infrastructure in 2010.

What is SCADA? Being one of the primary categories of control systems, SCADA systems are generally used for large geographically dispersed distribution operations, such as electrical power grids, petroleum and gas pipelines, water and sewage systems and other critical infrastructures (Stouffer, Falco, & Kent, 2006). They not only provide management with remote access to real-time data from Distributed Control Systems (DCSs) and Programmable Logic Controllers (PLCs) but also enable operational control center to issue automated or operator-driven supervisory commands to remote station control devices.

One of the enabling elements in SCADA systems is the set of various communication protocols employed within the hierarchical system (Anderson, 2010; Dzung et al., 2005; Krutz, 2006). Their functionalities range from processing raw data transmission to handling high-level exchange between different networks and domains. These protocols have strong implications on the security of SCADA system. We name a few most popular ones: Modbus,

Profibus, Distributed Network Protocol (DNP3) and Utility Communications Architecture (UCA), Foundation Fieldbus, Common Industrial Protocol (CIP), Controller Area Network (CAN), Object Linking and Embedding (OLE) for Process Control (OPC) and Inter-Control Center Communications Protocol (Krutz, 2006).

Most industrial plants now employ networked process historian servers storing process data and other possible business and process interfaces, such as using remote Windows sessions to DCSs or direct file transfer from PLCs to spreadsheets. This integration of SCADA networks with other networks has made SCADA vulnerable to various cyber threats. The adoption of Ethernet and TCP/IP for process control networks and wireless technologies such as IEEE 802.x, Zigbee, Bluetooth, WiFi, plus WirelessHART and ISA SP100 (Dzung et al., 2005; Krutz, 2006) has further reduced the isolation of SCADA networks. The connectivity and de-isolation of the SCADA system is manifested in Figure 1.

Furthermore, the recent trend in standardization of software and hardware used in SCADA systems (Krutz, 2006) potentially makes it even easier to mount SCADA-specific attacks[1]. Instances such as Siemens *Programmable Logic Controller* (PLC) and Vx-Works[2] vulnerability disclosures show the need to take security precaution in order to maintain the safety and performance of SCADA components and the overall system.

Moreover, a piece of sophisticated malware, such as Stuxnet, could take advantage of multiple Windows zero-day vulnerabilities and target the command-and-control software installed in industrial control systems world-wide, using a known default password that the software maker hardcoded into its systems. Stuxnet aims to sabotage facilities by reprogramming PLCs to operate as the attackers intend them, most likely out of their specified boundaries while its "misreporting" feature hides the incident from the network operations center (Falliere & Chien, 2011). Others like Duqu (Symantec, 2011) or Flame (CrySyS Lab,

Figure 1. Typical SCADA components; Source: United States Government Accountability Office Report GAO-04-354 (Pfleeger & Pfleeger, 2007)

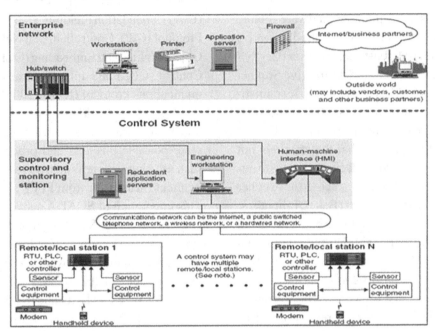

2012) have sought to infiltrate networks in order to steal data that can be useful in attacking the industrial control systems. As of April 21st. 2011, there were already more than 50 new Stuxnet-like attacks beckon SCADA threats discovered (Muncaster, 2011).

These attacks may disrupt and damage critical infrastructural operations, contaminate the ecological environment, cause major economic losses and, even more dangerously, claim human lives (Arnold, 2006; GAO, 2007). These likely "penalty costs" due to the lack of protection and our *aversion to loss* push us to consider protection measures with reasonable cost-effectiveness.

However, many factors, such as the *legacy issues* of the over 30-40 years old existing systems, the 24×7 *continuous availability* operation requirement, the *hard deadline* of heavy machinery and physical components, and the *low computation power* of the end devices, have been keeping ready security measures in the traditional IT from

direct implementation and immediate deployment to the large part of the current SCADA systems (GAO, 2004). Had we not started with the legacy systems but been freed from the difficulties such as interoperability (Lewis, 2006; Oman & Phillips, 2007) instead, we may apply and implement many known security measures directly, such as rigorous *access control*, end-to-end secure communication protocols with *full authentication*, *encryption* besides *key management systems* etc. (Anderson; 2010; Pfleeger & Pfleeger, 2007). Nevertheless, the method of an *intrusion alarm* coupled with a *security response* (Allen, 2000; Endorf, Schultz, & Mellander, 2004), a well-established approach in the traditional security field, has its special immediate appealing factors to securing SCADA systems (Anderson, 2010, Scarfone & Mell, 2007).

The ultimate goal of much needed work in this area is to achieve satisfactory control performance in a continuous 24×7, real-time, realistic environment, where normalized behavior co-exists with benign noises, honest mistakes, natural components and or systems faults plus potential malicious cyber intrusions. Thus we focus on SCADA-specific Intrusion Detection System (IDS) and resilient control strategies by surveying and evaluating a set of proposed SCADA-specific IDS in addition to our own approach that combines both intrusion detection and resilient control to address this challenge.

1.1 Why SCADA-Specific Intrusion Detection/Prevention Systems?

Security is not an end product but a process, let alone the legacy and backward compatibility issues in securing SCADA systems. Thus an all-encompassing and airtight prevention is not only extremely expensive both in economic and operational sense but also technically and socially infeasible. A sound implementation and viable deployment of one IDS and resilient control strategy can manifest itself as an add-on intelligence and resilient assurance component to the existing SCADA systems with minimum hardware cost or operational changes, leveraging many entrenched SCADA component infrastructures and technologies. To this end, the industrial and academic control security community has started to build IDS specifically for SCADA systems (Cheung et al., 2007; Moran & Belisle, 2008; Naess et al., 2005; Oman & Phillips, 2007; Robinson & Woodworth, 2008; Rrushi, Campbell, & di Milano, 2008; Tsang & Kwong, 2005; Tsang & Smith, 2008; Yang, Usynin, & Hines, 2005).

Nevertheless, it is important to realize that when we borrow tools from other fields, there are situations and conditions that our original set of assumptions might not hold. A SCADA system is different from the conventional IT system in the following ways (Stouffer, Falco, & Kent, 2006; Zhu, Joseph, & Sastry, 2011): it is a *hard real-time* system; its *timeliness* and *availability* at

all times is very critical and its terminal devices have limited computing capabilities and memory resources (DHS, 2005). Additionally, in the existing SCADA systems, there are weak authentication mechanisms to differentiate human users or privilege separation or user account management to control access and so on (Oman & Phillips, 2007). Such fundamental weakness in access control leaves the door open to attacks. These differences challenge design and implementation of SCADA-specific IDSs.

Meanwhile, among the attempts to date, some authors (Cheung et al., 2007) may consider that SCADA systems usually have a relatively static topology[3], a *presumably* regular network traffic[4] and the use of simple protocols, hence monitoring them may not be more difficult than doing so in enterprise systems. But such assumptions are not fully validated yet barely any mentioned work has been tested on real operational SCADA system network traffic. The related details are to be discussed in subsequent sections.

Furthermore, the cyber-physical security of real-time, continuous systems necessitates a comprehensive view and a holistic understanding of network security, control theory and physical systems (Zhu, Joseph, & Sastry, 2011). There are partial overlaps in the focus and terminologies by convention in each field, where in turn have their own field-specific interpretations for these overlapped lingoes. One of the barriers faced by researchers in IDS for SCADA is the occupational or the cultural and lingo differences between IT and control personnel. Thus this chapter aims to convey the idea of intrusion detection and prevention in the setting a SCADA system by leveraging the classic control engineering and theory view point. Towards concrete progress beyond generic discussions, it's important for us to survey and evaluate up-to-date research efforts in this area and reflect on the soundness of the overall methodologies. We may want to ask:

- Whether these techniques and approaches have addressed the specific needs of SCADA systems?
- Whether we are being simply handicapped by the special needs of current SCADA systems in terms of security engineering efforts? Or
- Whether we are leveraging the entrenched SCADA infrastructure components and technologies?

1.2 Contribution

Overall, we make the following contributions:

- First systematic and thorough effort in investigating and assessing the landscape of up-to-date SCADA-specific intrusion detection techniques and systems;
- Explain the nuance of SCADA-specific IDS and provide clear definitions plus a taxonomy and a set of metrics of SCADA-specific IDS;
- Ease the interoperability between conventional IT security and control systems research by framing the intrusion detection problem in a setting favorable to SCADA systems' continuous operation, withstanding the possible presence of adversary and unintentional faults;
- Bring in cross-discipline insights to tailor the special needs entailed by SCADA systems by leveraging entrenched SCADA components and technologies and provide future direction; In doing so, we show a prototype of our efforts in this arena.
- Offer a simplified taxonomy/comparison of change detection methods;
- Present a resilient and flexible estimation scheme *robustly* rectifies and cleans data upon both isolated and patchy outliers while maintain the optimality of the Kalman Filter under the nominal condition;

- Propose an online window-limited sequential *Robust Generalized Likelihood Ratio Test* (RGLRT) without any *a priori* knowledge of the occurrence time or the distribution of the outliers;
- The RGLRT bears an optimal stopping time, i.e., asymptotically shortest detection delay time while maintaining lowest false alarm rate.

1.3 Related Work

Since research on SCADA-specific IDS and resilience to cyber threats is of a rather new arena, we decide to resort to the classics in the standard IT field for references when it comes to classification and categorization.

As observed by John McHugh (2000) *"The point is that the taxonomy must be constructed with two objectives in mind: describing the relevant universe and applying the description to gain insight into the problem at hand."*

Both Stefan Axelsson (2000) and John Mchugh (2001) have thorough work on classification of intrusion detection systems. Many evaluation and assessment principles on SCADA-specific IDS are derived from their works.

Aside from the specific proposed systems that we will compare more in details in later sessions, we'd like to bring forward the ideas and methods that directly affect or relate to the technicalities of our own proposed approach.

A unified view is to consider intrusion detection as a signal detection problem as framed by Stefan Axelsson (2000), where we consider the normal network traffic as background data. If we view background data and responses as noise and attack data and responses as signal, the IDS problem can be characterized as one of detecting a signal in the presence of noise. This school of thought is much in line with the standard control theory (Callier & Desoer, 1991).

The CUSUM (Cumulative Summation) method and its variants are widely used for anomaly detection. As pointed out in (Basseville & Nikiforov, 1993; Soule, Salmatian, & Taft, 2005), its major drawback is that it requires *a priori* knowledge on information after change, i.e. the intensity of the anomaly etc. But in practice, such information is not predicable. Given that our work is closely related to CUSUM, sequential analysis and hypothesis testing in general, we deem that the related sequential testing approaches deserve a brief exposition in more details in the following Section 5.

To address robustness issues, Zhu et al (2002) proposed a filtering technique that ensures an estimation error variance with a guaranteed upper bound given the norm-bounded time varying parameter uncertainty in both the system state and output measurement matrices. Their focus doesn't include outlier detection though. Ting et al (2007)used a weighted least squares-like approach by introducing weights for each data sample. A data sample with a smaller weight has a weaker contribution when estimating the current time step's state. They treated the problem as an *expectation maximization* (EM) learning problem with maximization over all available data points at every time step while using a variational factorial approximation of the true posterior distribution to get analytically tractable inference. Jeong and Lee (2010) removed the drifting tracking points using the Kalman filter when the flow based tracking approach is possibly prone to outliers due to its aperture problem.

Hammes (2010) studied robust positioning algorithms for transmitter devices over wireless networks where the non-line-of-sight propagation effects lead to erroneous signal parameter estimates. The framework of an extended Kalman filter (EKF) is rewritten into a linear regression model at each time step while non-parametric pdf estimation is used for position estimation within a parametric signal model to solve for position and velocity of the user equipment.

1.4 Definitions and Difficulties from Ambiguities

To resolve the ambiguity of same terminologies that bear different meanings in control theory (including systems & control and fault detection & isolation) and in IT (particularly, operating system and security engineering), we intend to unify and broaden the terms to ease the misunderstanding and to highlight the end goal of providing engineers and researchers insights into the problems facing networked control systems (Zhu & Sastry, 2010).

- **Fault**: A non-hostility-induced deviation from the system's specified behavior including honest mistakes caused by honest people and component failures or defects.
- **Anomaly:** Refers to malicious and intrusive event plus abnormal yet non-intrusive behavior including (faulty and noisy/ messy) actions.
- **Misuse:** Includes both malicious and unintentional misuse.
- **Detection:** Alarm alerts issued in the presence of true anomaly or misuse.
- **False Alarm/Positive:** Alarm alerts issued in the absence of real anomaly and/or misuse when there is normal traffic/behavior only.
- **False Negative or Missed Detection:** Missed detection in the presence of a real intrusion.
- **Note**: Any large network is a very "noisy" environment even at the packet level.

This chapter is self-contained. The rest of it is organized as follows, Section 2 outlines real time intrusion detection types and proposed SCADA-specific Intrusion Detection Systems in the literature; Section 3 shows the comparison of surveyed systems by using a series of proposed metrics; Section 4 evaluates the proposed systems; Section 5 gives a brief exposition of hypothesis testing and a taxonomy/comparison of related work;

Section 6 states the problem formulation of our proposed methodologies including performance metrics; Section 7 presents the resilient estimation scheme; Section 8 describes the procedure for outlier detection; Section 9 shows simulation results, evaluation and discussion. Section 10 Concludes.

2 PROPOSED SCADA-SPECIFIC INTRUSION DETECTION/ PREVENTION SYSTEMS

We adapt a taxonomy of real-time intrusion detection to facilitate the choice for control's researchers as well.

2.1 On Real Time Intrusion Detection Types

In the early days of IDS research, two major approaches known as *signature detection* and *anomaly detection* were developed.

In between these two approaches, there lie the probabilistic- and specification based methods for intrusion detection. A *probabilistic approach* is also termed as a *statistical* or a *Bayes* method (Kruegel et al., 2003) with probabilistically encoded models of misuse. It has some potential to detect unknown attacks. A *specification-based approach* constructs a model of what is allowed, enforces its predefined policy and raises alerts when the observed behavior is outside this model. It has a high potential for generalization and leverages against new attacks (Balepin et al., 2003). This technique has been proposed as a promising alternative that combines the strengths of signature-based and anomaly based detection. Instead of finding the deviation and unknowns, specification-based method (Balepin et al., 2003; Ko, Ruschitzka, & Kevitt, 1997) defines what's allowable in terms of network traffic behavior/ patterns. This method sounds promising. But it might be tedious to enumerate all possibly allowable patterns.

Complementary to the above knowledge based classification; there are also *behavioral detection approaches*[5]. They capture behavior patterns associated with certain attacks which are not necessarily illegitimate in semantic sense. They may also abstract allowable normal interaction as well. Such methods are quite promising, especially in conjunction with other methods (Zanero, 2004) (See Table 1).

2.2 Model-Based IDS for SCADA Using Modbus/TCP

The group at SRI (Cheung et al., 2007) adapted the specification-based approach for intrusion detection to SCADA systems that rely on Modbus/ TCP. This work renders a multi-algorithm IDS appliance containing pattern anomaly recognition, Bayes analysis of TCP headers, and stateful protocol monitoring complemented with customized Snort rules. Alerts are forwarded to the correlation framework.

They offer three model-based techniques to characterize the expected/acceptable system behavior according to the Modbus/TCP specification and to detect potential attacks that violate these models.

2.3 Anomaly-Based Intrusion Detection

We discuss two anomaly-based intrusion detection systems in this section.

2.3.1 AutoAssociative Kernel Regression and Statistical Probability Ratio Test SPRT

Yang et al (2005) use the *AutoAssociative Kernel Regression* (AAKR) model coupled with the *Statistical Probability Ratio test* (SPRT) and apply them to a simulated SCADA system. The fundamental methodology is pattern matching. Predetermined features representing network traffic and hardware operating statistics are used

Table 1. Comparison of intrusion detection approaches

Knowledge based or behavioral based	Approach	Basis	Attacks Detected	Generalization
Knowledge	Signature	Misuse	Known	No
Knowledge	Anomaly	Learned models of normal	Must appear anomalous	Yes
Knowledge	Probabilistic	Model learning	Match patterns of misuse	Some
Hybrid	Specification	Construct normal model	Must violate specs	Yes
Behavioral	Behavioral	Capture behavioral pattern	Match patters of behavior	Yes

by the AAKR model to predict the "correct" behavior. Then new observations are compared with past observations denoted as normal behavior. The comparison residuals are fed into SPRT to determine whether is anomalous or not. Besides DoS attacks, ping flood, jolt2 attacks, bubonic attacks, simultaneous jolt2 and bubonic attacks, the authors also consider insider attack scenarios.

2.3.2 Multi-Agent IDS Using Ant Clustering Approach and Unsupervised Feature Extraction

Tsang and Kwong (2005) propose an unsupervised anomaly-learning model - the *Ant Colony Clustering Model* (ACCM) in a multi-agent, decentralized IDS to reduce data dimensionality and increase modeling accuracy. The idea is bio-inspired from nature to construct statistical patterns of network data into near-optimal clusters for classification.

2.4 Configurable Middleware-Level Detection

Næss et al (2005) presents a configurable *Embedded Middleware-level Intrusion Detection System* (EMISDS) framework. It's implemented within *MicroQoSCORBA*, a CORBA-based middleware framework, with high configurability achieved with the Interface Definition Language (IDL) compiler and code generation tools (McKinnon et al., 2003). The system model is comprised of

anomaly and misuse detection while leaving the flexibility to specify the interaction of middle-level information within the IDS.

2.5 Intrusion Detection and Event Monitoring in SCADA Networks

Oman and Phillips (2007) from the University of Idaho give a very clear exposition on the implementation of a SCADA power-grid testbed for intrusion detection and event monitoring. They are producing comprehensive intrusion signatures for unauthorized access to SCADA devices besides baseline-setting files for those devices.

2.6 Model for Cyber-Physical Interaction

2.6.1 Power Plant interfacing Substations through Probabilistic Validation of Attack-Effect Bindings (PVAEB)

Rrushi and Campbell (2008) look into the attacks on IEC 61850 (2004), the protocol used for communication between electricity substation and power plant (a nuclear power plant in the paper).

The authors present the semantic correlation between the dynamics of nuclear reactors in the power plant and those of the generated electricity provision in the substation through *Structural Equations Modeling* (SEM). For each logical node of IEC 61850, they apply *Bayesian Belief Networks* (BBN) to enumerate probability distributions attributed by its associated data individually. Then the authors use *Stochastic Activity Network* (SAN) to verify such bindings and to spot intrusions.

All constructions of attack-effects are based on *known* failure models.

2.6.2 Workflow-Based Non-Intrusive Approach for Enhancing the Survivability of Critical Infrastructures in Cyber Environment

Xiao et al (2007) proposed an approach based on workflow, a technique to automate existing processes to incorporate the detections of both known attack patterns and known unsafe states.

This work leverages the presumably existing survivability-related knowledge and protection scheme. They consider that each essential component in the physical layer has a corresponding node in the workflow. A simplified water treatment system is studied through simulation to illustrate the idea.

3 COMPARISON OF PROPOSED SYSTEMS

The overall comparisons of the proposed systems are listed in Table 2 and Table 3. The rationale behind choosing the features we used for comparison is out of operational concerns besides performance issues.

3.1 Intrusion Detection

Particularly, we'd like to look into the intrusion detection methods used in each system, seen in Table 4.

3.2 SCADA-Specific-Ness

We compare how SCADA's special needs are being addressed in each proposed system with results shown in Table 5.

Table 2. Comparison of intrusion detection system approaches

Name of System	Publ year	Degree of SCADA Specific	Specific Domain	Detection Prevention Principle	Malicious Intrusions only?	Threat model	Time of Detection	Security	Fallacy Analysis	Unit of analysis
PVAEB [67]	2008	high	electrical power	proba.	fault & intrusion	no	N/A	low	no	packet
IBM NADS [49]	2008	medium	N/A	anomaly, spec. behavioral	extensible	outsider not explicit	Non-real	low	no	flow-based
SRI Modbus [13]	2007	high	N/A	spec. proba.	extensible	outsider	real	medium	no	packet
WFBNI [87]	2007	high	water treatment system	signature	unintent. faults unsafe states	not explicit	on-line prediction	low	no	N/A
SHARP [19]	2008	medium	N/A	spec. encryp.	extensible	insider or outsider	on-line	high	no	N/A
IDEM [57]	2007	high	power grid	signature	yes	unauth. access	real	low	N/A	packet
AAKR-SPRT [89]	2006	high	no	anomaly	yes	insider & outsider	real	low	no	packet
EMISDS [52]	2005	low	N/A	anomaly, spec., signature	yes	N/A	real	low	no	procedural interval
MAAC-UFE [80]	2004	medium	N/A	anomaly	yes	both	real	N/A	yes	N/A

Table 3. Comparison of intrusion detection system approaches continued

Name of System	Data Proc.	Data Coll.	Scalab-ility	Granul-arity	Audit Source	Type of Response	Inter-oper.	Imple-ment.	Deploy. ment	Real traces
PVAEB [67]	centr.	centr.	medium	batch	host	passive	N/A	yes	no	testbed
IBM NADS [49]	centr.	dist.	high	cont.	network	passive	yes	yes	N/A	N/A
SRI Modbus [13]	dist.	dist.	high	cont.	both	active	yes	yes	no	testbed
WFBNI [87]	centr.	dist.	high	cont.	network	passive	maybe	yes	no	simulation
SHARP [19]	centr.	centr.	low	cont.	network	active	yes	no	N/A	N/A
DEM [57]	centr.	centr.	low	cont.	network	passive	yes	yes	no	testbed
AAKRSPRT [89]	centr.	centr.	low	cont.	host	passive	yes	yes	no	testbed
EMISDS [52]	dist.	dist.	high	batch.	both	N/A	N/A	no	no	simulation w/o intrusion
MAACUFE [80]	dist.	dist.	high	N/A	both	active	N/A	yes	no	KDD-cup

4 EVALUATION OF PROPOSED SYSTEMS

4.1 Design Pitfalls and Evaluation Criteria

Looking at IT standard IDSs, McHugh (2000) criticizes many aspects of the DARPA/LL evaluation. In terms of modeling, both signature and probabilistic IDSs model misuse, the *illegal* behavior of an intrusion. Anomaly-based IDSs empirically and statistically model normal system usage and behavior. Specification-based IDSs define what is allowable under protocol and policy specification. All these model-based approaches bear certain common drawbacks:

- Inaccurate models can lead to false alarms and/or missed detections.
- Modeling can be expensive and difficult if the system and/or user activity is complex.

Anderson (2010) states "In general, if you build an intrusion detection system based on data-mining techniques, you are at serious risk of discriminating."

Paxson has a similar argument, even more from a technical point of view (2001) that one of the pitfalls of machining learning based IDS techniques is the lack of illumination for the rationale behind many approaches on how they decide to take such approach; and why they succeed in doing so or why they fail in achieving.

According to Axelsson (2000), McHugh (2001), and Paxson (2001), we shall look for

- Soundness
- Completeness
- Timeliness
- Choice of metrics, statistical models, profiles
- System design
- Social implications
- Feedback: or how to decide actionable events

The SCADA-specific angles we look at are: What are their contributions, limitations or room for improvement, extensibleness in terms of

- How do they frame the work including assumptions, logics and conclusions?
- What kind of security properties do they want to achieve? Do they achieve and how?
- What are their trust model, threat model and attack scenarios? How plausible?
- What are the illuminations they bring into the problem space?
- What's the selling point of their approach?
- What kind of detection algorithms they've used that suit SCADA systems particularly well?
  - Either through leveraging the entrenched components and/or technologies used in the specific SCADA physical systems under their study;

Table 4. Comparison of intrusion detection method in each proposed system

Name of System	Detection Type	Intrusion only	Detection Method / Algorithm
PVAEB [67]	anomaly	fault intrusion	Structural Equation Modeling, Bayesian Belief Networks, Stochastic Activity Networks
IBM NADS [49]	anomaly, behavioral specification	N/A	net flow matching
SRI Modbus [13]	spec., prob.	extensible	descriptive statistics, simple rule based
WFBNI [87]	signature	fault intrusion	matching fault model
SHARP [19]	spec.	extensible	N/A
IDEM [57]	signature	yes	N/A
AAKRSPRT[89]	anomaly	yes	AAKR, SPRT, pattern matching
EMISDS [52]	anomaly, spec. signature	yes	simple rule based, sliding window
MAACUFE [80]	anomaly	yes	ACCM, PCA

○ Or restrict their attention to a more focused and potentially narrowed workspace that are more relevant to specific SCADA physical system under their study when applying generic methods.

• What are the subtle points they bring out that might have been simply left out by a non-SCADA-security expert?

• What's unique in the cyber-physical interactions?

• How is the detection performance in terms effectiveness and efficiency? Effectiveness is reflected through high detection rate and low false alarm rate; efficiency overheads.

4.2 Evaluation Results

4.2.1 Strength

The model-based system for SCADA system using Modubs/TCP addresses Modbus protocol encapsulated within TCP/IP. The idea can be generalized to other control system protocols as well.

Since SCADA networks are built of resource-constrained embedded systems, the IDS using the middleware-level detection has the advantage of directly accessing message signatures and parameter values without decoding the raw network packets. But there is a tradeoff in the risk involved in handling embedded responses to attacks.

Both model-based intrusion detection and middleware-level intrusion detection build models to specify the normal behavior of the network traffic and compare the SCADA traffic against these models to detect potential anomalous behavior. Model-based detection is an important complement to signature-based approaches.

The specification-based IDS has an inviting advantage to SCADA systems and networked control systems in general.

4.2.2 Weakness

Intrusion detection research for SCADA systems to date has been quite limited, with the three most prominent and critical deficiencies being:

• The lack of a well-considered threat model;

• The absence of addressing false alarm and false negative (mis-detection) rates; and

• The need to empirically ground the development of IDS mechanisms in the realities of how such systems operate in practice, including the diversity of traffic they manifest and the need to tailor IDS operation to different SCADA environments.

From the above evaluation of the current IDSs for SCADA systems, we can see that the current bottleneck problems faced by research and design henceforth implementation and deployment of

Table 5. Comparison of SCADA's specific deeds addressed in each proposed system

Name of System	Security Properties			Inter. oppp	Use of SCADA Components					Interaction between
	Time-liness	Availability			Domain/ Industry	HW	SW	communication		Cyber – Physical
		Self Security	Type Response					hardware	protocol	
PVAEB [67]		low	passive	N/A	electrical power			simulated IED	IEC 61850 DNP3	yes
IBM NADS [49]		low	passive	yes					Modbus	
SRI Modbus [13]		medium	passive	yes	N/A				Modbus	
WFBNI [87]		low	passive	N/A	water					yes
SHARP [19]		high	active	yes	N/A					
IDEM [57]		low	passive	yes	electrical power	yes				
AA KRSPRT [89]		low	passive	yes	N/A				SNMP	
EMISDS [52]	yes	low	passive	N/A	N/A					
MAACUFE [80]		N/A	active	N/A	N/A		yes			

IDS for SCADA are the scarcity in access to operational SCADA system (network traffic) traces and the lack of prudent yet novel threat models, or attack scenarios.

Barely any of these systems has a performance evaluation on the false alarms that it generates. However, given the availability demand of SCADA systems, we believe this is an issue that must be addressed well before IDS can be implemented and deployed in SCADA systems at a large scale.

Before presenting our approach, we give an overall review of its foundation – hypothesis testing, sequential analysis and detection, with a simplified taxonomy.

5 BACKGROUND ON HYPOTHESIS TESTING

Let $\mathfrak{M}$ $\mathfrak{M}$ be the set of probability measures on the real line $\mathbb{R}$ and let P_0, P_1 be two distinct elements of $\mathfrak{M}$, having densities p_0, p_1 with respect to some measure ω. Denote $\left\{z_k\right\}_0^m$ sequence of *identically independently distributed* (iid) observations of a random variable Z with distribution D. The testing problem is hypotheses

$$\begin{cases} H_0 & : \quad D = P_0 \\ H_1 & : \quad D = P_1 \end{cases} \tag{1}$$

Let p_{θ_i}, dependent on a parameter θ, be the respective densities of p_i for $i = 0,1$ with respect to some dominating measure ω.

To discriminate between the two we may either use the likelihood ratio test provided by the Neyman-Pearson lemmma, or Wald's sequential probability ratio test. Recall that *log-likelihood ratio* is defined as

$$\begin{cases} s(\theta, z, i) & = & \log \dfrac{p_{\theta_1}(z)}{p_{\theta_0}(z)} \\ S_n & = & \displaystyle\sum_{i=1}^{n} s(\theta, z, i) & = & \displaystyle\sum_{i=1}^{n} \log \dfrac{p_{\theta_1}(z_i)}{p_{\theta_0}(z_i)} \end{cases} \tag{2}$$

5.1 Fixed Sample Size Test

For the *Neyman-Pearson* test, the sample size is fixed and we reject hypothesis H_0 if S_n is too large.

5.2 Sequential Probability Ratio Testing

Wald's *Sequential Hypothesis Testing* (SHT), or the *Sequential Probability Ratio Testing*

(SPRT) scheme in 1947 not only enjoys the benefits of relatively smaller sampling size than that of single sampling schemes in the detection of large changes, but also retains a desirable expected sampling size before action is taken when dealing with small changes in magnitude (Page, 1954).

The task of SHT becomes

$$
\begin{cases}
S_0 & = & 0 \\
S_{k+1} & = & \log \dfrac{p_1(Z_k)}{p_0(Z_k)} + S(k) \quad k \geq 1 \\
N & = & inf\left\{ n \geq 1 : S_n \notin [L, U] \right\}
\end{cases}
\tag{3}
$$

The SHT decision rule follows,

$$
d_N = \begin{cases} H_1 & if & S_N \geq U \\ H_0 & if & S_N \leq L \end{cases}
\tag{4}
$$

where $L \approx \ln \dfrac{F_N}{1 - F_A}$ and $U \approx \ln \dfrac{1 - F_N}{F_A}$ with F_A being the predefined false alarm rate and F_N the predefined *false negative rate* or the missed detection rate upon user's choice and tuning.

Under the assumptions that hypothesis H_0 is of the distribution P_0 with a probability function p_0 and H_1 of P_1 and p_1. Pick 2 numbers a, b with $a < 0 < b$ and define the decisive sample number (the stopping rule or the detection rule)

$$
N = inf\left\{ n \geq 1 : S_n \leq a \, or \, S_n \geq b \right\}
\tag{5}
$$

with $inf \, 0 \neq \infty$

Wald (1947) proved that N is almost surely finite under both P_0 and P_1. The testing procedure is to stop at stage N and reject H_0 if $S_n \geq b$ and accept H_0 if $S_n \leq a$ (hence reject H_1). We denote this test $SPRT(a, b, P_0, P_1)$. The average sample numbers are $\mathbb{E}_j, j = 0,1$, where $\mathbb{E}_j$ denotes expectation under P_j. The error probabil-

ities are $\alpha = P_0 \, (S_n \geq b)$ and $\beta = P_1 \, (S_n \leq a)$. The *SPRT* is optimum in the following sense. Consider any other testing procedure with corresponding elements $\alpha', \beta', \mathbb{E}_0, \mathbb{E}_1$ (Lehmann & Romano, 2005), it holds that

$$
\begin{cases} \alpha' & \leq & \alpha \\ \beta' & \leq & \beta \end{cases} \Rightarrow \begin{cases} \mathbb{E}_0[N] & \leq & \mathbb{E}_0[N'] \\ \mathbb{E}_1[N] & \leq & \mathbb{E}_1[N'] \end{cases}
\tag{6}
$$

SPRT's major strength lies in two-fold that it's a recursive online scheme and optimal in sample size for both hypothesis with theoretical proof on performance bounds. However, it assumes θ_1, the distribution after change is known; while in reality, especially for the goal of this chapter, it is not.

5.2.1 Sequential Detection

Closely related to sequential testing theory is the theory of sequential change-point detection. Page (1954) and Shiryaev (1963) modified Wald's SPRT and developed the cumulative sum (CUSUM) (Page, 1958) and the Shiryaev-Roberts charts (Tsang & Kwong, 2005) respectively to improve the sensitivity of the Shewhart charts (1931). The goal of optimality in the *Shiryaev-Roberts-Pollak* (SRP) sense is to minimize the *worst-case average delay* subject to the upper bound of a false alarm whereas in *Lorden's* sense is to minimize the upper bound of the worst case delay subject the upper bound of a false alarm (Lorden, 1971).

The CUSUM (Basseville & Nikiforov, 1993; Montgomery, 2009) test is one of the most successful algorithms of sequential change detection. The CUSUM procedure developed in 1954 calculates the cumulative sum of samples from a process X_n with weights ω_n in the following fashion,

$$\begin{cases} S_0 &= 0 \\ S_{n+1} &= \max(0, S_n + X_n - \omega_n) \end{cases}$$

The stopping rule or the detection rule is that: when the value of S exceeds a certain threshold value, a change in value has been found[6].

Widespread applications and theory development in quality control (Lucas & Croser, 1982; Montgomery, 2009; Ryan, 2011), fault detection (Chiang, Russel, & Braatz, 2001; Willis, 2011), surveillance (Hutwagner et al., 1997; Jiang et al., 2011), anomaly detection (Siris & Papaglou, 2006; Mandjes & Zuraniewski, 2011) are stemmed from CUSUM and/or CUSUM alike procedures. Some of the methods proposed over the years were originally ad hoc procedures and were later proven to possess optimality properties including both Wald's SPRT and Page's CUSUM. Others remain popular though sub-optimal such as Shewhart (1931) and *Exponentially-Weighted Moving Average* (EWMA) (Roberts, 1959) control charts.

The overall comparison as a simplified taxonomy is summarized in Table 6.

For a more detailed review on sequential analysis or sequential change-point detection involving multivariate and dependent observations, interested readers please refer to (Lai, 2001) and (Basseville & Nikiforov, 1993), respectively.

6 PROBLEM STATEMENT

The uncertainties in the SCADA system including its components and the environment where it situates (Zhu, Joseph, & Sastry, 2011), can be benign component faults or malicious attacks and may skew the sensor measurements and thus the estimation and control command results. We need more than simply discard physical readings that are obviously "out of pre-specified boundaries" such as beyond a maximum allowed range but dynamically identify those stealthy ones which

gradually affect what PLCs and/or other controllers would process by adding more intelligence to the controller. Our way to achieve so is through the investigation of those outliers.

6.1 Why Outliers

What motivates us to address the issue of outlier-detection and -mitigation is multifaceted. First, outliers are often clear indications of the environmental noise level and potentially faults in sensors or malicious attacks in the system (Zhu & Sastry, 2011). As for their impact on the applications, in general the performance of linear least squares estimates, a fundamental building block of controllers' functionalities, is prone to noise and may degrade remarkably when plant or observation disturbances are non-Gaussian, particularly when the non-Gaussianness, i.e., outliers, are of a heavy-tailed variety giving rise to occasional very large values (Tukey, 1960; Huber, 1968; Huber, 1972). In light of its prevalent and broad usage among many decision making algorithms in engineering fields and in SCADA systems particularly, we are mostly interested in the skewing impact of outliers (Mehra, 1970) having on the Kalman filter, the optimal linear least square error estimator. The state estimation error can grow without bound because the estimate is a linear function of the observation noise. Such impact potentially leads to divergence (Fitzgerald, 1971) and instability (Sangsuk-Iam & Bullock, 1990) and destabilize the whole controller.

However, we need to point out that the online detection of outliers is difficult: moments-based procedures themselves are inherently *not* robust to outliers (Ben-Gal, 2005; Huber & Ronchetti, 2009). Additionally, that the adversaries have control over inputs further complicates the detection task. Especially in light of attacks similar to Stuxnet, which causes the operation and behavior of motors deviate from its nominal range, the approach that we advocate here would monitor the

Table 6. A simplified taxonomy/comparison of sequential analysis/ change point detection methods

Work Name	Observation Sequence	Statistical Parameter Knowledge			Problem Formulation	Optimality Criteria	Test Statistics	Key Point
		Occurrence Time	Q_0	Q_1				
Page '54 [58]	iid	unknown	known	known	minimax	Lorden	maximum likelihood	recursive CUSUM
Shiryaev '63 [74]	iid	geometric distribution	known	known	Bayesian	SRP		
Roberts '66 [66]	iid	unknown	known	known	Bayesian	SRP		
Lorden '71 [39] GLR	iid	unknown		unknown	minimax	Lorden	log-likelihood	one-sided SPRT
Wilsky-Jones '76 [86] Window-limited GLR		unknown	known	known			general likelihood	limited-window
Pollak '85 [62]	iid	unknown	known	known	Bayesian	SRP		almost minimax
Moustakides '86 [50]	iid	unknown	known	unknown	minimax	Lorden		
Lai '98 [35] Reduced-window GLR	dependent	unknown	known	known		change-of-measure		reduced window
Robust-GLR	dependent	unknown	known	unknown		change-of-measure		robust

payload and curtail such effect should it happen. Let's recap estimation and identification in state-space models and the statistical approach based on the Kalman filter and likelihood techniques.

6.2 A General State Space Model Setting

Let positive integer $k = 0, 1, \ldots$ denotes discrete time, then a stochastic state-space model in discrete time has the following form state:

$$x_{k+1} = F_k x_k + G_k u_k + w_k \tag{7}$$

observation:

$$y_k = H_k x_k + J_k u_k + v_k \tag{8}$$

where $x_k \in \mathbf{R}^n$ is the (hidden) internal state vector, $u_k \in \mathbf{R}^r$ is the input vector, $y_k \in \mathbf{R}^m$ is the output i.e. observation (measurement) vector. $w_k \in \mathbf{R}^r$, the process (plant) (7) noise vector, is a white Gaussian noise sequence with zero mean and covariance matrix $Q_k > 0$. $v_k \in \mathbf{R}^m$, the observation (measurement) (8) noise vector, is a white Gaussian noise sequence with zero mean and covariance matrix $R_k > 0$.

$\{F_k\}$, the state transition matrix, $\{H_k\}$, the observation matrix, $\{G_k\}$, and $\{J_k\}$, the control matrices are known sequences of matrices with appropriate dimensions. The initial system state vector x_0 is Gaussian with zero mean and covariance matrix P_0. We assume that the initial state x_0 and the two noise sequences w_k, v_k are mutually independent. We will use observation and measurement interchangeably.

In summary, (7) is a recursive state model of the linear dynamical process (plant), and (8), a linear observation model of the system. Note such a model (7)-(8) is a Markov model, namely the pair $(X_{k+1}; Y_k)$ is a Markov process.

6.3 Kalman Filter

The Kalman filter provides one particular estimate of the state x_k of the system (7)-(8). It's a *minimum variance* estimate of the state, i.e. the conditional mean[7] of x_k given the past observations $\{7\ 7; y_{k-2}; y_{k-1}\}$. We denote this *one-step ahead prediction* as $\hat{x}_{k+1|k}$. Formally, let vectors $\boldsymbol{y_k} = \{y_0, \ldots, y_k\}$, $\boldsymbol{u_k} = \{u_0, \ldots, u_k\}$ and denote $\mathbb{E}$ as the mean, we define: the *estimated state* $\hat{x}_{k|k} \triangleq \mathbb{E}[x_k \mid \boldsymbol{y_k}, \boldsymbol{u_k}]$, the *estimation error cova-*

riance matrix $P_{k|k} \triangleq \mathbb{E}[(x_k - \hat{x}_{k|k})(x_k - \hat{x}_{k|k})^T \mid \boldsymbol{y_k}, \boldsymbol{u_k}]$, the predicated state $\hat{x}_{k+1|k} \triangleq \mathbb{E}[x_{k+1} \mid \boldsymbol{y_k}, \boldsymbol{u_k}]$, the predication error covariance matrix $P_{k+1|k} \triangleq \mathbb{E}[(x_{k+1} - \hat{x}_{k+1|k})(x_{k+1} - \hat{x}_{k+1|k})^T \mid \boldsymbol{y_k}, \boldsymbol{u_k}]$, and the predicated observation $\hat{y}_{k|k} \triangleq \mathbb{E}[y_k \mid \boldsymbol{y_k}, \boldsymbol{u_k}]$.

As shown in Figure 2, the overall flow diagram of the Kalman Filter, it's an on-line recursive algorithm. To illustrate its recursion, we decompose its procedure into two phases, namely the *predication phase* and *measurement update phase*.

Figure 3 illustrates the recursive procedure of the Kalman filter, noting at each time step, only current and previous step are involved. That is to say no batch operation is required. This is precisely what makes the Kalam filter an *online* algorithm.

6.4 Outliers' Distribution Model

We shall point out that employing a outliers' distribution model only gives us a somewhat plausible and tractable model for generating outliers (Xu, Tomsovic, & Bose, 2005) and for illustrating the impact of outliers on estimation performance. That is not to say that our detection scheme is dependent on the outliers' distributions, otherwise it is not robust nor effective.

There are several types *heavy-tailed* or alternatively referred to as *fat-tailed* distributions[8] in wide use (Martin & Thompson, 1982). Alternatively, the *contaminated normal distributions* is one specific instance of the more generic mixture distribution model for outliers (Hadi, Imon, & Werner, 2009) which will suffice for purposes of our current exposition. To be more specific, the outliers are generated through the contaminated-normal distribution with *degenerate* central component (Martin & Thompson, 1982),

$$CN(t; \gamma, \sigma^2) = (1 - \gamma) N(t; 0, 0) + \gamma N(t; \gamma, \sigma^2)) \tag{9}$$

That is to say the process x_t is observed perfectly about $100(1 - \gamma)$ percent of the time and is corrupted by outliers about 100γ percent of the time, where usually $0.01 \leq \gamma \leq 0.25$.

6.5 Further Property Assumptions

Furthermore, for some integer d, let $(\boldsymbol{R}^d, \boldsymbol{B}, \lambda)$ be a measure space, where $\boldsymbol{R}$ is the real line, $\boldsymbol{B}$ the Borel σ-algebra, and λ the Lebesgue measure. Let $\boldsymbol{F}$ be a zero-mean probability measure on $(\boldsymbol{R}^d, \boldsymbol{B})$ such that $\boldsymbol{F}$ is absolutely continuous with respect to λ and admits the density f in accordance with Radon-Nikodym theorem. We have a sequence of identically *iid* observations $\left\{z_k\right\}_0^m$ of a random variable Z with a probability density $p_\theta(Z)$ that is dependent on one *scalar* parameter only. The parameter $\theta = \theta_0$ before an *unknown change time* ν and $\theta = \theta_1$ after ν. Note that change time ν is *unknown*. We either consider ν as a nonrandom unknown value or a random unknown value with unknown distribution. In other words, we deal with a nonparametric approach as far as this change time ν is concerned. In practice, either it is very difficult to have *a priori* information about the distribution of the change times, or this distribution is nonstationary (i.e. it doesn't have an invariant mean nor variance). This is particularly meaningful for our problem setting, given that we have no *a priori* knowledge of when the intrusion thus outliers or anomalies would occur at all. It's also the reason why certain basic tools can't directly suit our problem.

Our *security model* is that the SCADA center itself is secure and so are the core programs. We assume the attack is session based, should it arise over the network.

By "*resilient*", we stress the importance of the flexibility and parsimoniousness of the overall strategy. Without incurring too large overhead, it shall maintain the system's optimal performance under nominal conditions while strive for near

Figure 2. The Kalman filter flow chart

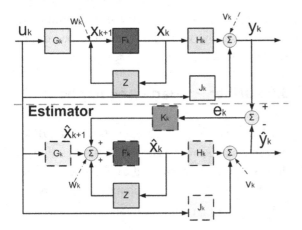

optimal performance should atypical situations arise without being unduly affected by spurious observations.

6.6 Meaningful Metrics for Recursive Robust Estimation

It's only appropriate to bring up the issue of the robustness of estimation schemes when we address outliers. Conceptually, the definition of robustness[9] we use here stipulates that small changes from an assumed nominal model would only introduce small changes in estimate, according to both Tukey (1960) and Huber (1974). Furthermore, *robust-resistant*, a purely data-oriented notion defined by Tukey (1977), refers that an estimate is called resistant if changing a small fraction of the data by large amounts results in little change to the estimate, i.e. the capability against gross error and outliers.

Formulation wise, while the minimax approach is pessimistic, it provides an optimum lower bound on performance. Let: $\mathfrak{T}$ be a class of estimates, $\mathfrak{F}$ a class of distributions, and $V(T, F)$ the asymptotic variance of $T \in \mathfrak{T}$ when the distribution is $F \in \mathfrak{F}$. Then the minimax robust estimate T_0 and its associated *least favorable distribution* F_0 satisfy

$$\min_{T \in \mathfrak{T}} \max_{F \in \mathfrak{F}} V(T, F) = V(T_0, F_0) = \min_{F \in \mathfrak{F}} \max_{T \in \mathfrak{T}} V(T, F) \qquad (10)$$

Naturally, this can be viewed as a game in which we choose $T \in \mathfrak{T}$, nature chooses $F \in \mathfrak{F}$ and $V(T, F)$ is the payoff. This game has a saddle point pair (T_0, F_0) if T_0 and F_0 satisfy the above (10). Furthermore, for multivariate, dependent Markovian (state space model) without process noises, analytically the *asymptotic variance* is still a good choice of performance measure (Mitter & Schick, 1993). The least favorable distribution is the member of F leading to the largest asymptotic variance[10] (or the Fisher Information). However, in the presence of process noises, the asymptotic variance no longer holds as a good performance measure (Schick & Mitter, 1994).

Plus, in this work, the goal is to achieve optimally estimating and tracking the state of stochastic time-variant linear dynamic system rather than obtaining the minimum asymptotic estimation error. Thus approximations of a conditional mean estimator, which is known for its unbiasedness and minimum error variance (Anderson & Moore, 1979), are targeted (Schick & Mitter, 1994).

6.7 Sequential Detection Performance Measure

6.7.1 False Alarm Constraints

Often the methodology of optimal change-point detection pursues stopping rules that achieve the best balance of the mean detection delay and the rate of false alarms or minimize the mean delay under a fixed false alarm probability (Baron & Tartakovsky, 2006). In order to establish a sound sequential detection performance measure, we must first lay out the associated false alarm probability constraints that the asymptotic lower bound for the detection delay is subject to.

Figure 3. The recursive operation of the Kalman Filter: a combination of the high-level diagram in Figure 2 and the formulations on section 6.3

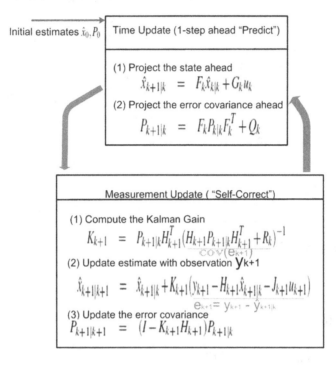

$$\mathbb{E}^{\nu}(T-v)_{1\{T\geq v\}} = \mathbb{E}^{\nu}(T-\nu)^{+} \qquad (11)$$

Accordingly, three related false alarm probability constraints in the ascendant order of stringency are listed as the following:

For *iid* observations, due to Shiryaev (1963), the *Bayesian* view concerns the *mean delay to detection* under the average false alarm

$$P\big(T<v\big) = \sum\nolimits_{k=1}^{\infty} \pi_{a}(k) P_{0}(T<k) \leq \alpha \qquad (12)$$

where π_{α} is *a priori* distribution of the change time v.

Whereas the (*Average Run Length*) *ARL* (Page, 1954) to false alarm constraint in a minimax formulation

$$\mathbb{E}_{0}\big[T\big] \geq \gamma \geq 1 \qquad (13)$$

is the worst case in Lorden's sense (1971), and is no smaller than a given number $\gamma > 1$ when the quality parameter remains fixed θ. The objective is to find the stopping rule that minimizes the worst case delay subject to an upper bound on the false alarm rate.

For non-independent observations, Lai (1998) proposed a *change-of-measure* argument, the most stringent one among the three, to guarantee a lower bound on the *window-limited* stopping time, or the detection delay:

$$sup_{v\geq 1} P_{0}\big(v\leq T<v+m_{\alpha}\big) \leq \alpha,$$

where

$$\liminf \frac{m_{\alpha}}{\log\alpha} > I^{-1} \quad but$$

$$\log m_\alpha = o\left(\log \alpha\right) as \, \alpha \to 0 \qquad (14)$$

The reason we choose the most stringent false alarm constraint, namely Lai's *change-of-measure* argument (14) lies in that it meets our desire to have as low as possible false alarm while achieving an asymptotic lower bound for the detection delay.

Correspondingly, as $\alpha \to 0$ for a positive integer I, the asymptotic lower bound for the detection delay is

$$\mathbb{E}^{\nu}\left(T - \nu\right)^+ \geq \left\{ \frac{P_0\left(T \geq v\right)}{I} + o\left(1\right) \right\} \left| \log \alpha \right|$$
$$uniformly \, in \, v \geq 1 \qquad (15)$$

7 RESILIENT ESTIMATION

Contaminated Observations with additive outliers
Suppose at an *unknown* time ν, the sensor measurement (observation) y_k (8) is subject to some *additive outliers* or *anomalies*, formally

$$\tilde{y}_k = y_k + y_{ao_k} 1\{k \geq \nu\} \qquad (16)$$

$$= H_k x_k + J_k u_k + \tilde{v}_k \qquad (17)$$

$$= H_k x_k + J_k u_k + v_k + y_{ao_k} 1\{k \geq v\} \qquad (18)$$

where $\tilde{y}_k$ is the observed data and the y_{ao_k} are the additive outliers $1\{k \geq \nu\}$, either in *isolation* or in *cluster*, $1\{k \geq \nu\}$ is a compact notion of an indicator function indicating the occurrence of the outliers (anomalies),

$$1 = \begin{cases} 1 & k \geq v \\ 0 & k < v \end{cases} \qquad (19)$$

Theorem 1.: A robust state estimate suffices above conditions is optimal in the min-max sense, i.e. having minimum variance over the least favorable contaminating distributions.

It can take the following form with $\breve{x}_{k|k} \triangleq \mathbb{E}[\tilde{x}_k \mid \tilde{y}_k]$, *compared to the original Kalman filter.*

$$\tilde{x}_{k+1|k} = F_{k+1} \tilde{x}_{k|k} \qquad (20)$$

$$\tilde{P}_{k+1|k} = F_{k+1} \tilde{P}_{k|k} F_{k+1}^T + Q_{k+1} \qquad (21)$$

$$\tilde{K}_{k+1} = \tilde{P}_{k+1|k} H_{k+1}^T \tilde{\sum}_{k+1}^{-1} \qquad (22)$$

$$\tilde{x}_{k+1|k+1} = \tilde{x}_{k+1|k} + \tilde{K}_{k+1}$$
$$\left(\tilde{y}_{k+1} - H_{k+1} \tilde{x}_{k+1|k} - J_{k+1} u_{k+1} \right) \qquad (23)$$

$$\tilde{P}_{k+1|k+1} = \left(I - \tilde{K}_{k+1} H_{k+1} \right) \tilde{P}_{k+1|k} \qquad (24)$$

with the robustified (censored) covariance matrix of the innovation (residual) becoming,

$$\tilde{\sum}_k = H_k \tilde{P}_{k|k-1} H_k^T + R_k^{\frac{1}{2}} W_k R_k^{\frac{1}{2}} \qquad (25)$$

where

$$W_k = diag\{w_{1k}, \cdots, w_{mk}\}$$

and $w_{1k}, \cdots, w_{mk}$ would be defined later in the proof.

Proof: We first show the result through construction. It is straightforward that the state estimator $\breve{x}_{k|k}$ corresponding to $\hat{x}_{k|k} = \mathbb{E}[x_k \mid y_k, u_k]$ of the original Kalman filter can be obtained by minimizing

$$\breve{x}_{k+1|k+1} =$$

$$argmin\left\{\left(\breve{x}_{k+1|k} - x_{k+1}\right)^T \left(P_{k+1|k}\right)^{-1} \left(\breve{x}_{k+1|k} - x_{k+1}\right)\right.$$

$$+ \left(\tilde{y}_{k+1} - H_{k+1}x_{k+1} - J_{k+1}u_{k+1}\right)^T R_k^{-1}$$

$$\left.\times(\tilde{y}_{k+1} - H_{k+1}x_{k+1} - J_{k+1}u_{k+1})\right\} \qquad (27)$$

with respect to $x_{k+1} \in R^n$, or equivalently

$$\breve{x}_{k|k} = \mathrm{argmin}\left\{\begin{array}{l}\sum_{i-1}^{n}\left(p_{ik} - a_{ik}x_k\right)^2 \\ +\sum_{j-1}^{m}\left(s_{jk} - b_{jk}x_k - q_{jk}\right)^2\end{array}\right\}$$
$$(28)$$

where

$$p_k = \left(P_{k|k-1}\right)^{-\frac{1}{2}}\breve{x}_{k|k-1}, s_k = \left(R_k\right)^{-\frac{1}{2}}\tilde{y}_k, q_k$$

$$= \left(R_k\right)^{-\frac{1}{2}}J_ku_k, a_k = \left(P_{k|k-1}\right)^{-\frac{1}{2}}, b_k$$

$$= \left(R_k\right)^{-\frac{1}{2}}H_k$$

so that p_{ik}, s_{ik} and q_{jk} are the i-th component of the vectors $p_k \in R^{n\times1}$, $s_k \in R^{n\times1}$ and $q_k \in R^{n\times1}$ correspondingly; $a_{ik} \in R^{1\times n}$ and $b_{ik} \in R^{1\times n}$ are the i-row vector of the matrix $a_k \in R^{n\times n}$ and $b_k \in R^{n\times n}$ correspondingly. In the case of M-estimation, the least squares solution is replaced by

$$\breve{x}_{k|k} = \mathrm{argmin}\left\{\begin{array}{l}\sum_{i=1}^{n}\left(p_{ik} - a_{ik}x_k\right)^2 \\ +\sum_{j-1}^{m}\acute{A}_j\left(s_{jk} - b_{jk}x_k - q_{jk}\right)^2\end{array}\right\}$$
$$(29)$$

where the $\acute{A}_j$ are suitable score functions with derivatives, i.e. influence function Ψ_j, or *psi*-function used in robust statistics. One of Huber's psi-function is

$$\Psi_H\left(Z\right) = \left\{\begin{array}{ll} Z & for \quad |Z| \le s \\ s\,sgn(Z) & for \quad |Z| > s \end{array}\right. \qquad (30)$$

is often used[11]. It gives robust estimates of location which are optimal in the min-max sense, having minimum variance over the least favorable contaminating distributions.

The normal equations for $\breve{x}_{k|k}$ corresponding to (29) have the form

$$\sum_{i=1}^{n}a_{ik}^T\left(p_{ik} - a_{ik}\breve{x}_{k|k}\right)$$
$$+\sum_{j=1}^{m}b_{jk}^T\Psi_j\left(s_{jk} - b_{jk}\breve{x}_{k|k} - q_{jk}\right) \qquad (31)$$

and can be solved explicitly only in some special cases. This is quite pragmatic as well; sensors are normally set with bounded values in practice.

Alternatively, one can use the approximated normal equations if we approximate[12],

$\breve{x}_{k|k}$ by $\breve{x}_{k|k-1}$ when using the weight function w_{jk} as the following:

$$\sum_{i=1}^{n}a_{ik}^T\left(p_{ik} - a_{ik}\breve{x}_{k|k}\right)$$
$$+\sum_{j=1}^{m}w_{jk}b_{jk}^T\left(s_{jk} - b_{jk}\breve{x}_{k|k} - q_{jk}\right) \qquad (32)$$

where the weight functions $w_{jk}, j = 1, \cdots, m$ are

$$w_{jk} = \frac{\Psi_j\left(s_{jk} - b_{jk}\breve{x}_{k|k} - q_{jk}\right)}{s_{jk} - b_{jk}\breve{x}_{k|k} - q_{jk}} \qquad (33)$$

Using (32) and some algebra, we obtain robustified (censored) covariance matrix of the innovation (residual),

$$\sum_{k}^{\sim} = H_k\tilde{P}_{k|k-1}H_k^T + R_k^{\frac{1}{2}}W_kR_k^{\frac{1}{2}} \qquad (34)$$

where $W_k = diag\{w_{1k}, \cdots, w_{mk}\}$.

8 ROBUST OUTLIER DETECTION

The overall procedure is shown as in Figure 4.

8.1 System Model with Outliers Contaminated Observations

Following the definition of the contaminated measurement $\tilde{y}_k$ (16-19), the state $\tilde{x}_k$, the estimate $\tilde{x}_{k|k}$, and the output residual $\tilde{e}_k$ of the Kalman filter upon the outliers occurred at time v can be expressed in the relations of their nominal counterparts, as

$$
\begin{aligned}
\breve{x}_{k|k} &= \hat{x}_{k|k} + \beta\left(k, v\right) y_{ao} \\
\tilde{e}_k &= e_k + \rho(k, v) y_{ao}
\end{aligned}
\tag{35}
$$

where the terms $\beta\left(k, v\right)$, $\rho(k, v)$ would be defined later.

Conditioned on the past outputs y_k and input signals u_k, the innovation e_k has the *conditional mean* $\mathbb{E}[e_k]$. Let's denote $\mu_k = \mathbb{E}[e_k]$, then

$$
\mu_k = \mathbb{E}[e_k] = \begin{cases} \rho(k, v) y_{ao_k} & k \geq v \\ 0 & k < v \end{cases}
\tag{36}
$$

where v, y_{ao} are unknown. The $\rho\left(k, t\right)$ are matrices that can be recursively evaluated after initialization $\rho\left(t, t\right) = 0, \beta\left(t - 1, t\right) = 0$,

$$
\beta(k, t) = F_{k-1}\beta\left(t - 1, k\right) + K_k\rho\left(k, t\right)
\tag{37}
$$

$$
\rho(k + 1, t) = -H_{t+1}F_k\beta\left(k, t\right) + I
\tag{38}
$$

where $\beta(k, t)$ and $\rho\left(k, t\right)$ are the difference of the estimate $\tilde{x}_{k|k}$, residual $\tilde{e}_k$ under outliers, comparing with their nominal counterparts as stated in

(35), to be evaluated recursively in parallel for $k \geq t$ and for every fixed t, one for each t within a moving window $t \in \{n - m, \cdots, n - m'\}$.

Meanwhile, the covariance matrix of the innovation is

$$
V_k = \mathbb{E}\left[\left(e_k - \mathbb{E}\left[e_k\right]\right)\left(e_k - \mathbb{E}\left[e_k\right]\right)^T\right]
\tag{39}
$$

$$
= \begin{cases} \tilde{\sum}_{k \geq v} \\ \sum_{k < v} \end{cases}
\tag{40}
$$

$$
= \tilde{\sum} k
\tag{41}
$$

It's easy to verify the design purpose, for $k < v$ weight functions $w_{jk} = 1$, $\forall j \in [1, m]$ thus

$$
\tilde{\sum}_k = \sum_k.
$$

8.2 Robust Sequential Probability Ratio Tests

According to Huber (1965), a statistical procedure is called robust if its performance is insensitive to small deviations of the idealized theoretical model. In terms of the robustness of a test, it shall withstand small arbitrary departures from both the null hypothesis (*robustness of validity*) and the specified alternatives (*robustness of efficiency*) (Huber & Ronchetti, 2009). When encountering deviation, the classical probability ratio test is *not* robust in the following sense: a single outlying data point thus deviating factor $p_1(x_j) / p_0(x_j)$ equal (or almost equal) to 0 or ∞ may unduly impact the test statistic $T\left(x\right) = \prod_1^n p_1(x_j) / p_0(x_j)$ therefore may totally skew the final hypothesis or probability test outcome. By censoring the single factors at some fixed numbers $c' < c''$ for sequential probability ratio test, one can replace the test statistic by:

$$T'(x) = \prod_1^n \pi(x_j)$$

where

$$\pi(x_j) = max\{c', min\{c'', p_1(x_j) / p_0(x_j) \}\}.$$

Note that we have precisely done so in the stage of resilient estimation that one of the key components of our test statistics, the covariance matrix of the innovation (residual), $\tilde{\Sigma}_k$ (34) or V (39), has been "censored".

8.2.1 Detection Rules

Without assuming any *a priori* knowledge of parameter η, the RGLR rule maximizes the log likelihood ratio over a window of inputs and decides the time to raise an alarm according to a certain rule, which we will state without formally proving as certain steps have showed by Huber (1965) and Quang (1985) in a sequential testing setting.

Theorem 2: The following stopping rule is optimal and robust

$$N_G = inf \{n : \max_{n-M \le t \le n-M'} sup_\eta \sum_{i=k}^n \log$$

$$[\frac{f\left(\tilde{\Sigma}_i^{-1/2}\left(e_i - \rho(i,t)\eta\right)\right)}{f\left(\tilde{\Sigma}_i^{-1/2} e_i\right)}] \ge c_\lambda\}$$

$$= inf\{n : \max_{n-M \le t \le n-M'}\left(\sum_{i=k}^n \rho^T(i,t)\tilde{\Sigma}_i^{-1} e_i\right)^T$$

$$(\sum_{i=k}^n \rho^T(i,t)\tilde{\Sigma}_i^{-1} \rho(i,t))^{-1}$$

$$\cdot(\sum_{i=k}^n \rho^T(i,t)\tilde{\Sigma}_i^{-1} e_i) / 2 \ge c_\lambda\} \qquad (42)$$

where $f(y) = e^{\frac{-\|y\|^2}{2}} / (2\pi)^{\xi/2}$ denotes the ξ dimensional normal density, $\xi = dim(\eta)$, and m'+1 $\ge \xi$ so that the matrix inversions in (42) are valid.

In essence, we are looking at an *optimal stopping time problem*: neither to stop too early hence a false alarm nor to stop too late hence missing a real anomalous event. Huber (1965) showed that in the neighborhoods of the idealized underlying distributions, which is the least favorable situation for both Type I (false alarm) and Type II (miss detection) error probabilities, the so called *censored probability ratio test* is most robust in a well-defined minimax sense.

In light that our test statistic has undergone the censoring processing at the robustified estimation stage, so our concerns translate into whether the corresponding sequential testing still are *least favorable* for errors.

Quang (1985) further proved that with the limiting maximum error probabilities being less than 1/2, such sequential test is also *least favorable* for *Average Sample Number* (ASN) and asymptotically minimax with respect to expected sample sizes.

8.3 Threshold and Window Size Choice

Note that (38) computes $\rho(t,k)$ recursively over each window. How to optimally choose $M, \tilde{M}$ and c_λ in general is a difficult problem (Basseville & Nikiforov, 1993) for online practices particularly due to the coupling effect between the threshold and window size on the asymptotical performance of the detection rule. But for off-line operations, the choice of window size is less demanding as all the data set is available, it's only a matter of computation time.

Figure 4. Block diagram of robust outlier detection and resilient estimation

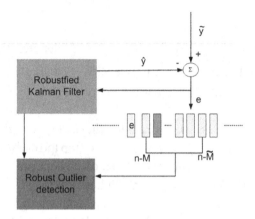

9 EXPERIMENTS AND EVALUATION

Currently, we are using synthetic data to conduct experiments. We model the discrete dynamics and two-dimensional measurement of the tracked object as

$$
\begin{cases}
x_{t+1} &=& A^e x_t + w_t \\
y_{i,t} &=& C_i x_t + v_{i,t}
\end{cases}
\tag{43}
$$

where w and v are white Gaussian noises with zero mean and covariance $Q^e = diag$

$(0.15^2, 0.15^2, 0.15^2, 0.15^2)$ and $R_i = R = diag(0.15^2, 0.15^2)$, and $\delta = 0.5$ is the sampling period.

$$
A^e =
\begin{bmatrix}
1 & 0 & \delta & 0 \\
0 & 1 & 0 & \delta \\
0 & 0 & 1 & 0 \\
0 & 0 & 0 & 1
\end{bmatrix}
C_i = C
\begin{bmatrix}
1 & 0 \\
0 & 1 \\
0 & 0 \\
0 & 0
\end{bmatrix}^T
\tag{44}
$$

The threshold c in the rule N_W subject to the false alarm probability criterion $P_0(N_W \leq m)$ can be computed by using Monte Carlo computation of $P_0(N_W)$ together with the method of successive linear approximation combined with bisection search for iterative solution of the equation $P_0\left(N_W \leq m\right)$. With the window size M, we have

$M \sim \alpha \log \gamma$ where $E_0(T) \sim \gamma$, and $a > \dfrac{1}{I(\theta, 0)}$.

The importance sampling procedure for Monte Carlo computation of $P_0(N_W \leq m)$ involves the following steps as shown in Algorithm 1.

Algorithm 1. Importance sampling for P_0

Note that $E_0\left(T\right) \sim \dfrac{m}{P_0(T \leq m)} \sim \log \gamma$, thus threshold c in the rule N_W subject to the false alarm probability criterion $P_0(N_W \leq m / \gamma)$ can be computed by using the above procedure for Monte Carlo computation of $P_0(N_W)$ together with the method of successive linear approximation combined with bisection search for iterative solution of the equation $P_0(N_W \leq m / \gamma)$.

The reason of employing such examples lies in that:

- Its multidimensionality suffices the complexity purpose
- Its generic enough to illustrate the impact of outliers

9.1 Resilient Estimation Performance

As stated in Section 6.6, we evaluate the estimation performance in terms of the error variance. Figure 5 shows that our resilient estimation scheme performs better than the standard Kalman filter in the presence of the randomly injected outliers while maintaining the latter's optimal performance under nominal conditions.

Figure 5. Tracking error comparison: The lower panel shows the performance of the resilient estimation is identical to that of the standard Kalman filter under nominal condition while having much smaller errors when outliers occur at time T = 10, 30, 60

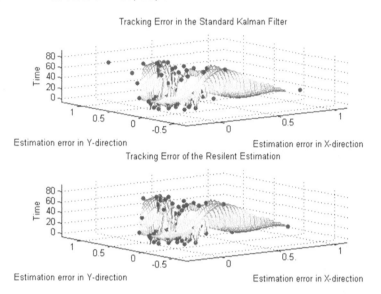

9.2 Robust Outlier Detection Performance

With randomly injected outliers and a false alarm constraint that is achieved through Monte Carlo simulation, our approach successfully detects multiple outliers as shown Figure 6.

9.3 Limitation and Discussion

As Pearson discussed in (2002), the MT-filter used in this work can be inapplicable when the covariance matrix on which the Kalman filter is based becomes singular. One way to deal with singular covariance matrices for the Kalman filter is to use *Singular Value Decomposition* (Xu, Tomsovic, & Bose, 2005).

10 CONCLUSION AND FUTURE DIRECTIONS

Given the increasing cyber attacks that are targeting SCAD systems, it's important to gear up for these threats and challenges. One aspect of

such security process is intrusion detection techniques that are specifically tailored for SCADA systems. In this self-contained chapter, to show the landscape, we enumerate and compare nine representative IDS that have been proposed in the research community to undertake this endeavor; to illustrate our design philosophy and the underlying approaches, we present our own ongoing project on this front. Generally speaking, on one hand, the lack of adequate false alarms analysis is prevalent in the IDS for SCADA systems that we've investigated. On the other hand, externally, the scarce access to the real operational SCADA system (network traffic) traces further compounds this issue for the research community[13]. However, we believe that SCADA systems' 27 × 7 availability demand entails a thorough study on false alarms generated by those IDS before they can be implemented and deployed in SCADA systems at a large scale. Another prominent shortcoming among the above mentioned IDS's is the deficiency in prudent yet novel threat models, or attack scenarios.

Ultimately, any viable technical solutions and research directions in securing SCADA systems

Figure 6. Detection of multiple outliers: a) detection of 3 outliers; b) detection of 4 outliers

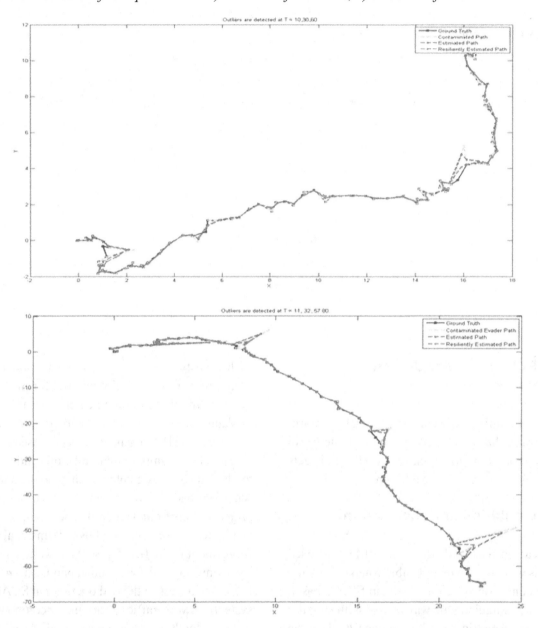

must lie in the conjunction of computer security, communication network and control engineering. However, the very large installed base of such systems means that in many instances we must for a long time to come rely on retrofitted security mechanisms, rather than having the option to design them in from scratch. This leads to a pressing need for deployable, robust, SCADA-specific IDS and resilient control strategies. As argued by Rakaczky (2005), the ease of deployment requires the intrusion detection/ prevention strategy to minimize the associated (personnel) overhead.

Towards the concept and realization of resilient control on top of intrusion detection, we start the first steps, namely resilient estimation, which stipulates to maintain the optimality of standard operations under the nominal conditions and to adapt abnormal situations through alleviating their impact. We address this issue as an optimal stopping problem, trying to find the balance between a low false alarm and a low miss-detection rate while arriving the decision as early as possible. We also present an online robust outlier detection scheme RGLRT that is optimal according to a stringent performance measure for SCADA systems and cyber-physical systems in general. Furthermore, this is accomplished without incurring large overhead. The strength of RGLRT lies in that it does not require *a priori* knowledge of the distributions of the attacks or benign anomalies, i.e., neither their mean nor their variance, if any, which is a clear advantage over SPRT in real world applications. Furthermore, its close relation with the state space setting and the Kalman filter offers it a more favorable position over nonparametric CUSUM in SCADA systems and in the engineering field. This algorithm can be applied from network traffic monitoring to application layer payload analysis and beyond to achieve intrusion detection and resilient control. We shall aim to capture the characteristics of a specific SCADA system under study with full situational awareness, including the dynamics of the physical plant being monitored, its communication patterns, system architecture, network traffic behavior, and specific application-level protocols used. Future work lies in the direction of implement these methodologies on real data.

REFRENCES

Allen, J. (2000). *State of the practice of intrusion detection technologies. Technical report.* DTIC Document.

Anderson, B., & Moore, J. (1979). *Optimal filtering.* Englewood Cliffs, NJ: Prentice-Hall Information and System Sciences Series.

Anderson, R. (2010). *Security engineering: A guide to building dependable distributed systems.* Wiley.

Arnold, C. (2006 June). *Cybersecurity of PCS/SCADA networks: Half-baked homeland security.*

Axelsson, S. (2000). *Intrusion detection systems: A survey and taxonomy. Technical report.* Sweden: Gteborg.

Axelsson, S. (2000). *A preliminary attempt to apply detection and estimation theory to intrusion detection.*

Baker, S., Filipiak, N., & Timlin, K. (2011). *In the dark crucial industries confront cyberattacks.* McAfee report.

Balepin, I., Maltsev, S., Rowe, J., & Levitt, K. (2003). Using specification-based intrusion detection for automated response. In *Recent Advances in Intrusion Detection* (pp. 136–154). Pittsburgh, PA: Springer. doi:10.1007/978-3-540-45248-5_8

Baron, M., & Tartakovsky, A. (2006). Asymptotic optimality of change-point detection schemes in general continuous-time models. *Sequential Analysis, 25*(3), 257–296. doi:10.1080/07474940600609597

Basseville, M., & Nikiforov, I. (1993). *Detection of abrupt changes: Theory and applications.* Prentice-Hall.

Ben-Gal, I. E. (2005). *Outlier detection.* Springer.

Callier, F., & Desoer, C. (1991). *Linear system theory.* Springer. doi:10.1007/978-1-4612-0957-7

Cheung, S., Dutertre, B., Fong, M., Lindqvist, U., Skinner, K., & Valdes, A. (2007). Using model-based intrusion detection for SCADA networks. In *Proceedings of the SCADA Security Scientific Symposium,* (pp. 127–134).

Chiang, L., Russell, E., & Braatz, R. (2001). *Fault detection and diagnosis in industrial systems.* Springer Verlag. doi:10.1007/978-1-4471-0347-9 complex environment. In *2010 IEEE International Conference on Robotics and Biomimetics (ROBIO)*, (pp. 938–943).

CrySyS Lab. (2012, May). *Skywiper (a.k.a. flame): A complex malware for targeted attacks.* Technical report. Cryptography and system security lab. Retrieved from http://www.crysys.hu/skywiper/skywiper.pdf

DHS (2005, October). *SCADA systems and the terrorist threat: Protecting the nation's critical control systems: Joint hearing before the subcommittee on economic security, infrastructure protection, and cybersecurity with the subcommittee on emergency preparedness, science, and technology of the committee on homeland security.* United States Congress-House Committee on Homeland Security, Subcommittee on Economic Security, Infrastructure Protection, and Cybersecurity (109-45).

Dzung, D., Naedele, M., Von Hoff, T., & Crevatin, M. (2005). Security for industrial communication systems. *Proceedings of the IEEE, 93*(6), 1152–1177. doi:10.1109/JPROC.2005.849714

Endorf, C., Schultz, E., & Mellander, J. (2004). *Intrusion detection & prevention.* McGraw-Hill Osborne Media.

Falliere, N. L. O. M., & Chien, E. (2011, February). *W32. Stuxnet dossier.* Retrieved from http://www.symantec.com/content/en/us/enterprise/media/securityresponse/whitepapers/w32 stuxnet dossier.pdf

Fitzgerald, R. (1971, December). Divergence of the Kalman filter. *IEEE Transactions on Automatic Control, 16*(6), 736–747. doi:10.1109/TAC.1971.1099836

GAO--United States General Accounting Office. (2004 March). *Critical infrastructure protection: Challenges and efforts to secure control systems, report to congressional requesters.* No. GAO-04-354.

GAO--United States General Accounting Office. (2007 September). *Critical infrastructure protection multiple efforts to secure control systems are under way, but challenges remain, report to congressional requesters.* No. GAO-07-1036.

Hadi, A. S., Imon, A. H. M. R., & Werner, M. (2009). Detection of outliers–overview. *Computational Statistics, 1*(1).

Hammes, U. R. (2010 February). *Robust positioning algorithms for wireless networks.* PhD thesis, TU Darmstadt.

Huber, P. (1968). Robust estimation. *Selected Statistical Papers*, 3–25.

Huber, P. (1972). Robust statistics: A review. *Annals of Mathematical Statistics, 43*(3), 1041–1067. doi:10.1214/aoms/1177692459

Huber, P. J. (1965, December). A robust version of the probability ratio test. *Annals of Mathematical Statistics, 36*(6), 1753–1758. doi:10.1214/aoms/1177699803

Huber, P. J. (1974). Roubst estimation of a location parameter. *Annnals of Mathmatical Statics, 35*.

Huber, P. J., & Ronchetti, E. M. (2009). *Robust statistics* (2nd ed.). Hoboken, NJ: Wiley. doi:10.1002/9780470434697

Hutwagner, L., Maloney, E., Bean, N., Slutsker, L., & Martin, S. (1997). Using laboratory-based surveillance data for prevention: An algorithm for detecting salmonella outbreaks. *Emerging Infectious Diseases, 3*(3), 395. doi:10.3201/eid0303.970322

IEEE PASSAT11, Boston, MA.

International Electrochemical Commission. (2004). *IEC TS 61850: Power systems management and associated information exchange–Data and communications security–Part 19.*

Jeong, J., & Lee, S. (2010 December).Outlier elimination method for robust visual servo control in

Jiang, W., Han, S., Tsui, K., & Woodall, W. (2011). Spatiotemporal surveillance methods in the presence of spatial correlation. *Statistics in Medicine, 30*(5), 569–583. doi:10.1002/sim.3877

Ko, C., Ruschitzka, M., & Levitt, K. (1997). *Execution monitoring of security-critical programs in distributed systems: A specification-based approach.*

Kruegel, C., Mutz, D., Robertson, W., & Valeur, F. (2003). Bayesian event classification for intrusion detection. In *Proceedings of the 19ᵗʰ Annual Computer Security Applications Conference (ACSAC '03)*. IEEE Computer Society.

Krutz, R. (2006). *Securing SCADA systems*. Indianapolis, IN: Wiley.

Lai, T. (2001). Sequential analysis: some classical problems and new challenges. *Statistica Sinica, 11*(2), 303–350.

Lai, T. L. (1998, November). Information bounds and quick detection of parameter changes in stochastic systems. *IEEE Transactions on Information Theory, 44*(7), 2917–2929. doi:10.1109/18.737522

Lee, D. (2012, May). *Flame: Massive cyber-attack discovered, researchers say.* Retrieved from http://www.bbc.com/news/technology-18238326

Lehmann, E., & Romano, J. (2005). *Testing statistical hypotheses*. Springer Verlag.

Lewis, T. (2006). *Critical infrastructure protection in homeland security: Defending a networked nation.* LibreDigital. doi:10.1002/0471789542

Lorden, G. (1971). Procedures for reacting to a change in distribution. *Annals of Mathematical Statistics, 42*(6), 1897–1908. doi:10.1214/aoms/1177693055

Lucas, J., & Crosier, R. (1982). Fast initial response for CUSUM quality-control schemes: Give your CUSUM a head start. *Technometrics, 24*(3), 199–205. doi:10.1080/00401706.1982.10487759

Mandjes, M., & Zuraniewski, P. (2011). M/G/transience, and its applications to overload detection. *Performance Evaluation, 68*(8).

Martin, R. D., & Thomson, D. J. (1982, September). Robust-resistant spectrum estimation. *Proceedings of the IEEE, 70*, 1097–1115. doi:10.1109/PROC.1982.12434

McHugh, J. (2000). Testing intrusion detection systems: A critique of the 1998 and 1999 DARPA intrusion detection system evaluations as performed by Lincoln laboratory. *ACM Transactions on Information and System Security, 3*(4), 262–294. doi:10.1145/382912.382923

McHugh, J. (2001). Intrusion and intrusion detection. *International Journal of Information Security, 1*(1), 14–35.

McKinnon, A., Dorow, K., Damania, T., Haugan, O., Lawrence, W., Bakken, D., & Shovic, J. (2003). A configurable middleware framework with multiple quality of properties for small embedded systems. In *Second IEEE International Symposium on Network Computing and Applications,* (pp. 197–204).

Mehra, R. (1970, April). On the identification of variances and adaptive Kalman filtering. *IEEE Transactions on Automatic Control, 15*(2), 175–184. doi:10.1109/TAC.1970.1099422

Mitter, S., & Schick, I. (1993). *Point estimation, stochastic approximation, and robust Kalman filtering*. Massachusetts Institute of Technology, Laboratory for Information and Decision Systems.

Montgomery, D. C. (2009). *Introduction to statistical quality control*. Hoboken, NJ: John Wiley & Sons, Inc.

Moran, B., & Belisle, R. (2008). Modeling flow information and other control system behavior to detect anomalies. In *Proceedings of the SCADA Security Scientific Symposium* 2008.

Moustakides, G. (1986). Optimal stopping times for detecting changes in distributions. *Annals of Statistics, 14*(4), 1379–1387. doi:10.1214/aos/1176350164

Muncaster, P. (2011 April). Stuxnet-like attacks beckon as 50 new SCADA threats discovered. Retrieved from http://www.v3.co.uk/v3-uk/news/2045556/stuxnet-attacks-beckonscada-threats-discovered

Naess, E., Frincke, D., McKinnon, A., & Bakken, D. (2005). Configurable middleware-level intrusion detection for embedded systems. In *25th IEEE International Conference on Distributed Computing Systems Workshops*, (pp. 144–151).

Oman, P., & Phillips, M. (2007). *Intrusion detection and event monitoring in SCADA networks* (pp. 161–173). Critical Infrastructure Protection. doi:10.1007/978-0-387-75462-8_12

Page, E. S. (1954). Continuous inspection schemes. *Biometrika, 41*, 100–114.

Paxson, V. (2001 November). *Topics in network intrusion detection*. In Tutorial, 8th ACM Conference on Computer and Communications Security (CCS-8).

Pearson, R. (2002, January). Outliers in process modeling and identification. *IEEE Transactions on Control Systems Technology, 10*(1), 55–63. doi:10.1109/87.974338

Pfleeger, C., & Pfleeger, S. (2007). *Security in computing* (*Vol. 604*). Prentice Hall.

Pollak, M. (1985). Optimal detection of a change in distribution. *Annals of Statistics, 13*, 206–227. doi:10.1214/aos/1176346587

Quang, P. X. (1985, June). Robust sequential testing. *Annals of Statistics, 13*(2), 638–649. doi:10.1214/aos/1176349544

Rakaczky, E. (2005). *Intrusion insights adapting intrusion prevention functionality for process control/SCADA systems*.

Roberts, S. W. (1959). Control chart tests based on geometric moving averages. *Technometrics, 1*(3), 239–250. doi:10.1080/00401706.1959.10489860

Roberts, S. W. (1966). A comparison of some control chart procedures. *Technometrics, 8*, 411–430. doi:10.1080/00401706.1966.10490374

Robinson, R. P. E., & Woodworth, B. (2008). *Security-hardened attack-resistant platform*. SHARP.

Rrushi, J., Campbell, R., & di Milano, U. (2008). *Detecting attacks in power plant interfacing substations through probabilistic validation of attack-effect bindings*. In SCADA Security Scientific Symposium.

Ryan, T. (2011). *Statistical methods for quality improvement* (*Vol. 840*). Wiley. doi:10.1002/9781118058114

Sangsuk-Iam, S., & Bullock, T. (1990, December). Analysis of discrete-time kalman filtering under incorrect noise covariances. *IEEE Transactions on Automatic Control, 35*(12), 1304–1309. doi:10.1109/9.61006

Scarfone, K., & Mell, P. (2007). Guide to intrusion detection and prevention systems (IDPS). *NIST Special Publication, 800*, 94.

Schick, I., & Mitter, S. (1994). Robust recursive estimation in the presence of heavy-tailed observation noise. *Annals of Statistics, 22*(2), 1045–1080. doi:10.1214/aos/1176325511

Schneier, B. (2003). *Beyond fear: Thinking sensibly about security in an uncertain world*. Springer.

Shewhart, W. A. (1931). *The economic control of quality of a manufactured product*. Princeton, NJ: Van Nostrand.

Shiryaev, A. (1963). On optimum methods in quickest detection problems. *Theory of Probability and Its Applications, 8*, 2246. doi:10.1137/1108002

Siris, V., & Papagalou, F. (2006). Application of anomaly detection algorithms for detecting syn flooding attacks. *Computer Communications, 29*(9), 1433–1442. doi:10.1016/j.comcom.2005.09.008

Soule, A., Salamatian, K., & Taft, N. (2005). Combining filtering and statistical methods for anomaly detection. In *Proceedings of the 5th ACM SIGCOMM Conference on Internet Measurement*, (p. 31). USENIX Association.

Stouffer, K., Falco, J., & Kent, K. (2006, September). Guide to supervisory control and data acquisition (SCADA) and industrial control systems security. *Recommendations of the National Institute of Standards and Technology Special Publication*, (pp. 800–82).

Symantec. (2011 November). *W32.duqu – The precursor to the next Stuxnet*. Symantec Security Response, [Online], *Accessed* 2011 November.

Ting, J.-A., Theodorou, E., & Schaal, S. (2007). A Kalman filter for robust outlier detection. In *IEEE/RSJ International Conference on Intelligent Robots and Systems, IROS 2007*, (pp. 1514–1519).

Tsang, C., & Kwong, S. (2005). Multi-agent intrusion detection system in industrial network using ant colony clustering approach and unsupervised feature extraction. In *IEEE International Conference on Industrial Technology, ICIT 2005*, (pp. 51–56).

Tsang, P., & Smith, S. (2008). Yasir: A low-latency, high-integrity security retrofit for legacy SCADA systems. In *Proceedings of the IFIP TC 23rd International Information Security Conference*, (pp. 445–459). Springer.

Tukey, J. (1960). A survey of sampling from contaminated distributions. In Olkin, I. (Ed.), *Contributions to probability and statistics essays in honor of Harold Hotelling* (pp. 448–485).

Tukey, J. (1977). *Exploratory data analysis*. Reading, MA: Addison-Wesley.

Wald, A. (1947). *Sequential analysis*. New York, NY: J. Wiley & Sons.

Willis, A. (2011). Design of a modified sequential probability ratio test (SPRT) for pipeline leak detection. *Computers & Chemical Engineering, 35*(1), 127–131. doi:10.1016/j.compchemeng.2010.06.009

Willsky, A., & Jones, H. (1976). A generalized likelihood ratio approach to the detection and estimation of jumps in linear systems. *IEEE Transactions on Automatic Control, 21*(1), 108–112. doi:10.1109/TAC.1976.1101146

Xiao, K., Chen, N., Ren, S., Shen, L., Sun, X., Kwiat, K., & Macalik, M. (2007). A workflow-based non-intrusive approach for enhancing the survivability of critical infrastructures in cyber environment. In *Proceedings of Third International Workshop on Software Engineering for Secure Systems (SESS'07)*. IEEE Computer Society.

Xu, L., Tomsovic, K., & Bose, A. (2005, April). Topology error identification using a twostage DC state estimator. *Electric Power Systems Research, 74*, 167–175. doi:10.1016/j.epsr.2004.10.005

Yang, D., Usynin, A., & Hines, J. (2005). Anomaly-based intrusion detection for scada systems. In *5th International Topical Meeting on Nuclear Plant Instrumentation, Control and Human Machine Interface Technologies (NPIC&HMIT 05)*, (pp. 12–16).

Zanero, S. (2004). Behavioral intrusion detection. *Computer and Information Sciences-ISCIS, 2004*, 657–666. doi:10.1007/978-3-540-30182-0_66

Zhu, B., Joseph, A., & Sastry, S. (2011). Taxonomy of cyber attacks on SCADA systems. In *Proceedings of the 2011 IEEE International Conference on Cyber, Physical, and Social Computing (CPSCom 2011)*. IEEE Computer Society.

Zhu, B., & Sastry, S. (2010). SCADA-specific intrusion detection/prevention systems: A survey and taxonomy. In *Proceedings of the First Workshop on Secure Control Systems (SCS'10)*, Stockholm, Sweden.

Zhu, B., & Sastry, S. (2011). Revisit dynamic ARIMA based anomaly detection. In *Proceedings of*

Zhu, X., Soh, Y., & Xie, L. (2002). Robust Kalman filter design for discrete time-delay systems. *Circuits, Systems, and Signal Processing, 21*(3), 319–335. doi:10.1007/s00034-004-7047-8

ADDITIONAL READING

Dimitriu, G. (2007). Using singular value decomposition in conjunction with data assimilation procedures. In *NMA 2006 LNCS 4310* (pp. 435–442). Berlin, Germany: Springer Verlag. doi:10.1007/978-3-540-70942-8_52

Grant, E., & Leavenworth, R. (1996). *Statistical quality control*. McGraw-Hill.

Kahneman, D., & Tversky, A. (1979). Prospect theory: An analysis of decision under risk. *Econometrica, 47*(2), 263–291. doi:10.2307/1914185

Nas, T. (1996). *Cost-benefit analysis: Theory and application*. Sage Publications, Inc.

Paxson, V. (1999). Bro: A system for detecting network intruders in real-time. *Computer Networks, 31*(23-24), 2435–2463. doi:10.1016/S1389-1286(99)00112-7

Tversky, A., & Kahneman, D. (1991). Loss aversion in riskless choice: A reference dependent model. *The Quarterly Journal of Economics, 106*(4), 1039. doi:10.2307/2937956

ENDNOTES

[1] In this chapter, we interchange the use of intrusion and attack equivalently.

[2] For example: US-Cert VU #840249 and US-Cert VU #362332.

[3] It's under the assumption that there is no wireless sensor network involved.

[4] Due to the scarce accessibility to operational SCADA traces known to the public, we are conservative at taking the leap of faith yet.

[5] A thoroughly stringent and meticulous categorization is not the focus of this paper. Interested readers may refer to (Axelsson, 2000; McHugh, 2001) for more detailed taxonomies on IDS.

[6] Note the above formula (7) only detects changes in the positive direction. When negative changes need to be found as well, the min operation should be used instead of the max operation, and this time a change has been found when the value of S is below the (negative) value of the threshold value.

[7]   Without assuming the noises to be Gaussian, the Kalman filter generates the minimum linear variance estimate of the state, i.e. the smallest unconditional error covariance among all linear estimates, which in general is not the conditional mean.

[8]   A fat tail is a property of some probability distributions (exhibiting extremely large kurtosis particularly relative to the ubiquitous Gaussian which itself is an example of an exceptionally thin tail distribution. Fat tail distributions have power law decay.

[9]   The word "robust" is loaded with many if not often inconsistent meanings.

[10]   Or the one minimizes the Fisher Information, provided that the Cramér-Rao lower bound is achieved.

[11]   The recommended choice of s in (30) is where is the -quantile of (e.g., $s = 1.883$ for a 3% contamination of data.

[12]   They can be considered as a recursive variant of the normal equations from the *Iterative Weighted Least Squares* IWLS method which is a popular algorithm for numerical calculation of M-estimates.

[13]   Particularly on this ground, we look forward to expositions on any commercial or proprietary IDS that are designed explicitly for SCADA systems in a specific domain.

Compilation of References

Aas, A. L., Johnsen, S. O., & Skramstad, T. (2009). Lecture Notes in Computer Science: *Vol. 5775. CRIOP: A human factors verification and validation methodology that works in an industrial setting. Safecomp 2009* (pp. 243–256). Hamburg, Germany.

Abrams, M., & Weiss, J. (2008). *Malicious control system cyber security attack case study- Maroochy Water Services, Australia.* Retrieved 2 January, 2012, from http://csrc.nist.gov/groups/SMA/fisma/ics/documents/Maroochy-Water-Services-Case-Study_report.pdf

Ackerman, S. (2010, 13 October). Doc of the day: NSA, DHS trade players for net defense. *Danger Room.* Retrieved on February 6, 2011, from http://www.wired.com/dangerroom/2010/10/doc-of-the-day-nsa-dhs-trade-players-for-net-defense/

AJ The Architects' Journal. (2012). *Oxford circus gets Japanese style 'desire-line' crossing.* Retrieved 9 August, 2012, from http://www.architectsjournal.co.uk/news/daily-news/-oxford-circus-gets-japanese-style-desire-line-crossing/5210489.article

Albert, R., Jeong, H., & Barabasi, A. L. (2000). Error and attack tolerance of complex networks. *Nature, 406,* 378–382. doi:10.1038/35019019

Alexander, G. K. (2010). *U.S. cybersecurity policy and the role of U.S. CYBERCOM.* Presentation to Center for Strategic and International Studies, 3 June.

Alexander, G. K. (2011). Building a new command in cyberspace. *Strategic Studies Quarterly, 5*(2), 3–12.

Allen, J., Christie, A., Fithen, W., McHugh, J., Pickel, J., & Stoner, E. (2000). *State of the practice of intrusion detection technologies.* Technical Report CMU/SEI-99-TR-028 ESC 99-028, Software Engineering Institute, Carnegie Melon University.

Allen, J. (2000). *State of the practice of intrusion detection technologies. Technical report.* DTIC Document.

American Gas Association (AGA). (2006). *AGA report No. 12, cryptographic protection of SCADA communications. Part 1 background, policies and test plan.* American Gas Association.

American Gas Association (AGA). (2006). *AGA report No. 12, cryptographic protection of SCADA communications. Part 2 performance test plan.* American Gas Association.

American National Standard (ANSI). (2007). *ANSI/ISA-TR99.00.01-2007 security technologies for industrial automation and control systems. International Society of Automation.* ISA.

American National Standard (ANSI). (2009). *ANSI/ISA–99.02.01–2009 security for industrial automation and control systems. Part 2: Establishing an industrial automation and control systems security program. International Society of Automation.* ISA.

American Petroleum Institute (API) energy. (2005). *Security guidelines for the petroleum industry.* American Petroleum Institute.

American Petroleum Institute (API) energy. (2009). *API standard 1164. Pipeline SCADA security.* American Petroleum Institute.

American Petroleum Institute. (2005). *Security guidelines for the petroleum industry,* 3rd ed. Retrieved October 15, 2011, from http://new.api.org/policy/otherissues/upload/Security.pdf

Amin, S., Sastry, S., & Cárdenas, A. A. (2008). *Research challenges for the security of control systems.*

Anderson, R. (2001). Why information security is hard: An economic perspective. In *Proceedings of the 17th Annual Computer Security Applications Conference* (pp. 358-365). Washington, DC: IEEE Computer Society.

Anderson, B., & Moore, J. (1979). *Optimal filtering*. Englewood Cliffs, NJ: Prentice-Hall Information and System Sciences Series.

Anderson, R. (2001). *Security engineering: A guide to building dependable systems*. Wiley & Sons, Inc.

ANSI. (2007). *TR99.00.01-2007, security for industrial automation and control systems, part 1: Terminology, concepts and models*.

ANSI/ISA. (2007). *TR99.00.01-2007, security technologies for industrial automation and control systems*.

ANSI/ISA. (2009). *TR99.02.01-2009, Security for industrial automation and control systems: Establishing an industrial automation and control systems security program*.

Arango, H. G., & Lambert-Torres, G. (2004). Spatial electric load distribution forecasting using simulated annealing. *WSEAS Transactions on Systems, 1*(3), 14–19.

Arnold, C. (2006 June). *Cybersecurity of PCS/SCADA networks: Half-baked homeland security*.

Arora, A., Krishnan, R., Nandkumar, A., Telang, R., & Yang, Y. (2004). *Impact of vulnerability disclosure and patch availability - An empirical analysis*. Paper presented at the Third Workshop on the Economics of Information Security, 2004, Minneapolis, MN.

Arulselvan, A., Commander, C. W., Elefteriadou, L., & Pardalos, P. M. (2009). Detecting critical nodes in sparse graphs. *Computers & Operations Research, 36*, 2193–2200. doi:10.1016/j.cor.2008.08.016

Asad, M. (n.d.). *Challenges of SCADA*. Retrieved from http://www.ceia.seecs.nust.edu.pk/pdfs/Challenges_of_SCADA.pdf

Ask, R., Røisli, R., Johnsen, S., Line, M., Ueland, A., & Hovland, B. Losnedahl, T. (2006). *Information security baseline requirements for process control, safety and support ICT systems*. ISBR. Retrieved January 1, 2011, from www.olf.no/no/Publikasjoner/Retningslinjer/Kronologisk/

Askwith, B. (2006, May). *WARP case study - Experience setting up a WARP*. Retrieved from http://www.warp.gov.uk/Index/indexarticles.htm

ASME. (2006). *RAMCAP: The framework (Vol. Version 2.0)*. Washington, DC: ASME Innovative Technologies Institute, LLC.

Assaf, D. (2008). Models of critical information infrastructure protection . In Shenoi, S., & Goetz, E. (Eds.), *International Journal of Critical Infrastructure Protection* (*Vol. 1*, pp. 6–14). Boston, MA: Springer.

Aviram, A. (2004). Network responses to network threats: The evolution into private security associations. *Florida State University College of Law Working Paper, (115)*.

Aviram, A., & Tor, A. (2004). Overcoming Impediments to Information Sharing. *Alabama Law Review, 55*(2), 231–280.

Axelsson, S. (2000). *A preliminary attempt to apply detection and estimation theory to intrusion detection*.

Axelsson, S. (2000). *Intrusion detection systems: A survey and taxonomy*. Götebrog, Sweden: Department of Computer Engineering, Chalmers University of Technology.

Bace, R., & Mell, P. (2002). *NIST special publication on intrusion detection system*. Retrieved October 15, 2011, from http://csrc.nist.gov/publication/nistpubs/800-31/sp800-31.pdf

Baigent, D., Adamiak, M., & Mackienwicz, R. (2004, November). *IEC 61850 communication networks and systems in substations: An overview for users*. Paper presented at the meeting of the Iberoamerican Symposium on Power System Protection, SIPSEP 2004, Monterrey, Mexico.

Bailey, W. J. (2010). *Hearts and minds, psuedo gangs and counter-insurgency: Based upon experiences from previous campaigns in Kenya (1952-60), Malaya (1948-60) & Rhodesia (1964-1979)*. Paper presented at the 1st Australian Couter Terrorism Conference, Perth, Australia.

Bailey, D., & Wright, E. (2003). *Practical SCADA for industry*. Burlington, MA: Newnes.

Baker, S., Filipiak, N., & Timlin, K. (2011). *In the dark crucial industries confront cyberattacks*. McAfee report.

Balepin, I., Maltsev, S., Rowe, J., & Levitt, K. (2003). Using specification-based intrusion detection for automated response . In *Recent Advances in Intrusion Detection* (pp. 136–154). Pittsburgh, PA: Springer. doi:10.1007/978-3-540-45248-5_8

Baran, P. (1964). On distributed communications networks. *IEEE Transactions on Communications Systems*, *12*, 1–9. doi:10.1109/TCOM.1964.1088883

Baron, M., & Tartakovsky, A. (2006). Asymptotic optimality of change-point detection schemes in general continuous-time models. *Sequential Analysis*, *25*(3), 257–296. doi:10.1080/07474940600609597

Baskerville, R., & Pries-Heje, J. (1999). Grounded action research: A method for understanding IT in practice. *Accounting Management and Information Technologies*, *9*(1), 1–23. doi:10.1016/S0959-8022(98)00017-4

Basseville, M., & Nikiforov, I. (1993). *Detection of abrupt changes: Theory and applications*. Prentice-Hall.

Baumeister, T. (2010). *Literature review on smart grid cyber security.* University of Hawaii, Department of Information and Computer Sciences. Retrieved January 23, 2012, from http://csdl.ics.hawaii.edu/techreports/10-11/10-11.pdf

Beattie, S., Arnold, S., Cowan, C., Wagle, P., Wright, C., & Shostack, A. (2002). *Timing the application of security patches for optimal uptime.* Paper presented at the Sixteenth Systems Administration Conference, Berkeley, CA.

Becker, E., Metsis, V., Arora, R., Vinjumur, J., Xu, Y., & Makedon, F. (2009). *SmartDrawer: RFID-based smart medicine drawer for assistive environments.* 2nd International Conference on PErvasive Technologies Related to Assistive Environments (PETRA '09). New York, NY.

Bellavita, C. (2009) 85% of what you know about critical infrastructure is probably wrong. *Homeland Security Watch*. Retrieved January 1, 2012, from http://www.hlswatch.com/2009/03/16/85-percent-is-wrong/

Bellovin, S. (2010). *Stuxnet: The first weaponized software?* Steve Bellovin's blog. Retrieved January 1 2012, from http://www.cs.columbia.edu/~smb/blog//2010-09-27.html

Bellovin, S. (2011, 18 November). Water supply system apparently hacked, with physical damage. *CircleID*. Retrieved on February 6, 2011 from http://www.circleid.com/posts/20111118_water_supply_system_apparently_hacked_with_physical_damage

Bendrath, R. (2001). The cyberwar debate: Perception and politics in U.S. critical infrastructure protection. *Information & Security: An International Journal*, *7*, 80–103.

Bendrath, R. (2003). The American cyber-angst and the real world–any link? In Latham, R. (Ed.), *Bombs and bandwidth: The emerging relationship between information technology and security* (pp. 49–73). New York, NY: The Free Press.

Ben-Gal, I. E. (2005). *Outlier detection*. Springer.

Benscath, B. (2011). *Duqu: A Stuxnet-like malware found in the wild*. Budapest, Hungary: Laboratory of Cryptography and System Security, Budapest University of Technology and Economics.

Berkeley, A. R. III, & Wallace, M. (2010). *A framework for establishing critical infrastructure resilience goals. Final report and recommendations by the council.* National Infrastructure Advisory Council.

Berman, O., & Krass, D. (2002). The generalized maximal covering location problem. *Computers & Operations Research*, *29*, 563–591. doi:10.1016/S0305-0548(01)00079-X

Berthier, R., Sanders, W., & Khurana, H. (2010). Intrusion detection for advanced metering infrastructures: Requirements and architectural directions. *First IEEE International Conference on Smart Grid Communications (SmartGridComm)*, (pp. 350-355). Gaithersburg, MD.

Bigham, J., Gamez, D., & Ning, L. (2003, September). *Safeguarding SCADA systems with anomaly detection.* Paper presented at the meeting of the Second International Workshop on Mathematical Methods, Models, and Architectures for Computer Network Security, St. Petersburg, Russia.

Bigham, J., Jin, X., Gamez, D., & Phillips, C. (2005). Hybrid workflow and Bayesian networks to correlate information in protection of large scale critical infrastructures. *Electronic Notes in Theoretical Computer Science*, *121*, 87–99. doi:10.1016/j.entcs.2004.10.009

Blank, S. (2008). Web war I: Is Europe's first information war a new kind of war? *Comparative Strategy, 27*(3), 227–247. doi:10.1080/01495930802185312

Boeing, A., Masek, M., & Bailey, B. (2008). *Protecting critical infrastructure with games technology*. School of Computer and Information Science, Edith Cowan University, Perth, Western Australia (9th Australian Information Warfare and Security Conference).

Bosch, O. (2002). *Cyber-terrorism and private sector efforts for information infrastructure protection*. International Institute for Strategic Studies.

Bosch, O. (2012). Critical information infrastructure and cyber-terrorism . In Reich, P., & Gelbstein, E. (Eds.), *Cyberwar, cyberterrorism and internet immobilization*. Hershey, PA: IGI Global.

Bossler, A. M., & Holt, T. J. (2009). On-line activities, guardianship, and malware infection: An examination of routine activities theory. *International Journal of Cyber Criminology, 3*(1), 400–420.

Bourgeois, P., Conesa, O., Grobauer, B., & Price, G. (2004). *EISPP common advisory format description*, version 2.0. Retrieved February 7, 2012, from http://www.cert-verbund.de/daf/documentation/eispp_v20.pdf

Boyer, S. A. (2010). *SCADA: Supervisory control and data acquisition. Iliad Development Inc*. ISA.

Brambley, M. R., Kintner-Meyer, M., & Katipamula, S. (2006). Wireless sensor applications for building operation and management . In Capehart, B. L., & Capehart, L. C. (Eds.), *Web based energy information and control systems: Case studies and applications* (pp. 341–367). Lilburn, GA: The Fairmont Press Inc.

Brenner, S. W., & Clarke, L. L. (2010). Civilians in cyberwarfare: Conscripts. *Vanderbilt Journal of Transnational Law, 43*, 1011–1076.

British-North American Committee. (2007). *Cyber attack: A risk management primer for CEOs and directors*. Retrieved 10 August 2012 from http://www.acus.org/docs/071212_Cyber_Attack_Report.pdf

Brito, J., & Watkins, T. (2011). Loving the cyber bomb? The dangers of threat inflation in cybersecurity policy. *Mercatus Center Working Paper No. 11-24* April.

Brownfield, M., Gupta, Y., & Davis, N. (2005). Wireless sensor network denial of sleep attack. *Sixth Annual IEEE Information Assurance Workshop* (pp. 356-364). West Point, NY: IEEE.

Brown, G., Garlyle, M., Salmeron, J., & Wood, K. (2006). Defending critical infrastructure. *Interfaces, 36*, 530–544. doi:10.1287/inte.1060.0252

Brown, I., & Sommer, P. (2010). *Reducing systemic cybersecurity risk*. Organisation for Economic Co-operation and Development (OECD) Multidisciplinary Issues; International Futures Programme on Future Global Shocks, Paris, France: Organisation for Economic Co-operation and Development

Brownlee, N., & Guttman, E. (1998, June). *RFC2350: Expectations for computer security incident response*. RFC. Retrieved from http://www.ietf.org/rfc/rfc2350.txt

Brunner, E., & Suter, M. (2008). *International CIIP handbook 2008/2009: An inventory of 25 national and 7 internation critical information infrastructure protection policies*. Zurich, Switzerland: ETH.

Bryes, E., & Hoffman, D. (n. d.). *The myths and facts behind cyber security risks for industrial control systems*. Retrieved 19 December, 2011, from www.isa.org/link/cyber_myth_fact

Buennemeyer, T., Jacoby, G., Chiang, W., Marchany, R., & Tront, J. (2006). *Battery-sensing intrusion protection system. In 2006* (pp. 176–183). IEEE Information Assurance Workshop.

Bühler, B., Rohrmair, G., Ifland, M., Lode, N., & Lukas, K. (2011). Ein standardkonformer Patch Management Prozess . In Schartner, P., & Taeger, J. (Eds.), *DACH security 2011* (pp. 248–258).

Buildings, A. com. (n.d.). *Networks*. Retrieved July 22, 2010, from http://www.automatedbuildings.com/frame_products.htm

Bumgarner, J., & Borg, S. (2009). Overview by the US-CCU of the cyber campaign Against Georgia in August of 2008. *US-CCU Special Report,* August.

Bundesamt für Sicherheit in der Informationstechnik. (2008). *IT-Grundschutz methodology.* BSI-Standard 100-2. Retrieved October 21, 2011, from https://www.bsi.bund.de/SharedDocs/Downloads/EN/BSI/Publications/BSIStandards/standard_100-2_e_pdf.pdf?__blob=publicationFile

Burton, E. (2008). *Final report into the loss of MOD personal data for Permanent Undersecretary Ministry of Defence.* Retrieved 10 December 2011 from http://www.mod.uk/nr/rdonlyres/3e756d20-e762-4fc1-bab0-08c68fdc2383/0/burton_review_rpt20080430.pdf

Bustillo, M. (2010, July 23). Wal-Mart radio tags to track clothing. *Wall Street Journal.* Retrieved February 18, 2011, from http://online.wsj.com/article/SB100014240527487044213045753832130611980900.html

Butler, B. S., & Gray, P. H. (2006). Reliability, mindfulness and information systems. *Management Information Systems Quarterly, 30*(2), 211–224.

Buttner, A., & Ziring, N. (2009). *Common platform enumeration (CPE) – Specification,* version 2.2. Retrieved October 20, 2011, from http://cpe.mitre.org/files/cpe-specification_2.2.pdf

Buzan, B., Wæver, O., & Wilde, J. D. (1998). *Security: A new framework for analysis.* Boulder, CO: Lynne Rienner Pub.

Callier, F., & Desoer, C. (1991). *Linear system theory.* Springer. doi:10.1007/978-1-4612-0957-7

Camp, L. J. (2006). The state of economics of information security. *I/S. Journal of Law and Policy, 2*(2), 189–205.

Cardenas, A. A., Amin, S., Lin, Z., Huang, Y., Huang, C., & Sastry, S. (2011). Attacks against process control systems: risk assessment, detection, and response. In *Proceedings of the 6th ACM Symposium on Information, Computer and Communications Security* (pp. 355-366). New York, NY: Association for Computing Machinery.

Cardenas, A. A., Roosta, T., & Sastry, S. (2009). Rethinking security properties, threat models, and the design space in sensor networks: A case study in SCADA systems. *Ad Hoc Networks, 7*(8), 1434–1447. doi:10.1016/j.adhoc.2009.04.012

Cardoso, J. M. P., & Diniz, P. C. (2009). Why both game theory and reliability theory are important in defending infrastructure against intelligent attacks game theoretic risk analysis of security threats. *International Series in Operations Research & Management Science, 128,* 1–11. doi:10.1007/978-0-387-87767-9_4

Carnegie Mellon Software Engineering Institute (CMSEI). (2012). *OCTAVE method.* Retrieved from http://www.cert.org/octave/octavemethod.html

Carr, J. (2011). *Inside cyber warfare: Mapping the cyber underworld* (2nd ed.). O'Reilly Media.

Cavelty, M. D. (2008). *Securing the homeland: Critical infrastructure, risk, and (in)security.* Hampshire, UK: Routledge.

Centre for the Protection of Critial Infrastructure (CPNI). (n.d.). *Meridian process control security information exchange (MPCSIE).* Retrieved from http://www.cpni.nl/informatieknooppunt/internationaal/mpcsie

Centre for the Protection of Critical Infrastructure (CPNI). (n.d.). *CPNI.* Retrieved from http://www.cpni.gov.uk/advice/infosec/business-systems/scada

Centre for the Protection of National Infrastructure (CPNI). (2005). *Firewall deployment for SCADA and process control networks.* Centre for the Protection of National Infrastructure.

Centre for the Protection of National Infrastructure (CPNI). (2011). *Configuring & managing remote access for industrial control systems.* Centre for the Protection of National Infrastructure.

Centre for the Protection of National Infrastructure (CPNI). (2011). *Cyber security assessments of industrial control systems.* Centre for the Protection of National Infrastructure.

Centre for the Protection of National Infrastructure (CPNI). (n.d.). *Process control and SCADA security- Good practice guidelines*. Retrieved from http://www.cpni.gov.uk/advice/cyber/business-systems/scada/

Centre for the Protection of National Infrastructure. (2006). *Good practice guide patch management*. Retrieved October 15, 2011, from http://www.cpni.gov.uk/Documents/Publications/2006/2006029-GPG_Patch_management.pdf

Centre for the Protection of the National Infrastructure. (2006). *Telecommunications resilience good practice guide*. London, UK: Centre for the Protection of the National Infrastructure.

Centre of Protection for National Infrastructure. (2009). *Risk assessment for personnel security*. Retrieved 22 January 2012 from http://www.dft.gov.uk/publications/personnel-security-resource-list/

CERT. (2003). *Advisory CA-2003-20 W32/Blaster worm*. Carnegie Mellon University's Computer Emergency Response Team. Retrieved January 23, 2012, from http://www.cert.org/advisories/CA-2003-20.html

Chaffey, N. (2011). *Cyber security: Managing people risk and the insider threat through strategic protective monitoring*. Retrieved 2 March 2012 from http://www.paconsulting.com/ our-thinking/managing-people-risk-and-the-insider-threat/

Channelnomics. (2010). *Cisco faces a tough 2011 in switching, routing*. Retrieved January 1, 2012, from http://channelnomics.com/2010/12/22/cisco-faces-a-tough-2011-in-switching-routing/

Charney, S. (2002). *Hearing before the Subcommittee on Government Efficiency, Financial Management and Intergovernmental Relations, Committee on Government Reform, House of Representatives. Critical Infrastructure Protection Significant Challenges Need to Be Addressed: Statement of Scott Charney Chief security strategist, Microsoft Corp*. Retrieved 20 December, 2011, from https://house.resource.org/107/org.c-span.171444-1.raw.txt

Chatham House. (2011). *About the Chatham House rule*. London, UK: Chatham House. Retrieved January 1, 2012, from http://www.chathamhouse.org.uk/about/chathamhouserule/

Chen, M., Gonzalez, S., Leung, V., Zhang, Q., & Li, M. (2010). A 2G-RFID-based e-healthcare system. *IEEE Wireless Communications*, *17*(1), 37–43. doi:10.1109/MWC.2010.5416348

Cheung, S., Dutertre, B., Fong, M., Lindqvist, U., Skinner, K., & Valdes, A. (2007). Using model-based intrusion detection for SCADA networks. In *Proceedings of the SCADA Security Scientific Symposium*, (pp. 127–134).

Chiang, L., Russell, E., & Braatz, R. (2001). *Fault detection and diagnosis in industrial systems*. Springer Verlag. doi:10.1007/978-1-4471-0347-9

Chien, E., & O'Gorman, G. (2011). *The nitro attacks: Stealing secrets from the chemical industry*. Retrieved 2 March, 2012, from http://www.symantec.com/content/en/us/enterprise/media/security_response/whitepapers/the_nitro_attacks.pdf

Church, R. L., & ReVelle, C. (1974). The maximal covering location problem. *Papers / Regional Science Association. Regional Science Association. Meeting*, *32*, 101–118. doi:10.1007/BF01942293

Church, R. L., & Scaparra, M. P. (2007a). Analysis of facility systems' reliability withn subject to attach or a natural disaster . In Murray, A., & Grubesic, T. (Eds.), *Reliability and vulnerability in critical infrastructure: A quantitative geographic perspective* (pp. 221–241). Heidelberg, Germany: Springer.

Church, R. L., & Scaparra, M. P. (2007). Protecting critical assets: The r-interdiction median problem with fortification. *Geographical Analysis*, *39*, 129–146. doi:10.1111/j.1538-4632.2007.00698.x

Church, R. L., Scaparra, M. P., & Middleton, R. S. (2004). Identifying critical infrastructure: The median and covering facility interdiction problems. *Annals of the Association of American Geographers. Association of American Geographers*, *94*, 491–502. doi:10.1111/j.1467-8306.2004.00410.x

CI2RCO Project. (2008). *Critical information infrastructure research coordination*. Retrieved from http://cordis.europa.eu/fetch?CALLER=PROJ_ICT&ACTION=D&CAT=PROJ&RCN=79305

Cisco. (2009). *Cisco 2009 annual security report* (Tech. Rep.). Cisco Systems Inc. Retrieved from http://www.cisco.com/en/US/prod/vpndevc/annual_security_report.html

Clarke, R. (2011, 15 June). China's cyberassault on America. *Wall Street Journal*. Retrieved February 6, 2011, from http://online.wsj.com/article/SB10001424052702304259304576373391101828876.html

Clarke, R. (2009). *War from cyberspace. The National Interest*. October/November.

Clarke, R. (2010). *Cyberwar: The next threat to national security and what to do about it*. Ecce Books.

Clarke, R. A., & Knake, R. (2010). *Cyber war: The next threat to national security and what to do about it*. New York, NY: HarperCollins.

Clinton, H. R. (2010). *Remarks on internet freedom*. Presentation to The Newseum [January.]. *Washington D., C*, 21.

Cobb, A. (1997). *Australia's vulnerability to information attacks*. Australian Strategic and Defense Studies Centre.

Cohon, J. (1978). *Multi-objective programming and planning*. New York, NY: Academic Press.

Colbourn, C. J. (1987). *The combinatorics of network reliability*. New York, NY: Oxford University Press.

Commission of the European Communities. (2004). *Communication from the commission to the council and the European parliament. Critical Infrastructure Protection in the fight against terrorism COM(2004) 702 final*.

Commission of the European Communities. (2004). *Communication from the commission to the council and the European parliament. Prevention, preparedness and response to terrorist attacks COM(2004) 698 final*.

Commission of the European Communities. (2004). *Communication from the Commission: Critical Infrastructure Protection in the Fight against Terrorism, COM(2004) 702 final*.

Commission of the European Communities. (2005). *Green paper on a European programme for critical infrastructure protection COM(2005) 576 final*.

Commission of the European Communities. (2006). *Communication from the Commission on a European programme for critical infrastructure protection COM(2006) 786*.

Commission of the European Communities. (2008). *Council decision on a Critical Infrastructure Warning Information Network (CIWIN) COM(2008) 676*.

Commission of the European Communities. (2008). *Council directive 2008/114/EC of 8 December 2008 on the identification and designation of European critical infrastructures and the assessment of the need to improve their protection*.

Commission of the European Communities. (2009). *Communication from the commission to the European parliament. Protecting Europe from large scale cyber-attacks and disruptions: enhancing preparedness, security and resilience*.

Commission of the European Communities. (2010). *Communication from the Commission: A Digital Agenda for Europe, COM(2010) 245*.

Commission of the European Communities. (2011). *Communication from the commission to the European parliament, the European economic and social commitee and the commitee of the regions. Achievements and next steps: towards global cyber-security*.

Committee on Homeland Security and Governmental Affairs. (2011). *Cyber security and American cyber competitiveness act of 2011 (S.21)*. 112th Congress, 1st Session, United States Senate, 25 January.

Committee on Homeland Security and Governmental Affairs. (2011). *Cyber security public awareness act of 2011 (S.813)*. 112th Congress, 1st Session, United States Senate, 13 April.

Committee on the Internet Under Crisis Conditions. Learning from September 11. (2003). *The Internet under crisis conditions: Learning from September 11*. Washington, DC: Computer Science and Telecommunications Board: National Research Council; National Academies of Science The National Academies Press.

complex environment. In *2010 IEEE International Conference on Robotics and Biomimetics* (ROBIO), (pp. 938–943).

Computerworld. (2011). *Lockheed Martin acknowledges 'significant' cyberattack*. Retrieved 1 January 2012, from http://www.computerworld.com/s/article/9217126/Lockheed_Martin_acknowledges_significant_cyberattack

Conte de Leon, D., Alves-Foss, J., Krings, A., & Oman, P. (2002, November). *Modeling complex control systems to identify remotely accessible devices vulnerable to cyber attack*. Paper presented at the meeting of the ACM Workshop on Scientific Aspects of Cyber Terrorism, SACT 2002, Washington DC, USA.

Conway, M. (2008). Media, fear and the hyperreal: The construction of cyberterrorism as the ultimate threat to critical infrastructures . In Dunn Cavelty, M., & Kristensen, K. S. (Eds.), *Securing the 'homeland': Critical infrastructure, risk and (in)security* (pp. 109–129). London, UK: Routledge.

Coole, M., & Brooks, D. (2009). *Security decay: An entropic approach to definition and understanding*. Paper presented at the 2nd Australian and Security conference, Perth, Australia.

Coole, M., & Brooks, D. (2011). *Mapping the organizational relationships within physical security body of knowledge: A management heuristic of sound theory and best practice*. Paper presented at the 4th Australian Security and Intelligence Conference, Perth, Australia.

Corley, H. W., & Sha, D. Y. (1982). Most vital links and nodes in weighted networks. *Operations Research Letters*, *1*, 157–160. doi:10.1016/0167-6377(82)90020-7

Cox, J. L. A. (2008). Some limitations of "risk = threat × vulnerability × consequence" for risk analysis of terrorist attacks. *Risk Analysis*, *28*(6), 1749–1761. doi:10.1111/j.1539-6924.2008.01142.x

Craig, P., Mortensen, J., & Dagle, J. (2008). *Metrics for the National SCADA Test Bed Program, PNNL-18-31*. Richland, WA: Pacific Northwest National Laboratory. doi:10.2172/963242

Creery, A. (2005). *Industrial cybersecurity for power system and SCADA networks*. 52nd Annual Petroleum and Chemical Industry Conference. Retrieved from http://ieeexplore.ieee.org/xpls/abs_all.jsp?arnumber=1524567

Crisis Resource Network. (2009). *Roundtable report: Network governance and the role of public- private partnerships in new risks*. 6th Zurich Roundtable on Comprehensive Risk Analysis and Management. Zurich: Crisis Resource Network.

Critical Infrastructure Information Act. (2002). Retrieved from http://www.dhs.gov/xlibrary/assets/CII_Act.pdf

CRUTIAL Project. (2006). *Critical utility infrastructural resilience*. Retrieved from http://crutial.rse-web.it

CrySyS Lab. (2012, May). *Skywiper (a.k.a. flame): A complex malware for targeted attacks*. Technical report. Cryptography and system security lab. Retrieved from http://www.crysys.hu/skywiper/skywiper.pdf

Curtis, K. (2005). *A DNP3 protocol primer (Revision A)*. Retrieved May 25, 2011, from http://www.dnp.org/AboutUs/DNP3%20Primer%20Rev%20A.pdf

Curtis, K. (2005). *DNP3 primer*. Revision A, 20 March 2005, DNP User's Group. Retrieved September 11, 2011, from http://www.dnp.org

Cutler, V., & Paddock, S. (2009). *Use of threat image projection (TIP) to enhance security performance*. 43rd Annual 2009 International Carnahan Conference Security Technology, 5-8 Oct. 2009.doi: 10.1109/CCST.2009.5335565

Daneels, A., & Salter, W. (1999). What is SCADA? *International Conference on Accelerator and Large Experimental Physics Control Systems*, (pp. 339-343).

Danyliw, R., Meijer, J., & Demchenko, Y. (2007). *The incident object description exchange format*. IETF Request for Comments (RFC 5070). Retrieved September 9, 2012, from http://www.ietf.org/rfc/rfc5070.txt

Dawson, J. (2009). *Identification of bad data*. TRUST Program, Jackson State University, 2009. Retrieved from http://www.truststc.org/reu/09/Reports/DawsonReport.pdf

Debrix, F. (2001). Cyberterror and media-induced fears: The production of emergency culture. *Strategies, 14*(1), 149–168. doi:10.1080/10402130120042415

Department of Defense. (2011). *Defence industrial base (DIB) Cyber security / information assurance (CS/IA) programme home – Program description*. Washington, DC: Department of Defense. Retrieved 1 January 2012, from http://dibnet.dod.mil/

Department of Defense. (2011). *Department of defense strategy for operating in cyberspace*. Washington, DC: Department of Defense.

Department of Energy (DoE). (2002). *Energy infrastructure risk management checklists for small and medium sized energy facilities*. Department of Energy.

Department of Energy (DoE). (2008). *Hands-on Control systems cyber security training of national SCADA test bed*. Retrieved from http://www.inl.gov/scada/training/d/8hr_intermediate_handson_hstb.pdf

Department of Energy (DoE). (2010). *Cybersecurity for energy delivery systems peer review*. Retrieved from http://events.energetics.com/CSEDSPeerReview2010

Department of Energy (DoE). (n.d.). 21 steps to improve cyber security of SCADA networks. *Department of Energy*.

Department of Energy (DoE). (n.d.). *Control systems security publications library*. Retrieved from http://energy.gov/oe/control-systems-security-publications-library

Department of Homeland Security (DHS). (2003). *Homeland Security Presidential directive-7*. Retrieved from http://www.dhs.gov/xabout/laws/gc_1214597989952.shtm#1

Department of Homeland Security (DHS). (2009). *Catalog of control systems security: Recommendations for standards developers*.

Department of Homeland Security (DHS). (2009). *National infrastructure protection plan: Partnering to enhance protection and resiliency*. Department of Homeland Security.

Department of Homeland Security (DHS). (2009). *Recommended practice: Improving industrial control systems cybersecurity with defense-in-depth strategies*. Department of Homeland Security.

Department of Homeland Security (DHS). (2011). *Cyber storm III final report*. Department of Homeland Security Office of Cybersecurity and Communications National Cyber Security Division.

Department of Homeland Security (DHS). (2011). *DHS officials: Stuxnet can morph into new threat*. Retrieved from http://www.homelandsecuritynewswire.com/dhs-officials-stuxnet-can-morph-new-threat

Department of Homeland Security. (2009). Cyber security procurement language for control systems. Retrieved October 16, 2011, from http://www.us-cert.gov/control_systems/pdf/FINAL-Procurement_Language_Rev4_100809.pdf

Dependability Development Support Initiative. (2002). *Roadmap for warning and information sharing*. Leiden, The Netherlands: RAND Corporation. Retrieved from http://www.ddsi.org/htdocs/Documents/final%20docs/DDSI_D4_WIS_roadmap_f.pdf

DePoy, J., Phelan, J., Sholander, P., Smith, B. J., Varnado, G. B., Wyss, G. D., et al. (2006). *Critical infrastructure systems of systems assessment methodology*. Livermore, CA: Technical Report SAND2006-6399, Sandia National Laboratories (October 2007).

DHS & DoE. (2007). *Energy: Critical infrastructure and key resources, sector-specific plan as input to the national infrastructure protection plan*. Department of Energy. Retrieved January 23, 2012, from http://energy.gov/oe/downloads/energy-critical-infrastructure-and-key-resources-sector-specific-plan-input-national

DHS (2005, October). *SCADA systems and the terrorist threat: Protecting the nation's critical control systems: Joint hearing before the subcommittee on economic security, infrastructure protection, and cybersecurity with the subcommittee on emergency preparedness, science, and technology of the committee on homeland security*. United States Congress-House Committee on Homeland Security, Subcommittee on Economic Security, Infrastructure Protection, and Cybersecurity (109-45).

Diaxion. (2010). *Understanding IT governance – Part two.* Retrieved from http://www.diaxion.com/blog/2010/05/04/understanding-it-governance-%e2%80%93-part-two/

DigitalBond. (n.d.). *DigitalBond.* ICS Security Tool Mail List. Retrieved from http://www.digitalbond.com/tools/ics-security-tool-mail-list

DnD. (2008. *Rosing ICT-Security award.* Retrieved October 10, 2010, from www.dataforeningen.no/it-sikkerhetsprisen.4796706-160557.html

Dondossola, G., Deconinck, G., Garrone, F., & Beitollahi, H. (2009). Testbeds for assessing critical scenarios in power control systems . In Setola, R., & Geretshuber, S. (Eds.), *Critical Information Infrastructure Security* (*Vol. 5508*, pp. 223–234). Lecture Notes in Computer ScienceBerlin, Germany: Springer. doi:10.1007/978-3-642-03552-4_20

Doyle, J. C., Alderson, D. L., Li, L., Low, S., Roughan, M., & Shalunov, S. … Willinger, W. (2005). The "robust yet fragile" nature of the Internet. *Proceedings of the National Academy of Sciences, 102*, 14497-14502.

Dunn Cavelty, M. (2010, 29 October). The real cyberwar is about beating the crooks and the spooks. *Parliamentary Brief Online*. Retrieved February 6, 2011, from http://www.parliamentarybrief.com/2010/10/the-real-cyber-war-is-about-beating-the-crooks-and-the#all

Dunn Cavelty, M., & Rolofs, O. (2011). *From cyberwar to cybersecurity: Proportionality of fear and countermeasures.* Presentation to Munich Security Conference, 5 February.

Dunn Cavelty, M. (2007). Cyber-terror—Looming threat or phantom menace? The framing of the US cyber-threat debate. *Journal of Information Technology & Politics, 4*(1), 19–36. doi:10.1300/J516v04n01_03

Dunn Cavelty, M. (2008). *Cyber-security and threat politics: U.S. efforts to secure the information age.* New York, NY: Routledge.

Dynes, S., Goetz, E., & Freeman, M. (2008). Cyber security: Are economic incentives adequate? In Shenoi, S., & Goetz, E. (Eds.), *International Journal of Critical Infrastructure Protection* (*Vol. 1*, pp. 15–27). Boston, MA: Springer.

Dzung, D., Naedele, M., Von Hoff, T. P., & Crevatin, M. (2005). Security for industrial communications systems. *Proceedings of the IEEE, 93*(6), 1152–1177. doi:10.1109/JPROC.2005.849714

Electricity Sector Information Sharing and Analysis Center. (2005). *Security guidelines for the electricity sector: Patch management for control systems*. Retrieved October 15, 2011, from http://www.esisac.com/Public%20Library/Documents/Security%20Guidelines%20for%20the%20Electricity%20Sector/Patch%20Management%20for%20Control%20Systems,%20Version%201.0.pdf

Elias, T. D. (1994, 2 January). Toffler: Computer attacks wave of future. *South Bend Tribune*.

Ellefsen, I., & von Solms, S. (2010). The community-oriented computer security, advisory and warning team. In *IST-Africa 2010 Conference Proceedings*. IIMC International Information Management Corporation.

Ellefsen, I., & von Solms, S. (2010). Critical information infrastructure protection in the developing world . In Moore, T., & Shenoi, S. (Eds.), *Critical Infrastructure Protection IV* (*Vol. 342*, pp. 29–40). Boston, MA: Springer. Retrieved from. doi:10.1007/978-3-642-16806-2_3

Ellefsen, I., & von Solms, S. (2010). C-SAW: Critical information infrastructure protection through simplification . In *What Kind of Information Society? Governance, Virtuality, Surveillance, Sustainability, Resilience* (*Vol. 328*, pp. 315–325). Boston, MA: Springer. Retrieved from. doi:10.1007/978-3-642-15479-9_30

Emond, J. P. (2008). Resolution and integration of HF and UHF . In Miles, S. B., Sarma, S. E., & Williams, J. R. (Eds.), *RFID technology and applications* (pp. 144–156). New York, NY: Cambridge University Press. doi:10.1017/CBO9780511541155.012

Endorf, C., Schultz, E., & Mellander, J. (2004). *Intrusion detection & prevention*. McGraw-Hill Osborne Media.

Energiened. (n.d.). *Energiened documentation*. Retrieved from http://www.energiened.nl/Content/Publications/Publications.aspx

ENISA. (2011, December). *Protecting industrial control systems: ENISA recommendations.* (R. Leszczyna, Ed.). Retrieved from https://www.enisa.europa.eu/activities/Resilience-and-CIIP/critical-infrastructure-and-services/scada-industrial-control-systems/

EPCglobal. (2008). *EPC™ radio-frequency identity protocols class-1 Generation-2 UHF RFID protocol for communications at 860 MHz - 960 MHz version 1.2.0.* EPCglobal, Inc.

Ericsson, G. (2001). *Managing information security in an electric utility.* Cigré Joint Working Group (JWG) D2/B3/C2-01.

Eriksson, J. (2002). Cyberplagues, it, and security: Threat politics in the information age. *Journal of Contingencies and Crisis Management, 9*(4), 211–222.

ESCoRTS Project. (2008). *Security of control and real time systems.* Retrieved from http://www.escortsproject.eu

ESCoRTS Project. (2009). *Survey on existing methods, guidelines and procedures.* eSEC. (n.d.). *eSEC.* Plataforma Tecnológica Española de Tecnologías para Seguridad y Confianza. Retrieved from http://www.idi.aetic.es/esec

European Commission. (2010). *Non-paper on the establishment of a European public private partnership for resilience.* Retrieved 1 January, 2012, from http://ec.europa.eu/information_society/policy/nis/docs/ep3r_workshops/3rd_june2010/2010_06_23_ep3r_nonpaper_v_2_0_final.pdf

European Commission. (2011). *Communication from the Commission to the European Parliament, the Council, the European Economic and Social Committee and the Committee of the Regions on Critical Information Infrastructure Protection: Achievements and next steps: Towards global cyber-security, COM(2011) 163 Final.* Brussels, Belgium: European Commission.

European Commission. (2012). *Proposal for a regulation of the European Parliament and of the Council on the protection of individuals with regards to the processing of personal data and on the free movement of such data (general data protection regulation) COM(2012) 11 final.* Brussels, Belgium:

European Commission European Network and Information Security Agency. (2009). *Good practice guide network security information exchanges*. Heraklion, Greece: ENISA. Retrieved 1 January, 2012, from http://www.enisa.europa.eu/act/res/policies/good-practices-1/information-sharing-exchange/good-practice-guide

European Court of Auditors and INTOSAI. (2012). *Audit of disaster preparedness*, Draft ISSAI SSXX. Retrieved from http://eca.europa.eu/portal/page/portal/intosai-aada/meetings/-SixthmeetingoftheINTOSAIWorkingGroup/Microsoft%20Word%20-%20Draft%20ISSAI%20on%20Disaster%20Preparedness%205.pdf)

European Network and Information Security Agency. (2010). *Incentives and challenges to information sharing.* Heraklion, Greece: ENISA. Retrieved 1 January, 2012, from http://www.enisa.europa.eu/act/res/policies/good-practices-1/information-sharing-exchange/incentives-and-barriers-to-information-sharing?searchterm=Incentives+and

European Network and Information Security Agency. (2011). *Protecting industrial control systems, recommendations for European and member states.* Retrieved 16 January, 2012, from http://www.enisa.europa.eu/activities/Resilience-and-CIIP/critical-infrastructure-and-services/scada-industrial-control-systems/protecting-industrial-control-systems.-recommendations-for-europe-and-member-states

European Network and Information Security Agency. (2011). *Co-operative models for effective public private partnerships.* Heraklion, Greece: ENISA. Retrieved 1 January, 2012, from http://www.enisa.europa.eu/act/res/other-areas/national-public-private-partnerships-ppps

European Network and Information Security Agency. (2011). *A flair for sharing - Encouraging information exchange between CERTs.* Heraklion, Greece: ENISA. Retrieved 1 January 2012, from http://www.enisa. europa.eu/act/cert/support/legal-information-sharing/ legal-information-sharing-1

European Network and Informations Security Agency (ENISA). (2010). *EU Agency analysis of 'Stuxnet' malware: A paradigm shift in threats and critical information infrastructure protection.* Retrieved from http:// www.enisa.europa.eu/media/press-releases/eu-agency-analysis-of-2018stuxnet2019-malware-a-paradigm-shift-in-threats-and-critical-information-infrastructure-protection-1

Evron, G. (2008). Battling botnets and online mobs: Estonia's defense efforts during the internet war. *Georgetown Journal of International Affairs, 9*(Winter/Spring), 121–126.

Ezell, B. C. (2007). Infrastructure vulnerability assessment model (I VAM). *Risk Analysis, 27*(3), 571–583. doi:10.1111/j.1539-6924.2007.00907.x

Ezell, B. C., Farr, J. V., & Wiese, I. (2000). Infrastructure risk analysis model. *Journal of Infrastructure Systems, 6*, 114. doi:10.1061/(ASCE)1076-0342(2000)6:3(114)

Fallere, N., Murchu, L. O., & Chien, E. (2011). *W32. Stuxnet dossier - Version 1.4.* Retrieved February 07, 2012, from http://www.symantec.com/content/en/us/enterprise/ media/security_response/whitepapers/w32_stuxnet_dossier.pdf

Falliere, N. (2010). *Stuxnet introduces the first known rootkit for industrial control systems.* Symantec Official Blog. Retrieved September 5, 2011, from http://www. symantec.com/connect/blogs/stuxnet-introduces-first-known-rootkit-scada-devices

Falliere, N. L. O. M., & Chien, E. (2011, February). *W32. Stuxnet dossier.* Retrieved from http://www.symantec. com/content/en/us/enterprise/media /securityresponse/ whitepapers/w32 stuxnet dossier.pdf

Falliere, N., Murchu, L. O., & Chien, E. (2011). *W32. Stuxnet dossier.* Symantec.

Farahani, S. (2008). *ZigBee wireless networks and transceivers.* Oxford, UK: Elsevier Ltd.

Farhangi, H. (2010). The path of the smart grid. *IEEE Power and Energy Magazine, 8*(1), 18–28. doi:10.1109/ MPE.2009.934876

Farwell, J. P. (2011). Stuxnet and the future of cyber-war. *Survival Journal, 53*(1), 23-40. Retrieved from http:// www.tandfonline.com/doi/abs/10.1080/00396338.201 1.555586

FERC. (2009). *Smart grid policy.* Federal Energy Regulatory Commission. Retrieved January 20, 2012, from http:// www.ferc.gov/whats-new/comm-meet/2009/071609/E-3. pdf

Fernandez, J. D., & Fernandez, A. E. (2005). SCADA system: vulnerabilities and remediation. *Journal of Computing Sciences in Colleges, 20*, 160–168.

Festinger, L. (1957). *A theory of cognitive dissonance.* Stanford, CA: Stanford University Press.

Firesmith, D. G. (2003). *Common concepts underlying safety, security, and survivability engineering. Technical note CMU/SEI-2003-TN-033.* Carnegie Mellon University.

Fischhoff, B., Slovic, P., & Lichtenstein, S. (1978). Fault trees: Sensitivity of estimated failure probabilities to problem representation. *Journal of Experimental Psychology. Human Perception and Performance, 4*(2), 330–344. doi:10.1037/0096-1523.4.2.330

Fisher, D. (2011, 20 October). Using Stuxnet and Duqu as words of mass disruption. *Threat Post.* Retrieved February 6, 2011, from http://threatpost.com/en_us/blogs/ using-stuxnet-and-duqu-words-mass-disruption-102011

Fitzgerald, R. (1971, December). Divergence of the Kalman filter. *IEEE Transactions on Automatic Control, 16*(6), 736–747. doi:10.1109/TAC.1971.1099836

Floyd, R. (2011). Can securitization theory be used in normative analysis? Towards a just securitization theory. *Security Dialogue, 42*(4-5), 427–439. doi:10.1177/0967010611418712

Forum of Incident Response Teams. (2007). *Common vulnerability scoring system (CVSS); FIRST*. Retrieved September 9, 2012, from http://www.first.org/cvss

Foster, J. S., Jr., Gjelde, E., Graham, W. R., Hermann, R. J., Kluepfel, H. M., & Lawson, R. L. … Woodard, J. B. (April 2008*). Report of the commission to assess the threat to the United States from electromagnetic pulse (EMP) attack*. Retrieved from http://www.empcommission.org/

Fulkerson, D. R., & Harding, G. C. (1977). Maximizing the minimum source-sink path subject to a budget constraint. *Mathematical Programming, 13*, 116–118. doi:10.1007/BF01584329

Gadzheva, M. (2008). Legal issues in wireless building automation: An EU perspective. *International Journal of Law and Information Technology, 16*, 1–17. doi:doi:10.1093/iijit/ean001

Gal-Or, E., & Ghose, A. (2005). The economic incentives for sharing security information. *Information Systems Research, 16*(2). doi:10.1287/isre.1050.0053

Gamez, D., Nadjm-Tehrani, S., Bigham, J., Balducelli, C., Burbeck, K., & Chyssler, T. (2000). Safeguarding critical infrastructures . In Diab, H. B., & Zomaya, A. Y. (Eds.), *Dependable computing systems: Paradigms, performance issues, and applications* (pp. 479–500). Hoboken, NJ: Wiley.

GAO--United States General Accounting Office. (2004 March). *Critical infrastructure protection: Challenges and efforts to secure control systems, report to congressional requesters*. No. GAO-04-354.

Garcia, M. L. (2001). *The design and evaluation of physical protection systems*. Boston, MA: Butterworth-Heinemann.

Garcia, M. L. (2006). *Vulnerability assessment of physical protection systems*. Burlington, MA: Elsevier Butterworth-Heinemann.

Gartner Group. (2011). *Gartner says worldwide operating system software market grew to $30.4 billion in 2010*. Stamford, CT: Retrieved 1 January, 2012, from http://www.gartner.com/it/page.jsp?id=1654914

Gartner. (2008). *Assessing the security risks of cloud computing*. Retrieved from http://www.gartner.com/DisplayDocument?id=685308

Gaylord, C. (2010, 16 February). Cyber shockwave cripples computers nationwide (sorta). *Christian Science Monitor*. Retrieved February 6, 2011, from http://www.csmonitor.com/Innovation/Horizons/2010/0216/Cyber-ShockWave-cripples-computers-nationwide-sorta

Gelbstein, E., & Kamal, A. (2002). *Information insecurity*. New York, NY: United Nations ITC Task Force.

German Association of Energy and Water Industries. (2005). Requirements for secure control and telecommunication systems, Version 1.0. Retrieved October 17, 2011, from http://www.vdew.net/bdew.nsf/id/52929DBC7CEEED1EC125766C000588AD/$file/Whitepaper_Secure_Systems_Vedis_1.0final.pdf

Gershwin, K. L. (2001). *Cyber threat trends and US network security: Statement of L.K. Gershwin, National Intelligence Officer for Science and Technology*. Retrieved 20 December 2011 from https://www.cia.gov/news-information/speeches-testimony/2001/gershwin_speech_06222001.html

Ghose, A., Balakrishnan, K., & Ipeirotis, P. (2008, June). *The impact of information disclosure on stock market returns: The Sarbanes-Oxley act and the role of media as an information intermediary*. Seventh Workshop on Economics of Information Security, Hanover, NH.

Gilchrist, G. (2008). Secure authentication for DNP3. *IEEE Power and Energy Society General Meeting - Conversion and Delivery of Electrical Energy in the 21st Century*, (pp. 1-3).

Gill, P., & Phythian, M. (2006). *Intelligence in an insecure world*. London, UK: Polity.

Ginter, A. (2010). *An analysis of whitelisting security solutions and their applicability in control systems*.

Gladwell, M. (2009). *The tipping point*. St Ives, UK: Abacus.

Glasstone, S., & Dolan, P. J. (1977). *The effects of nuclear weapons* (3rd ed.). Washington, DC: U.S. Government Printing Office. doi:10.2172/6852629

Glöckler, O. (2011). *IAEA coordinated research project (CRP) on cybersecurity of digital I&C systems in NPPs*. Retrieved from http://www.iaea.org/NuclearPower/Downloads/Engineering/meetings/2011-05-TWG-NP-PIC/Day-3.Thursday/TWG-CyberSec-O.Glockler-2011.pdf

Glover, P., & Bowyer, S. (2011). *Who will secure your organisation in the future? Selecting for cyber-security personnel.* Retrieved 20 April 2012 from https://cybersecuritychallenge.org.uk/files/info-downloads/Who_will_secure_your_organisation_in_the_future.pdf

Goméz, J. A. (2011). *III curso de verano AMETIC-UPM 2011 hacia un mundo digital: Las e-TIC motor de los cambios sociales, económicos y culturales.*

Goode, S., & Lacey, D. (2009, December). Social embeddedness and sharing security information: Bridging the cost benefit gap. *Proceedings of the 20th Australasian Conference on Information Systems,* Melbourne, NSW.

Gordon, L. A., Loeb, M. P., & Lucyshyn, W. (2003). Sharing information on computer systems security: An economic analysis. *Journal of Accounting and Public Policy, 22*(6), 461–485. doi:10.1016/j.jaccpubpol.2003.09.001

Graham, S., & Thrift, N. (2007). Out of order: Understanding repair and maintenance. *Theory, Culture & Society, 24*(3), 1–25. doi:10.1177/0263276407075954

Green, M., Drew, S., Carter, L., & Burnett, D. (2009, January). *Submarine cable network security.* Presentation delivered at the Asia Pacific Economic Forum Workshop on Information Sharing. Retrieved 1 January, 2012, from http://www.iscpc.org/information/Openly%20Published%20Members%20Area%20Items/Submarine_Cable_Network_Security_PDF.pdf

Griffith, T. (Ed.). (1997). *On war.* Chatham, UK: Wordsworth Editions Limited.

Grigg, C. Reliability Test System Task Force of the Application of Probability Methods Subcommittee. (1999). IEEE reliability test system – 1996. *IEEE Transactions on Power Systems, 14*(3), 1010–1020. doi:10.1109/59.780914

Gross, T. (2008). Internet failure hits two continents, and may last two weeks. *National Review.* Retrieved from http://tinyurl.com/87tuus2

Grove, C. (2012, February 29). Cut cable halts service to thousands of GCI customers. *Anchorage Daily News.* Retrieved from http://tinyurl.com/7yurj7f

Grubesic, T. H., & Matisziw, T. C. (2012). A typological framework for categorizing infrastructure vulnerability. *GeoJournal,* online before print. DOI: 10.1007/s10708-011-9411-0

Grubesic, T. H., & Murray, A. T. (2006). Vital nodes, interconnected infrastructures and the geographies of network survivability. *Annals of the Association of American Geographers. Association of American Geographers, 96*(1), 64–83. doi:10.1111/j.1467-8306.2006.00499.x

Grubesic, T. H., & O'Kelly, M. E. (2002). Using points of presence to measure city accessibility to the commercial internet. *The Professional Geographer, 54,* 259–278. doi:10.1111/0033-0124.00330

Grubesic, T. H., O'Kelly, M. E., & Murray, A. T. (2003). A geographic perspective on commercial Internet survivability. *Telematics and Informatics, 20,* 51–69. doi:10.1016/S0736-5853(02)00003-5

Gungor, V. C., Sahin, D., Kocak, T., Ergut, S., Buccella, C., Cecati, C., & Hancke, G. P. (2011). Smart grid technologies: Communication technologies and standards. *IEEE Transactions on Industrial Informatics, 7*(4), 529–539. doi:10.1109/TII.2011.2166794

Hadi, A. S., Imon, A. H. M. R., & Werner, M. (2009). Detection of outliers–overview. *Computational Statistics, 1*(1).

Hadnagy, C. (2011). *Social engineering: The art of human hacking.* Indiana: Wiley Hadnagy, C., & O'Gorman, J. (2011). *Social engineering: Capture the flag results.* Retrieved 4 January 2012 from http://www.social-engineer.com/downloads/Social-Engineer_Defcon_19_SECTF_Results_Report.pdf

Hahn, R. W., & Layne-Farrar, A. (2006). The law and economics of software security. *Harvard Journal of Law & Public Policy, 30,* 283–354.

Haimes, Y. Y., & Chittester, C. G. (2005). A roadmap for quantifying the efficacy of risk management of information security and interdependent SCADA systems. *Journal of Homeland Security and Emergency Management, 2*(2), 12. doi:10.2202/1547-7355.1117

Hammerli, B., & Renda, A. (2010). *Protecting critical infrastructure in the EU.* Task Force Report. Brussels, Belgium: Centre for European Policy Studies. Retrieved from http://www.ceps.eu/ceps/download/4061

Hammes, U. R. (2010 February). *Robust positioning algorithms for wireless networks.* PhD thesis, TU Darmstadt.

Hamoud, G., Chen, R., & Bradley, I. (2003). Risk assessment of power systems SCADA. *IEEE Power Engineering Society General Meeting.*

Hansen, L., & Nissenbaum, H. (2009). Digital disaster, cyber security, and the Copenhagen school. *International Studies Quarterly, 53*(4), 1155–1175. doi:10.1111/j.1468-2478.2009.00572.x

Harrison, J., & Townsend, K. (2008, December). An update on WARPs. *ENISA Quarterly Review, 4*(4), 13-14. Retrieved from http://www.warp.gov.uk/downloads/enisa_quarterly_12_08.pdf

Hauge, S., Johnsen, S. O., & Onshus, T. (2009). *Uavhengighet av sikkerhetssystemer/Functional independence of safety systems.* Sintef Report. Retrieved January 1, 2011, from www.ptil.no/nyheter/ny-rapport-om-sikkerhetssystemers-uavhengighet-article7292-24.html

Hawrylak, P. J., & Mickle, M. H. (2009). EPC Gen-2 standard for RFID. In Y. Zhang, L. T. Yang, & J. Chen (Eds.), *RFID and sensor networks: Architectures, protocols, security and integrations* (pp. 97-124). Boca Raton, FL: Taylor & Francis Group, CRC Press.

Hawrylak, P. J., Cain, J. T., & Mickle, M. H. (2008). RFID tags . In Yan, L., Zhang, Y., Yang, L. T., & Ning, H. (Eds.), *The internet of things: From RFID to pervasive networked systems* (pp. 1–32). Boca Raton, FL: Auerbach Publications, Taylor & Francis Group. doi:10.1201/9781420052824.ch1

Hawrylak, P. J., Ogirala, A., Norman, B. A., Rajgopal, J., & Mickle, M. H. (2011). Enabling real-time management and visibility with RFID . In Kolker, A., & Story, P. (Eds.), *Management engineering for effective healthcare delivery principles and applications* (pp. 172–190). Hershey, PA: IGI Global. doi:10.4018/978-1-60960-872-9.ch008

Heacock, R. (2009). *Internet filtering in sub-Saharan Africa* (Tech. Rep.). OpenNet Initiative. Retrieved from http://opennet.net/sites/opennet.net/files/ONI_SSAfrica_2009.pdf

Hendricke, U. (2011, July). *Germany's PPP for the protection of CII.* Presentation delivered at the Meeting of the Working Groups of the European Public Private Partnership for Resilience (EP3R) Brussels, 6th July 2011. Retrieved from http://ec.europa.eu/information_society/policy/nis/strategy/activities/ciip/impl_activities/ep3r_06_07_2011/index_en.htm

Hildick-Smith, A. (2005). *Security for critical infrastructure SCADA systems.* SANS Institute.

Hollnagel, E., Woods, D., & Leveson, N. (2006). *Resilience engineering.* Ashgate.

Holstein, D. C., Li, H. L., & Meneses, A. (2010). *The impact of implementing cyber security requirements using IEC 61850.*

Holstein, D. K. (2008). *P1711 "The state of closure".* PES/PSSC Working Group C6.

Holton, G. A. (2004). Defining risk. *Financial Analysts Journal, 60*(6), 19–25. doi:10.2469/faj.v60.n6.2669

Homeland Security Act. (2002). Washington, DC.

Homeland Security Newswire. (2011). *Greatest cyber vulnerabilities are people, says cybersecurity expert.* Retrieved 15 December 2011 from http://www.homelandsecuritynewswire.com/bull20111019-greatest-cyber-vulnerabilities-are-people-says-cybersecurity-expert

Hopkins, A. (2011). Risk-management and rule-compliance: Decision making in hazardous industries. *Safety Science, 49*, 110–120. doi:10.1016/j.ssci.2010.07.014

Hoque, E., Dickerson, R. F., & Stankovic, J. A. (2010). Monitoring body positions and movements during sleep using WISPs. *Proceedings of the 2010 International Conference on Wireless Health*, (pp. 44-53). New York, NY.

House Committee on Armed Services. (2010). *Statement of General Keith B. Alexander Commander United States Cyber Command.* United States House of Representatives, 23 September.

Howard, M., & LeBlanc, D. (2003). *Writing secure code.* Microsoft Press.

Hubbard, D. W. (2009). *The failure of risk management and what to do about it.* Hoboken, NJ: Wiley.

Huber, P. (1968). Robust estimation. *Selected Statistical Papers*, 3–25.

Huber, P. J. (1974). Roubst estimation of a location parameter. *Annnals of Mathmatical Statics, 35*.

Huber, P. (1972). Robust statistics: A review. *Annals of Mathematical Statistics, 43*(3), 1041–1067. doi:10.1214/aoms/1177692459

Huber, P. J. (1965, December). A robust version of the probability ratio test. *Annals of Mathematical Statistics, 36*(6), 1753–1758. doi:10.1214/aoms/1177699803

Huber, P. J., & Ronchetti, E. M. (2009). *Robust statistics* (2nd ed.). Hoboken, NJ: Wiley. doi:10.1002/9780470434697

Huntington, G. (2009). *NERC CIP's and identity management*. Huntington Ventures Ltd.

Hutchins, T. R., & Overbye, T. J. (2011). *The effect of geomagnetic disturbances on the electric grid and appropriate mitigation strategies.* North American Power Symposium (NAPS), 2011.

Hutwagner, L., Maloney, E., Bean, N., Slutsker, L., & Martin, S. (1997). Using laboratory-based surveillance data for prevention: An algorithm for detecting salmonella outbreaks. *Emerging Infectious Diseases, 3*(3), 395. doi:10.3201/eid0303.970322

IBM Global Services. (2007). *A strategic approach to protecting SCADA and process control systems.*

ICS-ALERT. (2011, 1 November). ICS-ALERT11-291-01E-W32.Duqu: An information-gathering malware. *ICS-ALERT.* Retrieved February 6, 2011, from http://www.us-cert.gov/control_systems/pdf/ICS-ALERT-11-291-01E.pdf

ICS-CERT. (2011, 8 November). JSAR-11-312-01-W32. Duqu-Malware. *Joint Security Awareness Report.* Retrieved February 6, 2011, from http://www.us-cert.gov/control_systems/pdf/JSAR-11-312-01.pdf

ICS-CERT. (2011, 23 November). Icsb-11-327-01-Illinois water pump failure report. *ICS-CERT Information Bulletin.* Retrieved February 6, 2011, from http://www.us-cert.gov/control_systems/pdf/ICSB-11-327-01.pdf

IEC 61508. (2010). *Functional safety of electrical/electronic/ programmable electronic safety-related systems.*

IEC 62443. (2008). *Security for industrial process measurement and control - Network and system security.*

IEC. (2003). *International Standard IEC 60870-5-101, second edition, Telecontrol equipment and systems - Part 5-101: Transmission protocols - Companion standard for basic telecontrol tasks.*

IEC. (2011). *IEC/TS 62351: Security.* Retrieved October 1, 2011, from http://www.iec.ch/smargrid/standards

IEEE PASSAT11, Boston, MA.

IEEE. (1992). *IEEE recommended practice for master/ remote supervisory control and data acquisition (SCADA) communications.*

IEEE. (2000). *IEEE recommended practice for data communications between remote terminal units and intelligent electronic devices in a substation.*

IEEE. (2006). *802.15.4-2006 wireless medium access control (MAC) and physical layer (PHY) specifications for low-rate wireless personal area networks (LR-WPANS).* Retrieved from IEEE 802.15 WPAN TG4: http://www.ieee802.org/15/pub/TG4.html

IEEE. (2007). *IEEE recommended practice for SCADA and automation systems.*

Igure, V. M., Laughter, S. A., & Williams, R. D. (2006). Security issues in SCADA networks. *Computers & Security, 25*(7), 498–506. doi:10.1016/j.cose.2006.03.001

Iinternational Atomic Energy Agency (IAEA). (2011). *IAEA technical meeting on newly arising threats in cybersecurity of nuclear facilities.* Retrieved from http://www.iaea.org/NuclearPower/Downloads/Engineering/files/InfoSheet-CybersecurityTM-May-2011.pdf

Inch, E. S., Warnick, B., & Endres, D. (2006). *Critical thinking and communication: The use of reason in argument* (5th ed.). Boston, MA: Allyn & Bacon.

Independent Oracle Users Group. (2009). *Security patching practices by Oracle customers.* Retrieved October 17, 2011, from http://ioug.itgonvergence.com

Indian Government. (2000, October). *Information technology act, 21 of 2000.* Retrieved from http://www.mit.gov.in/content/view-it-act-2000

Industrial Control Systems Cyber Emergency Response Team. (2011). *ICS-CERT incident response summary report.* Retrieved 20 July, 2012, from http://www.us-cert.gov/control_systems/pdf/ICS-CERT_Incident_Response_Summary_Report_09_11.pdf

Industrial Defender. (2011). *Managing automation systems: Critical infrastructure operators' challenges and opportunities.* Retrieved 20 July 2012 from www.industrialdefender.com/icsreport/ICSurveyReport.pdf

Information Sharing and Analysis Centre Council. (2009). *The role of information sharing and analysis centres in private/public sector critical infrastructure protection.* New York, NY. Retrieved 1 January, 2012, from http://www.isaccouncil.org

INSPIRE Project. (2008). *Increasing security and protection through infrastructure resilience.* Retrieved from http://www.inspire-strep.eu

Institute for the Protection and Security of the Citizen. (2006). *European SCADA and control systems information exchange.* Joint Research Centre of the European Commission. Ispra, Italy. Retrieved 1 January, 2012, from http://sta.jrc.ec.europa.eu/index.php/competitive-projects-/21-scni/8-e-scsie

Institute of Electrical and Electronics Engineers (IEEE). (1994). *IEEE standard C37.1-1994: Definition, specification, and analysis of systems used for supervisory control, data acquisition, and automatic control.* Institute of Electrical and Electronics Engineers.

Institute of Electrical and Electronics Engineers (IEEE). (2000). *IEEE PES computer and analytical methods subcommittee.* Retrieved from http://ewh.ieee.org/cmte/psace/CAMS_taskforce.html

Institute of Electrical and Electronics Engineers (IEEE). (2007). *IEEE standard for substation intelligent electronic devices (IEDs) cyber security capabilities.*

Institute of Electrical and Electronics Engineers (IEEE). (2008). *Transmission & Distribution Exposition & Conference 2008 IEEE PES: Powering toward the Future.* Institute of Electrical and Electronics Engineers. Institute of Electrical and Electronics Engineers (IEEE). *WGC1 - Application of computer-based systems.* Retrieved from http://standards.ieee.org/develop/wg/WGC1.html.

Institute of Electrical and Electronics Engineers (IEEE). (n.d.). *IEEE power & energy society.* Retrieved from http://www.ieee-pes.org

Institute of Electrical and Electronics Engineers (IEEE). *E7.1402 - Physical security of electric power substations.* Retrieved from http://standards.ieee.org/develop/wg/E7_1402.html.

Institute of Electrical and Electronics Engineers (IEEE). *WGC6 - Trial use standard for a cryptographic protocol for cyber security of substation serial links.* Retrieved from http://standards.ieee.org/develop/wg/WGC6.html

Intelligence Reform and Terrorism Prevention Act. (2004). House of Representatives. Washington, DC.

International Atomic Energy Authority. (2008). *Nuclear security culture.* Retrieved 10 August, 2012, from http://www-pub.iaea.org/MTCD/publications/PDF/Pub1347_web.pdf

International Electrochemical Commission. (2004). *IEC TS 61850: Power systems management and associated information exchange–Data and communications security–Part 19.*

International Electrotechnical Commission (IEC). (2007). *IEC TS 62351-1: Power systems management and associated information exchange – Data and communications security. Part 1: Communication network and system security – Introduction to security issues.* International Electrotechnical Commission.

International Electrotechnical Commission (IEC). (2007). *IEC TS 62351-3: Power systems management and associated information exchange – Data and communications security – Part 3: Communication network and system security – Profiles including TCP/IP.* International Electrotechnical Commission.

International Electrotechnical Commission (IEC). (2007). *IEC TS 62351-4: Power systems management and associated information exchange – Data and communications security – Part 4: Profiles including MMS.* International Electrotechnical Commission.

International Electrotechnical Commission (IEC). (2007). *IEC TS 62351-6: Power systems management and associated information exchange – Data and communications security – Part 6: Security for IEC 61850.* International Electrotechnical Commission.

International Electrotechnical Commission (IEC). (2008). *IEC TS 62351-2: Power systems management and associated information exchange – Data and communications security – Part 2: Glossary of terms.* International Electrotechnical Commission.

International Electrotechnical Commission (IEC). (2009). *IEC TS 62351-5: Power systems management and associated information exchange – Data and communications security – Part 5: Security for IEC 60870-5 and derivatives.* International Electrotechnical Commission.

International Electrotechnical Commission (IEC). (2010). *IEC 61850-7-2: Communication networks and systems for power utility automation – Part 7-2: Basic information and communication structure – Abstract communication service interface (ACSI)*. International Electrotechnical Commission.

International Electrotechnical Commission (IEC). (2010). *IEC TS 62351-7: Power systems management and associated information exchange – Data and communications security. Part 7: Network and system management (NSM) data object models*. International Electrotechnical Commission.

International Federation for Information Processing (IFIP). (n.d.). *IFIP TC 8 International Workshop on Information Systems Security Research*. Retrieved from http://ifip.byu.edu

International Federation for Information Processing (IFIP). (n.d.). *IFIP technical committees*. Retrieved from http://ifiptc.org/?tc=tc11

International Federation for Information Processing (IFIP). (n.d.). *IFIP WG 1.7 home page*. Retrieved from http://www.dsi.unive.it/~focardi/IFIPWG1_7

International Federation of Automatic Control (IFAC). (n.d.). *TC 3.1. Computers for control — IFAC TC websites*. Retrieved from http://tc.ifac-control.org/3/1

International Federation of Automatic Control (IFAC). (n.d.). *TC 6.3. power plants and power systems — IFAC TC websites*. Retrieved from http://tc.ifac-control.org/6/3

International Federation of Automatic Control (IFAC). (n.d.). *Working Group 3: Intelligent monitoring, control and security of critical infrastructure systems — IFAC TC websites*. Retrieved from http://tc.ifac-control.org/5/4/working-groups/copy2_of_working-group-1-decentralized-control-of-large-scale-systems

International Instruments Users' Association (WIB). (2010). *Process control domain - Security requirements for vendors*. EWE (EI, WIB, EXERA).

International Monetary Fund (IMF). (2012, April). *World economic outlook report*. Retrieved from http://www.imf.org/external/pubs/ft/weo/2012/01/pdf/text.pdf

International Organization for Standardization. (2005). *ISO/IEC 27002:2005. Information technology - Security techniques - Code of practice for information security management*.

International Society of Automation (ISA). (n.d.). *ISA99 Committee - Home*. Retrieved from http://isa99.isa.org/ISA99 Wiki/Home.aspx

International Telecommunication Union. (2010, November). *Facts and figures 2010*. Retrieved from www.itu.int/ITU-D/ict/material/FactsFigures2010.pdf

INTERSECTION Project. (2008). *Infrastructure for heterogeneous, resilient, secure, complex, tightly interoperating networks (INTERSECTION)*. Retrieved from http://www.intersection-project.eu

Interstate Natural Gas Association of America (INGAA). (2011). *Control systems cyber security guidelines for the natural gas pipeline industry*. Interstate Natural Gas Association of America.

IRRIIS Project. (2006). *Homepage of the IRRIIS project*. Retrieved from http://www.irriis.org

IsaSecure. (2010). *International Society for Automation, ISA Security Compliance Institute, North Carolina*. Retrieved January 1, 2011, from www.isasecure.org/

ISO 11064. (2000). *Ergonomic design of control centers*.

ISO/IEC 27001. (2005). *Information technology -- Security techniques -- Information security management systems*. Requirements, ISO.

Israeli, E., & Wood, R. K. (2002). Shortest-path network interdiction. *Networks*, *40*, 97–111. doi:10.1002/net.10039

Japkowicz, N., Myers, C., & Gluck, M. (1995, August). *A novelty detection approach to classification*. Paper presented at the meeting of the 14th International Conference on Artificial Intelligence, Montreal, CA.

Jara, A. J., Zamora, M. A., & Skarmeta, A. F. (2011). An internet of things-based personal device for diabetes therapy management in ambient assisted living (AAL). *Personal and Ubiquitous Computing*, *15*(4), 431–440. doi:10.1007/s00779-010-0353-1

Jeff Trandahl, C. (2001). *USA Patriot Act (H.R. 3162).* Retrieved from http://epic.org/privacy/terrorism/hr3162.html

Jeong, J., & Lee, S. (2010 December).Outlier elimination method for robust visual servo control in

Jewell, L. N., & Siegal, M. (1990). *Contemporary industrial organizational psychology.* St Paul, MN: West Publishing Company.

Jiang, W., Han, S., Tsui, K., & Woodall, W. (2011). Spatiotemporal surveillance methods in the presence of spatial correlation. *Statistics in Medicine, 30*(5), 569–583. doi:10.1002/sim.3877

Jin, X., Bigham, J., Rodaway, J., Gamez, D., & Phillips, C. (2006, March). *Anomaly detection in electricity cyber infrastructure.* Paper presented at the meeting of the International Workshop on Complex Network and Infrastructure Protection, CNIP 2006, Rome, Italy.

Johnsen, S. O., Bjørkli, C., Steiro, T., Fartum, H., Haukenes, H., Ramberg, J., & Skriver, J. (2011). *CRIOP – A scenario method for crisis intervention and operability analysis.* SINTEF. Retrieved February 10, 2011, from www.criop.sintef.no

Johnsen, S. O., Okstad, E., Aas, A. L., & Skramstad, T. (2010). *Proactive indicators of risk in remote operations of oil and gas fields.* SPE International Conference on Health, Safety and Environment in Oil and Gas Exploration and Production. DOI 10.2118/126560-MS

Johnson, M. E., & Goetz, E. (2007). *Embedding information security into the organization. IEEE Security & Privacy, 5(3).* Los Alamitos, CA: IEEE Computer Society.

Kabay, M. E. (2010). *Attacks on power systems: Data leakage, espionage, insider threats, sabotage.* Retrieved October 15, 2011, from http://www.networkworld.com/newsletters/sec/2010/ 090610sec2.html?page=1

Kahneman, D., & Tversky, A. (1979). Prospect theory: An analysis of decision under risk. *Econometrica, 47*(2). doi:10.2307/1914185

Kanabar, M., & Sidhu, T. (2011). Performance of IEC 61850-9-2 process bus and corrective measure for digital relaying. *IEEE Transactions on Power Delivery, 26*(2), 725–735. doi:10.1109/TPWRD.2009.2038702

Kaplan, S. (1997). The words of risk analysis. *Risk Analysis, 17*(4), 407–417. doi:10.1111/j.1539-6924.1997.tb00881.x

Kappenman, J. G., Radasky, W. A., Gilbert, J. L., & Erinmez, I. A. (2000). Advanced geomagnetic storm forecasting: A risk management tool for electric power system operations. *IEEE Transactions on Plasma Science, 28,* 2114–2121. doi:10.1109/27.902238

Khurana, H., Hadley, M., Lu, N., & Frincke, D. (2010). Smart-grid security issues. *IEEE Security & Privacy, 8*(1), 81–85. doi:10.1109/MSP.2010.49

Killcrece, G. (2004, August). *Steps for creating national CSIRTs.* Retrieved from www.cert.org/archive/pdf/NationalCSIRTs.pdf

Klaus, M. (2010, March). *MELANI: Information exchange –A story of success.* Presentation delivered at ENISA's Workshop on Information Sharing; Amsterdam. Retrieved 1 January, 2012, from http://www.enisa.europa.eu/act/res/workshops-1/2010/information-sharing-workshop/copy_of_agenda-of-the-information-sharing-workshop

Knapp, E. D. (2011). *Industrial network security: Securing critical infrastructure networks for smart grid, SCADA, and other industrial control systems.* Syngress Media.

Knorr, K. (2006, September). *Security monitoring for siemens products.* Paper presented at the 19th Task Force of Computer Security Incident Response Teams Meeting, Espoo, Finland.

Knorr, K. (2009, March). *Product vulnerability management - The Siemens CERT perspective.* Paper presented at the Workshop on the EU policy dimension of vulnerability management and disclosure process, Brussels.

Ko, C., Ruschitzka, M., & Levitt, K. (1997). *Execution monitoring of security-critical programs in distributed systems: A specification-based approach.*

Kolfal, B., Patterson, R., & Yeo, L. (2010, June). *Market impact on IT security spending.* Presentation at The Ninth Workshop on the Economics of Information Security Harvard, NH.

Korns, S. W., & Kastenberg, J. E. (2008). Georgia's cyber left hook. *Parameters,* (Winter): 60–76.

Kosut, O., Jia, L., Thomas, R. J., & Tong, L. (2010, March). *Limiting false data attacks on power system state estimation*. Paper presented at the meeting of the 2010 44th Annual Conference on Information Sciences and Systems, CISS 2010, Princeton, USA.

Krause, K. (2010). *The true size of Africa*. Retrieved from http://edge.org/documents/Edge-Serpentine-MapsGallery/high-res/Krause.pdf

Krebs, B. (2008, June 5). Cyber incident blamed for nuclear power plant shutdown. *Washington Post Online*. Retrieved October 17, 2011, from http://www.washingtonpost.com/wp-dyn/content/article/2008/06/05/AR2008060501958.html

Krebs, B. (2011, 22 November). DHS blasts reports of Illinois water station hack. *Krebs on Security*. Retrieved February 6, 2011, from http://krebsonsecurity.com/2011/11/dhs-blasts-reports-of-illinois-water-station-hack/

Kruegel, C., Mutz, D., Robertson, W., & Valeur, F. (2003). Bayesian event classification for intrusion detection. In *Proceedings of the 19th Annual Computer Security Applications Conference (ACSAC '03)*. IEEE Computer Society.

Krutz, R. L. (2006). *Securing SCADA systems*. Hoboken, NJ: Wiley Publishing, Inc.

Kujuro, A. (1990). *Trend of system technology in intelligent buildings in Japan*. Singapore: Asia-Pacific Exhibitions and Conventions Pte Ltd.

Kunreuther, H., & Heal, G. (2003). Interdependent security. *Journal of Risk and Uncertainty, 26*(2-3), 231–249. doi:10.1023/A:1024119208153

Lafontaine, J. (1999). *Intelligent building concept*. Ontario, Canada: EMCS Engineering Inc.

Lai, T. (2001). Sequential analysis: some classical problems and new challenges. *Statistica Sinica, 11*(2), 303–350.

Lai, T. L. (1998, November). Information bounds and quick detection of parameter changes in stochastic systems. *IEEE Transactions on Information Theory, 44*(7), 2917–2929. doi:10.1109/18.737522

Lambert-Torres, G., Rossi, R., Ribeiro, G. M., Valiquette, B., & Mukhedkar, F. (1992, August). *Computer program package for power system protection and control*. Paper presented at the meeting of the CIGRÉ Biennale Congress, Paris, France.

Langevin, R. J. R. (2008). *Securing cyberspace for the 44th presidency*. Washington, DC: Center for Strategic and International Studies.

Langston, C., & Lauge-Kristensen, R. (2002). *Strategic management of built facilities*. Boston, MA: Butterworth-Heinemann.

Lawson, S. (2010, 23 April). Cyberwar: We don't know what it is or if we're in one, but. *Forbes.com*. Retrieved February 6, 2011, from http://www.forbes.com/sites/firewall/2010/04/23/cyberwar-we-dont-know-what-it-is-or-if-were-in-one-but/

Lawson, S. (2011). Beyond cyber-doom: Cyberattack scenarios and the evidence of history. *Mercatus Center Working Paper, No. 10-77*.

Lee, D. (2012, May). *Flame: Massive cyber-attack discovered, researchers say*. Retrieved from http://www.bbc.com/news/technology-18238326

Lehmann, E., & Romano, J. (2005). *Testing statistical hypotheses*. Springer Verlag.

Leveson Inquiry. (2011). *Witness statement of Sienna Miller*. Retrieved 17 April 2012 from http://www.levesoninquiry.org.uk/wp-content/uploads/2011/11/Witness-Statement-of-Sienna-Miller.pdf

Leveson, N. (1995). *Safeware – System safety*. Addison-Wesley.

Lewis, J. A. (2010). *The cyber war has not begun*. Unpublished manuscript. Retrieved February 6, 2011, from http://csis.org/files/publication/100311_TheCyberWarHasNotBegun.pdf

Lewis, J. A. (2011). *Thresholds for cyberwarfare. IEEE Security and Privacy, 99*. PrePrint.

Lewis, T. (2006). *Critical infrastructure protection in homeland security: Defending a networked nation*. LibreDigital. doi:10.1002/0471789542

Lim, C., & Smith, J. C. (2007). Algorithms for discrete and continuous multicommodity flow network interdiction problems. *IIE Transactions, 39*, 15–26. doi:10.1080/07408170600729192

Lines, S. (2008, May). *Best practice for sharing threats and warning information between industry and the US government*. Presentation at the CSIIR Workshop Oak Ridge National laboratory, May 13 2008.

Liu, Y., Ning, P., & Reiter, M. K. (2009, November). *False data injection attacks against state estimation in electric power grid*. Paper presented at the meeting of the 16ᵗʰ ACM Conference on Computer Communications Security, CCS′09, Chicago, USA.

Liu, D., Wang, X. F., & Camp, J. (2008). Game-theoretic modeling and analysis of insider threats. *International Journal of Critical Infrastructure Protection, 1*, 75–80. doi:10.1016/j.ijcip.2008.08.001

Lorden, G. (1971). Procedures for reacting to a change in distribution. *Annals of Mathematical Statistics, 42*(6), 1897–1908. doi:10.1214/aoms/1177693055

Louthan, G., Hardwicke, P., Hawrylak, P., & Hale, J. (2011). *Toward hybrid attack dependency graphs*. Paper presented at the 7th Annual Cyber Security and Information Intelligence Research Workshop, Oak Ridge.

Lucas, J., & Crosier, R. (1982). Fast initial response for CUSUM quality-control schemes: Give your CUSUM a head start. *Technometrics, 24*(3), 199–205. doi:10.1080/00401706.1982.10487759

Luders, S. (2006). CERN tests reveal security flaws with industrial networked devices. *The Industrial Ethernet Book, 35,* 12-23. Retrieved May 12, 2009, from www.iebmedia.com

Luijf, E. (2003). *Critical information infrastructure in the Netherlands*. The Netherlands: TNO Physics and Electronics Laboratory.

Lundin, E., & Jonsson, E. (2002). *Survey of intrusion detection research*. Technical Report No. 02-04, Department of Computer Engineering, Chalmers University of Technology, Götebrog, Sweden.

Lund, J., & Aarø, L. E. (2004). Accident prevention. Presentation of a model placing emphasis on human, structural and cultural factors. *Safety Science, 42*(4), 271–324. doi:10.1016/S0925-7535(03)00045-6

Lynn III, W. J. (2011). *Remarks on the department of defense cyber strategy*. Presentation to National Defense University, 14 July.

Lynn, W. J. III. (2010). Defending a new domain: The Pentagon's cyberstrategy. *Foreign Affairs, 89*(5), 97–108.

Madsen, J. (2008). *The realization of intelligent buildings*. Retrieved May 28, 2010, from http://www.buildings.com/ArticleDetails/tabid/3321/ArticleID/5736/Default.aspx

Malcolmson, J., Brown, P., Way, R., Abdi, S., Brennen, S., & Walters, J. (2010). *Improving interoperability by understanding information-sharing culture: A scoping study.* QINETIQ/10/00888.

Mandjes, M., & Zuraniewski, P. (2011). M/G/ transience, and its applications to overload detection. *Performance Evaluation, 68*(8).

Manning, C. D., & Schütze, H. (1999). *Foundations of statistical natural language processing*. Cambridge, MA: MIT Press.

Mansfield, I. (2011, May). *Mobile banking surges as emerging markets embrace mobile finance*. Retrieved from www.cellular-news.com/story/49148.php

Markou, M., & Singh, S. (2003). Novelty detection: A review – Part 2: Neural network based approaches. *Signal Processing, 83*(12), 2499–2521. doi:10.1016/j.sigpro.2003.07.019

Marsh, R. T. (1997). *Critical foundations: Protecting America's infrastructures: The report of the president's commission on critical infrastructure protection*. Washington, DC: The White House.

Martinelli, M., Tronci, E., Dipoppa, G., & Balducelli, C. (2004, September). *Electric power system anomaly detection using neural networks*. Paper presented at the meeting of the 8th International Conference KES 2004, Wellington, New Zealand.

Martin, R. D., & Thomson, D. J. (1982, September). Robust-resistant spectrum estimation. *Proceedings of the IEEE, 70,* 1097–1115. doi:10.1109/PROC.1982.12434

Masek, M., Boeing, A., & Bailey, W. (2010). Critical infrastructure protection risk modelling with games technology. *What Kind of Information Society? Governance, Virtuality, Surveillance, Sustainability . Resilience, 328,* 363–372. doi:doi:10.1007/978-3-642-15479

Masica, K. (2007). *Recommended practices guide for securing ZigBee wireless networks in process control system environments.*

Masica, K. (2007). *Securing WLANs using 802.11i*. Draft. Recommended Practice.

Massoud Amin, S., & Wollenberg, B. (2005). Toward a smart grid: Power delivery for the 21st century. *IEEE Power and Energy Magazine, 3*(5), 34–41. doi:10.1109/MPAE.2005.1507024

Matisziw, T. C., Grubesic, T. H., & Guo, J. (2012). (in press). Robustness elasticity in complex networks. *PLoS ONE*. doi:10.1371/journal.pone.0039788

Matisziw, T. C., Murray, A. T., & Grubesic, T. H. (2009). Exploring the vulnerability of network infrastructure to interdiction. *The Annals of Regional Science, 43*, 307–321. doi:10.1007/s00168-008-0235-x

Matrosov, A., Rodionov, E., Harley, D., & Malcho, J. (2011, January). *Stuxnet under the microscope.* Retrieved from http://www.eset.com/us/resources/white-papers/Stuxnet_Under_the_Microscope.pdf

Mavridou, A., & Papa, M. (2011). A situational awareness architecture for the smart grid. *7th International Conference in Global Security Safety and Sustainability (ICGS3).* Thessaloniki, Greece.

McAfee Foundstone Professional Services and McAfee Labs. (2011). *Global energy cyberattacks: "Night dragon.* Santa Clara, CA: McAfee Foundstone Professional Services and McAfee Labs.

McAfee. (2011). *Global energy cyberattacks - Night Dragon.* Retrieved February 20, 2011, from www.mcafee.com/us/resources/white-papers/wp-global-energy-cyber-attacks-night-dragon.pdf

McConnell, M. (2010, 28 February). Mike McConnell on how to win the cyber-war we're losing. *Washington Post*, p. B01.

McDaniel, P., & McLaughlin, S. (2009). Security and privacy challenges in the smart grid. *IEEE Security & Privacy, 7*(3), 75–77. doi:10.1109/MSP.2009.76

McHugh, J. (2000). Testing intrusion detection systems: A critique of the 1998 and 1999 DARPA intrusion detection system evaluations as performed by Lincoln laboratory. *ACM Transactions on Information and System Security, 3*(4), 262–294. doi:10.1145/382912.382923

McHugh, J. (2001). Intrusion and intrusion detection. *International Journal of Information Security, 1*(1), 14–35.

McHugh, J., Christie, A., & Allen, J. (2000). The role of intrusion detection systems. *IEEE Software, 17*(5), 42–51. doi:10.1109/52.877859

McKinnon, A., Dorow, K., Damania, T., Haugan, O., Lawrence, W., Bakken, D., & Shovic, J. (2003). A configurable middleware framework with multiple quality of properties for small embedded systems. In *Second IEEE International Symposium on Network Computing and Applications,* (pp. 197–204).

Mehra, R. (1970, April). On the identification of variances and adaptive Kalman filtering. *IEEE Transactions on Automatic Control, 15*(2), 175–184. doi:10.1109/TAC.1970.1099422

Mé, L., & Cédric, M. (2001). *Intrusion detection: A bibliography*. France: SUPÉLEC.

Mell, P., Bergeron, T., & Henning, D. (2005). *Creating a patch and vulnerability management program*. NIST Special Publication 800-40 v2.0. Retrieved October 15, 2011, from http://csrc.nist.gov/publications/nistpubs/800-40-Ver2/SP800-40v2.pdf

Mell, P., Scarfone, K., & Romanosky, S. (2003). *A complete guide to the common vulnerability scoring system,* Version 2.0. Retrieved October 14, 2011, from http://www.first.org/cvss/cvss-guide.pdf

Meridian. (n.d.). *Meridian*. Retrieved from http://www.meridian2007.org

Microsoft. (2010). *Software vulnerability management at Microsoft*. Retrieved October 17, 2011, from http://www.microsoft.com/download/en/details.aspx?id=4372

Mills, E. (2010, 15 November). Symantec: Stuxnet clues point to uranium enrichment target. *CNET News.* Retrieved on February 6, 2011 from http://news.cnet.com/8301-27080_3-20022845-245.html

Mitchell, G. R. (2000). Placebo defense: Operation desert mirage? The rhetoric of patriot missile accuracy in the 1991 Persian Gulf War. *The Quarterly Journal of Speech, 86*(2), 121–145. doi:10.1080/00335630009384286

Mitchell, G. R. (2002). Public argument-driven security studies (review essay). *Argumentation and Advocacy, 39*, 57–71.

Mitchell, G. R. (2006). Team B intelligence coups. *The Quarterly Journal of Speech, 92*(2), 144–173. doi:10.1080/00335630600817993

Mitnik, K., & Simon, W. (2002). *The art of deception.* Indiana: Wiley Publishing.

Mitre, (2009) *Common vulnerabilities and exposures.* Retrieved 09th September, 2012, from http://cve.mitre.org/

Mitter, S., & Schick, I. (1993). *Point estimation, stochastic approximation, and robust Kalman filtering.* Massachusetts Institute of Technology, Laboratory for Information and Decision Systems.

Miyachi, T., Narita, H., Oguma, N., & Furuta, H. (2010, August). Consideration on vulnerability handling for control systems. *Proceedings of the SICE Annual Conference,* (pp. 1200–1203). Taipei.

Montgomery, D. C. (2009). *Introduction to statistical quality control.* Hoboken, NJ: John Wiley & Sons, Inc.

Moore, T. (2010, June). *Policy recommendations for cybersecurity.* Presentation delivered at the Ninth Workshop on the Economics of Information Security, Cambridge, MA (rump session presentation).

Moran, B., & Belisle, R. (2008). Modeling flow information and other control system behavior to detect anomalies. In *Proceedings of the SCADA Security Scientific Symposium* 2008.

Moteff, J. (2005). *Risk management and critical infrastructure protection: Assessing, integrating, and managing threats, vulnerabilities and consequences.*

Moustakides, G. (1986). Optimal stopping times for detecting changes in distributions. *Annals of Statistics, 14*(4), 1379–1387. doi:10.1214/aos/1176350164

Muncaster, P. (2011 April). Stuxnet-like attacks beckon as 50 new SCADA threats discovered. Retrieved from http://www.v3.co.uk/v3-uk/news/2045556/stuxnet-attacks-beckonscada-threats-discovered

Murray, A. T. (2012). An overview of network vulnerability modeling approaches. *GeoJournal.* doi:doi:10.1007/s10708-011-9414-z

Murray, A. T., & Grubesic, T. H. (Eds.). (2007). *Critical infrastructure: Reliability and vulnerability.* Heidelberg, Germany: Springer.

Murray, A. T., Matisziw, T. C., & Grubesic, T. H. (2007). Critical network infrastructure analysis: interdiction and system flow. *Journal of Geographical Systems, 9,* 103–117. doi:10.1007/s10109-006-0039-4

Myung, Y. S., & Kim, H. J. (2004). A cutting plane algorithm for computing k-edge survivability of a network. *European Journal of Operational Research, 156,* 579–589. doi:10.1016/S0377-2217(03)00135-8

Naedele, M., & Dzung, D. (2005). Industrial information system security part 1. *ABB Review, 2,* 66–70.

Naess, E., Frincke, D., McKinnon, A., & Bakken, D. (2005). Configurable middleware-level intrusion detection for embedded systems. In *25th IEEE International Conference on Distributed Computing Systems Workshops,* (pp. 144–151).

Nakashima, E. (2011, 18 November). Foreign hackers targeted U.S. water plant in apparent malicious cyber attack, expert says. *Washington Post.* Retrieved February 6, 2011, from http://www.washingtonpost.com/blogs/checkpoint-washington/post/foreign-hackers-broke-into-illinois-water-plant-control-system-industry-expert-says/2011/11/18/gIQAgmTZYN_blog.html

Nakashima, E. (2011, 25 November). Water-pump failure in Illinois wasn't cyberattack after all. *Washington Post.* Retrieved February 6, 2011, from http://www.washingtonpost.com/world/national-security/water-pump-failure-in-illinois-wasnt-cyberattack-after-all/2011/11/25/gIQACgTewN_story.html

Nath, C. (2011). *Cyber security in the UK.* Number 389 September 2011. Retrieved 2 August 2012 from http://www.parliament.uk/business/publications/research/briefing-papers/POST-PN-389

National Infrastructure Advisory Council. (2006). *Public-private sector intelligence coordination: Final report and recommendations by the council.* Retrieved 1 January, 2012, from http://www.dhs.gov/xlibrary/assets/niac/niac_icwgreport_july06.pdf

National Infrastructure against Cyber Crime. (2010). *United against cybercrime spring report 2010.* The Hague, The Netherlands. Retrieved 1 January, 2012, from http://www.samentegencybercrime.nl/UserFiles/File/NEW-lentebericht_2010-UK%20DEFINITIEF.pdf

National Infrastructure Security Coordination Centre (NISCC). (2005). *Firewall deployment for scada and process control networks. Good practice guide.* National Infrastructure Security Coordination Centre.

National Infrastructure Security Coordination Centre (NISCC). (2005). *Good practice guide on firewall deployment for SCADA and process control networks. British Columbia Institute of Technology*. BCIT.

National Institute of Standards and Technology (NIST). (2004). *NISTIR 7176: System protection profile - Industrial control systems*. Decisive Analytics.

National Institute of Standards and Technology (NIST). (2009). *NIST SP 800-53: Information security*. National Institute of Standards and Technology.

National Institute of Standards and Technology (NIST). (2010). *NISTIR 7628: Guidelines for smart grid cyber security. Smart Grid Interoperability Panel–Cyber Security Working Group*. SGIP–CSWG.

National Institute of Standards and Technology (NIST). (2011). *NIST SP 800-82: Guide to industrial control systems (ICS) security*. National Institute of Standards and Technology.

National Institute of Standards and Technology. (2009). *Recommended security controls for federal information systems and organizations*. NIST SP800-53, Revision 3. Retrieved from http://crsc.nist.gov

NC. (2011). *The National Commission on the BP Deepwater Horizon oil spill and offshore drilling's final report*. Retrieved February 1, 2011, from www.oilspillcommission.gov

NCS. (2004). *Supervisory control and data acquisition (SCADA) systems, technical information bulletin NCS TIB 04-1*. Arlington, VA.

NERC Steering Group. (2003). *Technical analysis of the August 14, 2003 blackout: What happened, why, and what did we learn?* Retrieved 10 December 2011 from http://www.nerc.com/docs/docs/blackout/NERC_Final_Blackout_Report_07_13_04.pdf

NERC. (2011). *Reliability standards for the bulk electric systems of North America*. Retrieved January 23, 2012, from http://www.nerc.com/docs/standards/rs/Reliability_Standards_Complete_Set.pdf

NETL. (2008). *Advanced metering infrastructure*. Retrieved January 23, 2012, from http://www.netl.doe.gov/smartgrid/referenceshelf/whitepapers/AMI%20White%20paper%20final%20021108%20%282%29%20APPROVED_2008_02_12.pdf

News, B. B. C. (2011). *150 officers warned over Facebook posts*. Retrieved 14 January, 2011, from http://www.bbc.co.uk/news/uk-16363158

Newton-Evans. (2008). *Market Trends Digest; Executive Summary of Findings From EMS, SCADA, DMS Study*. Ellicott City, MD: Newton Evans Research Company Inc.

Nichol, J. (2008). *Russia-Georgia conflict in South Ossetia: Context and implications for U.S. interests*. Washington, DC: Congressional Research Service.

Nickolov, N. (2005). Critical information infrastructure protection: Analysis, evaluation and expectations. *Information & Security, 17*, 105–119.

NIST. (2010). *NISTIR 7628, guidelines for smart grid cyber security*. National Institute of Standards and Technology.

North American Electric Reliability Corporation (NERC). (1989). *The 1989 system disturbances*. NERC Disturbance Analysis Working Group.

North American Electric Reliability Corporation (NERC). (2004). *Final report on the August 14, 2003 blackout in the United States and Canada: Causes and recommendations*. Retrieved from http://www.nerc.com/filez/blackout.html

North American Electric Reliability Corporation (NERC). (2009). *Categorizing cyber systems. An approach based on BES reliability functions. Cyber security standards drafting team for project 2008-06 Cyber security order 706*.

North American Electric Reliability Corporation (NERC). (2010). *CIP-001-1a: Sabotage reporting*. North American Electric Reliability Corporation.

North American Electric Reliability Corporation (NERC). (2011). *CIP-002-4: Cyber security — Critical cyber asset identification*. North American Electric Reliability Corporation.

North American Electric Reliability Corporation. (2010). *Critical infrastructure protection standards*. Retrieved October 17, 2011, from http://www.nerc.com/page.php?cid=2%7C20

Northcutt, S., & Novak, J. (2000). *Network intrusion detection–An analyst's handbook* (2nd ed.). Indianapolis, IN: New Riders Publishing.

Norwegian Oil Industry Association (OLF). (2006). *OLF guideline No. 104: Information security baseline requirements for process*. Norwegian Oil Industry Association.

Norwegian Oil Industry Association (OLF). (2006). *OLF guideline No.110: Implementation of information security in PCSS/ICT systems during the engineering, procurement and commissioning phases*. Norwegian Oil Industry Association.

Norwegian Oil Industry Association (OLF). (2009). *Information security baseline requirements for process control, safety, and support ICT systems*. Norwegian Oil Industry Association.

NTSB. (2002). *Pipeline rupture and subsequent fire in Bellingham, Washington, June 10, 1999*. (Pipeline Accident Report NTSB/PAR-02/02). National Transportation Safety Board.

NTSB. (2005). *National Transportation Safety Board safety study – Supervisory control and data acquisition (SCADA)*. (Report NTSB/SS-05/02).

Nye, D. E. (2010). *When the lights went out: A history of blackouts in America*. Cambridge, MA: MIT Press.

Oman, P. W., Risley, A. D., Roberts, J., & Schweitzer, E. O., III. (2002, April). *Attack and defend tools for remotely accessible control and protection equipment in electric power systems*. Paper presented at the meeting of the Texas A & M Annual Conference for Protective Relays Engineers, College Station, TX.

Oman, P., Roberts, J., & Schweitzer, E. (2001). *Obstacles to self-healing reliable complex control systems*. Fourth Information Survivability Workshop: Impediments to Achieving Survivable Systems. Retrieved December 6, 2011, from http://tinyurl.com/4x4wf33

Oman, P., Schweitzer, E., III, & Frincke, D. (2000). Concerns about intrusions into remotely accessible substation controllers and SCADA systems. *Twenty-Seventh Annual Western Protective Relay Conference*, (p. 160). Spokane, WA. Retrieved January 18, 2012, from http://www.selinc.com/literature/literature.aspx?fid=282

Oman, P., & Phillips, M. (2007). *Intrusion detection and event monitoring in SCADA networks* (pp. 161–173). Critical Infrastructure Protection. doi:10.1007/978-0-387-75462-8_12

Omer, M., Nilchiani, R., & Mostashari, A. (2009). Measuring the resilience of the global internet infrastructure system. In *Proceedings of 3ʳᵈ Annual IEEE Systems Conference*. Vancouver, BC: IEEE Computer Society

OPC Task Force. (1998). *OPC overview*. Retrieved June 7, 2011, from http://www.opcfoundation.org/Archive/72e9fbfa-6a89-4ef2-9b6d-3f746fd7eb05/General/ OPC%20Overview%201.00.pdf

Open Smart Grid. (n.d.). *Open smart grid*. Retrieved from http://osgug.ucaiug.org/default.aspx

*Oracle Security*1998O'Reilly *PLC manual*. (2011). Retrieved from http://www.plcmanual.com/

Oriyano, S. P., & Gregg, M. (2011). *Hacker techniques, tools and incident handling*. Jones and Bartlett Learning.

Page, E. S. (1954). Continuous inspection schemes. *Biometrika*, *41*, 100–114.

Parker, M. (2011, 12 December). Beyond Stuxnet and Duqu: Security implications to our infrastructure. *Symantec Connect*. Retrieved February 6, 2011, from http://www.symantec.com/connect/blogs/beyond-stuxnet-and-duqu-security-implications-our-infrastructure

Patterson, T. (2010, 15 October). U.S. electricity blackouts skyrocketing. *CNN.com*. Retrieved February 6, 2011, from http://www.cnn.com/2010/TECH/innovation/08/09/smart.grid/index.html?hpt=Sbin

Pawlak, Z. (1991). *Rough sets - Theoretical aspects of reasoning about data*. Dordrecht, The Netherlands: Kluwer Academic Publishers.

Paxson, V. (2001 November). *Topics in network intrusion detection*. In Tutorial, 8th ACM Conference on Computer and Communications Security (CCS-8).

Payne, J. W., Bettman, J. R., & Johnson, E. J. (1993). *The adaptive decision maker*. New York, NY: Cambridge University Press. doi:10.1017/CBO9781139173933

Pearson, R. (2002, January). Outliers in process modeling and identification. *IEEE Transactions on Control Systems Technology*, *10*(1), 55–63. doi:10.1109/87.974338

Peddabachigari, S., Abraham, A., Grosan, C., & Thomas, J. (2007). Modeling intrusion detection system using hybrid intelligent systems. *Journal of Network and Computer Applications*, *30*(1), 114–132. doi:10.1016/j.jnca.2005.06.003

Peoples, C., & Vaughan-Williams, N. (2010). *Critical security studies: An introduction.* London, UK: Routledge.

Perlner, R. A., & Cooper, D. A. (2010). *Quantum resistant public key cryptography: A survey.* National Institute of Standards and Technology.

Perrow, C. (1999). *Normal accidents: Living with high-risk technologies.* Princeton, NJ: Princeton University Press.

Peterson, D. G. (2011, 19 October). Duqu and ICS? *Digital Bond.* Retrieved February 6, 2011, from http://www.digitalbond.com/2011/10/19/duku-and-ics/

Pfleeger, S. L. (2010). Anatomy of an intrusion. *IT Pro, July/August 2010,* 21-28.

Pfleeger, C., & Pfleeger, S. (2007). *Security in computing* (*Vol. 604*). Prentice Hall.

Pietre-Cambacedes, L., Kropp, T., Weiss, J., & Pellizzoni, R. (2008, August). *Cybersecurity standards for the electric power industry – A survival kit.* Paper presented at the meeting of the 42nd CIGRE Biennale Conference, Paris, France.

Pietre-Cambacedes, L., & Chaudet, C. (2010). The SEMA referential framework: Avoiding ambiguities in the terms security and safety. *International Journal of Critical Infrastructure Protection, 3,* 55–66. doi:10.1016/j.ijcip.2010.06.003

Pollak, M. (1985). Optimal detection of a change in distribution. *Annals of Statistics, 13,* 206–227. doi:10.1214/aos/1176346587

Porteous, J. M. (1995). Intelligent buildings and their effect on the security industry. *Proceedings Institute of Electrical and Electronics Engineers 29th Annual 1995 International Carnahan Conference* (pp. 186-188). New York, NY: IEEE.

Poulsen, K. (2003). *Slammer worm crashed Ohio nuke plant network.* Retrieved October 13, 2011, from http://www.securityfocus.com/news/6767

Powell, A. (2010, March). *UK's information sharing national strategy.* Presentation delivered at ENISA's workshop on Information Sharing; Amsterdam. Retrieved 1 January, 2012, from http://www.enisa.europa.eu/act/res/workshops-1/2010/information-sharing-workshop/copy_of_agenda-of-the-information-sharing-workshop

Powell, R. (2007). Defending against terrorist attacks with limited resources. *The American Political Science Review, 101,* 527–541. doi:10.1017/S0003055407070244

Preece, J., Nonnecke, B., & Andrews, D. (2004). The top five reasons for lurking: improving community experiences for everyone. *Computers in Human Behavior, 20*(2), 201–223. doi:10.1016/j.chb.2003.10.015

President's Commission on Critical Infrastructure Protection. (1997). *Critical foundations: Protecting America's infrastructures.* Washington, DC: President's Commission on Critical Infrastructure Protection. Retrieved 1 January, 2012, from http://www.ciao.gov/CIAO_Document_Library/PCCIP_Report.pdf

PSA. (2010). Audit of BP Norge's follow-up of new work processes within drilling and well activities using information and communication technology (ICT). *PSA Journal,* 2010/1112. Retrieved January 1, 2011, from www.ptil.no/news/audit-of-bp-s-follow-up-of-new-work-processes-article7566-79.html

PSA. (2010). Audit of Norne 2010. *PSA Journal,* 2010/93. Retrieved January 1, 2011, from www.ptil.no/nyheter/tilsyn-med-beredskap-norne-fpso-article6834-24.html

PSA. (2010). *Safety system independence.* Retrieved January 1, 2011, from www.ptil.no/news/safety-system-independence-in-focus-article7293-79.html?lang=en_US

Quang, P. X. (1985, June). Robust sequential testing. *Annals of Statistics, 13*(2), 638–649. doi:10.1214/aos/1176349544

Rader, E., Wash, R., & Brooks, B. (2012). *Stories as informal lessons about security.* Symposium on Usable Privacy and Security (SOUPS). Symposium on Usable Privacy and Security (SOUPS) 2012, July 11-13, 2012, Washington, DC, USA.

Rakaczky, E. (2005). *Intrusion insights adapting intrusion prevention functionality for process control/SCADA systems.*

Ralston, P. A., Graham, J. H., & Hieb, J. L. (2007). Cyber security risk assessment for SCADA and DCS networks. *ISA Transactions, 46*(4), 583–594. doi:10.1016/j.isatra.2007.04.003

Raymond, D. R., Marchany, R. C., Brownfield, M. I., & Midkiff, S. F. (2009). Effects of denial-of-sleep attacks on wireless sensor network MAC protocols. *IEEE Transactions on Vehicular Technology, 58*(1), 367–380. doi:10.1109/TVT.2008.921621

Renn, O. (2005). *Risk governance – Towards an integrative approach*. White paper no.1. Geneva, Switzerland: IRGC.

Reyes, A., Barba, A., Callaghan, V., & Clarke, G. (2001). *The integration of wireless, wired access and embedded agents in intelligent buildings.* Paper presented at the The 5th World Multi-conference on Systemics, Cybernetics and Informatics, Orlando, Florida.

Rid, T. (2011). Cyber war will not take place. *Journal of Strategic Studies,* iFirst.

Rijksoverheid. (2009). *Scenario's nationale risicobeoordeling 2008/2009.* Retrieved from http://www.rijksoverheid.nl/documenten-en-publicaties/rapporten/2009/10/21/scenario-s-nationale-risicobeoordeling-2008-2009.html

Rinaldi, S. M., Peerenboom, J. P., & Kelly, T. K. (2001). Identifying, understanding and analyzing critical infrastructure interdependencies. *IEEE Control Systems Magazine,* (December): 11–25. doi:10.1109/37.969131

Riptech. (2001). *Understanding SCADA system security vulnerabilities.* Retrieved from http://www.iwar.org.uk/cip/resources/utilities/SCADAWhitepaperfinal1.pdf2001

Ritchie, B. (1993). *Ritchie and Marshall (1993) business risk management (Vol. 1).* London, UK: Chapman & Hall.

Roberts, S. W. (1959). Control chart tests based on geometric moving averages. *Technometrics, 1*(3), 239–250. doi:10.1080/00401706.1959.10489860

Roberts, S. W. (1966). A comparison of some control chart procedures. *Technometrics, 8,* 411–430. doi:10.1080/00401706.1966.10490374

Robinson, R. P. E., & Woodworth, B. (2008). *Security-hardened attack-resistant platform.* SHARP.

Rohrmair, G., & Knorr, K. (2007). Patch Management aus Sicht eines Herstellers . In Schartner, P. (Ed.), *DACH Security 2007* (pp. 248–258).

Rossi, R. (2000). *Systemic hierarchical classifier for high-voltage electric systems.* PhD Thesis, Itajuba Federal University, Itajuba, Brazil (in Portuguese).

Rosslin, J. R., & Choi, M.-K. (2009). Assessment of the vulnerabilities of SCADA, control systems and critical infrastructure systems. *International Journal of Grid and Distributed Computing, 2*(2).

Rousseau, D. M. (1989). Psychological and implied contracts in organizations. *Employee Responsibilities and Rights Journal, 2,* 121–139. doi:10.1007/BF01384942

Rowe, B. R., & Gallaher, M. P. (2006, June). *Private sector cyber security investment strategies: An empirical analysis.* Fifth Workshop on Economics of Information Security, Cambridge, UK.

Rrushi, J., Campbell, R., & di Milano, U. (2008). *Detecting attacks in power plant interfacing substations through probabilistic validation of attack-effect bindings.* In SCADA Security Scientific Symposium.

Rue, R., Pfleeger, S., & Ortiz, D. (2007, June). *A framework for classifying and comparing models of cyber security investment to support policy and decision-making.* Sixth Workshop on Economics of Information Security, Pittsburgh PA.

Ryan, T. (2011). *Statistical methods for quality improvement (Vol. 840).* Wiley. doi:10.1002/9781118058114

Saadwi, T., & Jordan, L., Jr., (Eds.). (2011). *Cyber infrastructure protection.* Retrieved from http://www.strategicstudiesinstitute.army.mil/pdffiles/PUB1067.pdf

Salmeron, J., Wood, K., & Baldick, R. (2009). Worst-case interdiction analysis of large-scale electric power grids. *IEEE Transactions on Power Systems, 24,* 96–104. doi:10.1109/TPWRS.2008.2004825

Sands-Ramshaw, L. (2010). *Creating large disturbances in the power grid: Methods of attack after cyber infiltrations.* Dartmouth College Computer Science Technical Report TR2010-668, Dartmouth College.

Sangsuk-Iam, S., & Bullock, T. (1990, December). Analysis of discrete-time kalman filtering under incorrect noise covariances. *IEEE Transactions on Automatic Control, 35*(12), 1304–1309. doi:10.1109/9.61006

SANS. (1989). *SCADA security advanced training.* Retrieved from http://www.sans.org/security-training/scada-security-advanced-training-1457-mid

SANS. (2011). *The 2011 Asia Pacific SCADA and Process Control Summit - Event-at-a-glance.* Retrieved from http://www.sans.org/sydney-scada-2011

Sasse, A. M., Ashenden, D., Lawrence, D., Coles-Kemp, L., Fléchais, I., & Kearney, P. (2007). *Cyber security KTN human factors white paper: Human vulnerabilities in security system.*

Scaparra, M. P., & Church, R. L. (2008). A bilevel mixed-integer program for critical infrastructure protection planning. *Computers & Operations Research, 35,* 1905–1923. doi:10.1016/j.cor.2006.09.019

Scaparra, M. P., & Church, R. L. (2008). An exact solution approach for the interdiction median problem with fortification. *European Journal of Operational Research, 189,* 76–92. doi:10.1016/j.ejor.2007.05.027

Scarfone, K., & Mell, P. (2007). Guide to intrusion detection and prevention systems (IDPS). *NIST Special Publication, 800,* 94.

Schick, I., & Mitter, S. (1994). Robust recursive estimation in the presence of heavy-tailed observation noise. *Annals of Statistics, 22*(2), 1045–1080. doi:10.1214/aos/1176325511

Schneider, D., & Rode, P. (2010, Spring). Energy renaissance. *High Performance Building Magazine,* 13-16.

Schneier, B. (2007) SCADA security hole. *Schneier on Security.* Retrieved 1 January, 2012, from http://www.schneier.com/blog/archives/2007/05/scada_security.html

Schneier, B. (1999). *Attack trees: Modeling security threats.* Dr. Dobb's Journal.

Schneier, B. (2003). *Beyond fear: Thinking sensibly about security in an uncertain world.* Springer.

Schryen, G. (2009). *A comprehensive and comparative analysis of the patching behaviour of open source and closed source software vendors.* Paper presented at the Fifth International Conference on IT Security Incident Management and IT Forensics, Retrieved February 6, 2012, from http://www.icsi.berkeley.edu/pubs/networking/comprehensiveand09.pdf

Secunia. (2010). *Secunia half year report 2010.* Retrieved October 17, 2011, from http://secunia.com/gfx/pdf/Secunia_Half_Year_Report_2010.pdf

SecureWorks. (2011, 26 October). Duqu questions and answers. *SecureWorks.com.* Retrieved February 6, 2011, from http://www.secureworks.com/research/threats/duqu/

Securities and Exchange Commission. (2011). *CF disclosure guidance: Topic No. 2 Cybersecurity.* Retrieved 09 September, 2012, from http://www.sec.gov/divisions/corpfin/guidance/cfguidance-topic2.htm

Senator Jean-Marie Bockel. (2012). *Rapport d'information on cyber defense.* Retrieved from http://www.senat.fr/notice-rapport/2011/r11-681-notice.html

Shapiro, R., Bratus, S., & Smith, S. (2011, March). *Assessing the vulnerability of SCADA devices.* Paper Presented at the Fifth Annual IFIP Working Group 11.10 International Conference on Critical Infrastructure Protection, Hanover, NH.

Sharples, S., Callaghan, V., & Clarke, G. (1999). A multi-agent architecture for intelligent building sensing and control. *Sensor Review, 19*(2), 135–140. doi:10.1108/02602289910266278

Shaw, E. D., & Stock, H. V. (2011). *Behavioral risk indicators of malicious insider theft of intellectual property: Misreading the writing on the wall.* Retrieved 15 December, 2011, from http://www.symantec.com/about/news/release/article.jsp?prid=20111207_01

Shaw, W. T. (2006). *Cyber security for SCADA systems.* PennWell Corp.

Shea, D. A. (2003). *Critical infrastructure: Control systems and the terrorist threat.* Retrieved 15 April, 2012, from www.fas.org/irp/crs/RL31534.pdf

Shewhart, W. A. (1931). *The economic control of quality of a manufactured product.* Princeton, NJ: Van Nostrand.

Shirey, R. (2000). *Internet security glossary.* Request for Comment 2828. Retrieved October 16, 2011, from, http://www.ietf.org/rfc/rfc2828.txt

Shiryaev, A. (1963). On optimum methods in quickest detection problems. *Theory of Probability and Its Applications, 8,* 2246. doi:10.1137/1108002

Shiu, S., Baldwin, A., Beres, Y., Duggan, G. B., Casassa Mont, M., Johnson, H., & Middup, C. (2011, June). *Economic methods and decision making by security professionals.* Tenth Workshop on the Economics of Information Security, George Mason University, NH.

Siponen, M., Pahnila, S., & Mahmood, M. A. (2010). *Compliance with information security policies: An empirical investigation.*

Siris, V., & Papagalou, F. (2006). Application of anomaly detection algorithms for detecting syn flooding attacks. *Computer Communications, 29*(9), 1433–1442. doi:10.1016/j.comcom.2005.09.008

SISCO - Systems Integration Specialists Company, Inc. (2005). *Overview and introduction to the manufacturing message specification (MMS)*. Retrieved October 12, 2011, from http://www.sisconet.com/downloads/mmsovrlg.pdf

Slay, J., & Miller, M. (2007). Lessons learned from the Maroochy water breach . In Shenoi, S., & Goetz, E. (Eds.), *International Journal of Critical Infrastructure Protection* (*Vol. 1*, pp. 73–82). Boston, MA: Springer. doi:10.1007/978-0-387-75462-8_6

Slovic, P. (1999). Trust, emotion, sex, politics, and science: Surveying the risk-assessment battlefield. *Risk Analysis, 19*(4), 689–701. doi:10.1111/j.1539-6924.1999.tb00439.x

Smart Accelerate. (n.d). *Intelligent building assessment methodology*. Retrieved May 24, 2010, from http://www.ibuilding.gr/definitions.html

Smart Grid Interoperability Panel (SGIP). (n.d.). *SGIP Cyber Security Working Group (SGIP CSWG)*. Retrieved from http://collaborate.nist.gov/twiki-sggrid/bin/view/SmartGrid/CyberSecurityCTG

Smith, S. S. (2006). *The SCADA security challenge: The race is on.*

Smith, S., Jamieson, R., & Winchester, D. (2007). An action research program to improve information systems security compliance across government agencies. *Proceedings of the Fortieth Annual Hawaii International Conference on System Sciences*, (p. 99).

Smith, T. (2001, 31 October). Hacker jailed for revenge sewage attacks. *The Register*. Retrieved 2 April, 2012, from http://www.theregister.co.uk/2001/10/31/hacker_jailed_for_revenge_sewage/

Snediker, D., Murray, A. T., & Matisziw, T. C. (2008). Decision support for network disruption mitigation. *Decision Support Systems, 44*, 954–969. doi:10.1016/j.dss.2007.11.003

Snyder, L. V., Scaparra, M. P., Daskin, M. S., & Church, R. L. (2006). Planning for disruptions in supply chain networks. *INFORMS Tutorials in Operations Research*, 234-257.

So, A. T. P., & Wong, K. C. (2002). On the quantitative assessment of intelligent buildings. *Facilities, 20*(7/8), 288–295. doi:10.1108/02632770210435206

Sommer, P., & Brown, I. (2011). *Reducing systemic cybersecurity risk*. Paris, France: OECD.

Song, S. (2011, October). *African undersea cables*. Retrieved from http://manypossibilities.net/african-undersea-cables

Soule, A., Salamatian, K., & Taft, N. (2005). Combining filtering and statistical methods for anomaly detection. In *Proceedings of the 5th ACM SIGCOMM Conference on Internet Measurement*, (p. 31). USENIX Association.

South African Government. (2002, August). *Electronic communications and transactions act, 25 of 2002*. Retrieved from http://www.acts.co.za/ect_act/

Spano, R., & Nagy, S. (2005). Social guardianship and social isolation: An application and extension of lifestyle/routine activities theory to rural adolescents. *Rural Sociology, 70*, 414–437. doi:10.1526/0036011054831189

Spellman, R., & Stoudt, M. L. (2011). *Nuclear infrastructure protection and homeland security*. Rowman & Littlefield.

Stajano, F., & Wilson, P. (2009) *Understanding scam victims: Seven principles for systems security*. University of Cambridge Computer Laboratory. UCAM-CL-TR-754

Stamp, J. (2003). *Common vulnerabilities in critical infrastructure control systems*. Albuquerque, NM: Sandia National Laboratories.

Standards Australia. (2004). *HB 221:2004 Business continuity management*. Sydney, Australia: Standards Australia International Ltd.

Standards Australia. (2004). *HB 436:2004 Risk management guidelines: Companion to AS/NZS 4360*. Sydney, Australia: Standards Australia International Ltd.

Standards Australia. (2009). *AS/NZS ISO 31000:2009. Risk management - Principles and guidelines: In context*. Sydney, Australia: Standards Australia International Ltd.

Standards Australia. (2010). *HB 327: 2010 Communicating and consulting about risk: Companion to AS/NZS ISO 31000:2009*. Sydney, Australia: Standards Australia, International Ltd.

Sternberg, E., & Lee, G. C. (2006). Meeting the challenge of facility protection for homeland security. *Journal of Homeland Security and Emergency Management, 3*(1), 11. doi:10.2202/1547-7355.1153

Stevens, W. R. (2005). *TCP/IP illustrated: The protocols.* Addison Wesley.

Stikvoort, D. (2009). *Trusted introducer information sharing traffic light protocol (ISTLP).* NISCC (UK). Retrieved 1 January, 2012, from https://www.trusted-introducer.org/links/ISTLP-v1.1-approved.pdf

Stohl, M. (2007). Cyber terrorism: A clear and present danger, the sum of all fears, breaking point or patriot games? *Crime, Law, and Social Change, 46*(4-5), 223–238. doi:10.1007/s10611-007-9061-9

Stouffer, K., Falco, J., & Kent, K. (2006, September). Guide to supervisory control and data acquisition (SCADA) and industrial control systems security. *Recommendations of the National Institute of Standards and Technology Special Publication,* (pp. 800–82).

Stouffer, K., Falco, J., & Kent, K. (2008). *Guide to supervisory control and data acquisition and industrial control systems security.* NIST Special Publication 800-82, USA.

Stouffer, K., Falco, J., & Scarfone, K. (2011). *Guide to industrial control systems (ICS) security.* NIST Special Publication 800-42. Retrieved October 15, 2011, from http://csrc.nist.gov/publications/nistpubs/800-82/SP800-82-final.pdf

Stouffer, K., Falco, J., & Scarfone, K. (2011). *NIST special publication 800-82: Guide to industrial control systems (ICS) security.* Retrieved February 7, 2012, from http://csrc.nist.gov/publications/nistpubs/800-82/SP800-82-final.pdf

Stouffer, K., Falco, J., & Ken, K. (2006). *Guide to supervisory control and data acquisition (scada) and industrial control systems security, Recommendations of the National Institute of Standards and Technology.* NIST.

Susman, G., & Evered, R. (1978). An assessment of the scientific merits of action research. *Administrative Science Quarterly, 23,* 582–603. doi:10.2307/2392581

Suter, M. (2007). *A generic national framework for critical information infrastructure protection.* Centre for Security Studies, Zurich University, Prepared for the World Summit on the Information Society and the International Telecommunications Union. Retrieved from http://www.itu.int/ITU-D/cyb/cybersecurity/docs/generic-national-framework-for-ciip.pdf

Suter, M., & Brunner, E. M. (2008). *International CIIP handbook 2008 / 2009.*

Swedberg, C. (2010). UC Davis winery tracks fermentation via RFID sensors. *RFID Journal.* Retrieved October 9, 2011, from http://www.rfidjournal.com/article/view/8033

Swedish Civil Contingencies Agency (MSB). (2010). *Guide to increased security in industrial control systems.* Swedish Civil Contingencies Agency.

Swiderski, F., & Snyder, W. (2004). *Treat modeling.* Microsoft Press.

Symantec. (2011 November). *W32.duqu – The precursor to the next Stuxnet.* Symantec Security Response, [Online], *Accessed* 2011 November.

Symantec. (2011). *W32.Duqu: Precursor to the next Stuxnet.* Mountain View, CA: Symantec.

Symantec. (2011). *W32.Stuxnet dossier.* Retrieved March 1, 2011, from www.symantec.com/content/en/us/enterprise/media/security_response/whitepapers/w32_stuxnet_dossier.pdf

Talbot, J., & Jakeman, M. (2009). *Frontmatter. Security Risk Management* (pp. i–xxiv). London, UK: John Wiley & Sons, Inc.doi:10.1002/9780470494974.fmatter

Taleb, N. (2010). *The black swan* (2nd ed.). New York, NY: Random House.

Taleb, N. N. (2007). *The black swan, the impact of the highly improbable.* Random.

Tech-Exclusive. (2010). India faces disrupted internet service due to undersea cable issue. *Tech-Exclusive.* Retrieved 1 January, 2012, from http://www.tech-exclusive.com/india-faces-disrupted-internet-service-due-to-undersea-cable-issue/

Technical Support Working Group (TSWG). (2005). *Securing your SCADA and industrial control systems.* Department of Homeland Security.

Techtarget.com. (2001). *IT-ISAC: A matter of trust.* Retrieved 1 January, 2012, from http://searchsecurity. techtarget.com/news/517824/IT-ISAC-A-matter-of-trust

Ten, C.-W., Liu, C.-C., & Manimaran, G. (2008). Vulnerability assessment of cybersecurity for SCADA systems. *IEEE Transactions on Power Systems, 23*(4), 1836–1846. doi:10.1109/TPWRS.2008.2002298

Thaler, R. H., & Sunstein, C. R. (2008). *Nudge: Improving decisions about health, wealth and happiness.* London, UK: Yale University Press.

The 451 Group. (2010). *The adversary: APTs and adaptive persistent adversaries.*

The White House. (1998). *Presidential decision directive 63- Fact sheet- Protecting America's Critical Infrastructures: PDD 63.* Retrieved 1 January, 2012, from http:// www.pub.whitehouse.gov/uri-res/I2R?urn:pdi://oma.eop. gov.us/1998/5/26/1.text.1

The White House. (2001). *Executive order 13231.* Retrieved from http://www.fas.org/irp/offdocs/eo/eo-13231. htm

The White House. (2006). *Homeland security presidential decision directive 7: Critical infrastructure identification, prioritization and protection.* (HSPD-7) Washington D.C. Retrieved 1 January, 2012, from http://www.dhs.gov/ xabout/laws/gc_1214597989952.shtm#0

The White House. (2007). *National strategy for information sharing.* Retrieved from http://georgewbush-whitehouse.archives.gov/nsc/infosharing/index.html

The White House. (2009). *60 day cybersecurity policy review: Assuring a trusted and resilient information and communications infrastructure.* Washington, DC. Retrieved 1 January, 2012, from http://www.whitehouse.gov/ assets/documents/Cyberspace_Policy_Review_final.pdf

The White House. (2009). *Cyberspace policy review: Assuring a resilient information and communications infrastructure.* Washington, DC: The White House.

The White House. (2011). *International strategy for cyberspace: Prosperity, security, and openness in a networked world.* Washington, DC: The White House.

Ting, J.-A., Theodorou, E., & Schaal, S. (2007). A Kalman filter for robust outlier detection. In *IEEE/RSJ International Conference on Intelligent Robots and Systems, IROS 2007,* (pp. 1514–1519).

Tipsuwan, Y., & Chow, M. Y. (2003). Control methodologies in network control systems. *Control Engineering Practice, 11,* 1099–1111. doi:10.1016/S0967-0661(03)00036-4

Todd, B. (2011, 18 November). Water pumping station hacked? *The Situation Room with Wolf Blitzer, CNN.* Retrieved February 6, 2011, from http://situationroom.blogs. cnn.com/2011/11/18/water-pumping-station-hacked/

Tolmasquim, M. T. (2009). *SIN - National interlinked system.* Retrieved October 15, 2011, from http://www. senado.gov.br/sf/comissoes/ci/ap/AP20091210_Dr_Mauricio_Tolmasquin.pdf

Tolone, W., Wilson, D., Raja, A., Xiang, W. N., Hao, H., Phelps, S., & Johnson, E. (2004). In Chen, H., Moore, R., Zeng, D., & Leavitt, J. (Eds.), *Critical infrastructure integration modeling and simulation: Intelligence and security informatics* (Vol. 3073, pp. 214–225). Lecture Notes in Computer ScienceBerlin: GermanyL Springer. Retrieved from.

Tom, S., Christiansen, D., & Berrett, D. (2008). *Recommended practice for patch management of control systems.* Retrieved October 14, 2011, from http://www.us-cert. gov/control_systems/practices/documents/PatchManagementRecommendedPractice_Final.pdf

Touré, A., et al. (2011). *The quest for cyberpeace.* International Telecommunications Union. Retrieved from http:// www.itu.int/pub/S-GEN-WFS.01-1-2011

TR1658. (2009). *Statoil governing document.* Technical Network and Security of Automation Systems.

Trebilcock, M., & Iacobucci, E. (2003). Privatisation and accountability. *Harvard Law Review, 116*(5), 1422–1453. doi:10.2307/1342731

Trusted Information Sharing Network. (2011). *Trusted information sharing network overview.* Canberra, Australia. Retrieved 1 January, 2012, from http://tisn.gov. au/www/tisn/rwpattach.nsf/VAP/(9A5D88DBA63D32A 661E6369859739356)~TISN+Overview+-+Fact+Sheet. PDF/$file/TISN+Overview+-+Fact+Sheet.PDF

Trusted Information Sharing Network. (2011). *Trusted information sharing network deed of confidentiality fact sheet.* Canberra, Australia. Retrieved 1 January, 2012, from http://www.tisn.gov.au/Documents/TISN+Deed+of+Confidentiality+-+Fact+Sheet.pdf

Tsang, C., & Kwong, S. (2005). Multi-agent intrusion detection system in industrial network using ant colony clustering approach and unsupervised feature extraction. In *IEEE International Conference on Industrial Technology, ICIT 2005,* (pp. 51–56).

Tsang, P., & Smith, S. (2008). Yasir: A low-latency, high-integrity security retrofit for legacy SCADA systems. In *Proceedings of the IFIP TC 23rd International Information Security Conference,* (pp. 445–459). Springer.

Tsang, R. (2009). *Cyberthreats, vulnerabilities and attacks on SCADA networks.*

TU. (2009). *Computer incidents may halt oil and gas production/Dataangrep kan stoppe Olje-Norge.* Retrieved from www.tu.no/it/article193101.ece

Tucker, A. (2003, October). *A model curriculum for K–12 computer science: Final report of the ACM K–12 task force curriculum committee.* Retrieved from http://csta.acm.org/Curriculum/sub/CurrFiles/K-12ModelCurr2ndEd.pdf

Tukey, J. (1960). A survey of sampling from contaminated distributions . In Olkin, I. (Ed.), *Contributions to probability and statistics essays in honor of Harold Hotelling* (pp. 448–485).

Tukey, J. (1977). *Exploratory data analysis.* Reading, MA: Addison-Wesley.

Turk, R. J. (2005). *Cyber incidents involving control systems.* Idaho National Laboratory. Retrieved 2 August, 2012, from http://www.inl.gov/technicalpublications/Documents/3480144.pdf

U.S. Government Accountability Office. (2011). *Cybersecurity guidance is available but more can be done to promote its use.* GAO 12-92. Retrieved from http://www.gao.gov/assets/590/587529.pdf

UK Centre for the Protection of National Infrastructure. (2010). *Good practice guide: Cyber security assessments of industrial control systems.* CPNI.

UK Centre for the Protection of National Infrastructure. (2010). *Good practice guide: Guide 2 – Implement secure architecture.* CPNI.

UK Centre for the Protection of National Infrastructure. (2010). *Good practice guide: Guide 3 – Establish response capability.* CPNI.

UK Centre for the Protection of National Infrastructure. (2010). *Good practice guide: Guide 4 – Improve awareness and skills.* CPNI.

UK Centre for the Protection of National Infrastructure. (2010). *Good practice guide: Guide 5 – Manage 3rd party risk.* CPNI.

UK Centre for the Protection of National Infrastructure. (2010). *Good practice guide: Process control and SCADA security.* CPNI.

UK Centre for the Protection of National Infrastructure. (2010). *Protecting against terrorism* (3rd ed.). CPNI.

United Nations. (2011, October). *World population prospects: The 2010 revision.* Retrieved from http://esa.un.org/unpd/wpp/index.htm

United States Computer Emergency Readiness Team (US-CERT). (n.d.). *Control systems security program: Industrial control systems cyber emergency response team.* Retrieved from http://www.us-cert.gov/control_systems/ics-cert/

United States Computer Emergency Readiness Team (US-CERT). (n.d.). *Control systems security program: Industrial control systems joint working group.* Retrieved from http://www.us-cert.gov/control_systems/icsjwg/index.html

United States Computer Emergency Readiness Team (US-CERT). (n.d.). *US-CERT: United States computer emergency readiness team.* Retrieved from http://www.us-cert.gov

United States General Accounting Office (GAO). (2004). *Critical infrastructure protection. Challenges and efforts to secure control systems.* United States General Accounting Office.

United States General Accounting Office. (2001). *Information sharing. Practices that can benefit critical infrastructure protection*. Washington, DC: General Accounting Office. Retrieved 1 January, 2012, from http://www.gao.gov/new.items/d0224.pdf

United States General Accounting Office. (2004). *Critical Infrastructure protection. Establishing effective information sharing with infrastructure sectors*. Washington, DC: General Accounting Office. Retrieved 1 January, 2012, from http://www.gao.gov/new.items/d04699t.pdf

United States General Accounting Office. (2004). *Critical infrastructure protection: Challenges and efforts to secure control systems*. Retrieved 7 January 2012 from www.gao.gov/new.items/d03233.pdf

United States General Accounting Office. (2007). *Critical infrastructure protection: Multiple efforts to secure control systems are under way, but challenges remain*. Retrieved 18 December 2011 from www.gao.gov/assets/270/268137.pdf

United States Nuclear Regulatory Commission. (2010). *Regulatory guide 5.71: Cyber security programs for nuclear facilities*.

US CERT. (2006). *Vulnerability note VU#190617: Live-Data ICCP server heap buffer overflow vulnerability*. Retrieved February 7, 2012, from http://www.kb.cert.org/vuls/id/190617

US Government Printing Office. (1997). *Critical foundations*. (Report 040-000-0699-1).

Verissimo, P., et al. (2006). *The CRUTIAL reference critical information infrastructure architecture: A blueprint*. Retrieved from http://homepages.gsd.inesc-id.pt/~mpc/pubs/04_Verissimo.pdf

Verton, D. (2003). Blaster worm linked to severity of blackout. *Computerworld*.

VIKING Project. (2008). *Vital infrastructure, networks, information and control systems management*. Retrieved from http://www.vikingproject.eu

Wald, A. (1947). *Sequential analysis*. New York, NY: J. Wiley & Sons.

Walt, S. M. (2010, 30 March). Is the cyber threat overblown? *Foreign Policy*. Retrieved February 6, 2011, from http://walt.foreignpolicy.com/posts/2010/03/30/is_the_cyber_threat_overblown

Water Sector Coordinating Council Cyber Security Working Group. (2008). Roadmap to secure control systems in the water sector.

Web application Security Consortium. (2009). *Web application firewall evaluation criteria*. Retrieved from http://projects.webappsec.org/w/page/13246985/Web Application Firewall Evaluation Criteria

Weiss, J. (2011, 17 November). Water system hack—The system is broken. *ControlGlobal.com*. Retrieved February 6, 2011, from http://community.controlglobal.com/content/water-system-hack-system-broken

Weiss, J. (2010). *Protecting industrial control systems from electronic threats*. Momentum Press, LLC.

Wentworth, F. (2000). *Critical infrastructure protection: Establishing an information sharing and analysis center (ISAC) can be like developing an organizational security policy* Global Information Assurance Certification Paper; SANS Institute. Retrieved 1 January, 2012, from http://www.giac.org/paper/gsec/155/critical-infrastructure-protection-establishing-information-sharing-analysis-center-be/100603

Wessel, R. (2007). RFID keeps cherries fresh. *RFID Journal*. Retrieved October 9, 2011, from http://www.rfidjournal.com/article/view/3554

West, A. (2008). *Securing DNP3 and Modbus with AGA12-2J*. IEEE Power and Energy Society General Meeting - Conversion and Delivery of Electrical Energy in the 21st Century, Pittsburgh, PA.

West, A. (n.d.). *SCADA communication protocols*. Retrieved from http://www.powertrans.com.au/articles/new pdfs/SCADA PROTOCOLS.pdf

West-Brown, M., Stikvoort, D., Kossakowski, K., Killcrece, G., Ruefle, R., & Zajicek, M. (2003, April). *Handbook for computer security response teams* (CSIRTs) (2nd ed., (pp. 15213-3890). Retrieved from http://www.cert.org/archive/pdf/csirt-handbook.pdf

White House Press Office. (2009, 29 May). Remarks by the president on securing our nation's cyber infrastructure. *White House Press Office*. Retrieved February 6, 2011, from http://www.whitehouse.gov/the_press_office/Remarks-by-the-President-on-Securing-Our-Nations-Cyber-Infrastructure/

Whitehouse, S. (2011, 7 March). Cybersecurity needs complete plan. *Politico*. Retrieved February 6, 2011, from http://dyn.politico.com/printstory.cfm?uuid=8D587513-F55D-BEB0-A25C03B5B2018326

WIB. (2010). *Cyber security standard to protect global critical infrastructure*. Press release. Retrieved from www.wib.nl/pressreleasenov2010.html

Wikipedia. (2012, July 20). List of countries by literacy rate. In *Wikipedia, The Free Encyclopedia*. Retrieved July 21, 2012, from http://en.wikipedia.org/w/index.php?title=List_of_countries_by_literacy_rate&oldid=503242769

Wikipedia. (2012, July 20). Flame (malware). In *Wikipedia, The Free Encyclopedia*. Retrieved 14:14, July 21, 2012, from http://en.wikipedia.org/w/index.php?title=Flame_(malware)&oldid=503359927

Willis, A. (2011). Design of a modified sequential probability ratio test (SPRT) for pipeline leak detection. *Computers & Chemical Engineering*, *35*(1), 127–131. doi:10.1016/j.compchemeng.2010.06.009

Willsky, A., & Jones, H. (1976). A generalized likelihood ratio approach to the detection and estimation of jumps in linear systems. *IEEE Transactions on Automatic Control*, *21*(1), 108–112. doi:10.1109/TAC.1976.1101146

Wilson, M., & Hash, J. (2003, October). *Building an information technology security awareness and training program*. Retrieved from http://csrc.nist.gov/publications/nistpubs/800-50/NIST-SP800-50.pdf

Wingfield, B. (2012, 13 January). Power-grid cyber attack seen leaving millions in dark for months. *Bloomberg*. Retrieved February 6, 2011, from http://www.bloomberg.com/news/2012-02-01/cyber-attack-on-u-s-power-grid-seen-leaving-millions-in-dark-for-months.html

Wojnarowicz, J., Klamra, M., Rzecki, K., & Romanska, A. (2005). *Security threats in open protocols for intelligent buildings*. Krakow, Poland: Cracow University of Technology.

Wollmer, R. (1964). Removing arcs from a network. *Operations Research*, *12*, 934–940. doi:10.1287/opre.12.6.934

Wood, A. J., & Wollenberg, B. F. (1996). *Power generation operation and control* (2nd ed.). Hoboken, NJ: John Wiley & Sons, Inc.

Wood, R. K. (1993). Deterministic network interdiction. *Mathematical and Computer Modelling*, *17*, 1–18. doi:10.1016/0895-7177(93)90236-R

Xiao, K., Chen, N., Ren, S., Shen, L., Sun, X., Kwiat, K., & Macalik, M. (2007). A workflow-based non-intrusive approach for enhancing the survivability of critical infrastructures in cyber environment. In *Proceedings of Third International Workshop on Software Engineering for Secure Systems (SESS'07)*. IEEE Computer Society.

Xie, L., Mo, Y., & Sinopoli, B. (2010, October). *False data injection attacks in electricity markets*. Paper presented at the meeting of the 2010 First International Conference on Smart Grid Communications, Maryland, USA.

Xu, L., Tomsovic, K., & Bose, A. (2005, April). Topology error identification using a twostage DC state estimator. *Electric Power Systems Research*, *74*, 167–175. doi:10.1016/j.epsr.2004.10.005

Yang, D., Usynin, A., & Hines, J. (2005). Anomaly-based intrusion detection for scada systems. In *5th International Topical Meeting on Nuclear Plant Instrumentation, Control and Human Machine Interface Technologies (NPIC&HMIT 05)*, (pp. 12–16).

Yang, A., Abbass, H. A., & Sarker, R. (2006). Characterizing warfare in red teaming. *IEEE Transactions on Systems, Man, and Cybernetics. Part B, Cybernetics*, *36*(2), 268–285. doi:10.1109/TSMCB.2005.855569

Young, S., & Aisle, D. (2002). *The hackers handbook: The strategy behind breaking into and defending networks*. Auerbach Publications.

Yu, X., Cecati, C., Dillon, T., & Simoes, M. (2011). The new frontier of smart grids. *IEEE Industrial Electronics Magazine*, *5*(3), 49–63. doi:10.1109/MIE.2011.942176

Zanero, S. (2004). Behavioral intrusion detection. *Computer and Information Sciences-ISCIS*, *2004*, 657–666. doi:10.1007/978-3-540-30182-0_66

ZDNet. (2010). 2015 the year of cyberwar: Gartner. *ZDNet*. Retrieved 1 January, 2012, from http://www.zdnet.com.au/2015-the-year-of-cyberwar-gartner-339307693.htm

Zhu, B., & Sastry, S. (2010). SCADA-specific intrusion detection/prevention systems: A survey and taxonomy. In *Proceedings of the First Workshop on Secure Control Systems (SCS'10)*, Stockholm, Sweden.

Zhu, B., & Sastry, S. (2011). Revisit dynamic ARIMA based anomaly detection. In *Proceedings of*

Zhu, B., Joseph, A., & Sastry, S. (2011). Taxonomy of cyber attacks on SCADA systems. In *Proceedings of the 2011 IEEE International Conference on Cyber, Physical, and Social Computing (CPSCom 2011)*. IEEE Computer Society.

Zhu, Q., McQueen, M., Rieger, C., & Basar, T. (2011, April). *Management of control system information security: Control system patch management*. Paper presented at the Workshop on Foundations of Dependable and Secure Cyber-Physical Systems, Chicago, Illinois.

Zhu, X., Soh, Y., & Xie, L. (2002). Robust Kalman filter design for discrete time-delay systems. *Circuits, Systems, and Signal Processing*, *21*(3), 319–335. doi:10.1007/s00034-004-7047-8

Zielstra, A., & Hafkamp, W. (2010, March). *Dutch cyber-crime information exchange: A public private partnership*. Presentation delivered at ENISA's workshop on Information Sharing; Amsterdam. Retrieved 1 January, 2012, from http://www.enisa.europa.eu/act/res/workshops-1/2010/information-sharing-workshop/copy_of_agenda-of-the-information-sharing-workshop

ZigBee Alliance. (2008). *ZigBee specification*. Retrieved September 17, 2011, from http://www.zigbee.org/Specifications/ZigBee/download.aspx

ZigBee. (n.d.). *ZigBee home automation overview*. Retrieved from http://www.zigbee.org/Standards/ZigBeeHomeAutomation/Overview.aspx

Zwan, E. v. (2010). *Security of industrial control systems, what to look for*. ISACA Journal Online.

About the Contributors

Christopher Laing is the Project Director of the nuWARP, Northumbria University, a not-for-profit organization, part of the UK government's Centre for the Protection of National Infrastructure initiative on securing data and network information infrastructures. He is also a consultant for the European Network & Information Security Agency, and he has worked with UK law enforcement agencies in the development of postgraduate computer forensics/digital security programmes. His research is focused on network infrastructures, in particular how the behaviour of complex network infrastructures may be used as a self-adapting defence mechanism.

Atta Badii, Founding Director of Intelligent Systems Research Laboratory, is a high ranking professor at the University of Reading, School of Systems Engineering. He holds the Chair of Secure Pervasive Technologies and has multi-disciplinary academic and industrial research experience in the fields of ICT Security & Trust Architectures and Distributed Intelligent Systems. Atta has made major contributions to over 25 large collaborative research projects to-date and has served as the Scientific and Technical Leader of several projects at both the national and international level; has over 180 publications; and has served on editorial and research steering boards as coordinator/technical leader/invited expert, e.g. as the Chair of the Security Architectures and Virtualisation Taskforce of the European Road Map Project SECURIST and as the Chair of the VideoSense: European Video-Analytics Network of Excellence.

Paul Vickers is a UK Chartered Engineer with a BSc degree in Computer Studies and a PhD in Software Engineering & HCI. He is currently Reader in Computer Science at Northumbria University. His research is in the computing domain, where it intersects with creative digital media with a particular emphasis on auditory display and how audio may be used in visualization for security applications.

* * *

Bill Bailey is currently a Researcher and Lecturer with Edith Cowan University, Security Research Centre, Perth, Australia. Specialising in: counter insurgency, terrorism, critical infrastructure protection, security management, business continuity, strategic risk, and emergency management. Bill served as an Inspector with the Royal Hong Kong Police, Tactical Unit and as a trained Negotiator before becoming a security and risk management specialist in Africa for the Oil and Gas industry. Extensive experience of security and disaster situations, including coup d'états in Equatorial Guinea 2004, Mauritania in 2004/2005 and a 'Hi-Jack' at Hong Kong Airport in 1978. Contracts include: Exxon Mobil in Kenya, Cameroon and Equatorial Guinea; Woodside Australian Energy in Australia, Mauritania and Senegal.

In Algeria, with Stirling FMC: First Calgary Petroleum, BP-Amoco, Bechtel, Halliburton Energy, and Amerada-Hess. Further contracts with: Control Risks Group, Triton Energy, Jet Air, Hess Energy; Pride Forasol, Virgin Atlantic, Schlumberger, ABB Group, and PTTEP.

Antony Bridges has been working in the security industry for thirteen years for a variety of Government Departments and commercial organisations. With a background in psychology, Antony has led projects designed to enhance overall security outcomes and organisational efficiency by addressing the human factor within the security system. Based in the United Kingdom at QinetiQ, his work in the UK and overseas has led to improvements in overall security system design and the selection, training and performance management of personnel. Antony draws upon academic research and his own practical operational experience to address the human factor within cyber security. He has a particular interest in creating an organisational culture that enhances security outcomes.

David Brooks is currently the Project Manager-Security for a green field mining project with a capital cost of over A$8 billion, responsible for the operational and regulatory design and implementation of the project wide Security System. David is a former Senior Security Science Academic with the Security Research Centre (SECAU), Edith Cowan University, Australia, where he conducted research in security risk, technology and management. He remains the Academic Chair of the SECAU annual *Security and Intelligence Conference* and is a member of the *Security Journal* Editorial Committee. David was previously employed by the Australian Defence Department as the West Australian Regional Plant and Equipment Contracts Manager. During this period, David was responsible for the implementation of the strategic process of facility plant maintenance.

Matthew Brundage is a second-year graduate student studying Computer Science at The University of Tulsa (TU) and is a Research Assistant with Dr. Mauricio Papa in the Critical Infrastructure Protection lab of The University of Tulsa's Institute for Information Security (iSec) Program. Matthew received his Bachelor of Science in Electrical Engineering and Bachelor of Science in Computer Science from the University of Tulsa in 2010. His primary research is in the design and development of a distributed, scalable monitoring system for ZigBee wireless networks. His graduate work resulted in a framework for development of sophisticated analysis tools to improve awareness of ZigBee network state and communication.

Maurilio Pereira Coutinho has B.S. (1981), M.Sc. (1998) and Ph.D. (2007) at Electrical Engineering by Itajuba Federal University (1981). Currently he is Associate Professor of Itajuba Federal University. He has experience in the area of Computer Science, with emphasis on Information Security Systems. Focused, mainly, in the subjects: critical infrastructures, critical infrastructures protection, electric power system, intrusion detection, and SCADA security. He is Coordinator of the Special Educational Program for Undergraduates Students of Electrical Engineering Course funded by Secretary of Undergraduation Courses of the Ministry of Education. He was Head of the Department of Electronic from 96-97 and Director of Electrical Engineering Institute from 1998-2004. He was member of the UNIBRAL Program with TU Dresden in the area of Data Protection and Data Security from 2003-2006. He was member of the UNIBRAL Program with TU Dresden in the area of Mechanical and Mechatronic Engineering from 2009-2010. He was the Brazilian Coordinator for the program from DAAD *Fachbezogene Partnerschaften mit Hochschulen in Entwicklungsländern – Technische Universität Dresden – Datenschutz und Datensicherheit* from 2007-2010.

Robert Doleman is attached to the Security Research Centre, Edith Cowan University (ECU), Perth, Australia, currently undertaking research in Facility Management, Risk, and Fire Safety. Recent publications include *Why are there systemic failures of fire protection equipment in Australian Aged Care Nursing Facilities: 2010, Vienna* and *A strategy to articulate the Facility Management knowledge categories within the built environment: 2011, Perth.* He lectures on Advanced Risk and Security within the School of Security Science, ECU. Robert is also the Risk and Engineering Manager for Fire Technologies Australia (FTA), one of the largest fire and blast product designers and installers within Australia. He is responsible for engineering risk analysis, design, and compliance of the fire blast systems and solutions.

Elyoenai Egozcue received his M.Sc. in Telecommunications Engineer from the UPNA University of Pamplona, Spain. He completed his Master Thesis on the study of integrated QoS in IP over WDM networks at the VUB University of Brussels, Belgium. From 2006 to 2008 he worked as a security researcher at S21sec, where he participated in several consultancy lead projects on RFID, MPLS and biometrics. From 2008 to 2011 he leaded or participated in several R&D projects at national and European level dealing with digital security of control systems being used in Critical Infrastructures (e.g. FP7 INSPIRE project). Since 2011, he has been S21sec's project manager of several R&D and customer-oriented projects on ICS/SCADA and Smart Grid security, including technical and compliance consultancies and security assessments for critical infrastructures in the energy sector. Recently, he has leaded S21sec's contribution to the studies of the European Network and Information Security Agency (ENISA) on ICS and Smart Grid Security.

Ian Ellefsen is a Senior Lecturer in the Academy of Computer Science and Software Engineering at the University of Johannesburg (UJ) in Johannesburg, South Africa. His current primary area of research is aspects relating to critical information infrastructure protection (CIIP) and other areas of information security.

Elke Franz studied Computer Science at the TU Dresden. Since she received her diploma in 1997, she has been a member of the privacy and security research group at this university. In 2003 she received her PhD at the same university. Her main research interests are steganography and privacy enhancing technologies, particularly their use within complex applications. She has been engaged in the project COMQUAD (founded by the German Research Foundation) and the European projects PRIME and ECRYPT (Network of Excellence) and participated in HEI cooperation projects with the UNIFEI in Brazil. Since 2006, she has been giving lectures about cryptography, data security, and steganography.

Eduardo Gelbstein has over 40 years experience in information and communications technologies (ICT), including the design of computer based automation systems, the project management of very large IT projects and several executive roles. Ed is a former advisor to the United Nations Board of and to the French National Audit Office. Prior to this he was the Director of the United Nations International

Computing Centre a service organization located in Geneva, New York and Brindisi, providing ICT services to the United Nations System. Prior to joining the United Nations in 1993, he was I.T. Strategy Manager and Chairman of the Business-IT Steering Group of the British Railways Board. He is the author of numerous articles and publications on information security and auditing as well as a regular speaker at international conferences on security and governance in Europe, the Middle East, and Africa. He also gives briefings on information security for the Geneva Centre for Security Policy.

Tony H. Grubesic is an Associate Professor in the College of Information Science and Technology and Director of the Geographic Information System and Spatial Analysis Laboratory (GISSA) at Drexel University. His research and teaching interests are in geographic information science, regional development, spatial epidemiology and public policy evaluation. Author of over 100 research publications, his recent work focuses on critical infrastructure vulnerability, alcohol-related morbidity, broadband deployment in the United States and air transportation systems. Grubesic obtained a B.A. in Political Science from Willamette University, a B.S. in Geography from the University of Wisconsin-Whitewater, a M.A. in Geography from the University of Akron, and a Ph.D. in Geographic Information Science from the Ohio State University.

Peter J. Hawrylak is an Assistant Professor in the Electrical Engineering department at The University of Tulsa (TU), is Chair of the AIM RFID Experts Group (REG), and chair of the Healthcare Initiative (HCI) sub-group of the AIM REG. Dr. Hawrylak is a member of The University of Tulsa's Institute for Information Security (iSec), which is a NSA (U.S. National Security Agency) Center of Excellence. Peter has six (6) issued patents in the RFID space and numerous academic publications. Peter's research interests are in the areas embedded system security, RFID, embedded systems, and low power wireless systems. He is Associate Editor of the *International Journal of Radio Frequency Identification Technology and Applications* (IJRFITA) journal published by InderScience Publishers, which focuses on the application and development of RFID technology.

Peter H. Jenney is a 30-year veteran in the software development, testing, and security space. Both a software developer and product manager, he has developed and managed software at leading edge companies including Dataware Technologies, where he invented CD-Record, the first commercial SCSI CD Recordable system and Rational Software where he drove Rational Testing products to over US$120M and managed technical relationships with Microsoft, IBM and others. In 2005 Mr. Jenney joined Security Innovation, Inc. as Vice President of Strategic Initiatives where he developed relationships and software in partnerships with global government and commercial organizations such as Cisco, Duma (China), CACI, USAF/AFIT, DOT, CERT, et al. Most recently, he entered into a new venture named SCADA Security Innovation where as co-founder and CTO, he creates and deploys novel cyber-defense software specifically focused at Industrial Control Systems and SCADA.

Stig O. Johnsen (M.Sc., PhD) is a senior researcher at SINTEF and NTNU (The Norwegian University of Science and Technology). He has been involved in safety and security research, resilience engineering in addition to a focus on human factors. He has been collaborating closely with the authorities in Norway and the oil and gas industry. In the last period he has been working with safety, security, and human factors issues related to remote operations, remote support, and integrated operations.

James Johnson is a first-year PhD student studying Computer Science at The University of Tulsa (TU), studying under Dr. Mauricio Papa in The University of Tulsa's Institute for Information Security (iSec) Program. James received his Master's degree in CS from the University of Tulsa in 2011, researching vulnerabilities in SCADA devices and developing a SCADA-oriented fuzzing framework for automated vulnerability analysis. He received his BS in Computer Science in 2009. His research interests include vulnerability analysis of embedded devices, security of automotive network systems, and native file redaction.

Konstantin Knorr started his information security career with a Diploma in Mathematics and continued his studies with a PhD in Information Security at the University of Zurich. Then, he joined a start-up company specializing in managed services for firewalls. For seven years Prof. Knorr was working for the Siemens Computer Emergency Response Team where he was leading a team of security experts focusing on cyber security for critical infrastructure projects in the energy and industry sector. Since January 2010 he is a professor for IT security at the University of Applied Sciences in Trier, Germany. His research interests encompass access control models, patch management, and security assessments.

Germano Lambert-Torres received the Ph.D. degree in Electrical Engineering from École Polytechnique de Montréal, Montréal, QC, Canada, in 1990, the B.S. and M.Sc. degrees in Electrical Engineering from Itajuba Federal University (UNIFEI), Itajuba, MG, Brazil, the B.S. degree in Economics from Faculty of Economic Sciences at South of Minas, and the B.S. degree in Mathematics from Itajuba Faculty of Sciences and Letters. From 1995 to 1996, he was a Visiting Professor with the University of Waterloo, Waterloo, ON, Canada. From 2000 to 2004, he was served as Pro-Rector of Research and Graduate Studies, UNIFEI. He is currently a Professor and Dean of the Electrical Engineering Department, UNIFEI. He serves on a number of committees related to intelligent systems, in IEEE and CIGRE. He also serves as a Consultant for many power industries in Brazil and South America. He is a member of Intelligent System Applications to Power Systems (ISAP) international board. He has been teaching many tutorials by IEEE in U.S., Europe and Asia. He served as General Chair for ISAP in 1999 and 2009, as well Vice-General Chair for ISAP 2001, LACTEC (Congress on Logic Applied to Technology) in 2003 and 2007. He has more than 70 Master and Doctoral thesis complete supervisions, and more than 400 journal and conference technical papers published. He is also author/editor and coauthor of nine books and more than 30 book chapters in intelligent systems and nonclassical logics.

Sean Lawson is Assistant Professor in the Department of Communication at the University of Utah. His research focuses on the relationships among science, technology, and security with an emphasis on new media, information, and communication technologies. Topics of interest include cybersecurity policy, surveillance, network-centric warfare, and military use of social media. In addition to his academic research on these issues, he is a contributor to *Forbes.com* and *CTOVision.com.* His Doctorate is from the Department of Science and Technology Studies at Rensselaer Polytechnic Institute. He has a Master of Arts in Arab Studies from Georgetown University and a Bachelor of Arts in History from California State University, Stanislaus.

Horst Lazarek is a Senior Lecturer of Computer Science at Technische Universität Dresden since 1980. His research interests include data protection, security, and risk management. He received Diploma in Mathematics and Physics (1967) from the Martin-Luther-University Halle-Wittenberg, the PhD (Dr. rer. nat.) degree in Numerical Mathematics from the University of Potsdam (1979) and the Habilitation in the field of "Computer in Developing Countries" from the Technische Universität Dresden (1990). From 1980 to 1984 and 1986 to 1987 he worked at the University of Angola; from 1994 to 1996 at the TU Wien. He was grantholder and coordinator in the TEMPUS-Project CD-JEP_24200-2003 TACIS (DASICURUDT 2005) and grantholder in the TEMPUS-Project CD-JEP-27173-2006 (UA) in the field of curriculum development in privacy and data security. From 2000 to 2006 he has been engaged in the scientific committee in the EU-ALBAN-project, participated in the scientific committee in European-Brazil-Windows I (ERASMUS MUNDUS) and in the steering committee in European-Brazil-Windows I and II and also in ACP-Program (ERASMUS MUNDUS). He was the German coordinator of the UNIBRAL Program between TU Dresden and UNIFEI in the area of Data Protection and Data Security from 2003-2006. He is member of the UNIBRAL Program between TU Dresden and UNIFEI in the area of Mechanical and Mechatronic Engineering from 2009-2010 and the German coordinator for the program from DAAD *Fachbezogene Partnerschaften mit Hochschulen in Entwicklungsländern – Technische Universität Dresden – Datenschutz und Datensicherheit* from 2007-2010.

Rafal Leszczyna is an Assistant Professor at Gdansk University of Technology, Faculty of Management and Economics. He holds the M.Sc. degrees of Computer Science and Business Management. In December, 2006 he earned a Ph.D. (with a distinction) in Computer Science, specialisation - Computer Security at the Faculty of Electronics, Telecommunications and Informatics of Gdansk University of Technology. Between 2004 and 2008 he worked in the European Commission Joint Research Centre, in the teams dealing with information security and the security of critical networked infrastructures. After his return to the university in 2008, from 2010 to 2012 he was seconded to the European Network and Information Security Agency (ENISA), where among the others he was responsible for coordinating the studies related to the security of industrial control systems and smart grids. His professional interests focus on the security of information systems, information security of critical infrastructures, and the issues relevant to information security management.

Anastasia Mavridou is a second-year graduate student studying Computer Science at The University of Tulsa (TU) and is a Research Assistant with Dr. Mauricio Papa in the Critical Infrastructure Protection lab of The University of Tulsa's Institute for Information Security (iSec) Program. Anastasia received her Dipl.-Ing degree in Electrical and Computer Engineering from the Aristotle University of Thessaloniki, Greece in 2010. Her research interests include information security, cyber-physical systems security, critical infrastructure protection, and rigorous system design.

Alan T. Murray is Professor, School of Geographical Sciences and Urban Planning, and a researcher in the GeoDa Center for GeoSpatial Analysis and Computation. He is currently an editor of *International Regional Science Review*, and former editor of *Geographical Analysis*. His formal training includes a B.S. in Mathematical Sciences (emphasis in operations research), an M.A. in Statistics and Applied Probability (emphasis in operations research) and a Ph.D. in Geography, all from the University of California at Santa Barbara. His research focuses on technical and application oriented topics in emergency service planning, crime, sustainability, transit, natural resource management, and infrastructure vulnerability. He is the author of two recent books, Critical Infrastructure: Reliability and Vulnerability (Berlin: Springer) and Business Site Section, Location Analysis, and GIS (New York: Wiley), and over 160 research articles, book chapters, and proceedings papers.

Mauricio Papa is an Associate Professor for the Tandy School of Computer Science at The University of Tulsa. He also serves as Faculty Director of the Institute for Information Security, which supports a multi-disciplinary program of study and research tackling cyber security issues on a global scale. Dr. Papa received his Bachelor of Science in electrical engineering from Universidad Central de Venezuela in 1992 and his Master of Science in Electrical Engineering and Doctorate degree in Computer Science from TU in 1996 and 2001, respectively. His primary research area is critical infrastructure protection. He also conducts research in distributed systems, network security, cryptographic protocol verification, and intelligent control systems.

Neil Robinson is a Research Leader at RAND Europe where he specialises in public policy research concerning cyber-security, CIIP, and cybercrime. Whilst at RAND Europe, Neil has conducted a number of research studies for the European Network and Information Security Agency (ENISA) into information sharing across a range of different contexts including the socio-economic barriers to information exchange and more recently issues affecting information exchange between Computer Emergency Response Teams (CERTs) and Law Enforcement Authorities (LEAs). Neil has also conducted research on a range of other cyber-security related topics for national governments in the United Kingdom, France and Sweden, as well as a number of EU institutions such as the European Commission and European Defence Agency.

Shankar Sastry is dean of the College of Engineering at UC Berkeley. Prior to serving as dean, he was director of CITRIS (Center for Information Technology in the Interests of Society), an interdisciplinary center spanning UC Berkeley, Davis, Merced, and Santa Cruz. In February 2007, he was appointed the Faculty Director of the Blum Center for Developing Economies. He chaired the Department of Electrical Engineering and Computer Sciences at UC Berkeley from January, 2001 through June 2004, he was director of the Information Technology Office at DARPA from 1999 to early 2001, and served as director of the Electronics Research Laboratory at Berkeley, conducting research in electrical, computer, and engineering sciences from 1996-1999.

Luiz Eduardo Borges da Silva received the B.S. and M.Sc. degrees in Electrical Engineering from Itajuba Federal University (UNIFEI), Itajubá, MG, Brazil, in 1977 and 1982, respectively, and the Ph.D. degree from École Polytechnique deMontréal, Montréal, QC, Canada, in 1988. He was a Visiting Professor with the University of Tennessee, Knoxville, in 1998. He is currently a Professor of the Electronic Engineering Department at UNIFEI. His research focuses on power electronics, electronic power systems, power converters, and applications of adaptive and intelligent control in industrial problems. He is the Head of Power Electronics at UNIFEI. He has directed many projects in the field of industrial electronics, and coauthored over 200 technical papers. He has supervised more than 30 Master and Doctoral thesis.

Sebastiaan von Solms is a Research Professor in the Academy of Computer Science and Software Engineering at the University of Johannesburg (UJ) in Johannesburg, South Africa. He is also the Director of the UJ Centre for Cyber Security. Prof von Solms is the Immediate Past President of the International Federation for Information Processing (IFIP) (www.ifip.org). He has been a consultant to industry on the subject of Information and Cyber Security for the last 20 years, and has consulted in this area locally and internationally. He is a Fellow of the Computer Society of South Africa, a Fellow of the British Computer Society and a Chartered Information Technology Professional (CITP).

Bonnie Zhu works on providing an integrated SCADA-specific cyber-physical security solution and reliable delivery of clean energy in smart grids. She holds a PhD in Electrical Engineering and Computer Science from Berkeley and a Certificate in Management of Technology from Haas Business School, among several graduate degrees. Her work on securing SCADA system has won Dr. Zhu, inter alia, multiple fellowships from National Science Foundation and the Sustainability Consortium. Dr. Zhu has also done research on cross-layer optimization for wireless sensor networks in addition to her 3-year EDA industry experience as a software developer for telecommunication equipment.

Index